EACH ONE TEACH ONE

Each One Teach One

Frank Laubach, Friend to Millions

BY

MARJORIE MEDARY

921

LONGMANS, GREEN AND CO.

NEW YORK · LONDON · TORONTO

C 1

LONGMANS, GREEN AND CO., INC.
55 FIFTH AVENUE, NEW YORK 3

LONGMANS, GREEN AND CO. LTD.
6 & 7 CLIFFORD STREET, LONDON W 1

LONGMANS, GREEN AND CO.
20 CRANFIELD ROAD, TORONTO 16

EACH ONE TEACH ONE

PUBLISHED SIMULTANEOUSLY IN THE DOMINION OF CANADA BY
LONGMANS, GREEN AND CO., TORONTO

FIRST EDITION MARCH 1954
REPRINTED DECEMBER 1954
OCTOBER 1957

LIBRARY OF CONGRESS CATALOG CARD NUMBER 54-5550

Printed in the United States of America

FOREWORD

A number of magazine articles have told in brief the remarkable story of Dr. Laubach's missionary campaigns for literacy, but when those words *missionary* and *literacy* come up in conversation, some people seem to shy away from them. In their minds a missionary seems to be a pious and impractical person trying to force Christianity upon peoples who hold other religious beliefs. And as for literacy, many say, "Why should a man wearing a loincloth and a few beads want to learn to read? And what will he read?"

Others who have heard a little about the Laubach methods and "lightning literacy" say incredulously, "But how can illiterate people learn to read faster than our youngsters learn to read a foreign language? If such speedy methods work, why aren't they used in our schools?"

Such questions, plus my enthusiasm for Dr. Laubach's work, led me to start writing this book. The quoted words of the new readers themselves in many different lands are sufficient answer to the first question. What they will read depends, as Dr. Laubach has been saying for years, on how much Americans, Europeans, and the literate people of lands largely illiterate are concerned over the problem.

The question about the Laubach methods is answered indirectly in the text but needs perhaps an explicit answer. The illiterate's speed is due to the fact that he is learning to read words he has heard all his life, whereas the American youngster studying French, Spanish, or German is usually trying to read a language quite foreign to his ears. Whether some of the Laubach devices might also be useful in foreign language classes is a matter educators may wish to explore.

Aside from answering the questions of doubters, another purpose urged me into writing. I felt that young people who in the next ten years will be making the choice of a career would like to know—indeed must know—what varied and vast opportunities for service are offered in the awakening lands all over this fast-changing world.

No one knows better than I what a hybrid kind of book has resulted from my efforts. It follows no pattern and probably cannot be classified. It is part biography, part social history, and part a career book. The plain facts are not embroidered with fiction. Except in one or two instances, all the dialogue is based on actual letters, journals, or speeches. Nothing has been added to lure readers in search of adventure, excitement, or mystery, and yet the book tells a story of world adventure and is full of the mystery of human personality and the excitement of a big idea.

It is my hope that it will lead many to read Frank Laubach's own books (see Bibliography), for they are aglow with his vision of what we Americans can do to help bring "peace on earth, good will toward men." Those who hear him speak from the pulpit or on radio or television never forget his personality and his voice, warm with the urgency of helping to satisfy the great hunger he has found among the illiterate millions.

To all who have helped with criticism, advice, encouragement in the completion of this book, I make grateful acknowledgment and to the following in special ways:

The *New York Times* for a part of the editorial "Literacy and Point Four" of July 22, 1949.

The *Christian Science Monitor* for an excerpt from the article "South Africa Unit Strives to Better Race Relations" by Glanville le Sueur, dated June 15, 1950.

Frank C. Laubach for unlimited permission to quote from unpublished letters and journals and from speeches, books, pamphlets, and other published material.

Robert S. Laubach (Bob, as he signs himself) for excerpts from the literacy *News Letters,* for the use of his pictures, and for helpful suggestions after his reading of the manuscript.

Alfred D. Moore, Executive Secretary, and Frederick J. Rex, Technical Adviser, of the Committee on World Literacy and Christian Literature, for much information about the work of the Committee.

Esther O. Hays and Madeline M. Beckmann for their cheerful co-operation in supplying material from the Committee files.

J. Maurice Hohlfeld, Ewing Gray, and June Dohse for excerpts from the literacy *News Letters.*

Edna Mendenhall Shaw, Dora Laubach Edson, T. C. Smith, Jennie Kline Hedden, and Martha Follmer Youmans, all of Benton, Pennsylvania, for reminiscences about the Laubach family.

The Committee on World Literacy and Christian Literature for the photographs by Robert S. Laubach, Arnold Maahs, Betty Mooney, Mary St. Albans, E. M. Stowe, and others. The Friendship Press for the charts from Frank C. Laubach's *The Silent Billion Speak.*

M. M.

To unknown missionaries and technical workers in many lands, whose spirit of service is helping to bring good will, justice, and peace in the world.

CONTENTS

ILLUSTRATIONS

PLATE 1

Dr. Laubach teaching a chief of the Medlpa tribe at a literacy conference in the mountains of New Guinea

PLATE 2

a) Young Moros were proud that letters regarding literacy came to Lanao from many parts of the world

b) Dr. Laubach teaches Twi chart at Akropong, Gold Coast

PLATE 3

a) Daughter teaching her mother to read Arabic in Algiers

b) Students receiving their diplomas at Dondi, in Angola

c) Woman in Tanganyika studying the first Cigogo chart

d) Dr. Laubach helping a teacher and a woman student at Dodoma, Tanganyika

PLATE 4

a) Learning to read in French Cameroun, West Africa

b) Setting type by linotype at Élat, French Cameroun

c) In the heart of Nigeria, Dr. Laubach teaches young and old to read their own language, Hausa

CHAPTER 1

A *Strange School*

"Has a dictionary of God's language ever
been written? *Need* is in His language. Millions who cannot read are calling for help."
—F. C. L.

A big Douglas airplane is headed toward the interior of New
Guinea, that vast island in the South Pacific where American
GI's fought in the jungle in the early years of World War II.
The time now is 1950. The airplane carries twenty persons.
That big man who wears a rough brown loincloth and, in
his nose, a flat white shell, is chief of a mountain tribe. He
has been to Lae on the northern coast of New Guinea to
beg these government people, teachers, and missionaries to
come and help his tribe. They are some of the uncounted
millions who live on the interior plateau. Most of them have
never seen a white man. Some are still cannibals.

The big mountain chief is talking to one of the travelers—
an American. He is Dr. Frank Laubach, friend to millions,
who has come to New Guinea to help start a literacy campaign. He is an expert in teaching the backward peoples of
the earth how to read, so that they can become more like
the people of progressive nations in their thinking, their
mode of life, and their ability to govern themselves.

At a narrow airstrip among steep mountains, the party
transfers to a smaller plane, to fly the last fifty miles to the

1

Oglebeng mission. The mountains are beautiful, but they make flying hazardous. It would not be pleasant to bail out into that wilderness below. It might be the Kukukuku country where the cannibals live. After a few minutes of flying, a landing field comes into view near a group of buildings surrounded by brilliant flower gardens. But see!—the flower beds are moving. They are people—hordes of them—wearing gorgeous headdresses made from plumes of the bird of paradise. And as the crowds gaze upward at the plane, now flying low, warning them to scatter, the travelers see that their faces are painted with red, yellow, green, and purple. They crowd so close to the landing strip, it will be a wonder if the pilot can land without accident.

Before the plane stops rolling, they are massed close around it, men, women, children, their dark bodies glistening with pig grease. They wear belts from which fall bundles of strings, and their necks and ears and noses are adorned with shells. In this land, shells are money and everyone is displaying his best today.

As the roar of the plane subsides, strange sounds fill the sudden stillness. Close at hand is the babble of voices, excited and happy. From beyond comes music—a loud rhythmic chant; hundreds of warriors are dancing around the field. Their brilliant headdresses and painted faces make a kaleidoscope of color. As the travelers step from the plane they can feel the ground quiver with the stamping of feet.

The crowd makes way for a man from the mission who comes to greet Dr. Laubach and his party. But they close in quickly again, and hundreds of painted faces with eager eyes watch every move Dr. Laubach makes. He is a man past sixty, of medium height, sparely built, with deep-set eyes and a warm smile. He wastes no time.

In front of a bamboo house he unrolls a big chart on which are drawn in large size some letters of the alphabet. Beside each is a picture, a syllable, and a word. Dr. Laubach smiles and, pointing to the first letter, says, "Ah. This man in the picture is saying 'ah.' You say 'ah.' "

He smiles and gestures at the nearest stalwart youth, and quickly the young man answers "ah." Then, surprised at his own audacity, he looks a little embarrassed and hides behind a friend. But Dr. Laubach goes on.

"Beside the man in the picture saying 'ah' is the letter *a*. It has its mouth open. It is saying *ah,* too."

The eager faces look a little puzzled. The missionary of this Oglebeng station steps forward and translates into their language what Dr. Laubach has just said. The bright head-dresses nod.

"Now all say 'ah,' " continues Dr. Laubach, and many of them shout "ah."

The first lesson goes on for an hour. There is a picture for each of the nine consonants in their language. After each one is a syllable and a familiar word beginning with that con-sonant. These lessons in the Medlpa language have been prepared at Lae with the help of native teachers, mission-aries, and government people. Even the Chief Administrator of Papua Territory, the head of the government, flew from Port Moresby on purpose to help. He is an educator and an expert in agriculture, eager to have his people be-come literate, for he knows that they can learn farming and all the ways of civilization much faster if they can read.

The sudden darkness of the tropics has come, but still the crowds linger. They do not want to leave. At last after prom-ises from the missionary that lessons will continue tomorrow, they scatter for the night.

Next morning soon after daylight the people gather again, thousands of them. This time the big bamboo-and-thatch church is opened, and hundreds sit cross-legged on the matted floor. The lesson charts are hung on the walls.

The eager pupils shout the answers together. Then a few of the nearest are invited to recite alone, and as fast as each one shows that he has learned the first lesson, he is sent to one of Dr. Laubach's helpers to continue with the next lesson. There are in all forty native teachers and missionaries and government people who have flown to the highlands to help. The groups of people gather about them in the big church and on the airfield just outside.

For three days the teaching goes on, and in that brief time thirty-six people have mastered the first little book of lessons. They can read! More than a hundred others are halfway through the book, and thousands know what reading means. On Sunday they hold a celebration. In the church they sing hymns set to their native tunes. The big chief who was in the plane makes a speech. Then diplomas are given to those who have finished the lessons, and certificates of service to those who have taught. They are told that the teaching will continue, and in another two weeks probably hundreds of them will be ready to receive diplomas. The campaign will go on until all the Medlpa people can read. The teachers will prepare more easy lessons and simply worded printed material which will teach them how to develop the best in their own culture and way of life and how to take their place in the modern world.

After church they hold a great sing-sing on the airfield. Six hundred painted warriors in their handsome headdresses dance while thousands watch.

And why are they so excited about learning to read? The

big chief on the plane said it this way when he asked Dr. Laubach and the others to come:

"We need the words of truth. Can words take legs and walk up those mountains alone? You white men can fly over the mountains. Come with your big bird planes and teach us how to worship God."

Of course, he spoke in his own language and it had to be translated, but it was a good speech in any language, for he had a big idea and said it clearly and forcefully.

To that man of New Guinea it was a wonderful thing to be able to read. The average American or European does not realize that the ability to read is a privilege. He has forgotten his lessons in history which described the life of his ancestors before the invention of printing, when books and reading were known only to the few. He is not greatly concerned when he learns that in vast areas of the world today books, magazines, and newspapers are still unknown. It takes an effort of the imagination to put oneself in the place of the illiterate—to picture what life is like for one who must get all his information by ear.

Frank Laubach is one man who understands. He learned through an experience twenty-five years ago while he was a teacher-missionary in Mindanao, southern island of the Philippines. The vision has controlled his life. In 1938, while attending a great International Council of missionaries near Madras, he wrote to friends in America:

"Eleven hundred million people, almost two-thirds of the world, had no delegate here at Tambaram, never have had a delegate anywhere, are voiceless, for they cannot read nor write nor vote. In Asia and Africa, over a billion people are illiterate, over half the human race, nine persons out of every ten. This cold paper cannot tell you what that means. You think it is a pity they cannot read, but the real tragedy is that they cannot *speak*; they are the silent victims, the forgotten men, driven like animals, mutely submitting in every age before and since the pyramids were built. The educated classes do not dream how they suffer. . . . They do not know enough to live without some leader to whom they are enslaved for life—more than half the human race are slaves yet, hungry, driven, diseased, afraid of this world, and of the demons in the next. This is the exact truth. They can be set free.

"I have not only seen these people across Asia and Africa, but have sat beside many of them and taught them one by one, and have seen a new light kindle in their eyes; love and hope dawn as they began to step out of blindness. I know that we can lift this tragic multitude out of their curse, easily, without great expense, by caring and knowing and doing our part."

Although most of these illiterates live in Asia and Africa and the islands of the South Pacific, some millions of them have homes in the Americas. They are not stupid people. They learn quickly when given a chance. And Dr. Laubach has invented a quick way of teaching them to read their own languages. This is the story of the man, his vision and his work.

CHAPTER 2

Seeking the Way

"Join me as together we go up toward those
heights we both see ahead of us."—F. C. L.

Frank Laubach was forty years old before his great idea
seized him. But he does not now speak of those earlier years
as wasted. While searching for his part in the world's work,
he learned a great deal that makes him understand others
who grope their way toward self-realization through service.

Frank Charles Laubach was born and grew up in Benton,
Pennsylvania, a small town on Fishing Creek, a branch of
the Susquehanna. It was a town of neat white houses, each
with a picket fence guarding the front dooryard and a big,
well-tended garden behind. Frank's father, Dr. John Brittain
Laubach, was a dentist, a lively, joke-loving man, who was
known to half the town as "Uncle Britt" or "Dr. Britt." His
mother was a woman of unusual ability and charm. Those
who knew her say that Frank looks like his mother, with the
same high brow and keen, deep-set eyes.

Harriet Derr Laubach had been a schoolteacher in Hughesville when the merry, brisk, middle-aged dentist began
courting her. In those horse-and-buggy days of the 1880's a
dentist often drove about the countryside like a doctor,
visiting his patients in their homes. He pulled teeth or filled
them or fitted new ones, as needed. "Dr. Britt" always had

7

a joke or a good story to help lessen the pain. He had started his practice in the days when roads were poor and the best means of travel was by horseback. Once he had even ridden as far as Virginia. He had many good tales to tell about the old settlers he had known.

By the time Frank was a small boy "Dr. Britt" was settled in Benton and had an office upstairs over a jewelry shop adjoining the big frame house where they lived. It stood on the main street of the village, close to stores and offices, easy to find when any of his country patients drove into town bringing a child with a swollen cheek or a raging toothache. After the trouble was attended to, "Dr. Britt" would say, like as not, "Better stay to dinner." Hattie Laubach would put on several extra plates, and round the table there would be much good talk and laughter.

Hattie Laubach was the kind of woman to whom neighbors turned in time of trouble. She was never too busy to put a shawl round her shoulders and hurry down the street to help ease the breathing of a croupy baby or to bring round a child half-drowned by falling into Fishing Creek. Her friends were legion. When she went back to Hughesville to visit, her fellow-teachers and old neighbors there gave her such a welcome that a young companion (now a Benton woman past eighty) still remembers wondering how it would feel to be eagerly greeted by so many friends. And yet Hattie Laubach was most of all a homebody. She always found time to read stories to Frank and later to talk with him about the books he had been reading for himself, drawn largely from a small library housed in the jewelry shop next door.

Once, when Frank was a small boy, a phrenologist came to Benton. In the 1880's it was believed that such a man could judge a child's mental power and aptitudes by the shape of his skull and the little "bumps" on it. Hattie Laubach, eager to guide the boy rightly, arranged for an examination by the phrenologist. The man, moving sensitive hands slowly over the child's head, said at last, "Ah, he has real intellectual ability. I advise you, madam, to have him become a lawyer."

Many years later Frank Laubach wrote that he was thankful his parents did not take that advice seriously. Being sensible folk, they gave their children every opportunity they could afford for education, but left them free to choose their own paths in life. Frank grew up much like other boys of that day in small towns all over America—weeding the garden, feeding the pigs, milking the cow, swimming below the dam in Fishing Creek, playing ball under the maples near the schoolhouse, helping with haying out at Uncle Clare's farm, studying his arithmetic under the big kerosene lamp in the living room, teasing his young sister, Bertelle, when she was trying to practice at the piano.

Then, as now, boys of twelve to fourteen had a gang. According to Benton legend, Frank's gang once found him guilty of violating one of their sacred rules. He had told his sister the exact spot in the woods above Fishing Creek where the gang usually met. In solemn conclave they found Frank guilty and declared that the punishment should be hanging. But the culprit, instead of protesting innocence or running away, freely admitted his guilt and agreed that the punishment would be just. Such an attitude took the court by surprise. The leader said, "Shucks! What's the fun if he ain't scared!" and the sentence was remitted.

A cousin remembers Frank as a bookworm. When he visited on their farm, he would always be found, sooner or later, stretched out on the floor with his nose in a book. His uncle said, "Frank'll be a smart man—or a lazy one."

By the time he had graduated from the Benton high school, Frank had decided he wanted to become a teacher. This early ambition, though it lasted only a few years, seems significant in the light of his present role of world teacher. Like many of his generation, he began his teaching in a one-room country school. It stood near a little railroad station called Laubach in the end of the valley where his ancestors had first settled.

The Laubachs had come to Pennsylvania from Germany about 1740. Fifty years later, in the days when Washington was President, a John Laubach had settled in the Fishing Creek valley. He was Frank's great-great-grandfather. With his neighbors he had established the first free public school in the county. From the first the Laubachs had believed in education.

On the rich acres cleared by John Laubach, Frank's grandfather, Andrew Laubach, had built a fine white house and big barns. He was a jolly, hospitable man known as Squire Andrew, farmer, storekeeper, postmaster, justice of the peace. By the time Frank began his teaching career Squire Andrew had died and an uncle was living on the farm. Frank boarded with a family beyond the old covered bridge over Fishing Creek. The schoolhouse, now changed into a dwelling, the old bridge, and the great house and barns of Andrew Laubach are still there in the valley, beautiful against the background of the enfolding hills.

Finding that he really liked teaching, Frank enrolled the following year in the Bloomsburg Normal School about fifty miles from home. One day at morning chapel the students were surprised to see a man in the blue dress uniform of the

United States Army seated on the platform beside the school president. Frank and all the other young fellows straightened their spines and squared their shoulders in unconscious imitation of his military bearing, and the girls fluffed up their pompadours and pulled down their shirtwaists because the soldier was handsome.

The buzz of talk subsided the moment the president rose. He introduced the visitor as Lieutenant Strong, who had a special message for student teachers.

Frank never forgot that brief message. It came from the lips of the young officer in terse, clipped sentences. The United States Government was needing recruits, not soldiers but teachers, because the Stars and Stripes had recently been raised over those islands called the Philippines, far across the Pacific. Everyone knew about Admiral Dewey's victory in Manila Bay, but few had any knowledge of the Filipinos' long struggle for freedom from Spain. They had been tragically oppressed; now they needed teachers. Who would go? Only men were wanted; no women volunteers were accepted (the girls sighed), because living conditions were likely to be hard. It would be a pioneering job; no cowards need apply. The Government wanted the best teachers that could be found, well-trained and physically strong. The service would be for two years.

The lieutenant closed with a personal anecdote: "I happened to be in the first boatload landed in Manila after the surrender. The streets were swarming with children. We couldn't understand them but they followed us, as children will. Pretty soon our chaplain found an empty schoolroom and began teaching the youngsters some English words. They caught on fast. Then along came General Merritt and stopped to see what the crowd was doing. He was pleased and said, 'Captain, I appoint you superintendent of schools. These people want books, not bullets. Carry on.' So that's what we're trying to do. Will you help?"

At the close of chapel the boys of the senior class volunteered to a man. All day the lieutenant held interviews with them, while the campus seethed with excitement. Who would be lucky enough to be chosen? In the evening came the news that two seniors had met the requirements. They were the two outstanding men in the class.

Frank Laubach was too young both in years and in training to volunteer. But how he envied those seniors! And the incident had its influence on the whole direction of his life.

After the next year, equipped with a grade-teacher's certificate, he applied for a position in the schools of Benton, and, young though he was, received the appointment. Everyone knew, of course, that "Dr. Britt's" son was a smart fellow. He was assigned to teach the sixth grade, and he proved to be a good teacher but not entirely successful as a disciplinarian.

Among the girls in the sixth grade was a young cousin of Frank's. One afternoon she was late getting home from school, and, when her mother asked why, she admitted that she had been kept for discipline.

"That mean old Frank!" she sputtered.

"But what did you do?"

"I was only drawing pictures, and—maybe I giggled a little."

"So, you deserved to stay after school," her mother admonished.

"But I've done the same things all the while and he never minded before," wailed the girl.

This state of affairs may have been duplicated in dozens

of schoolrooms supervised by youthful teachers, but, though not unusual, it reveals two aspects of Dr. Laubauch's personality—a certain sternness combined with a long, long patience.

A year or two of teaching made him realize his need for college training. He wanted to enter Princeton, but found that he could not meet the entrance requirements. Just then an opportunity came to attend Perkiomen Seminary as a student and part-time teacher. This famous "prep" school, founded by German Quakers at Pennsburg, was not far from home.

Was it at Perkiomen that he first caught the vision of world-service? Many years later in a letter from the Philippines, dated in June, 1932, he wrote: "It is a shock to learn of the death of Dr. Kriebel, the great president of Perkiomen, and one of the most loyal friends anybody ever had. . . I think that year at Perkiomen was the best year of my whole life, so far as intense work and real earnestness were concerned."

Another teacher who made that year memorable to Frank was the school football coach, Roy Strock. He astonished the boys by holding a mission-study class on Sundays after helping them win games on Saturdays. "It was the man's quiet heroism that impressed us," Frank wrote later. "Strock had lost an eye through an accident only a few months before, but that did not prevent him from playing a good game of tennis nor from volunteering to go to Africa as a missionary."

It was Strock who influenced Frank to join the Student Volunteers, that organization which in his generation was spreading the missionary zeal of Protestant churches among college students. Such men as John R. Mott and Bishop

Thoburn and Bishop Stuntz were even then talking in world terms, as if the earth housed a great family and it was the natural thing to move from room to room; as if missionaries' lives, far from being narrow and limited, were actually like windows opening upon the wide world.

Along with ideals of service, Frank Laubach was developing his scholarly instincts. After graduation from Perkiomen, he entered Princeton. A friend recalls that his letters were full of long words, and her mother teased her, saying, "Run for your dictionary. Here's another letter from Frank."

Nevertheless, no one loved fun better than Frank Laubach. The same friend tells of one of his pranks during a vacation. On the day he was expected home from Princeton, his mother was busy putting his room in apple-pie order to welcome him. The doorbell rang. Answering it, she found a middle-aged man with dark hair and a rather large mustache, who said he was the new Congregational minister in Jamison City, a town nine miles away. He knew friends of the Laubachs there and had come to Benton to have some dental work done by "Dr. Britt" but had missed the train home.

Mrs. Laubach, always hospitable, told him of course he was welcome to spend the night. She took him upstairs to Frank's room, saw that he was comfortable, and then went about her work.

It was nearly time for Frank's train. Soon she heard him come bounding up the porch steps in his usual exuberant way and she flew to the door. There was much to talk about with a boy just home from college, but presently she had to explain about the stranger in his room. Frank didn't mind; he would sleep in the back room.

"Dr. Britt" came home, welcomed Frank in his hearty

way, and then Mrs. Laubach, with supper ready to serve, called their guest. But he had disappeared! When she explained to her husband about him, the dentist said no such person had been in his office. He had never heard of a new minister from Jamison City. Frank asked questions, making her describe him in detail. Presently he left the room and returned wearing a dark wig and a large mustache. While his mother blinked and his father roared with laughter, he proceeded solemnly to ask the blessing before supper.

To help pay his college expenses, Frank sold aluminum ware by house-to-house canvassing during several summer vacations, and was a highly successful salesman. No doubt that skill in mimicry which fooled his mother served him well in the selling game.

After graduation from Princeton in 1909 he went on to Columbia University, where he earned a master's degree in 1912 and a Ph.D. in 1915. He lived and worked during one of those student years at Spring Street Settlement House and learned at first hand some of the problems of city slums.

In 1914 he held a job in the Charity Organization Society of New York and there became interested in the seemingly hopeless work with vagrants. It was the custom to require vagrant men, before they received food or a night's lodging, to do a certain stint of work on the woodpile, in the hope that they would be cured of expecting something for nothing. But over and over again the same vagrants appeared, and Frank Laubach made up his mind to find out why.

He persuaded a philanthropist to underwrite the rent of a large apartment, selected several vagrants most promising as case studies, found jobs for them, and persuaded them to become roomers in his apartment "dormitory." His efforts to rehabilitate them were not a hundred per cent successful, but they were sufficient to win him the name of "Dominie of the Woodpile." The results of his year's study of these men appeared in the thesis he submitted for a doctor's degree in sociology. It was entitled "Why There Are Vagrants."

During these same years the young social worker had been taking courses at Union Theological Seminary and had been ordained a minister of the Congregational Church. But something still more eventful had happened. A pretty, fair-haired neighbor in Benton, whom Frank had known all his life, had suddenly become very important to him. Her name was Effa Seely. She had been graduated from the nurses' training school of Presbyterian Hospital in Philadelphia and had been made night superintendent of nurses there. For a young nurse that was a big responsibility, requiring dignity and sometimes sternness; but it isn't hard to imagine that smiles replaced the stern looks when an old neighbor, now a handsome minister, came to call.

Frank and Effa were married on May 15, 1912. They had decided that they would become missionaries together. For ten years they had both been interested in the Philippines because a cousin of Effa's and another young man of Benton had gone to the Islands among the first groups of teachers sent by the United States Government. Their letters about the wild Moros of the southern island of Mindanao indicated that there might be plenty of adventure and no dull moments in the life of missionaries in that region. The United States Army had been trying to control those Moros ever since 1898. The officer who had accomplished all that military force could achieve was a man by the name of Pershing—a name that later became famous in World War I. Perhaps a nurse and a missionary who understood vagrants could do some good there. Frank and Effa Laubach were eager to go to Mindanao in the Philippines. Frank had already made a resolution which has held through a lifetime: he would go where the need was greatest. He would fight where the ranks were thinnest and the battle hottest. In 1915 the American Board of Commissioners for Foreign Missions of the Congregational Church decided to send the Laubachs to Mindanao.

A woman who was a small girl in Benton at that time remembers the flutter of excitement in the village on the day the Laubachs left. She watched as the dray with its big horses drew up at the hotel and the drayman loaded two huge trunks. Then she had a fleeting glimpse of the young couple when the family surrey rolled away toward the railroad station. They were going to a far-off spot on the map called the Philippine Islands. Would they ever come back to Benton? She had heard one of the neighbors say, "Those Philippine Islands are full of wild men with rings in their noses. Why doesn't Dr. Britt's son have sense enough to stay at home and become a good dentist like his father?"

CHAPTER 3

"Wild Men of Mindanao"

"The way to stop hatred is to start a back-
fire of love."—F. C. L.

A voyage across the Pacific means adventure to most people
even today. In 1915 it was much more thrilling because few
Americans traveled to the Orient. The memories of clipper
ships and the tea trade had faded. Most Americans considered the Philippine Islands as remote as the moon and much
less important. For a few, those far-off Islands "had come on
the map," as Frank Laubach once said, "on May 2, 1898—
the day after Admiral Dewey sank the Spanish fleet in
Manila Bay."

But American ideas about the people of the Philippines
were strangely distorted. During the few months of fighting
just after Dewey's naval victory, all sorts of fantastic stories
were published in this country. Sensational magazines pic-
tured the Filipinos as naked savages with shields and spears
and painted faces. People with lively imaginations assumed
they were cannibals, because it was known that a few cannibals did exist on other Pacific Islands.

Of course these were not the notions held by Frank and
Effa Laubach, when they sailed from San Francisco late in
1915. They knew more than most Americans about the Phil-

ippines; they had read missionary reports and letters from teachers, Effa's cousin and others.

On the long voyage they set about absorbing as much information as they could from books and from other travelers. They studied a fascinating map of the thousands of islands in the group called the Philippines. Effa would often put her finger on the big southern island, Mindanao, and note, with a little start each time, that it lay only ten degrees north of the equator. What was it going to be like keeping house in the tropics? Had they brought with them the right kind of clothes and furniture?

Frank was interested in the history of the Islands. He knew, of course, the main outline of facts: how Magellan, who set out to sail around the world under the Spanish flag in 1519, was killed in those far-off islands of the Pacific; how they were later named in honor of King Philip of Spain and brought under Spanish control. The Spaniards, who had been fighting the Moslems of northern Africa, dark-skinned men known as Moros (Moors), when they found dark-skinned people in the Philippines who were also Moslems, called them Moros and at once began to fight them. It was to the land of those Moros that the Laubachs were going.

The books did not tell much about them except that they were fierce fighters, and that an American Army Post called Camp Keithley was maintained on Lake Lanao. It was the rest of the Philippines with which Spain, and later the United States, had been most concerned.

In the sixteenth century Spain had sent priests and friars as well as soldiers to try to Christianize the island people just as she did the natives in all her American colonies. The friars had discovered that only the people of the southern

islands were followers of Mohammed. The others accepted
Christianity with little opposition, and it was not long before
the Spanish friars dominated the Philippines, except for
Mindanao and the Sulus at the south.

Until about 1890 the Filipinos had submitted to this Spanish rule without much question. As in the Americas, the rule
of Spain was autocratic, but it brought certain benefits. A
university was established in Manila. Sons of wealthy Filipinos were educated and even traveled in Europe. Women
were held in higher regard than in most other Oriental
lands.

But as always, too much power led to corruption. The
Spanish friars had gradually extended their control until
they claimed a tenth of the best land in the Philippines.
Educated Filipinos began to see that their own people were
being cheated of their rights. Slowly a spirit of independence developed, and then open rebellion. The Spanish government tried to put down the revolution by torture, imprisonment, and exile. In 1896, José Rizal, patriot hero of
the Islands, was executed. That was Spain's most tragic mistake. The people were completely aroused and under Emilio
Aguinaldo, they united to end Spanish oppression.

The people of Cuba were likewise fighting for independence from Spain. The intervention of the United States in
Cuba led to intervention in the Philippines as well. But our
leaders were not ready to govern those remote tropical
islands. They knew far too little about them, and the Filipinos knew even less about Americans. Misunderstanding
of motives on both sides led to months of needless fighting.

When at last peace was restored, President McKinley
appointed a commission to study the problems of the Philippines and to make recommendations. Frank Laubach

found one statement in the report of that commission that
interested him exceedingly because it outlined the policy
being followed by the American Government:

"The destiny of the Philippine Islands is not to be a state
or territory of the United States, but a daughter republic of
ours, a new birth of liberty on the other side of the Pacific,
a model of Christian democracy and a beacon of hope for all
the benighted millions of the Asiatic continent."

The books told how the improvement of sanitation and
health had been one of the first government projects. It was
estimated that over a third of the Filipino population in
1900 had tuberculosis. Under American supervision the
death rate was cut in half, and epidemics of smallpox,
cholera, leprosy, and bubonic plague were ended.

But it was the schoolteachers from America who had
made the greatest change of all in the Philippines. In 1900
the Government had sent out a call to colleges and normal
schools for volunteers to teach for two years. It was that
call which Frank had heard at Bloomsburg Normal School,
when two of the best men in the senior class were selected
to go. In 1901 the U. S. Transport *Thomas* had sailed for
Manila with six hundred teachers aboard. These men faced
pioneer conditions. In spite of precautions, some could not
adjust to the tropical climate. Some died of cholera; many
were laid low by malaria, but others came to take their
places. Of the two known to Frank and Effa Laubach, one
had married a Filipina and was making his home in the
Islands.

The school system set up by the Americans was winning
the confidence of the Filipinos. The curriculum included
agriculture, industrial arts, and physical education besides
English and other book subjects. In 1915 the younger gen-

eration were speaking English along with Spanish or one of the Filipino dialects. English was gaining ground as an official language beside Spanish, and most newspapers and magazines in the Philippines were in English.

Fortified with information and bursting with eagerness, Frank and Effa landed in Manila. Their brief stay verified much that the books had told. Manila was an American city set in Spanish background. It was not until they started southward that they felt they had reached the real Philippines.

They took passage on a small steamer bound for Cagayan, a city on the northern shore of the island of Mindanao. It was a journey of three days and nights. At once they were entranced by the scenery. The steamer skirted shores of strange wild beauty, where stately palms towered above the graceful foliage of bamboo and the dense green of mango trees. They had glimpses of terraced rice fields and of coconut groves; of little bamboo houses set high on posts and thatched with nipa palm leaves; of two-wheeled carts drawn by slow, wide-horned carabao.

At towns where the leisurely steamer docked to leave cargo, they sometimes went ashore. Once they rode about in a small carriage called a *calesa* drawn by a little horse hardly larger than a Shetland pony.

Among the passengers on the steamer was an American teacher, returning to Surigao, who told them strange tales of riding over the rough trails of Mindanao on such small horses. He described the mountain streams, which were sometimes dry and sometimes raging torrents, and had to be forded with caution. Often he had crossed a stream by clinging to his little horse's saddle or its mane or its tail, and once he had nearly drowned when the current swept him to the downstream side of the horse and he was deluged with water pouring over the animal's back.

Effa hoped that Frank's work would not involve much traveling, especially after she heard that some of the streams were infested with crocodiles. But the story that fascinated her most was one told by the traveler about a giant lizard he had seen one day as he was riding along a trail.

"It was like some prehistoric monster," he said, "fifteen feet long at least, and as high as a German shepherd dog. When it sat up on its hind legs to look at me, its head was higher than mine, although I was mounted on a small horse. We sat there staring at each other for fifteen minutes."

Effa shivered. "Weren't you scared?"

"Not till afterwards. When I moved, it went crashing away through the undergrowth; so I guess it was more scared than I."

On the steamer the Laubachs had an introduction to Filipino food. The meals were made up largely of rice served in various ways with fish or eggs, a few vegetables, and much fruit. They liked the sweet potatoes, called *camotes,* and the bananas of many different kinds. There were strange fruits, too—mangoes and guavas and pomelos.

When they reached Cagayan, they were warmly welcomed by the Reverend Frank J. Woodward and his wife, who had started a church and a small school for girls. Cagayan had been for many years a center of Spanish culture and was also known for its lively interest in music. The Woodwards said there were pianos in Cagayan which cost much more than the houses in which they stood.

It was a good place in which to adjust to life in the tropics. Frank and Effa enjoyed the work for several months, but they were eager to see Lanao, the land of the Moros. It was not far away. The Woodwards had a house at Camp Keithley, near Lake Lanao, where they went at times for rest and escape from the tropic heat, and the Laubachs joined them on their next trip.

They followed a road that went steeply up along a ravine hundreds of feet deep where the great trees were full of chattering monkeys. At one point they had a view of a glorious shimmering waterfall, the famous Maria Cristina Falls. When at last they came upon Lake Lanao, they were entranced. It lay like a jewel among towering mountain peaks. Along the shore were strange boats with their prows curiously carved and painted. The air was cool and invigorating after the heavy heat at sea level.

It was market day in the Moro town of Dansalan—"the chief social event of the week," said the Woodwards. Frank and Effa sniffed the strange mingled odors of fish and brown sugar and betel nuts and gazed at the crowd with fascinated eyes. Some of the poorer people were in rags of dirty muslin, but others, men and women alike, wore *malongs*, handwoven robes, usually in stripes of yellow, magenta, green, blue—all the colors of the rainbow. The men's were tucked up around their hips; the women's hung full length and sometimes covered the head. The men's turbans and fezzes added still more color, and so did their gay umbrellas. Some men wore white pantaloons and coats with many gold buttons; others a kind of tunic with a sash, and a dagger sticking in it.

"Ten years ago every Moro went armed," said Mr. Woodward. "Now only the fiercer *datos* (chieftains) carry weapons."

A strange mixture of Moro and American buildings made up the town of Dansalan. Moro houses, somewhat more substantial than the light bamboo structures elsewhere in the Islands, were built of roughly split timbers, with gables and beam ends often beautifully carved and decorated. Among them the plain concrete American buildings were a bit incongruous. But the Americans in the town and at the army post were young and gay, and Effa thought she would not be too lonely when Frank made arrangements to start work there.

During their vacation the Laubachs were to eat at the Officers' Club and to occupy the vacant house of one of the officers. At bedtime they were somewhat dismayed to find that all the locks had been removed from the doors, but they barricaded them with two chairs and some sticks of wood.

"There's really no danger," said Frank trying to sound reassuring.

In the dead of night they were wakened by a bugle sounding "To arms!" There was a scurrying of feet in the strange darkness, then silence.

"What is it?" whispered Effa.

"Nothing I hope. The colonel said the Moros have been restless, but—"

Quick, sharp, the report of a gun, then more silence!

Effa lay trembling. Frank peered from a window, but there was no light to be seen in the whole camp. Just as he lay down again, there was the sound of something scraping under the house. Was it a Moro?

They waited in silence for what seemed hours. At last came the bugle sound to disband, and they heard the men scattering across the camp grounds. But they did not sleep the rest of the night, and appeared at the Officers' Club for breakfast, limp and weary-eyed.

"What happened?" asked Frank.

"Oh, there have been threats," the C.O. answered, "so I ordered a call to arms, just to let the Moros know we are prepared. One of the men in loading his gun got excited and discharged it. It gave the governor such a fright that he ordered that soldier to load and unload his gun the rest of the day. He's at it now."

"But," said Frank, "we heard something under the house, rubbing against the posts."

"Goats," said the C.O., laughing. "They do that every night, but they aren't dangerous."

The Laubachs laughed, too, but the C.O. went on: "You know Lanao is still considered a danger zone. On the trails away from Dansalan and the camp, our men are sometimes shot at. You see, these tribes around Lake Lanao were the last to be subdued. Back in the hills there are still outlaw *datos*, suspicious of all Christians. A missionary would just add to our troubles."

He went on to explain that, ever since the time of Magellan, the Moros, like other Moslems, had hated and often fought against Christians—first the Spaniards and then the Filipinos who became Christian. For a hundred years or more they had made raids in their swift, bright-sailed ships on the coasts of the northern islands and carried off captives, much as did the old Vikings of the north Atlantic. For years watch towers were manned all along the coasts to warn of raids by the ferocious Moros.

After this piracy was quelled by gunboats, the Moros retired into the jungles of Mindanao, but at intervals they emerged to fight the Christians. It was part of their faith that anyone killed in fighting the enemies of Islam would go straight to the seventh heaven on a beautiful white horse.

Effa recalled that many letters from home had asked about the "wild men of Mindanao." Perhaps they were not so far wrong as she had supposed.

Reluctantly the Laubachs gave up their plans for starting a school at Dansalan, at least for the time being. They knew that Christian teachers had won the good will of the Moslems in Zamboanga and Jolo. When the time was ripe, they would do the same; they would return to Lanao.

Under the direction of the American Board they settled in Manila, where for a dozen years Dr. Laubach taught sociology, psychology, and education in Union College and Union Theological Seminary. The scholarly life suited him. He wrote several books about the Philippines and was altogether so successful that he was considered for president of the college and seminary. He failed of election by one vote. That apparent failure was momentous not only for him but for millions; if he had become president, probably he would never have returned to Lanao.

Of several children born to the Laubachs during these years, only one had survived the many health hazards in a tropical land, and that was probably because Effa had brought him home to Benton, Pennsylvania, to give him a start. He was named Robert but called Bob. Bob was twelve years old when his father decided to try again the opening of a school in Lanao.

CHAPTER 4

Each One Teach One

"I should rather make good Mohammedans
than bad Christians."—F. C. L.

In December, 1929, when Frank Laubach went back to
Lanao, this land of the Moros was still considered an out-
post, just on the edge of danger. He was hoping to start a
normal school to train teachers for Lanao Province, but to
his dismay he found that the number of educated young
people was far too few for such a school. Most of the population were still illiterate. To be sure, there was a high school
in Dansalan as in other Filipino towns, and the principal
took his meals at the Officers' Club where Frank also
boarded. But the public schools had not won the confidence
of the Moros as they had the people of Luzon and other
islands.

Although the sultans, the *panditas* (priests), and some of
the *datos* (chiefs) could read the Koran in Arabic, they did
little to encourage popular education. Women especially
suffered from ignorance and superstition. Marriageable girls
of wealthy families were at that time confined in towers to
become pale and beautiful and suitable as brides for sultans.
They were rarely seen even by relatives.

Unfortunately, some Christian Filipino teachers, who had
come to the public high school in Dansalan about five years
before, either did not know Moslem customs or chose to

28

flout them. They made love to some Moro girls who were
not kept so strictly confined. The wrathful fathers killed
several of the teachers and burned a number of school-
houses. After that, except for about fifty girls in a dormitory
in Dansalan, few were allowed to attend school.

Into this atmosphere of suspicion and explosive hate,
Frank Laubach walked unsuspectingly at the end of 1929.
He was alone, for it had seemed best that Effa and Bob,
for the time being, should stay at Baguio in the hills above
Manila.

Dansalan looked less prosperous than before. In 1918 the
American troops had been withdrawn from Camp Keithley,
and the Filipino constabulary had taken over, with a few
American officers. Now most of the Western-style buildings
were empty, and the whole place had an air of decline. Even
the Moro houses, with their beautifully carved beam ends
overhanging the street, looked neglected.

Frank Laubach, walking slowly along the familiar streets,
came suddenly upon the charred ruins of a building. It was
one of the schools burned by the angry Moros. Little remained but the concrete foundation, and that would soon be
hidden by clumps of fast-growing bamboo. It seemed like a
symbol of his wrecked hopes and plans. But he shook off
the mood of discouragement. Was he not a missionary bringing a gospel of good will? Surely even these fierce Moros
could not resist that!

Suddenly in the still air the Islam call to prayer rang out
from the mosque at the end of the street: "There is no God
but Allah, and Mohammed is his Prophet."

Resolutely Frank turned back and went into one of the
little shops, or bazaars, that he and Effa had delighted to
visit when they had come to the lake more than ten years

before. He hoped the proprietor might remember him. But in the dim little shop, smelling of oil and sandalwood, he did not find the old Moslem in green turban. A young man wearing a fez was just rising from his knees and rolling up a beautiful prayer rug. He answered Frank's questions briefly and at once turned away to talk with a yellow-turbaned *dato* in the corner, who was chewing betel nuts and spitting through blackened teeth. Frank could not understand their words, for as yet he knew the language only slightly, but from their glances in his direction he guessed they were talking of him. Their expressions were hostile.

While thinking what to say or do next, he stood examining a beautiful silver box inlaid with ivory and decorated with precious stones. The young proprietor said abruptly, "That is not for sale," and carried it into a back room.

Quietly Frank Laubach left the shop and set out for Camp Keithley, where he was to live in the Woodwards' cottage. It seemed to him that the monkeys chattering in the tree-tops were laughing at his discomfiture. But after dinner at the Officers' Club and some talk with the men there, he regained his spirits.

The next day and the next he returned to the town, trying to find old friends and to make new ones. In the bazaars and the market place he talked with men, whenever they would listen, about his plans for a school, about his recent visit to Dapitan, where the Filipino hero, José Rizal, had lived in exile and had started a school for boys. But the Moros listened coldly and turned away without answer.

At the end of a week he was deeply discouraged. After a month he acknowledged to himself that he was beaten. And this failure on the heels of the disappointment in Manila bit into his soul. Frank Laubach was not used to failure.

For several months he had been passing through a profound religious experience, seeking to know God and His will through persistent contemplation and prayer. Now he prayed with renewed fervor. Each evening at sunset, with only his little black dog Tip for company, he would climb Signal Hill behind the cottage. There a view of incomparable splendor lay before him—lakes and mountains and the distant sea. The beauty of sky and hills and shining waters sometimes eased the ache of failure and loneliness, and sometimes made it worse. Often he prayed aloud and then listened with all his soul for an answer to the prayer. One evening, when his despair was deepest, his lips began to move, and it seemed to him that God was speaking through his own voice.

"My child," the voice said, "you have failed because you do not really love these Moros. You feel superior to them because you are white. If you can forget you are an American, and think only how I love them, they will respond."

And Frank Laubach answered, "It is the truth, God. Drive me out of myself, and come and take possession of me and think Thy thoughts in my mind."

And the voice said again through his own lips, "If you want the Moros to be fair to your religion, be fair to theirs. Study the Koran with them."

The next day, when he told some *panditas* that he wanted to study the Koran, they crowded into his cottage eagerly, ready to make him a good Moslem. The man wearing the brightest-colored *malong*, with buttons of ten-dollar gold pieces, brought under his arm a pamphlet which listed the holy books of Islam. He read the titles impressively: the Torah, the laws of Moses; the Zabur, the psalms of David;

the Kitab Injil, the gospel of Jesus Christ; and the Koran of Mohammed.

Dr. Laubach said as best he could in their language, "From childhood I have studied the first three books on your list."

At once they found that there was much to discuss in their common knowledge. Partly in English, partly in the Moro tongue, the *panditas* talked of Jesus as the holiest prophet after Mohammed, and told how God had carried him up to heaven while he was praying in Gethsemane. Dr. Laubach bit his tongue and did not try to correct them. Instead he asked questions and found that several Old Testament patriarchs—Abraham, Noah, Jacob, David—were familiar to them under slightly different names.

After that discussion Frank Laubach realized that he needed to know more about the language spoken by his new friends. It is known as Maranaw. He asked an American officer whether he knew any Moro who could teach the language.

The officer grinned. "Yes, if you aren't too particular, I can recommend an ex-convict, a murderer. When he was sentenced to twenty years, I helped him to appeal his case because I thought the sentence too heavy, since he had killed in self-defense. Pambaya is now my loyal friend and will do anything I ask."

So Pambaya began to teach Maranaw to Frank Laubach and to his assistant, Donato Galia, a graduate of Teachers College, Columbia University, who had arrived to help in the normal school that did not yet exist.

There was no dictionary of the Maranaw language; in fact not a page of the language had ever been printed. The Koran and other books read by the *panditas* were printed in Arabic, using of course the Arabic alphabet. This was too difficult for most people to learn.

Dr. Laubach and his assistant decided that their first step should be to make a dictionary of Maranaw, using the Roman alphabet. But when they tried to write the words they heard, nobody could tell them where one word ended and the next began.

They would ask, "Pambaya, what is the word for *go*?"

Pambaya would shake his head.

"How do you say, 'Where are you going?' "

"Andakasoong," with a smile.

By trial and error they discovered that *anda* was *where*, *ka* was *you*, and *soong* was *go*.

It was slow work, but after six weeks they had a box filled with cards, on which were written thirteen hundred Maranaw words and their meanings.

Mr. Galia learned to speak the language very quickly because he was a native Filipino, and the Visayan dialect is not too different from the language of the Moros. But Dr. Laubach learned slowly at first, because all the Filipino languages seem to an American to say things backwards. Instead of "What have you?" they say "What is had by you?"

The spelling was a problem, too, because the men had decided to use just one letter for each sound and only one sound to each letter. They wanted to avoid the kind of confusion caused in English by *c* and *k* or by the vowels in such words as *wait* and *weight* with the varying spelling of the long *a* sound. Fortunately, Maranaw sounds required only twelve consonants; so there were some left over in the Roman alphabet for other uses. For example, they decided to use *w* (double *u*) for the sound usually rendered in English by *oo* (double *o*).

The *panditas* and a group of young Moros followed the work with great interest, and Frank Laubach eagerly accepted the opportunity to learn from them more about Mohammed. All during his period of discouragement he had been seeking to learn more about prayer and its power. When he told the *panditas* that he was trying to do the will of God every moment of the day, they said, "Any man who tries to do the will of God all the time is like Mohammed himself. We love to listen to you because you tell us beautiful things from the Koran."

And he would answer, "But I learned these things from Jesus."

The work on the dictionary was sometimes stopped altogether because so many Moros came to express their gratitude. "You are the first who has ever tried to appreciate us," they insisted, and would break in on his brief hours of rest to tell him that they feared he was overworking!

About this time he wrote to his father:

"Pioneering is the only life worth living. . . . Every day here has the zest of high adventure. I know perfectly well that there are dangers and near catastrophes, but we get by them and life is all the more thrilling because it is daring."

Trouble with outlaws had flared up again in the jungle, and there was news of fighting. The *panditas* had sometimes encouraged such rebellion, but this time they sent word to the outlaws to cease fighting for the welfare of Lanao. A new spirit was abroad. A Moro from the region of the fighting appeared one day, asking that a school be started there. He produced a New Testament and said he wanted a copy in Maranaw to study.

With the Moros so eager to learn to read their own language, a building for a school was needed, and also a printing press. It seemed as if these needs were met miraculously. A local merchant offered a building that had once been a dance hall and later a motion-picture theater. A friend in Cagayan wrote: "Do you need a press? We could sell two presses and lots of type for 250 pesos, and the printer would come with the outfit."

Frank Laubach nearly wept with joy when he read that letter, and his co-worker Galia whispered, "God is working ahead of us."

When the press arrived, they feared the floor of the old building would not support a thousand-pound machine. They would have to install some sort of foundation for it. But when they went to examine the floor more thoroughly, they discovered a concrete base exactly the right size and shape for the press. When had it been built and for what purpose? They could only guess and be thankful for what seemed another miracle.

Silvino, the printer, arrived and before long began setting up the type for the first page of Maranaw ever to be printed. But when the *panditas* saw the Roman type, they insisted that only Arabic letters would do because Arabic was the holy script of Mohammed. So Pambaya wrote the same sentences in Arabic script on a stencil, and the little sheet was printed with the Roman text on one side and the Arabic on the other. It was the first issue of a small newspaper. Here is a translation of the opening paragraphs:

This is the beginning of a story paper in the Moro language, to be distributed around the four sides of Lake Lanao. All Moros feel delighted because this paper is being started. The leading datos will furnish stories for the newspaper, telling of the famous ancestors of early days and of the events in Mecca and other important places.

Our paper will also be helpful for business. It will tell the price of rice, corn, beans, various kinds of cloth and thread, of silk and woven hemp, of lumber, brass, silver and gold articles, and betel nuts.

Frank wrote to his father, February 16, 1930:

"Tomorrow will be an important day in the history of this province, I believe, for we are going to distribute our first paper. . . . The Moros who have seen the proof are as pleased as though it were bound in gold!"

It was called the *Lanao Totwl* (*Progress*) and there was indeed great excitement the day it appeared. But no Moro except Pambaya could read the side printed in Roman letters, and at once all the young men clamored to learn. A leading *dato* brought a petition from fifteen young men for a night school where they might learn to read their own language.

Frank Laubach and Donato Galia set up their school without any formalities. They borrowed a box of hand-printing letters from the superintendent of schools and prepared charts full of short easy sentences in very large letters. They tried to teach the young Moros those sentences, but it was slow work. They shortened the charts and revised them, but still the process of learning to read was not easy.

They kept on working. They asked the Moros to help them find some "key words" which would make it easy for beginners to remember the letters and their sounds. At last they hit on three common words that contain all the Moro consonants:

Malabanga—the name of a town
karatasa—paper
paganada—to learn

From the syllables of these three key words could be made many other familiar words. For example, from Ma la ba nga

mama—man
ama—father
mala—large
ala—God
lama—yard
lala—to pat

Here was a scheme that would help beginners learn the letters easily. Laubach and Galia made some new charts and tried teaching from them. They worked like a charm! Once the pupil got the idea that certain letters represented certain sounds and these sounds were words he knew, the rest was easy. Maranaw has only four vowels and the remaining three were combined thus:

mi li bi ngi
mo lo bo ngo
mu lu bu ngu

From these syllables other words could be made; for example:

bibi—duck
lobi—coconut
luma—smooth

With these new charts the Moros were soon learning to read, not only words but sentences. In one short hour a man who had never known a letter could read a whole page of his own language. His delight was wonderful to see.

During the next few months Frank's letters to his father were full of stories of amazing experiences:

"A half dozen Moros interrupted this letter. They came in and said they could not wait until tomorrow but had to be taught right away. They had only an hour to spare and

FIRST MARANAW READING CHART
Lesson I

a	ma	la	ba	nga
i	mi	li	bi	ngi
o	mo	lo	bo	ngo
u	mu	lu	bu	ngu

ma ma man	a ma father	la la to pat	a la God	ma la large	la ma yard
mi. mi girl	a mi our	li li name	a li name	li ma hand	li o outside
mo mo chewed	a mo monkey	lo lo dull	a lo hello	ma lo pretty	o lo head
ba ba short	ba ba i woman	la ba profit	ba la pair	ba li a receipt	ba lo clang
bi bi duck	bi ba i push	la bi more	i bi itch	o bi a vegetable	lo bi cocoanut
bo bo to pour	ba bo aunt	la bo prefer	bo la ball	bu la wide	bu l smoke
nga nga open mouth	ba nga island	bo nga fruit	lu nga plural	ma nga a fly	o nga fruit
ngi ngi corner of mouth	la ngi wait	li ngi to turn	lu ngi allow	lu ma smooth	lu mi make flat

wanted all the education they could get in that time. So I have stopped this letter to teach them. While I concentrated on one of them, the rest listened. They have just left the house. I do not expect you to believe me, but here is the fact; this man had finished reading three pages of our newspaper and could read everything I put before him with fair speed. One hour!

"A Moro from a distant village came at five in the evening and I taught him in a half hour. He was unusually bright and very much pleased with himself, and I praised him and told him I wanted him to be a teacher in his village. When he had finished, he took me over where nobody else could hear us and said, 'You taught me to read and you are the best friend I have in the world. I want to do something for you. Is there anybody in Lanao you want me to put out of the way?' I said, 'No, thank you, brother. But you are certainly a very big-hearted man. Go home and teach others and that will make me happy.' The next day I learned that he is one of the outlaws."

At first all the teaching had been done by Laubach and Galia, but as enthusiasm grew, they began training others to teach. After a year they had nineteen paid teachers and a growing list of volunteers.

From the first these teachers were taught to follow the charts exactly. Success depended on their using the method step by step as it had been planned. They were trained to teach by questions, never telling the student what he could answer for himself, but never asking any question he couldn't answer from the chart.

An American lieutenant who saw what was being accomplished and how long it took to make the new charts by hand for each teacher, had two thousand printed in Manila at his own expense. These were soon put to use all over Lanao Province.

Frank often worked at the school and in the printing room from seven in the morning until six at night. Most of his writing he had to do in the evening when his Moro friends

were less likely to interrupt because after dark their fear of
balbal (ghosts) kept them at home. He wrote:

"On market day twice a week, I stand from seven to
twelve before a chart in the market place while people
crowd around trying to get near enough to learn to read,
almost pushing me off my stool in their eagerness to be next.
I do not see how my teachers get time to record the names of
their students; I seldom do."

"As I finished breakfast about six-thirty and arose from
the table, there came a knock at the door. I turned the knob
and there crowded into my little house sultans and *hadjis*
and *datos*; sixty tried to get in, but some had to stay outside
for want of room. They had hired a launch and had come
twenty miles to be examined for they had learned to read
Moro with English letters. We marched down the road a mile
to our school, and there we spent the whole forenoon in
joyously throwing compliments at one another. . . . On our
school wall is a motto: 'In five years Lanao the most literate
province in the Philippines.' These men declared, 'Less than
five years, much less.' "

One of the most successful young Moro teachers was Gani
Noor. He was nephew of a *hadji* who had been befriended
by General Bullard twenty-five years before. Gani Noor real-
ized what the printing press might mean to his people. He
began helping Dr. Laubach to collect and print many of the
Moro epic songs, especially those about their ancient hero,
Bantugan. Thousands of Moros knew the songs by heart.
They were sung at every fiesta and every wedding.

These songs about Bantugan are to Moros what the *Odys-
sey* has been to the Western world. To have them recorded
in print was very exciting to them and made the *Lanao
Progress* more popular than ever. The familiar words helped

to make reading easy, but also strengthened their habit of singing what they read. Effa Laubach, who had by that time joined her husband at Dansalan, recalls that one day, when she had started on a journey by boat, she heard a strange chanting from somewhere on deck, and found a man stretched out on some bags of copra, *singing* his newspaper to the sky and sea!

In the success of the reading campaign, Frank Laubach had not lost sight of his real purpose in Lanao. Reading was not an end in itself, but a means to an end. He had come to teach the Christian way of life and had begun, as all good missionaries do, by practicing it. He did not urge these Moslems to be baptized or to join his church, but they showed a growing interest in the services. Often the windows of the room that served as a church were crowded with faces of those watching from the outside. Sometimes, when invited by the *panditas*, Dr. Laubach worshiped with them in their mosques.

Each week at his own church services he talked about one of the prophets, or *nabis*, whose stories appear both in the Old Testament and the Koran. The Moros showed so much interest that he decided to print these talks in a series of pamphlets. Each began with what the Koran tells about the prophet and continued with the story as given in the Bible. The last of the series was about Nabi Isa, or Jesus.

For the eager new readers Donato Galia wrote and printed a little book of history from the Moro point of view. The doctors in the government hospital prepared a booklet of simple lessons in hygiene. All this printed matter was read almost before the ink was dry. The printing was slow work because of the limited supply of type at hand. After only a few pages were set, the printing had to be done and the

type distributed so that it could be used again. Frank wrote
to his father: "If you ever started a wagon down a hill and
then found it was getting away from you, you realize how
we feel with our press. We are behind the demand hopelessly."

A young Moro came to the school one day asking, "Have
you a new issue of the paper?"

"Not until next Monday."

He began to walk the floor. "What will the young ladies
do? They will be discouraged if they have nothing to read.
They will finish this paper in a day. Then what?"

"Will they do something desperate?" Frank asked, wanting to laugh at the young man's solemn concern. He was one
of the volunteer teachers who was having great success in a
neighboring *barrio* (village).

"No," he said, "the princesses will not poison themselves—
nor me either." He began to smile. "I could not blame them
if they did, however. I have played a trick on them." He
chuckled. "It was only to make them learn fast—but now the
joke is on me. I cannot keep up with them."

Frank begged him to tell what trick he had used.

"It was nothing—but it worked. The most beautiful *ba-i*
(princess) in the house of Sheik Borabong learned to read
very fast, but the others were indifferent. So I persuaded a
handsome young man to write a love lyric to the bright *ba-i*,
and I took it to her when I went to give the next lesson in
that household. It was—ah, a very fine lyric. It called her the
most charming lady in Lanao, not only beautiful but learned,
more lovely than the singing waters of the Maria Cristina
Falls, more to be desired than golden fruit. She read the
lyric to the other princesses, and at once they all desired
learning. I could not teach them fast enough. They devoured

the lessons. And now they wish a new paper, a new book every other day! What shall I do?" The look of distress reappeared on his face.

"Do?" Frank Laubach burst out laughing. "Just tell all the other teachers about your trick and find us some love lyrics so that we can print one in the *Lanao Progress* every week."

It was not long before six hundred women and girls had learned to read. Every week some high *dato* brought his daughter to Dansalan, begging that she be allowed to board at the *madrasa* while she studied, but the school was not yet equipped as a boarding school.

One morning a group of *datos* came to offer a piece of land for a girls' dormitory and school. It was beautifully situated near the lake, and the men said, "It is not for sale to anybody, but we give it to you without asking a cent."

Dr. Laubach thanked them and could not find it in his heart to tell them just then that there would be no money to put up a building on the land. The depression had struck America, and funds which had supported the work in Lanao were dwindling every day. He faced a bitter problem. Now, just when enthusiasm for learning was at its height, he must tell his new friends the budget would have to be cut in half. He would have to drop twelve of the staff and cut the small salaries of the rest.

As long as possible he put off telling the bad news, but finally came a day, July 26, 1931, when all those who had been teaching gathered to make their monthly reports. One man had taught forty-one women and seventy-one men to read in the past month. Realizing the hours of devoted work represented by such figures, their leader was sick at heart. As teacher after teacher reported his success, the room grew tense with excitement. When the names of the new readers had all been reported and counted, there were fifteen hundred and twenty-one in all, and three hundred of them were women.

At once fifty men arose and volunteered to become teachers. And Dr. Laubach sat there as if paralyzed, knowing he must soon break the bitter news about lack of funds. Somebody moved that a gigantic fiesta be held to celebrate the year's success. The sultans and *datos* voted with a roar that a month from that day they should hold such a fiesta as had never been seen in Lanao.

That afternoon Frank Laubach called in twelve of his paid teachers, one by one, and told them he could not pay them any longer. "It would be easier for me to jump into the lake than to face you with this news," he said.

Knowing the excitable nature of the Moros, he half-expected some of them to fly into a rage. All were dejected, some turned pale, but not a man showed resentment. They saw that their leader was deeply disturbed and they faced the disappointment with loyalty. Those who had any means of subsistence, even the slightest, volunteered to continue teaching without pay. By August the number of volunteer teachers had risen to a hundred and seventy-five.

True to their promise, the Moros went ahead with plans for a great fiesta to celebrate the growing success of the literacy campaign. It was held in a *barrio* situated near the lake among rich rice fields. The Laubachs had to walk for several kilometers along the rice terraces to reach the *barrio*. Just as they arrived it began to rain heavily, putting an end to the horse races and preventing the horse fight, which is an exciting part of any Moro fiesta. The Laubachs were not sorry, for they knew that horses are often killed in these fights.

The *barrio* was a kaleidoscope of gayly colored umbrellas, which Moros made by sewing yellow, orange, or magenta silk, bordered with silver beads, over the frame of an ordinary umbrella. These above the bright turbans and *malongs* seemed doubly brilliant in the rain.

The Laubachs were escorted to the largest house in the *barrio*, home of Kakai Dagalangit, a most important *dato*. Half the crowd tried to follow, all begging to learn to read and write. They sat in a close circle on floor mats in a large room which had been made ready for a crowd by drawing back the heavy cotton curtains that usually divide a Moro house into sections. Each wife and her children occupy a section, surrounded by great bags of corn and rice and by the wooden chests in which their personal belongings are kept. From the ceiling of the big room were hung gay banners, and the walls were bright with weaving done by the women.

Today the women and girls crowded around Effa Laubach. Many clamored to be taught to write their own names, while small boys and girls, many of them naked, crowded close, shouting letters of the alphabet to prove they were learning to read.

Suddenly the clamor was drowned by the booming crash of *agongs*, great brass gongs hung from the rafters and beaten like drums. Six old men were beating six *agongs*, and the tumult nearly shattered the Laubachs' nerves. It lasted for fifteen minutes; then the *agongs* were again hidden in their beautiful basket-and-cloth coverings, and women began bringing in food. They served it on low brass *tabaks* (tables), each a masterpiece of metalwork. Hard-boiled eggs in a nest of red rice made a festive dish.

All afternoon the rain drummed on the iron roofing of the house. More people kept crowding in. Some taught others to read. A priest recited part of the Koran, his tongue tripping off the words so fast that it was a marvel to hear.

At sunset the muezzin gave the familiar signal for the Moslem hour of prayer. Dr. Laubach was invited to go to the mosque, but first he had to follow the Moslem custom of washing hands and arms, face, head, and feet. Then with the others he entered the mosque barefoot. To his surprise, a priest's hat was put on his head and he was led to the front, where he knelt on a beautiful prayer rug beside the *dato* and an Arab sheik. In a high tremulous voice, the sheik chanted the service in Arabic. In spite of the strange language, which most of the worshipers, as well as he, could not understand, a sense of deep reverence filled the place. Laubach's respect for his Moslem friends grew. He wondered how long it would be before the whole world would come to understand that the God of this vast universe is the God of all men and all religions.

The worshipers went home to a hearty meal of beef and *camotes*, fruit, spices, and sweetmeats, after which Dato Dagalangit recited his genealogy, claiming to be descended from Mohammed on his mother's side and from Indra Patra on his father's side.

The Laubachs began to grow drowsy, but they soon learned that fiesta nights are not for sleeping. A young woman in a gold and purple *malong* began to sing a *bayok* (lyric) in a sweet, plaintive voice, and shouts of delight almost drowned her tones. Then at the opposite end of the room an older woman, her head covered with her *malong*, began another *bayok*. She sang with deep feeling; her beautiful voice seemed to express the tragedies of hundreds of women of Islam.

Back and forth the two women sang until midnight. Then the younger woman left, and an old sultan began one of the long *darangans* (epics) about the renowned Bantugan. It was taken up by the woman with the beautiful voice; and so on and on responsively the two sang through the night. Every little while the crowd would join in a familiar part of the long, long story. Three nights are required for singing the entire epic.

At daybreak the music ended, and the Laubachs prepared to leave. But before going they asked the *dato* to let them take some pictures of him and of his family. He was reluctant because devout Moslems have a great prejudice against pictures and images of every kind. At length he consented to pose with his favorite wife and their small son, probably because the pretty young wife was so eager to be photographed. As she stood under a palm tree in the early sunlight, she was very beautiful in her softly draped green and yellow *malong*; but what would she be like after twenty years if her life followed the usual pattern of Moro women? Would the changes that were starting in Lanao help to give her more freedom, wider horizons of thought, books and magazines to read?

Not long after the great fiesta, Kakai Dagalangit, having heard about the lack of funds for the literacy campaign, came to Dr. Laubach with his eyes glittering. "This campaign," he said, "shall not stop for lack of money. It is the only hope for Lanao. Everybody who learns must teach somebody else. If he doesn't I'll kill him!"

Smiling at the man's violent good will, Laubach was suddenly electrified by the idea. He saw that nothing could be better for a newly literate person than to try sharing his skill with a neighbor. It would be good for him and good for the neighbor. It would fix in the new reader's mind all that he had learned. It would give him a new feeling of importance and self-respect and, best of all, train him in the spirit of sharing. If every learner actually became a teacher, literacy could spread like a prairie fire.

Thus from the fierce loyalty of a Moro to his own people came the idea of "each one teach one"—a method which has helped to make Laubach literacy campaigns successful all over the world.

CHAPTER 5

A Bridge to the East

"The world is sick of hatred and crime, and yet it is afraid to trust love."—F. C. L.

By the fall of 1931 news of the remarkable things going on in Lanao had spread all over the Philippines. Teachers from neighboring provinces and government officials came to observe the Maranaw Folk School, or *madrasa*, as it was called, and were enthusiastic about what they saw. In response to a request, Dr. Laubach and Mr. Galia made charts with key words for teaching the Visayan dialect, spoken by the greatest number of people in the central islands. These charts worked so well when put to use that soon all the provinces in the Islands, speaking about fifteen different dialects, were clamoring for help.

The National Christian Council invited Dr. Laubach to come to Manila. There he was in demand to speak in churches and schools, before women's clubs and Boy Scouts. Students in agricultural schools and high schools volunteered to go home and teach their parents how to read and write their own language. The *barrio* schools were opened at night so that teachers might train others how to teach. The same key-word method was used in preparing charts in various dialects. Soon the volunteer teachers were reporting that as they went along the streets, children would sing out: "There go our teachers! Malabanga, Milibingi, Molobongo."

At one meeting held in a Y.M.C.A. building there was such a crowd that those at the back could not see the charts at all. Out of the crowd came a Chinese, who told how he had helped the famous Jimmie Yen (the man who simplified Chinese for coolies) to teach his own people in China. "We used lantern slides," said the man. After that, slides showing the charts in four dialects were made, and then it was easy for large crowds to watch a demonstration of teaching.

Besides helping to prepare the charts in the different dialects, Dr. Laubach began training a group of persons to teach the six thousand prisoners in old Bilibid prison. Always his thoughts turned to those most helpless or in greatest need.

When Governor General Theodore Roosevelt, Jr., stated there was some fear that the literacy campaigns might be used for Protestant propaganda, Dr. Laubach suggested that he appoint a non-sectarian committee to coordinate all the agencies interested in literacy. The director of the Bureau of Education gave his approval of the work started in the high schools, and the Philippine Education Company consented to act as a secular headquarters for the movement, and to print and sell packets of the necessary teaching materials.

Behind all this enthusiasm for education was a growing national pride. At the Muños Agricultural School, during Dr. Laubach's visit one of the teachers rose to speak to the students.

"Boys," he said, "do you remember how our national hero, Dr. José Rizal, risked his life to return to the Philippines during his exile and cut the cataracts from his mother's eyes to save her from blindness? You can all be Rizals and cut the cataracts of illiteracy from the eyes of your mothers and fathers and neighbors."

The students promised to a man that during the next vacation they would try to teach everyone in their own families to read.

Laubach sympathized thoroughly with the patriotic ideals of the Filipinos, but he had his eyes on still more distant goals. He had noted long before, while studying the history of the Philippines, that their role in the Orient was unique. They had been Christianized (except for the Moslems on Mindanao and Cebu) centuries before Western influence began to touch the rest of the Far East. Now if this wave of interest in literacy could also stir new zeal for the Christian way of life, this light might spread over the continent of Asia. The Philippines lie at its very doorstep. They have trade with China, Japan, Malay, Burma, Indonesia. If sixteen million Filipinos were to become literate and zealously Christian, what a golden link of good will and understanding they might create between East and West!

Returning to his work in Lanao, Dr. Laubach found that many young Moros, after learning to read their own Maranaw, were coming daily to the *madrasa* to try reading newspapers in English. Some had learned to read and write English in the public schools, but had lost these skills and were eagerly renewing them. Building on their interest, he began to organize English-speaking youth groups in various centers all over Lanao. The *Lanao Totwl*, which had grown to several pages, was now printed partly in English and partly in Maranaw.

Laubach's chief purpose in organizing the youth groups was to stimulate a spirit of service to their own communities, for that spirit seemed to be lacking in the training of Moslem young folk. Most of the people were self-centered and inclined to think anyone a fool who gave time, effort, or money for the common good. With the boys cooperating, nine ways were listed in which the new societies might serve:

1. By finishing the literacy campaign that had been started.

2. By helping to distribute the newspaper being published in Maranaw.

3. By helping the government, the Red Cross, and the Anti-Tuberculosis Society to educate the people.

4. By holding meetings at which experts on agriculture, animal husbandry, and health laws might speak.

5. By distributing new kinds of fruit, vegetables, and trees.

6. By fighting locusts, wild pigs, monkeys, rats, and other pests.

7. By studying the ideals of the Boy Scouts and the principles of ethics.

8. By promoting all sorts of recreation, such as baseball, volley ball, and other games.

9. By keeping peace and trying to reconcile enemies.

All this was Christianity in action. Without realizing it, the young Moros were putting into practice some of the teachings of their own prophet Nabi Isa (Jesus). Their interest in learning to read their own language had become a yeast to leaven the whole life of Lanao.

Some of the young men were even fired with the idea of going to other lands to teach the millions who cannot read. One day when the new governor general, Theodore Roosevelt, Jr., came to visit the *madrasa* they showed him a big map of the world which they had made with Lanao as its center. Whenever a letter came asking about the literacy campaign, they would fasten on a bright silk thread, running from the country whence the letter had come to Lanao. "We must go and help those other people," they would say.

They were delighted when Mr. Roosevelt, after studying the map, asked to have charts of the Maranaw lessons sent to Puerto Rico, where he had been governor general before coming to the Philippines.

Early in 1934 the United States Congress passed a bill providing a plan for Philippine independence. The Islands, after establishing a constitutional government, should become a self-governing commonwealth and after ten years an independent republic. Naturally the nationalist spirit increased rapidly. The Moros were worried for fear they might be ruined when the time came for independence. They were not yet allowed to hold elections because not enough of the population could read and write. They realized, therefore, the importance of literacy. They must be ready to choose their own leaders and to send representatives to the national government. Otherwise they might be governed by men from the other islands. Already hundreds of immigrants from the northern islands were taking up land in their province. They would be outnumbered if they did not soon win the right to hold elections.

The *Lanao Totwl* of June 1, 1934, carried a short article headed:

NEW PASSION FOR EDUCATION

The granting of independence to the Philippines has given a new impetus to the literacy campaign . . . because the Maranaw people are determined to become a regular province . . . When the signatures of 60,000 adults have been secured, a large book will be carried to Manila, and the Legislature will be asked to change Lanao from a special to a regular province.

Macaindeg, the head printer at the *madrasa,* used every opportunity to impress on the young people the importance of learning to read and write and of teaching others. He urged them to read the newspapers and keep informed concerning their own province, the government of the Philippines, and events in the United States and the whole world.

The *Lanao Totwl* by 1933 was like a small magazine of twelve to twenty pages, with an attractive cover of Moro design on colored paper, the arabesque border usually framing a picture of some person or event of recent interest. It was published twice monthly and carried local news such as the celebration of Garden Day by the schools; national news, such as the meeting of the Constitutional Convention; and international items about plans for a Pacific airline or a world peace and disarmament conference. It was full of significant items on the care of children, health, diet, agriculture—the value of tomatoes and of papayas in the diet, how to grow more rice per acre, soil erosion, using rice hulls for fertilizer. On the inside back cover Philippine laws regarding property and other matters were printed in English and Maranaw in parallel columns. On the outside of the back cover there was always part of a Maranaw epic poem.

The printing press in Dansalan was as busy as a press could be. Besides the newspaper, it turned out an English-Maranaw dictionary, the Gospel of Luke in Maranaw, and thousands of pamphlets on all sorts of subjects: "The New Miracle Rice," Motherhood and Baby Care," "Moro Folklore," "Life on Its Highest Levels," "Where Christians and Moslems Are Brothers."

And Frank Laubach, still experimenting with the power of prayer, knew in his heart that without the vision of God's will that had come to him in those prayerful hours on Signal Hill, none of these things would have come to pass.

When the new constitution for the Philippines was completed in 1935 and Constitution Day was celebrated in Dansalan, the Laubachs were on their way home on furlough. The government of the new Commonwealth at once established a Division of Adult Education, and took over responsibility for teaching people to read. Night schools were established all over the Islands and "literacy wagons" were sent out to attract the illiterate adults and give them lessons. In 1937 Tagalog was declared the national language of the Philippines, but of course this did not end the use of other dialects or the need for literacy work.

By 1941, when the tragedy of war struck the Philippines, the same Moros who had resented both United States soldiers and teachers were among the most loyal citizens in resisting the Japanese invasion. Ten thousand of them signed a pledge of loyalty, and most of these were men who had learned to read at the Lanao *madrasa.* The stories of their heroism during the war still remain largely untold. Perhaps among them and the other Filipinos will arise a poet or writer of fiction who will open the eyes of Americans and the whole world to the admiration they deserve. A collection of short stories called *Philippine Cross Section,* edited by Maximo Ramos and Florentino B. Valeros, and published in 1950, shows that Filipinos, writing in English, can create real literature in a language not their own. Some of them feel that English should be promoted as the language of the Philippines, because "a people will best understand the world of today in English, and they will best make themselves understood by the world in English."

This statement would probably not be accepted by most

Asians today in the face of the rising tides of national spirit and the suspicious attitude toward all influences from Europe and America. But the leadership of such men as Carlos Romulo, delegate from the Philippines to the United Nations, who served as President of the Assembly in 1949 and later as Ambassador to the United States, may yet show that, as Frank Laubach dreamed, the Philippines are truly a bridge between East and West.

CHAPTER 6

"Co-operative Discovery"

"It takes the revelation of all to make the fully rounded truth. Help us to remember, Lord, that Thy truth needs co-operative discovery, just as do all inventions."—F. C. L.

In the early 1930's teachers in mission schools in southern Asia began to hear about the new way of learning to read— the "each-one-teach-one" way in the Philippines. Letters reached Frank Laubach from missionaries in India—men who had struggled for years to lift the great wet blanket of illiteracy that hung over all their work.

But could lessons like those in Maranaw and the other Philippine dialects be made in languages not so phonetic— languages having several symbols for one sound? And would the each-one-teach-one idea work in other lands?

As to the second question, Dr. Laubach had little doubt. He was sure that he had found the best way to teach the millions of illiterates all over the world. Each new learner who became a teacher not only multiplied the numbers of new readers; he also remembered better whatever he tried to teach; he acquired new dignity by becoming a teacher; and he learned the joy of sharing.

But whether the charts based on key words could be made in languages with more complicated alphabets Laubach had some doubt. While he was wondering, his enthusiastic secretary, Minnie Schultz, who had come from the States in 1931, persuaded him to prepare a form letter to persons along the route he would travel when he started home on furlough. So confident was Miss Schultz that she mailed, not fifty, but five hundred of the letters. Invitations poured in from Singapore, Ceylon, various parts of India, Syria, Turkey, Palestine, Cairo. Since there was no money available for such undertakings except the travel allowance of a missionary and family on furlough, it was decided that Effa and Bob, who was just graduating from the Lanao Public High School, would stay in Lanao two months longer and meet Dr. Laubach after his visits in India.

When his Moro friends heard of these plans they were delighted. Would he not be carrying blessings to other Moslems in many lands? Hundreds escorted him to his steamer on January 20, 1935, and thronged aboard the ship. With glowing faces they listened till every *dato* had made a speech; then the sheik said: "We are going to pray for you." They were so crowded on the deck that they could not bow in the usual Moslem way; so they stood with hands extended, turning the palms now up, now down, while the priest prayed that the blessings of Allah should be upon their American friend as he carried the good work of Lanao to less fortunate nations.

In early February, 1935, a steamer from Singapore to Bombay plied its way swiftly across the Indian Ocean. In a corner of the deck, shielded from the tropical sun, three travelers, instead of lying relaxed in steamer chairs, were gathered around a table strewn with papers. On the papers were lists of letters and words that looked somewhat like the Maranaw reading chart, but the letters had strange shapes. The woman was bent over a thick book labeled Hindi-English dictionary.

"It looked so easy when I saw your Maranaw charts, Dr. Laubach," she murmured. She was a missionary returning to her station in India.

Dr. Laubach smiled ruefully. "I knew it would be different, Miss Pope. In Maranaw we had sixteen letters, but in Hindi there are fifty."

"Besides those that are split and spliced because of the vowel sounds being understood," said the dark-eyed man across the table. "But surely we can find some key words just the same. May I have the dictionary a moment?" He spoke English, like his companions, but with the accent of Oxford University. He was an Indian who had become interested in what his fellow travelers were trying to do.

All three bent again over the half-made charts, and for several minutes there was no sound but the splash of the waves. Then Frank Laubach leaned back with a sigh.

"Mr. Mehrotta," he said, "I'm going to cable my wife to come on the next ship. I'm going to sail right past India. I'm licked."

Mehrotta looked up with dismay in his eyes. "No, no, you can't! This is what India needs most of all. Our people are 90 per cent illiterate. We must find a way. Let's try again. Let's put the letters that sound alike in families—*p* and *b* in one family, *t* and *d* in another, and so on. Perhaps then we can find the right key words."

Again the two missionary teachers and the Indian bent over the papers. Suddenly the puzzle was solved. In half an hour they had arranged the letters in fifteen families and had found five good key words for the first chart. By the time they reached Bombay they had completed a set of key-word lessons—the first ever made in an Indian language. Frank Laubach was elated. Here was something hopeful to offer to discouraged workers among the illiterate millions of India.

He took the train to Nagpur where the National Christian Council was meeting, and was greeted with the exciting news that a friend had arranged for him to have an inter-view with Mahatma Gandhi the following week. Gandhi—the little man with the big heart, the Great Soul of India, beloved by the hungry multitudes! If he approved of this new way of teaching, it would be accepted almost without question. But there must be some lesson charts to show him.

Four Indian teachers offered to help prepare charts in Marathi. For six days they worked steadily putting lessons into the proper form. They even made them in color, so that they were truly beautiful.

At his little house in Wardha, the Mahatma dressed in *khaddar* (homespun cotton) received his American guest courteously but very simply. They sat on rugs, cross-legged in Indian fashion. Two disciples of their great leader hovered near. When Dr. Laubach unrolled the Marathi charts, Gandhi peered at them through his spectacles for a moment, then said abruptly, "I doubt whether India ought to become literate."

His guest could hardly believe his ears. Surely this man who had devoted twenty years to helping the poor could not have meant those words!

"Why do you say that?" he asked.

"The literature you publish in the West is not fit for India to read," said the Mahatma. "Look at what your people are writing and selling to us on any railway stand. And besides, many of the greatest benefactors of the human race have been illiterate—for example, Mohammed."

Frank Laubach did not reply at once. He was praying silently that his answer might be one full of truth and persuasion.

"Mr. Gandhi," he said slowly, "you are right. But on the other hand, millions of us admire *you* and have read your books with great blessing. If you had not written these books, and if we had not learned to read, we should never have heard of you."

The Mahatma dropped his head, saying meekly, "Still I think I would have done a little good."

Dr. Laubach, seeing that the way was open, went on. "I believe that the greatest single blessing that ever came to this world is the life and teaching of Jesus Christ. If accounts of his life had not been written and if we had not been able to read the Gospels, we would know very little about him."

The Mahatma moved his head up and down slowly and silently for a few moments, looking intently at his guest. At last he spoke. "I really do believe in literacy for India. Indeed, I myself have probably taught, indirectly, thirty thousand to read. But by far the largest question for India is how to feed her hungry multitudes."

"That is exactly why India needs to become literate," said Dr. Laubach earnestly. "The right way to lift the masses above hunger is to teach them to lift themselves. Your illiterates have been the victims of educated scoundrels, who have kept them in debt all their lives. Literacy is the only road I see to their complete emancipation."

But the Mahatma shook his head, and after a little talk of other matters, the interview ended. That evening as Dr.

Laubach rode back to Nagpur, his British companion remarked, "Gandhi thinks you are attempting the impossible."

" 'Fools rush in where angels fear—' " quoted Frank Laubach with a laugh, knowing in his heart there were many in India besides Gandhi who thought that his "lightning literacy" plan was hopeless and a little presumptuous. And he was not surprised, remembering the vastness of India, its seething millions, their long history, and their slow struggle for independence. Who was he to think that he could help this half-awakened giant?

In a mood of deep discouragement the following afternoon he boarded a train for the Mennonite mission at Dhamtari. Even at five o'clock in February the heat was stifling. He sank limply into a second-class compartment and watched the sweating crowd push toward the third-class coaches, their sandals and bare feet shuffling in the dust, the men's legs bare below the *dhoti* and cotton shirt, the women's graceful saris framing weary, patient faces. Into the second-class coach came a Moslem in a richly embroidered fez, then a well-to-do Hindu with a turban of brocaded silk and a long tunic over white-cotton jodhpurs. He was accompanied by his daughter in a soft rose-silk sari, and they were followed by a porter with a mountain of luggage on his head.

Watching the life about him, Frank Laubach thought of a day in Benton long ago when, stretched in the shade of an apple tree, he had spent a hot afternoon completely absorbed in Rudyard Kipling's *Kim*—the book that first made India live for him. Here after forty years were the same people, and he felt as if the red-headed waif Kim and the patient old Lama might appear at any moment.

When the tropic night descended swiftly, he stretched out in the bunk, and, finding no blankets, remembered he had been warned that travelers in India must carry their own bedding. What did it matter? The heat was still oppressive. Exhausted, he fell asleep. But at midnight he wakened with his teeth chattering. Luckily he had a light overcoat in his luggage. Putting it on, he lay down again and tried to get warm by thinking of the hot sun and soft breeze across the lake at faraway Lanao. Why had he ever left his friendly Moro people? Why had he dared to think he could help India? What if the lessons were a complete failure?

Before daybreak he tumbled wearily out onto the station platform at Raipur, expecting a tedious wait of three hours for the train to Dhamtari. Almost at once a Westerner in white shorts walked up to him and said:

"My name is Moyer. Are you Laubach?"

"Moyer! I thought you lived a hundred miles from here."

"I do, but I just drove in to meet you and take you down to the mission."

"And you got here at four A.M.! Did you get any sleep?"

"Yes, plenty. I slept on the station benches."

Laubach put a hand on his shoulder. "Man, if you hadn't been here, I might have taken the next train for Bombay. I'm scared about your expectations. We can't be sure these key-word lessons will work in India."

"Never mind," said Moyer. "We are all praying, and God, more than anybody else, wants us to win."

He led the way to a shabby-looking car and they were soon on the highway. It was still dark as they sped along a road through a dense jungle, and the lights of the car made the shadows seem even darker. Suddenly Mr. Moyer jammed on the brake. As the car slowed, Frank Laubach saw a great beast lying in the road just ahead.

"Tiger," said Moyer.

The big cat had evidently been asleep. It stretched, for all the world like a huge pet pussy, rose, and blinked into the headlights, then moved lazily aside, but stood peering not five feet from Dr. Laubach's elbow as the car picked up speed.

"Do you see them often?" he asked.

Mr. Moyer nodded. "But they've never leaped at a car yet."

So this was India—a sleeping tiger. But suddenly his anxiety about the lessons was gone.

> "Tiger, tiger, burning bright
> In the forests of the night,
> What immortal hand or eye
> Could frame thy fearful symmetry?"

Surely Moyer was right. It was part of God's plan that India should be literate.

For a month Dr. Laubach worked with American and Indian teachers in the Dhamtari mission, trying to improve the lessons in Hindi. Each evening they all went to a village near by to try out the lessons on some leather workers who were not only illiterate, but belonged to the class called "untouchables" according to the Hindu caste system. The lessons went so well that it was agreed they should be printed even though they were still far from perfect.

The following month Dr. Laubach traveled to South India and joined Dr. Mason Olcott, head of the Union Teachers' Training School near Katpadi, and a group of teachers who wanted to try making lessons in two other languages. Half of them worked on lessons in Telugu, a language beautiful in sound and spoken by over twenty-six millon people. The rest worked on Tamil which, some claim, is the world's oldest language. It is also spoken by millions. Dr. Laubach acted as adviser to both groups and in the evenings they would go out to one of the neighboring villages, gather the people from their low mud huts under a powerful Mazda lantern, and try teaching them to read. Then they would return and go to bed on pallets spread in one room of the schoolhouse. It was terribly hot, and often Frank longed to carry his pallet out of doors, but he was warned that panthers lived among the rocks close by.

After two weeks a third group of teachers arrived. They were from the Moslem Government School of Vellore and wanted to prepare lessons in Urdu. This is the language spoken by most of the Moslem population. With these Moslems, Dr. Laubach soon felt at home, but their zeal for work was so intense that he was almost exhausted by the time the president of the Arabic College in Madras came and took him home.

Missionaries and teachers, both Moslem and Hindu, gathered for demonstrations of the charts and were so enthusiastic about the lessons that Laubach was filled with misgivings.

"But they are not good enough yet," he kept warning them. He knew that months of patient work were needed to improve the charts.

"Yes, yes, of course," they said, and continued to put garlands of flowers around his neck and to praise him in grateful speeches.

Two months were gone. It was time to meet Effa and Bob and his diligent secretary at Colombo, chief port of Ceylon. As he turned his back on India, Laubach wondered whether he had done well or ill and whether his new friends there would ever want to see him again.

The next stop was in Cairo, Egypt, and there a surprise awaited him. A group of forty Christian workers had already gathered, eager to make lessons in Arabic.

"We have read about you and your Moro friends," the Egyptians among them said. "Do the same thing for us in Egypt that you did for them."

The secretary of the group had even provided a book called *Phonetics of Arabic* in which someone had arranged the letters in families just as Mr. Mehrotta had done in Hindi. The forty workers took turns in shifts of ten and had such fun finding key words and making charts that, in two days, they had put together a set of trial lessons.

A doctor in the hospital of Old Cairo invited them to try the lessons on some of his convalescent patients who could not read. All forty of the workers were so eager to see the magical results they had heard about that they volunteered to teach. Each went to sit beside a patient and start him on the road to learning. At the end of half an hour they returned with downcast faces. Only one or two reported any success at all. Some had discovered that their patients had poor eyesight; others that their own patience in teaching did not last ten minutes.

Then Dr. Laubach realized he had made a serious mistake. Making charts and teaching from them were entirely different jobs. He should have explained his method very carefully to each eager teacher. That method had grown slowly out of his own experience and was a necessary part of the whole scheme. Very early he had realized that almost every adult who could not read had a sense of inferiority. Consequently he had learned never to use a loud tone of voice, never a frown or rebuke. If the new reader was timid, he encouraged him, if slow, he took care never to show impatience. There were no embarrassing pauses, no nagging. Whatever the pupil did well he praised. He had found that a pat on the shoulder or a hearty "That's fine" seemed to work magic with even the slowest learner. All this he should have explained and demonstrated to the volunteer teachers.

Patience—long, long patience and constant good will would be necessary, no matter how cleverly they planned the lessons. That evening, standing by moonlight in the shadow of one of the great pyramids, Frank Laubach thought of the toiling slaves who had built that mass of masonry. Millions of their descendants all over the Middle East were still in bondage to ignorance and superstition. Was there any way to free them except with a patience which matched their own?

In Jerusalem a few days later he had to remind himself often of that lesson in patience, for a new problem arose concerning the charts. As he worked with the Director of Education for Palestine and his staff to improve the Arabic lessons, he was amazed to hear one of them say, "These key words will never do. They are not classical words; they are words from the street. If they are put into print, they will degrade the language."

"But people must first learn to read the words they hear," protested Dr. Laubach, "the common, everyday words."

"Never!" insisted the fastidious scholar. "Such degradation of our literature cannot be tolerated."

There was a hot debate, and it seemed as if plans for swift literacy among the Arabs would die then and there. At last a compromise was reached. The group agreed to find a list of pure classical words which were also words used in everyday talk by the masses of people.

The feeling of these Arab scholars about their language

may seem strange to Americans, but it is not unlike the
attitude of many people toward the new translation of the
Bible. They say, "It sounds like something you might hear
on the street, not like the Bible at all. I prefer the good old
King James version because it's literature." There are purists
in every language and their work is often valuable, but in
spite of them language grows and changes.

Two primary school teachers took the Arabic lessons, unclassical as they were, and tried them out on some Moslem
boys, in a village a few miles from Jerusalem. At Dr. Laubach's suggestion they experimented with the each-one-
teach-one plan. A teacher taught the first boy, who taught
the second, the second the third, and so on. The lesson
worked, and he moved on to Beirut in Syria with some hope
in his heart.

There he learned about some other problems of the Middle
East. When a talented woman teacher took the lessons to a
village, she was received with smiles at first because the
mothers thought she had come to teach the children. But
when she asked the men and women if they, too, did not
wish to learn to read, they were shocked. Had they not lived
many years without knowing how to read and write! And
the sheik shook his head. "Some are born to be educated like
the sheiks, and others must work and till the soil. What respect would the workers have for us, if they, too, could
read?"

Frank, remembering his democratic Moro friends far away
in the Philippines, wished he could command one of the
genii from the *Arabian Nights* with a magic carpet, and
whisk a dozen Moros, including a *dato* and a sultan, straight
to Syria. They might bring to that ancient land the new
vision they had caught for their own people and for all Islam.

Moving on into Turkey, Laubach found that vision already partly a reality. Under the dictator Kemal Atatürk, the difficult Arabic alphabet had been replaced in 1928 by a Roman alphabet, splendidly phonetic. Turkish teachers had been sent to gather new ideas from all over the world. Night schools for adults had been opened, and the government had announced that jobs would go only to those who could read and write. In four years two millions had become literate.

Now, in 1935, Frank found a welcome awaiting him in Istanbul, thanks in part to an old friend, John Kingsley Birge, with whom he had worked at the Spring Street Settlement House in New York during his student days. Mr. Birge had made a scientific word count to determine the one thousand "basic" Turkish words that would be needed to teach reading in the primary schools or among illiterate adults. The list of words was already in use, and government officials, accustomed to modern ideas in education, at once asked Dr. Laubach to make a set of lessons in Turkish, similar to those he had just been making in thirty languages across southern Asia. Turkey, already half-westernized, took this new step toward "streamlined literacy" with enthusiasm.

CHAPTER 7

India Shall Be Literate

"So holding this globe in my hand, I am
trying to help Thee reach hearts around the
whole earth."—F. C. L.

All this work on the way home for a furlough, Laubach had
done without any other funds than the usual missionary
allowance. Fortunately, his letters to friends in America had
aroused their interest in the whole immense problem of
world literacy. A few of them organized a World Literacy
Committee and raised funds to help him carry on the work
he had begun. After reaching home he undertook a speaking
tour, and everywhere audiences were astonished to hear that
three-fifths of the human race still could not read and write!

"Surely they must be stupid!" some listeners said.

But many of those who heard the story pitied the millions
in Asia and Africa less fortunate than themselves, and were
eager to help give them a start toward a better way of life.
As interest grew, the World Literacy Committee became the
Committee on World Literacy and Christian Literature and
a part of the Foreign Missions Conference of North America,[1] which is supported by more than a score of mission
boards.

Growing financial support made it possible for Frank Lau-

[1] Now the Foreign Missions Division of the National Council of Churches
of Christ in the United States of America.

bach, at the end of his furlough in 1936, after a brief stay in the Philippines, to return to India for further work. He was welcomed with both cheers and groans. The lessons in Tamil that he had helped to prepare had been a failure, but those in Telugu were fairly successful. Part of the failure was due to the use of words unfamiliar in everyday speech; part to the use of words from another dialect. The lessons had been prepared too hastily and in the border region between Tamil and Telugu. "But why should we expect success at the first attempt?" asked Mason Olcott, whose enthusiasm never seemed to flag. Cheerfully he gathered a committee and they all set to work to improve the Tamil lessons.

After a week of intense effort Laubach moved into the Telugu-speaking region where several leaders were eager to help revise the first charts. Among the workers was a woman whom he did not remember, but from her accent he knew she was Australian. Her name was Grace Chapman. After some years of teaching among Moslem women in India, she had gone home on furlough, intending to return by way of Mindanao, because she had read about Laubach's work among the Moslems there and she wanted to learn from him. No sooner had she reached Australia than she heard that he had returned to India. She had packed up and traveled back as fast as possible, without taking her furlough.

"The millions of illiterates in India are more important than my vacation," she said.

Her spirit and that of dozens of other teachers—Indian, English, and American—filled Frank Laubach anew with zeal and humility. Many of these persons had for years been trying different methods of teaching adults to read. Some had had success, but all their methods were slow and, among the millions of India, their work was like a drop in the ocean.

If now his key-word methods had given them new hope,
he felt that he must keep on trying until together they made
the very best lessons possible for each language in India.

A visit with an old friend gave him new courage. At a
college in Guntur he found as president, Dr. Roy Strock,
the very man who, back in his days at Perkiomen, had
coached football and taught the boys about foreign missions.
Strock had become secretary of the National Christian Council of India—a leader in his chosen work.

At the meeting in Guntur and at almost every meeting of
people interested in literacy there was much discussion concerning the best words to be used in the lessons. For example, in the Central Provinces, a leading educator had prepared a list of the thousand most-used Hindi words to guide
writers of primers for children. This list had been approved
by the government. But Laubach soon discovered that it
differed decidedly from a list of the words most often used
by illiterates. It represented the printed language but not
the daily speech of the people. If his key-word lessons were
to be useful in teaching adults, they must consist of the
words those people spoke and heard. But the Hindi scholars,
like the Arab scholars of Palestine, insisted that words from
the vernacular could not be tolerated. Their language,
directly descended from Sanskrit, would, they felt, be degraded. Nevertheless, one educator set to work making a list
of the words most often heard in the speech of illiterates,
and thus one step was taken toward preparing material for
them to read when the prejudice against the vernacular
should be conquered.

In one part of India that prejudice had already disappeared because of the work of a great poet. Rabindranath
Tagore, whose beautiful poems have been translated into

English and many other tongues, was using the common language of the masses of Bengal rather than the language of scholars. And so strong was his influence that the spoken Bengali was slowly taking the place of the old, stilted literary language.

Long before knowing about this problem of languages in India, Frank Laubach had been attracted by the poetry of Tagore and had read certain poems so often that he knew them by heart.

> "Here is thy footstool and there rest thy feet
> where live the poorest, and lowliest, and lost."

Such lines made him sure that in Bengal lived a man whose spiritual insight and compassion were like that of Jesus. He wondered if it would be possible to see and talk with him. In January, finding himself near Bolpur, he wrote asking for an interview with the poet. Back came a cordial invitation from Tagore himself, and Laubach accepted it at once.

There followed three memorable days at Santiniketan, the school founded by Tagore, embodying his dream for India. The poet, clad in the Bengali *chadar*, like a Roman toga, received his Western guest on the balcony of the guest house. Sensing no doubt that here was a mind akin to his own, he talked freely about his ideals and purposes in education. He had chosen a spot remote from the tumult of the city so that the students might know the beauty of dawn and dusk, of forest stillness and starlight during their years of study. The classes were held mostly out of doors. He wanted the school to be like the forest sanctuaries, the *ashrams*, where the wise men of ancient India had taught their followers. Santiniketan had been visited by educators of many lands and had become a meeting place for scholars from East

and West who sincerely desired to learn about the various
civilizations of Asia and Europe, and who believed, like
Tagore, that East and West each had some vision to offer
the other.

As he listened, Frank Laubach thought he had never heard
a voice so musical, so compelling, nor ever seen a face of
such nobility. The brilliant dark eyes shone with a beauty
not of this world but of a spirit that dwelt with God. In his
journal that week he wrote, "What is a man's best gift to
mankind? To be beautiful of soul and then let people see
into your soul. This is what I learned as I looked upon the
face of Rabindranath Tagore and listened to him."

Laubach talked also with several teachers in the school
and felt in them something of the same spiritual nobility.
Mornings and evenings he heard the boys singing the poet's
songs in the lilting Bengali rhythms or chanting ancient
Sanskrit prayers. He felt that the place was well named
Santiniketan, "House of Peace."

A month later he read in the papers that Tagore had been
invited to speak at the annual assembly of Calcutta University, an honor conferred only on distinguished scholars. The
poet in a brilliant speech discussed the influence of the West
on his native land, and he spoke in Bengali. This was an
innovation and proved beyond doubt that the everyday language of the people could become the general medium of
expression both practical and literary.

After that, whenever the words in his literacy lessons were
questioned, Laubach had a strong argument in favor of the
vernacular. He had only to refer to Tagore and his influence
as proof that the spoken language could be used by writers
with clarity and beauty; that the use of it need not degrade
the splendid literary traditions of India. He pointed also to

the fact that the beloved Mahatma Gandhi was using his own tongue (Gujerati), not a highly "literary" language, in his magazine *Harijan*.

In northern India one missionary, who had a talent for writing in direct and simple language, had translated the Gospel of Luke into the Hindi of the common people. He was merely doing, he said, what the writers of the New Testament had done in the first place, for they wrote the life of Jesus, not in classical Greek, but in the spoken Greek of their day.

Much of Laubach's speaking that year was done in the schools and colleges of India, and he found that students everywhere from the Punjab in the north to Madras in the south were awakening to the need of adult education in India and were eager to help. At the Agricultural Institute at Allahabad the importance of literacy was emphasized in a new way by its famous director, Sam Higginbottom. He and his colleagues had been working for several years to improve the cattle of India by crossbreeding them with cattle from other lands. Since cows are sacred, according to the Hindu religion, they are never killed, though many of them starve to death. India has more cattle than any other country in the world. In fact, it has about a third of all the world's cattle. Cows sometimes wander unhindered through the streets of cities, and in the villages the hour of dusk is called "cowdust time" because it is marked by the return of the cattle from the fields. They are used as work animals for pulling plows and carts, but they give little milk in comparison with such Western breeds as the Guernsey and the Holstein. If new cattle strains could be developed to provide more milk, they would help to solve the great food problem of India.

At the Agricultural Institute a start in successful breeding had been made, but it could not gain much headway until the millions of villagers understood the reason for it and were willing to cooperate. If only they could read, it would be easy to spread the information about the importance of milk as food and about the value of milk-producing cattle. But it would take years to go around the country and explain such matters to three hundred and forty-five million people by word of mouth!

When Laubach finished speaking about literacy at the Agricultural Institute, Higginbottom rose and said to the students, "There has never been a more important subject discussed in this college than the one you have just heard."

Another educational leader thanked Dr. Laubach in the name of all the poor debtors of India. Practically every person who cannot read is in debt to a *baniya* (moneylender). Since the illiterate cannot tell for himself how his account stands, he usually remains in debt all his life, just as his father and grandfather did before him. Moneylenders everywhere have the illiterate at their mercy. For example, a father in India borrows a hundred rupees for his daughter's dowry. He signs by thumbprint a note stating that he owes two hundred rupees and on that amount will pay interest at 30 per cent or even as high as 60 per cent. Soon he must sell his two bullocks, his only means of livelihood, in order to pay the interest. Then one by one all his possessions vanish as he struggles to meet the exorbitant demands of the moneylender. If he could read he would think a long time before selling himself into such slavery.

Besides the *baniyas* there are the *zamindars* (tax collectors) who claim a very large part of the crop so that families often are left without enough to eat. Literacy would help the people to end such injustice.

Wherever Dr. Laubach spoke to students he urged them to waken to their great opportunities; to learn how to teach illiterates and to write simply and clearly for the millions who would soon be starting to read.

In spite of the eager response of students, however, he felt that it would take years to make India literate unless lessons could be made simple enough to be used in each-one-teach-one campaigns, like those in the Philippines. Constantly he prayed that God would help him solve the problem for India. He was working on lessons in Gujerati (Gandhi's language) with the faculty of a teacher-training school at Godhra, north of Bombay. One night while he was praying a new idea burst upon him. It was based on some lessons he had seen in which pictures were used to help the memory. Fortunately, there was a good Indian artist teaching at the training school. After words were found that began with each of the Gujerati consonants, this artist drew a picture corresponding to each word—and a new method of teaching was begun. It was called the "picture-word-syllable" method. The pictures made the lessons easier for the new reader to master and to review by himself as well as to teach to another illiterate.

When the new chart was used in teaching some women, they were so fascinated that they waited on the doorstep each morning for more lessons. Much encouraged, Dr. Laubach returned to Allahabad to try using the new picture method in Hindi and in Urdu.

Ralla Ram, a Hindu leader of the Student Christian Movement, and Reyazul Hassan, an enthusiastic Moslem, with a group of other college-trained Indians, worked devotedly with Laubach for two weeks. They not only improved the

પાઠ

		કલમ	ખડીઓ	ગધેડું	ઘડો	ક k	ખ kh	ગ g	ઘ gh	
		ચકલી	છત્રી	જમાદાર	ઝભલું	ચ ch	છ chh	જ j	ઝ jh	
		ટપાલી	ઠગ	ડબ્બો	ઢબુ	ટ ṭ	ઠ ṭh	ડ ḍ	ઢ ḍh	
		તપેલી	થડ	દડો	ધજા	નગારૂં	ત t	થ th	દ d	ધ dh	ન n
		પગ	ફળ	બકરી	ભમરો	મરચું	પ p	ફ ph	બ b	ભ bh	મ m
		રસ્તો	ઇયળ	લસણ	વડ	ર ra	ય ya	લ la	વ wa	
		શકોરૂં	સસલું	હળ		શ sh	સ s	હ h	ળ ḷ	

Gujerati reading chart.

lessons in Hindi and Urdu, but had the pleasure of presenting them to Jawaharlal Nehru, who was already one of India's
great leaders. His home was in Allahabad. In his note of
thanks to Dr. Laubach he wrote:

"I am greatly interested in the literacy movement which
is gathering momentum in India. . . . I hope that the provincial governments, who are pushing this literacy campaign,
will take full advantage of your expert knowledge and experience."

Fired with enthusiasm because the new method brought
swift results wherever it was tested, Frank Laubach worked
like a dynamo for two weeks on other languages before
sailing for Africa. After six weeks there (see Chapter 11)
he was back in India for sixteen days, bringing with him

Marathi reading chart.

still better ideas for the new picture charts—ideas which he had experimented with in the African languages. More pictures and easier lessons!

Like a zealous whirlwind, he moved across India, working night and day to improve the earlier charts in Telugu, Tamil, and several other languages. His zeal was contagious. Coworkers caught fire, and when at the end of June, 1937, he sailed away to Lanao, he was confident that a great wave of interest in literacy would soon sweep over India.

He was absolutely right. When he returned in December, 1938, to attend the International Missionary Council at Madras, concern over literacy had become an epidemic. Instead of sluggish despair there was hope. Mahatma Gandhi, Mr. Nehru, and other leaders of the Congress Party were convinced that it was possible for India's millions to learn to read and write. The most enthusiastic believed it could be done in five years. Their figures were based on the each-one-teach one plan as follows:

Eight per cent were literate in 1938. If each of the 8 per cent would teach one that year,

16 per cent would be literate in 1939, and
32 "   "   "   "   "   " 1940, and
64 "   "   "   "   "   " 1941, and
128 "   "   "   "   "   " 1942!

The extra 28 per cent would take care of the increase in population, and that is no joke in India, where the population was then increasing five times as fast as literacy. Actually, literacy did increase from 7 per cent of the population in 1931 to 12 per cent in 1941, in spite of the population increase.

The great International Council at Tambaram, a suburb of Madras, was the first great Christian convention to give serious study to the problem of world literacy. Half the delegates were from the Orient and Africa, and they knew the great needs in their own lands. Between sessions of the conference they crowded into the literature room to see the lesson charts already prepared and in use in fifty different languages of Africa and Asia.

In spite of the lively interest in literacy, Frank Laubach felt that it was not enough. After the closing address by the great John R. Mott, a ringing challenge to the Christians of the world, Dr. Laubach wrote a long letter to his friends in the churches of America and India. Here is another paragraph from that letter, part of which is quoted in Chapter 1:

"As millions become literate there looms up the staggering task of providing them with enough good literature. These literacy campaigns are going to double the world's readers! Here in India where eleven out of twelve are illiterate, a mighty tide has begun to rise. Millions will be literate soon—before we are ready. In China ten out of twelve are illiterate. But a mighty tide has begun to rise. Millions will soon be reading—before we are ready. Are we going to give them reading matter, or who? Will it be clean or not? Will they be flooded with the message of Christ or with atheism? Will they read love or hate? Whatsoever is sown in their minds, the world will reap. . . . That is the most stupendous, the most arresting, the most ominous fact, perhaps on this planet. Nothing can stop it now."

As Laubach said, "a mighty tide had begun to rise." Before and after the Madras Council, forty conferences were held in various parts of India and these were attended by Hindus, Moslems, as well as Christians of all sects, by educators, premiers, vice-chancellors, political leaders, mayors, judges, social leaders. The movement for independence was gaining headway in India. The green and yellow flag of the Congress Party appeared more and more frequently. Women were wearing saffron-colored saris and men garments of *khaddar* (native cotton) to show their patriotism.

One of the first conferences was held at Mettur Dam in the hills of the Madras Presidency under the leadership of Dr. Mason Olcott. A hundred leading Hindus, Moslems, and Christians came together to wrestle with the problem of illiteracy. They discussed how to start a literacy campaign, how to find teachers, how to make people eager to learn. Would the each-one-teach-one plan work? Would people teach without pay?

Laubach had to explain many times that his method was based on Christ's teaching: "Thou shalt love thy neighbor as thyself."

"Were not adults too old to learn?" Here his friend Mason Olcott helped by quoting Professor E. L. Thorndike's book on *Adult Learning* to prove that a man of forty can learn more quickly than a child of six because he has a larger speaking vocabulary and he has learned how to reason. He does not lean on memory alone. Frequently, Dr. Laubach would demonstrate by finding an old man who was illiterate and persuading him to try the lessons. First he would test his eyesight by placing six dots close together like this : . : . and asking the man if he could tell how many dots there were. If he named the right number, his eyes were good enough for reading. Often in half an hour he could read the first chart and sometimes a short sentence. Usually the learner himself was as surprised as the audience.

Was it right for women to learn to read and had they the brains to do it? Usually some educated Indian women in the meeting were the answer to that question, and everyone had to admit that India would be better off if there were more women like them.

These college-bred women, dignified and lovely in their graceful silken saris, knew better than anyone else that the education of women was one of the most basic problems of their land. There is an old Indian proverb that asks: "Will learning help a woman to blow the fire?" It represents the prevailing attitude toward women, rich or poor, high caste or low caste. Only 4 per cent of India's women could read and write.

In the cities, of course, some of the younger generation had begun to adopt Western ways, but there was, and still is, sharp disapproval of the freedoms that American girls take for granted. And in the villages of India the ancient customs prevailed. A girl was married at ten or twelve and went to live with the young husband's family, where she was trained by her mother-in-law in all wifely duties. One of these was that she should never speak her husband's name or her own to a stranger. She rarely saw anyone outside the household. In most Moslem homes women maintained purdah, keeping themselves closely veiled except within the women's part of the house. Among Hindus a girl was expected to marry someone of her own caste. No girl, according to the law, could inherit property.

Many men, otherwise progressive in their thinking, who had caught the literacy fever and were eager to improve conditions in India, seemed unable to change their ideas about the education of women.

Another question that often arose was the familiar one: Was it right to teach the language of daily speech instead of the classical Hindi or Urdu or Tamil? The example of Tagore and Gandhi usually persuaded the questioners that their language would not be degraded.

But who would write interesting short informational articles to be read by the millions of new readers? That was the most serious question of all. Language experts were asked to prepare lists of words showing what illiterate adults were most interested in and talked about most. The lists included: debts and hate of moneylenders, cow dung for fuel, quarrels (especially of mothers and daughters), court trials, rice, cooking, Gandhi, pilgrimages and sacred shrines, jewelry for women's noses and ankles, riddles, ghosts, snake-charming, plague, purdah, caste, eye diseases, itch, rats.

Dr. Laubach visited many cities where literacy campaigns were in progress and saw classrooms packed with learners. In Bihar province he was taken to see a prison where the prisoners, instead of wanting to get out, were glad to be there because they were learning to read! The superintendent had started classes for them and also had established a system of self-government. For Dr. Laubach's visit the prison cabinet asked their best poet to sing in his honor. Here are some lines in translation from his poem:

"The spring season has set in for our souls;
The name of God has a new charm and the garden of my heart
a fresh beauty.

. . . . .

The days of my sighs and groans are over, and another voice is
in my life.
I was not free inside this jail, nor was I free even before I came;
But today there is a new longing in my heart.

. . . . .

Everybody is praying for the happiness of our guest,
But my prayer surpasses all others and exceeds all measure.
How fortunate we are that we should have him in our midst as
our guest.
For he hails from the land of the free."

In schools and colleges all over India, Laubach was welcomed. At Lahore in the Punjab he found a group of students so on fire with zeal that they had the Minister of
Education worried sick. They wanted to cut all red tape and
proceed at once to do three things:

1. Fifteen days of intensive propaganda with posters, radio broadcasts, leaflets from airplanes, processions.

2. A pledge from every literate man either to teach one
person each month or to pay a rupee a month until Lahore
was literate.

3. All schools to have vacations of three months, but every
student required to teach during school hours every day instead of studying.

When the vexed Minister of Education asked Dr. Laubach
what to do with these rash youths, he answered, "It seems
to me the safest thing is to give them all the rope they want
and then try to keep up with them!"

In contrast he thought of a visit to another school in central India, which was devoted to the training of princes of native states. Every one of the sixty princes wore a sky-blue turban. They all looked like princes in fairy tales with their handsome faces and great black eyes. And they all promised to try to make the people of their states literate, but there was no "passion for the poor in their eyes."

Laubach talked to gatherings of teachers and outlined for them his teaching method: "Never scold or frown. Pat the student on the back and tell him how bright he is. Treat him like a rajah."

This revolutionary idea always shocked the teachers. Some of them thought it might work with adults, but with children—never! In India they still followed the old maxim, "Spare the rod and spoil the child."

At some of the conferences they also discussed the question that Mahatma Gandhi had raised: Shall we first feed the hungry and give them better homes before trying to teach them to read? But the answer was unanimous: If we make people literate they will be able to help themselves.

One of Dr. Laubach's most spectacular days was spent at Kosamba where he had been invited to lead a joint conference of government teachers and missionaries. From the train, where he was strapping up his bedding in the early morning, he heard the sound of Scottish bagpipes. Looking out, he saw a band of young Indians dressed in plaid kilts and Scottish "bonnets" and behind them a vast throng of people. Wondering what celebrity was arriving—Gandhi or the Viceroy perhaps—he started to leave the train. In came a group of town officials, one of whom proceeded to make an address of welcome. Then followed a parade to the center of the city, where four thousand school children sang a song especially written for the literacy campaign. The refrain consisted of syllables from the lesson charts which the illiterates learned by chanting.

"All the boys are singing ka, ke, ki, ko, ku
All the girls are singing ka, ke, ki, ko, ku
All Baroda's singing ka, ke, ki, ko, ku."

Then there was a great feast at which all castes ate together. Everyone agreed that a new era was beginning in Baroda and indeed all over India.

Back and forth across the vast land Dr. Laubach traveled, from Assam close under the Himalayas to Lahore in the Punjab, up and down the great valley of the Ganges and across the plateau of South India, visiting cities and remote villages, helping to make lessons in other languages, speaking now to little groups of students and now to vast outdoor throngs gathered at a *mela* (religious festival). Sometimes he worked with committees far into the night. Often he could not sleep on the trains. At Indore in late March the thermometer stood at 102° day after day. But Frank Laubach did not falter. This was the great wave of literacy that he had hoped and prayed and worked for, and his heart was full of gratitude because others had caught the vision and now nothing could stop the miracle of India's awakening.

But as he was leaving that spring of 1939, Dr. Laubach wrote:

"And yet I was afraid of the thing I was doing in India—unloosing something that had been chained since the dawn of time. Nearly three-fifths of the human race might in a few years be throbbing with a new, nameless, terrible hope as were these people. If Christian missions can lead this new uprising, if the way can be opened for Christ to satisfy the hunger of these new literates, they will be the meek who will inherit and bless the earth. But if, after starting this thing, we allow the leadership to slip from the Christian brotherhood in all lands, if this unthinkably vast multitude become educated with pagan ideals, God pity the future."

That very year, in September, 1939, World War II broke out, and India, like every other country, was faced with many urgent problems. Under the leadership of Gandhi, the people continued their struggle for independence, and it was finally won in 1947.

In 1940 the book called *India Shall Be Literate*, prepared by Laubach in collaboration with others, was published in India. What progress in literacy he found when he was able to return to India, ten years later in March, 1949, you will read about in Chapter 12.

CHAPTER 8

Latin American Neighbors

"An effort to lift our entire planet to a new
economic, social, and health level, trusting God
and justice, will react in blessing upon America as well as upon all mankind."—F. C. L.

When war burst upon the United States in December, 1941,
Frank and Effa Laubach were at home on furlough. Bob had
just graduated from Wooster College in Ohio. Naturally they
were greatly concerned about their friends in the Philippines, but they could not return there nor could they continue work in India or Africa. Some people might have
thought it a good chance for a few years of home life and
a little rest, but not the Laubachs. Frank knew that the
Western Hemisphere had its backward areas, too—that there
were millions in Central and South America to whom he
might give help.

In all the countries of Latin America the percentage of
illiteracy was high. This was due partly to poor transportation, which left many communities isolated, and partly to
the fact that in most of the countries the Indian part of
the population still followed their traditional ways of life.
Pushed out of their lands by European conquerors, they had,
just as in North America, been at first exploited and then
ignored. Gradually they and their descendants had retreated

into the mountains or jungles, where they lived meager, half-starved lives in their dark adobe huts, sharing their crowded shelters with the family donkey, pig, and fowls.

Even among the people of Spanish blood and the *mestizos* (mixed Indian and white), education was largely for the wealthy and official classes. Under Spanish rule, splendid universities were established in Mexico City, Bogotá, Lima, Cuzco, and other cities, but book learning was considered superfluous for the great masses. This state of affairs continued even after the countries of Central and South America became independent in the early nineteenth century. Public schools and popular education as we understand it did not flourish among our southern neighbors.

In 1940 under the threat of war all the American countries were drawn together for common defense. Our own government established the Office of Coordinator of Inter-American Affairs in July, 1941, with Nelson A. Rockefeller as its head. When Dr. Laubach and the World Literacy Committee determined to see what could be done for literacy in Latin America, it was to the coordinators as well as to our ambassadors in the various countries that they turned for cooperation.

Dr. Laubach set out in the middle of October, 1942, and traveled most of the way by air. His first stop was at Barranquilla, Colombia, which most North Americans think of as the front door to South America. It is only about three hundred miles from the Panama Canal. There he was expected to make a speech in Spanish, replying to the welcome of government officials. He was "afraid he butchered the verbs sadly" but the Director of Education was kind and hospitable just the same. This educator was thrilled over the each-one-teach-one idea. "It is revolutionary!" he exclaimed. "The Latin people are *emocional* and if they become enthusiastic over such a movement, it will spread like fire."

With the help of a committee, lesson charts in Spanish were quickly made on Laubach's picture-word-syllable plan already successful in India, but with the pictures on the back of each page. The government agreed to pay half the expense of printing the lessons, and the Coordinator's office the other half. Dr. Laubach visited schools in four cities and trained students in the proper methods of teaching adults to read. Committees were organized to take charge of a literacy campaign. Everywhere there was enthusiasm. Dr. Laubach was impressed by the evident popularity of North Americans in Colombia and by the eagerness with which people—that is, those who could read—bought the Spanish edition of *Reader's Digest*.

He thought Colombia was the most air-minded country in the world. It was easy to see why when he looked down from the airplane on his way to the mountain capital, Bogotá. Seeing the winding Magdalena River, which cuts the country in two, he could easily understand why it took more than a week to travel up the river and over the mountains. By air it took only two hours. Air travel was new to him at that time, and he was thrilled to view lakes and valleys, roads looping and twisting around the mountains, patterns of fields in the great coffee plantations, and red-roofed houses clustered in towns and cities.

His next stop was in Guayaquil, Ecuador, that small country on the equator which furnishes most of the quinine the world needs and also much balsa wood for airplanes. Here again he found the Coordinator's office most helpful. It was headed by Alan Reed, known as a leader in the city for all kinds of good works. He at once made plans for printing the Spanish literacy charts in color.

Dr. Laubach next set out by train over the mountains for Quito, the capital. He was fascinated by the views of deep valleys and snow-capped peaks, and by the bright ponchos

	a la	a		pa to	pa
	ha cha	ha		ra ton	ra
	ma no	ma		ba lanza	ba
	sa po	sa		va ca	va
	za pato	za		ca sa	ca
	ta za	ta		ga to	ga
	na riz	na		cha leco	cha
	da do	da		fa rol	fa
	la piz	la		ja rra	ja
	lla ve	lla			

Spanish reading chart.

worn by Indian travelers, but after fifteen hours of looking over the precipices that the train skirted, he decided that airplane travel was far safer, or at least less nerve-wracking. The clear, cool air of the mountains was delightful after the sultry heat at sea level.

In ancient Quito, he found still another helpful representative of the Coordinator's office, C. W. Jones, who had started the "Voice of the Andes" radio broadcasts, heard all over the world. Here lessons were needed in the Indian dialect Quechua (pronounced Kechua), for the population is more than half Indian and at that time only one in a thousand could read and write. The committee of educators who gathered to prepare lessons under Dr. Laubach's direction had a hard time agreeing on the right words to be used, but otherwise the charts were easy to prepare because it is a language with only three vowels and twelve consonants.

Quechua, the language of the Incas, "children of the sun," was once spoken throughout their rich empire. As everyone knows, these Indians achieved a remarkable civilization before they were conquered by Pizarro in 1533. Their buildings, their pottery and weaving, their work in gold and silver, their feather mosaics are among the art treasures of the world. But they developed no system of writing, and their descendants are among the "silent billion" whom Dr. Laubach is striving to help. He described their condition as heartbreaking. The city of Quito, with its magnificent old Spanish buildings full of art treasures, towering above the low Indian adobe houses, seemed a symbol of the need for social progress.

The Quechuas also form a large element of the population of Peru, where he made his next stop. In the beautiful city of Lima, the capital, with its fine boulevards and lovely gardens, almost everyone can read and write. Only a few people seemed concerned over the fact that 85 per cent of their Indian countrymen were illiterate. Some of the educators thought the Indians should be taught to read, but in Spanish, not in their own tongue.

Dr. Laubach went on to the ancient city of Cuzco, once the capital of the Inca empire, and found there a hearty welcome and lively interest in his work. The people are mostly of Indian descent and know the problems of the Indians. Along the narrow cobbled streets, Quechuas still drive their llamas, those strange-looking beasts of burden which also furnish wool, hides, and meat for their owners. From llama wool the women weave the beautiful blankets and the striped red ponchos which the men wear and tourists delight to buy. His hosts took him to see the famous mountain fort which the Incas defended against the Spaniards with slingshots, bows and arrows, until their ammunition gave out. The walls, built of irregular, thirty-ton stones fitted tightly together, are considered an architectural marvel even in this day of technical triumphs.

More marvelous still to Dr. Laubach was the eagerness of eight present-day Quechuas in the Cuzco prison where he took the first Quechua lesson chart and began teaching one of them to read. The man mastered it in ten minutes and showed the same skill in teaching the next prisoner. As each one taught one, their faces glowed, and the men who had been helping Frank Laubach prepare the lessons were exultant. The most scholarly of these Peruvians came to the train to say farewell and embraced him in the warm fashion of South Americans.

Next Dr. Laubach took a steamer across Lake Titicaca, which lies among magnificent mountains more than two miles above sea level. He saw Indians skimming along in their little boats made of the bulrushes that grow along the shore, with sails of the same rushes. Their graceful shape was designed by the Incas centuries ago. From the other side of the lake a train took him to La Paz, capital of Bolivia. The Indians of that region are the Aymarás, the most powerful tribe conquered by the Incas. The Aymarás comprise 90 per cent of the population but are largely illiterate and work for a pittance mining the tin that constitutes much of the wealth of Bolivia.

Dr. Laubach attended a Quaker church in the Indian section of La Paz. He wrote:

"Tonight I had a spiritual experience which will echo through the rest of my life. It was the Aymará prayer meeting. There was nothing Quaker about it. Everyone prayed aloud at the same time. It began with a murmur; then women's plaintive wails were heard above the rest, and presently there was the sound of weeping. I heard the terrible cry of ages rising to God from broken hearts; and behind that I heard the bitter cry and anguish of all the illiterates in the world—the oppressed, the blind, the hopeless. . . . And it was three nights before Christmas!"

He returned to the same church for a Christmas program and was relieved to find the stolid faces smiling on that festive day. The street outside the church was swarming with Indians, some of the women with babies on their backs. Many of the laborers, he learned, spend their meager pay for coca, a drug like cocaine, which dulls the nerves and ultimately does harm to nerve cells and brain. At the mines they were sometimes given coca free so that they would work harder because their fatigue would be deadened by the drug. The sale of coca was said to be one of the chief sources of government revenue. That same year, following a strike, a committee of Bolivians and North Americans had been investigating the wrongs done to the miners and had reported that the Indians were badly exploited.

A group interested in their welfare made a series of lessons in Aymará under Dr. Laubach's direction, and then tried them out on several illiterates in the crowded market street. The government asked also for lessons to bridge their learning of Spanish later. In the Department of Education there was much talk about illiteracy, but no one was actively at work on the problem. One woman seemed likely, Dr. Laubach thought, to continue her interest in the wretched Indians, but at the United States Embassy he was told that a literacy campaign would probably fade out unless he remained to push it or sent someone to do so.

At his next stop, in Cochabamba, Bolivia, he found an interdenominational mission for the Indians and people actively interested in teaching them. A lively committee helped improve both the Spanish and Quechua charts and worked out a compromise in spelling between the system used in Bolivia and that favored in Peru.

He learned that the Indians in the jungles of eastern Bolivia are still savages. No one knows how many there are. At Roberé, where the plane made a brief stop, he met a young missionary from Michigan "with a far vision in his eyes," who had come to work among these savage tribes. There, on the headwaters of tributaries to the Amazon River, is a vast frontier, which may someday support great populations. Now the only sure means of travel from one small city to another is by air. Otherwise, the region is like the North American frontier two hundred years ago. Frontier justice prevails without recourse to courts of law. In Santa Cruz he learned that a doctor who oppressed the poor had been shot, but there was no attempt to bring the murderer to justice.

His plane was delayed two days by heavy rains, but on January 18 he finally reached Corumbá, a town just across the border in Brazil. The clerk at the hotel and everyone around him was speaking Portuguese instead of Spanish. At first Dr. Laubach felt lost, but very soon he was fascinated by this giant southern country, larger than our own, and in the six weeks he spent there, he fell completely in love with its people.

His first stop was at São Paulo (Portuguese for Saint Paul), the great industrial city of southern Brazil. There, with the help of a committee, he made the first picture-word-syllable lessons in Portuguese before setting out for Rio de Janeiro to get in touch with government groups who might be interested in literacy.

Landing at Rio, he was entranced, like all travelers, with its beauty. In a few days it was the kindness of the people that seemed to him even more remarkable than their city. Time after time, when he asked for information, strangers went out of their way to help him. He found there was an acute transportation problem. Cars, busses, trains jammed to the doors! Yet everyone was patient; there was no shouting and quarreling. He wrote: "This country has not only the natural resources to lead the world, but the joy, peace, kindness."

Another thing that struck him at once was lack of race prejudice. People of every shade and ancestry—black, dusky, red, white—mingled naturally. To be sure, there are few Indians in that coastal part of Brazil to complicate the problem. One man admitted that most of the Indians had been killed by white men's diseases and the cruelty of the early settlers.

Everywhere he saw evidence of the Good Neighbor program which had been started by the United States Government in the 1930's and had been gaining momentum under the stress of war. An American Technical Mission to Brazil had been organized during the summer of 1942 and was busy with various projects in cooperation with Brazilian technicians. Specialists in agriculture were studying what crops best suited different areas and the best methods of growing them—rice, cotton, sugar, maté, cocoa, coffee, citrus fruits, rubber. Mining experts were helping to develop the mineral resources of Brazil, which include the rarer metals— manganese, bauxite, tungsten, nickel, chromium, cobalt, as well as iron, coal, copper, gold, and oil. Industrial experts were studying problems of transportation and power and the best locations for mills and factories. A giant steel mill had already been started at Volta Redonda, northwest of Rio de Janeiro.

Laubach wrote: "I shall return home with a clear vision of how the United States can promote world peace. It will not be done by policing the world. That will only make us hated. It can be accomplished by a vast program of selfless service all over the world. . . . What we need is that rare combination of the dreamer and the doer—men who can see far and can also see the practical step to take now."

No figures regarding the numbers of illiterates in Brazil were available at that time, but later Laubach learned that the percentage of illiteracy was estimated at 70. He found, however, a number of Brazilian leaders already at work on the vast problem.

He was taken by an American, long a resident of Rio and Secretary General de Acção Social (Social Action), to see Don Gustabo Armbrust who was working with great zeal to extend education more widely in Brazil. The same day they called on a leading Brazilian educator, Don Lourenço Filho. He showed a lively interest in Laubach's easy chart lessons and said: "Our Institute for Pedagogical Research will publish them and try them all over Brazil the moment you have them ready. We are in the process of compiling a basic word list of two thousand words." He gave Dr. Laubach a copy of this tentative list and also a list of the two hundred most important Portuguese words, which might be useful in perfecting his charts.

The care Dr. Laubach takes to find exactly the right words for the lessons is shown by his experience with the Portuguese lessons. When the first chart was being copied by some students at Bennett College, one of them said: *"Ave* (meaning *bird*) is not the word most illiterates would use. They would use *pajaro* in talking of birds." So it was necessary to find another word for the vowel *a* and *asa* (meaning *wing*) was chosen.

As soon as suitable copies of the charts were ready, Dr. Laubach tried them on several illiterates. At one of his first demonstrations there were about fifty eager observers, and the pupil, a middle-aged Negro woman, became self-conscious and could only giggle nervously, insisting that she couldn't learn. It was Dr. Laubach's first complete failure, and he was deeply embarrassed. But, recovering quickly, he asked a young woman of the Salvation Army to take a lesson in teaching the chart. Then quietly he suggested, "Suppose you take the pupil into another room and try teaching her alone." Then he went on talking to the group about their proposed literacy campaign. In half an hour, the door opened and back came the Salvation Army lass and her pupil, their faces radiant. "She knows it," cried the teacher. "Yes, it's very easy," said the pupil, smiling and confident.

Dr. Laubach, though still ashamed of his own failure, felt that he could not have provided a better demonstration to emphasize the value of the each-one-teach-one plan and of gentleness and consideration in handling illiterates. Later at Salvador, in Baía, one of the most illiterate states of Brazil, he saw the each-one-teach-one plan work like a charm. It was at a settlement house in a slum district. A local teacher taught an illiterate woman the first lesson, she taught another woman, that woman a man, he another woman, and she a girl, five learning to read in an hour and a half.

Of course, there arose the inevitable question: What will these illiterates read after they have learned how? Laubach started plans for the writing of suitable short articles, informational and religious, and left what funds he could spare to help meet printing costs. And he constantly prayed that all the enthusiasm among government leaders, teachers, pastors, and church laymen wouldn't cool off before the job was completed.

He noticed in Brazilian cities, as in Spanish-speaking ones, how eagerly people bought their own foreign edition of *Reader's Digest*, called *Seleções*. And he found many bookshops in Rio and São Paulo, where shelves were filled with the world's classics —the writings of Marcus Aurelius, Kant, Plato, Cicero, Ruskin, Emerson, Tolstoy—in inexpensive editions. He decided that the Brazilian public could be trusted to desire something better than trash for its reading matter.

At Recife, a city at the eastern point of Brazil, Dr. Laubach had a heart-warming experience. He was visited by Gordon Woodward, son of his former fellow workers in the Philippines. He had not seen Gordon since he was ten years old; now he was thirty, married, father of a year-old baby, and teaching in a college about three hours' ride from Recife.

"The climate is very much like that of Lanao," Gordon reported. Dr. Laubach motored home with him through a land of palms and coconuts, sugar cane and cotton, and he gave a talk on literacy at the college.

The next stage of his journey took him to Belém, port city at the mouth of the mighty Amazon River. There he found a preacher who also held the office of chief of police! This man put him in touch with the Secretary of Education and he had a busy day speaking about and demonstrating the new literacy lessons. He had time for only a brief glimpse of the water front where the river boats transfer their cargoes of crude rubber, lumber, nuts, and alligator skins to ocean steamers. The harbor was quiet under the clouds of war, but he heard things about the giant Amazon and its basin that made him gasp. A river four thousand miles long, stretching seven-eighths of the distance across South America, with seven of its numerous tributaries over a thousand miles long! It drains an area almost as large as the continental United States. This great Amazon basin is the vastest unsettled fertile area in the world and by no means all jungle.

Dr. Laubach knew of the health work of the Rockefeller Foundation here in conquering snakebite and undertaking to stamp out malaria, yellow fever, and jungle fever. He heard much about Fordlandia, the great area where Henry Ford had planted rubber trees to help meet United States needs for rubber. He wished he had time to find out more about the scattered Indians of that vast area and about the *caboclo* (woodsmen) who do most of the work along the rivers, bringing in the supplies of balsa, rotenone, cocaine, quinine, curare, and rubber necessary to our modern world.

Reluctantly, on March 5, he said good-by to friendly Brazil and took a plane for Caracas, capital of Venezuela, beyond the Guianas and the vast jungles of the Orinoco River. At Caracas he was happy to find a letter telling him that five thousand of his lessons made for the Quechua Indians were already being put to use in Peru.

In Venezuela, prosperous because of its oil wells, he found the Department of Education itching for a literacy campaign. Several of the committee themselves helped prepare the lessons in Spanish to suit the needs of the country. When he left, he felt that Venezuela, like Brazil, would really see the campaign through.

At Barranquilla, Colombia, he rounded the circle of his South American journey of five months. Everywhere he had found people eager to learn, eager to improve their way of life. He wrote: "When we help God with the illiterates, everything is very providential. It was in Lanao; it is in South America. This is my testimony: The way to get God helping our work is to help His work."

With brief stops in the Panama Canal Zone and Costa Rica, he flew northward to Guatemala City, and landed at the most beautiful airport he had seen in Latin America. At once he was infatuated with Guatemala, as have been many other travelers, but it was not merely with the gorgeous flowers and magnificent mountains. He found the churches awake to their duties and opportunities to help the people, and the government with a lively interest in literacy under a very efficient president, Jorge Ubico. President Ubico, who found time to inspect every detail from road-building to student scholarships, wanted reading lessons made for the army. Since Guatemala required universal military training of one year he argued that literacy could be rapidly spread that way.

As in the South American countries, the Indians of Guatemala seemed to Laubach to need help more than any other part of the population. All the Indian languages in Guatemala are descended from the famous ancient Maya language, but they are by no means alike. Two of them, Quiché and Mam, spoken by Indians only fifteen miles apart, are as different as possible. For five days, Dr. Laubach worked intensively with two missionaries serving these mountain people. A language expert at the University of Chicago had called Mam the hardest language on earth with respect to phonetics. It consists largely of one-syllable words ending in consonants. But they soon made lessons in Mam, Quiché, and Conob, thanks to preliminary work by several missionaries.

Part of their work was done at a meeting place on the shores of Lake Atitlán, a lovely lake in the midst of waterfalls and volcanoes. One pair of missionaries had traveled two days from their home, where they had to ride burros or walk twenty miles to reach the nearest road. Another was just back from a thirty-mile hike up the mountains to a new church he had recently opened for the Indians. Dr. Laubach wrote:

"These Indians, supposed to be so stolid, rushed out of their houses to shake our hands. They are the friendliest, kindest people I ever saw . . . and they are proving bright at learning to read their own languages. One man learned the chart in the Cakchiquel language in sixteen minutes and then he taught another in an equally short time. Both were thrilled, and many people called it a *milagro* (miracle). But I have come to expect such miracles of these charts."

Returning to Guatemala City he found the Minister of Education keenly interested in the charts and in a literacy campaign. The Minister was an archaeologist and historian, who had written twenty-five books about the ruins of the Mayas and Aztecs in Guatemala and what they reveal of Indian civilization. Laubach urged him to have some of his articles put into simple language for the Indians so that they could read their own history and take pride in it.

Dr. Laubach held classes in a church twice a day for illiterates. One woman said with tears in her eyes, "I don't see why you pay any attention to a nobody like me. I have so longed to read the Bible where it tells about my Lord, but I thought I would never, never be able to read His words. Now I am on the way, and you are the one who took away my blindness."

During his last day in Guatemala, women who had learned in the past two weeks taught others to read while a hundred people looked on. Then at a closing session the leaders discussed what literature could be prepared for the new readers, what subjects would most interest them, and how to get writers to prepare material.

"The rising of this silent majority into literacy all around the world," Laubach told them, "is more important than the world war in its permanent effect upon world progress."

Next day on the plane to Mexico City he found in the March 29th issue of *Life* magazine an article about literacy achievements in Russia. A hundred million had learned to read since 1920! Six billion books had been printed! Newspaper circulation had increased twentyfold! It was to this that the Soviet government owed much of its technological progress and, in equal measure, said the article, the unity of its people during the war. Dr. Laubach wrote: "Never has a more vivid illustration of the transforming power of literacy been seen. But China is going to be as wonderful, and later on, India."

How tragic those words, written in 1943, look to our disillusioned eyes, ten years later. We know now that it makes a vast difference who teaches illiterates and what they are given to read. It is not too late to remember the millions of new readers awakening in India. Shall we let Soviet Russia supply their reading matter? Experts have figured that the cost of one bomber would finance a ten-year publishing program in almost any land.

Laubach's ten days in and near Mexico City passed in a whirl of activity—interviewing government officials and educators, visiting schools and settlements, making lesson charts and demonstrating them, being photographed and interviewed by newspaper reporters. He was impressed by the large number of Americans he saw everywhere and by the influence exerted by some of the best of them. They arranged for him an interview with the Minister of Education who said: "Dr. Laubach, you have arrived in Mexico at exactly the right moment, for we have a commission studying this subject of literacy. Will you please give us written permission to use your system? Then we will begin. We will solicit volunteers by high-pressure propaganda until everyone will teach."

Laubach knew that in Mexico this was not idle talk, for in that country after their revolution of 1917–20 there had been an energetic campaign to carry education into the more backward rural areas. Groups of teachers, forming "cultural missions," were sent out to establish schools and help communities achieve better homes, village sanitation, improved agriculture, new industries. In ten years nine hundred thousand Mexicans had learned to read, but the campaign had slowed down among the Indians, who do not speak Spanish. The teachers had tried to have them read Spanish without first teaching them to read their own language.

On April 11, Dr. Laubach took off by plane for Yucatán, that "thumb" of Mexico which extends northward into the Gulf directly south of New Orleans. No railroad connected it with the rest of Mexico and in those war days there was little steamship travel.

Yucatán is the land that supplies the world with chewing gum, made from the sap of the *sapote* tree. In the chief city, Mérida, Laubach was surprised to find thousands of windmills supplying power for various purposes. But the interest of Yucatán for him lay in the fact that it is the home of about fifty thousand descendants of the Mayas who once ruled parts of Mexico, Guatemala, and British Honduras. When they were conquered by the Spaniards in the early sixteenth century, the remnants of this remarkable people fled eastward. They still tend to distrust their Spanish-speaking countrymen.

He was welcomed by a group of persons who had already started work among these Mayas. After a short train ride and a five-mile walk in the tropical heat, they reached Xocenpich, the Maya center, and at once began work on lessons in that language. The committee consisted of five North Americans and about fifteen Mexicans, and proved to be the most expert he had encountered in all Latin America. They needed help chiefly with methods of teaching.

As soon as the first charts were ready, Dr. Laubach tried them on several illiterates with great success. At once there were requests that a class be held each Sunday morning for those who wanted to learn to read.

The state Director of Education called a meeting of teachers, and so many came that they could not all get in to University Hall. It was decided to have two thousand copies of the lessons printed at once.

One day out of the nine in Yucatán, Dr. Laubach took for sightseeing among the famous Mayan ruins. With friends he set out at dawn on the six-mile walk to Chichén Itzá, where the Carnegie Foundation has spent large sums in unearthing and restoring one of the Mayan cities buried in

the jungle. The Mayas, like the Aztecs, used hieroglyphics
to record their history and had invented a calendar more
perfect than ours. But the imposing pyramid, so often shown
in travel pictures, was the scene of human sacrifice. When
there was a drought, the priests, after elaborate ceremonies,
threw maidens into a horrible pit to appease the god of rain.
More cheerful to modern sightseers is a ball park where the
Mayas played a kind of basketball. The park retains its marvelous acoustical properties, so that you can speak in a quiet
voice at one end and be heard clearly at the other. Dr.
Laubach occasionally enjoys pausing to be a tourist, and
then he sometimes wonders why it is easier to raise funds to
unearth the dead past than to help the people living today.

On April 21, he made his last speech in Spanish for a
while; he was headed for Haiti, where the language of the
people is Creole, a dialect of French. En route across Cuba
by plane he wrote:

"The new world that we expected after the war has already
come; today Cuba is only ten minutes wide. . . . The world
is now smaller by air than the United States is by rail. . . .
Some magnificent thinking is being done about the details
of government needed for such a new world, but no world
structure, no matter how perfect technically, will stand upon
foundations of sand, nor upon the old selfish standards.
Henceforth we have got to come clean on the command
'Love thy neighbor as thyself.' My neighbor is myself, when
I do that. He is my larger self. And who is my neighbor?
Everyone who has fallen among thieves or is in trouble is
my neighbor, is myself. 'Mind my own business' is the attitude of the priest and Levite and it is wickedly dangerous
in this new world."

The Republic of Haiti is a good example of the man who

"fell among thieves" in the parable of the Good Samaritan, for it has had a tragic and discouraging history. It occupies the western third of the island of Hispaniola, where Columbus' *Santa Maria* was wrecked on his first voyage and where he established the first colony. The island was later claimed by France. About 95 per cent of its people are of pure African descent from the slaves who, under Toussaint L'Ouverture, declared their independence in 1804. Their struggle to establish a sound constitutional government has been a long, hard one. The land is poor. Two-thirds of it is mountainous. An area slightly larger than Vermont has to support three and a half million people. The capital and largest city is Port-au-Prince.

The language spoken by everyone is called Creole—a mixture of French, Spanish, African, and Carib (Indian), but the official language is French. French is taught in the schools; and even in the churches it has been used instead of Creole.

Dr. Laubach was met at the airport by the Reverend Ormonde McConnell, an Irish Methodist preacher, who had been working for five years to persuade people of influence that Haiti could quickly become literate if Creole were taught instead of French. Many people believed in the need for a literacy campaign, but only a few defended Creole, even though they all used it in their homes. Mr. McConnell was overjoyed to welcome an ally, especially the very man whose work had inspired his own. He took Dr. Laubach at once to the American Ambassador, who cordially offered to arrange an interview with President Élie Lescot.

Mr. McConnell had already taught some five hundred persons to read by making lessons like the earlier Laubach charts. He had used a system of phonetic spelling for Creole instead of the difficult French spelling. That very first evening he took Dr. Laubach, the Ambassador, and fifty other prominent men of Haiti a few miles out of the city to witness a demonstration of reading by men who, two months before, had been completely illiterate. The Haitians were impressed by their skill and Dr. Laubach was equally impressed by the tremendous influence of this preacher who had accomplished so much singlehanded.

The next day both the Minister of Education and the President endorsed the idea of teaching Creole, and at once a group of teachers and educators was gathered to help prepare picture-word-syllable charts. They worked with such enthusiasm that in three days the lessons were practically completed, and Dr. Laubach could proceed with demonstrations. A completely illiterate woman learned the whole chart so quickly that he was sure at once that the lessons were a success. At later demonstrations she was asked to teach others and did it so successfully that audiences were amazed.

An eminent Creole scholar and also an important archaeologist gave their approval to the phonetic spelling and agreed to start compiling a Creole-French dictionary which would be needed, of course, in preparing books and articles for the new literates to read. Dr. Laubach talked to the boys of the national school of agriculture and won their enthusiasm by teaching a fifty-year-old man to read in ten minutes. At a mass meeting of teachers in a big city theater, hundreds promised to teach adults as soon as the literacy campaign should get under way. In crowded churches he talked to other hundreds, demonstrating how to teach the lessons.

At a reception given by the American Ambassador one of the guests said to him: "Creole is really the language of the

Normans. I was born in Normandy and when I came to Haiti, I could understand the Creole at once. The Haitians have very foolishly despised a language which is as ancient and aristocratic as French."

The day before he left, Dr. Laubach was summoned to the Palace, which, he said, looks like the White House, to receive the National Order of Honor and Merit from the hands of President Lescot—the crowning event of an amazing ten days.

On the plane next day he wrote: "Pastor McConnell was almost too happy to speak. He has won his long hard battle. Now it seems certain that Creole, the language of the people, will become the official language of Haiti." The country needed other things besides literacy, he knew, to make it a happy, healthy, prosperous land, but a literacy campaign was a big step in the right direction.

CHAPTER 9

Highway to a Safe World

"Countries are engaged in what they call
'total war.' . . . Total Christianity as a world
experiment has not yet been tried. If we
should like to see it tried, we must begin by
trying it in ourselves."—F. C. L.

Back home after eight strenuous months of travel and teaching, Frank Laubach spent the summer lecturing and writing
about literacy. He completed his now famous book *The Silent Billion Speak.* When it was published, it began to win
many new friends among both church and government people for the cause of world literacy. A review of the book
by the Honorable Robert L. Owen, aged ex-Senator from
Oklahoma, was read in Congress and incorporated in the
Congressional Record of July 8, 1943. The United States
Government recognized that Dr. Laubach's work was forg-
ing a strong link in its Good Neighbor policy.

By November Dr. Laubach was off for Latin America
again. On this trip he revisited some countries to see how
his teaching might be improved and extended, but he also
started work in half a dozen new areas.

First of these was the island of Jamaica, a British crown
colony. A law had just been passed granting universal suffrage the following year, even though more than 60 per
cent of the people were still illiterate. That meant, of course,

that any election would be decided by an illiterate majority. Responsible leaders were worried.

The language of Jamaica is English. It offered a new challenge to Dr. Laubach. Would his phonetic system work in such an unphonetic language? A set of lessons prepared in New York before he left proved to be too difficult. There was another problem, too. English as spoken in Jamaica is rather different from that in New York, not only in pronunciation but in vocabulary, because of words of African origin. For example, Dr. Laubach listened to some young people rehearsing a play. It was called "What For To Do?" which sounded in their speech like "Wa Fe Do?" It began: "Alberta, yo is a silly girl. Yo shettin' up yo trunk, gwine away, leave yo dress behin' wen I tek arl de trouble fo get it ready."

What letters or symbols should be used so that an illiterate person could learn to read the language his ears heard? Should words be spelled in the usual English way or phonetically? There were English, Scots, Jamaicans, and North Americans on the literacy committee, and their pronunciations of the commonest words differed. Which sounds was it best to teach to the illiterates?

In spite of these tribulations, the group made a satisfactory set of lessons, though Dr. Laubach said it was "very, very much the most difficult task" in language he had yet undertaken.

After many interviews and meetings a lively literacy campaign was started, and Dr. Laubach spent a thankful and joyous Christmas with his fellow-workers. The Committee on World Literacy had provided him with two assistants on this second Latin American trip. The Reverend Theodore P. Fricke attended to all sorts of details about passports and visas, arranged interviews, consulted printers, drew pictures, and did a hundred things to help. Miss Maria Dayoan, who had headed a Literacy Committee in the Philippines, was also in the group. In her charming Filipino dress, she spoke at some of the meetings, and demonstrated by her presence that differences of color or race have no importance.

After a brief stop in Haiti, the group moved on to Santo Domingo, capital of the Dominican Republic, which occupies the eastern two-thirds of the island of Hispaniola. Here, illiteracy runs to 73 per cent. The government was already planning a literacy campaign to celebrate the centennial of their independence. As in Jamaica, the arrival of Dr. Laubach seemed providential. He wrote:

"This only proves that God is behind every door with His hand on the doorknob, ready to open it for those who are trying to do His will."

The Spanish lessons already used in a number of countries needed only a few changes to be useful in Santo Domingo. A good artist made scores of pictures to accompany the words and syllables.

Early in February the team went to Puerto Rico and found the Governor and the Commissioner of Education eager to cooperate. Although under the United States flag since 1898, the island still had a handicap in illiteracy; about 30 per cent of the people could not read. There, as in so many regions, poverty and illiteracy go hand in hand. Puerto Rico is seriously overpopulated—is, in fact, one of the most densely populated areas in the world.

While Dr. Laubach was teaching a man to print the letters as he learned them, the excited crowd applauded each letter. The pupil applauded with them, starting roars of laughter. The laughter seemed to help the learners, and Laubach de-

cided then and there that "keep 'em laughing" was a good
rule for literacy campaigns as well as for vaudeville.

There followed a busy six weeks in Colombia, Ecuador,
Peru, and Bolivia, where the work started the year before
was now showing splendid results. In Guayaquil, Ecuador,
for instance, the Writers' League had sponsored a big campaign. The Coordinator, Alan Reed, and his brother, who
owned a press, had printed thousands of the Laubach lessons
in color. Placards were posted everywhere urging everyone
to teach somebody to read. Cards about literacy were put
into matchboxes, cereal boxes, and other common purchases.
Newspapers gave much publicity and printed thousands of
lessons as supplements. So many illiterates learned to read
that the leaders lost track of the number. They were printing a booklet about the campaign to help other cities.

In Peru, where government and education officials had
been cool the year before, they welcomed Dr. Laubach so
warmly that he could hardly find time to work on the new
improved lessons. Although Miss Dayoan had remained in
Puerto Rico, fortunately Sherwood Reisner, a Yale divinity
student, had joined the group in Colombia. There, while
revising the Spanish lessons, they tried a new idea; above
each syllable in a sentence was placed the same picture that
the new reader had learned to associate with that syllable.
This method seemed at first to make the lessons even easier
than before, but it involved the drawing of more pictures
by the hundreds. When artists could not be found, Mr. Reisner and Mr. Fricke did the drawings and soon became expert
and swift. Later these pictures above the syllables were
abandoned because they interfered with progress in reading
for *meaning*, which must quickly advance beyond syllable
recognition.

In spite of his sixty years it was Dr. Laubach who set the pace for the group. He could not bear to waste time. When they were stranded for three days in Puno, Peru, because of a delayed visa, he started adapting the old Quechua lessons to the Indians of that area. He wrote:

"Puno is a city of Indians. The women nearly all have packs on their backs. They wring one's heart. . . . Tonight the lights are too dim to read or write, and it is cold with no fire. I feel like a caged lion. How people can enjoy doing nothing is beyond my comprehension."

He had already learned that almost all South Americans said, "*Mañana* (tomorrow)." But they responded to his enthusiasm, photographed him and his pupils for the newspapers, asked him to speak on the "Voice of the Andes." Priests and archbishops gave their approval of his work, proving that community activities in literacy developed good will and eased the tensions between Catholic and Protestant groups.

Laubach and his assistants moved on into Paraguay just before Easter. This little country south of Brazil, long known as the "hermit country" of South America, was new territory to the literacy expert. He had not visited any Paraguayan city the year before, but he knew something of the country's tragic history: how it was long ruled by dictators, one of whom led the nation into a war in the 1860's, in which its wealth was so depleted and so many men were killed that Paraguay has not yet recovered. There is little manufacturing or mining, and not much trade with the outside world, partly because the country is landlocked; it has no seaports.

The people are Catholic, and the United States Ambassador, misunderstanding Dr. Laubach's purposes, threw cold water on his plans, fearful that he would rouse latent antagonisms. People with whom Laubach talked disagreed about the amount of illiteracy in Paraguay. Some claimed there was none in the capital Asunción, where everyone spoke Spanish, but that outside the city, where an Indian tongue called Guaraní prevailed, there *might* be a *little* need for teaching. On the other hand, an officer at the military school reported, "A large number of our cadets cannot read or write. No matter what statistics say, illiteracy is enormous in Paraguay."

Dr. Laubach was used to such contradictions; he went quietly to work, calling on teachers and other leaders, visiting schools, asking questions. Fortunately, the new Minister of Education was young and wanted to make his mark; he set the wheels moving.

But Guaraní proved to be very different from other Indian languages, and it was slow work making the lessons. No one in the Office of Education offered to help, and no artist volunteered to draw the pictures. Easter was a holiday time and the weather was unseasonably warm. (It was autumn, of course, in the southern hemisphere.)

Then after two weeks of frustration (was it the heat or the *mañana* habit?) people began to wake up. The president of the Chamber of Commerce helped with the charts, and his daughter, an artist, came to do some of the drawings. Dr. Laubach was asked to speak on the radio, and a Spanish professor offered graciously to correct his prepared speech so that he should make the best possible impression. Students at the Normal School presented him with roses. The President offered to have the literacy charts printed at government expense, and the Ambassador reported that Frank

Laubach had won the hearts of the people of Paraguay as no other North American had ever done. The people there had won his heart, too, and he wished he could stay a year. He was thankful he had allowed over a month for the work in Paraguay. Much had been accomplished in good will as well as in literacy.

He was glad to return for a brief visit to Brazil, where his experiences had been so pleasant the year before. Dr. Lourenço Filho, the great educator, and his staff had been perfecting the Laubach lessons and had them ready for printing. When Dr. Filho saw the new lessons with their slightly different picture plan, his face fell. But after studying them, he agreed that they were better and that the new plan should be adopted even if it caused some delay. He was planning to print 250,000 copies. Dr. Laubach wrote:

"It was one of the happiest experiences of my life to hear the great and vital plan Dr. Lourenço Filho outlined for Brazil. I came away walking on air and sure that Brazil will have the greatest literacy campaign in the western hemisphere. She may well do so. The majority of her people are still illiterate; yet she is destined to become the world's greatest country, with twice the natural resources of any other country. She is mostly frontier even yet, as the United States of America was 150 years ago. It is a land for the future, the greatest future perhaps in the world."

The literacy team left beautiful Rio with regret. In a day's stop at Recife, which had become a great American army center, all three found old friends, one from the United States, one from China, one from the Philippines. In a visit to the Union Theological Seminary, Dr. Laubach gave a demonstration of teaching and to his own amazement found

PLATE 1

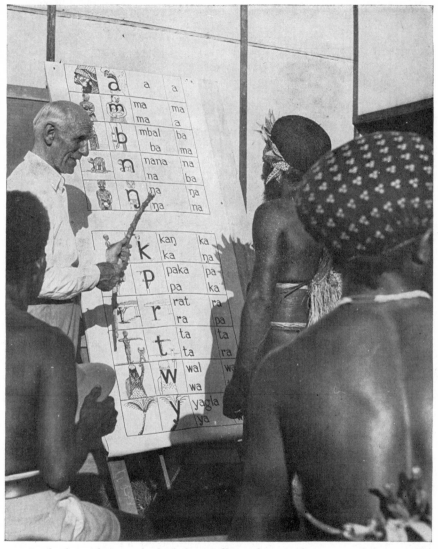

Dr. Laubach teaching a chief of the Medlpa tribe at a literacy conference in the mountains of New Guinea

PLATE 2

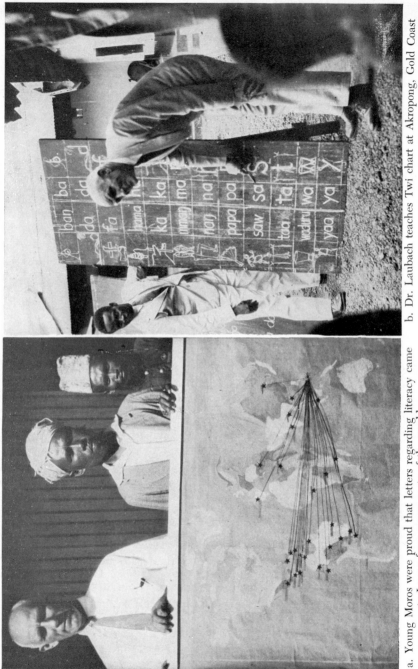

a. Young Moros were proud that letters regarding literacy came to Lanao from many parts of the world

b. Dr. Laubach teaches Twi chart at Akropong, Gold Coast

PLATE 3

a. Daughter teaching her mother to read Arabic in Algiers

b. Students receiving their diplomas at Dondi, in Angola

c. Woman in Tanganyika studying the first Cigogo chart

d. Dr. Laubach helping a teacher and a woman student at Dodoma, Tanganyika

PLATE 4

a. Learning to read in French Cameroun,
West Africa

b. Setting type by monotype at Élat,
French Cameroun

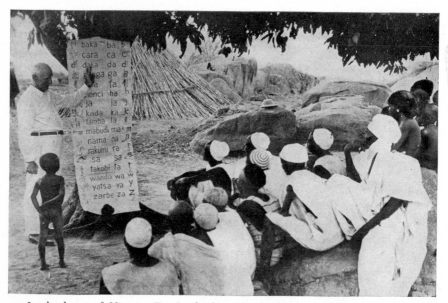

c. In the heart of Nigeria, Dr. Laubach teaches young and old to read their own
language, Hausa

PLATE 5

a. Testing the Hindi chart on the driver of a bullock cart, Marehra, U.P., India

b. Setting type by hand for Christian literature in India, in 1952

PLATE 6

a. Night student at Rajkat learning from
a new Gujerati chart

b. New readers selecting books from village library box in India

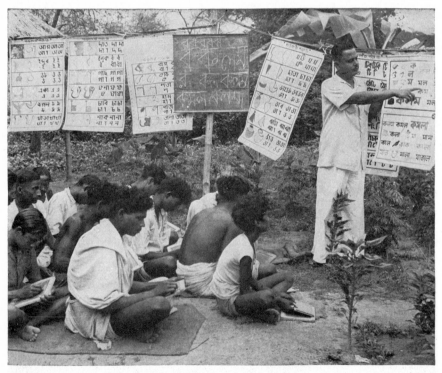

c. Bengali class using new charts at Birdwan, India

PLATE 7

a. Training teachers to use Hindi charts

b. Young Bible student at Taegu teaches an elderly Korean woman to read

PLATE 8

a. Woman teacher and pupil reading
   Creole in Haiti

b. New readers in Honduras

c. Dr. Laubach teaching in Mexico

himself speaking in Portuguese! He claims no special aptitude for languages, and of course does not try to master all
the languages in which he helps to prepare lessons. Some-
how he had imbibed Portuguese.

His next stop was Port of Spain, Trinidad, another British
crown colony, an island off the coast of Venezuela. It supplies the world with much sugar, oil, and especially asphalt
from its famous pitch lake. Dr. Laubach reached Trinidad
on May 31, and on June 6 he wrote: "The air is tense with
the invasion [of Normandy], news of which comes in over
the radio every hour. We prayed in silence at the outset of
our meeting this afternoon for the boys in that awful fight.
God hasten its end."

He revised the English lessons made in Jamaica to con-
form to the vocabulary of Trinidad. On the committee who
helped were three second-generation East Indians (that is,
from India), and he found that their people constitute
a third of the population of Trinidad. Churches, welfare
agencies, and government united in starting the literacy campaign. Dr. Laubach wrote: "No other government in this
tour showed keener eagerness to do a thorough job. One
gained increasing confidence that they will not only feel
deeply but will carry on to success."

Mr. Fricke and Mr. Reisner went on to Mexico, according
to previous plans, and Dr. Laubach flew to Havana, Cuba.
There he spent the busiest three weeks of the entire tour
and greatly missed his two assistants. He wrote:

"I cannot understand the packed churches every night,
for my talks are poor, unprepared. But the interest is intense . . . I wish there were in my party a natural born
writer who could keep close at my elbow and write the

many, many touching incidents of each day. I need a combination of photographer, artist, newspaper reporter, and manager for these trips."

In addition to promoting a literacy campaign he was conducting a kind of seminar for four observers, who had been assigned to learn his methods in order that they might carry on literacy work in other regions. He wrote:

"The only trouble has been that the dear Cuban people made such a heavy program that there has been no time for our seminar people to have conferences by ourselves. However, under that plan they would have missed seeing the tremendous pressure under which we usually hold our campaigns. If they didn't have lectures, at least they had first-hand experience. Cuba is the exciting climax of this eight months' tour."

Happy, but nearly exhausted, he flew home on June 30, 1944. Early in 1945 he went southward again for a month's strenuous work in Mexico and Honduras.

And what were the tangible results of these three tours of Latin America? Here are a few of the items of news that came to the attention of the Committee on World Literacy and Christian Literature in New York between 1944 and 1947, revealing how much Laubach's work had helped to stimulate social progress:

1944—"In August, President Avila Camacho of Mexico issued a decree requiring that everyone know how to read and write by February 28, 1946. Radio, newspapers, magazines, and posters are telling the reading public that each person between the ages of eighteen and sixty must teach at least one illiterate to read and write. Citizens are cooperating enthusiastically. President Camacho himself has a class of young people."

1944—"The President of Haiti offered $200 in prizes for the best folklore stories in Creole. One of the prize winners was a young man who had learned to read and write only three months before. The newspaper in Creole for new literates was printing a larger edition than any French newspaper in Haiti."

1946—"The government of Guatemala, in a four-year campaign, has undertaken to raise its literacy rate from 65 to 95 per cent. Nearly four hundred persons from every walk of life have volunteered to teach in the night schools, where two thousand are enrolled. One penny will buy a copy of the magazine for new literates entitled *Pan* (Bread). It is printed in large type and contains information on agriculture and health, as well as spiritual helps."

1946—"*Selecciones of the Reader's Digest* published a pamphlet *Como Ensenar a Leer por el Metodo de Laubach* (How to teach reading by the Laubach method) in an edition of a million copies to be distributed free throughout Latin America. Governments were ordering them faster than they could be delivered."

1946—"In La Paz, Bolivia, plans were made at a conference of missionaries for conducting a literacy campaign in Spanish, Quechua, and Aymará. Their slogan was, 'Reading opens the windows of the soul!' "

1947—"The government of Brazil in April launched an immense literacy campaign using a million and a half Portuguese charts based on the Laubach method, with teaching to be done by primary- and secondary-school teachers, assisted by volunteers. The first booklet was called *Ler*. When a new adult reader mastered that, he was ready for *Saber* and *Viver*, two booklets discussing everyday needs and an individual's relation to family, community, state, and world.

Dr. Lourenço Filho said: 'Undoubtedly a new spirit in favor of fundamental education is being established in our country.' "

Most important in its world influence was the fact that in 1946 the newly organized UNESCO in the United Nations placed literacy as the first educational project to be considered at its meeting in Paris, and asked Dr. Laubach for a report on techniques and methods useful in promoting literacy campaigns.

Meanwhile, was Frank Laubach resting on his laurels? Of course not. In 1945 and 1946 he conducted Literacy Institutes at four colleges in the United States, explaining his techniques and methods to missionaries at home on furlough and to young people planning to go out to mission fields. This teaching was later taken over by Dr. J. Maurice Hohlfeld of the Hartford Seminary.

Dr. Laubach also prepared a book, *Streamlined English Lessons,* and these were tested in experiments at Teachers College of Columbia University and in the Adult Education Department of the New York public schools. Then, as second readers for new literates, he wrote *The Story of Jesus,*[1] a series of booklets telling the most important episodes in the life of Jesus. These were written in simple English with phonetic helps so that new literates could begin to read the Scriptures at once. Such booklets were also prepared in simple Spanish. And to go along with them, Dr. Laubach and others wrote a book called *Making Everybody's World Safe* which, in easy-to-read sentences, explains the fundamental ideals of democracy and of the United Nations.

And as if all this were not enough to keep a man busy,

[1] *The Story of Jesus* gives the life and teachings of Jesus from the four Gospels in a vocabulary of 1500 words. It has been translated into forty languages.

Page from Brazilian primer.
Primeiro guia de leitura, *Ler*.

Dr. Laubach with collaborators prepared a handbook for literacy workers everywhere called *Teaching the World To Read* (1947). He was becoming known as the Apostle of Literacy.

As the world slowly recovered from six years of war, it seemed as if an era of opportunity for all backward peoples was about to begin and an awakening to the true message of Christ—a time of "peace on earth, good will toward men."

In October, 1946, Frank and Effa Laubach returned to the Philippines for several months. When they reached Mindanao, they found the city of Cagayan in ruins. This was not so much through enemy attack as because of the "scorched-earth" policy used in the American withdrawal in 1941. Most of the old stone or concrete foundations of buildings were intact, and on these the people had built houses of nipa palm or were living under American canvas. Everywhere there were Army jeeps. But travel was difficult because many bridges had been bombed.

Up in the hills at Lanao the destruction was less evident. Their former home and the church and school were intact, but the things they had left, including all Dr. Laubach's research concerning the old Maranaw songs and legends, were gone. The orange groves they and their friends had planted were ruined.

As in other parts of the Philippines, any Americans who did not escape before the Japanese attack had gone into hiding, but they had been protected by Filipino friends, often at great risk. The Laubachs heard many tales of danger and of heroism during their months in Lanao.

CHAPTER 10

"The Directed Will"

> *"Religion seems to me today to be not doctrine or faith primarily, but primarily the directed will. That is my task, to hold my will to the current of power and let Thee sweep through endlessly."*—F. C. L.

When a man close to the age of retirement goes about his work with superb efficiency and also with the enthusiasm of youth, people begin to ask, "How does he do it? What is the source of his energy?"

Frank Laubach is now well past sixty, white-haired and somewhat bald, still lean of build; he works too hard and moves too fast to gather any extra flesh. His face has mellowed, as all kind faces do. The eyes twinkle sometimes, but often there is in them the look of the seer and the prophet. Indeed, Frank Laubach is known, among an inner circle of friends, as a mystic of mystics. Since that hour on Signal Hill he has become increasingly sure of the guidance of God, sure that God has a purpose in the world, and that it is every man's privilege to cooperate in attaining that purpose.

For many years he has kept a journal of his experiences in trying to do the will of God. He believes that people should share such experiences with one another in order to gain strength. A Moslem once quoted to him from the Koran the same idea: "One hour spent talking about God is better than seventy years spent in prayers alone." But Dr. Laubach understands the general American reluctance to speak of such personal matters. In 1930 he wrote: "I think the average man doesn't speak of his feeling about God because it isn't done outside of church and Sunday school. He fears being called either a goody or a hypocrite."

To break down this reluctance in himself he has written frankly and freely to his family and friends about his own spiritual struggles, combining news about such matters with accounts of his work and the humdrum of daily living. In 1937, Constance E. Padwick of Cairo, Egypt, compiled excerpts from the letters in a small book entitled *Letters by a Modern Mystic*, which has gone into a fourteenth printing.

Not long after his experience on Signal Hill in Lanao, Frank Laubach wrote:

"The sense of being led by an unseen hand which takes mine, while another hand reaches ahead and prepares the way, grows upon me daily. I do not need to strain at all to find opportunity. It piles in upon me as the waves roll over the beach, and yet there is time to do something about each opportunity."

When someone asked him once, "Is it necessary to pray?" his answer was:

"No, prayer is not necessary; it is a privilege. Beauty is not necessary if you prefer ugliness. . . . Refusal to pray is a form of insanity, and it means that the spirit is committing suicide."

Dr. Laubach believes in prayer, not only in church or at certain hours of the day, but during every waking hour. In 1942, while in Rio de Janeiro he wrote: "To ask: 'What next, who next, where next, Lord?' and training one's thoughts to follow God's leading is the hardest, deepest discipline any man can have and the most rewarding." Through the years he has trained himself by a "game with minutes" to follow this discipline.

He believes that the answer to prayer comes very clearly when one's will is completely attuned to God's will: "I feel that if life is wholly yielded to God it becomes like a violin fitting into the music of an orchestra, only this music has a purpose which pierces eternity."

He believes in praying for others. He is confident that in what we call mental telepathy we have a clue to the reality and power of thought waves; that true prayer represents the use of these thought waves under God's guidance; and that we have barely begun to use the power of prayer. His book on prayer, published in 1946 is called *Prayer: the Mightiest Force in the World.* In a later book, *Wake Up or Blow Up,* (1951) he urges all who believe in prayer to pray often for persons in positions of responsibility, especially for those who represent us in the United Nations.

No one who has followed Frank Laubach's career will ever again confuse the word *mystic* with mere piety or dreamy wishful thinking. Like most of the world's renowned mystics, Dr. Laubach is strenuous. All who have gone with him on literacy tours agree that he can outwork any of them. His energy and fortitude are phenomenal. In African equatorial heat or in the frigid altitudes of Afghanistan he pushes ahead, making new lessons in various languages and dialects, planning and writing for illiterates as if fatigue were an unknown word. He attributes it all to God's power working through him and is sure that anyone can have the same dynamic energy who keeps the Divine current turned on through prayer.

Not everyone, of course, is gifted with Dr. Laubach's intellect and originality. Only a fine mind, well-trained, could master the intricacies of language as he has done. Only an original thinker could have developed the key-word plan for teaching Maranaw in the first place. Only originality and patience made possible the continued improvement of the charts and their adaptation to each new language problem.

Dr. Laubach is a rare combination of mystic and scientist. In his book *India Shall Be Literate,* a handbook for literacy workers, published in India in 1940, he wrote in answer to those who asked "What is your method?"

"We have no final method yet, excepting to be forever dissatisfied, to study all methods, to try those that look most promising, to adopt what is best, to improve on them where possible, and to throw them away the moment something better appears. . . . There are those who say that several methods are equally good and that 'the will to learn is what really matters.' This simply is not the whole truth nor half of the truth. Easy lessons with interesting content will beget the will to learn, while over-difficult lessons with no meaning will discourage the stoutest heart. . . . We must beware of deciding [on the method] by logic or argument. Only experience is reliable. 'Nobody knows which is the best lesson but the illiterate.'"

This is the scientific approach. Always his attitude is: "If we aren't sure, let's experiment and find out." The persons with whom he has least patience are those who waste months and years surveying problems, discussing them, but doing nothing.

We have seen how, after starting with the key-word method in the Philippines and finding that it was only partly

		a	i	o	u
amo		a	i	o	u
mama		ma	mi	mo	mu
sapi		sa	si	so	su
karabao		ka	ki	ko	ku
tali		ta	ti	to	tu
babak		ba	bi	bo	bu
lapad		la	li	lo	lu
nanas		na	ni	no	nu
papanok		pa	pi	po	pu
gantang		ga	gi	go	gu
dado		da	di	do	du
rantai		ra	ri	ro	ru
ngari		nga	ngi	ngo	ngu

Maranaw picture-chain chart.

successful in India, he began to combine pictures with the key words. Then, because the new lessons did not lend themselves to the each-one-teach-one plan, he and others at Godhra developed the picture-word-syllable method. Even though the lessons built by this method were received with enthusiasm, he continued experimenting, and on his return to the Philippines developed "picture-chain" charts, which were still easier for illiterates to use because the chain of pictures helped the memory. This method also proved successful in India and elsewhere because illiterates usually have excellent visual memories. Later came the idea of using pictures that suggest the shapes of the letters. Each picture is thus a key to the sound that begins a word, and a key to the word itself. (*See the chart in the illustration on plate 1.*) This method has proved useful with Arabic, Persian, Korean, and other alphabets as well as with our Roman alphabet. Dr. Laubach is daringly experimental.

Another quality that impresses those who work with him is his amazing adaptability. After a lively discussion with scholars concerning alphabets, syllabaries, phonetics, or reformed spelling, he can sit down beside an unlettered Indian of the Andes or a Negro in the Congo area and quietly give him, not only a lesson in reading, but a new feeling of self-confidence and pride.

One of Dr. Laubach's associates who has watched him at work in varied surroundings said: "After all it is the Christlike spirit in him that is more important than any of his methods. That is why he is accomplishing so much while other groups discuss and survey but do little or nothing about this problem of world literacy."

The Christlike spirit also reveals itself in his honest humility. An old friend in Benton likes to tell about the day when Dr. Laubach, at home for a few weeks from his world travels, was visiting with a group of men whom he had known for years. They talked of business, farming, politics, church and school problems—all the things in which different ones were interested. During a sudden pause Frank heaved a long sigh and remarked, "I wish I knew something!" The other men stared at him incredulously and then burst out laughing. It was fantastic to hear such a remark from the language scholar, world missionary, and statesman; and yet they were sure he meant exactly what he said.

Opinions about a man in his old home town are often an acid test of character—both of the man and of the town. Many "a prophet is not without honor save in his own country." But the town of Benton both honors and loves Frank Laubach. A woman of the younger generation there expressed the general attitude when she said: "While I was growing up, I knew just three places in the world—Benton, our neighboring city, Wilkes-Barre, and the Philippines where the Laubachs had gone."

In spite of long absences, the Laubachs have kept in close touch with the home folks and are welcomed as belonging to Benton whenever they return. When plans were developing for a new window in the Methodist church to harmonize with a beautiful one installed some years earlier, Frank Laubach was one of the first to contribute. And he made the wise suggestion that the young people of the Sunday school be asked to choose the subject to be represented in stained glass. In order to make their choice they would have to think about the Scriptures, the purpose of stained-glass windows in a church, the beauty of the older window. They would learn much. The following winter they received from England an old engraving which showed Christ in the attitude of prayer. Dr. Laubach, in the midst of busy days abroad, had found time to send a picture which he thought might help the young people in choosing the subject for the window.

When a school building was ready to be dedicated in Benton, a member of the school board asked advice of Frank Laubach about the program of dedication. In a few days he received some typewritten pages headed DEDICATORY RESPONSIVE. Copies were printed and ready for the hundreds who gathered to dedicate the new building.

DEDICATORY RESPONSIVE

Everyone is requested to join in the responses.

Leader. To the spirit of warm friendship and cooperation which binds this community—

People. We dedicate this building.

Leader. To the building of men and women who shall continue and enrich this community spirit in the years to come—

People. We dedicate this building.

Leader. To the type of education which combines culture with efficient service in the vocations to which youth is called—

People. We dedicate this building.

Leader. To the lifting of agriculture from dreary guesswork to the inspiring plane of science and professional skill—

People. We dedicate this building.

Leader. To help transform housekeeping into the art of homemaking—

People. We dedicate this building.

Leader. To the habit of patient, persistent, purposive toil, without which no worthy achievement is possible—

People. We dedicate this building.

Leader. To supplying a long-felt need for a center ror community activities—

People. We dedicate this building.

Leader. To furnishing those whose formal school days are ended with library and laboratory facilities for adding to their knowledge—

People. We dedicate this building.

Leader. To join hands with the home and the church in building characters sensitive to the will of God and the needs of men—

People. We dedicate this building.

Leader. To the enkindling of a noble passion for individual and civic righteousness—

People. We dedicate this building.

Leader. To prepare youth for enlightened citizenship by acquainting it with the affairs of our nation and the world—

People. We dedicate this building.

Leader. To the help of our new neighbors who have come from distant places to live and labor among us—

People. We dedicate this building.

Leader. To the dawning of a generous toleration and the dissipation of blind and poisonous prejudice—

People. We dedicate this building.

Leader. To the great vision of working together for a better world; to the promotion of peace, good will, and human brotherhood—

People. We dedicate this building.

Surely no school ever had a more auspicious opening than that given by reverent voices joined in this litany, enabling the audience to share in the dedication. It was just like Frank Laubach to remember that such participation is important.

CHAPTER 11

Africa Awakens

"Oh, spirit of Livingstone, how can I best
help the land you opened, the land where you
perished?"—F. C. L.

Through the years Frank Laubach had felt the challenge of
the great continent of Africa. En route home after his first
visit to India he had stopped briefly in Cairo and made some
lessons in Arabic, more or less as an experiment. In the
spring of 1937 he spent fifty strenuous days in East Africa
and learned much about the need for literacy work and the
problems involved. But he did more than make a survey;
for wherever Dr. Laubach sees a need, he has an urge to
do something about it at once.

Landing at Mombasa, principal port of Kenya, a British
protectorate, he took an evening train for Nairobi, the capital. Like all travelers, he was fascinated next morning by
glimpses of zebras, giraffes, antelope, wildebeests, grazing
on the veldt, the grassy plain that is a wild-game preserve
extending for hundreds of miles along the railway. The animals seemed symbolic of the vastness and wonders of the
African continent.

The Director of Education in Nairobi sent him on to Ki-
sumu, a lovely town on the shore of Lake Victoria, where
he found the teachers in a school for boys eager to try lessons in the Luo language. There he was amused to discover

that his sleeping room was on one side of the equator and his workroom on the other side. One evening, just for fun, he stepped back and forth across the equator a thousand times, which, he maintained, established some sort of world record.

Making lessons in Africa proved to be much simpler than in India because the languages are more nearly phonetic, but three problems at once arose. First, what spelling to use? Europeans, encountering the unwritten languages of Africa, had spelled them like their own languages—Italian, German, French, Portuguese—without much regard for simplicity. Kikuyu, for example, spoken by over a million people, was spelled like Italian in North Kenya and somewhat like German in other sections. In such cases, it was necessary to choose which spelling, and Dr. Laubach asked three educated Africans to make the decision.

A second problem arose when he encountered sounds for which we have no letters in the Roman alphabet. The Zulus, for example, have three sounds somewhat like the cracking sound one makes in the back of the mouth when saying "get up" to a horse. What letters should represent these sounds? Kq? kqx? qxg? Or some entirely new symbols?

The third and biggest problem in Africa was what language to teach in certain sections. There are three main language groups: Bantu, Hamitic, and Nilotic or Sudanic, but there are hundreds of languages and dialects, some spoken by several million people, some by a few thousand. Where dialects are similar it would save time and money to prepare only lessons that could be used by large numbers. The missionaries agreed to make word lists and to have the best scholars compare these lists. A year would be needed for such work.

Dr. Laubach next went southward along the coast to Zanzibar, which had once been the center of the Arab slave traders. When it became a British protectorate in 1890, that trade was abolished, largely because the great David Livingstone had roused the conscience of mankind, but the slave drivers' language survived. It is called Swahili and is a kind of *lingua franca* (common tongue) all over East Africa. Laubach and an energetic committee quickly made lessons in Swahili, in two sets, one with Roman letters, the other with Arabic. Then at Dar es Salaam, capital of Tanganyika, he tried a new experiment with the Swahili lessons. An African boy made pictures, not only for all the consonants with one vowel: *ba, ma, sa,* etc., but for all the consonants with every vowel: *ba, be, bi, bo, bu.* This change involved hours of labor, but it made the lessons much easier for the learner because, once he got the idea, he could go on discovering the sounds of letters for himself. At the first trial of this new kind of chart, Dr. Laubach reported:

"One young fellow, learning the syllables, suddenly discovered that he could pronounce new words alone. With victory gleaming in his eye, he shouted, 'Give me a book! I can read!' And he did, as elated as Columbus when he first sighted the coast of the New World."

It was the women of Africa who especially roused Dr. Laubach's sympathy. He saw lines of women trudging up the steep hills, bent under two-hundred-pounds packs held by straps around their foreheads. He was told that girls of certain tribes were trained in early childhood for this heavy work. The government had tried to discourage the practice by making sixty pounds the legal load for women as for men. But the women refused to obey, saying "Who are we that we should be limited to the load that a man is able to carry?"

In the cities he saw women with far different problems. They were the thousands whose men had left the tribal life to work in modern industry. They lived in crowded quarters, and the women, though well clothed and fed, had nothing to do, their minds untrained and their hands idle. They flocked to the literacy classes held in a girls' school and begged to have lessons on Saturday as on other days.

When Dr. Laubach left Africa on June 1 that year, he hoped to return soon; but plans for a visit in 1940 were interrupted by the war. However, through the war years he received word that at least forty mission stations developed lessons like those begun in 1937 and that they were bringing good results. A chaplain serving with East African troops in 1942 wrote:

"You would be amazed at the sale of literature among African soldiers. I simply cannot keep pace with the demand. When work is over, a walk around the camps shows groups of Africans reading, singing, and some studying, the place littered with books."

In January, 1947, Dr. Laubach went back to Africa, but this time to Egypt, that puzzling land of extremes—fertility and desert, wealth and poverty, proud past and uncertain future. Its people were 90 per cent illiterate. He found government representatives quite as eager as the mission groups of all denominations to unite in the common cause of nation-wide literacy.

The Laubach lessons were copied by the best calligrapher in Cairo, with the ancient Arabic script down one side of a page and opposite it the modernized letters designed by a young Moslem architect named Khattar. His "unified" Arabic alphabet had been endorsed at a UNESCO conference in the Middle East. He had reduced the necessary symbols from five hundred to thirty, so that, it was hoped, the new learners would be able to read and write in about a tenth of the time formerly needed. Follow-up books, *Four Friends of Egypt*, *The Story of Jesus*, and *Helping the United Nations*, were prepared.

Later two young women distributed these books through Upper Egypt in a way that might make any adventurous girl want to be a missionary. These two traveled up and down the Nile in a houseboat, an old sailing vessel equipped with living quarters. At strategic points they moored the houseboat and used a bookmobile, converted from an army ambulance, to travel to the little country churches. There they talked with the village people, especially the women, and added a few books to a library shelf of perhaps twenty or thirty volumes. Needed most of all were simple books on child care, homemaking, family life, community service. There in the land of Cleopatra, women, perhaps descended from her slaves, were awakening and eager to escape from their bondage of ignorance.

All through the Middle East, governments were aroused to the need of doing something for their people. In May, 1947, Dr. Laubach went to Ethiopia, a Christian country since the fourth century, but one that has remained almost solidly illiterate. Working with Emperor Haile Selassie's educational adviser, he helped to simplify another alphabet, this time in the Amharic language. The government ordered typewriters and linotype dies in the simplified alphabet and planned that hundreds of boys from the Emperor's schools should return to their villages and teach the adults to read and write.

The following month Dr. Laubach spent in Syria, Lebanon, and Iran, countries that had won new political independence, which made more education urgent. Everywhere he made sure that committees were organized to prepare reading matter for the new learners—reading matter that was practical, democratic, and Christian.

In October, 1947, he spoke at a series of missionary conferences in London. At nearly the same time Mr. Alfred D. Moore, the new executive secretary of the Committee on World Literacy and Christian Literature, stood before the UNESCO Conference in Mexico City and demonstrated the Laubach literacy methods to delegates from all the members of the United Nations. Literacy had become a problem to be shouldered by governments as well as by Christian missionaries. Dr. Laubach and his Committee had emerged as world statesmen.

Late in 1947 he returned to Africa, and this time the wish he had voiced in Cuba was realized. He had an assistant who could help report the human-interest aspects of the work. His son Bob was with him as reporter, typist, and photographer. Bob was by this time in his late twenties. His hobby was photography and he had also, like his father, a knack with words. His pictures added a vivid new touch to the letters they sent in from the field. These letters, reproduced by offset printing, were subscribed to by hundreds of interested readers in all the churches supporting the Committee. They have become an important feature of the literacy work.

The "literacy team," 1947–48, included, besides Dr. Laubach and Bob, Mr. and Mrs. S. Herold Olsen of Denmark, who had offered their services without salary. Mr. Olsen, an entomologist by profession and also a competent artist, did the thousands of drawings needed for the charts and lessons. With Bob presiding over the mimeograph, they turned out lesson sheets at a dizzy speed. They had to, for in Liberia alone, they prepared lessons in eight different languages in two weeks.

From November, 1947, to June, 1948, the team visited Sierra Leone, Liberia, the Gold Coast, the Belgian Congo, the Cameroons, Nigeria, Northern and Southern Rhodesia, and the Union of South Africa. A look at the map of Africa will show what a stupendous task they had undertaken.

The story of this one tour would fill a good-sized book. The days were crammed with incident. In Nigeria one of their interviews was with a chief who sat on his throne under a royal umbrella. After four of his men had learned the first chart in a few minutes, he directed them to teach others at once. All of them began bowing with their faces to the ground in front of Dr. Laubach, but this sort of ceremony he couldn't stand. He begged them with gestures to rise, and showed them how to say their thanks in American style by shaking hands.

In Liberia one of the demonstrations was held at the executive mansion of President Tubman—with his illiterate waiters acting as pupils. A mission worker later reported that Dr. Laubach's visit opened her eyes to the possibilities of cooperation not only with other missions but also with the government. She wrote:

"The people have a great respect for the word of their leader, the President. Everyone wants to learn to read, especially in the first flush of enthusiasm. But it is good to have the President remind the people, when they get weary, that he desires and commands them all to learn to read and to teach others."

In Northern Rhodesia Dr. Laubach wrote:

"One of the top experiences of my life was to stand under the colossal monument of David Livingstone as he gazes across Victoria Falls, first seen by him among all white men, in 1855. He died just seventy-five years ago. . . . Livingstone came here to free the slaves, but the Africans will not be free from the worst slavery until they can read, and know the freedom which Jesus Christ gives."

The British government invited Dr. Laubach to observe the mass literacy campaigns already started in the Copper Belt, a chain of six or seven mines, where thousands of workers live in great company compounds. Experiments among them had shown that they learned best when taught individually by a friend or relative—a method suggested by Dr. Laubach's each-one-teach-one plan. It had worked like magic. Thousands of the workers had already become literate. Dr. Laubach found that fairly good lessons were in use, but was able to show how they could be streamlined. The government at once adopted the changes, published the lessons in newspapers, and proposed to teach them by radio broadcasts. The craving for literacy was also keen in remote villages, where women wanted to learn to read and write letters, in order to keep in touch with absent husbands and sons.

While in Rhodesia, Dr. Laubach was pleased to have news that the Swahili lessons he had helped to make in the Congo could be printed on a new offset press in Nairobi so cheaply that they could be sold for five cents each. "The illiterate can now begin his education for a nickel," he wrote, "with volunteer teaching by the each-one-teach-one method (tuition free)."

As he traveled southward, he was troubled by evidences of the race problem:

"Southern Rhodesia is already a white man's country. . . . I suppose nothing short of Heaven can stop the tide which creeps up from the south of Africa, which means that Africa is becoming the white man's garden—unless the white race annihilates itself meanwhile with its civilization-destroying wars.

"The strategy now for the African is to achieve just as much culture, and make just as great a contribution as he can, and so win the admiration of the white man.

"I think we are doing the one thing that can help the Negro of Africa. We are helping him to enlarge his vision, to understand the world problem, and to make a greater contribution toward world welfare. Literacy is helping him to help himself. Christian missions are helping him to catch the spirit of Jesus, without which no education of any kind is safe."

CHAPTER 12

Amazing Contrasts

"Literacy is building a bridge to ten million
minds a year. . . . We cannot destroy that
bridge, but we can cross it with a great army
of books and papers."—F. C. L.

In 1949 Dr. Laubach and a literacy team visited the Far
East. Of all his journeys to date, it was the most spectacular
because of its contrasts. Imagine going from Bangkok with
its ornately spired Buddhist temples and ancient, exquisite art
of the dance, to India in a ferment of progress following its
achievement of independence, thence to the highlands of
New Guinea, still inhabited by cannibals, and then to South
Korea, at that time a land just freed from Japanese occupation and vibrant with hope.

The letters from the literacy team tell of tea in the King
of Siam's garden; a sing-sing by thousands of New Guinea
warriors clad in pig's grease and bird-of-paradise feathers;
a Korean prayer meeting in a former Shinto school overlooking the city of Seoul. Bob Laubach's pictures plus Phil
Gray's drawings made the series fascinating to their many
American readers.

The invitation to visit Thailand (formerly known as Siam)
shows how Dr. Laubach's reputation had mounted during
the years. At the UNESCO meeting in Mexico City late in
1947, where Alfred Moore of the Literacy Committe dem-

onstrated the Laubach methods, the Director of Adult Education for Thailand was present. Mr. Boon Chuey Sombongse was so impressed that, after a little consultation with Mr. Moore, he asked that Dr. Laubach should visit his country and cooperate with his government and UNESCO in organizing literacy campaigns.

Dr. Laubach and Bob left New York by airplane in the midst of a snowstorm, and a week later, in spite of four days' delay in Karachi, they were enjoying the balmy air of Bangkok, the beautiful capital of Thailand. The artists of the literacy team, Phillip and Ewing Gray, arrived by boat two days later. This young couple had been fired with interest in Laubach's work when they heard him speak in an Ohio church. Their hobby was art, and when they learned that their talents in drawing could be used in making attractive lessons for the illiterates they decided to join the team.

They were all received by Mr. Boon Chuey and other government officials as if they were visiting royalty. Movies were made of all their first public appearances and were widely shown in order to publicize the literacy campaign throughout the country. Dr. Laubach wrote that the expectations of the Siamese were so high that he was frightened for fear of disappointing them. The Siamese language, he knew, is a difficult one with a long and complicated alphabet. As always, he enlisted the cooperation of everyone who had previously worked in promoting literacy. The Department of Education had already prepared some lessons based on well-known Siamese proverbs. He added the scheme of teaching the letters by associating the shape of each letter with the picture of an object, the word for which began with that letter. Two experts, a Siamese named Saranya and the Reverend Paul Eakin, who had worked for years with the language, helped prepare these alphabet lessons, the Grays and some native artists drew hundreds of pictures, and Bob prepared stencils for the mimeograph.

The lessons were used at a teachers' institute, organized somewhat on the American plan. About two hundred teachers and school inspectors from all over Thailand gathered for a month in Bangkok and were trained how to teach the lessons. They took turns demonstrating, while the others in the class criticized them on the basis of courtesy, patience, and good humor. At first these teachers were slow to join in discussion in the democratic way, but Dr. Laubach gradually persuaded them to question him and to express their own opinions. Each day they also listened to lectures by government leaders on better nutrition, child care, farming, and other practical matters. Each was asked to write in simple words and sentences an article on some subject that would be of interest to new literates. These articles were used to make the second lesson book.

Every afternoon the teachers went to a neighboring small town and practiced their skill on a class of illiterates. The same kind of institute was held the following two weeks in the village of Jaw Haw, in a rural region where the language and the needs of the people were somewhat different.

It was hoped that these two "pilot projects," demonstrating how and what to teach, would enable the teachers to start such projects all over the country. As more and more people learned to read, they would more quickly assimilate all the new knowledge of health, sanitation, nutrition, and agriculture, which a progressive government was trying to spread before them.

Some of the articles written in the class at Jaw Haw were pasted on the wall under the title *Good News*. This "wall newspaper" proved so effective that it was decided to publish a regular newspaper for new literates, in very simple language, using the nine hundred words they would know after mastering their two books.

Exceptionally good news from the United States reached the literacy team in Thailand—the news of President Truman's call for a "bold new program" of technical assistance to areas needing help, the government program which has come to be called Point Four.

In the book *Wake Up or Blow Up,* published two years later, Dr. Laubach told how a talk of his own was partly responsible for President Truman's plan. Several years before, in a New York church, he had been telling about some of his experiences in helping illiterates. The rector's wife, whose father was a United States Senator, was so inspired by what he told that she called her father in Washington and said she wanted the President to hear Dr. Laubach's story. A few days later a conference was arranged. Laubach, accompanied by the Reverend Sam Shoemaker and Senator Alexander Smith, went to the White House, and described to the President the sorry plight of illiterates and how grateful they always are to those who help them. He explained his belief that if America would share her technical knowledge and skill with these people, they would no longer be fooled by communist propaganda.

The President listened intently but made no promises. He said the country needed more religion before it was ready for such a plan. From his words Laubach felt he had been thinking about the matter for a long time and listening to similar advice from other men, among them Dr. Norris Dodd, the agricultural expert. About two years later, in his inaugural address of January 20, 1949, President Truman suddenly called for a "bold new program . . . for the improvement and growth of undeveloped areas."

Dr. Laubach in Thailand saw the news spread across the front page of a newspaper and was jubilant. He wrote:

"People were amazed and thrilled. Point Four shot new hope into the veins of the disintegrating world."

The campaign in Thailand revealed unusually fine cooperation between government officials and missionaries. A number of missionaries visited the two teachers' institutes, and Dr. Laubach spent several days with a group of them discussing the special problems of a Buddhist country. He wrote:

"Buddhism is such a gentle and kindly religion that it is not as easy here as in Africa to demonstrate the superiority of Christianity over their native religion. Buddhists strive for spiritual perfection as Christians do. But there is one great difference: A Christlike person is burning with zeal to help other people, as Jesus did every moment of his life. The perfect Buddhist, on the other hand, is concerned with achieving perfection within himself; and he exceeds the requirements of his religion when he makes great effort to help others. This literacy campaign will suceed, therefore, if it makes the unique spirit of Jesus an evident necessity for the progress of Siam. . . . These kindly Siamese do better than their religion, and when they see that the Way of Christ exceeds the way of Buddha in service they will be impressed."

The Siamese were wonderfully kind and generous in entertaining their Western guests. Dinners, music, plays, dancing, pantomime—each evening something was done to give them pleasure. Bob wrote that during the Jaw Haw project "boys and girls of the schools demonstrated fancy marching

drills and calisthenics, cadets of the Air Corps did gym-
nastics and tumbling, and other students demonstrated Siamese boxing, in which one boxes with feet, elbows, and
knees as well as fists. In the evening three large movie screens
entertained the thousands gathered in the school grounds."

He also described the farewell dinner given by the Minister of Education on the lawn in front of the education
building:

"It was a Chinese dinner, complete from shark fins soup
to birds' nest pudding (with lotus blossoms floating in it),
and nine courses in between. Afterwards, the Minister presented each of us with a lovely gift, decorated with classical
Siamese art. There was a program of Siamese dancing. At
one point two dozen little girl dancers showered the guests
with rose petals."

The literacy team flew from Bangkok to Calcutta. The
next three strenuous weeks in India and Pakistan were both
joyous and disappointing. Much had happened since Dr.
Laubach's last visit ten years before. India had won in her
long struggle for independence, but not exactly in the way
her great leader, Mahatma Gandhi, had hoped. In spite
of his best efforts to keep Hindus and Moslems united,
they had formed separate governments—India and Pakistan.
Gandhi himself had been killed by a fanatic of his own
people.

During the tragic riots between Moslems and Hindus,
when millions were refugees from their homes, the Christians of India had helped all alike, and this service had increased their popularity in many parts of the land. But Dr.
Laubach was sadly disappointed to find that the Christian
churches had not continued their leadership in the program
of literacy for India. Instead, it was the government that

was now most active in promoting literacy; which meant, of course, that the teaching did not always include the Christian message, and might be used to spread an opposing philosophy of life. He found dozens of young Hindus and Moslems passionately eager to help lift their people to new standards of living and sure that literacy was the key to their progress. Such enthusiasm warmed his heart, as did the welcome from many old friends who were still on fire with their zeal for literacy. But some missionaries had found the lessons too hard to be successful by the each-one-teach-one method; and many clung to the old-fashioned idea that they should teach reading first to those who had already become Christians.

"No! Not first," cried Dr. Laubach, "but simultaneously! Many in America say: 'We must make America really Christian before we send out missionaries to other countries.' No, not before, but at the same time. Everyone and especially missionaries should know that literacy is the best of all missionary avenues in this mighty world upsurge of education."

He was heartened by news from home which showed that his pleas had not fallen on deaf ears. Syracuse University had decided to give courses in its school of journalism especially designed for missionaries and young Christians of other lands, to train them "to write simply and fascinatingly" for new literates.

As always, Dr. Laubach set to work in India improving the lessons of ten years before. Government officials at both New Delhi and Madras said: "We liked your other lessons, but if you have new ideas, we want the latest." They agreed also to his suggestions for a second reader of one-page ar-

ticles giving practical information and for a weekly digest
of valuable information, which would gradually build up
the new literates' reading ability. He advised them to ask
the editor of our American *Readers' Digest* to send one of
his skilled writers to teach Indians how to start a *Hindi
Digest* for new Hindi readers.

A missionary at Amritsar in northwest India transported
the literacy team across the border to Lahore in Pakistan.
It took nearly three hours to go from one country to the
other because they were stopped nine times by police or
customs officials.

At Forman Christian College near Lahore they made lessons in Punjabi, using Roman letters for the first time instead of the more difficult Persian letters, and found that
the lessons could be learned in about a quarter of the time.
But with all the new eagerness for education it was startling to find that the woman holding the office of Deputy
Minister of Education maintained constant purdah; outside
her home she was always veiled, like most Moslem women,
from head to foot, with just a peephole through the lace-
work over the eyes. Her aim was to prove that Moslem
women could be educated and take part in the progress of
their country without violating purdah.

Hastening back to Calcutta, the "literacy tramps," as the
Laubachs and Grays called themselves, caught an Australian plane, which in two days' flight took them to Darwin
on the northern coast of Australia. Here they were met by
several missionaries who had flown more than a thousand
miles to learn how to teach reading to the aborigines scattered over that vast section of their southern continent. The
group all together made sets of lessons in four languages in

four days. It meant that the artist, Phil Gray, "worked like a slave. But his pictures got better with every new set of lessons," wrote Dr. Laubach.

Darwin itself, although it had suffered from air raids during the war, looked prosperous and enterprising, with a very modern hospital, a radio station, and most hopeful of all, Dr. Laubach thought, a church bearing the sign, "Methodist, Presbyterian, Congregational *United.*"

As they flew to Brisbane, across eighteen hundred miles of sparsely populated country, they were glad to learn that Australia was letting down its immigration bars to admit European refugees. It has a population of only seven and a half million in an area about the size of the United States.

In Brisbane there were tedious details about the visas and permits necessary for flying to Papua—New Guinea. The travelers landed first at Port Moresby, on the south coast, only ten degrees south of the equator. Their host was a missionary who had succeeded James Chalmers after that hero of Congregational-mission history was eaten by cannibals in 1901. The last of those cannibals had died only the year before, and Dr. Laubach saw half a dozen of their children, now living in Port Moresby.

New Guinea was a land of many surprising contrasts. Women in grass skirts riding about in jeeps; native teachers aboard the airplane, their eyes shining with the thrill of their first flight while their big bare toes gripped the foot rests; the church in Lae jammed with people who spoke in five different languages; a "human pipe organ" consisting of conch shells, one to a man, each man making the single note of his shell blend into the harmonies of familiar hymns; a radio station where newscasters in grass skirts broadcast word of the literacy team's arrival in pidgin, the common tongue of New Guinea. One speech began:

"*I gudpela samting turu sapos yumi ken sikul kuik long rid na rait.* [It's a very good thing to suppose we (you-me) can quickly learn to read and write.] *Long onem liklik taim baimbai igat sampela titsa i kam bilong long-wei peles, Amerika.* [In (long) a little time soon a teacher fellow will come from a faraway place, America."]

If you read the strange-looking words aloud you will find that they sound somewhat like English, though they represent New Guinea patterns of thought.

In Lae they made lessons in pidgin as well as in thirteen other languages with the help of missionaries and native teachers. Dr. Laubach described the Administrator of Papua-New Guinea as "the most sincere and hard-working governor I have seen in any colony in the world."

You have read in the first chapter of this book about his amazing visit to the New Guinea highlands where big chiefs for miles around had come in paint and feathers with thousands of their people to learn the white men's secret for better ways of living. When they found that Dr. Laubach and his helpers could not stay and visit all their tribes, one chief begged, "Then go to the white man's countries and tell many more missionaries to come here and teach us to do right."

Dr. Laubach wrote:

"As we flew back to the south coast of New Guinea, we saw a great clearing in the midst of the jungle. The steward told us that is the Kukukuku country, where no white man has ever yet gone and returned alive. 'Cook-you-cook-you' seemed like a good name for those cannibals. I was told that they are hostile because the first whites to visit them were policemen who shot them. Now the Lutheran mission is trying to overcome with love the hatred aroused in that tribe by earlier bad treatment."

They returned to Australia to report to large and interested crowds about their remarkable days in New Guinea. Their next destination was Korea, but news had come that, because Shanghai was closed, they would have to go by way of Tokyo. A military permit to enter Japan usually required weeks. Dr. Laubach sent a personal appeal to General MacArthur, and the permit came by the time they had reached Bangkok. Dr. Laubach wrote:

"We travelers strongly favor a world government for purely personal reasons, for we waste so much time getting passports, visas, injections, and permits, going through customs, and dodging wars."

They were welcomed in Seoul by a woman missionary, nearing seventy, but driving her own jeep like a youngster. She had read Dr. Laubach's book, *The Silent Billion Speak*, and had roused the interest of everyone around her in literacy. With the help of two Korean professors of language, Dr. Laubach soon had a primer of sixty pages ready to be mimeographed. He found the staff of the United States Information Service ready to cooperate in publishing the material and distributing it.

The conferences held in Seoul, Chongju, and Taegu were most enthusiastic, for the South Koreans had many strong Christian churches. Christianity has had a longer history in Korea than many of us realize. It began in the late sixteenth century when a few priests arrived during a Chinese invasion. By the middle of the nineteenth century there were more than twenty thousand converts to Christianity. They were cruelly persecuted until 1882 when Korea made its first treaties with Western powers. By 1944 the Christians of Korea numbered well over half a million. After the partition of the country at the 38th Parallel, streams of refugee Christians from the north had poured into South Korea. There were huge congregations in all the churches, and they kept saying: "Each-one-teach-one-and-win-one-to-Christ is our hope. We must make all Korea Christian. We must convert the Communists."

Tension and fear of the future were apparent everywhere. In Seoul for three days the streets were blocked by marching people, with banners begging America not to leave Korea undefended. On one of the mountains that surround the city, people prayed night and day for a peaceful settlement between North and South.

Among the illiterates who flocked to the churches eager to learn were many women, some young mothers with babies on their backs, some gray-haired grandmothers. In Korean fashion they left their shoes at the door and sat or squatted on the floor beside their teachers. When they found how easily they could learn to read, their gratitude was pathetic. One said, "All my life I have been despised because I could not read. Now I have read this book. You see I am not dumb after all." Another old woman said: "I came many miles to this class, and I have slept every night in this church. I have done nothing but study this book, and now I can read it all. I thank God that you came and that I came."

These women expressed the pathos of illiteracy in that ancient land, where paper was manufactured as early as 618 A.D. and where printing with movable types was practiced in 1403, several decades before Europeans had ever seen a printed paper book!

Dr. Laubach found that the chief problem in Korea was

not literacy itself so much as the need for simple literature. At least half the people could already read, but could not understand the material printed in most newspapers, magazines, and books. He gathered a crowd of writers and used all his eloquence to persuade them to write for the new literates.

Korea has the most scientific alphabet in the world. It is completely phonetic and dates from 1443, about the time that printing first began in Europe. This alphabet was designed to make the writing of everyday Korean words possible for anyone. But because Chinese was considered aristocratic and scholarly, educated people chose to use Chinese characters in their writing. Today most writers still use many of the Chinese characters along with the Korean letters. Dr. Laubach tried to make them realize that, by using symbols unfamiliar to the common people, they were reaching only the well-educated fifth of the population, while the Communists were writing easy material for the great majority.

Two colleges, one for women and one for men, agreed to establish jointly a school of journalism to train young people to write simply and interestingly for the millions of newly literate. They also agreed to prepare the "second readers" needed in the literacy campaigns, and a series of graded books to follow them.

Back in New York in August, after a brief stop in Japan, Dr. Laubach received word that the United States Information Service was printing fifty thousand copies of the primer for the literacy campaign.

Then, less than a year later, in June, 1950, came the dreaded attack from North Korea and war. American boys were called to fight beside South Koreans and many are buried in that far-off tragic land. Someday perhaps we shall learn how many of those Koreans, so eager to learn, and those who had caught the vision of helping their neighbors have survived the holocaust.

Dr. Laubach wrote soon after his return that year:

"Technicians will not bless the world unless they are strong in Christian love and ideals. The world needs Christ more than it needs skills. It will not accept Christ unless we offer it help with these other things. But if we give skill without character, we make the world only more powerful to do itself harm. The really greatest thing we can export to the world is our best Christ-filled men and women, with the technical skills to help materially and spiritually.

"We are foolish, incredibly foolish, not to take the world for Jesus Christ, when we know the way. We have the money, we have the knowledge, we have the magnificent people—more of each than perhaps all the rest of the world put together. Yet we are losing the world! The atom bomb, communism, and the rise of multitudes are all part of God's challenge. Awake, Christians, awake, and join this mighty march.

"God is calling us. It is we who must lead the world. Not rule it—serve it! And so lead it to Christ."

CHAPTER 13

"Mender of Old Baskets"

"Literacy is one of the thousands of skills
which we in America may share with the
world."—F. C. L.

In January, 1950, the Laubach literacy team was back in
Africa. It included, besides Dr. Laubach and Bob, Phillip and
Ewing Gray, the artists who had worked with them in the
Orient the year before, and also Dr. J. Maurice Hohlfeld,
specialist in phonetics, and his wife Emma.

At their first stop, which was in Angola, or Portuguese
West Africa, Bob wrote:

"Have you ever had the sensation of coming on a scene
you feel sure you have seen before? Though this is our first
visit to Angola, we find here the same eagerness of the
crowds to learn to read that we have seen in many countries
around the world. As we look at these earnest illiterates here
at Quessua, we need only to change in our minds the style
of their clothing and the tint of their skins, and they might
well be some of the Siamese, Indians, Koreans, or New
Guineans whom we saw last year.

"For everywhere the scene is similar in this respect: the
illiterates come by the hundreds, usually twice as many as
we expect; they come early in the morning, listen in rapt
attention to the lessons from the big chart, and spend their
noon hour and evenings reviewing the charts and booklets.

In every country the illiterates' enthusiasm to learn is keen. And the thrill for us is always high as we watch hundreds of men and women start up the ladder of literacy."

The literacy campaign in Angola was typical of large campaigns under church auspices in many lands. The campaign was directed by Dr. John Tucker, Secretary of the Evangelical Alliance of Angola, whom Dr. Laubach described as a "missionary statesman." Lessons were needed both in Portuguese and in Kimbundu, the native tongue.

The travelers were greeted on a Sunday afternoon at the seaport of Luanda by a crowd of twelve hundred that jammed the church to the doors, their faces shining with eagerness as they listened to greetings from each of the team, ending with Dr. Laubach, whom they dubbed *"ohosi"* (the lion, or leader). When he had finished, they shouted *"Cada um ensina um e ganha um para Cristo"* (Each one teach one and win one for Christ) which had been chosen as watchword for the campaign.

Early Monday morning the party boarded a rail motor car for Malange, located on a high plateau beyond the jungle. The trip was planned to avoid the time of day when the dreaded tsetse fly is active, but en route they saw some larger creatures of the jungle—two deer, and a young buffalo followed by a leopard and then a lion.

At a Methodist mission in Quessua, they found hundreds of people waiting to be taught. Phil Gray prepared large wall charts in both languages, and with these they began training teachers. Then teachers and students were paired off and together they bent their heads over the lesson sheets that Bob had mimeographed. Meanwhile others of the team were translating the "second reader," *The Story of Jesus,* into simple Portuguese and Kimbundu.

At the end of ten days about a hundred and fifty eager students were examined and found ready to receive diplomas because they could read the first book in one language or the other. The governor of the province came to present the diplomas and was surprised and pleased to find his own servant among the new readers. He also gave certificates of Christian service to those who had been teachers. Dr. Laubach wrote: "Those who had learned to read danced with joy all the way out the front door, waving their diplomas in the air."

Next the party traveled in a car over rough roads to another mission at Dondi. En route they had to cross a flooded river by ferry. It consisted of a pontoon pulled on a cable by African boatmen, who sang as they worked. The song, carried by soloist and chorus in antiphonal fashion, went like this when translated:

Solo: Is the white man a good one?

Chorus: Good one he is.

Solo: Will the white men give a good tip?

Chorus: A big tip they will give, surely.

Solo: Shall we make the crossing all right?

Chorus: Yes, we will indeed.

The tip was a good one, of course, and the travelers wished their whole fourteen hours of dusty, jolting travel could be to the same music.

At Dondi they found a larger mission which, with its old Spanish-type buildings, reminded them of California. A four-mile square of land included schools for boys and girls, a teacher-training school and seminary, a hospital and nurses training school, the whole cooperatively run by the Congregational Church of the United States and the United Church of Canada.

The team had arrived a few days ahead of schedule so that they had time to prepare charts and lessons before the multitudes of learners arrived. Six or seven hundred, three times the number expected, flocked to the mission. Many of them were unfamiliar with the ways of civilization, and it took some careful management to keep the gathering from becoming like a huge circus. With about four hundred teachers and pastors, besides regular workers at the mission, it meant that twelve hundred people had to be *fed and housed* every day—a stupendous job in itself.

Each day's program began with a half hour of singing and devotion. The Umbundu people loved to sing. The great hall, overflowing at doors and windows, rang with a hymn written especially for the occasion by one of the missionaries, Dr. Ralph Collins of Canada. It was called "Song of the Emancipated." It had a marching rhythm and the crowd sang it in Umbundu and English at the same time: *"Tua Pandula a Suku yetu"* (Thanks to Thee our God and Heavenly Father).

After a day of training the teachers, the excitement began. Each teacher took one or two illiterates out under a tree and began the lessons in reading, using mimeographed sheets as usual. But there remained about two hundred of the crowd with no teachers. Some of them had walked several days to get there; they could not be left untaught. So they were gathered into classes in front of the big charts, and several missionaries taught these larger groups as best they could.

Bob Laubach wrote: "On any afternoon while the students were scattered far and wide under the trees, it reminded me of a big college campus in the States, on the first warm day of spring when the students flock outside.

But the intense concentration of our Angola students upon their books undoubtedly far exceeded the average college student's interest in his texts.

"In the number of lessons turned out for the students, we set a new record. For several days we had five mimeographs going full blast, for 65,000 individual sheets had to be run off on short order to meet the demand. A dozen missionaries and Africans co-operated to make our workshop look like the press room of a daily paper."

The teaching and study continued for six days, interrupted only by big assembly meetings morning and afternoon for singing and worship. On the fifth day the teachers began to present their students for examination. Five "examining boards" were necessary. Students who failed the first time would study some more and return the next day. Three persons were kept busy making lists of those who passed, and filling out diplomas for them and certificates for their teachers. Others were at work preparing the first pages of the "second reader," *The Story of Jesus*, to present to each graduate.

Graduation day was the grand climax with rain threatening and more than eight hundred students and teachers lined up for the ceremonies. But the rain held off for two hours, just long enough for all to file past the altar and receive the coveted symbol of a new kind of life. Waving their diplomas over their heads, they sang again: *"Tua Pandula"* in loud, ringing voices:

"Thanks to Thee, our God and Heavenly Father
    For the light that shone upon our darkness;—"

After this big successful campaign in Angola the literacy team divided. The Grays remained in Angola to finish the thousands of pictures needed for lessons and second readers. The Laubachs, accompanied by Dr. Tucker, took a boat around the Cape of Good Hope to Mozambique, Portuguese East Africa. The Hohlfelds went to the Belgian Congo, Nigeria, and Liberia to follow up the work begun there by Dr. Laubach in 1948.

The Hohlfelds wrote from Leopoldville in the Congo:

"Everywhere we went we found the enthusiasm of the 1948 campaign still high. What a joy it was to hear the folks speak of Dr. Laubach as *Okombekombe* (mender of old baskets)! That was the name they gave him in 1948, and while they may forget the name Laubach, they vividly recall Okombekombe.[1] It is gratifying to learn the results of the each-one-teach-one campaign. One woman went home and taught her husband. The man did not go to sleep nights until he had learned to read every word on the Laubach charts. Many of the mission stations have now printed the primers in permanent form, and some have *The Story of Jesus* printed. There is a great need for more Christian literature.

"Everywhere we find missionaries keenly interested in the tonal analysis of African languages. These languages are similar to Chinese in that several words may be spelled alike and yet have different meanings. The only difference in pronunciation is that one word is given a different tone from another word. Several of the missions have wire recorders, and we are using these helpful devices to aid in the language-learning program."

On the short ocean voyage Dr. Laubach had a few days

[1] The older people who were illiterate felt that they were useless "like old baskets full of holes." When Dr. Laubach taught them to read, they said, "He patches up the holes in our heads just the way the basket mender does with old baskets."

of much needed rest and a chance to finish his book of "streamlined" English lessons, revised after they had been tested, for which United States publishers were waiting.

In Mozambique, Dr. Tucker proved to be a great help because he spoke Portuguese fluently. There, for the first time, Dr. Laubach found active government opposition against the missions and their educational work, but even so, the each-one-teach-one plan could be used; the authorities made no objection if an eager learner was taught by a friend.

There, as everywhere else, he found the people pathetically grateful for the hope he brought them. At Beira, after the literacy meetings, an old man came to him and said: "We cannot find words to tell you what you have done for us. We feel like a dog which cannot speak, but can only wag its tail. But we will thank the Lord for you every day. May God keep you well to help the whole world as you have helped us."

As the Laubachs moved into Nyasaland, they found themselves again on the trail of David Livingstone. They crossed the broad Zambesi River, which the great explorer had traced, and held their conference in Blantyre, where he had founded a mission named for his own birthplace in Scotland. Besides making lessons in another language and demonstrating how to teach them, Dr. Laubach led the discussion as usual to the all-important problem of producing enough good reading matter for the awakened people. Some of the people in Nyasaland are Moslems, and he had an exhilarating session with their chiefs, who proved as responsive as his old friends in Mindanao.

When it was time to go into Tanganyika, it seemed to him that the Lord himself planned a way. Bob had tried to book air passage weeks ahead, but in vain. The very day they wanted to leave, the air office phoned that a plane was making its first trip by a new route, and two seats were available because of cancellations!

At Dodoma, in Central Tanganyika, the Grays joined them, and they rapidly made lessons in Cigogo (pronounced Cheegogo). After they had prepared the usual phonetic charts, they made short reading lessons to provide repetition of the words, trying always to inject a bit of humor. For example, one story ended thus:

The man saw the lion.	The man ran away.
The woman saw the lion.	The woman ran away.
The boy saw the lion.	The boy ran away.
	The lion ran away.

Dr. Laubach wrote:

"The Cigogo language has a word for everything you can think of, and thousands of words you would never think of. The names for people with peculiar habits are very apt and could well be introduced into the States. You may know a person who fits each of these words:

mumagamagama—one who loses other people's things.

muwavi—a good-looking woman who can't cook.

muvumizi—one who constantly grunts to show his endorsement of what people say—a yes man.

muwandoloci—one who growls when waked up in the morning."

The literacy team next visited Uganda, traveling forty hours by steamer on Lake Victoria, which is almost as large as Lake Superior. They had been invited to Uganda by the Department of Public Welfare, and were not surprised to find that adult education already had a big start in that prosperous and progressive country. The King of Uganda, a graduate of Cambridge University in England, conferred with them. They visited seven busy literacy centers, and watched demonstrations by teachers who a few months before had been illiterate themselves. They were using lessons modeled on those made in India in the 1930's. Dr. Laubach persuaded the parliament that a program of "each-one-teach-one" based on the easier new lessons would bring results, and that more and simpler reading matter was needed. He impressed on them the importance of training young writers who would prepare easy-to-read informational material for the new literates.

Again he noted the good character of British colonial policy. A super highway was being built from the beautiful city of Kampala to Nairobi in Kenya, printing center of East Africa. On their trips through Uganda they saw everywhere wonderful fields of cotton, sugar cane, coffee, tea, cassava, bananas, pyrethrum. The people were prosperous and, instead of expecting gifts, wanted to give presents to these visiting white people. They loaded them with pineapples, a half dozen chickens, and a sheep!

A short flight took them southward to the twin kingdoms of Ruanda-Urundi at the northern tip of Lake Tanganyika, not far from the spot where Stanley found Livingstone. That dramatic meeting of 1871 publicized by the New York *Herald* probably made more Americans look at the map of Africa than has any event before or since. But too many Americans think that nothing has changed in Africa since that day.

At a Quaker mission in the hills, only two degrees from the equator but seven thousand feet above sea level, the literacy team held a pleasant conference with teachers from several missions of different denominations. They made lessons in the Kirundi language and experimented with them, changing words that were not perfectly familiar to the illiterates. Dr. Laubach wrote:

"The reactions to the charts were all joyous. The women babbled and giggled among themselves. One man was so excited that we could not stop him, so he read the whole first book through in one forenoon. One principle we observe is: 'Never hold a hungry student back.' Before me are two pages of themes to be used for preparing pamphlets in Kirundi. A few of them might surprise you: Why Keep Flies Out of Baby's Eyes? (they don't); Itch; Lice; Jiggers; Witchcraft; Gossip; Worms; Boil All Your Water."

They learned that the people of Urundi are of three types: the pygmies, the middle class, and the very tall slim aristocracy who according to tradition came from Ethiopa. Bob Laubach took some fascinating pictures and reported picturesque glimpses of two of these groups:

"The last afternoon we were in Kivimba we heard a far-away murmur in the valley, like distant thunder. A few minutes later the rhythms were more distinct. Around the edge of our hill came walking a dozen of the King's best drummers, with an excited crowd following behind. Each drummer had a heavy, four-foot wooden drum balanced on his head, playing it as he walked along.

"Soon the King arrived, and the Belgian guests. With the drums placed upright the thunderous serenade began. One after the other, the experts took charge of the lead drum, thumping it vigorously. The drum chorus in the background kept the rhythm going. The experts jumped high in the air, danced around the enclosure, or drummed with one hand and performed fancy gyrations with the stick in the other hand.

"By contrast, we were quiet as church mice on our Sunday morning visit to the pygmy village. The ashes still smoldered where they had been baking their pots—an art reserved for the pygmies in Urundi. Dr. Rawson wound up his tiny phonograph and set it on the ground. The clear notes of a gospel hymn in their own Kirundi floated out of the machine. The villagers crowded closer. Men in simple gowns of bark cloth elbowed among women with suckling babes. Naked children peered between their parents' legs. After a couple of records Betty Cox gave them a short talk. Then, with a closing prayer, we stole away as silently as we had come, knowing that some seed had been planted in the hearts of these shyest of Africa's peoples."

The "literacy tramps" were delayed twice in getting to French Cameroun because air travel in Africa was so popular and so unpredictable. But Dr. Laubach used the delays, as always, to get in touch with a local mission and make some new lessons or improve some old ones.

However, when they finally reached Yaoundé, capital of French Cameroun, he was shaking and burning with malaria. One of the missionaries promptly drove him to the big Presbyterian mission at Élat and left him in the hospital, where, he said, "Dr. George Thorne had me feeling like a new man in three days."

This Élat mission, begun in 1902 with a church of four members, now has a regular church congregation of over two thousand five hundred and twenty branch churches; an industrial school teaching carpentry, masonry, auto mechanics, electrical work, and other trades; an agricultural school;

a normal school; a theological seminary; a press; a hospital; and a dental clinic and school. All this development in a region where fifty years ago several of the tribes were cannibals and all were primitive savages!

They did not become civilized or Christian over night, as people sometimes imagine. One former savage said: "I believed in God ten times before but it never stuck. Please remember this across the seas, for it is a shame in my heart. But now I have found Him at last."

Bob Laubach visited the dental clinic and had some necessary work done in a unique place—the only school in all Africa where an African can be trained in dentistry. He wrote:

"Almost within earshot of the chattering monkeys in the nearby jungle is the whirr of the dentist's drill. Cameroun is the great center for gorillas and all kinds of monkeys, birds, and leopards. Every day we spent some time chatting with several dozen gorillas and chimpanzees which two Americans had collected. The natives catch them in the forests when they are babies and sell them to the collectors. A baby gorilla in America is said to be worth five thousand dollars. They have to love these gorillas and give them plenty of company or they will die of homesickness. The smallest ones jump up in your arms and hug you like a baby. But don't let a four-hundred-pound adult gorilla hug you. He doesn't know when he's being rough!"

Even from a hospital bed Dr. Laubach helped prepare lessons in another language, Bassa, and do "the spade work" for lessons in five other languages. And Phil Gray made beautiful new pictures and charts for the first lessons in Bulu. These had been made in 1948 and were already in use.

Each picture suggests the shape of a letter and the meaning of a word; *da* means "to step."

French government officials, interested in adult literacy because of a visit by a UNESCO delegation the year before, came to Élat to see the Laubach work and invited them to give a demonstration at the government teachers college in the capital. Their final day in Africa was, therefore, spent at Yaoundé, a city with modern streamline government buildings overlooking banana and papaya groves and groups of native huts.

Back home, after a brief visit to UNESCO headquarters in Paris, Dr. Laubach summed up the situation in Africa in statesmanlike terms:

"The masses of Africa are coming up—either by the communist way of revolt and class war, or by the Christian way of education of mind and heart. Africans grow ever more restive, ever more determined to better their condition, ever more desirous for education because they think that education will help them. The best missionary efforts, enlightened industrial programs, wise educational programs by several governments—Uganda and Liberia outstanding among them—are lifting thousands of Africans in a Christian and democratic fashion.

"Since education is the leading passion of Africa, missions will do the most for Africa and for Christ by making every effort to help the adults as well as the children learn to read. . . .

"We know the very things which they need to know. But our educated people need bridges to convey their knowledge to these illiterates. Our literacy and Christian literature program is a bridge. For example, our agriculturists know how to make the soil more productive; we can give the new literates that information in simple words in their own language. The backward areas need to know the laws of health, child care and dietetics, ideals of freedom and responsibility. All these literacy can convey to them.

"Twenty African countries in which we worked openly urge the church to make people literate. Some countries now ask the missions to make them Christian. In the light of the United States' and the United Nations' proposals to help the retarded areas with our know-how, literacy looms as one of the greatest challenges in the world."

In June, 1950, a special correspondent of the *Christian Science Monitor,* reporting from Pretoria on the excellent work of the South African Institute of Race Relations, concluded as follows:

The institute has decided that as far as the non-Europeans themselves are concerned, all the trouble starts with illiteracy, or, at any rate, that literacy is the road leading to progress in all directions. For this reason it has established, with the aid of a government subsidy, literacy classes for adult Africans in many of the locations and mine compounds.

Here servant girls, store boys, and mine laborers begin for the first time to decipher the printed word that images the sounds they make in their own native tongues. Through the method introduced by an American professor, Dr. Laubach, and adapted by Mrs. Maida Whyte, wife of the present director and the institute's adult education officer, they soon learn to read the vernaculars.

It is one of the most hopeful signs in a land where there often does not seem much hope. If Africans all over the continent can acquire, rapidly, the ability to read their own languages, as well as some of the European languages, they will sooner be in a position to understand the nature of the changes going on all around them.

CHAPTER 14

Why Not Try Christian Service?

"The true way to peace and survival is precisely the Way of Christ."—F. C. L.

By late 1950, Dr. Laubach began to feel that the real problems of literacy lay, not in Africa or India, but in prosperous America. Each year he came home from his strenuous work among the hungry millions to find thousands of his fellow Americans totally unaware of any world beyond their own county or state. Then when trouble broke out in Korea, everyone began to ask "Why?"

"It's all the fault of the Kremlin and the Communists," was the ready answer of many speakers and writers.

As the tension between East and West increased, Laubach saw that far too many Americans did not know the complete answer. He felt that they would be glad to help if only they understood; and so he wrote the book with a startling title—*Wake Up or Blow Up*. Its first chapter is headed: "You Can't Win a Cold War with Hot Weapons; Let's Try Christianity." In a hundred and sixty eloquent pages he tried to make Americans see that the only way to stop communism is to offer assistance to the depressed milions—not in the form of charity but in all the various ways that will enable them to help themselves. That little book has been steadily gaining new readers. Many other writers

171

and speakers are saying in different ways the same thing
Laubach said.

He found time, as usual, to speak in churches and colleges
about the problems of literacy and their relation to the
hunger and poverty of the world. He challenged college
students to prepare themselves for service in needy areas by
learning how to write and to teach others to write for the
millions who will soon be literate. He emphasized the fact
that in Arabic lands and in India there are far too few who
know how to write simple, direct articles of information for
the great masses of their people. They need teachers to train
them in that kind of journalism. Hundreds of students wrote
to ask about such training and were told about the courses
offered at the University of Syracuse.

In January, 1951, the Committee for World Literacy celebrated, at a dinner in New York, Dr. Laubach's twenty years
of work. Between 1930 and 1950 he had started literacy campaigns in sixty-three countries and had helped to make lessons in over two hundred languages. Among those who spoke
at the dinner in praise of his achievements were men from
the United States Department of State and from the United
Nations. Both of them said literacy is absolutely essential
if underprivileged peoples are to attain the better life they
covet. The help we offer them in better farming methods,
good practices in sanitation and health, industrial progress,
will bring results ten times as fast if the people are able
to read.

Dr. Laubach's own speech at that dinner was a call for
"A War of Amazing Kindness." He pointed out that America's budget for war was fifty billions, two thousand times
as much as for the Point Four Program; that, even so, the
war of force was failing; that a campaign of good will was

Africa and even into Spain, where the Moslems ruled until they were driven out about the time of Columbus. Islam, sometimes called "the religion of the sands," is still the dominant religion of North Africa, except where a few missionaries keep the lights of Christianity burning. Dr. Laubach wrote:

"My heart is very heavy for missionaries who are keeping on in spite of everything . . . in this Moslem region where missions face one of the most difficult tasks in the world. . . . We came to give something to these missionaries, but they have given me far more than I can give them."

Algiers, largest French city outside of France, with its fine harbor, chic dress shops, and electric busses, seemed a pleasant place to the literacy team until they threaded the narrow winding streets of the "Kasbah," the Arab section huddled under the walls of an old castle. There they saw the other Algiers, where children in cold dark alleys watched for the coming of the milk peddler and his donkey loaded with brass buckets.

A committee of missionaries had sent out a call for everyone interested in literacy to come to a series of public meetings. Government officials, university professors, and other laymen, as well as pastors and missionaries, came. They included French, Arabs, and Kabyles and represented about ten different church denominations. Two men came from Tunisia, and four from Morocco. More than fifty remained to help prepare the lessons and learn to teach according to the Laubach method.

Lessons were prepared in Arabic, French, Spanish, and Kabyle. The Arabic lessons were ready first for Dr. Laubach's demonstration. Among the teachers he trained was Jasmina, an educated girl who had discarded her veil. When it came time for her to demonstrate her teaching skill, her own mother was among the veiled women who were the pupils. Swathed from head to foot in robes and veils with only a tiny peephole for the eyes, they sat in front of the Arabic charts, docile, hidden, and quiet as Moslem women have been for generations. At first their responses were timid and slow, but as the lesson continued, their voices betrayed their excitement. They read words, then sentences, then a whole page with no trouble! Jasmina's mother was quickest of all, and the daughter's lovely face glowed with delight.

Twenty-two teaching centers were planned for future work. A start was made in writing simple literature for the new readers. Much remained to be done, but the group of workers were jubilant, because, for the first time, several permanent interdenominational committees were established. Everyone felt that with this new spirit of cooperation they had taken a big step toward literacy in North Africa.

In the middle of February the Laubachs took a plane for Tripoli, the capital of Libya, where the Department of Education had asked for help. Libya, that former Italian colony where occurred some of the fiercest fighting of World War II, was preparing for independence in January, 1952, under the supervision of the United Nations. Everyone realized the need for literacy work in a country where less than 5 per cent of the adult men could read and not even 1 per cent of the women. Mussolini had built magnificent hotels, boulevards, and promenades in the city of Tripoli, but education for Arabs had been blocked during the thirty years of Italian control. There was scarcely an educated leader among the Arabs, now planning to become a free and independent nation. But Dr. Laubach found the Director

of Education and the Arab inspectors of schools full of enthusiasm and very teachable. They were grateful when the
only four missionaries in the country offered their help. One
of these, a doctor, was eager to work with the literacy committee in preparing simple pamphlets on health.

In the midst of their intense work the literacy team were
entertained almost every day by various officials, from the
governor down. They were invited also to the American air
base on the outskirts of Tripoli, where the chaplain gave a
party in their honor. Bob showed some of his film strips,
which delighted the eighty children of the families living
there.

Bob Laubach and Phil Gray took a day for sightseeing
among the famous Roman ruins at Leptis Magna, where the
Emperor Septimius in the second century built a city that
rivaled Rome itself. There, too, Christianity had flourished
during the centuries when North Africa was the garden of
the Roman Empire.

Effa Laubach visited two schools for girls. She was happy
that, through the zeal of a Libyan woman educated in
Damascus, there were two thousand girls enrolled in government schools in Tripoli. Knowing much of Moslem customs and homes, she was amazed by what this one educated
woman had accomplished. The teachers were alert, too; they
promised to show the fifth- and sixth-grade girls how to use
the new Laubach lessons in teaching their mothers at home.
Providing for the education of women is one of the most
difficult problems in Moslem lands and one of the most important. As a perceptive woman of India said before the
Adult Education Conference in 1939: "When we educate a
man, we educate but a single individual, whereas when we
educate a woman, we educate a whole household."

From Tripoli the literacy team flew to Cairo across the deserts where camel caravans still travel the sandy wastes, loaded with dates and oil, rice and wheat, and where in favored spots water for irrigation is still pumped by man power or by oxen in the ancient way. In Cairo the team worked with a UNESCO committee, government leaders, and the Inter-Mission Council. The government literacy campaign, of which Dr. Laubach had such high hopes in 1947, had petered out, but through the church campaign many people had learned to read and there was a new spirit of unity among Christian teachers.

From them he learned a dramatic story of the kind that is common in Christian missions, but can never be told too often—how a little seed planted in good ground almost always bears much fruit.

Davida Finney, one of the women who carried books to little churches up and down the Nile valley, had reared an Egyptian girl named Halana Mikhail. Halana had helped make Arabic lessons and later had traveled through Egypt organizing women to teach illiterates. She even went to the Sudan and started a campaign there. So successful were her efforts that in 1950 she was asked by the United Nations Relief and Rehabilitation Administration to help in the immense Arab refugee camp at Gaza. It sheltered part of the tragic multitude forced to flee from their homes during the Arab-Jewish struggle in Palestine. They were being fed and housed in tents by the United Nations, but they merely existed in hopeless despair. Halana started a literacy campaign among them, depending entirely on volunteer teachers. Hope began to brighten the sad faces. The news spread to other refugee camps, and soon Halana was going from camp to camp throughout Jordan and Syria, training teachers and organizing campaigns. The gratitude of the refugees is shown by a typical letter, written by a woman after two weeks of study. It was in Arabic, of course. Translated it reads:

My dearly beloved Miss Halana,

I am writing to you the first letter after I learned reading and writing.

I send you every thanks for your work for our fatherland and I ask God to keep you and to help you in this good work which the method of Master Laubach has given us.

I have come from darkness into light.

                              Signed, The Faithful Anma

The UNRRA asked Dr. Laubach to make a tour of the camps and give advice regarding the literacy work. For six days he traveled in a UN car with a group of Christian Arabs, visiting Amman, the new capital of the Arab state of Jordan, Gaza, and other camps in the valley of the Jordan River and near Bethlehem. The ruins of war seemed doubly tragic in the very land where Jesus taught: "Thou shalt love thy neighbor as thyself." But as always, Dr. Laubach found things to make him optimistic. He wrote:

"At one of the big refugee camps, we listened to a 50-year-old man read after two weeks of study. His 12-year-old son had taught him! Both were full of delight, and with good reason, for the man did well. There is a great demand for the few available books, and the teachers report boundless eagerness to learn."

Books were far too few because almost all UNRRA funds had to be used for food. So he wrote to the Technical Co-operation Administration in Washington, explaining the need and asking that money be sent for books.

In Beirut, the port and capital of Lebanon, he spoke at the American College and suggested it would be an excel-

lent center for training young people to teach and to write
for the new literates—a good place to establish a school of
journalism for the Near East. In Lebanon the population is
half Christian. Beirut has long been a center of education
both Moslem and Christian, a meeting place of East and
West ever since the time of the Crusades. In the days of
Richard the Lionhearted, Europe learned much from the
Middle East, for Arab scholars led the world in philosophy,
mathematics, and medicine. How fitting it would be if the
West could now repay its debt by spreading freely through
these Moslem lands our technical skills and practical knowledge of health and sanitation, agriculture and conservation,
along with literacy and democratic ideals of freedom!

On February 21 the literacy team headed for India, flying
from Cairo to Bombay. They spent three weeks at an important conference held at the Spiritual Life Center at Nasra-
pur, not far from Bombay. There a beautiful estate between
two rivers had been turned into a gathering place for missionaries and other leaders, much like similar "camps" in the
United States. Here were gathered delegates from every important language area of India studying what to write and
how to write for the millions learning to read. The articles
must be full of practical information but also interesting, for
new literates, like most people, are persuaded not by reason
as much as by their emotions—by stories that arouse admiration, laughter, ambition, pity. Dr. Laubach wrote: "The
Indian people are wonderful storytellers, but for the life of
them they can't write what they have said. The next time
we make a trip we are going to take a tape recorder along
and record their delightful stories. This material, carefully
edited, printed in large legible type, and attractively illustrated, will help to keep India's new literates interested."

One delegate, Dr. Gladys Rutherford, working with the India Village Service, had such a happy faculty for presenting health facts in graphic form that some of her lectures were recorded just as she gave them, to be made into booklets for new readers.

All the delegates tried their hands at writing and went home loaded with material on village life, agriculture, and health, prepared to write booklets in the language each knew. These would then be edited and published by the National Christian Council, under the direction of Ruth Ure, a veteran in the field.

At another conference, in Poona, Dr. Laubach led a discussion about the training of writers and the need for schools of journalism in India. Plans were already under way for such a school at Hislop College in Nagpur, to be established in 1952 by Professor Roland Wolseley of Syracuse University.

When he reached New Delhi, capital of the Republic of India, Dr. Laubach found the very air electric with ideas and plans for making democracy a reality in that ancient land. The Secretary of Education seized on his suggestion for putting up phonetic charts in all the villages so that illiterates would begin to learn without any formal teaching, just depending on their neighbors to give them a start. He talked with a young woman sent by UNESCO to help prepare health pamphlets for India. He visited a *Maylah*, or village fair, sponsored by the Department of Education, where entertainments and exhibits drew the people together, taught them how to improve village life, and prepared them to respond when the village teachers launched a literacy campaign.

Everywhere he heard people discussing the relations of India and the United States. He wrote:

"One of the best suggestions I have heard is that in return for one million tons of wheat (sent by the United States), India be required to release seventy million dollars for technical assistance in India, so that these famines will not recur. That is very far-sighted statesmanship, and is received with favor here in India. We must help countries to help themselves."

In April the team was off for Afghanistan, this time traveling by automobile. Their route lay first through the famous Khyber Pass which Frank Laubach confessed he had wanted to see ever since reading Kipling's stories in his youth. Through this gateway from the Middle East to India conquering armies have passed since the time of Alexander the Great, and camel caravans loaded with the riches of the East have traveled westward. Now there are separate roads for trucks and camels; but the narrow pass is still scenic and the towering cliffs are a little sinister.

At the Afghan border the travelers were joined by a new member of the team, Professor J. Christy Wilson of Princeton Theological Seminary, who could speak Persian and who acted as interpreter. They were also met by the young Afghan Director of Primary Education, who drove them the remaining two hundred miles to Kabul, the capital, over a mountain road so steep and twisting that it made them dizzy.

Kabul, in its wide mountain valley dominated by snow-capped peaks, reminded them of Denver as it must have been in frontier days, with muddy streets and no sidewalks and new buildings going up every day. A broad new avenue leads to the site of a developing university, which will include a technical school, staffed and equipped by Americans, and a college for women. Double-decked buses, overflowing with people, baggage, and mail, blare their way past horse-drawn carts, an occasional camel caravan, and plodding donkeys. Bob Laubach wrote: "Donkeys in this country carry everything from chickens to whole families."

The streets looked gay, he said. The women, all in purdah, wear single-pieced gowns, called *burkahs*, which are of every color of the rainbow. These are matched by the brilliant shawls which the men wrap around head and neck in cold weather.

And cold it was! Spring had not yet reached this mountain land, and the visitors, though wearing winter underwear and sweaters, had to live in their overcoats both indoors and out. The only heat in most buildings came from tiny stoves that gave off more smoke than warmth.

Even before their bags were unpacked, the team set to work making lesson charts in Persian and in Pushtu, the official Afghan language. Yakub Hasan, a highly educated Moslem in the Department of Education, was assigned to help them. He is a gifted linguist who has taught many of the leaders of Afghanistan to speak English. He decided the best trial pupils were the young soldiers in a neighboring camp. If they learned to read, they could teach their families in remote mountain villages after their military training was over.

So every day fifty soldiers with their officers marched into the new library of the Department of Education and sat on the floor in front of the charts. At first they were stolid and unbelieving. Their officers, too, and a score of local schoolteachers watched Dr. Laubach skeptically. Could he actually teach these raw recruits to read in a few days?

But, as always, Dr. Laubach performed the miracle. By the end of the second lesson the soldiers were eager, alert, their eyes agleam with triumph. In a few days they were reading sentences; and they shouted with excitement the day some little books were put into their hands. To be sure, most of them had to be shown how to hold the books and turn the pages. These pages were the first part of the primer which the literacy team had been busy preparing.

It was printed on a new government offset press and artist Phil Gray had outdone himself in making attractive pictures. The same press was printing sets of the big teaching charts to be posted in villages all over the land.

Mr. Wilson later wrote that Dr. Laubach had disproved the old saying "that you can't hurry the East." In his quiet way he had done the impossible. "He gives us no time to sit lazy," remarked Mr. Hasan, laughing, but added, "He is the kindest person in the world."

Dr. Laubach was invited to have an audience with the king, Mohammed Zahir Shah, who, though seldom seen by his people, is greatly concerned about progress for Afghanistan. During a visit to UNESCO Headquarters in Paris he had learned about the Laubach method of "lightning literacy" and urged that it be tried. Dr. Laubach found him a quiet man with simple democratic ways, very grateful for the help offered to his people.

There were strenuous sessions with teachers and representatives of UN and UNESCO and the American Embassy planning the second book to supply the new literates with reading matter. All the technicians agreed they were baffled by the problem of teaching health and sanitation, agriculture and engineering to people who couldn't read. In collaboration these technical advisers began writing articles, and a book took shape rapidly.

Besides the officials, Dr. Laubach found a colony of about thirty Americans and British in Kabul who were eager to cooperate. They had been holding church services each week in one of the homes, and welcomed the literacy team to an Easter service there. No preaching or teaching of the Christian faith is attempted among the Moslems of this ancient land. What they learn about the Christian way of life, they learn only by the example of Europeans and Americans who are working there.

Dr. Laubach found that a dozen or more Americans were teaching in the government schools. He also talked with engineers of an American construction firm that, at the king's request, is building dams to irrigate half a million acres and to supply electricity to most of Afghanistan. They had already completed one dam, besides miles of roads and canals. "They are the best missionaries in the world," wrote Dr. Laubach. "When that vast area is irrigated, the nomads can give up their tents and settle down to become farmers as well as shepherds. Then schools can be established for their children, and health centers and modern ways of living."

As always Dr. Laubach was reluctant to leave his new friends. On the trip out of Afghanistan, they met thousands of the nomads returning from Pakistan to their native hills. At one point the car had to stop while a caravan of camels, donkeys, sheep, and people plodded slowly past. Bob wrote:

"The very young and the very old (both men and animals!) were privileged to ride the camels and donkeys. One camel would have a dozen or more newborn lambs on its

back in a box, with a white tent to protect them from the
sun. Almost every donkey and camel had a baby strapped
on with a blanket. From beneath the blankets of one camel
we saw the bare legs of a little boy or girl swinging to and
fro. I saw one old withered grandmother, tied on a camel
with a big shawl, and holding tight with both hands and
with a rope in her teeth. With every lurch of the long-legged
animal the old woman shook violently.

"While I kept my cameras busy, Mother and Dad took the
census of the caravan—475 camels, well over 600 donkeys,
nearly 4,000 people. At the very rear came the herds of
sheep—untold thousands of them, with their winter-fattened
tails plumping absurdly along behind them."

On their last night in Afghanistan the literacy team saw
a bit of its summer beauty, when they stopped at a government resthouse at Jalalabad. There under tall palms and
stately cypress trees they found a garden filled with the
scent of roses and orange blossoms, exquisitely refreshing
after their miles of rugged travel.

After a day's stop in Lahore, Pakistan, not for rest but to
help with some new Urdu charts, the team flew to New
Delhi. There they were joined by Dr. Frederick Rex, an expert in adult literacy work in Latin America and one who
knows the world problem from several years' association
with UNESCO.

On April 26 they flew to Rangoon, Burma, that little land
between India and China and Thailand which became a
republic in 1948, after long years as a British dependency.
Probably no land of the Orient is more familiar to the West,
at least in name, because of several romantic incidents and
associations. There runs "the road to Mandalay" known the
world over. There, too, from Lashio in Burma to Kunming

in South China runs the famous Burma Road, built by the toil of thousands of peasants during World War II, when the Japanese had overrun eastern China and a back-door route had to be made to the capital at Chungking. Rangoon is also known in missionary history because it was there that the pioneer missionary, Adoniram Judson, began his work, and there that Judson College became one of the great Christian centers in the Orient. It is now a part of the government university. But most of all, Burma is known in America today through the book *Burma Surgeon*, by Dr. Gordon S. Seagrave, a descendant of two missionaries who pioneered in Burma with Judson. Dr. Seagrave's graphic story of medical work in North Burma, of the war service of his hospital unit when Burma was invaded, and of their heroic retreat through the jungle to India with General Stilwell represents for many one of the most dramatic missionary sagas ever written. When Burma was shattered by civil strife the year after declaring its independence, and Dr. Seagrave was accused of treason and imprisoned as one of the rebels, thousands of readers felt that a personal friend was in danger. Dr. Seagrave appealed for a retrial, which the supreme court had allowed at the time the Laubachs reached Rangoon in May, 1951. Dr. Laubach wrote:

"The open war has stopped, but the strained relations still exist. There seem to be five different insurgent groups, and the Communists are taking as much advantage of this inner discord as they can. Bandits are a constant menace outside the city of Rangoon. Few people abroad and perhaps even few people in Burma understand the meaning and the depth of the conflict between the eight million true Burmese and the two million tribal peoples. But that it is deep and serious nobody will deny."

However, groups representing several different languages and dialects welcomed the literacy team with enthusiasm and started making lesson charts. Since Burmese had been declared the national language, Dr. Laubach concentrated first on that. It proved to be as irregular in spelling as English, and the committee had a real struggle making easy lessons. They did it at last, and produced a primer of twenty-two lessons which some illiterate patients in a hospital mastered so fast that they kept Phil Gray and three Burmese artists and Bob and his helpers at the mimeograph on the jump to supply new material.

The Burmese alphabet is like no other in the world. Bob wrote:

"I haven't made any real research, but I wouldn't be surprised to hear that the man who invented the Burmese alphabet was the same fellow who invented the compass— that instrument to make circles. For the Burmese alphabet is made up almost entirely of circles, parts of circles, circles on top of circles and circles overlapping circles. You have to go around in the right circles in Burma to be able to read!"

Most of the other languages of Burma use the Roman alphabet, and making lessons in them was easier. There was time for some of the groups to translate chapters of *The Story of Jesus* and work on the second reader to supply practical information for the new literates. As usual, Dr. Laubach conferred with experts in health and medicine, child care, and agriculture, asking each one: "What do you know that you wish the illiterates and new literates to know?" Also, as usual, their answers were full of technical terms, which the committee must put into simple phrases.

A scheme had been growing in Dr. Laubach's mind. Instead of little articles such as, "You should have a garden,"

or "You should raise milk goats," he planned a book of
stories called *U Sein the Wise Man*. The hero, U Sein, first
learned to read and then did all the things a good citizen
should do to build better ways of living for his family and
community. At the end, U Sein was recognized as a very
wise man, a benefactor, and a leader. If the new literate,
reading these stories, became really interested in U Sein,
reasoned Dr. Laubach, he might go and do likewise. Moreover, a series of such Wise Man stories could be adapted to
any newly literate region in the world simply by changing
the name of the hero to Juan or Akbar or Anand or whatever name was most common in the native language.

The literacy team was scheduled for a campaign in Indonesia starting June 1. Dr. Rex went ahead to help arrange
the program, and the rest of the team spent a week in
Malaya. Only a week, but of course they were not idle. In
Singapore, that fascinating cosmopolitan city at the tip of
the Malay Peninsula, they were eagerly welcomed by the
Christian Council and also by the governor of Singapore.
Officers of the government, Malay teachers, and missionaries
all agreed that the spread of literacy was essential to help
the people of Malaya resist the false promises of communism.

Twenty Malay scholars joined Dr. Laubach at the University of Singapore, and as fast as they chose the right
words for lessons, Phil Gray began his drawings. Since
Malay belongs to the same group of languages as do the
Philippine languages, the work seemed easy to Dr. Laubach. He found old friends among the missionaries and
some were still using lessons he had helped to make sixteen
years before.

Taking the first of the new charts with him and leaving the rest of the party in Singapore, Dr. Laubach flew north to Kuala Lumpur, capital of the Federation of Malaya. There, in a round of meetings and conferences, he again drew together all the different groups interested in literacy —Moslem government leaders, Christian workers, the Rotary Club, and the British commissioner. Besides what he accomplishes in literacy, Dr. Laubach's spirit of hope and good will is always like a powerful catalyst in chemistry, producing a quick reaction of cooperation and the state of mind "it-can-be-done."

Back in Singapore he reported to the head of the United States Information Service the widespread eagerness he had found not only for literacy in Malay but for lessons in English. His *Streamlined English* lessons, published in New York, would be useful if only they could be made available. The USIS agreed to see what could be done.

On June 1 the literacy team took off for Java, that thickly populated island which is the center of the new Republic of Indonesia. They landed at Jakarta, the capital city, which was formerly known as Batavia when the islands were the Netherlands Indies. They were met by Dr. Rex and representatives of the government and the Christian Council. They found that the Ministry of Education had already published attractive books for new literates, giving information about their new government and the duties of citizenship. This youngest republic of the Far East, born late in 1949, was very busy at the task of making democracy work among a people only 7 per cent literate. The leaders were on the job. One of them, with the long name Simandjoentak took Dr. Laubach and Dr. Rex to meet President Achmed Soekarno. Dr. Laubach wrote:

"We were charmed by his irresistible graciousness. The

people all fall under his fascination as did we. At the end of forty minutes he invited us to come to a shadow play or *wayang*, which he was giving that evening in his palace. There we saw an astonishing exhibition. One man manipulated the puppets, dozens of them, and talked and sang the parts for all of them, for both men and women. An orchestra of forty players accompanied the performance on gongs, xylophones, and stringed instruments. A bright light was arranged so that the shadow of the puppets fell on a large white screen. From one side you could only see the "movies" or shadows of the puppets, but from the other side you could see the puppets and orchestra as well. The President received us cordially and told us to wander about as we pleased. The show was to last all night, as it told a long legend which originated in India centuries ago. We left before midnight, as we had to get a plane at 6 A.M. for Sumatra.

"My heart goes out to this government, with all its tremendous problems in education and everything else. They know full well that, in the words of President Soekarno to me that evening: 'Democracy with illiterate people is humbug.' If Indonesia can keep its government honestly and sincerely working for the welfare of its people, I believe and pray that it will make the grade as a Republic."

On the great island of Sumatra, which stretches for a thousand miles across the equator, they worked for a week among the Bataks, a Christian people in a Moslem land. Their language, Dr. Laubach found, is even closer to the Philippine languages than is Malay, and he was convinced that at least part of the Filipino people must have come from Sumatra centuries ago. When the Batak people gathered for their religious services, he found a fourth of the congregation were Moslems, who seemed to have no objection to joining in Christian worship. He felt that the genuine fervor of the Batak Christians might account for the impression they had made on their Moslem neighbors. Here was something new in the world—and surely a hopeful sign for the future of the seventy-five million people of Indonesia.

Although Dr. Laubach works gladly with national government groups and representatives of the United Nations, with everyone, in fact, interested in literacy, he is happiest, he confesses, when working with Christian churches around the world. While open-minded about all other religions, he is also convinced that the Christian way is the best. But it is the Christian ideal of service that he stresses, not Christian dogma. He wants all the new literates to have, along with their books of practical information, the story of Jesus, simply told. Thus they will learn the Christian way from the greatest of all Teachers.

Back home in the late summer of 1951 Dr. Laubach wrote: "As I think back over this last tour, I'm more certain than ever that there is only one solution for the world's misery, and only one way that will beat communism. That is Christian service. We saw it working. We saw how the masses love you when you help them. In Asia the masses are desperately determined to better their condition and the governments are desperately worried. Where our missions and our government are giving enough service, we are saving Asia. Where we are not helping people, we are losing them. You who know this should shout it from the housetops. For America is thinking in a cloud. Say it clearly, say it loudly, say it constantly!"

CHAPTER 15

Millions of Voters Learn To Read

"When we say 'education' we must mean honor, justice, love of fellow-man—all that is implied in the phrase 'training for democracy.' "—F. C. L.

In October, 1951, Dr. Laubach was awarded one of the three Medals of Honor given annually by the Theodore Roosevelt Memorial Association to outstanding American citizens. He was chosen for distinguished service in the advancement of social justice. It was estimated that by his method, whether taught by him or by others, sixty million persons had learned to read. Still more significant, his achievements had made men believe, for the first time, in the possibility of world-wide literacy.

At sixty-seven Frank Laubach had become the world's foremost literacy expert. More and more often his name was appearing in news headlines. Nationally-read magazines such as *Collier's*, *Life*, and the *New Yorker* published feature articles about him and his work. The *New York Times* made his literacy campaigns the subject of an editorial, stressing how closely his work ties in with the purposes of the Point Four program. It read in part:

The achievement of large-scale literacy is not an end in itself. An association with so-called primitive peoples will readily demonstrate that there is no necessary connection between literacy and intelligence, and an association with those who are most literate will likewise show that there is no necessary connection between literacy and human happiness or greatness of spirit. But literacy itself is a tool and an exceedingly useful one. It can be made to serve a wide variety of good purposes and it can facilitate accomplishment in many fields.

It is much easier, for example, to hold an election if the voter can read the names of the candidates on a ballot. It is easier to put issues before him if he can read a definition of them. It is easier to conduct a public health program if persons can read the label on a bottle. It is easier to preserve and to disseminate a lofty tradition or a valuable innovation if it can be committed to a form in which it is made readily familiar. Perhaps, above all, it is easier to break down the barriers between groups of persons, and hence individuals, if their means of intercommunication are improved.

Dr. Laubach has always maintained that literacy is merely a means to many good ends. And these ends are not only the immediate practical ones, enabling men to raise more food, live in more decent homes, or have more leisure from the grind of toil. Literacy also gives a voice to the "silent billion," a voice in world affairs. Only a literate people can have a truly democratic government.

The elections held in the new Republic of India from October, 1951, to January, 1952, provided a remarkable demonstration of the problems caused by illiteracy in carrying on the democratic process of voting. India, declared a republic in August, 1947, held its first country-wide elections in 1951–52. Since the new constitution gave the franchise to all adults of sound mind, 176 million were eligible to vote, but by far the great majority of these could not read or write. In some sections of the country illiteracy ran as high as 90 per cent. These millions could not be reached by newspapers, or radio, and did not attend election rallies. How could candidates for the offices in the nine states and for the House of the People in the national government influence this vast electorate, and how could the voters who could not read cast their ballots?

Elaborate plans had to be made. First, a symbol was chosen for each party—the picture of something that a voter would recognize as belonging to the candidate he wished to vote for. A team of bullocks was the symbol of the Congress Party, a tree that of the Socialist Party, an ear of corn with a sickle that of the Communists. A camel, a lantern, a boat, a rising sun were used as symbols by other parties or by independent candidates. In one section a candidate while campaigning rode from village to village on a camel to make his symbol familiar to the people.

When each voter (man or woman) reached the polling place on election day, his left forefinger was marked with indelible ink to prevent voting twice. Then he was handed as many paper ballots as there were offices for which he was entitled to vote. He did not need to read and mark a ballot. Behind a curtain he found a row of ballot boxes each labeled with the symbol of a candidate. He put a ballot into the box of each candidate he wished to vote for. By this simple process he cast his first vote in the biggest general election ever held in the world.[1]

On the whole this system of voting by symbols worked better than anyone had dared to hope. The masses of illiterate voters proved that they understood the purpose of voting and the issues at stake far better than was expected. To be sure, there were mistakes. One man, aged 105, who had

---

[1] "Unprecedented Experiment in Democracy" by Robert Trumbull, *The New York Times Magazine*, January 20, 1952.

promised his vote to all twelve candidates in his district, tore his ballot paper into twelve pieces and put a piece in each candidate's box. Of course he lost his vote, but he went away smiling because he had kept his promise. Another man, wishing to vote for a candidate with the lamp as a symbol, thrust his ballot into the flame of the lantern which lighted the polling booth. But voting mistakes are not confined to the inexperienced. Even in highly literate countries like our own, many ballots are invalidated by errors during every election. Men and women who have been reading all their lives do not always follow printed directions.

The results of the elections in India returned to power the leaders of the Congress Party, which had been largely responsible for winning the country's independence. Some skeptical observers said the results indicated that the elections were a mere form and did not represent the real wishes of the majority. But persons long familiar with India claim that the Congress Party which, on the whole, follows a middle-of-the-road policy, includes the group best-fitted to hold the reins of power as trustees until such time as the people have a full understanding of democracy.

The Communists won a number of offices in the 1952 elections, especially in sections of extreme poverty. We know, of course, how active Communists are in promising better living to the poor, and how their promises lead in the end to loss of freedom. The next general election will be held in 1956. Who will win the battle for men's minds in the intervening years? Will the groups in India interested in literacy and democracy awaken the masses to the danger of these false promises and to the real and more lasting benefits of democracy?

Many Americans besides Dr. Laubach, who have visited

India, are telling us that it is foolish to expect starving people, ill-housed and poorly clothed, to be interested in democratic freedoms. We must first show them how to find freedom from want. Then they will probably be interested in freedom of speech, of the press, and all the freedoms that well-fed people prize so highly.

A disciple of Gandhi, the saintly Vinoba Bhave, has been walking all over India, penniless, persuading wealthy landowners to give some of their land for distribution to the poor. By 1952 three hundred thousand acres had been given; among the donors was Nehru.

The government of India has adopted several measures designed to correct the food shortage: irrigation, reclaiming of marginal lands, lowering of excessive taxes, buying out big landlords and distributing the land to the peasants, a grow-more-food campaign. It has been estimated that an increase of 10 per cent in production can give India enough food for her millions. The United Nations, the British commonwealths, and our own government are giving technical assistance.

One trouble is that India and her problems are so vast that the average person cannot comprehend them. The land itself is truly a subcontinent, larger than the continent of Europe exclusive of Russia. And as to population—if all the people in the world were passing in review, one out of every five would be an Indian. The most recent census showed that the increase in population since 1940 had been forty-two million.

On returning to India in January, 1952, Dr. Laubach wrote that the feeling toward Americans was much better than the year before. He felt that the change was due in part to the fact that they liked our Ambassador, Chester

Bowles, and that he and Prime Minister Nehru had signed an agreement granting to India some millions of Point Four money for technical assistance. Part of this money is being used in a great Village Development Program, whereby the people are helped by experts to increase production on their farms, learn home industries, improve their health, and become literate. The Indian government asked the famous American county agent, Horace Holmes, to act as head of this village project. The story of how Holmes rolled up his sleeves in good American fashion and worked with a group of Indian students demonstrating how to double their crops of wheat and potatoes, how to improve their tools and their soil, has been told in many American newspapers and magazines. (If you have not read it, see *Life* for December 31, 1951.)

Mr. Holmes at once asked Dr. Laubach's help in finding teachers for the literacy part of the village-improvement scheme. He also ordered three thousand copies of the newest literacy primers and copies of the new colored charts that Phil and Ewing Gray had been perfecting.

The Grays and Dr. Laubach were working in several villages of North India, demonstrating teaching methods and helping to train literacy teachers, writers, and illustrators. Ewing Gray wrote:

"Since 1948 when Phil and I started trailing the alphabet with Dr. Laubach, we have been in many strange and exciting places, but none more interesting, and I might say, more romantic than here at Marehra. Our headquarters, furnished us by the India Service Workers, is in a Mohammedan home, a part of which was built in the seventeenth century and abandoned during those terrible days following the partition of India in 1947, when great numbers of Moslems fled to Pakistan to escape persecution. All around us are ancient mosques, temples, and crumbling buildings whose thick brick and mud walls surround little courtyards with many shrines. Beautifully carved doors are rotting on rusty hinges as they swing open to admit monkeys, stray goats, and sacred cows.

"We have set up the various departments of our work in the courtyards, since the weather is cool and the sunshine never penetrates the dark inner rooms. Someone must be on guard at all times to prevent the monkeys from taking over. The art department seems to be especially fascinating to monkeys. Just now I can count seven watching for a chance to investigate the new color charts.

"Our Moslem cook, Sabir, makes delicious curries and *chapatis*. All milk comes from the water-buffalo cows. Our water supply is carried in a goatskin bag from a nearby well. 'Boiled water' has become an important command.

"Mornings are spent in the preparation of books on child care, agriculture, citizenship, etc., for different stages of teaching the illiterates. Phil and I are making on canvas large charts in color which are to be printed on some indestructible material for wide use in India's villages.

"At twelve-thirty each day we go into a typical rural village to teach. The villagers are thrilled over our gaily colored charts. The main idea of this particular project is to demonstrate teaching methods whereby the illiterate can be taken from the primer stage to functional literacy in seven weeks."

A missionary doctor who was helping to prepare the lessons in health described the village classes at Marehra thus:

"It was easy to see that the method was working. The

faces of old men would light up as they began to realize that reading is not hard after all. After the charts, the primer was used, and one who could just read was set to teach the next person. At that point groups of two or three would gather under the trees, working out the shapes and sounds of letters. The third stage sees the new literate copying the shapes with his finger in the sand. Now he can write also! I saw this happening almost as quickly as I can write an account of it."

While the Grays continued work on the Hindi primer at Moradabad, Dr. and Mrs. Laubach had gone to Katpadi Agricultural Institute in South India to a literacy conference. They found themselves in one of the worst famine areas, where farming was practically abandoned because the monsoon rains had failed for five successive years. People were dying of starvation, and Indian scientists and government leaders were desperately seeking new ways to bring water to the thirsty lands. Communists as usual were active among the hungry peasants.

Dr. Laubach helped the conference groups translate into Telugu and Tamil the little book of practical knowledge which he had devised in Burma the year before. He called it *Anand the Wise Man.*

An official of the Point Four program came to Katpadi to observe the literacy work. His report must have been favorable, for soon news arrived that S. K. Dey, head of the joint Indo-American Village Development Program, was putting literacy ahead of everything else. Then came a request from headquarters of the Technical Co-operation Administration in New Delhi for a consultation. At the office Dr. Laubach was told that they had cabled his name to Washington, recommending that he and his team direct the literacy part of the Village Program. If he agreed their work would start July 15.

Other gratifying news arrived. Professor Roland E. Wolseley, who had developed the courses in journalism for literacy workers at Syracuse University, had been awarded a Fulbright professorship to start a department of journalism at Hislop College, affiliated with Nagpur University. This meant young Indian journalists could receive training in their own land. It was the fulfillment of one of Laubach's dreams.

Part of that dream Bob Laubach was bringing into reality. He had remained in the United States as a student and assistant in journalism at Syracuse. Because of his experience with new literates in many countries, he was giving invaluable aid in the courses in simple journalism while working for an advanced degree.

In answer to appeals Dr. Laubach found time for two weeks in Pakistan, where likewise the burning problem was how to produce simple reading matter for the new literates, especially the women. As usual he went to the heart of the problem by consulting with the faculties of two colleges, urging that courses in practical journalism be added to their curriculums. Also he talked with missionary doctors and nurses about writing a simple book on health, and he arranged to have *Anand the Wise Man* translated into Urdu.

Urgent requests had come from Malaya for the help of the literacy team; so in spite of news about bandits harrying that country, the Laubachs and the Grays flew to Kuala Lumpur, the capital. Their work in lesson-making took them to several of the fenced villages where missionaries were helping people resettled for protection from the bandits.

The British High Commissioner was encouraging all phases of mission work—medical, educational, and religious—as the best hope for the country.

While in Malaya the Laubachs celebrated their fortieth wedding anniversary. At Manila, their next stop, pleasant reunions awaited them. A crowd of old friends were gathered at the airport; letters and telegrams from Mindanao said, "Welcome! Come on down. We love you." They could not take time to go to Lanao, but they found among the delegates to the literacy conference several former students of the Maranaw Folk School, now holding positions of leadership in church and government.

They helped to make new lessons in Tagalog and Ilocano and started a Philippine version of the second reader to be called *Juan the Wise Man*. The lessons were printed with astonishing speed, thanks to the efficiency of Doris Hess, one of the first missionary graduates of the courses in simple journalism at Syracuse.

Besides the church conference on literacy, the government Department of Education had summoned the superintendents of schools of all the provinces to meet Dr. Laubach in Manila. They discussed many aspects of adult education. He wrote:

"We were greatly surprised at the tremendous recovery Manila has made from the frightful war destruction we had seen four years before. . . . I was impressed also by the new spirit of optimism in the Filipinos. . . .

"It gave me keen satisfaction to reread the final chapters of my book, *The People of the Philippines*, printed in 1925. I had made a daring, and as nearly all Americans thought, fantastically over-optimistic prophecy of the future of the Philippines. . . . I said in my final sentence (and this is what brought guffaws twenty years ago), 'Perhaps the success of the Philippines is to be a factor in settling the fate of the world.'

"The Philippines of 1952, with all their problems and defects, are beginning to fulfill the prophecies which many people then called fantastic. That is why for me it was the grand climax and the most hopeful experience of our tour. This is what makes a man's soul sing—when his dreams come true for a people he loves dearly!"

CHAPTER 16

"A Sower Went Out To Sow"

"And as he sowed . . . other seeds fell into good soil and brought forth grain, growing up and increasing and yielding thirtyfold and sixtyfold and a hundredfold."—Mark iv: 3-8.

Like the sower of old, Laubach has scattered seeds far and wide—seeds of good will and of literacy. He has been too busy sowing to worry much about whether all the seed took root. Some "fell on rocky ground" and some "among thorns" but the seed that "fell into good soil" has begun to yield its harvest.

The time is February, 1953; the place, Allahabad Agricultural Institute in India, the same famous school where Laubach made a convincing talk to students in 1937. That remarkable missionary, Sam Higginbottom, is no longer the principal, but the Institute continues its splendid work. Since the war it has, in fact, enlarged its program through an Extension Department, which includes three hundred neighboring villages. Forty men and women at a time live and work in these villages, returning to the Institute every two weeks for three days to study their problems together. Now new buildings are going up. A grant from the Ford Foundation has made it one of five Indian centers of training in social education and especially in literacy work.

Today one of the new buildings is crowded. Under Dr.
Laubach's direction groups are writing new stories about
Anand in various languages. The place buzzes like the Tower
of Babel. The Tamil committee is massed at one end of the
veranda, the Hindi at the other end, while Gujerati flourishes around Dr. Laubach's desk, and Telugu is crowded into
his secretary's tiny office. The pretty American secretary has
recently arrived from the New York office to help Dr. Laubach with a mountain of paper work. As part of American
TCA, he is now responsible for the literacy end of the vast
Village Development Program. It includes not only preparing charts, primers, and second readers in eleven languages,
but training teachers and discovering and training writers
to prepare periodicals for the new literates.

Dr. Laubach is beaming. He is never happier than when
challenged by a huge job. He is sure now that the Hindi
lessons, with Phil Gray's attractive pictures, are exactly right.
After his long struggle for perfection he is satisfied to recommend them to the government of India as the best possible
device for teaching adults to read. Nearly every state of
India has invited the team to come and start a campaign.

The program has been streamlined through long experience. A month before a literacy push in any area, the big
charts are pasted on village walls so that illiterates, with a
little encouragement from some leader in the village, can
learn the letters easily through the bright pictures. When
the literacy classes start, those who know the letters dash
through the primer in a week. Interest rises as they start the
second reader, *Anand the Wise Man.*

Our scene changes from Allahabad to a village. Teachers
from the training school are arriving in a jeep—nine persons
in the two narrow seats. Dick Cortright, trained in literacy

techniques at Hartford Seminary, and Betty Mooney, graduate in simple journalism at Syracuse, are the leaders. It is evening, for few classes can be held during the day when the men are busy in the fields. Moonlight sheds a mysterious beauty over the mud houses. Fires of cow dung glow in the dusty shadows. The people of this village are slightly better off than those of many villages; they are gathered around several kerosene lanterns instead of tiny oil lamps or candles. Two homes even have cement walls and real gardens.

Voices in the dusk cry "Salaam," and children crowd around the jeep. One of the leading men comes forward to greet the teachers. He escorts two of them to his veranda, where he has lamps ready. The older girls say eagerly, "Come, sister," and crowd around Betty. Older women surround one of the Indian student teachers.

"Here are my three annas," says one. "Write my name in the book."

The men gather more slowly. One with the help of his own tiny lamp studies the big chart on the wall. Several with copies of the primer gather about Dick. A bright-eyed young man proudly demonstrates that he can read the very last lesson. Dick, who speaks Hindi slowly, suggests that he help an older man who is just starting the primer.

A gray-haired man and a woman with wrinkled face sit in front of their house a little apart. "We are too old to learn," the man says when a student teacher approaches them.

She answers softly, "Dr. Laubach who invented these lessons is also a *baba* (venerable old man). If he wasn't too old to make the books, surely you are not too old to read them."

The man nods his head and the woman smiles timidly. They follow the teacher slowly to the wall chart, where they soon discover that each picture in the shape of a letter suggests a word they know.

Dick Cortright is giving the eager young man a copy of *Anand the Wise Man*. His eyes glow as he opens the book. At the edge of the circle of lamplight, he sits motionless, completely absorbed in the first story.

Anand is a sort of superman whose successes parallel those now possible to each villager. They are described in easy words and sentences, with much repetition of both words and ideas to drive home the information that every farmer needs. First, Anand learns to read. Then he reads how to make a good garden and makes one. Another story tells how to raise better chickens; others how to abolish rats; why the drinking water should be boiled. Anand teaches his wife Revati to read, and she learns what to feed the baby, what vegetables to eat, how to make potato *chapati*. Anand is soon admired and consulted by his neighbors. He reads about his government; in the last chapter he even goes to New Delhi. There a friend who has sent him books takes him to visit the Directors of Agriculture, of Health, of Education. Each one praises him for helping India.

Anand is truly the hero of literacy campaigns because it has been discovered that the book about him solves a baffling problem—the reluctance of Indian farmers to adopt new ideas. They are suspicious of all strangers and especially of an educated person who offers help, because they and their forebears have been victimized for so long. They may watch patiently a demonstration of better ways to plow and plant, but after the expert has gone, most of them return to their old ways. However, they have deep respect for the printed page. They believe that what is in black and white must be true; print is a marvel they hold in awe. So when a farmer learns to read well enough to follow the stories of Anand, he will nod and say, "If Anand boiled the drinking water for his family, it must be right. I will do that, too." Then he is ready to cooperate when an expert in village sanitation or an agricultural demonstrator arrives.

The Anand book is proving so successful that the Laubach team has prepared a second volume of more interesting stories—stories involving trouble, conflict, crises, and success, the plots devised by Margaret Lee Runbeck, an experienced writer who recently went to India to start a course in journalism at Isabella Thoburn College in Lucknow. According to Dr. Laubach, she puts "the zing" into stories contributed by students in the literacy training courses. They concern Anand's family and neighbors as well as Anand himself, and have enough action and suspense so that new readers will be carried along by pleasant anticipation, much as listeners follow, day by day, the fortunes of their favorite radio-serial family. There is a difference, however, for Anand's adventures are full of practical information for the improvement of family and village life.

Anand's troubles begin when he proposes that women may be elected to the village *panchayat* (council), quoting the new constitution for India in support of the change. When he saves a foolish neighbor from falling into the clutches of an unscrupulous moneylender, he barely escapes the villain's revenge. Later his son welcomes a *Harijan* (formerly untouchable) girl who wants to learn to read, and all the neighbors boycott the class in spite of the teachings of the beloved Gandhi that there are no longer any untouchables. But the good work of Anand and his son in showing how to fight a plague of locusts and in improving the village school finally wins over old prejudices. In the end the son marries the *Harijan,* and when, after a disastrous village fire, Anand and his son build a new house of bricks with a tile roof, they start another new custom by building a room which the young couple can have as their own.

Another part of the story centers around a young neighbor, Gopi, whose mother is jealous of his wife and her new ways. He is tempted to move to the city when he hears that there it is easier to make money with less hard work.

"Shanti [the young wife] took him by the hand, and they went together through the sleeping village. They could see the fields in the light of the moon. The sky was filled with stars around the moon. Through the trees, the stars looked like fruit. She said nothing at all. She let all the beautiful things do the talking for her. Gopi looked around them at the moon and the stars and the trees. Then he smiled with happiness.

" 'Farming is best,' he said. 'It feeds a man's body and his soul. It is the hope of India.' "

Later when Shanti saves Gopi's life by knowing what to do when he is bitten by a poisonous snake, the mother is reconciled to her modern daughter-in-law. Throughout these episodes the information is specific about how to destroy locusts, how to make bricks and plan a house, how to cauterize a snakebite.

A pleasanter problem involves a lovely village girl who is wanted in marriage by three boys whose family rivalry is setting the village at odds. A newcomer suggests:

" 'Why don't we go back to the old customs? Let the boys who want to marry Phulmati come together in a village festivity. Let each tell why he is the one Phulmati should marry. Then let the girl put a garland of white flowers on the one boy she wants for a husband. That was the custom among our old rulers. We can use it for a festivity because now we are all our own rulers.' "

The families agree to this new-old custom of letting a girl decide for herself, but suspense continues through three chapters telling what each boy does to win her favor. The richest suitor throws a party including music and a cinema in a big tent (and incidentally the reader learns what makes movies seem to move). The second suitor, who is fond of reading, starts a library for the village (and its organization is given in some detail). The third suitor, when a famine threatens, offers to his neighbors part of the wheat he has saved for seed and leads a movement for improving the next harvest with better seed.

At the festivity Phulmati makes her choice among the suitors wisely, as did Shakespeare's Portia.

"Anand asked the three boys who loved Phulmati to stand in a row. They were all laughing and talking, but their hearts were very much excited. Rama, the son of the rich family, was in fine new clothes, with gold around his neck and gold on his hands. The neighbors said to themselves, 'This is to tell Phulmati that if she chooses him, she will be able to wear gold.'

"Vishwa-Nath, the boy who had given the town its library, had a book in his hand. The neighbors said to themselves, 'This is to tell Phulmati that their life together will be filled with education, if she chooses him for her husband.'

"But Ishwar, the boy who was helping the village get better crops from its fields, had nothing in his hands. His face held the only riches he had brought. For his face was filled with love for Phulmati.

"Suddenly everyone stopped speaking, for Phulmati, wearing a veil over her pretty face, came near. Her mother walked beside her. Phulmati had in her hands a long garland of white flowers.

"They walked slowly to the three boys. Everyone was too excited to say a word. . . . Then she raised her arms and put the garland around the neck of Ishwar.

"Everyone was surprised. All had thought she might choose

Rama, the son of the rich family, with his gold. But she had chosen the boy who had great riches of love in his heart. She had chosen the boy who loved to help other people make life good. She knew she would make a good life with this husband."

These samples from the second Anand book show how the new reader (and his wife) can be led easily to attain reading skill, at the same time imbibing much valuable information. It is an old device, and the lessons taught by the stories may seem too obvious to experienced readers; but they will fascinate the great new reading public in the Indian villages. They present adult problems with honesty and sincerity, and the very simplicity of the language gives them much of the dignity and beauty of folk literature.

From the true-to-life fiction of Anand, devised to meet a literacy problem, the scene again shifts—this time to New Delhi. In the TCA office Laubach and an official of the Indian Government are conferring with a publisher about the cost of printing more charts and books for the vast literacy campaign. The publisher is an American who owns two newspapers and a big comic-strip color printing press. He understands mass production and is here to give technical assistance. A press in Bombay has been doing the charts with handsome color work, and other presses in India have printed most attractive books with the Grays' pictures in color, but there aren't enough large presses to meet the demand.

The American publisher looks admiringly at one of the big charts. "How many of these will you need?" he asks.

"There are five hundred thousand villages," answers Laubach. "At least one set of four to six charts for each village."

The publisher measures the chart and looks more closely at the colors. Then his pencil works busily setting down some figures. "Hm—let's see. Roughly I'd say about twenty cents a set. Might be able to shave that a trifle."

"The charts are not all exactly the same as these," puts in the Indian official. "The charts for each language are different, and the campaigns are in eleven languages."

"That makes it harder to cut the cost," says the American. "What about these little books?" He leafs through a Hindi primer.

"We'll need about three hundred million," says Laubach.

"Twice the population of the U.S.A.!" The publisher looks a bit startled.

"In eleven languages," the Indian reminds him.

"But not that number of each," adds Laubach. "Say a printing of from three hundred thousand to nine hundred thousand to start with in each language."

Again the publisher does some rapid figuring. "One and a half cents a copy," he concludes.

"That's wonderful." Laubach smiles. "Two cents has been the lowest estimate considered possible. At a cent and a half for a printing of three hundred thousand, we could get going with forty-five hundred dollars—that is, for each language."

"And that is very much money," says the Indian, "but in many states the governments are already planning to provide the money."

"When I was at home in December," says Laubach, "some good friends of the Literacy Committee offered funds for small demonstration editions in all the languages. If we can sell each book for three cents, the returns can be used for larger and larger editions. But time is important. We need to start with big printings. We need more presses, faster presses, bigger presses. Besides the charts and primers, there are the second readers, *Anand the Wise Man,* you know, and there should be third readers, and village newspapers, and—"

"Many, many books and magazines, and libraries as in all towns in America, not just in our great cities," says the Indian.

"Your program is stupendous," says the American publisher. "I'm used to talking about big orders, but this—well, it's a bit staggering."

"Yes, India and its needs leave everyone gasping," remarks Laubach. "Until I heard your estimate I saw only little peanuts to feed an elephant. Now I think I see how to satisfy the elephant—provided enough Americans and Indians see it, too."

The scene shifts again like an endless movie—to Tanganyika, to Egypt, to Brazil, to Cuba—wherever men and women inspired by Laubach's vision and technique are carrying on active work for literacy. One of the most promising campaigns is in Middle Egypt, directed by veteran Davida Finney, with local leaders and trained teachers in charge of the follow-up work. The new political leaders in Egypt want the help of a literate populace in building a prosperous country.

Dr. Laubach's work and its influence are best judged in the light of world events of the past twenty-five years and world problems of today.

In 1929 and 1930, when most people in the United States were in a panic from the stock-market crash and the ensuing depression, Frank Laubach was working himself out of his personal depression by making friends with the hostile Moros and teaching them how to read.

In 1937, when Americans and Europeans were casting frightened glances at the war clouds rising out of Germany,

Frank Laubach was busy in India and East Africa planting seeds of interest in literacy which flowered into great enthusiasm before and after World War II.

During the war years, while most Americans not actually engaged in military life were engrossed in war activities, Frank Laubach was fighting his special war against illiteracy in Latin America.

And in the later 1940's, while almost everyone sat back with sighs of relief and relaxed, showing now and then a spark of interest in the new United Nations, Frank Laubach was flying to all the backward lands of Africa and Asia, quick to see the needs of the millions who had been awakened by winds of change all over the world. Like a true statesman he foresaw what this vast awakening would mean long before the spread of communism made it clear to political leaders.

By 1950 many governments appreciated the importance of literacy and, as we have seen, sought for help from Dr. Laubach. UNESCO of the United Nations embarked upon a program of fundamental education—a program of which literacy is a basic part. Our own United States government launched its Point Four program of technical assistance to undeveloped areas.

Importers and manufacturers also have come to see practical reasons why it is important for men living in the jungle to know how to read. The industrialist may be depending on that jungle man for balsa wood. He is far less likely to harm himself or a valuable piece of machinery if he can read the safety signs posted in the timber area or at the loading wharf.

One person reading of Dr. Laubach's work remarked, "He is a striking example of what an individual moved by the force of a big idea can accomplish—one person daring to challenge the illiteracy of millions. To be sure he has not reached the goal, but he has made the world believe that it can be done. And what a demonstration of the power of the individual at the very time when totalitarian philosophy would have us believe that the state is supreme, the individual nothing."

In our practical American way we sometimes say, "Figures talk." A few figures taken from the financial report of the Committee on World Literacy and Christian Literature tell in their graphic way the story of Dr. Laubach's work.

In 1937 the total receipts of the committee, largely personal gifts, amounted to a sum just under $3,200; the expenditures, a sum just over $2,500. Fifteen years later, in 1952, the committee, now a part of the Division of Foreign Missions of the National Council of the Churches of Christ in the U.S.A., was operating on a budget of $203,540. The money, contributed by forty-five different Protestant organizations, was designated for literacy work in thirteen different countries.

If figures talk, a budget multiplied by eighty in fifteen years bespeaks a remarkable growth in both interest and activity. But these figures by no means tell the whole story. They do not mention the seventy-five or more countries in which Dr. Laubach has worked or the two hundred and thirty languages, not counting dialects of Spanish and Arabic, in which he has helped to make lessons. They do not tell of the projects undertaken in collaboration with other organizations and governments, or of those inspired by his example now being carried on under the auspices of the United Nations or of individual nations. Figures cannot describe the tremendous impetus his work has given to other missionary efforts, nor the courage and hope planted in millions of hopeless hearts all over the world.

Nor do the figures reveal anything of the careful but unspectacular work of the executive secretary, Alfred Moore, and his staff of assistants, who labor faithfully in their crowded New York office to keep the wheels turning smoothly.

The figures do tell something about the cooperative efforts of a number of churches in their support of the committee. Dr. Laubach, wherever he goes, brings together all those interested in promoting literacy—laymen as well as clergymen and missionaries, civil servants, military men, and government officials. This cooperative effort is the very spirit of world service which his work so well symbolizes.

A new plan close to his heart is outlined in one of the last chapters of *Wake Up or Blow Up*. It is a plan for selecting from churches all over America outstanding Christian leaders in middle life who would be willing to go to underdeveloped areas and give technical advice and help in any lines in which they are expert. Dr. Laubach feels that men and women who have reached the peak of their careers would welcome the chance to share the riches of their experience to help lift the world out of its misery. It is not enough, he says, to send mere technicians. Those who represent us and our democratic ideals to others should be, above all, men and women of character, of complete integrity, eager to help, educated in both mind and heart.

Saddened by revelations about the black market in goods sent through UNRRA to help Filipinos who had suffered in the war, he said:

"We ought never to loan or give money or charity of any kind to a country until we have conscientious men and

women with a missionary spirit, who speak the language of
the country, who have exact knowledge of the situation, and
who are capable of seeing that the money is not misused or
misappropriated."

Such persons, he believes, can be found in our churches
among those who are also equipped to give the technical
help needed in underdeveloped areas. Characteristically, he
at once organized a training center for such men and women
at Koinonia, one of the Camps Farthest Out, planned for
developing spiritual leaders.

He made, also, a challenging appeal for technical aid in
the literacy program to a group of journalists, following a
dinner at Riverside Church in New York:

"I shall give you what your foreign correspondents never
give you, a worm's idea of the problems which baffle us in
Asia. Your correspondents constantly consult the men at the
top. I live in daily contact with the illiterate men at the
bottom. They outnumber those at the top in Asia fifty to
one—in some areas ninety-nine to one. I am today talking for
a billion people who, I think, are going to determine the fate
of Asia and perhaps of the world."

After outlining the literacy work already begun, he continued:

"It is obvious that to feed the minds of three hundred
million new literates, a vast amount of simple literature must
be prepared. But as you well know, reading matter does not
write itself. It requires know-how and sweat. . . . In Nagpur, India, is being started this summer the first school of
simple journalism in Asia. . . . We shall need more of these
schools in India and also in Malaya, Indonesia, Siam, Burma,
the Philippines, and the countries of the Near East. I see no
other way to break this bottleneck. . . .

"We are pioneering in the production of a new type of reading, simpler than you men now produce for a level of mind lower than any of you now reach. We are lonesome pioneers in that field. We are not satisfied with our work. We need the help of superb journalists and editors like you. . . .

"I think there has never in history been such a group of wizards at writing with a punch as you and others like you in America today. . . . I plead with you to devote some of that genius to saving the two-thirds of the human race from following a false messiah in communism. . . .

"Just how would you begin? You would first need to train native writers who have facility with their own language. You would have to send those writers down among new literates just as you now have reporters among the leading people of the country. There you could mold opinion as swiftly and effectively as the Communists are doing it now. It is a disgrace that the Communists are winning Asia when the greatest script writers are in America, unaware that they could save the world if they poured their genius into the dialects of Asia. . . . Once Communists start their blood purges, there is no pathway back to democracy. . . .

"I am not asking for your money, but for your brains. . . . I appeal to the strongest men in journalism to come out to Asia and write to beat the devil. Up to this moment the devil is beating us."

The new school of journalism at Nagpur, India, graduated its first class in the spring of 1953. A third of the students were experienced journalists who wrote for the Nagpur newspapers during their year of study. The group especially interested in social education experimented with writing for new literates and produced, by cooperative work, a Manual which will serve as a text for future classes. Pioneer work on such a Manual had already been done at Syracuse.

The group at Syracuse under Bob Laubach produced an experimental edition of a simple newspaper, which they called *One Step Forward,* and also an attractive small magazine (twenty-four pages) called *Read.* These were devised as models for such periodicals in any country where they are needed. The printing was done also as a pilot project, to show what can be produced with inexpensive equipment, such as might be obtainable in underdeveloped lands. The students in the group were from different countries and will carry their skills back home to serve their own people in their own languages.

So will other seeds fall into good soil and bring forth grain.

CHAPTER 17

Lending a Hand

"Let us all stop being God's problem and become His answer."—F. C. L.

Since the governing law of Dr. Laubach's life is to meet needs, wherever he finds them, with loving service, it seems fitting to close this account of his work with the question: How can we help?

Many older people feel, since there are so many needs close at hand, it is best to help our neighbors, our own community, and perhaps the underprivileged of our own country, and not worry about the rest of the world. "Charity begins at home" is their motto.

The only weakness in this point of view is that airplanes and radio have made the world so small that today everybody is our neighbor. That Malay girl in a sarong and that Afghan herder in sheepskin cap are no longer two months' travel away. They are at our very doorstep, and what they do and think and say affects our lives as much as if they lived across the street, sometimes more—for the clamoring need of the hungry millions in Asia may determine whether we have peace or war in this generation.

But fear is not a good motive for service. Only good will can inspire real help for our neighbors' need, whether they be near or remote. The eighty-year-old philosopher, Bertrand Russell, said recently, in an interview broadcast from his English home, that he believes the doctrines of Karl Marx cannot help the world to achieve the good life because they are not based on a kindly feeling toward people. Only good will (plus intelligence, of course) will solve the world's problems.

Some people, however, find it hard to have a kindly feeling toward strangers far away. They do not wish them ill, but neither do they care enough to will them good. Their feelings are neutral. If you are one of these, and especially if you are a young person, you have within yourself many allies for building good will. One of them is your natural curiosity. Do you not wonder what it would be like to be a young person growing up today in Northern Rhodesia or Iran or Burma or Brazil? If you don't have that curiosity, you had better wake up, for plenty of young people in those lands are wondering about you and the rest of the world. They may outstrip you, for curiosity is a powerful drive toward achievement.

Another possible ally within us all is a sense of gratitude. Too seldom do we pause to consider what part of our heritage of science, mathematics, medicine, art, religion we owe to those ancient lands which we sometimes count as backward. Where did our alphabet come from? The Phoenicians of the eastern Mediterranean shores. Where did Europeans learn the art of papermaking? From China, but the Chinese themselves recognized that paper made in Korea was superior to all other. And in Korea men were printing with movable types as early as 1403—a generation before Gutenberg in Europe. Where was the first printing done in the Americas? In Mexico City. Who invented our system of numbers? The Arabs. Who first measured the earth's circumference? An Egyptian, named Eratosthenes. Whence came Judaism and Christianity, the dominant faiths of the Western world? From the Middle East.

The list of our debts to the people of other lands would fill volumes—debts that no one of us can ever repay except in gratitude. But that gratitude, if genuine, can build good will toward the people now needing help in those lands. And good will sooner or later finds a way to help. As Dr. Laubach says in *Wake Up or Blow Up:* "A good neighbor doesn't lend money; he goes and lends a hand."

If you have an aptitude for languages and a liking for all sorts of people, you might prepare yourself to help the campaign for world literacy. Teachers and writers will be needed by the hundreds as the desire to read snowballs in all lands where illiteracy has prevailed.

Ultimately, such writers will develop among the people of each language group, but at first someone must lead the way. Journalists, editors, illustrators, engravers, publishers, printers, pressmen, booksellers, librarians—all will find work waiting for them. In the newly wakened lands the next fifty years may parallel the fifty years that followed the invention of printing in Europe, when books first became available to the common man. In those fifty years over eight million books were printed. The multitudes of new readers in Asia and Africa will demand many times that number. Engineers, agriculturists, doctors, public health nurses, chemists, bacteriologists are also needed. The world is full of ringing challenge today for young people who have the spirit of adventure.

An English missionary in Tanganyika, inspired by Dr. Laubach's visit in 1950, described in recent letters to him the literacy work which she and a team of nine educated Africans were doing among the people of the Wagogo tribe.

In great crowds they came streaming across the plains as soon as they heard news of the teaching. Most of the men were plastered with red mud, their hair plaited in fantastic style, with beads around their necks and dangling from their ears. But some of them set new records of speed in learning to read. One of the brightest, whenever he opened his primer, would solemnly put on the white frames of an old pair of glasses—minus the lenses. The teacher, each time she saw him, wanted to laugh and to weep, for the man seemed a symbol of all illiterates in the more primitive tribes—so eager for the good things of civilization that they sometimes mistake its claptrap for the essentials of progress.

Each of us can help to make sure that such people—our distant neighbors—are offered the essentials, the lenses as well as the frames, the opportunity to learn to read, and the books and magazines in which they can find both practical information and the truths that undergird our civilization.

BIBLIOGRAPHY

Laubach, Frank C.: *The Silent Billion Speak.* Friendship Press, 1943

——: *Teaching the World to Read.* Friendship Press, 1947

——: *Wake Up or Blow Up.* Fleming H. Revell Company, 1951

——: *Prayer, the Mightiest Force in the World.* Fleming H. Revell Company, 1946

——: *Letters by a Modern Mystic.* Student Volunteer Movement, 1937

——: *The People of the Philippines.* George H. Doran Co., 1925

——: *Seven Thousand Emeralds.* Missionary Education Movement, 1929

——: *Lanao Progress.* 1933–1940 newspaper files in library of the American Board of Commissioners for Foreign Missions, Boston

——: *India Shall Be Literate.* National Christian Council, Nagpur, 1940

——: *Streamlined English Lessons.* Committee on World Literacy and Christian Literature, 1945 and The Macmillan Company, 1951.

——: *The Story of Jesus, Retold from the Bible.* Committee on World Literacy and Christian Literature, 1946

——: *Making Everybody's World Safe.* Committee on World Literacy and Christian Literature, 1947

——: *You Are My Friends.* Harper and Brothers, 1942

225

Andrews, C. F.: *Mahatma Gandhi's Ideas.* The Macmillan Company, 1929

Collier, John Jr. and Burtrón, Amíbel: *The Awakening Valley.* Chicago University Press, 1949

Cooke, Morris Llewellyn: *Brazil on the March.* Whittlesey House, 1944

Douglas, William O.: *Strange Lands and Friendly People.* Harper and Brothers, 1951

————: *Beyond the High Himalayas.* Doubleday and Company, 1952

————: *North from Malaya.* Doubleday and Company, 1953

Fischer, John: *Master Plan, U. S. A.* Harper and Brothers, 1951

Fischer, Louis: *Life of Mahatma Gandhi.* Harper and Brothers, 1950

Goodfriend, Arthur: *The Only War We Seek.* Farrar, Straus and Company, 1951

Hanson, Earl Parker: *New Worlds Emerging.* Duell, Sloan and Pearce, 1949

Hewitt, Gordon: *Nothing Can Stop It Now.* Lutterworth Press, 1947. Reprinted by Committee on World Literacy and Christian Literature, 1950

Lesný, V.: *Rabindranath Tagore, His Personality and Work.* Allen and Unwin, 1939

Masani, Minoo: *Our India.* Oxford University Press, 1942

Michener, James A.: *The Voice of Asia.* Random House, 1951

Muehl, J. F.: *Interview with India.* John Day, 1950

Osgood, Cornelius: *The Koreans and Their Culture.* Ronald Press Company, 1951

Paton, Alan: *Cry, the Beloved Country.* Charles Scribner's Sons, 1948

Pearson, W. W.: *Shantineketan, the Bolpur School of Rabindranath Tagore*. The Macmillan Company, 1916

Ramos, Maximo and Valeros, Florentino B., Editors: *Philippine Cross-Section*. The Bardavon Series of Philippine Literature, A Barangay Writers' Project, 1950

Rau, Santha Rama: *Home to India*. Harper and Brothers, 1945

Rhys, Ernest: *Rabindranath Tagore, a Biographical Study*. The Macmillan Company, 1915

Singh, R. Lal and Lownsbery, Eloise: *Gift of the Forest*. Longmans, Green and Company, 1942

Sharing Skills—Stories of Technical Assistance. United Nations Department of Public Information, 1953

Wiser, William W. and Charlotte V.: *Behind Mud Walls*. Agricultural Missions, Inc., 1951

Wyckoff, Charlotte Chandler: *Jothy*. Longmans, Green and Company, 1939

PREACHING IN ENGLAND
IN THE LATE
FIFTEENTH AND SIXTEENTH
CENTURIES

**Gallicantus Iohannis alcok epi Eliensis ao cō
fratres suos curatos in sinodo apud Bernwell.
xxv. die mensis Septembris. Anno millesimo.
CCCC.nonagesimo octauo.**

The bishop preaches to his priests in synod. Woodcut from the title page to
John Alcock, *Gallicantus Iohannis alcok episcopi Eliensis ad confratres suos curatos
in sinodo apud Bernwell*, (London, [1498]).

(Reproduced by permission of the Bodleian Library).

PREACHING IN ENGLAND

in the late Fifteenth and
Sixteenth Centuries

A Study of English Sermons 1450—c.1600

by J. W. BLENCH

Lecturer in English, University of Aberdeen

NEW YORK
BARNES & NOBLE INC.
1964

First Printed 1964

PRINTED IN GREAT BRITAIN

PREFACE

The present work is based on a dissertation submitted some years ago at Cambridge for which the degree of Doctor of Philosophy was granted. Since then, however, I have thoroughly revised and enlarged it and have made use of new material.

I should like to acknowledge the generous help which I have received in the preparation of this study. My college, St. John's Cambridge, awarded me a Research Exhibition, which enabled me to begin work upon the subject. I am deeply indebted to the late Professor G. R. Owst who read this work in its various stages, offering most valuable comments, and who with unfailing courtesy and sympathy gave me richly of his ripe scholarship and wisdom. Miss E. E. H. Welsford allowed me to draw on her unparalleled knowledge of sixteenth century literature and guided me in the difficult early stages of research, while expert help with Canon Law references was afforded by Dr. W. Ullmann. Mr. Hugh Sykes Davies, and later Professor W. L. Renwick and Professor G. I. Duthie gave me their stimulating interest and encouragement.

I must also express appreciation of the help and service given me by the Librarians and staffs of many libraries—of the University Library Cambridge, the Bodleian, the University Libraries of Edinburgh and Aberdeen, of the British Museum, the National Library of Scotland, the Lambeth Palace Library, and the Cathedral Libraries of Lincoln, Peterborough and St. Paul's.

My thanks are due to the editors of the *Review of English Studies* and the Oxford University Press for permission to make use in this book of material which first appeared in a rather different form in an article on John Longland and Roger Edgeworth (April, 1954).

Finally, I should like to thank the University of Aberdeen and the Carnegie Trust for the Universities of Scotland for providing the subsidy required for the publication of this book.

J. W. BLENCH

King's College
University of Aberdeen
6 November, 1963

CONTENTS

ABBREVIATIONS

A.J.P.	*American Journal of Philology.*
C.H.	*Church History.*
C.H.E.L.	*The Cambridge History of English Literature*, ed. A. W. Ward and A. R. Waller, 14 vols. (Cambridge, 1907–16).
C.P.	*Classical Philology.*
C.S.	Camden Society.
D.N.B.	*Dictionary of National Biography*, ed. L. Stephen, 63 vols. (London, 1885–1900).
D.R.	*Dublin Review.*
E.C.	*Essays in Criticism.*
E.E.T.S.	Early English Text Society.
o.s.	Original series.
e.s.	Extra series.
E.H.R.	*English Historical Review.*
H.J.	*Hibbert Journal.*
H.L.Q.	*Huntington Library Quarterly.*
H.T.R.	*Harvard Theological Review.*
J.H.I.	*Journal of the History of Ideas.*
L. & P.M.E.	G. R. Owst, *Literature and Pulpit in Medieval England*, 2nd edn., (Oxford, 1961).
Loeb.	The Loeb Classical Library.
M.L.R.	*Modern Language Review.*
M.P.	*Modern Philology.*
M.S.R.	Malone Society Reprints.
P.G.	J. P. Migne, *Patrologiae Cursus Completus . . . Series Graeca*, 104 vols. (Paris, 1857–60).
P.L.	J. P. Migne, *Patrologiae Cursus Completus . . . Series Latina*, 221 vols., (Paris, 1844–80).
P.M.E.	G. R. Owst, *Preaching in Medieval England* (Cambridge, 1926).
P.M.L.A.	*Publications of the Modern Language Association of America.*
P.S.	Parker Society.
Q.J.S.	*Quarterly Journal of Speech.*
R.E.S.	*Review of English Studies.*
S.M.	*Speech Monographs.*
S.P.	*Studies in Philology.*

S.T.C.	A. W. Pollard and G. R. Redgrave, *A Short Title Catalogue of Books Printed in England, Scotland, and Ireland and of English Books Printed Abroad*, 1475–1640, (London, 1926).
T.B. cum gloss. ord., etc.	*Textus biblie, cum glosa ordinaria, Nicolai de Lyra postilla, moralitatibus eiusdem, Pauli Burgensis additionibus, Matthie Thoring. replicis*, 6 vols. (Basel, 1506–8).
T.B. cum post. Hug. Card.	*Prima (-septima) pars huius operis: continens textum Biblie cum postilla domini Hugonis Cardinalis*, 7 vols. (Basel, 1498–1502).
T.F.T.	Tudor Facsimile Texts.
T.L.S.	*Times Literary Supplement.*
Vg.	Vulgate Bible.

NOTE ON QUOTATIONS

In the quotations I have throughout preserved the original spelling, except that in the case of printed books I have rendered the black letter thorn ɲ by ' th '. In the case of manuscripts, however, I have retained the thorn. All contractions and signs of abbreviation have been silently expanded except the ampersand (&). I have retained the original use of capitals in the case of printed books, with the exception of the *Sermones* of Stephen Baron, where it is extremely careless and irregular. In this last instance, and in the case of manuscripts I have introduced a few capitals in the interest of clarity. I have completely modernized the punctuation of the manuscripts, and have modernized that of the printed books to the extent of replacing oblique lines (/) by commas, and brackets round quotations by italics, while in a few instances I have added commas to make the meaning clear. All scriptural references are to the Authorized Version, except where it is indicated that they are to the Vulgate, or Douay Version.

INTRODUCTION

It is a matter for considerable surprise that hitherto there has not been undertaken a systematic study of preaching in England from the ' Eve of the Reformation ' to the period of the early Anglican maturity at the close of the reign of Elizabeth I. For the medieval period there are the admirable volumes of G. R. Owst, *Preaching in Medieval England* (Cambridge, 1926) and *Literature and Pulpit in Medieval England* (Cambridge, 1933; 2nd edn., Oxford, 1961), together with his lecture, *The Destructiorum Viciorum of Alexander Carpenter* (London, 1952). For the seventeenth century we have the learned study of W. F. Mitchell, *English Pulpit Oratory from Andrewes to Tillotson* (London, 1932), although this is concerned purely with style. However, for the sixteenth century, the work done has been quite fragmentary. Apart from stray chapters in larger works and a few magazine articles,[1] there are indeed four books to consult, but none aims at any completeness. The first, A. F. Herr's *The Elizabethan Sermon* (Philadelphia, 1940), is a brief treatment of the Elizabethan preachers; it is a book concerned more with ' background ' and the preaching scene than with the sermons themselves, and is offered only as an initial survey. The second is a mid-nineteenth century compilation by J. O. W. Haweis, *Sketches of the Reformation and Elizabethan Age taken from the Contemporary Pulpit* (London, 1844), which consists largely of loosely grouped excerpts from some of the preachers, illustrating various rather unrelated aspects of the life and thought of the time. The third is the very useful and frequently entertaining *The Paul's Cross Sermons* 1534–1642 (Toronto, 1958) by Millar Maclure, which however confines itself to this particular group of sermons. The last is F. Pützer's *Prediger des englischen Barock* (Bonn, 1929), which includes criticism of the style of some sixteenth century preachers, but does not deal with any other aspect of their work. It seemed therefore that a detailed examination of all classes of the extant material would be of value for two reasons.

[1] As G. P. Krapp, *The Rise of English Literary Prose* (New York, 1915) ch. iv, pp. 153–217; *C.H.E.L.*, vol. IV, ch. xii, pp. 224–41; W. E. Campbell, ' Sermons and Religious Treatises,' in E. M. Nugent, *The Thought and Culture of the English Renaissance. An Anthology of Tudor Prose* 1481–1555 (Cambridge, 1956), pp. 305–25; T. E. Bridgett, ' The Bristol Pulpit in the days of Henry VIII,' *D.R.*, 3rd series, i (1879), pp. 73–95; Dom Hilary Steuert, ' The English Prose Style of Thomas Watson, Bishop of Lincoln, 1557,' *M.L.R.*, xli. 3 (1946), pp. 225–36; J. L. Lievsay, ' " Silver tongued Smith," Paragon of Elizabeth Preachers,' *H.L.Q.*, xl. 1 (1947), pp. 13–36.

First, an unfortunate gap in English literary history would be filled;[2] secondly, fresh light would be thrown on the tone and temper of the religious life of the country at a crucial period in church history and this would in turn help us to gauge more accurately the spiritual quality of the times.[3] I hope therefore that the following chapters will be of interest to the ecclesiastical historian as well as to the student of literature.

Reference to the pages of Bale and Pits shows of course that many of the sermons of the late fifteenth and early sixteenth centuries have unfortunately perished.[4] However, sufficient material remains from this part of the period selected for study on which to base valid conclusions. On the other hand, a higher proportion of texts has survived from the mid-sixteenth century, while for the Elizabethan period there is a positive *embarras de richesse*.

The lines of approach adopted (explained at greater length at the beginning of each chapter), are those which I found most rewarding and which grew naturally out of the subject itself. Thus I begin, as do nearly all preachers, with scriptural interpretation; I then examine the various forms of sermon construction (rhetorical *Dispositio*) used within the period, and follow this with a detailed study of style, (rhetorical *Elocutio*). As the sixteenth century witnessed the rise of humanistic culture in England, the questions suggested themselves; what use do the preachers make of classical allusion, what authors do they quote, and from which sources? I therefore next attempt an answer to these questions. I then deal with the sermon themes, and through them trace the development of the English religious sensibility from the morbid piety of the ' waning of the Middle Ages ', through the turbulence of Reformation and Counter-Reformation,

---

[2] It is particularly surprising that Krapp's remark that ' a complete study of early Reformation preaching is much to be desired', (*The Rise of English Literary Prose*, p. 187, n. 58) should not have stimulated a previous student to undertake this rewarding task.

[3] Most studies of sixteenth century church history are, I believe, vitiated by neglect of the detailed evidence provided by the sermons about the ' spiritual climate ' of the times. For example, even fairly recent studies, as P. Hughes, *The Reformation in England*, 3 vols. (London, 1950–4) or T. M. Parker, *The English Reformation to* 1558 (London, 1950) make little use of the sermon material, while P. Janelle (*L'Angleterre Catholique à la veille du Schisme*, Paris, 1935, pp. 19–22) confines his attention to such well known manuals as the *Festiall* and the *Quartuor Sermones* of John Mirk, the *Pupilla Oculi* and the *Exornatorium Curatorum*.

[4] For example, the *Conciones ordinariae* and the *Conciones extraordinariae* of Dean Colet, as well as the *Sermones elegantes* of Bishop Tunstall are no longer extant; (see John Bale, *Scriptorium Illustrium maioris Brytanniae quam nunc Angliam and Soctiam uocant: Catalogus*, Basel, 1557, pp. 649, 714) while the *Conciones ad utrumque statum* of the Augustinian hermit Thomas Pemchett as well as the *Conciones* of the Carthusian martyr John Houghton have not survived (see John Pits, *Relationum Historicarum de Rebus Anglicis tomus primus*, Paris, 1619, pp. 675, 724).

to the serene and wholesome spirit of devotion found in Hooker and Andrewes. Finally, as the hearing of sermons was an important aspect of life throughout the period studied, J end by suggesting the influence of the various sermon themes on poetry and drama.

Following what I believe to be the sound practice of G. R. Owst and G. G. Coulton, I give many quotations from little-known sources; as merely to give references detracts very much, in my view, from the interest and value of the discussion.

Much of the material used is previously unexamined, and although many of the forgotten preachers dealt with are in themselves of minor stature, nevertheless significant patterns do emerge from the study of them as groups. I have given detailed treatment to two major neglected preachers of Henry VIII's reign, John Longland, Bishop of Lincoln, and Roger Edgeworth, Canon of Bristol, whose work can, I think, give the modern reader not a little pleasure.[5] In the case of more familiar preachers, as Latimer (some passages of whose sermons have indeed attained a classical status) or Henry Smith, or Hooker, I have fitted the different aspects of their achievements into a new and complete framework—and I found in each instance that there were still several fresh things to say about them. Although in general I stop at 1603, I include Andrewes, because a fair number of his sermons were delivered in Elizabeth's reign, and there are, I believe, certain aspects of his achievement which have not hitherto received the attention which is their due.

[5] For a brief treatment of these two preachers see my article ' John Longland and Roger Edgeworth, Two Forgotten Preachers of the Early Sixteenth Century,' *R.E.S.* new series, v. 18 (1954) pp. 123–43.

CHAPTER I

SCRIPTURAL INTERPRETATION

WHILE it is too narrow a view to regard preaching merely as a branch of hermeneutics, nevertheless the Bible has nearly always given at least the starting point, if not the main subject to the sacred orator. Between the mid-fifteenth century and the close of the sixteenth century there are highly significant variations in the theory and practice of scriptural interpretation, and an examination of these as found in the English preachers, forms an illuminating chapter in the history of the religious thought of the times.

I

THE PRE-REFORMATION CATHOLIC PREACHERS, INCLUDING THE CONSERVATIVE HENRICIANS (1450–1547)

Tyndale's racily depreciatory description of the methods of interpretation used by the exponents of ' Old Learning ' has often been noticed:

> They divide scripture into four senses, the literal, tropological, allegorical, and anagogical. The literal sense is become nothing at all: for the pope hath taken it clean away, and hath made it his possession. He hath partly locked it up with the false and counterfeited keys of his traditions, ceremonies, and feigned lies; and driveth men from it with violence of sword: for no man dare abide by the literal sense of the text, but under a protestation, 'If it shall please the pope'. The tropological sense pertaineth to good manners (say they), and teacheth what we ought to do. The allegory is appropriate to faith; and the anagogical to hope, and things above.[1]

It is interesting to turn from this account to the evidence of the sermons, to see how far in them the charge that ' the literal sense . is become nothing at all ' is borne out, and to determine the quality of the spiritual interpretations offered. Before proceeding to the texts themselves however, it is necessary to notice that in the Middle Ages there was no uniformly received teaching about the

---

[1] *Doctrinal Treatises*, ed. H. Walter, (Cambridge, 1848) P.S. *The Obedience of a Christian Man*, ' The Four Senses of the Scripture,' p. 303.

precise content of the terms ' letter ' and ' spirit '. The classical exposition of St. Thomas Aquinas was by no means adhered to by all exegetes. This states that the ' letter ' is the whole meaning intended by the inspired writer, and subsumes both literal and figurative verbal expressions, while the ' spirit ' is founded upon the persons, things and events mentioned in the sacred history related by the writer, the significance of which was known at the time only to God.[2] There was too the older and more confused principle found in the Alexandrian and Latin Fathers, and exemplified clearly in Paschasius, which has behind it the theory of ' verbal dictation '. This indeed recognises the presence of the ' literal sense ' in metaphor and prophecy, but it founds the spiritual sense upon the basis of the verbal expression, even in the case of figurative expression.[3] This we shall see is the principle behind most spiritual interpretations in the sermons delivered in England during the period 1450–1547. The English preachers have less affinity with the Angelic Doctor than with the ' Biblical-moral ' School of Peter Comestor, Peter the Chanter, and Stephen Langton.[4] This school attached considerable importance to allegories based upon the natural properties of things mentioned in the text, whether the passage in which the thing occurred was in the language of ' statement ' or in that of ' symbol '. The exposition of these natural properties was facilitated by spiritual dictionaries, or *distinctiones*, in which any word which required elucidation could be looked up.[5] Interpretations of natural properties after this manner in the more learned preachers will be noticed later.[6]

Is then the account of Tyndale justified by the texts which remain to us? At the outset it may be stated that it is largely true of the conservative Catholic preachers who stand by the 'Old Learning', although the spiritual value of many of the expositions of the more learned among them is far from nugatory. However there is too within this period another group of preachers, who, while remaining Catholic in doctrine, nevertheless are influenced by the humanistic approach of Colet and Erasmus, and provide predominantly literal
. expositions.

When we approach the first of these groups, we find however,

---

[2] *Summa Theologica*, I, 2, 1, a. 10; (*Sancti Thomae Aquinatis Opera Omnia*, 25 vols., Parma, 1852–73, vol. I, pp. 6–7) *Quaestiones Quodlibetales*, VII, a. 14–16 (ibid. vol. IX, pp. 562–5). The novelty of this solution is brought out well by Beryl Smalley, *The Study of the Bible in the Middle Ages*, 2nd edn. (Oxford, 1952) p. 300.
[3] *The Study of the Bible in the Middle Ages*, pp. 41–2.
[4] See ibid. pp. 196–242.   [5] Ibid. pp. 246–9.   [6] See *post*, pp. 8–9, 15–16, 35.

that in some of the ruder *De Tempore* sermons of the late fifteenth century, there is no scriptural interpretation at all. An unlearned collection, perhaps from the Worcester diocese (MS. Hatton 96, ff. 10–91), consists merely of a crude catalogue of marvels drawn ultimately from that favourite source book, the *Legenda Aurea*. These almost sub-Christian hagiographical panegyrics are doubtless typical of much of the instruction given to rustic audiences, but their subject matter is more fittingly considered later in the chapter on Themes.[7] The interpretation which does occur in popular *De Tempore* sermons bears out to a considerable extent Tyndale's account. In two collections (MSS. Harleian 2247, [a late fifteenth century revision of Mirk's *Festial*][8] and Lambeth 392) Old Testament incidents are usually allegorized. Abraham and Isaac (Gen. xxii), says one homilist quoting Grosseteste, are types of God the Father and Christ.[9] The plagues sent to Egypt and the sprinkling of the blood of the Paschal lambs on the doorposts of the Israelites' houses (Exod. vii–xii) receive too a spiritual exposition. In the world with its manifold miseries (Egypt) dwell good men (Israel) who escape God's anger by mortifying the mind, will, and reason, and by anointing these faculties with the Passion of Christ (sprinkling the doorposts).[10] The poetic expression of prophecy receives similar treatment at the hands of another preacher; Isaiah's ' Every valley shall be exalted, and every mountain and hill shall be made low ' (Isa. xl. 4), probably following St. Gregory, is moralized into ' be þe valei is þe meke man vndirstonde þat schal ben maad hiȝ in euerlastynge ioie, & bi montayns ben vndirstondyn proud men & hiȝe men þat in þe ende schul be lowyd in euerlastynge dampnacion.'[11]

In these two collections, the Gospels of the Day are indeed usually paraphrased briefly, but the interpretations offered are again spiritual. Thus the historical narrative of the wedding feast at Cana (John ii. 1–11, the Gospel for Epiphany II) gives the preacher scope to declare that ' in þis gospel tweie þingis forsoþe whe schulde take

---

[7] See *post*, pp. 257–8.

[8] This collection was probably made about 1483; it contains many new sermons. See Lilian L. Steckman, 'A Late Fifteenth century revision of Mirk's Festial,' *S.P.* xxxiv (1936), pp. 36–48)

[9] MS. Harl. 2247, f. 91r. Cf. *Glossa Ordinaria*, P.L., cxiii. 218; *Glossa Interlinearis*, in *T.B. cum gloss. ord.*, etc., vol. I, f. 146v.

[11] MS. Lambeth 392, f. 151v. Cf. *Glossa Ordinaria*, P.L., cxiii. 1281; *Glossa Interlinearis*, in *T.B. cum gloss. ord.*, etc., vol. IV, f. 70r; *Nicolai de Lyra postilla*, (ibid.); Hugh of St. Chre, *T.B., cum post. Hug. Card.*, vol. IV, sig. n3v.

hed to; þe firste is what is betokenyd be þis weddynge, þe secunde is what betokenyþ þes sixe water pottis.'[12] The wedding signifies first the union between the Son of God and mankind in the Incarnation,[13] and the pots are the six things which made Him assume flesh, and which are manifested in the Incarnation; ' mildenes ', ' mercy & pite ', 'meknesse', 'porenes', 'pees & pesiblenes ', ('þat he schulde putte pees betwixe vs & God þe fadir, & also betwixe vs & aungels, betwene whom was discord for the firste synne of man ') and finally ' loue & charite '.[14] However the water pots can have another meaning, they can represent the six ' heuynesses ' which the Apostles experienced during the Passion: when ' Crist seide to hem þat oon of hem schulde bitraie him '; ' whan Iudas took him to þe Iewis & [he] was kissid of Iudas þat traitour '; then the ' smytyng of buffetis, þe heed & þe chekis of Ihesu Crist her loue '; ' þe scornyng of þe Iewis ' (' prophetize to vs who is he þat smytiþ þee '); ' þe spoiling of his cloþis & of þe departynge of hem', and finally 'his crucifyinge '.[15] In accordance with this interpretation the miracle of the changing of the water into wine has its spiritual meaning too; ' þes sixe water pottis, þat is of heuynes, ben turnyd into wyn of comfort & ioie in þe resurrection of oure Lord.'[16] Secondly however, the wedding is that ' betwene God & ich feiþful soule ' effected by the sacraments.[17] Three stages in earthly marriage—' suraunte of þe concent', 'solempnyte in þe chirche' and 'knowynge eiþer of oþer '—symbolise three parts in the soul's life; ' baptemys of innocents', 'verri penaunce doynge' and 'euerlastynge ioie'.[18] Now the water pots are made to represent six miseries in the state of sin, ' þe trespas don aȝens þe spouse Ihesu Crist', 'þe defoulynge & forsakyng of Ihesus', 'þe leesynge of þat tyme', 'þe quenchynge & vndoyng of þe gode dedis don before in charite', 'þe obligacion þat man þorouȝ synne byndith hym to hell peynys', and lastly 'the lesynge of the grace of God'. However by 'þe weddyngis of penaunce ' (confession and the new infusion of grace) these sorrows are changed into the ' gostli wyne of comfort'.[19] Again, the incident of the strewing of branches of palm before Christ at His entry into

---

[12] MS. Lambeth 392, f. 168r.
[13] Ibid., cf. Hugh of St. Cher, *T.B.*, *cum post. Hug. Card.*, vol. VI, sig. T6r.
[14] MS. Lambeth 392, ff. 168r-v.　　[15] Ibid. f. 169r.　　[16] Ibid.
[17] Ibid. cf. St. Bernard, *Sermones de Tempore*, Dominica prima post octavam Epiphaniae, serm. ii. (De spiritualibus nuptiis) *P.L.*, clxxxiii. 158–60; Hugh of St. Cher, *T.B.* *cum post. Hug. Card.*, vol. VI, sig. T6r; both authorities mention the marriage between God and soul, but not specifically by means of the sacraments.
[18] MS. Lambeth 392, ff. 169r-v.
[19] Ibid. f. 170r. Cf. Hugh of St. Cher, *T.B.*, *cum post. Hug. Card.*, vol. VI, sig. T6v, V1r-v, (a partial parallel).

Jerusalem on Palm Sunday (Matt. xxi. 8, from the Gospel for Advent I) provides this spiritual interpretation:

þe gospell sayeth not þat þei brought drye stikkes that bene roten, but bowes of treis þat were grene & fresh. Cause whi, vnto clere vnderstanding that is full notable. For it is to witt that a palme tre, with bowes be grene in euery tyme of þe yere; þat is [to] sey in vere, in hervest, sommer and wynter. Bi vere, þat is whan levis springe, it signifieth yonge age in which all creatures floryssh & floureth. Bi hervest is vnderstond age, when the levis fall of mannes welfare for age. Bi somer prosperite. By wynter adversitee. So then he is a plentevous palme þat his hert neuer dryeth bi dedely syn, but euer is grene. In youth by gode life & clennes. In age by perseverance in godenes. In prosperite by measure in temperaunce, in adversitee by perseverance & paciens. *Vnde in Psalmo: Iustus ut palma florebit* [Ps. xvi. 13 (Vg.)].[20]

Less happy is the exposition of the symbolic language of the Gospels, seen in this treatment of the Parable of the Labourers in the Vineyard (Matt. xx. 1–16; the Gospel for Septuagesima). The perverse elaboration of this unhappy piece of exegesis is best seen in an extended quotation which allows its characteristic properties fully to be savoured:

This gode husband & householder it is oure souereyn lorde allmyghti God þat enteryth in to þe vyne yerd of mannes soule by inward inspiracion of grace. But it is to wit þat a vyne yerd is called vj maner wise in scripture & vndirstande more þan bi mannes soule.

Ther is oon called þe vyne of synnes & of wicked men þat haue no grace nor power to amend þem. But þat vyne is not Goddes vyne: but rather þe develles vyne. And for to plant in þis vyne yerd, þe devylle gothe oute & bryngeth in werke men after his deuice and plesure & hireth þem with a sory ledyn peny; þat is, euerlasting dampnacion. He bringeth in prowde men, envious, irous, covetous, slouthfull men, glotonous men, vicious men, avouterers, fornicatouris, lecherous ly[u]ers, disclaunderers, bakbyters, extortioners, oppressioners of pore men, thevis, misodomites, & all cursed, wicked & fals felishippes, & all such myschevis men, of whom it is writ *Deutronomij xj, vua eorum vua fellis & botrus amarissimus.* [see Deut. xxxii. 32]. The grape & þe clustre þat commyth of þis cursed vyne, it is bitter as gall for it bryngith men to endeles dampnacion. . . .

Ther is an oþir vyne, þat is þe vyne of holy chirche & of tru

[20] MS. Harl. 2247, ff. 4ᵛ–5ʳ.

Cristen men, which is called Goddes vyne; whereof Dauid þe prophete said to oure lorde God þus: *vineam de Egipto transtulisti.* [Ps. lxxix. 9 (Vg.)]. A gode Lorde, quod *Dauid*, þou haste remevid & take[n] þe vyne from Egypt, þat is to say from þe develles power & made it þe vyne of holy chirch. God our souereyn lorde planted þis vyne of holy church with his holy handes, & plentevously hath watrid hit with [his] sacred blode in his precious & peynefull passion, & þe laberous workmen in þis vyne yerd be gode men & gode women þat se God by þeire verrey feyth & gode werkes, lyving after Goddes wyll & keping his preceptes.

There is þe þird vyne tree which is mannes soule in clennes of life redemyd & bought with Cristes precious blode, þat is also Goddes vyne; whereof þe gospell spekith þis day. And as a vyne muste be vndir sette & knytte to rayles & roddes þat it fall not to þe grounde, to be stroyed & trode vndir fote, right so must þis vine, mannes soule, be knytt vnto byndynges of Goddes commandments, & be vndir sett with iij principalles, þat is to say, feith, hope & charite, & þan closed aboute with þe perfite pale of þe xij articles of þe feith nayled with vij principall virtues, contrary to þe vij dedely synnes; & vndir pynned with þe dedis of mercy to kepe þe vyne of mannes soule close from þe venemous byting of ravenous bestes; þat is to say from þe sottell suggestions of þe worlde, þe flesh, and þe devell, þat euer be besy to destroy þe precious vyne of mannes soule, redemyd by Goddes blessid blode.

The 4.vyne is þat vertuous virgine, our lady seint Mary, which is Goddes owne vyne. . . Wele may þen þat merciful modir of God be called a vertuous vyne, þat brought forth Criste Ihesu, þe grape of excellent swetnes & mercy to synfull mannes socoure.

The v vyne is oure souereyn Criste Ihesu. *Iohannes, xiv. Ego sum vitis vos palmites* [John xv. 5]. . . The swete wyne of þis precious vyne Criste Ihesu, is Cristes blode, shed in his precious passion for mannes redempcion. . . This precious vine Criste Ihesu yeveth redily mercy and grauntith perdon & grace bothe to yonge & olde, riche, pore, as well þei þat cum first as þei þat cum last. . . .

The vj vyne, and þe last, is likened to a peny þat þe tru laborere shall have for his reward for by þis peny is vnderstond þe blisse of God in heven; for as a peny is rounde withoute ende, so is þe blisse of God in hevyn endeles þat euer shall endure. This precious vine, þe blisse of heven, bringeth forth clere wyne of euerlasting saluacion. . . This clere wyne of endurying ioye & gladnes is withoute dregges of doole, sorowe, or tribulacion.[21] The real point of the parable is missed, that those converted later in life receive the reward of heaven, just as do those who for long have led a godly life; while the vineyard, which doubtless signifies the Church, in which the faithful labour, is made to represent a number of other things which obscure the true significance of the story. The Parable of the Sower (Luke viii. 4–15, the Gospel for Sexagesima) even although it is expounded by Our Lord Himself, receives also allegoric interpretation from this homilist. The whole is declared to deal with alms-giving; as ' oure soueryn saviour Criste Ihesu is þe way, þat is to sey to hevyn', we are told that 'that sede þat fallith beside þe way is he þat yeveth not his almous bot for pompe & veyne glory of þe worlde, and than he lesith his merite.' Similarly the seed which falls on stony ground is he who gives alms to rich men, but that which falls on good earth is the man who gives his alms to poor needy men.[22]

However, it may be seen that the interpretation given in popular *De Tempore* sermons was not always predominantly allegorical for in a late fifteenth century collection preserved in Lincoln Cathedral Library (MSS. Linc. Cath. Libr. 50 and 51) simple literal expositions and unforced moral applications of the Gospel of the Day considerably outnumber far-fetched spiritual interpretations.[23]

On the other hand strained allegory in popular instruction survives well into Henry VIII's reign; an anonymous preacher who defends the use of images adds an allegorical exposition of the second commandment: ' Thou shalt not make to thyself any graven image, nor the likeness of anything that is in heaven above, or in the

[21] Ibid. ff. 34ᵛ–6ʳ. Cf. Hugh of St. Cher, *T.B.*, *cum post. Hug. Card.*, vol. VI, sig. k 5ʳ, (God enters man's soul by grace); St. Thomas Aquinas, *Catena Aurea*, [Origen, ' Tr.' 10 in Matt.,'—the penny signifies salvation; St. John Chrysostom, ' Super Matthaeum, Hom. 34, ex Op. Imperfecto,'—the wage signifies eternal life] *Opera Omnia*, vol. XI, pp. 229, 230.

[22] MS. Harl. 2247, f. 37ʳ. Cf. *Nicolai de Lyra postilla*, in *T.B.*, *cum gloss. ord.*, etc., vol. V, f. 146ʳ; Hugh of St. Cher, *T.B.*, *cum post. Hug. Card.*, vol. VI, sig. C5ʳ. (Both parallel only in mentioning alms giving.) The expositions in these English *De Tempore* collections are of similar type and quality to the earlier examples cited by Owst, *L. & P.M.E.*, pp. 58–66.

[23] For example, of the few spiritual interpretations which occur, one might instance: St. John the Baptist in prison (Matt. xi. 2) figures sinners in the bond of sin (sermon for Advent III, MS. Linc. Cath. Libr., 50, f. 15ᵛ); the feeding of the five thousand (John vi. 1–14) signifies the Blessed Sacrament (sermon for Lent IV, ibid. ff. 125ʳ–6ᵛ); the deaf and dumb man (Mark vii. 31–7) signifies the sinner who does not recognise his sin (sermon for Trinity XII, MS. Linc. Cath. Libr. 51, f. 6ʳ); the dropsical man (Luke xiv. 2–4) signifies covetous people (sermon for Trinity XVII, ibid. f. 42ᵛ); the man sick of the palsy (Matt. ix. 1–8) signifies the sinner (sermon for Trinity XIX. ibid. f. 53ʳ).

earth beneath, or in the water under the earth. Thou shalt not bow down to them nor worship them.' He relates the three parts of man, the head (the seat of intelligence), the breast (the seat of will or desire) the belly (the seat of carnal concupiscence) to the ' heaven above ', the ' earth beneath ', and the ' waters under the earth ' respectively. To make idols of anything in the various regions thus becomes in the first, intellectual pride, setting private wisdom against the teaching of the Church; in the second, loving worldly things better than God; and in the third, indulging in gluttony and lechery.[24] The worshipping of the golden calf (Exod. xxxii) is a figure of this last, for just as at the outset the Israelites sat down to eat and drink and then rose to play, so lechery follows gluttony and drunkenness; and as the ear-rings of their wives, sons and daughters were melted down to make the calf, so are whole estates and the portions of the other members of the family devoured by fleshly sin.[25] The laughter of Erasmus at far-fetched allegories and tortured exegesis, found in the *Praise of Folly*,[26] would certainly have been called forth also by some of these English examples!

If such interpretation predominates among the popular preachers of the Old Learning, what of the exposition of its more sophisticated adherents? As already briefly stated, in kind it is similar, but the quality is usually (although not invariably) intellectually and spirit-ually superior. Thus Dr. John Taylor, Master of the Rolls, preaching in 1508 on a text from the Gospel of the Day for Candlemas ('And when the days of her purification according to the law of Moses were accomplished, they brought him to Jerusalem, to present him to the Lord; as it is written in the law of the Lord, Every male that openeth the womb shall be called holy to the Lord; and to offer a sacrifice according to that which is said in the law of the Lord, A pair of turtledoves, or two young pigeons.' Luke ii. 22–4), does indeed mention that pigeons were the offering of the poor, and exhorts his audience to follow the Divine humility, but most of his sermon is a moralization of the properties of the birds, in the manner of the *distinctio*.[27] The pigeon or dove (*columba*, Vg.) signifies simplicity and meekness, while the turtle (*turtur*, Vg.) represents chastity.[28] We should offer these qualities to Our Lord, but alas! those whose lives are evil, neither ' offyr vppe turtyl nor yit pygyon, but radyr a

<hr>

[24] MS. Bodley 119, ff. 4ʳ–7ᵛ.   [25] Ibid. ff. 8ʳ–9ʳ.

[26] See ' Μωρίας 'Εγκώμιον Stultitiae Laus,' *Desiderii Erasmi Opera Omnia*, ed. J. LeClerc, 10 vols. (Leyden, 1703–6) vol. IV, 476A, B; 493A–6A.

[27] See *ante*, p. 2.

[28] MS. Harl. 131, f. 3ᵛ. Cf. *Glossa Interlinearis*, in *T.B. cum gloss. ord.*, etc., vol. V, f. 131ʳ.

caren crow.'[29] Further, the pigeon betokens ' them that opynly doth penance ' and the turtle ' them that secretly wepe & sorow for ther synys'.[30] Yet again, says Dr. Taylor, 'the dowve [or pigeon] techys vs the examplys of vij virtues by vij propyrtyes the which be in the dowve.' First, this bird 'lackyth a gal', so should we have no rancour; secondly, 'sche lyffyth not by caren nor wormys', so should we not live in sin; thirdly, ' sche fedyth apon corn & specially the best corns', so should we live by God's word; fourthly, 'sche hath a lamentable voyce as hyt war wepyng for hyr song'; so ' blessed are they that mourn '; fifthly, ' oftyntyme sche norysshys a nodyr dowve byrde', so we should be merciful; sixthly, 'sche delytyth to syt apon water syde ' and can see the shadow of her enemy coming, so over the ' watyrs of holy scripture every feythful sowle schuld syt & be wele war of the commyng of hys enemye that lyeth aweyt for hym; as the dowve as sone as sche aspyeth the shado of the hawk hyr enemye sche flyth away & skysyth for hyrself.' Finally, ' sche dothe byld in holys of stone or in the holys as you know of the dowvehouse', so ought the Christian to place his abode in the five wounds of Our Lord.[31]

John Alcock, Bishop of Ely, in an exhortation to the Carthusians of St. Anne's Coventry, declares (following the *Glossa Ordinaria*) that God's advice to Lot, *in monte salvum te fac* (Gen. xix. 17; ' save thyself in the mountain', Douay) may be interpreted as an admonition to flee to the security of the religious life, where salvation is sure: for

> experyence sheweth that a grete habundance of waters destroyed all thynge that groweth in the vale at many seasons. The contrary is in suche thynges that ben in the hygh mountayns. The herbes & floures there growyng ben of more vertue by the reasons that they ben more cocte & nourysshed by the sonne than the herbes or floures growynge in the vale. For as Iohan Crysostom sayth The higher the hylle be, the nerer is it to heuen. And so a place of more quyetnes prayer & perfeccion in token [of which] our sauyour Cryst Ihesu *In monte solus orabat*. [Matt. xiv. 23].[32]

Similarly, in another sermon, expounding the fact that Joseph went to Bethlehem to make his profession where he was born, Alcock declares:

> Bedlem frendes *interpretatur domus panis* & it sygnefyeth to euery man his parysshe chirche whiche is the place of his regeneracion where he shall be fed with the brede of Bedlem

---

[29] MS. Harl. 131, f. 4r.   [30] Ibid. f. 4v.   [31] Ibid. ff. 4v-7r.
[32] *Mons perfectionis, otherwyse in Englysshe, the hylle of perfeccyon* (Westminster, 1501 sig. Aiir; Cf. *Glossa Ordinaria, P.L.*, cxiii. 131.

Cryst Ihesus & with his sacraments whiche hath *omnem dulce-dinem* to saluacion of men.[33]

Again, in this sermon the bishop declares that five occasions on which Our Lord raised his voice, are five proclamations, which if men will not hear, they lose eternal life. These signify the five obligatory sacraments. First is the Parable of the Sower, *Iesus clamabat: Qui habet aures audiendi audiat*, (Luke viii. 8, ' Jesus cried out: He that hath ears to hear, let him hear', Douay) which represents the Blessed Sacrament, for the ' word ' transforms the bread; second is the reference to the waters of life, *Si quis sitat, veniat ad me et bibat*, (John vii. 37, 'If any man thirst, let him come to me, and drink', Douay) which represents the Precious Blood and water which flowed from Our Lord's side at the Passion, from which flow all the sacraments, and here Baptism is specially intended; third is the cry to the dead Lazarus, *Laʒare veni foras*, (John xi. 43, ' Lazarus, come forth', Douay) which betokens Penance; fourth is the prayer to forgive the Jews, *Dimitte illis*; *non enim sciunt quid faciunt*, (Luke xxiii. 34, ' Father, forgive them, for they know not what they do', Douay) which signifies Extreme Unction, and the last is the shout which will be heard at Doomsday, *Ecce sponsus venit exite obviam ei*, (Matt. xxv. 6, ' Behold, the bridegroom cometh, go ye forth to meet him', Douay) which represents Confirmation.[34] Not only does the sacred text lend itself to such torturing; it has, Alcock tells the Carthusians, a quasi-miraculous power of radiating holiness even to those who do not fully understand it: then let a less learned religious be consoled, for:

> though thou haue not the hole perfyte intellect therof, yet rede & here it. For ryghte as [a] man beynge in a place full of swete oynements & herbes odoryferous, feleth the swetnes of them though nother he se them nor vnderstonde theyr nature, Ryght so the vertue of the worde of god & his scrypture gyueth an Influence of grace to hym that hereth & redeth it though he vnderstondeth it not & be in synne or wretchednesse.[35]

[33] *Sermo . . . Qui habet aures audiendi: audiat, Luc. viii.* (Westminster, n.d.) sig. Bvᵛ. For the interpretation of ' Bethlehem', see St. Jerome, Epist. CVIII, *P.L.*, xxii. 885, ' Comment. in Michaeam,' lib. II. cap. v, *P.L.*, xxv. 1197; St. Gregory the Great, ' XL Hom. in Evangelia,' lib. I, Hom. viii, *P.L.*, lxxvi. 1104; St. Isidore of Seville, ' Etymologiae,' lib. XV, cap. i, *P.L.*, lxxxii. 530; *Glossa Ordinaria, P.L.*, cxiv. 73; Hugh of St. Cher, *T.B.*, *cum post. Hug. Card.*, vol. VI, sig. a6ᵛ.

[34] *Sermo . . . Qui habet aures audiendi: audiat*, sig. Aiiʳ et seq. Cf. Hugh of St. Cher, *T.B. cum post. Hug. Card.*, vol. VI, sig. FF3ᵛ. (*Laʒare veni foras* signifies Confession.)

[35] *Mons perfectionis*, sig. Aviʳ. Cf. the earlier opinion that the layman will get good from hearing the Latin Gospel at Mass, *even if he does not understand it*, just as an adder is affected by the charm pronounced over her, though she does not understand the words. (G. G. Coulton, *The Roman Catholic Church and the Bible*, Medieval Studies, no. 14(a) 2nd edn. London 1921, pp. 24–5.)

Richard Fitzjames, Bishop of London, also favours spiritual interpretation. He speaks of the three Jesuses of the Old Testament, *Jesus filius Nave* (Josuah), *Jesus filius Josedech* (Josuah the son of Josedech, the high priest, Haggai i. 12–15; Zech. iii. 1 ff., vi. 10 ff.), and *Jesus filius Sirach* (to whom the authorship of the book of Ecclesiasticus is attributed), saviours by power, obedience and wisdom respectively, and declares them to be figures of Our Lord, *Jesus filius Dei*, who is perfect Power, Obedience and Wisdom.[36] Again, Cain after the murder of his brother Abel, a sin which violated the law of nature, fled to ' Nayde ' [Nod] (Gen. iv. 16) which, says Fitzjames, following traditional interpretation, signifies instability.[37]

St. John Fisher, Bishop of Rochester, who in his sermons belongs to the Old Learning, like his medieval predecessors shows no historical sense; he speaks of David's manslaughter of the ' good knyght Urye '[38] [Uriah] and of Martha as ' a woman of noble blode to whom by inheritance belonged the castel of bethany'.[39] His exegesis too is highly allegorical. The four rivers of Paradise (Gen. ii. 10–14) signify the cardinal virtues ' ryghtwysnes, temperaunce, prudence, and strengthe, wherewith the hole soule myght be wasshed and made pleasaunt lyke as with so many flodes.' Alas, however, from the Devil's paradise of ' bodyly and sensuall pleasure ' issue four rivers ' ferre contrary vnto the other, that is to saye the flode of couetyse contrary to Iustyce, the flode of glotony agaynst temperaunce, the flode of pryde agaynst prudence, and the flode of lechery agaynst strength', and, ' who so euer be drowned in any of these flodes it is harde for them to be tourned to god by true contrycyon, the ragynge of them is so great and ouer flowynge'.[40] Again, says the bishop, 'the mounte or hyll named Syon, sygnefyeth the chyrche of crysten people, lyke as the mounte Synay betokeneth the synagogue of Ieues ',[41] while the goal of the Christian life is ' the heuenly cyte Iherusalem prepared in the moost hygh mountaynes,

[36] *Sermo die lune in ebdomada Pasche,* (Westminster, 1405) facsimile by Francis Jenkinson (Cambridge, 1907) sig. Aiiv–Bviv. Cf. W. O. Ross, *Middle English Sermons, edited from British Museum MS. Royal* 18B. *xxiii* (London, 1940) E.E.T.S. o.s. 209, pp. 3–4.
    [37] *Sermo die lune in ebdomada Pasche,* sig. Cvir. Cf. *Glossa Ordinaria, P.L.,* cxiii. 100.
    [38] *The English Works of John Fisher,* Part I, ed. John E. B. Mayor, 2nd edn., (London, 1935) E.E.T.S., e.s. xxvii, p. 6.
    [39] Ibid. p. 290. Cf. Owst, L. *& P.M.E.,* 114–16, for earlier examples of unhistorical treatment of Biblical characters.
    [40] *English Works,* Pt. I, pp. 34–5. Cf. *Glossa Ordinaria, P.L.,* cxiii. 87; *Glossa Interlinearis,* in *T.B., cum gloss. ord.,* etc., vol. I, f, 37r; Hugh of St. Cher, *T.B., cum post. Hug. Card.,* vol. I, sig. b2v.
    [41] *English Works,* Pt. I, p. 167. Cf. *Glossa Ordinaria* on Matt. xxi. 5, *P.L.,* cxiv. 152; Hugh of St. Cher on Ps. ii. 6, *T.B., cum post Hug. Card.,* vol. II, sig. a5v. (Sion signifies the Church).

which place without doubte is promysed to all good and ryghtwyse people for a rewarde of theyr good lyuynge in this transytory worlde, lyke as therthly Iherusalem a place of rest & peas was promysed to them that suffred pacyently the grete labours & stormes in goynge ouer the reed see, and also toke grete payne in deserte.'[42] The story of Jonah provides a notable tropological exposition; for, says Fisher, the ' vij degrees of the fall of Ionas from god by brekynge his commandement, sygnefy vnto vs the dyuers fallynges downe of the synner, whereby he gooth lower & lower from one degre to an other in to dyuers perylles of depnesses.'[43] In answer to a possible objector to this interpretation the bishop declares:

> It forceth not for our purpose at this season though Ionas in holy scrypture sygnefy Cryst. For one & the same thynge by a dyuers consyderacyon may be taken figuratyuely for two contraryes. Somtyme in holy scrypture the lyon sygnefyeth Cryst, and sometyme by the lyon is sygnefyed the deuyll, as in the epystle of saynt Peter. *Tanquam leo rugiens circuit.* [1 Pet. v. 8]. It sygnefyeth Cryst as in the appocalypse. *Vicit leo de tribu Iuda.* [Rev. v. 5].[44]

Fortified by this, Fisher finds that Jonah fleeing from his mission to Nineveh (Jonah i. 3) figures ' concent of the mynde ' to sin;[45] his hiring a ship at Joppa ' the study & besy serchynge for tyme & oportunyte ' to fulfil the sinful desire,[46] his actual hiring of the ship going to Tarsus, the sinner's ' fulfyllynge of his purpose that he hath ben about so longe to accomplysshe'.[47] Further, the sleep of Jonah in the ship signifies the sinking into the habit of sin (Jonah i. 5); his being cast into the sea (Jonah i. 15), the stage when he ' reioyseth & maketh boste of the synne that he commytted, where of very ryght he sholde be ashamed, and fere the paynes of the lawe ordeyned for open synners.'[48] The swallowing of Jonah by the whale (Jonah i. 17) figures that dire degree when ' the synner wyl defend his errour & impugne ayenst vertue, they haue so longe made theyr vaunte of theyr so doynge, that it semeth to them as no synne, by all means that may be founde, procure & be aboute to cause al other to thynke the same.'[49] Finally, if Jonah had not been ' socoured by the grete mercy of our lorde ':

> I beseche you who coude haue saued hym from turnynge a parte in to the whalles nature by dygestyon, & the resydue to haue ben voyded out through his guttes lyke dunge in to the

[42] *English Works*, Pt. I, p. 167.   [43] Ibid. p. 201.   [44] Ibid.
[45] Ibid. pp. 201–2.   [46] Ibid. pp. 202–3.   [47] Ibid. pp. 203–4.
[48] Ibid. pp. 205–6.   [49] Ibid. p. 206.

depe see, wherby we may wel perceyue that a synner fallynge downe from one degre of synne in to an other without he shortly returne to the state of grace amendynge his lyfe, call to almyghty god his maker for helpe & haue a full trust in that mercyfull lorde shall at the laste by despayre be incorporate to the substaunce of the deuyll, so shall be conueyed thrugh his bely & fall downe in to the depe pyt of hell.[50]

However as Jonah cried out to God and was delivered (Jonah ii.), so the penitent sinner will be restored to grace.[51]

Similarly the story of Adam (Gen. ii. 8–iv.) represents that of every sinner. Adam signifies the soul, and Eve the body; while the fruit of the tree of life, which ought to be eaten, that of the tree of knowledge which it is forbidden to eat, and that of the other ordinary trees in Eden, which it is indifferent to eat, represent three kinds of pleasure to be had in the world: that which, when we fast and pray, comes from Our Lord, who has the words of life; that deadly pleasure which comes from sin; and that neutral pleasure which comes from necessary eating, drinking, and sleeping. Eve, the body, tempts Adam, the rational soul, who can either consent or refuse. Alas! Adam, as all too many sinners, never touched the tree of life! As Adam was excluded from the earthly paradise for disobedience, so those in sin are excluded from heaven, and no man is admitted there before justification. Thus the Cherubim and the flaming sword outside Eden have an allegorical meaning too; the sword is two-edged, and signifies mortal sin, which slays body and soul; the burning flame betokens the fire of purgatory, which scours venial sin, while the Cherubim are strict examiners who admit to Paradise only those who have due provision of good works.[52]

Fisher subjects New Testament history to similar treatment; the episode of Christ sleeping in the ship while the tempest raged, and calming it at the earnest petition of the disciples (Matt. viii. 23–7; the Gospel for Epiphany IV in the Sarum Missal), signifies how troubled is the conscience of the sinner abandoned by God, and what great peace and joy comes from forgiveness.[53] Again, the miracle at Cana yields the significance that in marriage ' moche of the

---

[50] Ibid. p. 208.   [51] Ibid.

[52] *Here after ensueth two fruytfull sermons, made and compyled by the ryght Reuerende father in god, Iohan Fyssher—Doctour of Dyuynyte and Bysshop of Rochester*, (London, 1532) sig. Ei^r–Hii^r. [These interesting sermons, both on Matt. v. 20, are not, unfortunately, included in the E.E.T.S. edition of Fisher.] Cf. *Glossa Interlinearis*, in *T.B.*, *cum gloss. ord.*, etc,. vol. I, f. 41^v; (the body tempts the soul); Hugh of St. Cher, *T.B.*, *cum post. Hug. Card.*, vol. I, sig. b4^v; (the Cherubim's sword as temporal punishment).

[53] *English Works*, Pt. I, p. 12. Cf. Hugh of St. Cher, *T.B.*, *cum post. Hug. Card.*, vol. VI, sig. f2^r.

waterynes of carnalitie between the maried persons, by vertue of the sacrament is changed into the wine of merite.'[54]

The poetic expressions of the Penitential Psalms allow the bishop to give many spiritual interpretations of the traditional kind. In the verse *Domine, ne in furore tuo arguas me: neque in ira tua corripias me* (Ps. vi. 1, ' O Lord, rebuke me not in thy indignation, nor chasten me in thy wrath', Douay), *furor* signifies hell, and *ira* purgatory:[55] the *lectus* of *lavabo per singulas noctes lectum meum* (Ps. vi. 7 Vg., ' every night I will wash my bed', Douay) is the voluptuousness of the body and the reminiscence of sin;[56] while the *inimici* of *Erubescant et conturbentur vehementer omnes inimici mei* (Ps. vi. 11 Vg., ' Let all my enemies be ashamed, and be very much troubled', Douay) are the devils.[57] In *Nolite fieri sicut equus et mulus quibus non est intellectus* (Ps. xxxi. 9 Vg., ' Do not become like the horse, and the mule, who have no understanding', Douay) the horse signifies wilful sinners and the mule those who through bad upbringing have long continued in sin;[58] *Quia cinerem tanquam panem manducabam* (Ps. ci. 10 Vg., ' For I did eat ashes like bread', Douay) is interpreted, 'I ofte called to remembraunce my synnes with contrycyon & penaunce',[59] while the hyssop in *Adsperges me hysopo, et mundabor* (Ps. l. 9 Vg., ' Thou shalt sprinkle me with hyssop, and I shall be cleansed', Douay), used in Jewish ceremonial purification, is ' an herbe of the grounde that of his nature is hote, and hath a swete smell, sygnefyenge Cryst whiche meked himselfe to suffre deth on the crosse', so that 'we myght saye. Lorde our faith is so clere and vndoubtefull by the meryte of the passyon of thy sone our lorde Ihesu cryst whiche by the effusyon of his holy blode hath gyuen so grete effycacy and strength to the holy sacramentes of his chirche, that when we receyue ony of them we shall be sprencled and made clene by the vertue of his precyous blode lyke as with ysope'.[60] The three parts of the Sacrament of Penance, contrition, confession and satisfaction, are found in the parallelism of the Hebrew poetic idiom in the first two verses of Psalm xxxi. (Vg.): ' *Beati quorum remisse sunt iniquitates*

---

[54] *English Works*, Pt. I, p. 472.
[55] Ibid. p. 9. Cf. Hugh of St. Cher, *T.B.*, *cum post. Hug. Card.*, vol. II, sig. b6ʳ.
[56] *English Works*, Pt. I, pp. 17–18. Cf. *Glossa Ordinaria*, *P.L.*, cxiii. 352; Hugh of St. Cher, *T.B.*, *cum post. Hug. Card.*, vol. II, sig. b6ᵛ.
[57] *English Works*, Pt. I, p. 22. Cf. *Nicolai de Lyra postilla*, in *T.B.*, *cum gloss. ord.*, etc., vol. III, f. 94ᵛ.
[58] *English Works*, Pt. I, pp. 38–8.
[59] Ibid. p. 157. Cf. *Glossa Ordinaria*, *P.L.*, cxiii. 1012; Hugh of St. Cher, *T.B.*, *cum post. Hug. Card.*, vol. II, sig. P2ᵛ.
[60] *English Works*, Pt. I, pp. 110–11. Cf. *Glossa Ordinaria*, *P.L.*, cxiii. 919; *Glossa Interlinearis*, in *T.B.*, *cum gloss. ord.*, etc., vol. III, ff. 157ᵛ–9ʳ.

['Blessed are they whose iniquities are forgiven', Douay] . . .
Beholde fyrst the remyssyon of synne by contricyon. *Et quorum
tecta sunt peccata.* ['and whose sins are covered'] Blyssed be they
whose synnes be hydde and put out of knowledge, whiche is done
by confessyon. *Beatus vir cui non imputavit dominus peccatum* ['Blessed
is the man to whom the Lord hath not imputed sin'] . . . Beholde
the thyrde tyme the hole & perfyte doynge away of synne by satys-
faccion.'[61] The three-fold joy of Penance is found in the eleventh
verse of the same psalm:

> *Letamini in domino et exultate iusti: et gloriamini omnes recti
> corde.* ['Be glad in the Lord, and rejoice, ye just, and glory, all
> ye right of heart', Douay]. He reherseth thre maner of Ioyes.
> Fyrst they be Ioyfull whose synnes be done away by contricyon,
> whiche may be called the inwarde Ioye for the graunte of theyr
> petycyon. Secondly they be more glad whan theyr synnes be
> couered & put out of knowledge by confessyon, & this may be
> called the Ioye shewed outwardly by Ioyfull mouynge of the
> body. And thyrdly they be moost gladde whan thyer synnes be
> so clene done away by satysfaccion, that no token may be seen
> or knowen of them, & this may be called the Ioye euer to be
> exercysed in the laude & prayse of god for his mercyful good-
> nes.[62]

In the manner of the *distinctio*, yet another representation of the
parts of Penance is found in the natural properties of the pelican,
night crow and sparrow, in the similes in *Similis factus sum pellicano
solitudinis, factus sum sicut nycticorax in domicilio, vigilavi et factus sum
sicut passer solitarius in tecto* (Ps. ci. 7–8 Vg., 'I am become like to a
pelican of the wilderness; I am like a night raven in the house. I
have watched, and am become as a sparrow all alone on the housetop', Douay):

> The pellycane as saynt Iherome wryteth in an epystle vnto a
> certayne decon called Presidius is of this condicyon, whan she
> fyndeth her byrdes slayne & destroyed by a serpent, she mourn-
> eth, she wayleth and smyteth herselfe vpon the sydes, that by
> the effusyon and shedynge of her blode, her deed byrdes may be
> reuyued. Truly they that are very contryte be of lyke condy-
> cyon. For whan they serche theyr conscyence & fynde theyr
> chyldren, that is to saye theyr good werkes slayne & destroyed
> by the serpent deedly synne, than they mourne & wayle sore,
> they smyte themselfe vpon the breste with the byll of bytter

[61] *English Works*, Pt. I, pp. 24–5. Cf. Hugh of St. Cher, *T.B.*, *cum post. Hug. Card.*,
vol. II, sig. 16ᵛ–m1ʳ.
[62] *English Works*, Pt. I, 43.

sorowe, to thentent the corrupte blode of synne may flowe out.
. . .

    The nyght crowe or the oule as sayth saynt Iherome is of
this condycyon, that as longe as it is daye she abydeth preuely in
the walles or secrete corners of some hous & wyll not be seen.
But whan the sonne is downe & is derke as in the nyght, anone
she sheweth herselfe & cometh out from that secrete place with
a mournynge crye & myserable, & sorrowful lamentacyon, she
neuer seaseth so cryenge vnto that it be day agayne. [So those
who lose the security and sunshine of baptismal grace mourn in
Penance until new grace is infused into their souls.]
   . . . Whan the sparowe suspecteth . . . snares or trappes be
layde for her on the grounde, anone she fleeth vp to the couer-
ynge of the hous or to the hous eues, and yf at ony tyme she be
constrayned by the reason of hunger to come downe agayne,
yet for fere she wyll shortely returne vp, so that thyder she wyl
flee for socour & surete in her daunger and peryll, there she
wypeth and seteth her byl, there she proyneth & seteth her
feders in ordre, there also she bryngeth forth byrdes, & there
restynge maketh mery as she can after her maner. [So we must
fly from the snares of worldly pleasure to the contemplation of
heavenly things, and there bring forth our birds (good works),
for we may 'rest in heaven' in this life by hope and trust,
always praising God. If we do these things, then indeed we
shall make satisfaction for our sins.][63]
    Similarly an image from the Song of Solomon, *Quae est ista quae
progreditur quasi aurora consurgens*? (Can. vi. 9 Vg., 'Who is she that
cometh forth as the morning rising?' Douay) signifies the Blessed
Virgin, the dawn before the full sun of the righteousness of
Christ.[64]
    Like the popular preachers, Fisher gives allegoric interpretations
of the parables. As the prodigal son (Luke xv. 11–end) each sinner,
by following worldly vanities, goes into a far country; he destroys
his substance by misusing God's gifts; he is crucified with hunger
by setting his appetite to use transitory pleasures. The citizens of the
far country are devils; the sinner keeps hogs when he would satisfy
himself in unclean concupiscence, and he eats husks, when, despising
the holy food of celestial doctrine, he desires the unclean pleasures of
the body. When, however, the penitent sinner recalls God's good-

---

[63] Ibid. pp. 151–4. For the pelican see St. Jerome, *Operum Mantissa*, Epist. XVIII,
P.L., xxx. 192–3; for the night crow see St. Jerome, Epist. CVI, P.L., xxii. 858–9; for
the sparrow see ibid., also *Glossa Ordinaria*, P.L., cxiii. 1012.
  [64] *English Works*, Pt. I, pp. 44–9. Cf. Hugh of St. Cher, *T.B.*, *cum post. Hug. Card.*,
vol. III, sig. v1^r.

ness, his Heavenly Father's grace prevents him, and the returned son is made partaker of the slain calf of our Saviour.[65] In the Parable of the Sower, the ground which brings forth fruit a hundred-fold is virginity, in which spiritual fruit is most abundant; that which brings forth sixty-fold is widowhood, where some weeds of carnality spring up too; while that which brings forth only thirty-fold is marriage, in which the weeds flourish more than the corn (see Matt. xiii. 8).[66]

Disregarding St. Thomas's admonition that doctrine can be founded only on the literal sense,[67] and following older practice here, Fisher attempts to refute Luther by spiritual interpretations. In his first sermon against the German reformer, preached at Paul's Cross during the octave of the Ascension 1521, at the burning of Lutheran books, the bishop attempts to prove the primacy of the Pope by the ' shadowe ' of Moses and Aaron leading the Israelites through the desert to the promised land. Moses is a figure of Christ, and Aaron of St. Peter the first Pope, while the journey represents that of Christians through the desert of this world to heaven. Just as Moses went up into the mountain to speak with God, while Aaron remained behind to instruct the people (Exod. xxiv. 14), so Christ ascended into heaven, and left Peter behind to teach the faith.[68] These interpretations aroused the stern indignation of Tyndale, who, while not denying typical significance to Moses and Aaron, declares that they figure Christ and every faithful preacher— although, he adds, in St. Paul, the High Priest is a figure of Christ. Aaron however, when he allowed the golden calf to be made (after Moses had ascended the mountain [Exod. xxxii. 1–6]) represents all false preachers and idolaters, as the Pope himself—so ironically Rochester's interpretation *is* right after all.[69]

Fisher's method is, notwithstanding, similar in his second sermon against Luther, preached at Paul's Cross on Quinquagesima Sunday

[65] *English Works*, Pt. I, pp. 235–6. Cf. *Glossa Ordinaria*, P.L., cxiv. 312 (one of the citizens signifies the prince of this world, the prodigal in the far country subjection to the desire of worldly things, feeding hogs unclean joys); *Nicolai de Lyra postilla*, in T.B., *cum gloss. ord.*, etc., vol. V, f. 155ʳ (feeding hogs signifies evil living); Hugh of St. Cher, T.B., *cum post. Hug. Card.*, vol VI, sig. R4ᵛ (the citizen signifies the devil; keeping hogs, luxury).

[66] *English Works*, Pt. I, pp. 468–72. Cf. St. Jerome, 'Adversus Jovinianum ', lib. I. 3, P.L., xxiii. 213, Epist. XXII, P.L., xxii. 403, Epist. CVII, ibid. 877; *Nicolai de Lyra postilla*, in T.B., *cum gloss. ord.*, etc., vol. V, f. 44ʳ; Hugh of St. Cher, T.B., *cum post. Hug. Card.*, vol. VI, sig. h3ᵛ.

[67] See *Summa Theologica*, I Q.i. a. 10 ad 1um (*Opera Omnia*, vol. I, p. 7); also *Quodlib.* VII. a.14 ad 4um (Ibid. vol. IX, p. 563).

[68] *English Works*, Pt, I. pp. 315–17.

[69] *Doctrinal Treatises*, ' The Obedience of a Christian Man,' pp. 208–9.

C

1526, when Robert Barnes and some Steelyard Lutherans, having abjured their heretical opinions, bore their faggots. The blind man in the Gospel for the Day (Luke xviii. 31–43) is the heretic, who cannot see spiritually. He is separated from the multitude, as the heretic by his singularity of opinion is cut off from the society of true believers. Those who walk in the right way before Our Lord are the Fathers of the Old Testament, and those who follow after, the members of the Christian Church. The manner in which the blind man was restored to sight signifies the way a heretic may be restored to the faith; he must hear from the multitude where Jesus is, that is, hear the truth in the Church; he must cry for mercy, that is, be reduced to the ways of the Church; and finally he must desire his sight with his whole will; that is, assent to the doctrine of the Church.[70] Similarly, the Parable of the Sower (Luke viii. 4–15) is made to support the Catholic position; the sower is Christ, and the seed the word; faithful preachers are ' but as the cophyns and the hoppers wherein the seed is couched '. The seed of the word is one; first, because it is ' sortable and agreable and lyke vnto itself in euery parte. As whan we se an heape of wheate, that is clene and pure wheate, without any diuers medlyng of cockel or of any other noughty and euyll sede, though there be many diuerse cornes, yet for as moche as they be all of one kynde, we say it is all one sede.' In the word there is no mixture of error or wicked doctrine. On the contrary Luther's doctrine is ' a medley made of many diuerse colours: & of dyueres patches & hathe a partye coote '; it is a mixture of Scripture with falsehoods.[71] Secondly the word is consistent, ' ther is in it no discord, no repugnancy, no contradiction, of one part of it with another ':

> It is lyke of it & of a songe, where be many syngers, that diuersely descant vpon the playne songe: but for as moche as they all agree without ony gerryng, withouten any mystunynge, they make al but one songe, and one armony. In lyke maner it is of the scriptures of god, and of the doctryne of the churche. There be many syngers, & some synge the playne songe, and some synge the descant, saynt Mattheu, saint Marke, saynt Luke, saynt Iohane, saynt Peter, saynt Paule, saint Iames, saint Iude syng the playne songe. Than be there a great nombre of the doctours which descant vpon this playne songe: but for bicause ther is no discorde, no repugnancy, no contradiction amonge them, at the leest in any poynt concernyng the substance

---

[70] *English Works*, Pt. I, pp. 436–42.
[71] Ibid. pp. 447–54. Cf. *Glossa Ordinaria*, *P.L.*, cxiv. 272 (the sower is Christ).

of our faithe: all their voyces make but one songe, & one armony.[72]
In contrast to this Luther disagrees with the Fathers and with himself, and the heretics wrangle amongst themselves.[73] Thirdly, Scripture itself is a unity:

> Though there be many bokes of scripture, both in the olde testament and in the newe also, yet all these bokes be so fully agreed by the expositions and interpretations of the holy doctours, that they make but one boke, and one body of scripture: and haue in them all but one spirite of lyfe: that is to saye, the spirite of Christe Iesu.[74]

Finally, the 'conditions' of the good men in the parable (Hi sunt, qui in corde honesto et bono, Luke viii. 15, 'they who in good and perfect heart, [hearing the word, keep it.]' Douay) are interpreted as referring to Catholics. In corde, is of one heart and mind in the faith; honesto, is fair with the beauty which comes to the heart enlightened by faith, and bono indicates 'the towardnes of a good wyll to bringe forthe the fruyte of goode workes'.[75]

It is interesting to notice here that a later representative of the Old Learning, William Peryn, preaching in St. Anthony's Hospital, London, at the close of Henry VIII's reign, on Transubstantiation in the Blessed Sacrament, is much more cautious than Fisher in the introduction of spiritual interpretations in theological argument. The declaration that the words Hoc est corpus meum are intended literally and the urging of the glosses of the Fathers which support Catholic doctrine on key New Testament texts occupy a more important place in his reasoning than does the mention of Old Testament 'types'—the bread and wine brought forth by Melchizedek (Gen. xiv. 18 and see Heb. vii.), the Paschal Lamb (Exod. xvi. and see John vi. 49–50, 58); or the reference to prophetic expression, as 'in every place incense shall be offered unto my name and a pure offering' (Malachi i. 11).[76] Protestant polemic had by then rendered it impossible to rely so confidently on the acceptance of positions supported by allegories.

Another habit of Fisher, which Tyndale finds peculiarly vicious, is his method of alleging fragments of texts in argument, while

---

[72] English Works. Pt, I, p. 455. Tyndale uses this illustration of ' descant ', however, in a derogatory manner; ' twenty doctors expound one text twenty ways, as children make descant upon plain song.' (Doctrinal Treatises, ' The Obedience of a Christian Man,' p. 307.)
[73] English Works, Pt. I, p. 455.   [74] Ibid. pp. 456–7.   [75] Ibid. pp. 462–4.
[76] Thre godlye and notable sermons of the moost honorable and blessed Sacrament of the Aulter (London, 1545) ff. 27ʳ et seq.

ignoring the context to suit his purpose. Probably this practice comes less from the dishonesty of which the reformer accuses the bishop, than from the ' verbal dictation ' theory which could be taken to mean that even in incomplete snatches the sacred text yields instructive meaning.[77] Thus Fisher quotes ' In the latter days some shall depart from the faith, giving heed unto spirits of error and devilish doctrine ' (1 Tim. iv. 1) and applies it to the Lutheran movement:[78] but as Tyndale points out:

> . . . it followeth in the text: ' Giving attendance, or heed unto the devilish doctrine of them which speak false through hypocrisy, and their consciences marked with a hot iron, forbidding to marry, and commanding to abstain from meats, which God hath created to be received with giving thanks.' Which two things who ever did, save the pope, Rochester's god?[79]

Tyndale quarrels with another half text used by Fisher, *fides que per dilectionem operatur* (Gal. v. 6 ' faith that worketh by charity ', Douay) which the bishop renders ' faythe whiche is wrought by loue' and by which he seeks to prove that faith springs from charity.[80] But this, protests the reformer, ' maketh a verb passive of a verb deponent. Rochester will have love to go before, and faith to spring out of love. Thus antichrist turneth the roots of the tree upwards.'[81] Tyndale disagrees too with Fisher's interpretation of the literal sense of St. Paul, *State et tenete traditiones quas didicistis sive per sermonem sive per epistolam nostram* (2 Thes. ii. 14, ' stand fast; and hold the traditions which you have learned, whether by word, or by our epistle ', Douay) which the bishop understands to refer to the Catholic ' traditions ', corresponding to the Jewish ' cabala ';[82] but, says the reformer, Paul's ' traditions were the gospel of Christ, and honest manners and living, and such good order as becometh the doctrine of Christ '.[83]

John Longland, Bishop of Lincoln, and Confessor to Henry VIII, another upholder of the Old Learning, has scarcely less predilection for spiritual interpretation than has Fisher. He is indeed

---

[77] Cf. the notion of St. Bonaventure, that even in a single letter, Scripture begets a multiform wisdom, referred to by F. W. Farrar, *History of Interpretation* (London, 1886) p. 295; and the same doctor's acceptance of the supernatural infallibility of every word of Scripture (Ibid. p. 272).

[78] *English Works*, Pt. I, p. 337.

[79] *Doctrinal Treatises*, ' The Obedience of a Christian Man,' p. 214.

[80] *English Works*, Pt. I, p. 331.

[81] *Doctrinal Treatises*, ' The Obedience of a Christian Man,' pp. 221–2.

[82] *English Works*, Pt. I, pp. 333–6.

[83] *Doctrinal Treatises*, ' The Obedience of a Christian Man,' p. 219.

loud in his praise of the sacred volume, and urges its diligent study in this passage from one of his *Sermones* on the Penitential Psalms, [which in common with all his preaching except three Good Friday sermons, is extant only in a Latin translation by Thomas Key—and which (as in the case of all such subsequent quotations from Longland) I now re-translate]:

. . . let us search the Scriptures, where the little infant has milk prepared, where the boy may learn what he should praise and admire, the youth what he should correct, the young man what he should follow after, the aged what he should pray for and seek from God, all what they should believe. In that inexhaustible treasury men may find piety, women may learn modesty, widows devotion, the wealthy liberality, the poor a consolation for their poverty.

. . . To this alone I think our whole study and industry should be applied; for nowhere else than in this volume is there to be had fully and abundantly that which contrives, premeditates, and suffices for the salvation of our souls, and without the safeguards of which it cannot but be that the people must miserably perish.[84]

However, as we learn from one of his Lenten sermons for 1517, his attitude is that of the medieval learned clerk, who despises the literal sense:

A nut has a rind, a shell and a centre or kernel. The rind is bitter, the shell is hard, but the centre is sweet and full of nourishment. So in Scripture the exterior part, that is the literal sense and the surface meaning, is very bitter and hard, and seems to contradict itself. But if you crack it open, and more deeply regard the intention of the spirit, together with the expositions of the holy doctors, you will find the kernel and a certain sweetness of true nourishment.[85]

---

[84] *Expositio Concionalis Quinti Psalmi Poenitentiales prefati Ioannis Longlondi, coram maiestate regia Annis do.* 1523, 1524, 1525, 1526, 1527, 1528, 1529, (London, 1532?) f. 661ᵛ. Cf. too ibid. ff. 657ᵛ–8ʳ. [The *Expositio Concionalis* is part of Longland's series of expository *Sermones* on the Penitential Psalms which were issued in successive years, but with consecutive pagination (see Bibliography, p. 357). I refer to this volume henceforward as *Sermones*.]

[85] *Quinque Sermones* (London, 1527?) f. 61ᵛ. These 'five sermons' preached before the king on the Fridays of Lent 1517 are included in the same volume with consecutive pagination as *I. Longlondi Dei gratia Lincolniensis Episcopi tres conciones* (London, 1527?)
The simile of Scripture as a nut is found in St. Jerome, Epist. LVIII, *P.L.*, xxii. 585: ' Totum quod legimus in scriptura nitet quidem et fulget in cortice, sed dulcius in medulla est: qui edere vult nucleum frangat nucem. *Revela* (inquit David) *oculos meos et considerabo mirabilia de lege tua.*' [Ps. cviii. 18, Vg.] It occurs also in St. Bonaventura; ' sub cortice literae occultatur mystica et profunda intelligentia'; quoted by Farrar, *History of Interpretation*, p. 295. Longland had his D.D., which was obtained largely by hearing and delivering lectures on the Bible, *biblice*, (that is, text by text with glosses); perhaps he felt proud of his privileged knowledge. (For the D.D. course at this time, see J. H. Lupton, *A Life of John Colet, D.D.*, new edn., London, 1909, p. 59.)

Using the same illustration when preaching against Luther, Longland goes even so far as to attribute harmful qualities to the literal
sense:

> For Scripture is like a nut, which has a rind, a shell and a
> kernel. The bitter rind is harmful, the hard shell is distasteful,
> only the kernel is abundantly pleasant and nutricious. So also
> is sacred Scripture, if you follow only the grammatical sense
> which appears on the outside surface like the rind, you will find
> no sap, no profit and no sweetness.[86]

Only Catholic theology holds the key to interpretation; otherwise
following the grammatical sense, errors are made like that of the
Jews, who misunderstood Our Lord's warning, ' Except ye eat the
flesh of the Son of Man, and drink his blood, ye have no life in you '
(John vi. 53).[87] Holding such a narrow view of the denotation of
the ' letter ', it is little wonder that the bishop declares: ' Take the
life from a body, and the body becomes still and inert: take the
inward and spiritual sense from Scripture, and it becomes dead and
useless.'[88]

The ecclesiastical students at Cardinal College, Oxford, (later
Christ Church) were however to be instructed in the old sound
method. Preaching at the laying of the foundation stone of the
college in 1525, Longland declares that on Wisdom's table (Prov.
ix. 2) they were to be served with courses of history, tropology,
allegory, and anagoge. History, he maintains, is but ' for the nourishment of babes, simple ones and those recently come to the faith:
to whom is suited milk and not solid food '. Tropology too is
indeed not denied to ' the unlearned mob ', but allegory is food for
' apter wits ', who ' from one thing collect another meaning to the
building up and increasing of the Christian faith '; it is the crown of
sacred studies.[89]

Holding such extreme notions, what then is Longland's practice?
It is seen at its most distinguished in the sermon at Cardinal College
just quoted, on the text ' Wisdom hath builded her house, she hath
hewn out her seven pillars: she hath killed her beasts: she hath

---

[86] *Tres Conciones*, f. 50ᵛ. The literal sense was considered particularly untrustworthy
after the Lollard upheaval; cf. M. Deansley, *The Lollard Bible* (Cambridge, 1920) p. 288,
where Thomas Palmer is quoted against the Lollards, as stating that the Church should
interpret the Bible ' sometimes morally, sometimes allegorically, sometimes anagog-
ically, and not according to the literal meaning of the words.' Cf. further, ibid. pp.
416–18; where the text of William Butler's *Determinatio* against Bible translations
is given. Butler speaks too (p. 418) of the *cortex literae*. Longland is of course following
earlier preachers, as Robert Rypon, Subprior of Durham (see Owst, *L. & P.M.E.*,
p. 61), in declaring that biblical literalism led to heresy.
[87] *Tres Conciones*, f. 47ᵛ.   [88] Ibid. f. 48ʳ.   [89] Ibid. ff. 33ᵛ–4ʳ.

mingled her wine, she hath also furnished her table ' (Prov. ix.1–2). This is built on two series of ' types ', in each of which the house in the text is equated with Solomon's temple. In the first, Solomon is a figure of Christ, Who is the true wisdom; and the Queen of Sheba who visits him (1 Kings x. 1–13; 2 Chron. ix. 1–12), is the human soul, which will find far greater wonders in Christ, than did the queen in Solomon.[90] The corruptible temple which Solomon built is a figure of the eternal Church which Christ built, being fashioned of living stones, Christ Himself being the Corner Stone.[91] The seven pillars signify the seven sacraments; the table the Catholic faith, and the courses set on it the bread of eternal life. The victim in the Church is the Sacred Host, the wine the Precious Blood. The queen marvelled at the dwellings of the ministers in the temple, so will the soul be overcome by the many mansions of heaven. The temple was a unity, so is the Catholic Church; in both are found ministers, while in heaven are the servants of God. The ministers in the temple wore rich vestments; the ministers of Christ should be clothed in the radiance of many virtues. In the temple were sacrifices; in the Church is the Sacrifice of the Mass, and the personal sacrifices of those consecrated to virginity.[92] In the second series of types Solomon figures Wolsey, the founder of the college, as originally preached by Longland, although after the cardinal's downfall this was altered to Henry VIII for prudential reasons.[93] The college too is a ' temple '; the seven pillars now are the seven arts, the sacrifices offered are the education of the students and the maintenance of the Fellows; the table is Scripture on which are served the four-fold courses, and the ' wine ' is the sweetness of Scripture which gladdens the mind.[94]

In his *Sermones* on the Penitential Psalms Longland does not entirely neglect the literal sense, but gives, like Fisher, many spiritual interpretations, which although of a similar traditional character, (and frequently based on the poetic verbal expression) are usually different in actual content from those given by Fisher. Thus the *ossa* of *quoniam conturbata sunt ossa mea* (Ps. vi. 3, Vg., ' for my bones are troubled ', Douay) signify interior firmness;[95] in the verse *Laboravi*

---

[90] Ibid. f. 15ʳ.   [91] Ibid. f. 22ʳ.   [92] Ibid. f. 24ʳ.

[93] See ibid., f. 32ᵛ; two versions of f. 13ᵛ (containing the Division) are found in the Cambridge University Library copy, the first referring to Wolsey, the second to the king; although only the second version of f. 32ᵛ is extant, it is obvious that the first version of this also referred to Wolsey.

[94] Ibid. ff. 33ʳ–4ᵛ.

[95] *Sermones*, f. 20ʳ. Cf. *Glossa Interlinearis*, in T.B., *cum gloss. ord.*, vol. III. f. 94ʳ; Hugh of St. Cher, T.B., *cum post. Hug. Card.*, vol. II, sig. b6ᵛ.

in gemitu meo, lavabo per singulas noctes lectum meum, lacrimis meis stratum meum rigabo (Ps. vi. 7, Vg., ' I have laboured in my groanings, every night I will wash my bed: I will water my couch with my tears', Douay) the *gemitus* is grief of heart,[96] the *lacrimae* signify confession,[97] the *lectus* is conscience,[98] *rigare* signifies attrition, and *lavare* contrition.[99] Similarly the *cicatrices* of *putruerunt et corruptae sunt cicatrices meae* (Ps. xxxvii. 6, Vg., ' My sores are putrified and corrupted ', Douay) are remembrances of past sins,[100] while the natural properties of the pelican, owl and sparrow provide once more an opportunity for allegory in *Similis factus sum pellicano solitudinis, factus sum sicut nycticorax in domicilio, vigilavi et factus sum sicut passer solitarius in tecto* (Ps. ci. 7–8, Vg., ' I am become like to a pelican of the wilderness: I am like a night raven [owl] in the house ', Douay). The pelican, says the bishop, lives alone in the desert; the owl in holes in walls, and the sparrow, although lustful by nature, sometimes remains alone chaste on the rooftop, so: ' by these three birds, living in lonely habitations, three orders of true penitents are signified. The first, in doing penance, completely leaves the world; the second leaves it only partly, while the third, remaining in the world, seeks salvation there; with periodic groanings and sighs of repentance. This three-fold penance is proper to three states of men. The first is that of solitaries, of anchorites or hermits; the second that of monks living in a convent; the third that of those who live well in the world.'[101]

Longland's treatment of the psalms is similar in his Good Friday sermons (which, as has been pointed out, alone of his works are extant in English). He expounds *redemisti in bracchio tuo populum tuum, filios Iacob et Ioseph* (Ps. lxxvi. 15, Vg., ' With thy arm thou hast redeemed thy people, the children of Jacob and of Joseph ', Douay) as follows:

---

[96] *Sermones*, f. 35ᵛ.   [97] Ibid. f. 37ʳ.
[98] Ibid. f. 38ʳ. Cf. *Glossa Ordinaria*, P.L., cxiii. 852; Hugh of St. Cher, T.B., *cum post. Hug. Card.*, vol. II, sig. b6ᵛ.
[99] *Sermones*, f. 38ʳ.
[100] Ibid. f. 132ʳ. Cf. *Glossa Ordinaria*, P.L., cxiii. 898.
[101] *Sermones*, f. 405ᵛ. Some parallel may be found in *Glossa Ordinaria*, T.B., *cum gloss. ord.*, etc., vol. III, f. 236ʳ. (the pelican signifies hermits, but the owl those asleep to the world); also in Hugh of St. Cher, T.B., *cum post. Hug. Card.*, vol. II, sig. P2ʳ⁻ᵛ (the pelican signifies hermits, but the owl those who live well in the world and the sparrow those in convents).
    Longland allegorizes the titles of the psalms too in the traditional way. Thus *pro octava* (Ps. vi) refers to the Last Day (*Sermones*, f. 1ᵛ.); cf *Glossa Ordinaria*, P.L., cxiii. 851, Hugh of St. Cher, T.B., *cum post. Hug. Card.*, vol. II, sig. b5ᵛ; the *recordatio Sabbati* (Ps. xxxvii. Vg.) is the examination of conscience and amendment of life (ibid. ff. 109ʳ–11ʳ); cf. *Glossa Ordinaria*, P.L., cxiii. 898, Hugh of St. Cher, op. cit. vol. II, sig. o7ᵛ; the *oratio pauperis* (Ps. ci. Vg.) is the prayer of the penitent sinner (ibid. ff. 362ᵛ–3ʳ); cf. Hugh of St. Cher, op. cit. vol. II, sig. P1ʳ.

Iacob is called Israel, and signifieth the people of Israel, the Israelites. Ioseph is interpretate *augmentum siue crescens*, . . . and signifieth the gentiles whiche were added & ioyned to the Israelites in fayth, and electe to be with them the veraye people of saluation, and to be redemed by Christe, for he redemed all.[102] Similarly dealing with David's hope in God, *Speravit anima mea in Domino. A custodia matutina usque ad noctem speret Israel in Domino* (Ps. cxxix. 5–6, Vg., ' My soul hath hoped in the Lord. From the morning watch even until night, let Israel hope in the Lord ', Douay), the bishop asks:

> How longe good prophete hast thou hadde this hoope? . . .
> I have hadde it *A custodia matutina*, sithe I haue hadde any yeres
> of discrecion: & shall haue *usque ad noctem* till my liues ende.
> And so this penitent prophet hauynge this great confidence,
> this highe truste, & affians in god: exhorteth all the worlde to
> the same sayenge, *Speret Israel in domino*. Lett all Israel, lett al
> the chirche mylytant of Christe, lett all faythefull Christen
> people, haue this fyrme & stedfaste hoope in this mercyfull
> lorde God.[103]

Longland's treatment of Old Testament poetic imagery may however perhaps be seen at its most felicitous in this interpretation of a simile in Job, [*Dies mei*] *pertransierunt quasi naves poma portantes*, (Job ix. 26, ' [My days] have passed by as ships carrying fruits ', Douay):

> But why should he speak of ships carrying apples? He does
> so assuredly because such ships scatter a certain perfume over
> the places they pass, which at the same time is drawn along
> with them. So also, we in our lives, scatter perhaps the frag-
> rance of our reputation, of our learning, abilities, nobility and
> power, which suddenly entirely vanishes along with our life.[104]

Like Fisher, Longland gives allegoric interpretations of episodes in New Testament history. The incident of Our Lord washing St. Peter's feet (John xiii. 5–9) is regarded as a mystery:

> What is all this? Mysterys, mysterys, secretys, archans,
> hydd thynges, and thynges, than, oonly known to god. For
> Christe sayd playnly. *Quod ego facio, tu nescis modo, sciens autem
> postea.* Thou knowyste not yete Petur what this matter meanys,

---

[102] *A Sermond spoken before the kynge at Grenwiche vppon good fryday MCCCCCxxxvj* (London, 1536?) sig. Biii^r. For the interpretation of ' Joseph', see e.g. St. Augustine, ' In Psalmum LXXIX Enarratio,' *P.L.*, xxxvi. 1021; St. Isidore of Seville, 'Etymologiae,' lib. VII. cap. vii, *P.L.*, lxxxii. 282.

[103] *A Sermond made befor the kynge at Rychemunte, vppon good fryday MCCCCCxxxvj* (London, probably 1535; see *T.L.S.*, 31 Dec. 1931) sig. Aiv^r. Cf. *Nicolai de Lyra postilla*, in *T.B.*, *cum gloss. ord.*, etc., vol. III, f. 283; Hugh of St. Cher, *T.B.*, *cum post Hug. Card.*, vol. II, sig. Bb3^v.

[104] *Sermones*, f. 396^v. Cf. Hugh of St. Cher *T.B.*, *cum post. Hug. Card.*, vol. I, sig. nn5^v.

but her after thou shalte knowe. What is this than to say, if I washe not thou shalte haue noo parte with me? Nought els, but if that god dothe not washe vs within our soulys, we shall neuer be saued.[105]

St. Peter's subsequent request to Christ: ' Lord, not my feet only, but also my hands and my head ' (John xiii. 10) allows further spiritual interpretation:

> What is this that Petur sayd, washe bothe feete, handes and hedd? Verely to open the matter clerely vnto you, by thes handes ar vnderstand *opera hominis*, the workes and deades of man. For the handes ar the principall instrumentes whereby man doys worke and labur. Therfor by the handes are vnderstand here, workes & deades. Thes thy euyll workes muste be washid clene by penans or thou goo to the greate mawndy of god, or that thou receiue thy maker. And not oonly thy handes thy workes, but also thy hede: wherby is vnderstand all thy fiue sensys, thy fiue wittes, for in thy hedd are all thy sensys. Ther is thy sight, thy heringe, thy smellinge, thy tastinge, and thy touchinge. Thes senses other wysse callid thy fyue wittys, muste also be, by penauns washid.[106]

Similarly the details of the procedure which took place at Our Lord's burial (John xix. 38–42) yield moral admonition:

> O thou christen man, lerne howe to burye thy lorde & God. Fyrste take hym reuerently downe from the crosse. But howe shalte thou take hym frome the crosse? Suerly by hauynge in thy deuoute and pitiouse remembraunce, his deathe. To remembre particulerly euery parte of his passion. . . . Thenne laye hym in a cleane fyne Syndon, in a cleane wyndinge shete. That is, to see thy conscience to be pure and cleane. . . . Thenne sprynkle and caste vpon hym plentyfully bothe myrre and aloes. Myrre is bittur, & is a dryer and a consumer of humors and a preseruer frome corrupcion. And signifyeth *Timorem domini*, the feare & dread of God, whiche dryeth vppe the humour of synne, whiche defendeth man frome thacte of iniquyte and preserueth hym in grace and in fauour of God. . . Thenne take aloes, whiche is also bittur of it selfe but it is pleasaunte in sauour, pleasaunt in smelle. And lykewyse purgeth humors & conserueth the bodie frome putrefaction: and signifyeth veraye contricion, whiche thoughe itt be of it selfe bittur and displeasaunte, yett itt dothe merueloussely

---

[105] *Sermond at Rychmunte*, sig. Fi[v]. Cf. *Glossa Ordinaria*, *P.L.*, cxiv. 405; *Nicolai de Lyra postilla*, in *T.B.*, *cum gloss. ord.*, etc., vol. V, ff. 224–5; Hugh of St. Cher, *T.B.*, *cum post. Hug. Card.*, vol. VI, sig. GG6[r] (quoting *Gloss. Ord.*, as above).

[106] *Sermond at Rychemunte*, sig. Fii[r]. Cf. Hugh of St. Cher, *T.B.*, *cum post. Hug. Card.*, vol. VI, sig. GG6[r].

purge and clense man frome the humor of synne, and con-
serueth hym graciously in the fauour of God, & preserueth
hym frome all inconueniences of the soule. . . . Thenne put this
body in to the sepulture, this sepulture is thy soule, thou
puttyste hym into the sepulture, whenne thou doeste receyue
hym, burye hym in this sepulture of thy soule, kepe hym ther,
lett hym reste wythin the, laye a stone vpon this sepulcre. This
stone is *constantia, perseuerentia,* the vertue that is called con-
stancye, perseueraunce, to be constaunte and permanente in
that godly penitent lyffe that thou haste nowe taken vpon the,
and to continue in vertue.[107]

Again, the temerity of the servant of the High Priest who struck the
Sacred Head (Matt. xxii. 67; Mark xiv. 65; Luke xxii. 63–4), allows
a warning that: ' He strykes god oon the face, that wyttyngly dothe
impugne truths. He strykes god on the face that letteth iustice, that
wrongeth the innocent that oppresseth the poore wretched person.
. . .'[108]

The language of St. Paul too receives allegoric interpretation.
' We have an altar, whereof they have no right to eat which serve
the tabernacle ' (Heb. xiii. 10) refers, says Longland, if we ' enquire
and serche *Non literam occidentem, sed spiritum viuificantem*: not the
letter but the spiryte: not the bare grammatical sence, but the spirituall: not the carnall vnderstandynge, but the inwarde thynge mente
therby ', to those who serve the body before God, and are unworthy
receivers of Holy Communion.[109]

Thus Longland, in spite of the fact that Thomas Robertson
dedicated to him his works on grammatical interpretation,[110] and
that St. Thomas More declared that the bishop, ' a second Colet ',
used to say that he had gained more light on the New Testament
from Erasmus's writings than from almost all the other commentaries
he possessed,[111] belongs in the scriptural interpretation of his
sermons whole-heartedly to the Old Learning. He looks backwards
to the Middle Ages, and it is significant that the commentary which

---

[107] *Sermonde at Grenwiche,* 1536, sig. Iiiᵛ–Iiiiʳ.

[108] *Sermond at Rychemunte,* sig. Oivᵛ. Cf. *Glossa Ordinaria,* on Matt. xxvi. 67–8,
P.L., cxiv. 171–2, on Mark xiv. 65, ibid. 235, on Luke xxii. 63–4, ibid. 343; Hugh of
St. Cher, on Mark xiv. 65, *T.B., cum post. Hug. Card.,* vol. VI, sig. s1ᵛ, on Luke xxii.
63–4, ibid. sig. Q2ᵛ.

[109] *A Sermonde made before the Kynge at Grenewiche, vpon good Frydaye, M.D.xxxviij*
(London, 1538?) sig. Diiʳ et seq. Cf. *Glossa Ordinaria,* P.L., cxiv. 669; *Glossa Interlinearis,*
in *T.B., cum gloss. ord.,* etc., vol. VI, 161ᵛ; Hugh of St. Cher, *T.B., cum post. Hug. Card.,*
vol. VI, sig. R7ᵛ.

[110] See J. Pits, *Relationum Historicarum de Rebus Anglicis, tomus primus,* p. 704.

[111] See the article on Longland in *D.N.B.*

he acknowledges most in quotation is none other than the *Glossa Ordinaria*.[112]

There is however, as stated at the beginning of this chapter, another group of preachers within this period, whose interpretation is predominantly literal, and whose work now demands attention. The services of John Colet and Erasmus to exegesis, in the consecutive exposition of the literal sense by the use of humanistic methods of criticism and the application of historical information, are well known. In his lectures on St. Paul's Epistles Colet breaks with medieval tradition, especially in employing the grammatical method of St. Jerome and Lorenzo Valla instead of the dialectical method of Peter Abelard.[113] As J. W. H. Atkins well puts it: ' Colet attempts an interpretation of St. Paul's Epistles by an application of the historical method, his main object being to explain their real meaning by viewing them against their historical background. Regarding them as letters of the first century A.D., written by a real teacher for contemporary readers under certain definite conditions, he resorts to Suetonius and others for light on the society and conditions of the time; and with this as the key to understanding of the works he succeeds in bringing out their main drift and their bearing on human life. . . . He also reveals in part the art underlying the Epistles, as well as certain aspects of the personality of the writer himself.'[114] Similarly, in the *Letter to Radulphus*, Colet sees in the first chapter of Genesis the theme of the ' one God as Creator set forth with the help of allegory, " after the manner of a popular poet ".'[115] Erasmus, in his preface to the *Novum Instrumentum* (1516) follows Colet's method and applies it to the Gospels;[116] in his *Paraphrases* (1517–24) it was his aim, in the words of F. W. Farrar, ' to brighten the meaning of words which had been partly deadened by familiarity, partly perverted by mistaken applications '.[117] In *Ecclesiastes* (1535), his work on preaching, Erasmus points out the need in exegesis to understand the figurative use of language, and stresses the importance of following the native sense of Scripture. He warns against allegories which are against the native sense, adding that the Fathers are sometimes guilty of this. Allegories are

[112] The parallels noted in the preceding notes suggest of course Longland's frequent use of the Gloss, although without acknowledgement. However it is also the commentary he actually acknowledges most in quotation. See e.g. *Quinique Sermones*, ff. 67r, 55v, 86r.
[113] See P. A. Duhamel, ' The Oxford Lectures of John Colet,' *J.H.I.*, xiv. 4 (1953) pp. 493–510.
[114] J. W. H. Atkins, *English Literary Criticism—the Renascence* (London, 1947) p. 58.
[115] Ibid. p. 59.   [116] Ibid.   [117] *History of Interpretation*, p. 320.

not to be made, he advises, unless the literal sense is first understood, and they must not be used to prove dogmas.[118] While it would be a mistake to neglect the influence on both Colet and Erasmus of Valla and Pico della Mirandola, and aspects of earlier authorities as St. Jerome, St. John Chrysostom and St. Gregory of Nyssa,[119] nevertheless their achievement represents the full efflorescence of a type of exegesis hitherto little practised in the Latin Church—the earlier literal school of Antioch (fourth century A.D.) having had but little influence in the West.[120]

Unfortunately, as distinct from his Oxford lectures, the full text of only one sermon of Colet is extant—the famous address to the Convocation of 1512.[121] The exposition in this is literal, with the application of St. Paul's admonitions in the text ('And be not conformed to this world: but be ye transformed by the renewing of your mind, that ye may prove what is that good, and acceptable, and perfect will of God', Rom. xii. 2), to the state of the church in Colet's own day. It is likely that the exposition given in his sermons preached in St. Paul's Cathedral when Dean, was also predominantly literal. Although we do not have the texts of any of these, Erasmus tells us that Colet ' would not take isolated texts from the gospels or apostolic epistles, but would start with some connected subject, and pursue it right to the end in a course of sermons: for example, St. Matthew's Gospel, the Creed, or the Lord's Prayer '.[122] These sermons were attended approvingly by Lollards,[123] and it is reasonable to suppose that they bore many affinities with the Oxford lectures.

With the work of Colet and Erasmus should be associated that of George Stafford, Fellow of Pembroke Hall, Cambridge, (d. 1529) who lectured on the Scriptures in the University in the 1520s,

---

[118] *Desiderii Erasmi Roterodami Ecclesiastae sive de Ratione Concionandi Libri Quatuor*, ed. F. A. Klein (Leipsig, 1820) lib. iii, pp. 544–622.

[119] J. W. H. Atkins, *English Literary Criticism—the Renascence*, p. 58.

[120] F. W. Farrar, *History of Interpretation*, pp. 210–12, 222, 239–240, 250. On the exegesis of Colet and Erasmus, see further, J. H. Lupton, *Life of Colet*, pp. 59–87; 246–52: also the introductions to his admirable editions of *Ioannis Coleti Enarratic in Epistolam S. Pauli ad Romanos* (London, 1873) and *Ioannis Coleti Enarratio in Primam Epistolam S. Pauli ad Corintios* (London, 1874): see too F. Seebohm, *The Oxford Reformers of* 1498 2nd edn., (London, 1869) pp. 29–90; 320–37; 391–407; G. V. Jourdan, *The Movement towards Catholic Reform in the early XVI century* (London, 1914) chs. i and ii, pp. 1–44; and E. W. Hunt, *Dean Colet and his Theology* (London, 1956) pp. 88–102.

[121] The text is given in Lupton, *Life of Colet*, pp. 291–304.

[122] See Erasmus, *The Lives of Jehan Vitrier . . . and John Colet*, tr. J. H. Lupton (London 1883) p. 24. (*Opus Epistolarum Des. Erasmi Roterodami*, ed. P.S. and H. M. Allen, and H. W. Garrod, 12 vols., Oxford. 1906–47, vol. IV, no. 1211, p. 516.)

[123] See J. Foxe, *Acts and Monuments [of Matters happening in the Church,]* ed. J. Pratt, 8 vols., (London, [1877]) vol. IV, p. 246.

adopting the new type of literal approach.[124] Although opposed at
first, Latimer shortly firmly approved of him, while in a sermon
preached in Edward VI's reign, he quotes an illustration remembered
from Stafford's exposition of St. Paul's Epistle to the Romans.[125]
Thomas Becon, in *The Jewel of Joy* (probably written 1547-8, first
extant copy 1553), quotes as ' a common saying which remaineth
unto this day, " When Master Stafford read, and Master Latimer
preached, then was Cambridge blessed ".'[126] He commends Stafford's
learning in Hebrew, Greek and Latin, and declares:

I doubt whether he was more bound to blessed Paul for
leaving those godly epistles behind him to instruct and teach
the congregation of God, whereof he was a dear member, or
that Paul, which before had so many years been foiled with the
foolish fantasies and elvish expositions of certain doting doctors,
and, as it were, drowned in the dirty dregs of the drowsy
duncers, was rather bound unto him, seeing that by his industry,
labour, pain, and diligence, he seemed of a dead man to make
him alive again, and putting away all unseemliness to set him
forth in his native colours; so that he is now both seen, read,
and heard not without great and singular pleasures of them
that travail in the studies of his most godly epistles. And as he
beautified the letters of blessed Paul with his godly expositions,
so likewise did he learnedly set forth in his lectures the native
sense and true understanding of the four evangelists, vively
restoring unto us the apostle's mind, and the mind of those holy
writers, which so many years before had lien unknown and
obscured through the darkness and mists of the Pharisees and
papists.[127]

Stafford's work was done, of course, after the Lutheran revolt, and
the orthodox found elements of danger in it. Thus George Joye
upbraids Stephen Gardiner with having sought to make Stafford
tone down his expositions: 'Ye wrote', he declares, 'to maister
George Stafforde to give hym warninge when he was complained of to
the Cardinall for readynge, and declarynge truly and feithfully
thepistle to the Romains, and shewed him howe he sholde temper
his lection.'[128] However there is no doubt that his lectures were
influential, particularly amongst the young.

[124] H. C. Porter, *Reformation and Reaction in Tudor Cambridge* (Cambridge, 1958)
p. 42.
[125] See Foxe, *Acts and Monuments*, vol. IV, p. 656; *Sermons*, pp. 440-1.
[126] T. Becon, *The Catechism*, etc., ed. J. Ayre (Cambridge, 1844) P.S., ' The Jewel
of Joy,' p. 425.
[127] Ibid. p. 426.
[128] Foxe, *Acts and Monuments*, vol. IV, p. 754.

The cause of the New Learning was aided also by various changes at Oxford and Cambridge. Richard Fox, Bishop of Winchester, founded Corpus Christi College Oxford for this purpose (1516) together with a Readership in Greek,[129] while at Cambridge Fisher encouraged the study of Greek and Hebrew, a Readership in Greek being founded in 1519.[130] In 1535 the Royal Injunctions to Oxford and Cambridge stopped the study of Canon Law, and replaced the study of the *Sentences* of Peter Lombard and the medieval commentators by that of Scripture 'according to the true sense thereof'.[131] At Cambridge the Regius Professorships of Greek and Hebrew were founded in 1540 and those at Oxford in 1546.[132]

The fruits of the example given in literal interpretation by Colet, Erasmus and Stafford, of the admonitions of Erasmus's *Ecclesiastes*, together with the changes at the two universities, are found in some preachers of the later part of Henry VIII's reign. The set of postils issued in 1540 by Richard Taverner, provides a series of brief, predominantly literal, consecutive expositions, with moral applications, of the Epistles and Gospels for the Sundays and Major Festivals throughout the year,[132a] The simple literal interpretations of the Parable of the Labourers in the Vineyard (Matt. xx. 1–16; the Gospel for Septuagesima)[133] and of the Parable of the Sower (Luke viii. 4–15; the Gospel for Sexagesima)[134] may be contrasted with the fancifully allegoric expositions offered in the earlier *De Tempore* collection (MS. Harl. 2247) already noticed.[135] The injunction that English Bibles should be placed in the churches had been issued in 1538,[136] and it is interesting to note that the postil on the Epistle for Advent II (Rom. xv. 4–13), recommends that all should have some knowledge of Scripture:

> My brethren and sisters the Epistle of S. Paule whych ye haue herde teacheth vs aboue al thinges to imbrace, loue, and

---

[129] C. E. Mallet, *A History of the University of Oxford*, 3 vols. (London, 1924–7) vol. II, pp. 20–5.

[130] J. B. Mullinger, *The University of Cambridge*, 3 vols. (Cambridge, 1873–1911) vol. I, p. 528.

[131] C. E. Mallet, *A History of the University of Oxford*, vol. II, pp. 62–3; J. B. Mullinger, *The University of Cambridge*, vol. I, p. 630.

[132] Mullinger, op. cit. vol. II, p. 52; Mallet, op. cit. vol. I, p. 71.

[132a] Taverner himself was of course a Lutheran, but these sermons which he edited are conservative in doctrine, and should be considered here. (See *Postils on the Epistles and Gospels compiled and published by Richard Taverner in the year* 1540, ed. E. Cardwell, Oxford, 1841, pp. ix, 181–8, 228–9.)

[133] *Postils* pp. 99–101.

[134] Ibid. pp. 105–9.   [135] See *ante*, pp. 5–7.

[136] See *Documents of the Christian Church*, selected and edited by Henry Bettenson (Oxford, 1950) pp. 325–6.

haue in reuerence all holy scriptures and not wythout cause, for they be the vndoubted wordes of God and not of men. And all that be in them wrytten be wrytten for our learnyng and instruction. But what learnynge? Surely heauenly learnynge, spirituall learnynge, learnynge of lyfe: as it is wrytten in the fourth chapter of saynt Mathew: Man lyueth not onely wyth breade but he lyueth of euery worde that commeth from the mouthe of God. [Matt. iv. 4.] The holy scripture then is the true breade of vnderstanding of ghostly learnyng, it is the true feading of the soule. Wherfore euery man ought to enforce hymselfe for to haue parte of it and to know it, to the intent that he maye lyue in soule and spiritually. . .[137]

However, private interpretation is not contemplated, and the series makes frequent use of the interpretations of the early Fathers, especially those of St. John Chrysostom, St. Jerome, St. Ambrose, St. Augustine and Origen; and in addition, particularly in the sermons for saints' days, of the *Paraphrases* of Erasmus. Also, some of these interpretations are allegoric, as that of St. Augustine on the five barley loaves at the feeding of the five thousand (John vi. 9) as representing ' the fyue bokes of Moses ',[138] or that of certain ' holy doctours ' on the passage where Christ sends two of the disciples for the ass and the ass's foal, before His entry into Jerusalem on Palm Sunday (Matt. xxi. 1–2), where the disciples are interpreted as ' the holy shewers of hys commynge as well of the olde testament as of the newe ', the ass as ' the people of Jury vpon whome God had of olde set and rested hymselfe by the lawe ', and the ass's foal as ' the Gentyles, vpon whom God had not sette nor restyd hym, which were oute of the lawe and mysbeleuers '.[139]

An anonymous set of postils on the Sunday Gospels and Epistles (1540–3?) offers the same kind of interpretation as Taverner's collection, although the individual sermons are not identical.[140] Significantly, this set pronounces against that allegorization of parables, which, as we have seen, was favoured by the Old Learn-

[137] Taverner, *Postils*, pp. 6–7.
[138] Ibid. p. 516. Cf. St. Augustine, ' Tractatus 24 in Joannem,' *P.L.*, xxxv. 1594; *Glossa Ordinaria, T.B., cum gloss. ord.,* vol. V. f. 204ʳ.
[139] Ibid. p. 4. Cf. St. Ambrose, ' Expos. Evang. sec. Luc.,' lib. ix, *P.L.*, xv. 1794; *Glossa Ordinaria, P.L.,* cxiv. 152; *Nicolai de Lyra postilla,* in *T.B., cum gloss. ord.,* etc., vol. V, ff. 63–4; St. Thomas Aquinas, *Catena Aurea,* [St. Jerome and Rabanus] *Opera Omnia,* vol. XI, p. 239.
See further, Taverner, *Postils,* pp. 472–3, 222, 476, 78, 554.
[140] Title-page missing; colophon runs; ' The ende of this brefe Postyl, vpon the Epistles and Gospelles of all the Sundayes in the yeare.' This interesting volume, which bears the device of Grafton (R. B. McKerrow, *Printers' and Publishers' Devices in England and Scotland* 1485–1640, no. 88) is not noticed by the *S.T.C.*: it is in the possession of Mr. J. I. Bromwich of St. John's College, Cambridge.

ing.[141] Again, Cuthbert Tunstall, Bishop of Durham, preaching on Palm Sunday 1536, on the Epistle of the Day (Phil. ii. 5–11), is largely content to give a rendering of the literal sense concerning Our Lord's humility and obedience.[142] He does however allow himself an allegoric interpretation against the primacy of the Pope: '. . . I will exalt my throne above the stars of God. . . . I will ascend above the heights of the clouds; I will be like the most High', (Isa. xiv. 13–14) spoken literally by Lucifer, is taken to signify the way in which the Popes exalt themselves above the angels (stars); above the prophets of the Old Testament, above the preachers and apostles of the New (clouds), and make themselves like God.[143]

Roger Edgeworth, that neglected but vigorous Henrician preacher, in his delightful series of sermons on St. Peter's first Epistle, delivered in the newly constituted Cathedral of Bristol, of which he was a prebendary,[144] goes through the Epistle, making the literal meaning clear, and expatiating, as to a lesser extent Colet had done in his lectures, on any important matters suggested by the text.[145] Thus St. Peter's reference to ' an inheritance incorruptible, and undefiled, and that fadeth not away, reserved in heaven for you ' (1 Pet. i. 4), allows Edgeworth to deal at length with the transience of this world, and the stable joys of heaven;[146] while the Apostle's admonitions to wives (1 Pet. iii. 1–6) occasions a tirade against cosmetics and the vanities of dress.[147] He provides too some ' background ' information about the Mediterranean area, likely to appeal to the sailors in his audience; as dealing with the entrance to the sea at the straits of Gibraltar, he speaks of ' Calys Malys ', a mountain in Granada (the Rock of Gibraltar?):

    Ill Calys, becaues of a great multitude of ragged rockes liyinge in the thresholde or bottom of the saide gate, so that

---

[141] Ibid. f. 123ᵛ; cf. ante, pp. 5–7.

[142] A sermon of Cuthbert Bysshop of Duresme, made vpon Palme sondaye laste past, before the maiestie of our souerayne lorde kynge Henry the VIII (London, 1539) sig. Aiiʳ–Bvʳ.

[143] Ibid. sig. Bvi–vii. Cf. St. Augustine, ' Enarr. in Psal. xlv ', P.L., xxxvi. 520.

[144] Sermons very fruitfully, godly and learned, preached and sette forth by Maister Roger Edgeworth, doctoure of diuinitie, (London, 1557) ff. 148ᵛ–317ʳ. All the sermons in this volume except the last three on St. Peter's first Epistle were preached in Henry VIII's time: Edgeworth informs us at the beginning of the eighteenth sermon on this Epistle (f. 279ʳ) that he had abstained from preaching for five or six years, i.e., during the reign of Edward VI, and that this particular series is resumed after a break of eight or nine years.

[145] Colet reflects, in passing, on the state of the ecclesiastical courts, when dealing with Rom. v; (the passage quoted in Lupton, Life of Colet, pp. 68–70, from the Expositio Literalis on Romans [found too in Ioannis Coleti Opuscula Quaedam Theologica, ed. with tr. by J. H. Lupton, London, 1876, pp. 162–3]. See further the passage quoted, Life of Colet, pp. 72–4).

[146] Sermons, ff. 120ʳ et seq.   [147] Ibid. ff. 198ᵛ–202ᵛ.

D

when any ship shall passe in or oute at the saide streicte, the
mariners must be sure of an highe water, and a measurable
winde, els they shall finde it an yll passage and perilous.[148]
Similarly Edgeworth can bring home to his audience the volume of
vice and sin, together with diversity of opinions in the Rome of
St. Peter's time by referring to contemporary conditions in cosmopolitan cities (as Bristol itself), for:

> . . . as we see by experience, where little concourse of straungers
> is, there is playne maner of liuynge, and after one manner, but
> in townes they be of another sort. The Germayns and Saxons
> brynge in their opinions. The Frenchmen their new fashions.
> Other countreis geuen to lechery runne to the open bars or
> stues. And for suche confusion of the inhabitantes.[149]

His view of the content of ' the letter ' is wide, resembling that of
St. Thomas Aquinas rather than that of Longland.[150] We see this
when he refuses to accept the Jewish tradition that there was a
particular stone ' which the builders rejected ' (Ps. cxviii. 22) when
preparing the materials for the temple in King David's time, about
which the king had a revelation that it would become ' the head of
the corner ' when the temple was built in Solomon's time, and which
in fact *was* placed at the top of the building;[151] on the contrary:

> . . . because the narration hath no euidence of scripture, it is
> not beste to grounde anye scripture vpon it, and specially this
> scripture that is so often in the mouth with our Sauiour Christ,
> and with the evangelists, and in the Apostolical epistles. But
> we must take the said wordes of the psalme *Lapidem quem
> repro[bauerunt]* spoken originally, and to the letter of Our
> Sauiour Christ selfe, and so he alledgeth the same wordes.
> Mat. xxi. [42–4].[152]

Again, Edgeworth declares that by ' ye are a chosen generation, a
royal priesthood ', (1 Pet. ii. 9) St. Peter does not mean that all
Christians are kings and priests in the ordinary sense, but that they
are so, only after a spiritual manner; by means, he suggests, of
Baptism and self-sacrifice.[153] However, occasionally we do find
allegoric interpretations of the older kind; as this passage on the
significance of the Flood:

> This blessed Sacramente of baptisme, by whiche we be
> regenerate and gotten agayne to God, was signified by the
> water that drouned the earth, and earthly carnall people, and

---

[148] Ibid. f. 108r.
[149] Ibid. f. 106r.　　[150] See *ante*, pp. 2, 22.　　[151] *Sermons*, ff. 150v–6r.
[152] Ibid. f. 156r. Cf. the discussion about a real stone [*Pauli Burgensis*] *Additio*
3, *T.B., cum gloss. ord.*, etc., vol. V, f. 67r.
[153] *Sermons*, ff. 167r–9r.

saued the eyght liues that then were saued. And that the water
of the sayde flud saued none that were oute of the shippe,
signifieth that all heretikes that be out of the common receaued
fayth of the churche, althoughe they be cristened, and glorieth
to be called christen men, yet by the same water they shall be
drouned into hell, by which the ship, the catholike churche was
lifte and borne vp into heauen and saued, as the materiall
shippe of Noe was lifte vp into the ayre aboue grounde, and
saued by water.[154]

Similarly, the natural properties of the *lepusculus* [rabbit or hare] in
lepusculus plebs invalida, qui collocat in petra cubile suum (Prov. xxx. 26,
'The rabbit, a weak people, which maketh its bed in the rock',
Douay) yield an interpretation in the manner of the *distinctio*:

Here is some diuersitie of translations, for that in our text is
called *lepusculus*, in other is called *herinacius*, and *hericius* & *Mus*.
And in psalm ciii it is sayd, *petra refugium herinacijs* [Ps. ciii. 18
(Vg.)], the rocke is a refuge, a place of safe garde and defence
for that beast. It is a little rough beast, and buildeth in the
rockes in Palestine, in the holy lande. I thinke we haue none of
them here with vs. For the same our translation in the prouerbs
of Solomon putteth *Lepusculus* an Hare or Leueret. This worde
Saplian in the Hebrewe hath dyuers significations, of which
one is a Hare, and so it is put in our common translation. A
Hare is a weake beast and a fraiful, euer running away, more
trusting to her feete, and to her form or resting place, then to
her owne strength. Sometimes she maketh her forme in olde
grofes, rockes, or quarryes, spent, lefte, or forsaken, and
signifieth the weake good Christen people that seke not to
reuenge the wrong done vnto them, and hath this pointe of
prudence and wisedome, not to truste in theyr owne strength,
but to putte theyr trust principally in our redemer & Sauioure
Iesus Christe, sygnefied by the stone or rocke, in whiche (as it
is sayde here) the Hare maketh his bed or forme.[155]

Also, being a Conservative Henrician, Edgeworth will not admit
any gloss which militates against Catholic doctrine, and in spite of

---

[154] Ibid. f. 226[r]. Cf. *Glossa Ordinaria, P.L.*, cxiii. 105, 107; *Glossa Interlinearis*, in
T.B., cum gloss. ord., etc., vol. I, f. 150[v]; Hugh of St. Cher, *T.B., cum post. Hug. Card.*,
vol. I, sig. c1[r].
[155] *Sermons*, f. 226[r]. Cf. *Glossa Ordinaria, P.L.*, cxiii. 1113–44. See too *Sermons*,
ff. 248[v]–9[r]. Commenting on Job xii. 7 ('But ask now the beasts, and they shall teach
thee'), Edgeworth gives the *rationale* of this type of interpretation: 'Then it may be
sayde that we aske these dumme creatures questions to learne witte by them, when we
consider theyr naturall operacions, examinyng and discussing and searching out theyr
natural operacions and vertues. And then they answer vs and teache vs, when by
consideracion of them we ascende and rise vp to the knowledge of god, or to som
learning to which we come by consideration of their properties.' (ibid., f. 246[v]).

theoretical approval, he distrusts in practice Bible reading by the laity; his own words on this topic are distinctly *piquant*:

> I haue euer bene of this minde, that I haue thought it no harme, but rather good and profitable that holie Scripture should be hadde in the mother tong, and with holden from no manne that were apte and mete to take it in hande, specially if we coulde get it well and truely translated, whyche will be verye harde to be hadde. But who be meete and able to take it in hande, there is the doubte.[156]

Edgeworth is indeed particularly concerned about the multitude of ignorant lay-people who take advantage of the Bibles actually current to become amateur exegetes: the physician, the carpenter and the smith are left to their own business, but, laments the preacher, echoing the language of St. Jerome:

> The facultie of Scripture onely, is the knowledge that all menne and women chalengeth and claymeth to them selfe and for theyr owne, here and there, the bablynge Sophister, and all other presumeth vppon thys facultye, and teareth it, and teacheth it afore they learn it. Of all suche greene Diuines as I haue spoken of, it appeareth full wel what learnynge they haue, by thys, that when they teache anye of their Disciples, and when they gyue anye of theyr bookes to other menne to reade, the fyrste suggestion why he shoulde laboure suche bookes is because by this (say they) thou shalt be able to oppose the best priest in the parish and to tell him he lieth.[157]

Some amateur theologians, says Edgeworth, neglect their secular work for unseasonable scripture study, with unhappy results:

> I haue knowen manye in this towne, that studienge diuinitie, hath kylled a merchant, and some of other occupations by their busy labours in the scriptures, hath shut vp the shoppe windowes, faine to take sainctuary, or els for mercerye and groserye, hath be[ne] fayne to sell godderds, [drinking cups] steanes [earthen jars or pots, usually with two handles] and pitchers and suche other trumperye.[158]

Very similar to Edgeworth in exposition are two other preachers of the same ecclesiastical party, William Chedsey, Fellow of Corpus Christi College Oxford and chaplain to Bonner, Bishop of London; and Cuthbert Scott, who became Bishop of Chester in Mary's reign. Both give historical ' background '; Chedsey, that the Pharisees and Herodians who came to Christ in an attempt to trap Him in His speech by asking if it was lawful to give tribute to Caesar (Matt. xxii.

---

[156] Ibid. f. 32r.   [157] Ibid. f. 36r. Cf. St. Jerome, Epist. LIII, *P.L.*, xxii. 544.
[158] Ibid. f. 43v.

15–16) were enemies, united on this occasion only by a common hatred of Him:[159] Scott, that the Jews accepted a prophecy that they would have a ruler of the ' house of Iudas ' [Judah] until the Messiah came; and as in the time of Our Lord, Palestine was divided into four parts ruled by aliens appointed by the Romans, the Jews were then *expecting* a Messiah.[160] Scott shows too some psychological insight, when he points out that when the Jews asked St. John the Baptist ' Who art thou? ' (John i. 19) it was a temptation for him to declare that he was equal to his Master.[161] However, on the other hand, for Chedsey the Pharisees represent ' singularitie ' and the Herodians ' subtlete ';[162] while Scott not only condemns private interpretation,[163] but also offers two allegories of the old kind: that the ' way ' in ' Blessed are the undefiled in the way ' (Ps. cxix. 1) is this earthly life, and also the moral law as given in the Decalogue;[164] and (from history) that Pompey, who polluted the temple in Jerusalem and caused unworthy persons to be made High Priest, betokens covetousness which permits simoniacal appointments in the Church.[165]

II

THE EARLY REFORMERS (1547–1553)

After demolishing the position held by the partisans of the Old Learning,[166] Tyndale proceeds to give what he takes to be the correct ideas on interpretation:

Tropological and anagogical are terms of their own feigning, and altogether unnecessary. For they are but allegories, both two of them; and this word allegory comprehendeth them both, and is enough. For tropological is but an allegory of manners; and anagogical, an allegory of hope. And allegory is as much

---

[159] *Two notable sermones lately preached at Paules crosse. Anno* 1544. *Ouerseen and perused by the byshop of London* (London, 1544) sig. Bviii^r–Ci^r. The first sermon is by Chedsey, the second by Scott. Cf. *Glossa Ordinaria, P.L.,* cxiv. 156 (disagreement between the Pharisees and Herodians over the payment of tribute).

[160] *Two notable sermones,* sig. Fiv^v.

[161] Ibid. sig. Hi^r.

[162] Ibid. sig. Ciii^r: ' The pharisey, by interpretation is he that is sequested and diuyded from other: and by him I vnderstand *Singularitie.* The Herodian after Christes own wordes is he, that hath the foxes crafte: and by him I meane *Subtlete:* Two shrode companions syngularyte and *subtlete.*' (For the interpretation of ' Pharisee ' as *divisus,* see e.g. Rabanus Maurus, ' De Universo,' lib. IV, cap. ix. *P.L.,* cxi. 95.)

[163] *Two notable sermones,* sig. Hviii^r–viii^v.

[164] Ibid. sig. Kv^r. Cf. *Glossa Ordinaria, T.B., cum gloss. ord.,* etc., vol. III, f. 262^v; *Glossa Interlinearis,* and *Nicolai de Lyra postilla,* ibid.; Hugh of St. Cher, *T.B., cum post. Hug. Card.,* vol. II, sig. X4^v.

[165] *Two notable sermones,* sig. Gvi^r.   [166] See *ante,* p. 1.

to say as strange speaking, or borrowed speech: as when we say of a wanton child, ' This sheep hath magots in his tail, he must be anointed with birchen salve '; which speech I borrow of the shepherds.

Thou shalt understand, therefore, that the scripture hath but one sense, which is the literal sense. And that literal sense is the root and ground of all, and the anchor that never faileth, whereunto if thou cleave, thou canst never err or go out of the way. Neverthelater, the scripture useth proverbs, similitudes, riddles or allegories, as all other speeches do; but that which the proverb, similitude, riddle, or allegory signifieth, is ever the literal sense, which thou must seek out diligently: as in English we borrow words and sentences of one thing, and apply them unto another and give them new significations.[167]

Illustrating this, the reformer gives some racy examples of non-scriptural ' borrowed speech ', amusingly directed against the Catholics:

When a thing speedeth not well, we borrow speech, and say, ' The bishop hath blessed it '; because that nothing speedeth well that they meddle withal. If the porridge be burned too, the meat over-roasted, we say, ' The bishop hath put his foot in the pot ', or, ' The bishop hath played the cook '; because the bishops burn whom they lust, and whosoever displeaseth them. ' He is a pontifical fellow '; that is, proud and stately. ' He is popish '; that is, superstitious and faithless. ' It is a pastime for a prelate.' ' It is a pleasure for a pope.' ' He would be free, and yet will not have his head shaven.' ' He would that no man should smite him, and yet hath not the pope's mark.' And of him that is betrayed, and wotteth not how, we say, ' He hath been at shrift '.[168]

Thus Tyndale refuses to admit the separate existence of a ' spiritual sense ' in Scripture; indeed he declares: ' God is a spirit, and all his words are spiritual. His literal sense is spiritual, and all his words are spiritual.'[169]

The placing of figurative language within the literal sense is of course not new; it is in accordance with the view of St. Thomas Aquinas, whose conception of the content of ' the letter ' is wider than that of some other Catholic interpreters, as Bishop Long-land.[170] However, the denial of the existence of the spiritual senses marks a departure from traditional exegesis, and is in agreement with the outlook of the continental reformers. For example, Luther

---

[167] *Doctrinal Treaties*, ' The Obedience of a Christian Man,' pp. 303–4.
[168] Ibid., pp. 304–5.   [169] Ibid., p. 309.   [170]See *ante*, pp. 2, 22.

declares that ' the literal sense of Scripture alone is the whole essence of faith and of Christian theology '; and further, that ' in the schools of theologians it is a well-known rule that Scripture is to be understood in four ways, literal, allegoric, moral, anagogic. But if we wish to handle Scripture aright, our one effort will be to obtain *unum*, *simplicem*, *germanum*, *et certum sensum literalem.*' 'Allegorizing,' he points out, ' may degenerate into a mere monkey-game.'[171] Luther believed, like Melancthon, that, as F. W. Farrar puts it, ' the pretence of a *multiplex intelligentia* destroyed the whole meaning of Scripture, and deprived it of any *certain* sense at all, while it left room for the most extravagant perversions, and became a subtle method for transferring to human fallibility, what belonged exclusively to the domain of revelation.'[172]

However, something relating to the spiritual senses is allowed by Tyndale; accommodations or applications may be made from the sacred text, even although they are not part of its proper significance:

> Beyond all this, when we have found out the literal sense of the scripture by the process of the text, or by a like text of another place, then go we, and as the scripture borroweth similitudes of worldly things, even so we again borrow similitudes or allegories of the scripture, and apply them to our purposes; which allegories are no sense of the scripture, but free things besides the scripture, and altogether in the liberty of the Spirit.[173]

These applications must however be controlled by the new doctrinal positions:

> Which allegories I may not make at all the wild adventures; but must keep me within the compass of the faith, and ever apply mine allegory to Christ, and unto the faith.[174]

When we turn to the sermons of the early reformers in England, do we find that their practice follows the new theory of interpretation? We find first, that the allegorizing of the figurative expression of the poetic and prophetic books of the Old Testament, favoured by the Old Learning, disappears completely.[175] Secondly,

---

[171] Farrar, *History of Interpretation*, pp. 327–8.
[172] Ibid. Harry Caplan writes that Melancthon regards the use of the four senses ' as the trifling and vicious recourse to a monstrous metamorphosis on the part of inept illiterates who have no science of speaking, and who do not even appreciate that ἀναγωγία meaning *petulantia*, may not be used for ἀναγωγή.' (' The Four Senses of Scriptual Intepretation and the Medieval Theory of Preaching,' *Speculum*, iv. 3 (1929) p. 289.) [Caplan quotes in a footnote Latin passages to this effect from Melancthon's *Elementa Rhetorices, De Elocutione, II*, ' De Quatuor Sensibus Sacrarum Scripturarum.']
[173] *Doctrinal Treatises*, ' The Obedience of a Christian Man.' p. 305.
[174] Ibid.
[175] Cf. *ante*, pp. 3, 14–16, 23–5.

we notice a concern for the native and original meaning of biblical expressions depending upon a knowledge of the original languages of the sacred books. Following Luther, John Bradford, Fellow of Pembroke Hall Cambridge, and Chaplain to Nicholas Ridley, Bishop of London, stresses that μετάνοια, 'repentance', means a 'forethinking', and carries no connotation of the Roman 'penance'.[176] Similarly he declares that St. Paul's ἀπολογία, (2 Cor. vii. 11) means not ' satisfaction ' but ' defence ' or ' answering again ' [A. V. ' clearing of yourselves '].[177] Again, Thomas Lever, Fellow of St. John's College Cambridge, shows that the Apostle's ' Let every soul be subject to the higher powers ' (Rom. xiii. 1) is a metonymy meaning ' let every person be subject to the higher powers ', for here St. Paul makes use of the Hebrew idiom, as found in ' the soul that sinneth it shall die ' (Ezek. xviii. 4) which places the most important part of man, the soul, for the whole man, just as in English idiom the body, the worse part (as in ' everybody ') is placed for the whole man.[178] Similarly, Roger Hutchinson, also Fellow of St. John's College Cambridge, dealing with the institution of the Eucharist, quotes, ' He took bread and blessed, and brake it ' (Mark xiv. 22) and proceeds:

Here we say, that ' to bless ' is to give thanks to God for all his innumerable benefits, and namely for our redemption through Christ. No, saith the papist: ' to bless ' is to make a sign of the cross on the sacrament. And to defend this interpretation they allege St. Paul's authority, who saith, " Is not the cup of blessing which we bless, partaking of the blood of Christ? " I answer: the Greek word, in these two texts which they allege for their crossing is εὐλογία which word cannot signify ' to cross '. For whereas Paul termeth it " the cup of blessing which we bless ", the Greek is, τὸ ποτήριον τῆς εὐλογίας ὅ εὐλογοῦμεν. And for the English, " he blessed and brake the bread ", Mark saith in the Greek tongue, in which he wrote his Gospel, λαβὼν ἄρτον εὐλογήσας ἔκλασε: which word, I say, cannot signify ' to make the sign of the cross '.[179]

The Catholic interpretation is, says Hutchinson, ' to make the Scripture a nose of wax, a tennis ball, and to wrest them to every purpose.'[180]

[176] The Writings of John Bradford, ed. A. Townsend, 2 vols. (Cambridge, 1848–53) P.S., vol. I, p. 45. Cf. Luther, Letter to Staupitz, in B.L. Woolf, Reformation Writings of Martin Luther (London, 1952) vol. I, pp. 56–60.
[177] Writings, vol. I, pp. 50–1.
[178] Sermons, ed. E. Arber (Westminster, 1895) p. 26.
[179] The Works of Roger Hutchinson, ed. J. Bruce (Cambridge, 1842) P.S., p. 226.
[180] Ibid.

Further, in the sermons of Hugh Latimer there is considerable simple re-telling of Old Testament history. The story of the usurpation of Adonijah (1 Kings i–ii) is recounted, as are those of Solomon's judgement to divide a child between two harlots who each claim that it is theirs (1 Kings iii), of Josiah (2 Kings xxii–xxiii), and of Samuel's sons who accepted bribes, but were disowned by their father (1 Sam. ii–iii) contrasted with the evil sons of Eli, condoned by their father (1 Sam. viii).[181] This kind of instruction was doubtless necessary at a time when the vernacular Bible had only recently been allowed to the laity. Also, the Catholic preachers had tended to quote more the poetic, prophetic and sapiential books of the Old Testament; for example Fisher and Longland choose the Penitential Psalms as subjects for exposition, Edgeworth quotes the psalms, prophets and wisdom books to a popular audience, as does Baron to a learned, but all seldom refer to the historical books, while the authors of the ruder *De Tempore* series similarly neglect Old Testament history. Thus the historical books would be comparatively unfamiliar even to regular sermon-goers.

It is interesting too to note that Latimer does not build farfetched allegories upon those Sunday Gospels which he treats. The Parable of the Labourers in the Vineyard (Matt. xx. 1–16; the Gospel for Septuagesima) is expounded without any of the misplaced subtlety which was noticed in a late fifteenth century treatment;[182] for, declares Latimer:

> ... every parable hath *certum statum*, ' a certain scope ', to the which we must have a respect; and not go about to set all words together, or to make a gloss for the same: for it is enough for us when we have the meaning of the principal scope; and more needeth not.[183]

Thus he finds that it shows ' that all Christian people are equal in all things pertaining to the kingdom of Christ.'[184] Similarly the Parable of the Sower (Luke viii. 4–15; the Gospel for Sexagesima) is treated simply, with due regard to Our Lord's own explanation of it.[185]

The English reformers recommend Bible-reading to the laity. The noble exhortation of the first sermon of the First Book of Homilies ('A fruitful exhortation to the Reading of Holy Scripture ',

---

[181] *Sermons*, pp. 113–17; pp. 125–6; pp. 176–7; 187–92.
[182] See *ante*, pp. 5–7.
[183] *Sermons and Remains of Hugh Latimer*, ed. G. E. Corrie (Cambridge, 1845) P.S., p. 199.
[184] Ibid. [185] Ibid. pp. 209–16.

probably by Cranmer) overthrows the notion that only the learned clerk is fit to gather doctrines from the sacred pages:

Unto a Christian man, there can be nothing either more necessary or profitable than the knowledge of holy Scripture; forasmuch as in it is contained God's true word, setting forth his glory, and also man's duty. And there is no truth nor doctrine, necessary for our justification and everlasting salvation, but that is, or may be drawn out of that fountain and well of truth. . . . These books, therefore, ought to be much in our hands, in our eyes, in our ears, in our mouths, but most of all in our hearts. For the Scripture of God is the heavenly meat for our souls, the hearing and keeping of it maketh us blessed, sanctifieth us, and maketh us holy; it turneth our souls; it is a lantern to our feet; it is a sure, steadfast, and everlasting instrument of salvation; it giveth wisdom to the humble and holy hearts, it comforteth, maketh glad, cheereth, and cherisheth our conscience; it is a more excellent jewel, or treasure than any gold or precious stone; it is more sweet than honey or honeycomb; it is called *the best part* which Mary did choose, for it hath in it everlasting comfort.[186]

John Hooper, Bishop of Gloucester (1550) and later of Worcester (1552), clearly regards his audience as Bible readers; he frequently refers them to places to look up afterwards; as to read Genesis x on Nineveh[187] and ' Gen. vii of the flood, Gen. xix of Sodom, Exod. xiv of Pharao ' on God's wrath against unrepentant sinners.[188]

Some of the liveliest polemic of the Reformers is directed against Catholic allegoric glosses; these they will under no circumstances admit. Latimer waxes indignant over Cardinal Pole's alleging, in support of the primacy of the Pope, the passage where Our Lord preaches to the people from Peter's boat, and then commands the nets to be lowered, with the result that a miraculous draught of fishes is taken (Luke v. 1–7). 'It is', declares the Reformer, ' a text that he doth greatly abuse for the supremacy: he racks it, and violates it, to serve for the maintenance of the bishop of Rome.'[189] However Latimer seeks to demolish the position that there is any allegoric

[186] *Certain Sermons Appointed by the Queen's Majesty to be declared and read by all Parsons, Vicars and Curates, every Sunday and Holiday in their Churches,* . . . ed. G. E. Corrie, (Cambridge, 1850) pp. 1–3. Of the First Book of Homilies, Cranmer is credited with nos. 1, 3, 4, 5, and 9; Thomas Becon with 7 and 11; Edmund Bonner with 6; Latimer with 12, and John Harpesfield with 2, while the writers of nos. 8 and 10 are unknown. (J. T. Tomlinson. *The Prayer Book, Articles and Homilies,* London, 1897, pp. 232–5.)
[187] *Early Writings of John Hooper,* ed. S. Carr, (Cambridge, 1843) P.S., p. 447.
[188] Ibid. pp. 449–50.
[189] *Sermons,* p. 198. *The Glossa Ordinaria* sees in Peter's boat a reference to the Church (*T.B., cum gloss. ord.,* etc., vol. V, f. 138ᵛ) while Hugh of St. Cher adds to this that the Church was given to Peter to rule, (*T.B., cum post. Hug. Card.,* vol. VI, sig. z6ʳ.)

significance in Christ's choosing Peter's boat rather than another
by a reference to every-day experience:

> Well, he comes to Simon's boat, and why rather to Simon's
> boat than another? I will answer, as I find by experience in
> myself. I came hither to-day from Lambeth in a wherry; and
> when I came to take boat, the watermen came about me, as the
> manner is, and he would have me, and he would have me: I
> took one of them. Now ye will ask me, why I came in that boat
> rather than in another? Because I would go into that I see stand
> next me; it stood more commodiously for me. And so did
> Christ by Simon's boat: it stood nearer for him, he saw a better
> seat in it. A good natural reason. Now come the papists, and
> they will make a mystery of it: they will pick out the supremacy
> of the bishop of Rome in Peter's boat. We may make allegories
> enough of every place in Scripture: but surely it must needs
> be a simple matter that standeth on so weak a ground.[190]

Further, the papists see a mystical sense in *Duc in altum*, ' launch out
into the deep ' (Luke v. 4); their argument is, ' he spake to Peter
only, and he spoke to him in the singular number: *ergo* he gave him
such pre-eminence above the rest.' For this Latimer has the utmost
scorn: 'A goodly argument! I ween it be a syllogismus, *in quem
terra, pontus* '; because Christ said to Judas, when he was about to
betray him, *Quod facis fac citius* (John xiii. 27; ' That thou doest, do
quickly ',) speaking in the singular number, in the presence of the
other disciples, did He give *him* some pre-eminence? ' Belike he
made him a cardinal; and it might be full well be, for they have
followed Judas ever since.'[191] As for the argument itself, Latimer
returns to ordinary experience to refute it:

> I dare say there is never a wherryman at Westminster bridge
> but he can answer to this, and give a natural reason of it. He
> [Christ] knoweth that one man is able to shove the boat, but
> one man was not able to cast out the nets; and therefore he said
> in the plural number, *Laxate retia*, ' Loose your nets '; and he
> said in the singular number to Peter, ' Launch out the boat '.
> Why? Because he was able to do it. But he spake the other in
> the plural number, because he was not able to convey the boat,
> and cast out the nets too; one man could not do it. This would
> the wherryman say, and that with better reason, than to make
> such a mystery of it, as no man can spy but they.[192]

Similarly, dealing with the Catholic apology for the immunity of
the clergy, Latimer declares:

[190] *Sermons*, pp. 205–6.   [191] Ibid. pp. 210–11.
[192] Ibid. p. 211.

And to maintain this they alleged many scriptures as thus, *Nolite tangere Christos meos*; which is ' Touch not mine anointed or consecrated people ' [1 Chron. xvi. 22].

Which words the Lord spake by the Israelites in Egypt, warning king Pharao to leave and cease from persecuting the Israelites: and it maketh as much for our clergy's immunity and proveth it as well, as if a man alleged, *Quem terra pontus*, to prove that an ape hath a tail.[193]

Sometimes the accommodations of the Reformers consist merely of the general application of Scripture texts to a contemporary situation, as when Latimer applies a passage on the character of a king from Deuteronomy (Deut. xvii. 14–20) to the youthful Edward VI in the first two of the ' Seven Sermons '.[194] However, in certain cases, although the theory may be quite different, the actual effect of the use of accommodation approaches the old type of allegory.[195] Thus Lever expounding the miraculous feeding of the multitude with the five barley loaves and two small fishes (John vi. 5–14) applies it to England; the king is equated with Christ, the nobles with the Apostles, and the people with the multitude.[196] Philip becomes those members of the Council who say that it is hard to make provision for the people, and tempt the king to live a life of ease ' in hauking, hunting, or gamnyng '.[197] Andrew represents those who put the good of the common people before their own advantage and who say: ' Here is a boye: Here be seruantes and retainers of ours, which haue fyue loaues and two fyshes, many benefyces, some prebendes, with dyuers offices: yea, and some of vs ourselues haue mo offyces then we can discharge. Pleaseth it your maiestie to take these into your handes, which haue ben kepte for vs, that they nowe in this great nede, may be better disposed amongst your people. *Quid hoc inter tantos?* '[198] The counsel of Judas is not mentioned in the parable; so, says Lever, let not the king listen to covetous councillors.[199] The people sat down to be fed, so those who are peaceful receive God's blessings, but those who are ' vnpacient, vnquiet, and full of busynesse ' suffer His vengeance.[200] The Apostles ministered to the people before gather-

---

[193] Ibid. p. 297. Richard Kedermyster, Abbot of Winchcomb, Gloucestershire, alleged this text in support of Benefit of Clergy in a debate of divines, following his Paul's Cross Sermon in 1515. (See G. Burnet, *The History of the Reformation of the Church of England*, ed. N. Pocock, 7 vols., (Oxford, 1865) vol. I, p. 40.
[194] *Sermons*, pp. 87–128.
[195] This point has been made by Maurice Evans in an article, ' Metaphor and Symbol in the Sixteenth Century,' *E.C.*, iii. 3 (1953) pp. 268–76.
[196] *Sermons*, p. 59.   [197] Ibid. pp. 71–2   [198] Ibid. pp. 72–4.
[199] Ibid. pp. 73–4.   [200] Ibid. p. 75.

ing up the crumbs, so should the nobles minister to the people, each one in his own vocation, before gathering rents and taxes from them.[201] Finally, Christ converted more by His miracles than by His preaching, so ' a meane learned person, keping an house in his parysh, and kepynge of godly conuersacion, shall perswade and teach mo of his parishioners with communicacion at one meale, than the best lerned doctor of diuinite keping no house, can perswade or teache in his parish by preaching a dosen solemne sermons ',[202] and similarly, ' the gentle man that kepeth a good house in his countrey, shall be in better credit with the people for his liberalitie, than the best oratour or lawyer in England, for all his eloquence.'[203]

Even more like the old manner of allegory is Hooper's treatment of Jonah. At the outset of his series of sermons he explains to his audience, that he has undertaken the interpretation of this prophet for two causes:

> The one, to declare unto the king's majesty and his most honourable council, that the doctrine we preach unto his majesty's subjects is one and the same with the prophets' and the apostles', and as old as the doctrine of them both, and not new as the papists, and new learned men of papistry, would bear the people in hand. The second cause is to declare which ways the sinful world may be reconciled unto God.[204]

From this approach it follows that he ' gathers ' from the ancient story the Lutheran scheme of salvation and various points against Catholic doctrines, as well as some general moral instruction. From God's anger against Nineveh (Jonah i. 2) we learn that God sees and is displeased with sin; that the people must amend or perish when the preacher comes, but that God is patient with sinners.[205] From the mariners' fear during the tempest (Jonah i. 5) we learn the state of those who lack faith,[206] while from Jonah's sleep (Jonah i. 5) we learn ' that when we think ourselves most at rest, then be we most in danger ' and also we are shown ' the nature of sin: '[207]

> While it is a committing, the prick and danger thereof is not felt, but it delighteth rather man. . . . And because God out of hand punisheth not our sin, the devil bewitcheth our minds and wits, and beareth us in hand that he will never punish, and that God seeth not our sin, nor is not so grievously offended with our sins. So yet sleepeth the sin at this day, of them that

[201] Ibid. p. 84.   [202] Ibid. p. 88.
[203] Ibid.   [204] Early Writings, p. 445.   [205] Ibid. pp. 449–50.
[206] Ibid. p. 453.   [207] Ibid. p. 454.

persecute God and his holy word; the sins of false or negligent bishops and priests, the sin of the corrupt judges, and seditious people: but it will awake one day, as ye may read Gen. iv and here by our Jonas. At the hour of our death sin will awake and with our own sin the devil will kill us eternally, except we awake betimes.[208]

The mariner's request that Jonah should pray to his God (Jonah i. 6) declares, says Hooper, that:

> . . . all idolatry and superstitious persons think one God to be stronger than the other; as it is to be seen in papistry at this present day, whereas it is disputed which lady is best, our lady of Bullayne, or our lady of Rome; Saint James in Italy, or Saint James at Compostella. Farther this text declareth that idolaters always seek new gods, where as their old god deceiveth them. So is it among Christians; when the matter is plain desperate, they lot the matter between three or four idolatrical pilgrimages which one of them shall be the patron of his health. Where as the word of God is known, there is no suit but unto God by the mediation of Christ, beside whom there is no health.[209]

Just as the captain of the ship found Jonah, the cause of the trouble (Jonah i. 7), so must the king and Council search out trouble-makers within the ship of the state.[210] Jonah's confession ' I am a Hebrew ' (Jonah i. 9) means for the audience ' I am a Christian and will forsake my sin '.[211] The mariners rebuked Jonah for leaving his mission (Jonah i. 10), so the leaving of preaching is worthy of the rebuke of all men.[212] Jonah's ' take me and cast me into the sea ' (Jonah i. 12) shows how the penitent judges himself worthy of pain and punishment,[213] while the act of the mariners in throwing Jonah into the sea (Jonah i. 15)[214] shows that although both the good and the bad are afflicted in the world,[215] the good are amended and the evil ' apeyred '[216] [made worse]. The belief of the Ninevites in God (Jonah iii. 5) allows Hooper to introduce his beliefs about Holy Communion;[217] their fasting, his ideas on the reasonable subjection of the body of the soul,[218] and their repentance, to declare that penitence consists of outward signs of heaviness, calling upon the Lord, leaving a wicked and accustomed evil life, and trust and confidence in God's mercy.[219] The gourd which springs up, and is

---

[208] Ibid.   [209] Ibid. pp. 454–5.
[210] Ibid. pp. 458–62.   [211] Ibid. pp. 469–70.   [212] Ibid. pp. 470–1.
[213] Ibid. pp. 471–2.   [214] Ibid. pp. 480–3.   [215] Ibid. pp. 490–1.
[216] Ibid. p. 509.   [217] Ibid. pp. 513–37.   [218] Ibid. pp. 538–9.
[219] Ibid. pp. 539–45.

shortly destroyed (Jonah iii. 6–7), is the symbol of the vanity of earthly things,[220] while God's rebuke of the prophet for sorrowing over the loss of a plant, and yet willing the destruction of a great city (Jonah iii. 9–11) leads to the ' general and universal doctrine, that God will save all penitent sinners, 1 Tim. ii ', and the corollary that true repentance necessitates restitution to God and man.[221] While this interpretation is doubtless nearer to the text than that of Fisher noticed earlier,[222] nevertheless it does start with a theological position which it proceeds to find in the words of the sacred writer; it is very far removed from anything resembling the later ' higher criticism '.

It is interesting also to notice that Latimer, while he will not admit pro-Catholic allegories, nevertheless introduces anti-Catholic accommodations. Thus he draws a parallel between the Pharisees and the monks and ' hollow-hearted papists ',[223] while those who were asleep when the enemy came and sowed tares (Matt. xiii. 25) are the ' bishops and prelates, the slothful and careless curates and ministers: they with their negligence give the devil leave to sow his, for they sow not their seed, that is they preach not the word of God; they instruct not the people with wholesome doctrine; and so they give place to the devil to sow his seed '.[224] Similarly, the labourers who murmur against the Lord of the vineyard because those hired late in the day receive the same wage as they do, are the ' merit-mongers, which esteem their own work so much, that they think heaven scant sufficient to recompense their good deeds; namely for putting themselves to pain with saying of our lady's psalter, and gadding on pilgrimage and such-like trifles '.[225]

There are finally, in Latimer, certain older elements, stemming doubtless from the fact that he belongs to the first generation of the Reformers. Unhistorically he calls Jairus a ' churchwarden ',[226] as Fisher had spoken of Uriah as a knight.[227] Also, in the older style of allegory, the giants who infested the world before the Flood (Gen. vi. 4) represent ' covetousness ',[228] while the incident of the calming of the storm by Christ when He was in a ship with the disciples (Matt. viii. 23–6) deals with ' the congregation of Christ and his church. The disciples being in the ship are preserved by Christ: so

---

[220] Ibid. pp. 552–3.   [221] Ibid. pp. 553–8.
[222] Cf. *ante*, pp. 12–13.   [223] *Sermons*, p. 287.
[224] *Remains*, p. 189. Cf. St. John Chrysostom, ' In Matt. Hom. xlvi al. xlvii,' *P.G.* lviii. 475–6. *Glossa Ordinaria*, *P.L.*, cxiv. 132; St. Thomas Aquinas, *Catena Aurea* [St. Augustine, ' Liber Unus Quaest. XVII in Matt. 11 '] *Opera Omnia*, vol. XI, p. 170.
[225] *Remains*, p. 220.   [226] *Sermons*, p. 533.   [227] Cf. *ante*, p. 11.
[228] *Sermons*, p. 245.

all those which are in the church of Christ shall be saved and preserved by him. The others, which are without this church, shall be damned and perish.'[229] From the miracle at Cana, we may learn that:

> when Christ is bidden to our marriage, there shall lack nothing; for he will turn the sour water into sweet wine. For water signifieth all such anguishes, calamities and miseries as happen by marriages: and all such kind of water, that is, all such calamities and miseries, he turned into wine; that is he sendeth comfort, he sendeth his Spirit, that maketh those miseries, that were before very bitter, most sweet and pleasant, the same spirit of God comforteth the heart, and keepeth it from destruction. Also, we may learn here by this marriage to keep a good order in our business: here, as one appointed had the oversight of all, so we may not let everybody be rulers; but to keep good order in all our business, let some rule, and some be ruled.[230]

Again, Latimer does not hestitate to quote medieval authorities if they give interpretations which suit his purpose, although indeed he expresses surprise at finding such expositions in these authors. Thus he adduces Nicholas Gorrham's comment that the eagerness of the crowd which rushed to hear Our Lord preach (Luke v. 1) contrasted with the tepidity of the Scribes and Pharisees who neglected Him, parallel the simple devotion of the lay-folk contrasted with the mediocre piety of the clergy.[231] Similarly, in a characteristically racy passage, Latimer quotes in support of the principle of the sufficiency of Scripture, a comment of Dionysius Carthusianus on ' He sat down and taught the people out of the ship ' (Luke v. 3), a place where we are told that Christ instructed the people without being given an account of this particular discourse:

> Oh, there is a writer hath a jolly text here, and his name is Dionysius. I chanced to meet with his book in my lord of Canterbury's library: he was a monk of the Charterhouse. I marvel to find such a sentence in that author. What taught Christ in this sermon? Marry, saith he, it is not written. And he addeth more into it; *Evangelistae tantum scripserunt de sermonibus et miraculis Christi quantum cognoverunt, inspirante Deo, sufficere ad aedificationem ecclesiae ad confirmationem fidei, et ad salutem animarum.* It is true, it is not written; all his miracles were not written, so neither were all his sermons written: yet for all that, the evangelists did write so much as was necessary. 'They wrote

---

[229] *Remains*, p. 182.   [230] Ibid. p. 165.   [231] *Sermons*, pp. 199–200.

so much of the miracles and sermons of Christ as they knew by God's inspiration to be sufficient for the edifying of the church, the confirmation of our faith, and the health of our souls.' If this be true, as it is indeed, where be unwritten verities? I marvel not at the sentence, but to find it in such an author. Jesus! what authority he gives to God's word! But God would that such men should be witness with the authority of his book, will they, nill they.[232]

III

THE PREACHERS OF MARY'S REIGN (1553–1558)

Before the restoration of Catholicism in England under Mary, the Council of Trent had in 1546 promulgated its decree on Holy Scripture. This states that the Church, following the examples of the orthodox Fathers, receives and venerates with an equal affection of piety and reverence all the books both of the Old and the New Testament, seeing that one God is the author of both; and also that the unwritten traditions are similarly received, as well those appertaining to faith as to morals.[233] Furthermore, it is proclaimed that the Synod:

> in order to restrain petulant spirits . . . decrees that no-one, relying on his own skill, shall—in matters of faith and of morals pertaining to the edification of Christian doctrine— wresting the sacred Scriptures to his own senses, presume to interpret the said sacred Scripture contrary to that sense which holy mother Church—whose it is to judge of the true sense and interpretation of the holy Scripture—hath held and doth hold; or even contrary to the unanimous consent of the Fathers . . .[234]

In the light of this statement it is not surprising to find James Brooks, Master of Balliol College Oxford, and shortly to be Bishop of Gloucester in succession to Hooper, declaring in a sermon at Paul's Cross at the beginning of the reign:

> . . . our mother the holie catholike Churche in that shee hath to her milke the true sence of the worde of God, shee hath likewise aucthorite to iudge & decide all matiers of controuersy in religion. For if the scripture of tholde lawe in Moses tyme was not made the highe iudge of controuersies (beying a thing it selfe in diuerse pointes called in controuersie) but aucthorite of Iudgement was giuen alwaies by goddes owne mouth to the

---

[232] Ibid. pp. 209–10.
[233] *The Canons and Decrees of the Sacred and Oecumenical Council of Trent*, tr. J. Waterworth (London, 1888) p. 18.
[234] Ibid. p. 19.

E

learned, and elders of the Sinagog, to whose iudgement all
were bounde to stande, and that vnder peine of present deth, as
appeareth in the booke of Deuteronomi [see Deut. xvii. 8–13], if
we Christians will not be counted in woorse state, and condicion,
then the Iewes were, nedes must we graunt to the catholike
Churche like aucthorite of Iudgement for the decision of al
controuersies in our Religion: whome if God didde not assist
euermore, with the true intelligence of Scripture, then should
the scripture stande the Church in as good stede as a paier of
spectacles shoulde stand a blynde Frier.[235]

Similarly Cardinal Pole, in his vernacular homilies, indeed approves
of the desire of laymen to study Scripture, but, he warns:

God forbedd that it should be permitted to all such that
show this desyr, to satisfye the same by what meanes they lyke
and think best themselffes: for this desyr must be directed, and
the wytt of man that seeketh and coueteth knowledge must be
limited; which, because it is nott, all these disordres and
inconuienences doth follow that we daylie do see.[236]

The laity should remember that if they have the Scriptures in their
hands, which the Church ' hath approued and geuen vnto ' them,
they ought to heed the interpretation of their father the Pope and
their mother the Church. ' You should nott', the Cardinal urges his
audience, ' be your owne masters, whiche were as much to make
yourselffes father and mother to your self. But that as you take the
booke of your mothers hand so also to take the interpretatyon of the
same of your mother and father and nott of yourselffe.'[237]

Further, says Pole, the student of Scripture must be grounded
in Catholic doctrine before approaching the sacred text: he ' must
learne besyde the booke, and wythout booke, afore he com to the
reading of Scripture, or at leaste whilest he readeth it; or ellse
reading shall profyte hym lyttle to take those fruytes of Scripture
that the prophet . . . sayd were *Desiderabiles super aurum et lapidem
preciosum multum, et dulciores super mel et fauum*.[238] [See Ps. xviii. 11
(Vg.)]. For, as St. James describes Scripture itself—*Quae autem
desursum est sapientia primum quidem pudica est, deinde pacifica, modesta,
suadibilis, bonis consentiens, plena misericordia et fructibus bonis, non
iudicans, sine simulatione*—[James iii. 17: ' But the wisdom, that is
from above, first indeed is chaste, then peaceable, modest, easy to be

---

[235] *A sermon very notable, fruictefull, and Godlie, made at Paules crosse the xii daie of
Nouembre, in the first yere of the gracious reigne of our Souereigne ladie Quene Marie* . . . *by
Iames Brokis Doctor of Diuinitie*, (London, 1553) sig. Biv[v]–v[r].
[236] MS. Vat Lat. 5968, f. 416[r]. (There is a microfilm of this manuscript in the
Bodleian Library.)
[237] Ibid. f. 427[r].   [238] Ibid. ff. 428[v]–9[r].

persuaded, consenting to the good, full of mercy and good fruits, without judging, without dissimulation ', Douay] so the Scripture scholar:

> shuld bryng wyth hym, *animum pudicum*, *deinde pacificum*, *modestum in moribus*, and nott contentiouse in wytt, but *saudibilis*, agreeing euer to the beste sorte; and as touching his works they must be full of mercyfull dedes and good fruits, makeng hymselfe no iudge of what he heareth of this doctrine, but receiue it in simplicity wythout all dissimulation . . . wherebye we may perceiue that it is nott so muche readeng that maketh vs good scholers or masters to learne or teache scripture, butt that this lesson learned wythout booke is it that healpeth vs moste to that end.[239]

Stubborn pride in private judgement will never bring a right understanding of Scripture, nor is diligence in reading of any avail, unless the student becomes humble like those ' that Scripture itself doth signifie vnto vs to be furthest from wytt, and most vnlike to get things furth by dilligence of readeng, which be *paruuli*, that is to saye, lyttle babes '.[240] So, declares the Cardinal: he ' who wyll take fructe of Scripture other by readeng or heareng the wordes thereof, or ells by any declaration made thereupon, he must furst be made *paruulus*, without the whiche Scripture is not onelie vnprofitable but it is noysome and perniciouse '.[241] The teacher of Scripture must be duly called to this office by the Church; even Our Lord ' made himself no open preachour and teachour, nor yett priuate afore he was called therunto, afore the father himselfe declared him what he was, and dyd bid all men to heare him.'[242] However, men can be saved without reading Scripture, ' as the moste parte of Christen men be '[243]—and, says the Cardinal, ceremonies give more light than the disobedient reading of Scripture; while the prime way to God is not by reading, but by the taking away of sins in Penance.[244]

Other preachers of Mary's reign stress the importance of the Church's interpretation; Thomas Watson, Master of St. John's College Cambridge and Dean of Durham, Bishop of Lincoln from 1556, declares:

> The scripture without the consent of the church is a weapon as mete for an heretike as for a catholike, for Arius, Nestorius, and such other heretikes dyd alledge the scripture for their

---

[239] Ibid. f. 431ʳ.   [240] Ibid. f. 435ʳ.   [241] Ibid. f. 435ᵛ.   [242] Ibid. f. 430ᵛ.
[243] Ibid. f. 431ʳ.
[244] ' Cardinal Pole's speech to the citizens of London, in behalf of religious houses,' in John Strype, *Ecclesiastical Memorials*, 6 vols. (Oxford, 1822) vol. III, pt. 2, 'A Catalogue of Originals,' no. LXVIII, pp. 503–4.

opinions, as the catholikes did: but theyr alledging was but the abusyng of the letter, whiche is indifferent to good and euil, & deprauinge of the true sense, which is only knowen by the tradition and consent of the catholike church: so that the one without the other is not a direction, but a seduction to a simple man, because the very scripture in dede, is not the bare letter, as it lieth to be taken of euery man, but the true sense, as it is delyuered by the vniuersal consent of Christes churche.[245]

Similarly, John Harpesfield, Archdeacon of London, in one of the homilies set forth by Edmund Bonner, Bishop of London, adduces the testimony of Scripture and St. Irenaeus against private interpretation.[246]

Following from this position, it is not surprising to find that in the two sets of dogmatic homilies of the reign, Bonner's[247] and Watson's,[248] Scripture is not so much expounded for itself, as used as an arsenal of illustrative texts to illuminate and confirm Catholic doctrine. In these sermons ' the Faith ' is preached with occasional reference to the Bible; there is no attempt at general exegesis of any portions of Scripture.

In the exegesis actually given in the sermons of this reign, literal interpretation does not predominate. With the exception of Edgeworth's last three sermons on St. Peter's first Epistle, belonging to a series begun in Henry VIII's reign,[249] I have not found consecutive literal exposition in the sermons of this time. In a Paul's Cross sermon by Hugh Glasier, one of Mary's chaplains, there is indeed no allegorical interpretation, and the story of the Publican and the Pharisee who went to the Temple to pray (Luke xviii. 9–14; the Gospel for Trinity XI) is applied in a straightforward fashion to the England of the day,[250] but this is not typical of the majority of the sermons of this period.

[245] *Twoo notable sermons, made the thirde and fyfte Fridayes in Lent last past, before the Quenes highness, concerninge the reall presence of Christes body and bloude in the blessed Sacrament: and also the Masse, which is the sacrifice of the newe Testament* (London, 1554) sig. Bvii[r].

[246] *A profitable and necessarye doctryne, with certayne homelies adioyned thervnto set forth by the reuerende father in God, Edmonde, byshop of London,* (London, 1555)—'An Homelye declaring how the redemption in Chryst is appliable to vs,' ff. 19[r]-20[r]: Harpesfield alleges 2 Pet. i. 19–21, and iii. 16–17; 2 Tim. iii. 14, and St. Irenaeus, *Contra Haereses,* lib. III, cap. iv, *P.G.,* vii. 855–7. Polemic against indiscriminate and disobedient reading of Scripture is also to be found in the tract by J. Standish, *A discourse wherein is debated whether it be expedient that the scripture should be in English for al men to reade that wyll,* 2nd edn. (London, 1555).

[247] As above, n. 246.

[248] *Holsome and Catholyke docrtyne concerninge the seuen Sacraments of Chrystes Churche . . . set forth in the maner of short sermons to bee made to the people,* (London, 1558).

[249] See *ante,* p. 33, n. 144.

[250] *A notable and very fruictefull sermon made at Paules crosse the xxv day of August . . . .* (London, 1555).

On the contrary, the interpretation which we find in the preachers of Mary's reign is frequently allegoric in the manner of the Old Learning, although it eschews the extravagances of some of the late medieval examples already noticed.[251] Thus much use is made of Old Testament ' types '; Hugh Weston, Dean of Westminster, refers to the restoration of Catholicism as ' rebuilding the walls of Jerusalem ';[252] while Brooks enumerates the figures of the Church: the Bride of the Canticles whom Christ calls *amica mea, formosa mea columba mea* (Can. iv. 1); the chaste turtle-dove who will receive no other mate (Can. vi. 9); the mother of all the faithfull (Gal. iv. 26); the garden so enclosed that no wild boar may easily enter and destroy the flowers (Can. iv. 12); the vineyard which brings forth sweet wine (Isa. v. 1–2); the well-spring of clear water running to give everlasting life (Can. iv. 15); the keeper of the carcass (truth) to which the eagles (the doctors) repair (Matt. xxiv. 28); the pillar of truth (1 Tim. iii. 15); the mystical body (Coloss. i. 18); the seamless coat of Christ (John xix. 23); the hen which keeps her chickens safe under her wings (Matt. xxiii. 37) and Noah's ark (Gen. vii) within which ' is life and safetie ', but outside of which ' is present death & drowning '.[253] Similarly, the figures of the Mass, the Paschal Lamb (Exod. xii) and the incident of Melchizedek bringing forth bread and wine (Gen. xiv. 18) are referred to by Watson[254] and by Leonard Pollard, Prebendary of Worcester.[255] John Harpesfield declares that there are two commonwealths in Scripture, that of the Jews and that of the Christians, the latter being foreshadowed by the

---

[251] Cf. *ante*, pp. 3–8.
[252] ' Magistri Hugonis Westoni, decani Westmonasterii, oratio, coram patribus et clero in synodo congregatis habita,' in Strype, *Ecclesiastical Memorials*, III. 2, ' Catalogue of Originals,' no. VIII, p. 187.
[253] *A sermon very notable, fruictefull, and Godlie*, sig. Ciii⌄–Cv⌄. Cf. [on Can. iv. 1] *Glossa Ordinaria*, P.L., cxiii. 1146, Hugh of St. Cher, *T.B., cum post Hug. Card.*, vol. III, sig. s2⌄; [on Can vi. 8 Vg.] *Glossa Ordinaria*, P.L., cxiii. 1159, *Nicolai de Lyra postilla*, in *T.B., cum gloss. ord.*, etc., vol. III, f. 364⌄, Hugh of St. Cher, op. cit., vol. III, sig. t6⌄; [on Gal. iv. 26] *Glossa Ordinaria*, P.L., cxiv. 158; [on Can. iv. 12] *Glossa Ordinaria*, P.L., cxiii. 1150, Hugh of St. Cher, op. cit., vol. III, sig. t1ʳ; [on Isa. v. 1–2] Hugh of St. Cher, op. cit., vol. IV, sig. b5⌄; [on Can. iv. 15] *Glossa Ordinaria*, P.L., cxiii. 1151, Hugh of St. Cher, op. cit., vol. III, sig. t2ʳ; in the case of 1 Tim. iii. 15 and Coloss. i. 18, Scripture itself refers to the Church; cf. [on John xix. 23] *Glossa Ordinaria*, P.L., cxiv. 121; [on Gen. vi] *Glossa Ordinaria*, P.L., cxiii. 105–6, *Glossa Interlinearis*, in *T.B., cum gloss. ord.*, etc., vol. I, f. 50⌄, Hugh of St. Cher, op. cit., vol. I, sig. b7⌄, [and on Gen. vii] ibid., sig. c1⌄.
[254] *Twoo notable sermons*, sig. Oiv̇ʳ.
[255] *Fyue homilies of late made by a ryght good and vertuous clerke, called master Leonarde Pollarde, prebendary of the Cathedrall Churche of Woster* . . . (London, 1556) sig. Eiʳ–Ei⌄, as marked; counting from the first page, sig. Fiiʳ–Fii⌄. (See Bibliography, p. 353.) For these interpretations cf. [on Exod. xii. 2–4] *Glossa Ordinaria*, P.L., cxiii. 217; [on Gen. xiv. 18] *Glossa Ordinaria*, P.L., cxiii. 120. *Glossa Interlinearis*, in *T.B., cum gloss. ord.*, etc., vol. I, f. 64ʳ.

former.[256] Thus he speaks of the passage of the Red Sea (Exod. xiv) as a figure of Baptism,[257] and (like Fisher) of Moses and Aaron as types of Christ and St. Peter.[258] Again, Harpesfield declares that in the Old Testament, God appeared to men under different forms; as with two angels to Abraham, when all seemed like men (Gen. xviii), or to Moses as fire (Exod. iii); while to Christians Jesus Christ, God and Man, appears under the forms of bread and wine in the Blessed Sacrament.[259] For Cardinal Pole, Jacob's ladder (Gen. xxviii. 12) is a figure of the Church, with the Apostolic Succession of pastors ascending to Christ Himself.[260] He builds an entire homily upon Psalm cxxi (Vg.) *Laetatus sum*, in which he finds that David had a vision of the Church under the ' type ' of the house of God or of Jerusalem.[261] In a city there is unity among the citizens (v. 3), so in the Church there is unity of faith and government: Our Lord is the builder of the celestial Jerusalem, the Church, while the foundation stone is St. Peter, the first Pope: the tribes went up to the terrestial Jerusalem (v. 4), so do all, both Jews and Gentiles, come into the Church.[262] The ' seats of judgement ' (v. 5) in the Church are the powers of binding and loosing given to her officers,[263] while Christ the builder perpetually prays for the peace and prosperity of His city[264] (cf. vv. 6–9). Not all the citizens however, adds the Cardinal, enjoy the benefits of citizenship, only those who fight concupiscence, and after a fall in the spiritual combat, rise again by Penance, participate fully in the joys won for them by Our Lord.[265]

Apart from using typology, these preachers of Mary's reign allegorize the verbal expression of Scripture. ' To awaken out of sleep ' (Rom. xiii. 11) is, for Stephen Gardiner, Bishop of Winchester, to leave both worldly things, and the late schism;[266] ' better a live dog than a dead lion ' (Eccles. ix. 4) means for John White,

---

[256] *A notable and learned Sermon or Homilie, made vpon Saint Andrewes daye last past* 1556 *in the Cathedral churche of S. Paule in London* . . . (London, 1556) sig. Av[r].

[257] Ibid. sig. Avi[r]. Cf. *Glossa Ordinaria, P.L.,* cxiii. 225; Hugh of St. Cher, *T.B., cum post. Hug. Card.,* vol. I, sig. m1[r].

[258] *A notable and learned Sermon vpon Saint Andrewes daye,* sig. Aviii[r]. See. *ante,* p. 17.

[259] 'An Homelye of Transubstantiation,' in Bonner's *A profitable and necessarye doctryne, with certayne homelies adioyned thervnto,* f. 58[r].

[260] MS. Vat. Lat. 5968, ff. 302[v]–3[r].

[261] Ibid. f. 282[r]. Cf. *Glossa Ordinaria, P.L.,* cxiii. 1043.

[262] MS. Vat. Lat. 5968, ff. 282[v]–4[v].

[263] Ibid. ff. 285[v]–6[r]. Cf. *[Pauli Burgensis] Additio, T.B., cum gloss. ord.,* etc., vol. III, f. 278[v].

[264] MS. Vat .Lat. 5968, f. 287[r].   [265] Ibid. ff. 288[r]–90[v].

[266] *Excertpa per R.D. Archdiac. Cantuariensis ex Concione quam Reverendus D. Episcopus Vintoniensis Cancellarius Regni Angliae habuit prima Dominica Adventus Londini in Coemeterio D. Pauli in maxima populi frequentia presentibus serenis. Rege, & Reverendo Legato,* (Rome, 1555) sig. Aii[r].

who succeeded Gardiner in the see of Winchester, 'Better is one lively preacher in the church, that dareth to bark against sin, blasphemy, heresy; better is one lively officer or magistrate in the commonweal, that dareth to speak against injuries, extortions, seditions, rebellions and other discords, than the dead lion: that is to say, men, perhaps of great dignity and vocation, who dare not open their mouths and bark; but suffereth, while al goeth to ruin, to the decay of Christian religion, and the subversion of the public wealth.'[267]   Similarly White allegorizes *Vae autem praegnantibus et nutrientibus in illis diebus! Orate autem ut non fiat fuga vestra in hieme vel sabbato* (Matt. xxiv. 19–20: 'Woe to them that are with child, and that give suck in those days. But pray that your flight be not in the winter, or on the sabbath', Douay); for he says, referring to Queen Mary, who died in December, that this

> saying if it be literally to be taken, in what case is this good lady, which is like now in winter, and this very day, being the shortest day of all the year, to be buried, and creap into the ground. For an answer, understand, Right Honourable, that winter here mentioned consisteth not in cold weather, short days, and long nights, but in cold zeal and affection, and in short devotion towards God, and in cold love and charity towards our neighbours.[268]

Similarly, by the Sabbath we are to 'understand [not] therby the Sabboth-day of the Jews, which was al in supersticion, [but] vacation from good works with murmuring against the merciful and wonderful works of God'.[269]   Also, says the bishop, the Scripture seems to threaten 'women dying in child-bed. Among whom, nevertheless, an opinion hath obtained, that to dye *in the bond*, as they cal it, of *our Lady*, and travail of child, hath some furtherance to the favour of God's mercye, in consideration of the travail, pain and burden wherwith the mother dyeth. And of that opinion am I, and agree with them therein. . . .'[270]   So the solution is that Scripture here intends to refer to one who is 'great and puffed up with pride, replenished with wrath, malice, ambition and covetousness, that shal have *oculos adulterii plenos*, his eyes ful of concupiscence, his tongue swelling with words of blasphemy, al his mind and body ful

---

[267] 'A sermon preached at the funerals of Queen Mary: by the Bishop of Winchester,' in Strype, *Ecclesiastical Memorials*, III. 2, 'A Catalogue of Originals,' no. LXXXI, p. 544. Cf. Hugh of St. Cher, *T.B., cum post. Hug. Card.*, vol. III, sig. o3ʳ.
[268] 'A sermon preached at the funerals of Queen Mary,' pp. 548–9. Cf. *Glossa Ordinaria, T.B., cum gloss. ord.*, etc., vol. V, f. 74ʳ.
[269] 'A Sermon preached at the funerals of Queen Mary,' p. 549. Cf. *Glossa Ordinaria*, as in n. 268, above.
[270] 'A Sermon preached at the funerals of Queen Mary,' p. 549.

of thoughts and actions of sin and disobedience '.[271] Again, White interprets, in the light of Catholic dogma, a text from Ecclesiastes— *laudavi magis mortuos quam viventes et feliciorem utroque iudicavi qui necdum natus est* (Eccles. iv. 2–3 ' I praised the dead rather than the living: and I judged him happier than them both, that is not yet born', Douay)—which on the surface, he says, seems to be partly incredible and partly pagan. Although God saw that all He made was good, to be born in Original Sin is bad, and when Job cursed the day of his birth (Job. iii, esp. v. 3), what he cursed was birth in sin.[272] Further, the bishop continues:

> . . . I infer to have a being is not evil, but to be, as indeed Judas was, a traytor to this Maker, that is evil. To be born in Christ's church, and not to abide therein; to promise and not to perform; to promise penance here, and not to practise; to hear the truth, and not to believe; to be daily taught and never to learn; ever to be warned and never to beware; that is horrible, execrable, cursed, and damnable. I am born into this world to this end, to serve God, and to be saved. I shal be dampned, not because I was borne, but because I served not [God].[273]

Also, the state of those dead in Christ, is better than that of those struggling amongst the miseries of this temporal life.[274]

Finally, in these preachers of Mary's reign, there are several striking ' accommodations ' to be noticed. Brooks, taking the words of Jairus, ' my daughter is even now dead: but come and lay thy hand upon her and she shall live ' (Matt. ix. 18), informs his audience that:

> sithen it may bee doen without preiudice to the letter, for the aduancement of Gods worde, gods truth, gods glorie, and may make the more to edification, I intende by gods grace, at this present, tapplie the same in a mistical sence, as spoken of an other person, that is to wit, of our mother the holy catholike church, for the spiritual reviving of her spiritual doughter spiritually deceased, this particulare churche of Englande.[275]

God's reviving hand is now, says Brooks, in this happy time of Queen Mary laid upon the English Church.[276] Again, John Harpes-

[271] Ibid.
[272] Ibid. pp. 536–7. Cf. *Glossa Ordinaria*, P.L., cxiii. 759; Hugh of St. Cher, *T.B.*, *cum post. Hug. Card.*, vol. I, sig. mm2ᵛ–mm3ʳ.
[273] 'A Sermon preached at the funerals of Queen Mary,' pp. 537–8. Cf. *Glossa Ordinaria*, P.L., cxiii. 1121.
[274] 'A Sermon preached at the funerals of Queen Mary,' pp. 540–1. Cf. *Glossa Ordinaria*, as above, n. 273.
[275] *A sermon very notable, fruictefull, and Godlie*, sig. Aiiʳ.
[276] Ibid. sig. Iiiʳ. The Protestants said (rather unfairly) of this sermon, that in it Brooks likened himself to Jairus, England to his daughter, and Queen Mary to Christ. (See M. Maclure, *The Paul's Cross Sermons* 1534–1642, p. 196.)

field compares Mary not only to the Old Testament women liberators Judith, Esther, and Deborah, and to Mary in the Gospel, who ' chose the better part ' (Luke x. 42), as did the queen, by her choice of a godly life; but even to the Blessed Virgin herself, with whom being chosen too by God because of her virtues, she can sing: *Ecce ex hoc beatam me dicent omnes generationes quia fecit mihi magna qui potens est & sanctum nomen eius.*[277] In very different vein however, is Dr. Richard Smith's application of 1 Cor. xiii. 3 (' though I give my body to be burned, and have not charity, it profiteth me nothing ') to the burning of Latimer and Ridley at Oxford for heresy (1555) on the principle that ' the goodness of the cause, not the order of death makes the holiness of the person.'[278]

IV

THE ELIZABETHAN PREACHERS (1558–1603)

The theoretical position of the early Anglicans on scriptural interpretation is given by the controversialist William Whitaker, Master of St. John's College, Cambridge, in his disputation with Cardinal Bellarmine and Thomas Stapleton. First, he outlines the position of his opponents with its manifold ' senses ':

> The Jesuit [Bellarmine] divides all these senses into two species; the historic or literal, and the mystic or spiritual. He defines the historic or literal, as that which the words present immediately; and the mystic or spiritual, that which is referred to something besides what the words express; and this he says is either tropological, or anagogic or allegorical.[279]

Against this he sets the Anglican attitude:

> These things we do not wholly reject: we concede such things as allegory, anagoge, and tropology in scripture; but meanwhile we deny that there are many and various senses. We affirm that there is but one true, proper and genuine sense of scripture, arising from the words rightly understood, which we call the literal: and we contend that allegories, tropologies, and anagoges are not various senses, but various collections from one sense, or various applications and accommodations of that one meaning.[280]

[277] *Concio quaedam admodum elegans, docta, salubris, & pia, magistri Iohannis Harpesfeldi, sacrae Theologiae baccalaurie, habita coram patribus et clero in Ecclesia Paulina Londini.* 26 Octobris 1553, (London, 1553) sig. Aiii^r-v.

[278] Foxe, *Acts and Monuments*, vol. VII, p. 548.

[279] *A Disputation on Holy Scripture against the Papists, especially Bellarmine and Stapleton* tr. and ed. W. Fitzgerald. (Cambridge, 1849) P.S., p. 403.

[280] Ibid. p. 404.

Argument must be based only on the literal sense,[281] and while we should follow the Holy Spirit in our interpretation, the Church of England believes that He speaks to each devout reader, rather than to ' the Church' as the Council of Trent declares.[282] Also, adds Whitaker, the Roman ' consent of the Fathers ' is largely chimerical, for in fact, they seldom agree.[283]

This position (which is similar to that of Tyndale already noticed)[284] is taken later by the Puritan William Perkins, Fellow of Christ's College Cambridge, in *The Art of Prophecying*, his handbook for preachers. The preacher must, says Perkins, ' proceed to the reading of the Scriptures . . . using a grammaticall rhetoricall and logicall Analysis, and the helpe of the rest of the Arts '.[285] In interpretation, which is ' the *Opening* of the words and sentences of the Scripture, that one entire and naturall sense may appeare', there is ' one onely sense, and the same is the literall.' The Catholic ' four senses ' are once again dismissed, and ' applications ' substituted for them. Perkins, like Tyndale, stresses the importance of the ' analogie of faith ', and he points out the importance of the context of any text.[286] However, a ' crypticall or darke ' place in which the natural sense of the words disagrees with the analogy of faith, must be interpreted in some way which is in accordance with the analogy of faith, and ' clear places '.[287] Also, the figurative language of Scripture is to be paraphrased into the language of statement.[288]

These principles are most fully put into practice by the extreme Puritans who had before them also the example of the literal exegesis of Calvin.[289] Perkins himself, in his Lectures on the first three chapters of Revelation, gathers doctrines and ' uses ' immediately from the words of the inspired writer.[290] Similarly Thomas Cartwright, the notable Cambridge exponent of Presbyterian government for the Church of England, in his exposition of St. Paul's Epistle to the Colossians, having explained the occasion of the writing of the epistle, goes through each verse drawing out the literal meaning.[291] John Rainolds, Fellow and later President of Corpus Christi College Oxford, Dean of Lincoln from 1593–8, and

[281] Ibid. p. 409.   [282] Ibid. p. 410.   [283] Ibid. p. 414.   [284] Cf. *ante*, pp. 37–8.

[285] *The Works of that famous and worthy Minister of Christ in the Vniuersitie of Cambridge M. William Perkins*, 3rd. edn., 3 vols. (London, 1631) vol. II, p. 650.

[286] Ibid. p. 651.   [287] Ibid. p. 654.   [288] Ibid. pp. 656–7.

[289] See Farrar, *History of Interpretation*, pp. 342–54.

[290] *A godly and learned Exposition or Commentarie vpon the three first Chapters of the Revelation. Preached in Cambridge by that reverend and judicious Divine Mr. William Perkins, Anno Dom.* 1595 (*Works*, vol. III, pp. 207–370).

[291] *A Dilucidation, or Exposition of the Epistle of St. Paul the Apostle to the Colossians, delivered in sundry sermons*, ed. A. B. Grosart (Edinburgh, 1864).

chief speaker for the Puritans at the Hampton Court Conference of 1604, in his ' opening ' and application of the minor prophets Obadiah and Haggai, is concerned to give a clear rendering of the literal sense of the text.[292] Edward Deringe, a supporter of Cartwright, in his exposition of part of the Epistle to the Hebrews, preached when he was Divinity Reader at St. Paul's, expatiates freely on what he takes to be the follies and evils of Catholicism as his text provides occasion[293] while Anthony Anderson, for long Rector of Medbourne, Leicestershire, in his series of sermons on the *Nunc Dimittis* introduces many castigations of the frivolities and vices of the England of his day.[294]

Other preachers too, not extreme Calvinists, give a consecutive literal exposition of portions of Scripture, with lengthy applications. Edward Topsell, Rector of East Hoathly, Sussex, and later Perpetual Curate of St. Botolph's Aldersgate, author of two manuals of Zoology, uses the verses of Joel to introduce declamations on the shortcomings of his own generation.[295] George Abbot, Master of University College Oxford, and later to become Archbishop of Canterbury (1611), in his treatment of Jonah, follows the literal

---

[292] *The Prophecy of Obadiah opened and applied in sundry sermons,* ed. A. B. Grosart (Edinburgh, 1864). *The Prophecy of Haggai interpreted and applied in sundry sermons,* ed. A. B. Grosart, (Edinburgh, 1864).

[293] *XXVII Lectures or readings vpon part of the Epistle written to the Hebrues* (London, 1590): as sig. Giv[r], dealing with Heb. ii. 4 (' God also bearing them witness, both with signs and wonders, and with divers miracles, and gifts of the Holy Ghost, according to his own will ') Deringe hits at miracles in the Roman Church: 'A miracle made St. Peter to be crucified at Rome; for as Ambrose reporteth it, when he fled away, Christ met him at the gate, at whose sight Peter being astonished, talked with him, and perceiued that Christ wold haue him goe backe, and bee crucified, and so hee died at Rome: then because Ambrose saith: *Vbi Petrus, ibi ecclesia*: . . . euer since the Pope hath been head of the Church. When this was gotten by a miracle, then all things came apace by many miracles; wee learned *transubstantiation,* and the sacrifice of the Masse, praier for the dead, going a pilgrimage, holie water, holie bread, oyle, candles: to bee short, all and for euerie poynt of Poperie sundrie miracles done; yea the verie dregges of miracles in milke pans, and greasie dishes, by Robin Goodfellow, and Haggs, and Fayeries, all wrought somewhat for their idle superstitions, that at this day we should knowe their mysteries, by their lying wonder.' See too, for example, ibid. sig. Xii[r]–Xiii[r]; on Heb. v. 1, Deringe introduces polemic against the Mass, the doctrine of Mary as Mediatrix of Graces, and the intercession of the saints.

[294] *The Shield of our Saftie: Set foorth by A. Anderson, vpon Symeons sight, in hys Nunc dimittis,* (London, 1581)—as sig. Siv[r]–Tiv[v], on 'A light to lighten the Gentiles ' (Luke ii. 32) having adduced a concordant text, John iii. 19 ('And this is the condemnation, that light is come into the world, and men loved darkness rather than light, because their deeds were evil ') Anderson launches out into a tirade against the manifold sins of England.

[295] *Times lamentation: or An Exposition on the prophet Ioel, in sundry Sermons or Meditations* (London, 1599); as pp. 24–5, on Joel i. 2, (' Hear this, ye old men, and give ear, all ye inhabitants of the land,') Topsell introduces a complaint that preachers are disregarded: or pp. 113–14, on Joel i. 8, (' Lament like a virgin girded with sackcloth for the husband of her youth ') Topsell points out that our affections in heavenly things must be as passionate as in earthly—but how seldom this is so!

historical method; he suggests what plant the gourd (Jonah iv. 6 ff.) might have been,[296] and is generous in the provision of applications and illustrative narrations.[297] John King, too, Archdeacon of Nottingham, a Chaplain to the Queen, and later Bishop of London (1611), is interested in Jonah's gourd,[298] and quotes Pliny on the whale as a piece of information concerning natural history.[299]

Some of the Elizabethan preachers declaim against the Catholic theory of four-fold interpretation. John Chardon, of Exeter College Oxford, later to be Bishop of Down and Connor, inveighs against the denigration of the literal sense, as ' the dead letter ', together with the solemn citation of the glosses of the Doctors.[300] Thomas Drant, Chaplain to Edmund Grindal when Bishop of London, and Divinity Reader at St. Paul's, is particularly severe on the Vulgate, which he sees as the great source book of Roman errors:

> Touching the vulgar translation, that is the matrixe and conceptorie place of verie error, & ignorance. Hence *Dunce*, hence *Dorbell*, hence *Houlcotte*, *Bricot*, *Tapper*, *Capper*, *Ecchius*, *Pighius*, *Coclaeus*, and *Hofmeister* haue founde, and finde out many a fonde argument. Hence wrangle the Iesuites, hence wrastle the Sorbonistes, hence the horn of Rome is most loftilie exalted. This is thrust vpon the world by the Inquisitors of Spaine: dubbed onelie good and authenticall by the Council of Trent, and whosoeuer will not receyue this, he standeth accurssed from the face of the saide Councell, with the fierce thunder-bolt of Anathemysation. Besides that, this translation taketh away and addeth to the text, moe then many hundreds of words. There is no leafe throughout the whole Testament, but it hath in this translation some great and greeuous error. Whereas the Hebrue translation sayth: *Melchisedec protulit panem*, and so sayth *Ambrose, He brought forth bread*; Iosephus sayth, *He ministered bread*. The vulgar translation

---

[296] *An exposition upon the prophet Jonah*, ed. Grace Webster, 2 vols. (London, 1845) vol. II pp. 289–93. After much learned discussion Abbot decides for the plant *ricinus*, which the ' Christian philosophers and physicians of late time commonly term . . . *Palma Christi*, ...'
[297] As ibid. vol. I, pp. 10–11, on Jonah i. 2, Abbot introduces a passage on the value of preaching: pp. 176–7, on Jonah i. 15, he remarks that the mariners, according to the comment of St. Jerome, took up Jonah in an honourable manner, but alas! our preachers are not reverenced: vol. II, 132, on Jonah iii. 6, he introduces a vigorous complaint on the vanities of dress: vol. I, pp. 53–7, on Jonah i. 4, speaking of the power of evil spirits to raise storms, he gives some strange narrations of such occurrences.
[298] *Lectures upon Jonah, delivered at York, in the year of our Lord*, 1594, ed. A. B. Grosart (Edinburgh, 1864) p. 290.
[299] Ibid. p. 142.
[300] *Fulfordo et Fulfordae. A sermon Preached at Exeter in the Cathedrall Church, the sixth day of August commonly called Iesus day* 1594 . . . (London, 1595) p. 13.

sayth: *He offered vp bread*: and heere vpon they would deuise their Masse offertorie. The Hebrue translation sayth *Osculemini filium*: kisse the sonne. The vulgar translation *Apprehendite disciplinam*: Take ye discipline.[301]

Again, Drant refuses to accept a gloss complimentary to the religious orders on Can. vi. 2 (' My beloved is gone down into his garden, to the beds of spices, to feed in the gardens, and to gather lilies ') which equates the spices with monks, and the lilies with nuns.

   . . . first concerning that clause that he came among the beds of his spicerie, *Hugo*, *de Lira* and *Gilbertus*; and euen with as good iudgement might I, or any other call Lilies Nunnes, and so the great Misterie of Christes comming downe into the earth, and the absolute pleasaunce of his refreshing, should be abridged in this, that Christe sometimes kept within Monkes cloysters, and sometymes went abroade to gather vp Nunnes, and so then should be nothing but a sely cloysterer, and a sely Nunne gatherer: and so Monkes should be spice, and Nunnes lilies: Monkes should please the mouthe of the beloved, and Nunnes the nose of the beloved. But this to thinke, is to thinke a worlde of absurdities, and to be short and sharpe, *Lira*, *delirat*, and *Gilbardus est bardus*, *Lyra* doteth and *Gilbardus* is a dolt.[302]

However he does accept the gloss of St. Jerome on this verse, which is still allegoric, if less exclusive: ' But S. Hierome and the better sort thinke that the beds of spicery are most of all men that be Gods elect, that those be Gods spices, these be Gods Lilies and Gods flowers.'[303]

Many of the Elizabethan preachers whose exegesis is predominantly literal, nevertheless make moderate use of typology. Thus Thomas Becon, following traditional interpretation, states that the ass on which Our Lord rode into Jerusalem on Palm Sunday signifies the Jews, and the colt the Gentiles, both to be included in the Church.[304] John Foxe, the martyrologist, declares that Samson overwhelming the Philistines is a figure of Christ conquering the powers of darkness.[305] Thomas Holland, Rector of Exeter College

   [301] *Three godly and learned Sermons, very necessarie to be read and regarded of all men* . . . (London, 1584) sig. Biiᵛ–Biiiʳ.
   [302] Ibid. sig. Eiʳ. Cf. Hugh of St. Cher, *T.B.*, *cum post Hug.. Card.*, vol. III, sig. t6ʳ; *Nicolai de Lyra postilla*, in *T.B.*, *cum gloss. ord.*, etc., vol. III, f. 364ʳ.
   [303] *Three godly and learned Sermons*, sig. Eiᵛ.
   [304] *A new postil, conteinyng sermons vpon all the Sonday gospelles*, 2 vols. (London, 1566) vol. I, f. 5ʳ. Cf. the references given *ante*, p. 32, n. 139
   [305] *A sermon of Christ crucified preached at Paules Crosse the Friday before Easter, commonly called Goodfryday* (London, 1570) f. 41ʳ. Cf. on Judges xvi. 30, *Glossa Ordinaria*, P.L., cxiii. 532; on Judges xiv. 5, Hugh of St. Cher, *T.B.*, *cum post. Hug. Card.*, vol. I, sig. G8ʳ.

Oxford, and Regius Professor of Divinity, sees in the visit of the Queen of the South to Solomon (1 Kings x) the foreshadowing of the coming of the Gentiles to Christ,[306] while Edwin Sandys, successively Bishop of Worcester and London and Archbishop of York, follows traditional interpretation in taking the vineyard in the Canticles (e.g. Can. ix. 6) as a figure of the Church,[307] and the foxes which destroy the vines (Can. ii. 15) of her enemies.[308] John Jewel too, Bishop of Salisbury, in his predominantly expository sermons, occasionally makes use of types, which are however usually actually referred to as such in Scripture. ' God ', he declares, ' opened his mind sometimes not by words, but by some notable kind of deed; and the people heard God speak to them, not with their ears, but with their eyes.'[309] So the water from the rock (Exod. xvii. 6) is a figure of the blood of Christ (see 1 Cor. x. 4), the manna (Exod. xvi. 15) of His body (see John vi. 31, 49, 58; Rev. ii. 17) and the serpent of brass raised on the pole (Num. xxi. 9) of the crucifixion[310] (see John iii. 14). Just as the material Jericho was overthrown by Joshua (Josh. vi), so the spiritual Jericho, the forces of falsehood and evil, are destroyed by God.[311] Henry Smith, Lecturer at St. Clement Dane's, although his interpretation is usually literal, also makes occasional use of types. The serpent in Num. xxi. 8 ('And the Lord said unto Moses, Make thee a fiery serpent, and set it upon a pole: and it shall come to pass, that every one that is bitten, when he looketh upon it, shall live ') is a type of Christ,[312] while the repentance of the Ninevites at the word of Jonah (Jonah iii. 5–9) ' after that he had been three days and three nights in the whale's belly ', signifies ' the calling of the Gentiles by Christ, after he had been three days and three nights in the bowels of the earth '.[313]

---

[306] Πανηγυρις D. Elizabethae, Die gratia Angliae, Franciae, and Hiberniae Reginae. A sermon preached at Pauls in London the 17 of November Ann. Dom. 1599 . . . (Oxford, 1601). Cf. Glossa Ordinaria, P.L., cxiii. 601; Nicolai de Lyra postilla, in T.B., cum gloss. ord., etc., vol. II, f. 146ᵛ.

[307] Sermons by Archbishop Sandys, ed. J. Ayre (Cambridge, 1841) P.S., p. 57. Cf. Glossa Ordinaria, P.L., cxiii. 1131; Hugh of St. Cher, T.B., cum post. Hug Card., vol. III, sig. q4ʳ.

[308] Sermons, pp. 62–5. The Glossa Ordinaria and Hugh of St. Cher interpret the foxes as heretics. (P.L., cxiii. 1141, T.B., cum post. Hug. Card., vol. III, sig. r7ʳ.)

[309] The Works of John Jewel, Bishop of Salisbury, ed. J. Ayre, 4 vols. (Cambridge, 1845–50) P.S., vol. II, p. 968.

[310] Ibid. p. 969.

[311] Ibid. p. 970. Cf. Glossa Ordinaria on Josh. vi. 20, P.L., cxiii. 511; Nicolai de Lyra postilla, in T.B., cum gloss. ord., etc., vol. II, ff. 10ᵛ–11ʳ.

[312] The Sermons of Mr. Henry Smith Gathered into one Volume. . . . and the life of Mr. Henry Smith, by Tho. Fuller B.D. (London, 1657) p. 193.

[313] Twelve Sermons, preached by Mr. Henry Smith (London, 1657) p. 775; [the pagination of this volume is consecutive with that of The Sermons, referred to in the previous note]. See too ibid. pp. 678–82, (a catalogue of the types of the casting off of the Jews and

Again (as in the case of the preachers of Edward VI's reign), accommodations, resembling in effect the older type of allegory, are frequently found in the sermons of this time.[314] For example, one ' H.B. ' moralizes the golden image with the feet of clay (Dan. ii. 31–5) in this manner; [as the image was overthrown]:

Euen so all your golden heads, that is al your honours and great glorie: all your siluer shoulders, that is, all your beaute and your brauerie: all your brasse bellies, that is all your pleasures and worldly treasures: all your yron legges, that is all your strength, youth and health, all stands vpon earthie, clayie, fickle feet, and a little stroke of death shall hit vpon their earth and clay, and footing fails and downe fals al.[315]

Anthony Anderson, after a literal exposition of the Parable of the Unfruitful Figtree in the Vineyard (Luke xiii. 6–9) in which he points out that the figtree represents the Jews,[316] proceeds to apply this place to his audience. The figtree becomes England, set in the vineyard of the Universal Church,[317] and Anderson is enabled to speak of the fruits which Englishmen should bring forth, their short comings in this respect, and their need for amendment.[318]

The sermons of Richard Hooker, in many ways so individual, are saturated with citations from Scripture, usually simply alleged in their literal sense. These sermons exemplify the result of that deep and reverent reading of Scripture recommended by the Homily 'A fruitful Exhortation to the Reading of Holy Scripture ';[319] Hooker has indeed ' ruminated, and as it were chewed the cud of them ' and has obtained ' the sweet juice, spiritual effect, marrow, honey, kernel, taste, comfort, and consolation of them.'[320] However behind his interpretation lies ' the analogy of faith '. After subtle analysis he finds that Habbakuk has not lost justifying faith by declaring ' the law is slacked and judgement doth never go forth ';[321] (Hab. i. 4): by the use of the distinction between the righteousness of justification and the righteousness of sanctification he harmonises the *dicta*

the calling in of the Gentiles) and ibid. p. 762, (the goats brought to Aaron that he might cast lots to see which were to be killed as scapegoats and which spared [Lev. xvi. 8 ff.] as types of Christ).

---

[314] Cf. *ante*, pp. 44–7.

[315] *A verie profitable sermon preached before her Maiestie at the Court about xiij yeares since by H.B.* (London, 1593) pp. 18–19.

[316] *A sermon preached at Paules Crosse, the 23 of Aprill, being the Lords day, called Sonday*, (London, 1581) sig. Aiv^r.

[317] Ibid. sig. Bi^r.   [318] Ibid. sig. Cviii^v–Hv^v.   [319] See *ante*. pp. 41–2.

[320] *Certain Sermons Appointed by the Queen's Majesty.* 'A fruitful Exhortation to the Reading of Holy Scripture,' p. 10.

[321] *The Works of that Learned and Judicious Divine, Mr. Richard Hooker*, ed. J. Keble, 2nd. edn., 3 vols. (Oxford, 1841) vol. III, p. 469–81.

of St. Paul and St. James on faith and works (Rom. iv; Jas. ii), for, says Hooker:

> except there be an ambiguity in some term, St. Paul and St. James so contradict each other; which cannot be. Now there is no ambiguity in the name either of faith or of works, both being meant by them both in one and the same sense. Finding therefore that justification is spoken of by St. Paul without implying sanctification, when he proved that a man is justified by faith without works; finding likewise that justification doth sometimes imply sanctification also with it; I suppose nothing more sound, than so to interpret St. James as speaking not in that sense, but in this.[322]

Hooker finds also that the Roman glosses are erroneous, and sorrowfully exclaims: ' O that the church of Rome did as soundly interpret those fundamental writings whereupon we build our faith, as she doth willingly hold and embrace them!'[323] He himself will however admit anti-Roman glosses; ' God hath spoken by his angel from heaven concerning Babylon (by Babylon we understand the church of Rome): " Go out of her my people, that ye be not partakers of her sins, and that ye receive not of her plagues." '[324] (see Rev. xviii. 4.)

Not all the Elizabethan preachers however, follow the theory of Whitaker and Perkins. Thomas Playfere, Lady Margaret Professor of Divinity at Cambridge (although indeed he opposed in debate Dr. John Overall's ' popish ' views on purgatory)[325] frequently returns in his sermons to the old allegoric methods. He allegorizes poetic verbal expression: ' the heads of the dragons are broken in the waters ' (see Ps. lxxiv. 13), he interprets, ' very strong vile sins are weakened and washt away with teares '.[326] The ' lilies of the field ' (Matt. vi. 28) are, says Playfere, ' the millions of the angels; or of al those which lead a pure & an angelicall life.'[327] A simile from the Canticles, ' Thy two breasts are like two young roes that are twins, which feed among the lilies ' (Can. iv. 5), allows him to declare:

> The breasts of the Church are the two testaments; out of which we that are the children of the church, suck the pure milk of the word of God. These testaments feede among the lilies.

[322] Ibid. pp. 506–7.   [323] Ibid. p. 501.   [324] Ibid. p. 496.
[325] See H. C. Porter, *Reformation and Reaction in Tudor Cambridge*, pp. 404.
[326] *The whole sermons of That Eloquent Diuine of Famous Memory: Thomas Playfere, Doctor in Diuinitie* (London, 1623) ' The Meane in Mourning,' p. 10. For the pagination of this volume, see Bibilography, pp. 354–5.
[327] Ibid. ' Hearts Delight,' pp. 19–20.

Because they treate and discourse especially of Christ, who saies, I am the lilly of the valleyes. These testaments also are like two young roes that are twins, because twins (as we reade of Hippocrates twins) when they goe, they goe together, when they feede, they feede together. And after the same fashion, the two testaments, being the two breasts of the Church, goe together, like two young roes that are twins feeding among the lilies.[328] A vision of Zechariah, 'What are these two olive trees upon the right side of the candlestick and upon the left side thereof. . . . What be these two olive branches which through the two golden pipes empty the golden oil out of themselves?' (Zech. iv. 12–13) is interpreted by Playfere (after St. Jerome) as a figure of Christ shining in the hearts of men through the word (the two Testaments) with the oil of gladness and goodness.[329] The allegorical glosses of the Fathers are indeed much to Playfere's taste: St. Jerome is behind his exposition of Num. xxxiii. 9: 'and they removed from Marah, and came to Elim: and in Elim were twelve fountains of water and threescore and ten palm trees: and they pitched there ':

All the while they were in Marah, which signifieth bitterness, they saw no fountains, no palme tree. But when they came to Elim, which signifieth rams, then they found twelue fountaines and seauentie palme trees. This iourney of the Israelites did intimate thus much: That the Church of Christ should neuer leaue iourneying on forward, till it came from Marah to Elim. That is from the Iewes, whose mouthes are full of cursing and bitterness, to the Gentiles, which are the true flocke and sheepfold of Christ. Here, the Church findeth twelue fountaines, and seauenty palme trees, twelue apostles, and seauentie Disciples. Which twelue Apostles, as twelue fountaines, haue flowed more generally ouer the face of *all* the earth to renewe it, then Noahs flood did to destroy it. And the seauenty Disciples, seauentie palme trees, haue flourished and spread branches ouer *all* the world, so that, as the Psalmist speaketh. The hills are couered with the shadowe of them, and the boughs thereof are like goodly Cedar trees. [Ps. lxxx. 10].[330]

Even Philo is quoted on Gen. xxiii. 19: 'Abraham buried Sarah his wife in the cave of the field of Machpelah ':

The Patriarch Abraham buried Sarah in the caue of Macpelah, that is, in a double sepulchre. He that buries his minde

---

[328] Ibid. ' Difference between the Law and Gospell,' p. 230.
[329] Ibid. p. 231. Cf. St. Jerome, ' Comment. in Zachariam,' lib. I, cap. vi, *P.L.*, xxv. 1446.
[330] *The whole sermons*, ' Difference betweene the Law and Gospell,' pp. 237–9. Cf. St. Jerome, Epist. LXXVIII, Mansio vi, *P.L.*, xxii. 703–4.

in knowledge onely, without any care of bringing forth fruit, he buries Sarah in a single sepulchre, as Philo Iudaeus doth allegorize vpon this stone; but he that burieth his minde as well in the performance and practise of religion (which is all in all) as in the knowledge and vnderstanding of it, he buries Sarah in a double sepulchre.[331]

Again, using patristic lore, Playfere gives a fanciful gloss on the language of St. Peter's first Epistle (1 Pet. v. 4: '. . . ye shall receive a crown of glory that fadeth not away '):

And this crowne, as St. Peter saith is vndefiled, which neuer fadeth away. The Greeke words which S. Peter vseth, are Latine words also: and they are not only appellatiues, beeing the epithetes of this crowne, but also propers, the one a proper name of a stone, the other of a flower. For *Isidore* writeth there is a precious stone called *Amiantus*, which though it be neuer so much soyled, yet it can neuer at all bee blemished. And beeing cast into the fire, it is taken out still more bright and cleare. Also *Clemens* writeth, that there is a flower called *Amarantus*, which beeing a long time hung vp in the house, yet still is fresh and greene. To both which, the stone and the flower, the Apostle, as I am verily persuaded, alludeth in this place.[332]

Lancelot Andrewes too, Bishop of Winchester (1619) and an early High Churchman, favours the old allegoric method.[333] His subtle breaking down and extraction of every ounce of meaning from scriptural texts has often been noticed,[334] but not, as far as I have found, his frequent return to the method of ' spiritual ' exegesis favoured by the Latin Fathers. On a text from Isaiah (Isa. lxiii. 1, ' Who is this that cometh from Edom, with dyed garments from Bozrah ? . . . ') Andrewes repeats the old imagery about the uselessness of the letter:

Goe we then to the kernell, and let the huske lye: let goe the dead letter, and take we to us the spirituall meaning that hath some life in it. For what care we for the literall *Edom* or *Bozrah*, what became of them: what are they to us ? Let us compare

---

[331] *The whole sermons,* ' Good Ground,' p. 188.

[332] Ibid. ' Glorie waighes doune the Crosse,' pp. 42–3.

[333] As a general rule the preference of the Catholic-minded for ' spiritual ' interpretations is noteworthy: Cardinal Newman speaks of ' the connexion of heterodoxy with Biblical criticism ' and declares that by the appearance of both in some of the Antiochene exegetes, ' it may be almost laid down as in historic fact that the mystical interpretation and orthodoxy will stand or fall together.' (Quoted by Farrar, *History of Interpretation,* p. 211.)

[334] See T. S. Eliot, *For Lancelot Andrewes, Essays on Style and Order* (London, 1928) pp. 24–7; W. F. Mitchell, *English Pulpit Oratory from Andrewes to Tillotson,* pp. 161–3; J. N. D. Bush, *English Literature in the Earlier Seventeenth Century* 1600–1660 (Oxford, 1945) p. 300.

spirituall things with spirituall things: that is it must doe us good. I will give you a key to this, and such like scriptures. Familiar it is with the *Prophets* (Nothing more than) to speake to their People, in their owne language; than to expresse their ghostly enemies, the both mortall and immortall enemies of their soules, under the titles and termes of those Nations and Cities as were the knowne sworne enemies of the Common-wealth of *Israel*.[335]

One form of the ' four senses ' is still valid for him; on ' Thou hast ascended on high, thou hast led captivity captive ' (Ps. lxviii. 18), he declares: ' Our bookes tell us, the *Scripture* will beare foure senses: All foure be in this; and a kind of ascent there is in them '.[336] Thus, as Sinai is mentioned in the preceding verse [' The chariots of God are twenty thousand, even thousands of angels: the Lord is among them, as in Sinai, the holy place '] there is literally, a reference to Moses receiving the law, and leading the Israelites away from their Egyptian bondage. By analogy, King David applies the verse to himself, to refer his carrying the Ark to Sion: 'As *Moses* to *Sinai*; so *David* to *Sion*.' Morally, we learn that when God's people are oppressed and cry ' Let God arise, let his enemies be scattered ' (v. 1), He rises up and judges the wicked. Prophetically, there is a reference to the Ascension and the sending of the Holy Spirit.[337]

Again, Andrewes allegorizes the ' pillars ' in the verse ' The earth and all the inhabitants thereof are dissolved: I bear up the pillars of it ' (Ps. lxxv. 3). Turning to Gen. xxxii. 28 ('And he said, Thy name shall be called no more Jacob, but Israel: for as a prince hast thou power with God and with men, and hast prevailed '), he extracts ' the *strength* of *Iacob* ' and ' the strength of *Israel* ': '(1) Of Iacob, sup-planting, or prevailing over men: (2) and of Israel, prevailing with GOD '.[338] Hence the pillars become human strength and God's strength, or Justice and Religion. So returning to the first two verses of the psalm (' Unto thee, O God, do we give thanks, unto thee do we give thanks: for that thy name is near thy wondrous

[335] *XCVI Sermons by the Right Honourable and Reverend Father in God, Lancelot Andrewes, late Lord Bishop of Winchester*, 2nd edn., (London, 1632) p. 568. For the imagery of husk and kernel see *ante*, pp. 21–2. Both the *Glossa Ordinaria* and Hugh of St. Cher refer on Isa. lxiii. 1, to Christ's victory and Ascension (*P.L.*, cxiii. 1306; *T.B., cum post. Hug. Card.*, vol. IV, sig. z3r).
[336] *XCVI Sermons*, p. 663.
[337] Ibid. For the literal sense as given by Andrewes, cf. *Glossa Ordinaria, P.L.*, cxiii. 943; for the ' prophetical ' cf. *Glossa Ordinaria* (ibid.); *Glossa Interlinearis*, in *T.B., cum gloss. ord.*, etc., vol. II, f. 178r; Hugh of St. Cher, *T.B., cum post. Hug. Card.*, vol. II, sig. A8v–B1r.
[338] *XCVI Sermons*, p. 265. Cf. *Glossa Ordinaria, T.B., cum gloss. ord.*, etc., vol. I, ff. 96r-v; Hugh of St. Cher, *T.B., cum post. Hug. Card.*, vol. I, sig. g8r.

works declare. When I shall receive the congregation I will judge uprightly '), Andrewes expounds: ' (1) *Celebrabimus IEHOVA* in the *first*: and (2) *Iusticias iudicabo*, in the *second.* GOD, and *Right*, the Pillars: The worshippe of GOD; and the execution of *Iustice* or *right*.'[339] These pillars are found too, later in the psalm; Religion in v. 9 (' But I will declare for ever; I will sing praises to the God of Jacob '); and Justice in v. 10 ('All the horns of the wicked also will I cut off; but the horns of the righteous shall be exalted ').[340] There is, finally, a moral application—the ruler in the Christian state must support the pillars, as did David; he must not weaken them as did Saul.[341]

Also, Andrewes moralizes the properties of things, in the old manner.[342] One of the most striking and spiritually profound instances of this occurs in an Ash-Wednesday sermon where he correlates with repentance the birds in Jerem. viii. 7: ' Yea the stork in the heaven knoweth her appointed times; and the turtle and the crane and the swallow observe the time of their coming; but my people know not the judgement of the Lord.' After noticing the rebuke to mankind that the birds and the beasts should be set up as examples to us,[343] Andrewes continues in his best manner:

> The lesson with these foure (all of them from the *Storke* in the toppe of the firre tree to the *Swallow* that buildeth under every penthouse) would take us forth, is, that which they themselves are so perfect in, that they may be professors of it. And, it is of foure sorts: (1) *They have a time, to retourne in.* (2) That time, is certaine and certainly knowne. (3) *They know it.* (4) *They observe it.*
>
> (1) *They have a time.* The place, the climate, which the cold of the weather maketh them to leave, they faile not but find a time to turne back thither againe. This they teach us, first: Who, in this respect lesse carefull and more senseless than they, find a time, and times many, oft and long, to take our flight from GOD, occasioned, by no cold or evile weather, for commonly, we doe it *when times are best and fairest*; but we can find no time, not so much as *halfe a time*, to make our returne in . . .
>
> (2) *They have a time certaine*: when if you wait for them, you

---

[339] *XCVI Sermons*, pp. 265–6.   [340] Ibid. p. 266.   [341] Ibid. pp. 268–71.
[342] Cf. *ante*, pp. 2, 5, 8–9, 15–16, 24, 35.
[343] *XCVI Sermons*, p. 199. Quoting Job xii. 7, ' But ask now the beasts and they shall teach thee . . . ', and Matt. vi. 26, ' Behold the fowls of the air . . . ', Andrewes continues: ' Well; this *Interrogate Iumenta* in the Old; this *Respicite Volatilia* in the New, this *Apostrophe*, thus sending us to *beasts*, and *fowles* to schoole; setting them before us, as patternes; setting them over us as *Tutors*, to learne of them how to carry ourselves is certainely a bitter *Apostrophe*, a great upbraiding, to us; a great aggrieving our sinne, or our folly, or both.'

shall be sure to see them come; and come at their appointed
season: they will not misse. It will not be long, but you shall
see the *Swallow* here againe. This they will teach us, second: Vs,
who have sometime some little perswasions *In modico* (like
Agrippa's) to doe as Christian men should doe, but (as Felix)
we can never εὐκαιρῆσαι find a *convenient* set time for it. *Returne*
we will, that we will; but, are still to seeke for our season: and
ever, we will doe, and never we *doe* it. . . .

(3) They have their certaine time, *and they know it.* What
time of the yeare the time of theire *returne* is, is commonly
knowen: who knowes not, when *Swallowes* time is? And our
ignorance in not discerning this point, doth GOD justly
upbrayd us withall; and bids us, if we know not what time to
take, to get up to these fowles, and to take their time, the time
they *returne* at; (that is) now, even this time, this season of the
yeare. . . .

(4) The last lesson is, *to observe it.* Opportunity (it selfe) is a
great favour, even to have it; but a second grace it is, to dis-
cerne it, to observe and take it.[344]

There are however more lessons still to be learnt:

. . . There want not, that stretch it farther: that by these
foure fowles, there is not only taught the *time*, but even the
manner also, how to performe our Repentance.

(1) That *vox turturis*, which is *gemebam*, an mournefull note;
(2) That very name and nature of the storke, הסידה of הסד full
of *mercy* and *compassion*: (3) That the *Swallowes nest, so neere the
Altar of GOD* (Psal. 84). (4) That the painfull *watching*, and
abstinence of the *Crane* specially when they take flight, so
credibly recorded in the Naturall *Histories*: that these (*Embleme-
wise*) teach us the:

(1) *Mournefull bewailing* of our life past;
(2) *the breaking of our former sins, by workes of mercy*;
(3) *the keeping neere this place,* the house, and *Altar* of GOD;
(4) the *abstinence* and *watching* to be performed, during this
time of our *returne*:

That is, that all these are allyed to the exercise of our *Repentance*,
and are meet vertues to accompanie and attend the practice of
it.[345]

Then finally in a passage of the greatest power and beauty, Andrews
applies the lesson of the birds to his audience: let them take the time
spoken of in the text for *their* repentance:

And that *time*, is at this *time*, now: Now, doe these fowles
returne: Who knoweth whether he shall live to see them *returne*

344 Ibid. pp. 199–200.   345 Ibid. p. 200.

any more? It may be the last spring, the last *Swallow*-time, the last *wednesday*, of this name or nature, wee shall ever live, to hear this point preached. Why doe we not covenant then with our selves not to let this time slip? Surely, lest no time should be taken the *Prophet* pointeth us at this; and (ensuing the *Prophet's* mind) the Church hath fixed her season at it. And nature it selfe seemeth to favour it, that at the *rising of the yeare*, we should *rise*; and *returne*, when the Zodiake returneth to the first signe.[346]

[346] Ibid. p. 202

CHAPTER II

FORM (Dispositio)

FROM the time of the Fathers until perhaps the beginning of the present century, the sermon has been regarded by all except the least cultivated or the most self-consciously Puritan preachers as a sacred oration, governed by the rules and embellished by the ornaments of rhetoric. The successors of the famous Fourth Book of St. Augustine's *De Doctrina Christiana* have been numerous, and the *Ars Praedicandi* is quite as much an Art as the *Ars Poetriae*.[1] The aim of preaching, says St. Augustine, is ' to teach, to delight and to move ', (*docere, delectare et movere*)[2] and in this art of preaching, the arrangement or disposition of the material is of paramount importance, if the preacher's message is to make its full effect in ' teaching ' and ' moving ' the audience. An examination of the various ' schemes ' of construction (rhetorical *dispositio*) employed during the period of this study, will provide us with further knowledge of the influence of formal rhetoric on the prose of this era.

I

THE PRE-REFORMATION CATHOLIC PREACHERS, INCLUDING THE CONSERVATIVE HENRICIANS (1450–1547)

In the Middle Ages there were two types of sermon construction, the ' ancient' and the ' modern '.[3] The ' ancient ', which was descended from the homilies of the Fathers, is without any elaborate

---

[1] Apart from those medieval and sixteenth century *artes* to be mentioned in the following chapter, and such well known later works as J. Claude's *Traité de la composition d'un sermon* [in *Les Œuvres posthumes de Mr Claude*, ed. I. Claude, 5 vols. (Amsterdam, 1688–9) vol. I, pp. 163–492], there is the host of largely forgotten medieval tractates listed by Th. M. Charland, *Artes Praedicandi, Contribution à l'histoire de la Rhétorique au Moyen Âge* (Paris and Ottawa, 1936) pp. 21–106, and by Harry Caplan, *Mediaeval Artes Praedicandi, a Hand-list* (Ithaca, N.Y., 1934) and *Mediaeval Artes Praedicandi, a supplementary Hand-list* (Ithaca, N.Y., 1936); there is too the multitude of tractates fom the sixteenth to the twentieth century noted by Caplan and by Henry M. King, ' Latin Tractates on Preaching: a Book-list,' *H.T.R.*, xlii. 3 (1949) pp. 185–206; ' Italian Tractates,' *S.M.*, xvi. 2 (1949) pp. 243–52; 'Spanish Tractates,' *S.M.*, xvii. 2 (1950) pp. 161–70; 'French Tractates,' *Q.J.S.*, xxxvi. 3 (1950) pp. 296–325; ' Scandinavian Tractates,' *S.M.*, xxi. 1 (1954) pp. 1–9; ' Dutch Tractates,' *S.M.*, xxi. (1954) pp. 235–47; and the tractates included in the same authors' ' Pulpit Eloquence; A list of Doctrinal and Historical Studies in English,' *S.M.*, xxii. 4, Special issue (1955); and ' Pulpit Eloquence; A list of Doctrinal and Historical Studies in German,' *S.M.*, xxiii. 5, Special issue, 1956, pp. 1–106. [2] *De Doctrina Christiana*, lib. IV, cap. xvii, P.L., xxxiv. 104–5.
[3] In what follows I am indebted particularly to W. O. Ross, *Middle English Sermons*, pp. xliii–li; C. Smyth, *The Art of Preaching, a Practical Survey of Preaching in the Church*

scheme of arrangement peculiar to sermons, and consists either of the explication and application of a passage of Scripture (often the Gospel or Epistle of the Day), *secundum ordinem textus*; or of the topical treatment of any subject, according to reason and Scripture. The ' modern ', which was the product of the university schools, shows the influence of Aristotelian logic rather than that of the form of the ancient classical oration.[4] Although there are slight differences between the Paris and the Oxford variants of this form, (in general the Parisian technique being less complicated and more concrete)[5] and the full rules for either are quite detailed, the essentials are the same, and it will be convenient to summarize these here, pointing out any differences between early fourteenth century practice (as found in the treatises of Thomas Waleys and Robert de Basevorn) and late fourteenth and fifteenth century practice (as found in the treatise of ' Henry of Hesse ' and the pseudo-Aquinas tract). In place of the usual six parts of the classical oration, Exordium, Narration, Division, Confirmation, Confutation and Conclusion,[6] the ' modern ' style consists of the following parts: the Theme; the Exordium or Protheme or Antetheme; the Prayer; the Introduction of the Theme; the Division (with or without Subdivision); and lastly the Discussion. Of these, the Exordium, Protheme or Antetheme may be omitted, while the Introduction of the Theme is not found in later practice.[7] The Theme is a text from Scripture, from which three main ideas may be extracted, and it forms the basis of the sermon. The Exordium which leads to a bidding Prayer (although its *purpose* in later practice is not to introduce this prayer),[8] is based either on part of the main Theme not to be treated in the body of the sermon, or on another text, the Protheme or Antetheme, allied to the main Theme by one of its words. After the Prayer, the Theme is again given out for the benefit of latecomers, and the preacher, in earlier practice, proceeds

of England 747–1939 (London, 1940) pp. 19–35; and Charland, *Artes Praedicandi*, pp. 111–226 (an analysis of the methods of construction) and pp. 233–403 (the texts of two handbooks of the ' modern style ', Robert de Basevorn, *Forma Praedicandi*, and Thomas Waleys, *De Modo Componendi Sermones*).

---

[4] See H. Caplan, ' " Henry of Hesse " on the Art of Preaching,' *P.M.L.A.*, xlviii. 2 (1933) pp. 343–4; ' Classical Rhetoric and the Mediaeval Theory of Preaching,' *C.P.*, xxviii. 2 (1933) pp. 85–8; E. Gilson, ' Michel Menot et la technique du sermon médiéval,' (*Les Idées et les Lettres*, Paris, 1932, pp. 93–154).

[5] See Charland, *Artes Praedicandi*, pp. 133–4, 145, 174, 178 and 181–7 (a specimen of the Paris style, from Basevorn, cap. 36–7).

[6] See *Rhetorica ad Herennium*, lib. I, cap. iii. 4, (ed. and tr. H. Caplan, London, 1954, Loeb, pp. 8–10); Cicero, *De Inventione*, lib. I, cap. xiv, (ed. and tr. H. M. Hubbell, London, 1949, Loeb, p. 41)

[7] Ross, *Middle English Sermons*, pp. xliv–vi.   [8] Ibid. p. xlv.

to the proper Introduction of the Theme, by Narration or Argumentation. If he chooses Narration, he proceeds by analogy, or quotation of a secular author, to explain the meaning, or provide a key to the Theme; if he chooses Argumentation, he employs an argument, the conclusion of which is the Theme itself. Then follows the Division of the Theme into three parts; this may be intrinsic if the sermon is *ad clerum*, and should be extrinsic if *ad populum*. The former follows either the order of the words as they appear, or the order of the grammatical structure, or the logical order of the ideas. The latter uses any ideas outside the text and applies them to it. Each part of the Division must be supported by other scriptural authorities, found the more easily, of course, by the use of a Concordance as that of Hugh of St. Cher. These parts are either simply amplified, or from them comes the Subdivision, by which various subordinate topics are extracted from the principal words or phrases of the Theme, as interpreted by the members of the Division which correspond to them, or new divisions are based upon the authorities cited to confirm the original Division of the Theme. In a treatise of the late fifteenth century, the *De Modo Componendi Sermones* of the Augustinian Thomas Penketh (ob. 1487) various methods of subdivision are used to give form to the sermon: in this way there may be ' pyramidal ', ' plane ', ' cubical ', and ' circular ' sermons.[9] Both the Division and the Subdivision must, if the sermon (as is usual) is in Latin, be enunciated with assonance and cadence.[10] Finally comes the Discussion, which is a dilation of these Subdivisions, aided by various devices, summarized by W. O. Ross as Discussion of a word; Argument; Multiplication of Authorities; Discussion of natural qualities; Use of Quadruplex Exposition; and Presentation of Cause and Effects.[11] These devices of amplification are, of course, used in the ' ancient ' form also.

Both these methods of construction are found in the sermons of this period. The ' ancient ' is used in the manuscript *De Tempore* collections; with complete simplicity in MS. Hatton 96, ff. 10–91; but with occasional faint echoes of the ' modern ' style, by at times grouping topics in threes or fours, in MS. Harleian 2247 and MSS. Lincoln Cathedral Library 50 and 51. For example, in a sermon for Advent I, the homilist of MS. Harleian 2247 points out that before the coming of Christ men erred and went from the right way: (i)

---

[9] Ibid. p. xlix.
[10] See the example given by Charland, *Artes Praedicandi*, pp. 321–2 (from Basevorn, *Forma Praedicandi*, cap. 1).
[11] *Middle English Sermons*, pp. l–li.

' bi instigacion of þe deuell, bi his deceytes wrenchis & wyles, by
þe way of pride & elacion ', (ii) ' bi sturinge of the worlde whiche
is ricches, bi the wey of covetise & auarise ', (iii) ' bi þe deceyvable
fragilite & freelnes of thys fykell flesh, be þe way of delytes &
vnclennes ': so Christ came to combat these: (i) ' in þe wey of
obedyence, mercy & mekenes ', (1) ' before his precious passion he
was obedient vnto his fadir in heven ', (2) ' to *Ioseph* þat lyved bi
craft of carpentrye & to his pore modir he was sogette ', (ii) ' in þe
wey of pacience & pouerte ', (iii) ' in þe wey of contynence &
clennes '.[12] Similarly, in a sermon for Sexagesima in the same
collection, the preacher, having pointed out the shortness of men's
life in these latter days, declares that we can still serve God, and earn
His reward, if we: (i) ' suffir tribulacion mekely '; (ii) ' do almos
dedes discretely '; (iii) ' voyde & for sake syn specially '.[13] Then
again, the homilist of MS. Lincoln Cathedral Library 51 in a sermon
for Trinity XXIV, warns us that we must be mindful of death for
three reasons: (i) ' þe vncerteyne tyme of dethe '; (ii) ' the tyme of
dethe is so peynefull '; (iii) ' þe dredeful syȝte of devylls that man
schall see in þe tyme þat þe sowle and þe body schall departe '.[14]

Employed with distinction by Colet in his Lectures on St. Paul's
Epistles, the ' ancient ' form was favoured too by the Dean in his
sermons at St. Paul's.[15] Taverner's *Postils* provide a notable example
of the ' ancient ' form, giving simple explanations of the Gospels
and Epistles throughout the year, and pointing out the lessons
which should be drawn from them. Edgeworth also adopts the
ancient form; as has been noticed, he proceeds in his series of
sermons on St. Peter's First Epistle to expound it *secundum ordinem
textus*, with considerable moral application.[16] In his series on the
Gifts of the Holy Ghost, he accords a simple topical treatment to
each;[17] in his ' Homily on Ceremonies ' he argues straightforwardly
by ' heads ';[18] while in his ' Homily on the Creed ' he goes through
each article consecutively (following the tradition that each apostle
contributed an article), expounding and applying the meaning.[19]
Again, Bishop Alcock in his sermon to his priests in synod, takes
the words of the *Regula Apostolica, Oportet ergo episcopum irrepre-
hensibilem esse, unius uxoris virum, sobrium, prudentem, ornatum, pudicum,*

[12] MS. Harl. 2247, ff. 1r–2r.   [13] Ibid. ff. 36r–7r.
[14] MS. Linc. Cath. Libr. 51, f. 78v; cf. too the similar examples ibid. ff. 10r, 35v,
58r, 72r; and MS. Linc. Cath. Libr. 50,, ff. 30v, 47v.
[15] See Erasmus, *The Lives of Jehan Vitrier . . . and John Colet*, tr. J. H. Lupton, p. 24,
(*Opus Epistolarum*, ed. Allen, vol. IV, no. 1211, p. 516) quoted *ante*, p. 29.
[16] See *ante*, p. 33.   [17] *Sermons*, ff. 1r–70v.   [18] Ibid. ff. 88r–98r.
[19] Ibid. ff. 71r–87v.

hospitalem, doctorem, non vinolentem, non percussorem, sed modestum, non litigiosum, non cupidum, sed suae domui bene praepositum . . . non neophytum, (1 Tim. iii. 2–6, ' It behoveth therefore a bishop to be blameless, the husband of one wife, sober, prudent, of good behaviour, chaste, given to hospitality, a teacher, not given to wine, no striker, but modest, not quarrelsome, not covetous, but one that ruleth well his own house, . . . not a neophyte ', Douay) and shows how the priestly character should be founded on these qualities.[20] Similarly, in his sermon to the nuns at the time of their consecration, the bishop takes as the basis of his delineation of the virtues of the true Religious, titles derived from those of Christ the Spouse, as *Nazarenus,* with its interpretation, ' Nazarei candidiores niue interpretantur, virgulti vel floridi, siue custodientes, aut separati a mundo, vel vncti, siue sancti, aut consecrati . . .'[21] So the nun must be *Nazarena, Custos, Uncta* and *Sancta*; and as Christ was called *Flos campi* (Can. ii. 1) so must the consecrated virgin be called; and as she carries a light during the service of profession, so must she be a *Lumen* in her life.[22] Also ancient in form is the sermon of exhortation to ordination candidates by William de Melton, Chancellor of York. He proceeds by topical sections: (A) the dignity of the priesthood and the need for humility in those seeking holy orders;[23] (B) standards of intelligence and learning necessary to a priest;[24] (C) canonical impediments to ordination—only the competent to be ordained;[25] (D) address to those admitted to the subdiaconate, to follow virtue and to avoid in particular five vices—(a) luxury and impurity, (b) anger, (c) avarice, (d) drunkenness, (e) vanity.[26]

Longland's series of sermons on the Penitential Psalms is also ' ancient ' in form; after a short Exordium he goes through the psalm verse by verse, expanding the literal meaning, adding ' spiritual ' interpretations, and dilating on various favourite topics arising from the text, as the vanity of life, and the horrifying evil of sin. Thus in the sermon on Ps. ci (Vg.) the bishop begins with an Exordium on Providence and the remedial effects of adversity;[27]

---

[20] *Gallicantus Iohannis Alcok episcopi Eliensis ad confratres suos curatos in sinodo apud Bernwell XXV die mensis Septembris Anno millesimo CCCC nonagesimo octavo,* (London, 1498).
[21] [*Desponsacio virginis christo Spousage of a virgin to Cryste.*] *An exhortacyon made to Relygyous systers in the tyme of theyr consecracyon by the Reuerende fader in god Iohan Alcok bysshop of Ely,* (Westminster, n.d.) sig. Aiii[r]. See Lam. iv. 7; Num. vi. 2; also St. Jerome, ' Comment. in Amos,' lib. I, cap. ii, *P.L.,* xxv. 1008;Epist. XLVI, *P.L.,* xxii. 491.   [22] Ibid. sig. Aiii[r]–Biii[r].
[23] *Sermo exhortatorius cancellarij Eboracensis hijs qui ad sacros ordines petunt promoueri* (Westminster, [1510?]) sig. ai[r]–aiii[r].
[24] Ibid. sig. aiii[r]–aiv[v].   [25] Ibid. sig. aiv[v]–avi[r].   [26] Ibid. sig. avi[r]–aviii[r].
[27] *Sermones,* ff. 353[r]–62[r].

proceeding to the psalm, he points out the necessity for prayer and repentance;[28] then, to select certain verses, the birds of verses 7–8 ('I am become like to a pelican of the wilderness: I am like a night raven in the house. I have watched and now become as a sparrow all alone on the housetop', Douay) allow him, as noticed earlier, to give spiritual interpretations;[29] the sad reflections of verses 4 and 12 ('For my days are vanished like smoke: and my bones are grown dry like fuel for the fire. . . . My days have declined like a shadow, and I am withered like grass', Douay) allow him to indulge in declamations on the transience of all worldly things;[30] the expression of the misery of sin in verse 5 ('I am smitten as grass, and my heart is withered: because I forgot to eat my bread', Douay) allows him to speak of sin's gravity and evil effects;[31] while verse 21 ('That he might hear the groans of them that are in fetters: that he might release the children of the slain', Douay) gives him occasion to detail the sins of youth and age.[32]

Fisher also in his series on the Penitential Psalms adopts the 'ancient' method; although where possible, as the basis of his treatment, he divides the psalm into its parts, which he often manages to make the favourite number of three. Thus he divides Ps. vi into: (A), a petition of mercy; (B), the reasons to move God to mercy; (C), David's thanks for forgiveness.[33] Similarly, he divides Ps. l (Vg.) into two main parts: (A), verses 1–10 and (B), verses 11–12. He then subdivides (A) into: (a) [David] 'enduceth and bryngeth in his petycyon whiche euery penitent persone may make apte and conuenyent to hymselfe', (b) 'he sheweth by many reasons his petycyon to be graunted', (c) 'he promyseth very true and vndoubtefull hope to hymselfe of the desyre that he asketh':[34] and (B) is subdivided into: (a) 'our prophete maketh a newe petycyon, (b) 'he sheweth the entent of his petycyon, whiche is that he may please god', (c) 'he teacheth that his desyre is the chefe thynge wherby euery man may please god and make recompense for synne.'[35] Again, dividing Ps. ci (Vg.) into two parts: (A), verses 1–13, and (B), verses 14–19; he subdivides (A) into: (a) 'the prophete maketh his petycyon and desyreth mekely to be herde of almyghty god', (b) 'he sheweth openly his owne wretchednes', (c) 'he remembreth hymselfe what he may do and how moche to obteyne mercy and grace', which he treats as in the person of all present:[36] while he

---

[28] Ibid. ff. 362�v–92�v.   [29] Ibid. 405�v–53ʳ; see *ante*, p. 24.
[30] Ibid. ff. 392�v–8�v, 490�v–502ʳ; see *post*, p. 230, n. 5.
[31] Ibid. ff. 398�v–403�v.   [32] Ibid. ff. 704ʳ–5ʳ.   [33] *English Works*, Pt. I, p. 8.
[34] Ibid. p. 94.   [35] Ibid. p. 115.   [36] Ibid. p. 137.

subdivides (B) into: (a) an exposition of the spiritual significance of Sinai, Sion, and Jerusalem, leading to an explanation of the full meaning of verse 14 (' Thou shalt arise and have mercy on Sion: for it is time to have mercy on it, for the time is come ', Douay);[37] (b) we are taught that we must move God's goodness to mercy by the remembrance of His benefits;[38] (c) we are taught to pray that God will uphold His Church Militant, that it may the sooner ascend to heaven.[39] Fisher will, however, on occasion introduce some extraneous material only loosely connected with the psalm he is treating. In the sermon on Ps. xxxvii (Vg.) he speaks of the Nativity of the Blessed Virgin; seeing a reference to Mary in Can. vi. 9 (' Who is she that cometh forth as the morning rising? ' Douay), he finds three parallels between the morning and Our Lady. First, the morning is mild and quiet; secondly, it puts away the black cloud of night, and thirdly it is clear without mists; so Mary is mild without the storms of wrath; she enhanced herself above sin's darkness, breaking the serpent's head; and she is without the darkness of ignorance.[40] On the contrary sinful men have three wretchednesses opposite to these virtues: they are shaken by fear, they are in bondage to sin, and blinded by ignorance,[41] which three wretchednesses Fisher finds in the psalm (Ps. xxxvii. 1–4; 5–7; 8–10 and all three in 11).[42] In the sermon on Ps. cxxix (Vg.) Fisher begins with an allegoric interpretation of the story of Jonah and extracting the three parts of Penance (contrition, confession and satisfaction) from the three days spent by the prophet in the whale, he proceeds to find these too in the beginning of the psalm.[43] An allegorization of the Parable of the Prodigal Son opens the sermon on Ps. cxlii (Vg.): four points are noted in the Prodigal and found also in the psalm; the going away (Luke xv. 11–16; Ps. cxlii. 3 Vg.): the manner of his return (Luke xv. 17–19; Ps. cxlii. 1–2 4–6); what he asks of his father (Luke xv. 20–1; Ps. cxlii. 7–9) and the reward which he receives (Luke xv. 22–4; Ps. cxlii. 10–12).[44] Longland adopts an even looser construction in the last three sermons of *Quinque Sermones*; the first half being on the Gospel of the Day, and the second on some of the Fruits of the Holy Spirit, which he had begun to expound in the second sermon. In this case the two halves tend to fall apart, and all sense of form is lost.[45] However, that the

[37] Ibid. pp. 164–83.   [38] Ibid. p. 183.   [39] Ibid. p. 191.   [40] Ibid. p. 52.
[41] Ibid.   [42] Ibid. pp. 53–70.   [43] Ibid. pp. 200–10.   [44] Ibid. pp. 234–67.
[45] In the second sermon (*Quinque Sermones*, ff. 64ʳ–73ʳ) on a text from the Gospel of the Day (Matt, xxi. 43) Longland deals with Charity, Joy and Peace; in the third (ibid. ff. 13ʳ–86ᵛ) he speaks first of the Gospel of the Day (John iv. 5–42) then after

' ancient ' construction can be simply and yet elegantly employed is shown by Tunstall's Palm Sunday sermon of 1536. Here the bishop takes the Epistle of the Day (Phil. ii. 5–11) and treats three things: first, ' the lytteral sence thereof conteinyng the infinite and inestimable humilitie and obedience of our sauioure Iesu Christ '; secondly, the ' disobedience of men by pryde done to man ageinst goddis lawe '; the thirdly the ' disobedience of al men by pride done to almyghty god ageynste goddis lawe. And howe that maye be amendid.'[46] The second section allows for polemic against the primacy of the Pope and papal intrigue against England,[47] and the third for a brief exposition of the moral law together with a short attack on the doctrine of Justification by Faith.[48] Tunstall concludes with a brief passage urging the worthy reception of Holy Communion at Easter, and the necessity of fasting, alms deeds and prayer.[49]

The ' modern ' style in a late form is found with all its elaboration in the series of learned Latin sermons by Stephen Baron. After announcing the Theme from the Song of Moses, *Utinam saperent et intelligerent ac novissima providerent* (Deut. xxxii. 29, ' O that they would be wise and would understand, and would provide for their last end ', Douay), Baron proceeds through an Exordium on the text *Multi sunt vocati, pauci vero electi*, (Matt. xx. 16, ' Many are called, but few are chosen '), to the Prayer and Division. On the Theme he will base, he declares, two parts: *Prima erit salutis querende inductiua. Secunda vie tenende directiua* [' The first will be inductive, concerning salvation to be sought; the second directive concerning the way to be followed '].[50] He divides each part into three; the first into *Preteritorum memoria, Presentium intelligentia*, and *Futurorum prouidentia*, according to the words of the Theme, *Vtinam, inquit, saperent preterita: et intelligerent presentia: ac novissima prouiderent id est futura*;[51] for the second, says Baron: *vere sapienti et intelligenti ac sue saluti prouidere cupienti iusticie via eligenda est* [' By the man who is truly wise and understanding and desirous of providing for his salvation, the way of justice (or righteousness) is to be chosen '], so he will deal with man's duty: *Deo, Sibi, Proximo*.[52] From these main divisions an apology for the break in construction (ibid. f. 76ᵛ) he deals with Peace, Patience and Longanimity; in the fourth (ibid. ff. 86ᵛ–97ᵛ) he speaks first of the Gospel (John xi. 1–45) then of Goodness, Benignity and Mildness; while in the fifth (ibid. ff. 97ᵛ–109ᵛ) after dealing with the Gospel (John xi. 41–54) he speaks of Modesty, Continence and Chastity.

[46] *A sermon . . . made vpon Palme sondaye laste past*, sig. A iiʳ⁻ᵛ.
[47] Ibid. sig. Bviᵛ–Eivʳ.   [48] Ibid. sig. Eivʳ–Fiiᵛ.   [49] Ibid. sig. Fiiᵛ–Fviiʳ.
[50] *Sermones*, ff. 2ʳ⁻ᵛ.   [51] Ibid. f. 2ᵛ.   [52] Ibid. f. 4ᵛ.

stems an extraordinary ramification of subdivisions, proliferating throughout the series of fifteen sermons.

The ' modern ' scheme is found too with considerable elaboration in the vernacular sermon preached on Easter Monday 1495 at Paul's Cross by Bishop Fitzjames. The Theme is from the Gospel of the Day, *Ipse Ihesus appropinquans ibat cum illis*, (Luke xxiv. 15, ' Jesus himself also drawing near, went with them ', Douay), from which as an initial Division the preacher immediately extracts two propositions; first, that Jesus ' nighed ' to mankind, and secondly, that He ' hath walked with mankind '.[53] The Exordium then deals with the three Jesuses of the Old Testament, *Jesus filius Nave* (Joshua), a saviour by power, *Jesus filius Josedech*, a saviour by obedience, and *Jesus filius Sirach*, a saviour by widsom, who are figures of *Jesus Filius Dei*, the perfect Power, Obedience and Wisdom.[54] Fitzjames then repeats his first Division and adds a corollary, that Christ has brought man to everlasting rest in heaven, and is thus the True Saviour.[55] This Division is now fused with the members of the Exordium: (A) Jesus ' nighed ' to man by His power, (B) He walked with man by obedience, (C) He brought man to bliss by wisdom.[56] (A) is subdivided, by showing that this ' nighing ' was (a) by Christ's part in Creation, (b) by His birth, (c) by His ministry.[57] Of these, (a) is subdivided into: (i) wherein stands the act of Creation, (ii) that Christ exercised this act on man as well as on all other creatures, (iii) how, in performing this act, He nighed to man.[58] Then (iii) is subdivided into: (1) Christ nighed to man generally, by leaving a *vestigium* of His handiwork in Creation; (2) He nighed specially, by, α making man in His image, β making man God's servant, γ inspired Grace—the Law of Nature—special graces, δ Circumcision, ε the written Law, ζ the light of Prophecy.[59] Further, (b) is subdivided into: (i) wherein stands the act of Incarnation, (the Second Person of the Holy Trinity took on our nature); (ii) it is an act of the almighty power of God, (but the Blessed Virgin Mary consented); (iii) how by this act Christ ' nighed ' to men, (by assuming human nature).[60] Similarly (c) is subdivided into the bodily and spiritual ministry, bringing: (i) light, (ii) healing, (iii) the sacraments.[61] Again, (iii) is further subdivided into: (1) why Christ instituted the sacraments, (2) what sacraments He instituted, (3) how he ' nighed ' to mankind in the same.[62] So, (1) gives the reasons why the sacra-

---

[53] *Sermo die lune in ebdomada pasche*, sig. Aii[r].   [54] Ibid., sig. Aii[v]–Bvi[v].
[55] Ibid. sig. Bvi[v].   [56] Ibid.   [57] Ibid. sig. Ci[r].   [58] Ibid. sig. Ci[v].
[59] Ibid. sig. Cii[r]–Dii[v].   [60] Ibid. Div[v]–Dvi[v].   [61] Ibid. sig. Ei[r].
[62] Ibid. sig. Evi[r].

ments were instituted (from the Master of the Sentences): α for man's
' humylyacion ', (to seek spiritual help through material things), β
for man's ghostly erudition, (they are effectuous signs), γ for man's
' exercytacyon ', (that man should be continually occupied in God's
service), δ for man's salvation.[63] (2) declares that there are seven
sacraments, but of these three only are necessary: α Baptism, which
is of necessity simple, β Penance, which is of necessity conditional,
(as it remits actual sins committed after Baptism), γ the Holy
Eucharist, which is of necessity convenient, (being spiritual food).[64]
(3) shows that Christ nighed to mankind: α in Baptism by taking
away Original Sin, β in Penance by restoring lost grace, γ in the
Holy Eucharist by coming in Sacramental Communion.[65] (B) is also
subdivided; Christ was obedient: (a) to His friends and the ' prelates', (b) to the Law, (although He ignored the Talmudic additions),
(c) to the Passion and Death, (for man's sake).[66] The third main
division (C), remains however undivided, and is merely elaborated
in meaning.[67]

The modern scheme was however intended for learned sermons
ad clerum, and when used *ad populum*, is found more usually without
elaborate subdivision, and often with some modification of form.
Thus in a Boy Bishop's sermon of Henry VII's reign, the Theme is
Laudate pueri Dominum (Ps. cxi. 1 Vg.) which is introduced after an
Exordium on the need for God's help in directing man's life to its
proper end, particularly in the case of children who lack reason.[68]
After the Prayers comes the Division; Christians must be children
not in wit, but in purity of heart; so the preacher may say: (A)
Laudate, pueri, Dominum in infantia; (B) *Laudate Dominum in adolescentia*; (C) *Laudate Dominum in perseverante etate humana*.[69] These
three ages may be likened to three laws: (A) to the Law of Nature,
(B) to the Written Law, (C) to the Law of Grace.[70] Then the way in
which we should love God in these three ages is given by ' a prety
conceyte of oure comyn Kalender ': (A) ' By *Kalendas* is understande
Childehode: *Kalendae* is as moche to saye *quasi colendo*, for the *con-
suetudo* of the Romaynes was, the fyrste daye of the moneth that is
called *Kalendas* falleth, to solempnyse to ther goddes Hely, Juno, and
Jupyter. So verely the childehode of man is dedycate to devocyon ';
(B) ' By Nonas I understande the seconde age, that is called *Juventus*

---

[63] Ibid. sig. Eviᵛ–Fiʳ.　　[64] Ibid. sig. Fiʳ–Fiiiʳ.　　[65] Ibid. sig. Fiiiʳ–Fivʳ.
[66] Ibid. sig. Fivᵛ–Givʳ.　　[67] Ibid. sig. Gvᵛ–Gviʳ.
[68] *In Die Innocencium Sermo pro Episcopo Puerorum*, ed. J. G. Nichols, Camden Society
Miscellany, vol. VII (London, 1875) Camden New Series, XIV, pp. 1–3.
[69] Ibid. p. 5.　　[70] Ibid.

Youthe. *Nonae dicuntur quasi nundinae*, as moche as to saye as a fayer, for in that tyme they occupied themself in fayers and marchaundyses'; (C) ' By the *Ydus*, the whiche is as moche to saye as *divisio*, a depart-ynge . . . I understande the latter age of man, in the whiche man is dyvyded from the worlde by dethe, to the ende for to receyve good or evyll as he hath deserved in this present lyfe.'[71] But, says the Boy Bishop, let us all serve God in each age; and if we fall, repenting, rise again; thanking God for His pardon in the words of the Theme, *Laudate pueri, Dominum*.[72]

Fisher, in his sermon (of 1521) against Luther takes as Theme the beginning of the Gospel of the Day, *Cum venerit Paraclitus, quem ego mittam vobis a Patre, Spiritum veritatis qui a Patre procedit, ille testimonium perhibet de me* (John xv. 26, ' But when the Paraclete cometh, whom I will send you from the Father, the Spirit of truth, who proceedeth from the Father, he shall give testimony of me ', Douay; from the Gospel for the Sunday within the Octave of Ascension). The Exordium consists of the drawing of the parallel between the obscuring of the sun followed by the coming of a thunderstorm (with the consequence that ' the weyke soules and feble hertes be put in a grete fere and made almost desperate for lack of comforte ') and the rise of heresies in the Church, with the consequence that ' many a weyke soule hathe myscaryed therby '. However, Christ foreseeing such tempests, uttered the words of the Theme *Cum venerit Paraclitus*, etc.[73] After the Prayer, Fisher draws two ' instructions ' from this, adds the third from the next sentence of the Gospel (*Et vos testimonium perhibebitis, quia ab initio mecum estis*; John xv. 27, 'And you shall give testimony, because you are with me from the beginning ', Douay), and concludes with a fourth instruction which attempts to refute the defenders of Luther.[74]

Fisher's Good Friday sermon[75] provides another modification of the modern form. The Theme is from Ezekiel, *Lamentationes carmen et vae* (Ezek. ii. 9, ' Lamentations and canticles and woe ', Douay), the words which the prophet saw written in the book of which he said, *factum est in ore meo sicut mel dulce* (Ezek. iii. 3, ' it was sweet as honey in my mouth ', Douay).[76] This book may be taken for us, says Fisher, as the Crucifix,[77] and for an Exordium

[71] Ibid. pp. 9–11.   [72] Ibid. pp. 12–13.
[73] *English Works*, Pt. I, pp. 311–13.   [74] Ibid. pp. 314–48.
[75] 'A Sermon verie fruitfull, godly, and learned, vpon thys sentence of the Prophet Ezechiell, *Lamentationes, Carmen, et vae*, very aptely applyed vnto the passion of Christ. Preached vpon a good Friday.' (ibid. pp. 388–428).
[76] Ibid. p. 388.   [77] Ibid.

G

(using an extended figure), he proceeds to draw an elaborate parallel between a book and the Crucifix: the boards, the arms of the cross; the leaves, the members of the Precious Body; the words written, the Divine Word; the letters, the marks of the scourge; and the capitals, the Five Wounds.[78] After the Prayer Fisher shows how the words of the Theme are written in the book of the Crucifix: ' Fyrst is lamentation, and this verie conuenientlye is written in thys booke of the Crucifixe. For whosoeuer will ioye with Christ, must first sorow with him. And by sorowe and lamentation hee may come vnto ioye: But hee that will not sorrowe and lament with Christ heere in thys lyfe, hee shall come fynallye to the place where is euerlastynge woe, I saye woe that shall neuer haue ende. Heere therfore is written all these three, lamentation, songe, and woe. '[79] Subdividing, the bishop shows how: (A) lamentation arises from: (a) fear, (b) shame, (c) sorrow, (d) hatred.[80] So, (a) we should fear hell, (b) feel shame that the Passion was occasioned by our sins, (c) sorrow over Our Lord's suffering, (d) hate sin, the cause of that agony.[81] Then follows (B): a song is for love, hope, joy or comfort; so here is a great matter: (a) for the love of all Christians, (b) for hope of heaven, (c) for joy, for: (i) by the cross we are reconciled to God; (ii) by the cross, the power of our enemies is broken; (iii) by the cross the account of our sins is erased; (d) for comfort for sinners who although they deserve everlasting shame, have been saved from it by the shame suffered by Christ.[82] In conclusion: (C) ' woe ', is the pains of hell which will be suffered by the impenitent. This is subdivided into ten parallels between the pains of the Passion which lasted but for a time, and the pains of hell which will endure for ever: (a) Christ was stripped, His hands and feet pierced with nails, but in hell is a more painful couch than the cross where moths shall gnaw the sinner and worms and serpents crawl over him; (b) hanging on the cross was painful to Christ's tender body, but the sinner hanging on the gibbet of hell will suffer even more grievous torments; (c) Christ endured extreme heat so that He sweated water and blood, but this is nothing compared to the heat of hell-fire; (d) Christ heard opprobious words, in hell the damned hear the cries of the devils and the other lost souls; (e) Christ wept for others' sins, the damned, having refused to weep cleansing tears on earth, weep scalding tears in hell; (f) Christ suffered extreme thirst, but the thirst of the damned is more terrible still; (g) Christ

[78] Ibid. pp. 393–6.   [79] Ibid, pp. 396–7.
[80] Ibid. p. 397.   [81] Ibid. pp. 397–407.   [82] Ibid. pp. 407–20.

was in great heaviness, but the despair of the damned is immeasurable; (h) Christ felt desolate on the cross, but the damned are forsaken by God for ever.[83]

Longland's Good Friday sermons too are based on a modification of the modern style, but are long and rather amorphous. For example that of 1535 is on the Theme *Quia apud Dominum misericordia et copiosa apud eum redemptio* (Ps. cxxix. 7, Vg., ' Because with the Lord there is mercy: and with him plentiful redemption ', Douay), which, after an Exordium on the certain trust in God's mercy which the penitent may have,[84] is divided into two: (A) God's mercy, (B) His redemption through Christ.[85] (A) is subdivided into seven kinds of Divine mercy: (a) a calling mercy, which is: (i) secret, as in the case of the publican in the temple; (ii) public, by the Word and preaching;[86] (b) a rewarding mercy, which gives men the gifts of: (i) nature, (ii) fortune, (iii) grace;[87] (c) a sparing mercy;[88] (d) a defending mercy—because of this we are not utterly destroyed by the Devil or mischance, although we deserve destruction on account of our heinous sins, in particular: (i) non-observance of the Sabbath Day, (ii) blasphemy, (iii) presumption, (iv) inobediency;[89] (e) a punishing mercy;[90] (f) a remitting mercy, in the forgiveness of sins;[91] (g) a crowning mercy, in the joys of heaven.[92] In (B) Longland declares that: (a) all went to hell before Christ's Passion, but God's mercy is wonderfully manifested in that Christ chose a hard and painful death (*mortem singularem*).[93] He follows this by: (b) the reasons why Christ celebrated the Last Supper before His Passion: (i) to show that there was no way to heaven but by (1) death, (2) passion, (3) tribulation; (ii) to show the mysteries of the Pasch (recalling the deliverance of the Israelites by the angel); (iii) to show His own passing out of the world, and to show that the world itself is passing away (we are now, says Longland, living precariously in the sixth and last age of the world); (iv) to inaugurate the New Law; (v) to institute the Holy Eucharist; (vi) to show that He would accept death willingly; (vii) to give an example to the Apostles and to all Christians: (1) to render lauds and thanks to God, (2) to teach them patience, (3) to teach them charity, (4) to teach them humility.[94] Then follows, (c) a mystical exposition of

---

[83] Ibid. pp. 420–8.   [84] *Sermond at Rychemunte*, 1535, sig. Aii^r–Aiv^v.
[85] Ibid. sig. Aiv^v.   [86] Ibid. sig. Bi^r–Biii^r.   [87] Ibid. sig. Biii^v–Biv^v.
[88] Ibid. sig. Ci^r.   [89] Ibid. sig. Ci^v–Ciii^v.   [90] Ibid. sig. Civ^r.
[91] Ibid. sig. Civ^v.   [92] Ibid. sig. Di^r.   [93] Ibid. sig. Di^r–v.
[94] Ibid. sig. Di^v–Fi^r. In the original text subdivisions (iii)–(vii) are marked as (i)–(v) but this does not accord with the actual form of the sermon.

St. Peter's request to Christ to wash not his feet only, but his hands and his head also (John xiii. 9): (i) the hands represent evil works and deeds which must be washed by Penance; (ii) the head is the seat of six faculties which must be washed by Penance: (1) the eyes—sight —unclean looks, (2) the ears—hearing—listening to unclean words, (3) the nostrils—smell—inordinate delight in sweet smells, (4) the mouth—taste—gluttony, (5) the tongue—speech—vain words, (6) touch—unclean touching; (iii) the feet represent affections and inclinations to sin which must also be washed by Penance.[95] Then follows: (d) a tract on the Last Supper and Transubstantiation in the Blessed Sacrament. The Holy Eucharist was instituted: (i) as a memorial of Christ's Passion; (ii) for the consolation of the Church; (iii) for our singular comfort; (iv) for our inward consolation; (v) for heavenly food.[96] Then follows: (e) the many ways in which Christ has shown and will show Himself: (i) as a natural man born of a maiden; (ii) to the Apostles *in quarta vigilia noctis* (Mark vi); (iii) in the Transfiguration to Peter, James and John (Matt. xxvii); (iv) to St. Mary Magdalene after the Resurrection (John xx); (v) to the eleven Apostles in the house in Jerusalem (Luke xxiv); (vi) to St. Thomas (John xx); (vii) to St. Stephen (Acts vii); (viii) to Christians in the Blessed Sacrament (as to the Apostles at the Last Supper); (ix) He will show Himself directly to the Blessed in heaven.[97] So: (f) we must examine ourselves carefully before receiving Holy Communion remembering all our past life, and grieving over our sins in the periods of our: (i) *pueritia*, (ii) *adolescentia*, (iii) *iuuentus*, (iv) *virilitas*, (v) *senectus*.[98] (g) Is our repentance fruitful? Let us remember the repentance of: (i) St. Peter, (ii) St. Mary Magdalene, (iii) the good thief.[99] (h) We must make our Confession, which should be: (i) *vera*, (ii) *simplex*, (iii) *aperta*, (iv) *integra*, (v) *accusatoria*, (vi) *fidelis*, (vii) *assidua*, (viii) *humilis*, (ix) *lachrymabilis*.[100] (i) We must in future: (i) flee dangerous occasions, (ii) use sobriety, (iii) remember Lot's wife;[101] (j) before receiving Holy Communion we must abstain from the act of marriage.[102] (k) If our reception is unworthy we merit damnation.[103] (l) The fruits of worthy reception are: (i) grace, (ii) pardon for venial sins, (iii) perhaps the remission of some temporal punishment.[104] (m) Then follows an enumeration of the causes of Christ's sorrow during His Passion: (i) the resistance of the sensual part of His human nature, during the Agony in the Garden,

[95] Ibid. sig. Fiv–Fiiir.   [96] Ibid. sig. Fiiir–Giiv.   [97] Ibid. sig. Giiv–Iir.
[98] Ibid. sig. Iiir–Iiiiv.   [99] Ibid. sig. Iivr-v.   [100] Ibid. sig. Kiv–Kiiiv.
[101] Ibid. sig. Kiiir–Liv.   [102] Ibid. sig. Liv.   [103] Ibid. sig. Liir–Livv.
[104] Ibid. sig. Livv.

(ii) the weakness of the Disciples, (iii) the future unkindness of Christians, (iv) the pitifully small fruit of the Redemption in heathens and bad Christians.[105] (n) Christ prayed, and so must we; let us each remember: (i) *quis*—I am a sinner, (ii) *cui*—I pray to God, (iii) *quomodo*—I must know God and myself truly, while my prayers must be: (1) humble, (2) faithful, (3) fixed on God, (4) devout and tearful, (5) charitable; (iv) *quando*—I must pray nearly always, (v) *quid*—I must seek God's will for me, as Christ submitted to the will of the Father at the Passion, (vi) Christ prayed *three* times; so let us *continue in* prayer.[106] (o) Let us consider the pains of the Passion: (i) the inconsistency of the Disciples, (ii) Christ was brought: (1) to Annas's house, (2) to Caiaphas, (3) to Pilate, (4) to Herod, (5) to Pilate once more, (6) to the 'Yelde hall', (7) to another house for scourging, (8) to the 'yelde hall' again, (9) to Calvary. Here note fourteen things about the crucifixion: α Christ's forgiveness of the Jews—*Pater dimitte illis*; *non enim sciunt quid faciunt*; β the words of the thief—*Si tu es Christus, salvum fac temetipsum et nos*; γ Christ's cry *Sitio*; δ Christ's commending of His soul to the Father—*Pater, in manus tuas commendo spiritum meum*; ε the darkness; ζ the rending of the veil in the Temple; η the earthquake; θ the stones rushing together and breaking; ι the rising of the dead; κ their appearance in the streets; λ the words of the centurion—*Vere hic homo Filius Dei erat*; μ the remorse of the Jews, who went about striking their breasts; ν the piercing of Christ's side with the spear. From the sacred stream that issued thence flow the seven sacraments: Baptism, Confirmation, Penance, Order, Matrimony, Extreme Unction, the Holy Eucharist; ξ the burial of Christ by Joseph of Arimathea.[107] In conclusion, Longland urges his audience to meditate on the entombment, bringing *pietas, devotio* and *oratio*. Let them go to the sepulchre with the three Marys and regard Our Lord's body, now indeed risen but on Good Friday contemplated in death.[108]

It is only with the advent of the sixteenth century that treatises on the art of preaching make any real adaptation of classical rhetoric to sermon construction. Classical influence in this matter is evident in Reuchlin's *Liber congestorum de arte praedicandi* (1503) and Erasmus's *Ecclesiastes* (1535).[109] There is no English sermon of this period, however, which I have seen, which is built on the full scheme of the

<hr/>

[105] Ibid. sig. Mi^r–Mii^v.   [106] Ibid. sig. Miii^r–Ni^v.
[107] Ibid. sig. Ni^v–Riii^v.   [108] Ibid. sig. Riv^r–v.
[109] See Reuchlin, *Liber congestorum de arte praedicandi*, (*De Arte Concionandi formulae, vt breues, ita doctae and piae. Iohanne Reuclino Phorcensi, anonymo quodam rhapsodo, Philippo Melancthone, D. Ioanne Hepino, autoribus* ... London, 1570, sig. Av^r–Bvii^r); Erasmus,

classical oration. On the other hand, the *Ecclesiastes* of Erasmus was written at the instigation of Fisher,[110] and it is interesting to note that in his two funeral sermons, the bishop does borrow certain classical devices. The sermon for Henry VII is built on the scheme of the ' secular oratours ' in their funeral orations; (A) the commendation of the dead, (B) the stirring of the hearers to have compassion on him, (C) the comforting of them again, which, declares Fisher, are found in this order in the first psalm of the Dirge (Ps. cxv. Vg.) which he will expound.[111] Each of these is however subdivided in the medieval manner: (A) into the ways in which the king made a virtuous end: (a) in the true turning of his soul from the world to God; (b) in his confidence in prayer; (c) in his belief in God and in the sacraments; (d) in his diligent asking of mercy;[112] (B) into the reasons why we should have pity on the king: (a) for the sorrows of death in his body; (b) for the fear of judgement; (c) for this world's miseries; (d) for his sorrowful cry to God for help;[113] (C) into the grounds of comfort, that God is: (a) merciful, (b) He has taken the king into His custody, (c) He has delivered him from all evil, (d) He will hence forward continue His favour to him.[114] In the sermon for the Month's Mind of the Lady Margaret, Fisher borrows the classical scheme for the praise of a great personage; before life, in life, and after death. The orator was expected to praise the ancestors, the gifts of body, fortune and mind, of the subject of his discourse, together with his noble deeds and glorious death.[115] Thus Fisher speaks of Lady Margaret's noble family, her exemplary manners, her gifts and virtues, her ascetical practices and good works, her painful but holy death, and the hope of her salvation.[116] However, this occurs only in a subdivision, and otherwise the construction is a modification of the medieval ' modern ' style.

Ecclesiastes, pp. 210–43, 402–4. See too H. Caplan, 'Classical Rhetoric and the Mediaeval Theory of Preaching,' *C.P.*, xxviii. 2 (1933) p. 95; 'A Late Mediaeval Tractate on Preaching, the Pseudo-Aquinas Tract,' (in *Studies in Rhetoric and Public Speaking in honour of James Albert Winans*, New York, 1925, p. 69)

[110] *Ecclesiastes*, pp. 6–7.   [111] *English Works*, Pt. I, p. 269.   [112] Ibid. p. 271. [113] Ibid. p. 276.   [114] Ibid. p. 281.

[115] Cf. Quintilian, *Institutio Oratoriae*, lib. III, cap. vii. 10–19; (ed. and tr. H. E. Butler, 2 vols., London, 1920–2, Loeb, vol. I, pp. 468–72); also C. S. Baldwin, *Medieval Rhetoric and Poetic*, (New York, 1928) pp. 30–2, for the lists of topics given by Hermogenes, Aphthonius and Menander.

[116] *English Works*, Pt. I, pp. 290–303.

II

THE EARLY REFORMERS (1547–1553)

It is noteworthy that the Reformers completely discard the elaborate ' modern ' style, and use various simple methods of construction. Their concern is to be direct and forcible, rather than to be subtle and learned. The ' First Book of Homilies ' provides short topical treatments of its subjects without anything of the old method of ' divisions '. For example, the first homily 'A Fruitful Exhortation to the Reading and Knowledge of Holy Scripture ' (attributed to Cranmer), is constructed as follows: Part I shows why a knowledge of Scripture is necessary and profitable to all men, and that by true knowledge of it, the most necessary points of man's duty to God and to his neighbour are known;[117] Part II shows how the excuses put forward by some that they dare not read Scripture [(a) that they are afraid of falling into error, and (b) that Scripture is so hard, it should be read only by learned men] are invalid, and ends with an exhortation to partake of the deep joy of reading the Bible.[118] Lever too adopts a very simple scheme in his sermons; after a brief Exordium he reads a passage of Scripture from the Gospel or Epistle of the Day, which he expounds and applies to his audience *secundum ordinem textus*. The ' Sermon in the Shrouds at St. Paul's ' is constructed as follows: the Exordium deals with England's need to repent if she is to escape God's vengeance, in particular the sin of covetous ambition must be eschewed;[119] then the text, the Epistle for Epiphany IV (Rom. xiii. 1–7) is read and applied to the audience; poor men have been rebels and rich men alas! have not done their duty.[120] The ' Sermon before the King ' once more takes for an Exordium England's need for repentance if the Divine wrath is to be warded off;[121] the text, the Gospel for Lent IV (John vi. 1–14) is read, and applied to the various orders in the commonwealth.[122] The ' Sermon at Paul's Cross ' takes as Exordium the treason of Londoners to God and the king;[123] then the text, the Epistle for Advent III (1 Cor. v. 1–5) is read, and applied to castigate covetousness, unworthy clergy and corrupt officers, to lament the decay of the universities, and to detail the duties of the various orders in the kingdom.[124] The famous sermon preached at Court by Bernard

---

[117] *Certain Sermons appointed by the Queen's Majesty*, pp. 1–5.
[118] Ibid. pp. 5–10.   [119] *Sermons*, pp. 21–5.   [120] Ibid. pp. 25–51.
[121] Ibid. pp. 55–9.   [122] Ibid. pp. 60–90, see *ante*, pp. 44–5.
[123] Ibid. p. 101.   [124] Ibid. pp. 102–43.

Gilpin, the 'Apostle of the North', a great nephew of Tunstall, is also simply constructed; the preacher gives out his text, 'Know ye not that I must be about my Father's business?' (Luke ii. 49) and outlines its occasion,[125] after which comes an application—very few do God's will in the commonwealth, either in the Church or in civil occupations.[126] Ecclesiastical abuses are detailed and castigated, as are the sins of the nobles, magistrates and public officers.[127]

The sermons of Bradford also are quite simply constructed. That on the Lord's Supper consists of an Exordium, a Division into three topics and an amplification of the members of the Division.[128] Perhaps in this simplification of the 'modern' scheme, which approximates to the essentials of the classical oration, we may see the influence of the arrangement recommended by Melancthon and Erasmus.[129] In the Exordium Bradford declares that there are but two sacraments, Baptism and the Lord's Supper, and on this occasion he will expound the Supper.[130] To do this he will consider three things: *who*, *what*, and *wherefore*: (A) who did institute this thing which we are about to celebrate; (B) what the thing is which is instituted; (C) wherefore and to what end it was instituted.[131] Although there is no technical 'subdivision' of any of these, in (B), however, nine reasons against Transubstantiation are given,[132] and in (C) five benefits of worthy reception of Communion are outlined.[133] The 'Sermon of Repentance' is looser in construction, but again is without formal elaboration. The text is, 'Repent ye for the kingdom of heaven is at hand' (Matt. iii. 2), and after an Exordium on the thankfulness which we should render to God for the gift of life and sundry other benefits,[134] Bradford divides the text into: (A) a command to repent: 'Repent ye'; (B) a showing of the cause why we should repent: 'for the kingdom of heaven is at hand'.[135] From these we should note: (a) the corruption of our nature—we need something to urge us to do right, the reward of heaven; (b) we must repent for the corruption of nature, and for our sins; (c) each member of the audience must regard this command and repent personally.[136] The main body of the sermon is not concerned however with any of these divisions; it is an exposition of the three parts of Penance according to Protestant teaching: (A)

---

[125] *A godly sermon preached before the court at Greenwhich* . . . 1552, (London, 1581) pp. 1–5.   [126] Ibid. pp. 5–9.   [127] Ibid. pp. 13–16.
[128] *The Writings of John Bradford*, vol. I, pp. 82–110.   [129] See *ante*, p. 85, n. 109.
[130] *The Writings of John Bradford*, vol. I, pp. 82–3.   [131] Ibid.
[132] Ibid. pp. 85–91.   [133] Ibid. p. 99.   [134] Ibid. p. 43.
[135] Ibid. pp. 43–4.   [136] Ibid. p. 44.

contrition, (B) faith, (C) newness of life.[137] The conclusion shows in a practical manner how repentance is obtained: looking into God's law and seeing how we have transgressed gives us knowledge of sin, for which we can repent in the way expounded before.[138]

Latimer's sermons, which show some variety of arrangement, are nevertheless also simple in construction. The celebrated sermons of the Card are ' figure sermons ' built on the game of Triumph, (a forerunner of whist). The text of both sermons is from the Gospel for Advent IV: *Tu quis es?* (John i. 19) and in an introductory passage Latimer tells his audience that, although by nature they are children of wrath, by Baptism each man's answer must be ' I am a Christian man '. The Christian has his ' rule of life ', just as the Friars have; it consists of the ten Commandments, the works of mercy and so on, but as it is near Christmas, the preacher will express this rule in cards.[139] Latimer deals his first card, ' Thou shalt not kill ' and adds Christ's spiritual extension of the meaning of this, to include all anger. Each man must put his trump card, his heart, on this and win salvation.[140] The second sermon deals a second card, of the same suit; a text from St. Matthew's Gospel ' Therefore if thou bring thy gift to the altar, and there rememberest that thy brother hath ought against thee; leave there thy gift before the altar, and go thy way; first be reconciled to thy brother, and then come and offer thy gift ' (Matt. v. 23–4). Let each man cast his trump, his heart, on these two cards, and then indeed he will win salvation.[141] However, adds Latimer in conclusion, the oblation will not be accepted by God unless the necessary works of mercy have been performed.[142]

The sermon to Convocation (1537), which falls into two parts (one delivered in the morning, the other in the afternoon), is simply and straightforwardly arranged. The text is, ' The children of this world are in their generation wiser than the children of light ' (Luke xvi. 8), and after a short Exordium[143] Latimer goes to the beginning of the parable in which these words occur to establish that the ' rich man ' is Christ, and the steward represents the clergy.[144] A steward should be faithful, but have the clergy of England been faithful to their calling? Have they not rather perverted the Gospel for gain; so that the papists have been wiser in their generation than the truly faithful ministers?[145] In the second sermon Latimer declares

---

[137] Ibid. p. 45; developed, ibid. pp. 45–79.   [138] Ibid. pp. 79–81.
[139] *Sermons*, pp. 3–8.   [140] Ibid. pp. 9–16.   [141] Ibid. pp. 17–22.
[142] Ibid. pp. 22–4.   [143] Ibid. pp. 33–4.   [144] Ibid. pp. 34–5.   [145] Ibid. pp. 36–40.

that the children of the world are the children of the Devil, not laymen: nor are the children of light the clergy, for some bishops are children of the world. The deeds of the children of the world declare them, no matter what they may profess—for what have the Convocations done in seven years? They have burnt a dead man, intrigued against Latimer himself, and tried to secure the condemnation of Erasmus as a heretic. The children of this world extol voluntary works, and all the profitable abuses from Rome, especially purgatory pick-purse.[146] Latimer then enumerates and castigates the abuses in England: in the Court of the Arches, the Consistory courts, in Ceremonies, holidays, images, relics, false miracles, the use of Latin in Baptism and Matrimony, and the selling of masses.[147] Finally comes the natural conclusion in an exhortation to love the light and preach the word diligently.[148] Canon Charles Smyth has written of Latimer's method: ' He does not begin by laying down dogmatic propositions which he then proceeds to illustrate by examples: he begins by indicating briefly what he has to say, and then works up to it through a concrete illustration or series of concrete illustrations ',[149] and as an example of this he analyses the beginning of the Sermon of the Plough.[150] This is true also of the sermons on the Lord's Prayer,[151] and of those on various Gospels and Epistles preached in the country.[152] For example, in the sermon at Stamford on Matt. xxii. 21, *Reddite ergo quae sunt Caesaris Caesari et quae sunt Dei Deo* (from the Gospel for Trinity XXIII; ' Render therefore unto Caesar the things which are Caesar's; and unto God the things that are God's '), Latimer uses the incidents of the Gospel as the basis of his generalizations. He begins with a brief statement:

> For the better understanding of this place, ye shall understand, Christ came to bring us out of bondage, and to set us at liberty, not from civil burdens, as from obeying the magistrates, from paying tax and tribute; but from a greater burthen, and a more grievouser burthen, the burthen of sin; the burthen not of the body, but of the soul; to make us free from it, and to redeem us from the course and malediction of the law unto the honourable state of the children of God. But as for the civil burthens, he delivered us not from them, but rather commanded us to pay them.[153]

Latimer then indicates the necessity of regarding the circumstances going before the speaking of this text; ' Who spake these words: to

146 Ibid. pp. 41–51.   147 Ibid. pp. 52–6.   148 Ibid. p. 57.
149 *The Art of Preaching*, p. 111.   150 Ibid. pp. 111–13.
151 *Sermons*, pp. 326–446.   152 Ibid. pp. 282–308; 447–551; *Remains*, p. 1–216.
153 *Sermons*, p. 282.

whom they were spoken, upon what occasion and afore whom?'[154] The disciples of the Pharisees accompanied by the Herodians, spoke these words to Christ, seeking to trap Him in his speech, to destroy Him; but Christ's reply is ' doctrine unto us that are Christ's disciples '.[155] Then after the Prayers, Latimer shows how the beginning of the Gospel, *Tunc abeuntes*, hangs on the preceding Parable of the Marriage Feast, which he expounds briefly as an encouragement to preachers who must call the laity to the Gospel, but are not to be blamed if they refuse to come.[156] So, proceeding *secundum ordinem textus*, Latimer draws out the application of this Gospel; the Council of the Pharisees allows him to speak of the shortcomings of General Councils: ' More credence is to be given to one man having the holy word of God for him, than to ten thousand without the word', and alas! how much wickedness is done by the papists *in nomine Domini*![157] The Pharisees and Herodians were enemies but agreed to destroy Christ; ' So many nowadays of our Pharisees, papists, in destroying the truth they agree wondrous well, whereas in private matters they hate one another as a toad '.[158] Then from the behaviour of the questioners we learn the craft of hypocrites; they say ' Master we know that thou art Tom Truth ', and indeed Christ taught the plain truth, as must preachers without the ' mingle mangle of man's traditions '.[159] Thus patrons must bestow benefices on true preachers, for preaching is the office of salvation.[160] This allows Latimer to sketch the properties of a true preacher, who must preach the Gospel and not dreams of men, and also must never be a flatterer.[161] Christ's answer to the subtle question showed supernatural wisdom; so are preachers given wisdom when papists seek to entrap them; as indeed was Latimer himself, when he was examined in King Henry's time.[162] From Christ's answer *Reddite ergo*, etc., Latimer draws the lesson ' Make not a mingle-mangle of them; but give to God his own, give to Caesar his own. To God give thy soul, thy faith, thy hope, thy obedient mind, to keep his word, and frame thy life thereafter: to Caesar give tribute, tax, subsidy, and all other duties pertaining to him; as to have him in thy honour and reverence, and to obey his just laws and righteous commandments, etc.'[163]

In the afternoon Latimer completes his application; Christ made the Pharisees answer their own question, as He had done shortly

[154] Ibid. pp. 282–3.   [155] Ibid. p. 283.   [156] Ibid. pp. 284–6.
[157] Ibid. pp. 287–8.   [158] Ibid. p. 289.   [159] Ibid. pp. 289–90.
[160] Ibid. pp. 290–2.   [161] Ibid. p. 292.
[162] Ibid. pp. 293–5.   [163] Ibid. p. 295.

before, when they asked Him by whose authority he taught. He had
asked them again whether John had authority of God or man;
which forced them to reply ' We do not know, we cannot tell '—for,
adds Latimer, ' These arch Pharisees thought nothing might be
done or taught without their license, nor otherwise but as they
pleased to interpret. They were like our religion and clergy, that
thought nothing might be taught but as they pleased.'[164] As
Christ said ' Give unto Caesar that which is Caesar's ', so must
Englishmen fulfil all their civil duties; especially tax paying.
Similarly they must not neglect their duty to God, keeping the
Commandments and paying tithes. Many however, alas! give their
heart to Caesar, and to God only an outward service with vain
ceremonies.[165] But let us keep faithfully this command of Christ,
for so shall we be blest in this life and rejoice evermore in the
next.[166]

However, most of Latimer's sermons suffer from looseness of
structure and are encumbered with digressions. The famous ' Seven
Sermons ' before the King take as text St. Paul's words, ' Whatsoever things were written aforetime were written for our learning
that we through patience and comfort of the scriptures might have
hope ' (Rom. xv. 4), to allow the preacher freedom in his choice of
topics.[167] Thus with the exception of the seventh sermon, which
is for Good Friday,[168] the series is built on four main passages of
Scripture, the treatment of which overlaps into the following
sermons—frequently necessitating recapitulation at the outset.
These are, first, Deut. xvii. 14–20: the duties of a king, which
Latimer applies to Edward;[169] secondly, Luke xviii. 2–5: the Parable
of the Importunate Widow, which allows him to expatiate on
corruptions in justice;[170] thirdly, 1 Samuel viii: the episode of the
Israelites asking the aged Samuel for a king, as his sons are mis-
governing, which he uses to castigate corrupt officers;[171] and
fourthly, Luke v. 1–3: the occasion when Christ taught the people
from Simon's boat, which provides a starting point for a dis-
quisition on the importance of preaching and the necessity for hearing sermons quietly without ' huzzing and buzzing '.[172] However
within this framework Latimer introduces many disgressions: he
gives his version of the *scala coeli* (the knowledge and following
of the Scripture), with its five steps;[173] he defends himself against

[164] Ibid. pp. 296–7.   [165] Ibid. pp. 298–305.   [166] Ibid. pp. 306–7.
[167] Ibid. p. 85.   [168] Ibid. pp. 216–38.   [169] Ibid. pp. 87–103, 112–22.
[170] Ibid. pp. 128, 142–50.   [171] Ibid. pp. 173–93.
[172] Ibid. 198–204.   [173] Ibid. pp. 97, 123, 178.

critics;[174] attacks the Lord Admiral;[175] brings notable instances of the miscarriage of justice to the king's notice;[176] inveighs against whoredom and recommends the wholesome exercise of shooting.[177] The last sermon before Edward, the *Ultimum Vale*, is equally rambling; its effectiveness depends upon its vigour and sincerity, not upon any skill in arrangement. This great sermon against covetousness is constructed as follows. The text is ' Take heed, and beware of covetousness: for a man's life consisteth not in the abundance of the things which he possesseth ' (Luke xii. 15). In the first part, Latimer, after an Exordium which points out that Jonah preached to the Ninevites and they heard him, but the English do not listen to the preachers, although their state is worse than that of the Ninevites,[178] proceeds to a digression on marriage.[179] He then introduces the main topic, covetousness, the root of all evil at which the preachers must strike.[180] Then follow two further digressions, on women,[181] and on the duties of great men to rise early and hear suitors.[182] The Division of the text is then squeezed in before the second part; *Quis dicat*; *quid dicat*; *cui dicat*; *et quare dicat*.[183] The second part begins with the context of the words of the text, Christ was sowing seeds of doctrine,[184] viz., (a) ' Beware ye of the leaven of the Pharisees, which is hypocrisy ' (Luke xii. 2); (b) ' For there is nothing covered that shall not be revealed; neither hid that shall not be known ' (ibid.), so let those make restitution who ought to do so; (c) 'And I say unto you my friends, do not be afraid of them that kill the body, and after that have no more that they can do. But I will forewarn you whom ye shall fear: fear him, which after he hath killed hath power to cast into hell; yea, I say unto you, fear him ' (Luke xii. 4–5); (d) ' Whosoever shall confess us before men, him shall the Son of man also confess before the angels of God ' (Luke xii. 8); (e) ' Unto him that blasphemeth against the Holy Ghost it shall not be forgiven ' (Luke xii. 10); (f) 'And when they bring you unto the synagogues, and unto magistrates, and powers, take ye no thought how or what thing ye shall answer, or what ye shall say: for the Holy Ghost shall teach you in the same hour what ye ought to say ' (Luke xii. 11–12); (g) ' Give and it shall be given unto you ' (Luke vi. 38—not spoken by Christ on *this* occasion!)[185] Then follows the true *matter* of the sermon, the evil of covetousness, the need for preaching, the need for promoters,

---

[174] Ibid. pp. 134–41, 154–5.   [175] Ibid. pp. 161–4.   [176] Ibid. pp. 127–8. 189–91.
[177] Ibid. pp. 196–8.   [178] Ibid. pp. 239–42.   [179] Ibid. pp. 243–4.
[180] Ibid. pp. 354–6.   [181] Ibid. pp. 252–4.   [182] Ibid. p. 255.
[183] Ibid. p. 256.   [184] Ibid. pp. 256–8.   [185] Ibid. pp. 258–70.

the wickedness of regraters and the folly of setting one's heart on riches.[186]

It is interesting to notice that the form of construction which was to become standard with the Elizabethan Puritans is used in this reign by Hooper in his series on Jonah. This form consists of the exposition of a passage of Scripture, *secundum ordinem textus*, by gathering ' Doctrines ' or lessons from each verse, and adding the ' Uses ' or moral applications of these.[187] Hooper's method is to give a short Preface to each sermon, and then to present the Doctrines and Uses arising from the portion of Jonah which he is expounding. Thus in the second sermon, in the Preface Hooper speaks of vocation, which can be godly or against God's word. It is a sin (a) to bear the name of a vocation and not to perform the duties connected with it, or (b) to do what ought not to be done by one in that vocation. Jonah avoided *his* vocation, and fell into danger. God alone saves men from danger, not the saints, so let the king see that true religion is taught in England! In their difficulty the mariners did not only pray, they laboured also, as must all men.[188] In the main body of the sermon, Hooper deals with several verses, extracting the Doctrines and Uses: from Jonah i. 7 ('And they said everyone to his fellow, Come, and let us cast lots, that we may know for whose cause this evil is upon us. So they cast lots and the lot fell upon Jonah ') we learn that the cause of disaster is sin, that if sin remains hidden for a time, yet it will eventually come to light, and also we are taught how troubles in a kingdom may be appeased —by casting out Jonahs.[189] So, in application, the preacher urges that to assuage the troubles in England the bad members of each order should be punished.[190] From the next verse, Jonah i. 8 (' Then said they unto him, Tell us we pray thee, for whose cause this evil is upon us; what is thine occupation? and whence comest thou? What is thy country? and of what people art thou? ') we learn that we should behave with humanity towards afflicted persons and that no man should be condemned without examination. So in application, Hooper points out that only those wicked persons who disturb the state are to be punished; such men must be diligently examined, and the innocent acquitted.[191]

---

[186] Ibid. pp. 270–81.   [187] See *post*, pp. 101–2.
[188] *Early Writings*, pp. 456–8.   [189] Ibid. pp. 458–9.
[190] Ibid. pp. 459–61.   [191] Ibid. pp. 461–2.

III

THE PREACHERS OF MARY'S REIGN (1553–1558)

The restoration of Catholicism witnesses the revival of the ' modern style ', albeit in modified form. John de Feckenham, Dean of St. Paul's (later last Abbot of Westminster) in a funeral sermon for the Queen of Spain (1555) takes the same text as Baron had used in his learned university sermons, *Gens absque consilio est et sine prudentia. Utinam saperent et intelligerent ac novissima providerent* (Deut. xxxii. 28–9, ' They are a nation without counsel, and without wisdom. O that they would be wise and would understand, and would provide for their last end ', Douay)[192], and divides the text at the outset: (A) *sapere*; be wise, refers to the past; (B) *intelligere*; understand, to the present; (C) *novissima providere*; to the future, to the provision for things to come.[193] This is supported by a text from Proverbs, *Acceptus est regi minister intelligens, iracundiam eius inutilis sustinebit* (Prov. xiv. 35, 'A wise servant is acceptable to the king: he that is good for nothing shall feel his anger ', Douay.)[194] After the Prayers Feckenham exhorts his audience to know: (A) that life passes, (B) the miseries thereof, (C) the sentence of death pronounced to every man: which correspond to the Division of the text.[195] Memory of these things brings: (a) the destruction of pride, (b) the quenching of envy, (c) medicine for malice, (d) the driving away of lechery, (e) the extirpation of worldly boast, (f) the recovery of everlasting life.[196] But alas! how long will men be *gens absque consilio*?[197] Feckenham concludes with an outline of the four last things: (a) Death, (b) Judgement, (c) Hell, (d) Heaven, and of the provision which all men must make against them: (a) that we may finish life and die well, (b) that we may receive merciful judgement, (c) we must make provision *here*, and avoid the pains of hell, (d) we must so provide here to live as not to lose heaven.[198] The various orders in the commonwealth must make diverse provision: the priests must teach good doctrine; the people must listen to the voices of their shepherds; the noblemen must see that due provision is made for the church; the married must remember their duties, as must masters

---

[192] See *ante*, p. 78.

[193] *A notable sermon made within S. Paules church in London, in the presence of certen of the kinges and Quenes moost honorable priuie counsell at the celebration of the exequies of the right excellent and famous Princesse, Lady Ione, Quene of Spayne, Sicilie and Nauarre etc., the XVIII of Iune, Anno* 1555 (London. 1555) sig. Aiiᵛ–Aiiiʳ.

[194] Ibid. sig. Aiiiʳ. [195] Ibid. sig. Avʳ– Biiiᵛ. [196] Ibid. sig. Bivʳ.
[197] Ibid. sig. Bvʳ. [198] Ibid. sig. Ciiiᵛ-Civʳ.

and servants. Due provision in these matters leads to a happy death.[199]

Pollard, in his homily ' Of fayth and knowledge of God ', does not use a text on which to build the sermon, but nevertheless employs an elaborate arrangement reminiscent of the modern scheme. At the outset he declares, ' I wyll shewe you ' (A) ' what fayth is ', (B) ' howe fayth must be used ', (C) ' howe it must be defended, that we do not erre or be deceaued therein '.[200] Each of these is extensively subdivided, although without cadence and assonance in the enunciation. (A) Faith is: (a) trust in the promises of God, (b) the assuredness which we have of things beyond sense.[201] On these matters of faith Pollard desires the audience to mark: (i) ' who is the reporter ', (ii) ' what be the thynges that are reported ', (iii) ' what they must be to whom this report is made '.[202] Thus, (i) God is the reporter, so that we must note: (1) 'the mercifull goodness of GOD, who doth so vouchsafe to teache such sory and wretched creatures '; (2) ' howe happy be we that haue such a master '; (3) ' howe safe and holsome are those lesson[s] which we lerne of him, the which thynge yf we dyd pythely consyder: O howe they wolde make oure stonye hartes to melte '.[203] Then (ii) the things reported are: (1) the Scriptures, (2) the sacraments, (3) the Christian duties, and the reward promised if these are performed:[204] while (iii) those to whom the report is made must be obedient to such a master in: (1) soul, (2) body, (3) goods;[205] so that we should consider: α ' how hard a thing it is to be a true student or scholar of fayth ', β ' what reuerence they that be faithfull do giue to God who subdue senses & reason ', γ ' how all faithless people especially heretics do blaspheme God who credit reason & senses more than God '.[206] Further, (B) faith must be used in the spirit of little children who have: (a) simplicity, (b) who ask and receive all things of their parents, (c) who are ruled by their parents by love, or if necessary by fear.[207] Of these, (b) is further subdivided into: (1) our dignity —God lets us speak to Him; (ii) how peaceful we could be, if we followed His will; (iii) how wholesome are the things which our Father gives us, and on the contrary how dangerous are the things given us by the Devil.[208] Then follows (C), we must beware lest the

[199] Ibid. sig. Civ^v-Dvi^r.
[200] *Fyue homilies*, sig. Ciiii^v, as marked, counting from the first page, sig. Eiv^v.
[201] Ibid. sig. Ciiii^v-Civ^r, (Eiv^v- Fi^r).   [202] Ibid. sig. Civ^r, (Fi^r).
[203] Ibid. sig. Ci^r-v, (Fi^r-v).   [204] Ibid. sig. Di^r-Dii^r, (Fii^r-Fiii^r).
[205] Ibid. sig. Dii^r, (Fiii^r).   [206] Ibid. sig. Diiv-Diii^r, (Fiii^v-Fiv^r).
[207] Ibid. sig. Diiii^r-Div^v, (Fiv^r- Gi^v).   [208] Ibid. sig. Div^v-Ei^r, (Gi^v-Gii^r).

Devil deceive us, by keeping in the house of our Father: (a) for these reasons: (i) the keeper is so strong that none can overthrow Him and spoil His house; (ii) the house is built on a rock, and the gates of hell will never prevail against it; (iii) those inside the house cannot be deceived by error, because they have the Spirit of all truth as a schoolmaster.[209] (b) How then shall we find this house? (i) It is the first built; (ii) it is large; (iii) it enjoys unity of faith.[210] This last is further divided to answer an objection that the Doctors disagree amongst themselves: (1) the Doctors' disagreement is in details only, not in essentials; (2) no Doctor is universally deceived; (3) the Doctors have corrected each other's errors.[211]

Most of the preachers of Mary's reign do not however use the 'modern' scheme with such elaboration; they content themselves with an Exordium, Prayer, Division into (most frequently) three topics (which usually do not depend on the words of the text) and Confirmation of the Division with little if any subdivision. So, as in the case of Bradford,[212] we may perhaps see the influence of Renaissance *artes praedicandi* as the *Ecclesiastes* of Erasmus. Brooks, in his Paul's Cross sermon, has an Exordium on the application he gives to the raising of Jairus's daughter; the desire of the Mother Church of Rome to revive from spiritual death the daughter Church of England together with an expatiation on the qualities of the Catholic Church and its survival of persecution.[213] After the Prayer comes the Division; England is dead for three causes: (A) for lack of unity with the church; (B) for lack of faith; (C) for lack of charity and good living.[214] Brooks then confirms (B) and (C), for he declares, (A) has already been dealt with in the Exordium.[215] Glasier's Paul's Cross sermon takes as text the Gospel for Trinity XI (Luke xviii. 9–14, the story of the Pharisee and the Publican who went up to the temple to pray) and after an Exordium which shows that Christ in this parable goes about to cleanse us of self-love and confidence in ourselves,[216] proceeds to the Prayers and Division: *Part I*; (A) ' I doe consider howe these two men went, of whom the gospell speaketh '; ['they did go together '] (B) ' I do consider whither they went '; [' they went to the temple '] (C) ' I do consider wherfore they went '; [' they went to pray ']; *Part II*: ' I . . . consider particularly their seuerall praiers '; (A) ' by themselfe ', (B) ' with the issue

---

[209] Ibid. sig. Eiᵛ-Eiiᵛ, (Giiᵛ-Giiiᵛ).   [210] Ibid. sig. Eiiʳ-Fiʳ, (Giv--Hiiʳ).
[211] Ibid. sig. Fiᵛ-Fiiʳ, (Hiiᵛ-Hiiiʳ).   [212] See *ante*, p. 88.
[213] *A sermon very notable, fruitefull, and Godlie*, sig. Aiiʳ-Diᵛ.
[214] Ibid. sig. Diᵛ-Diiʳ.   [215] Ibid. sig. Diiʳ.
[216] *A notable and very fruitcefull sermon made at Paules crosse*, sig. Aiiʳ-Aiiiʳ.

H

and the effecte thereof '.[217] In the development of Part I, Glasier includes under (A) three great offences prevalent in the realm at the time, (a) lack of reverence for the Blessed Sacrament, (b) rebellion, (c) lying;[218] but this forms only part of his treatment of this section, while (B) and (C) are simply developed.[219] In the development of Part II, Glasier considers (A) and (B) first with reference to the Pharisee's prayer and secondly to the Publican's prayer.[220]

A modification of the ' modern ' scheme is found also in John Harpesfield's two formal sermons. In that preached in Latin *ad clerum* at St. Paul's in 1553, Harpesfield takes a text from the Acts of the Apostles, spoken by St. Paul, *Attendite vobis et universo gregi, in quo vos Spiritus sanctus posuit episcopos regere ecclesiam Dei, quam adquisivit sanguine suo* (Acts xx. 28, ' Take heed to yourselves, and to the whole flock, wherein the Holy Ghost hath placed you bishops, to rule the church of God, which he hath purchased with his own blood ', Douay), and after a Ciceronian apology for his personal inadequacy proceeds to the Division: (A) *primum, quam bene Paulus (cuius haec sunt verba) & sibi & gregi attenderit*: [' first, what good heed Paul, whose words these are, takes to himself and the flock '] (B) *secundum, quam male, nostris hisce temporibus, pastores in utroque, se cura gesserint*: [' secondly, how badly, in these our times, pastors in general execute their cure '] (C) *tertium, qua via sit ingrediendum ut et nobis et nostro gregi deinceps bene attendamus*: [' thirdly, what way should be entered upon, so that we in turn should take good heed to ourselves and the flock '].[221] These are expanded in the main body; (A) has a little subdivision: St. Paul warns us against three pests: (a) adulation, (b) avarice, (c) vainglory;[222] while he warns Timothy to have care: (a) in doctrine, (b) in defending the flock from wolves, (c) in providing worthy ministers.[223] (B) and (C) are however more simply confirmed. In (B) the evils of Edward's reign are lamented, [224] and in (C) the preacher exhorts his clerical audience to be firmer in their stand for the faith now than they were under Edward.[225]

In his English sermon preached in St. Paul's on St. Andrew's Day 1556, Harpesfield in the Exordium divides Ps. cxvii (Vg.) into four parts; in it David declares: (A) he had been in peril of life and grief of soul; (B) God of his mercy delivered him; (C) those vexations were a scourge for sin; (D) he thanks God his deliverer and exhorts

---

[217] Ibid. sig. Aviiir-Bir.   [218] Ibid. sig. Bviiiv-Cviiv.
[219] Ibid. sig. Cviiir-Dviiv.   [220] Ibid. sig. Dviiv-Eviir.
[221] *Concio . . . habita coram patribus et clero in Ecclesia Paulina Londini*, sig. Aiir-v.
[222] Ibid. sig. Avr.   [223] Ibid. sig. Aviiiv-Bir.   [224] Ibid. sig. Bivr-Bviv.
[225] Ibid. sig. Bviv-Bviiiv.

others to do likewise.[226] These are briefly expanded, and then applied to the feast on which the sermon is being preached: (A) let us remember the miserable state of late years; (B) how God has delivered us; (C) that we suffered those miseries for our sins; (D) let us render thanks.[227] However, adds Harpesfield, he will expand only the first two.[228] After the Prayers he proceeds to confirm these without further subdivision.[229]

Watson, in his learned sermons on the Blessed Sacrament, allows the confirmation of part (C) of the Division in the first sermon to form the Exordium of the second. In the first sermon he declares that three things hold him to the old faith regarding Transubstantiation: (A) plain Scripture; (B) the uniform authority of the Doctors; (C) the consent of the Church;[230] but he deals with (A) and (B) only in this sermon,[231] while in the main body of the second he seeks to prove the sacrifice of the Mass by: (A) the institution of Our Lord; (B) the prophecy of Malachi; (C) the ' figure ' of Melchizedek.[232] To this he adds three ways in which Christ offered Himself in sacrifice; (A) really and corporally on the cross; (B) figuratively in the Paschal Lamb; (C) continually in heaven;[233] and three ways in which He is offered by men: (A) figuratively in the Oblations of the Old Testament; (B) mystically in the Mass; (C) spiritually, whenever we meditate on the Passion;[234] while finally in each Mass there is: (A) Consecration; (B) Oblation; (C) Participation.[235]

The simple ' ancient ' form is found too in this reign in Bonner's *Homilies*, which are similar in method to those of Edward's reign. For example John Harpesfield's ' Homily of Transubstantiation ' adopts a simple topical treatment: (A) in the Blessed Sacrament, the substance of the bread and the wine is changed, only the ' fourmes ' remain;[236] (B) in the Old Testament, God appeared to man under various forms—as with two angels to Abraham, like men, or to Moses as fire.[237] Yet this is difficult to explain! so: (C) Our Lord

[226] *A notable and learned Sermon or Homilie, made vpon Saint Andrewes daye last past* 1556 *in the Cathedral churche of St. Paule in London, by Mayster Iohn Harpesfield doctour of diuinitie and Canon residenciary of the sayd churche, Set forth by the bishop of London* (London, 1556) sig. Aii[r-v].
    [227] Ibid. sig. Aii[v]-Aiv[v].   [228] Ibid. sig. Aiv[v].   [229] Ibid. sig. Av[r]-Ciii[r].
    [230] *Twoo notable Sermons*, sig. Bvii[r].
    [231] Ibid. sig. Bviii[v]-Lii[v]; (C) is expanded as the Exordium of the second sermon, ibid. sig. Liii[r]-Niv[r].
    [232] Ibid. sig. Oiv[r]; confirmed, sig. Oiv[v]-Riii[v].   [233] Ibid. sig. Riv[r-v].
    [234] Ibid. sig. Rvi[r]-Rviii[v].   [235] Ibid. sig. Yi[r].
    [236] *A profitable and necessarye doctryne, with certayne homelies adioyned therevnto*, f. 58[r].
    [237] Ibid. f. 58[v].

appears as bread and wine in the Blessed Sacrament, because He is there our spiritual food,[238] (D) the writings of the Fathers confirm the doctrine of the Real Presence;[239] (E) also ' bread ' in Scripture means ' food '—both of the body and the soul.[240] Watson's ' Sermons on the Sacraments ' give straightforward topical treatments also, although that on the Gifts of the Holy Ghost is built on the traditional scheme of parallels between the capital vices, the Gifts, the opposite virtues, and the petitions of the *Pater Noster*:

	Vice	*Gift*	*Virtue*	*Pater Noster*
(A)	Pride	Holy Fear	Humility	' Hallowed be thy name.'
(B)	Envy	Pity (Piety)	Meekness	' Thy Kingdom come.'
(C)	Ire	Knowledge	Mourning	' Thy will be done.'
(D)	Sloth	Fortitude	Thirst for Righteousness	' Give us this day our daily bread.'
(E)	Covetousness	Counsel	Mercifulness	' Forgive us our trespasses.'
(F)	Gluttony	Understanding	Cleanness of Heart	' Lead us not into temptation.'
(G)	Lechery	Wisdom	Making peace	' Deliver us from evil.'[241]

Simple also in construction are Feckenham's ' Two Homilies on the first, second and third articles of the Creed', [242] which are similar in method to Edgeworth's ' Homily on the Creed ', expounding the articles in order.[243]

IV

THE ELIZABETHAN PREACHERS (1558–1603)

In this reign three methods of construction may be differentiated: the ' ancient ' form, the new Reformed arrangement of Doctrines and Uses, and the ' modern style ' so modified as to approximate to the true classical form with its variations. First, the ' ancient ' form is found once more in Becon's *Postils* which follow the method of those of Taverner in brief exposition of the sum of the Gospels and Epistles.[244] The series on Jonah by Abbott[245] and that by King;[246]

[238] Ibid. ff. 58ᵛ-9ʳ.   [239] Ibid. ff. 59ʳ-60ᵛ.   [240] Ibid. ff. 60ᵛ-61ᵛ.
[241] *Holsome and Catholyke doctryne concerning the Seuen Sacraments*, ff. 29ʳ-35ᵛ. Cf. Ross, *Middle English Sermons*, pp. 10-11, 49, 341, 346.
[242] *Two Homilies vpon the first, second, and third articles of the Crede, made by maister Iohn Feknam, Deane of Paules* (London, [1555?]).
[243] See *ante*, p. 74.   [244] See *ante*, ibid.
[245] *An Exposition upon the Prophet Jonah.*   [246] *Lectures upon Jonah.*

that on the *Nunc Dimittis* by Anthony Anderson;[247] that of Deringe on Hebrews;[248] and that on Obadiah and Haggai by Rainolds,[249] like that of Edgeworth on St. Peter's First Epistle, proceed *secundum ordinem textus* to expound and apply the meaning.[250] The ' Second Book of Homilies ', like the First, provides short topical expositions of the subjects treated;[251] the ' Homily against Gluttony and Drunkenness ', (attributed to Pilkington, although most of it is a translation of Peter Martyr's *Commentary on the Book of Judges*) is constructed as follows: (A) all kinds of excess displease God;[252] (B) He punishes such excess grievously;[253] (C) noisome diseases and great mischiefs follow upon excess.[254] Similar topical expositions are found in the sermons of Richard Greenham (successively Rector of Dry Drayton, Cambridgeshire, and preacher at Christ Church, Newgate),[255] and also in many of the sermons of Henry Smith.[256]

Secondly, the new Reformed method, which we have noticed in the sermons of Hooper, [257] is found in the Lectures of the extreme Puritans. Popularized by the Latin commentaries of Musculus (Wolfgang Muesslin, 1497–1563),[258] this form is outlined in Perkins's *Art of Prophecying*: the preacher is: (1) ' to reade the Text distinctly

[247] *The Shield of our Safetie.*
[248] *XXVII Lectures or readings vpon part of the Epistle written to the Hebrues.*
[249] *The Prophecy of Obadiah opened and applied in sundry sermons; The Prophecy of Haggai interpreted and applied in sundry sermons.*
[250] See *ante*, p. 74.   [251] See *ante*, p. 87.
[252] *Certain Sermons appointed by the Queen's Majesty*, pp. 298–310. In the Second Book of Homilies, Jewel is credited with nos. 1, 2 (showing the influence of Bullinger), 3, 7, 9, 15, 16, 19; Grindal with 4 (although somewhat altered); Pilkington with 5 (partly from Peter Martyr) and 6; Taverner with 13 and 14; Parker with 17; while part of 10 is taken from Erasmus; 18 from St. John Chrysostom and Veit Dietricht, and three quarters of 20 from R. Gualter (Tomlinson, *The Prayer Book, Articles and Homilies*, pp. 244–6).
[253] *Certain Sermons appointed by the Queen's Majesty*, pp. 301–3.
[254] Ibid. pp. 304–8.
[255] *The Workes of the Reverend and Faithfull servant of Iesus Christ. M. Richard Greenham . . . collected into one volume) . . . The Third Edition. . .* (London, 1601); 'Seven Godlie and Fruitfull Sermons, vpon sundrie portions of the holie Scripture: . . .' pp. 45–96.
[256] Those of Smith's sermons which are 'ancient' in form are as follows: *Sermons:* 'The Christians Sacrifice,' 'The true trial of the Spirits,' 'The Wedding Garment,' 'The way to walk in,' 'The honour of Humility,' 'The Young-mans Task,' 'The Christians practice,' 'The Art of Hearing, in two sermons,' (second sermon), 'The trial of Vanity,' 'The banquet of *Jobs* children,' 'A Caveat for Christians,' 'A memento for Magistrates,' 'The Lawyers Question,' 'The Law-givers Answer, to the Lawyers Question,' 'The censure of Christ upon the Answer;' *Twelve Sermons:* 'Two Sermons of the Song of Simeon,' 'The Calling of Jonah,' 'Jonahs punishment,' (two sermons), 'The trumpet of the Soul,' 'Maries Choice;' *Three Sermons made by Mr. Henry Smith* (London, 1642): 'The Benefit of Contentation,' 'The Affinite of the Faithfull,' 'The lost sheepe is found.'
[257] See *ante*, p. 94.
[258] As for example *In Epistolam Apostoli Pauli ad Romanos: Commentarii Wolfgangum Musculum Dusanum* (Basel, 1555); Observations, Questions and Answers are marked as such assiduously in the margin.

out of the Canonicall Scriptures '; (2) ' to give the sense and vnderstanding of it being read, by the Scripture it selfe '; (3) ' to collect a
few and profitable points of doctrine out of the natvrall sense ';
(4) ' to apply (if he have the gifte) these doctrines rightly collected
to the life and manners of men in a simple and plaine speech '.²⁵⁹
The sermons of those who use this scheme proceed according to the
order of the text, to give Doctrines, Uses, Objections and Answers,
marked as such in the margin, with no attempt at the formal symmetry of the classical scheme.   Found in its purity in the sermons of
Cartwright,²⁶⁰ this form becomes unbearably tedious to the modern
reader after but a few pages.   However, that it does not inevitably
lead to dullness is shown by the lively series on Joel by Topsell,²⁶¹
where within this framework extended disquisitions on contemporary manners and morals are introduced, thus alleviating the
monotony of the method itself.²⁶²

Thirdly, the vast majority of the Elizabeth preachers adopt a
modified version of the ' modern style ' approximating to the
classical form, although they use it with some freedom.   The
classical arrangement, as we have seen, was advocated by Reuchlin
and Erasmus,²⁶³ and the version of the ' modern style ' found in the
treatise of Hyperius of Marburg (Andreas Gerhard, 1511–64), The
Practice of Preaching (' Englished by Iohn Ludham ' 1577),²⁶⁴ reaches
out to the true classical form.   The parts of the sermon as detailed
by Hyperius are: (A) ' Reding of the sacred scripture '; (B) ' Inuoca-
tion '; (C) ' Exordium '; (D) ' Proposition or division '; (E) ' Confirmation '; (F) ' Confutation '; (G) ' Conclusion ';²⁶⁵ and of these
the last five are of course stock parts of the classical oration.   The
Confutation is not always necessary in preaching, and frequently it is
omitted from those sermons which otherwise adhere to this scheme.
Certain of the sermons of Jewel are notable examples of the short
but elegant use of this arrangement; for example that on Haggai
i. 2–4 (' Thus speaketh the Lord of hosts, saying, This people say,
The time is not come, the time that the Lord's house should be built.
Then came the word of the Lord by Haggai the prophet saying, Is

    ²⁵⁹ Works, vol. II. p. 673.   Perry Miller writes interestingly on the influence of Ramus
on the form of the Puritan sermon, which in his opinion was created de novo from the
principles of the French logician. (The New England Mind: the seventeenth Century, New
York, 1939, pp. 338–9).
    ²⁶⁰ A Dilucidation, or Exposition, of the Epistle of St. Paul the Apostle to the Colossians.
    ²⁶¹ Times lamentation.
    ²⁶² See the references given post, pp. 302, n. 382, 307 n. 408, 310 n. 422.
    ²⁶³ See ante, pp. 85, 88.
    ²⁶⁴ The practis of preaching, otherwise called the pathway to the pulpit. . . Written in Latin
by . . . A. H., and Englished by I. Ludham (London, 1577).   ²⁶⁵ Ibid. f. 22ʳ.

it time for you, O ye, to dwell in your ceiled houses, and this house
to lie waste? ') recalls in the Exordium the occasion of the speaking
of the words; the Jews were captive in Babylon, the Temple was
desolate, and its ornaments were removed by the conqueror.
Darius however conquered the Chaldees and allowed the Jews to
return to Palestine and rebuild the Temple, but alas! many would
not return, preferring ease in a heathen land. Queen Elizabeth is
like Darius, continues Jewel: she has restored the Gospel; do not
let the audience say ' The time is not yet come. . . .'[266] Then follows
the Division: (A) ' Wherefore, first, I will prove, by God's grace,
that our church hath been overgrown with errors and abuses, as
then the temple of Hierusalem was defaced by the Chaldees '; (B)
' secondly, I will shew what things they be that do stay men from
re-edifying this temple '; (C) ' last of all, after what sort this church
ought to be builded, and so I will leave you to God '.[267] After the
Prayers, Jewel confirms as follows: (A) Christ foretold the ultimate
success of the Gospel but also at times the decay of the Church.
Romanism is such a decay, for there are many differences between it
and primitive Christianity, as: (a) in the Holy Communion the
Romans took away from the laity reception under both kinds, and
also the use of the vernacular in the celebration; (b) images were
introduced; (c) the marriage of the clergy was forbidden; (d) private
masses were introduced; (e) the Mass and the Primacy of the Pope
bear up the whole of the religion of late times and neither is primitive.[268] (B) Men do not build up the Church of England, because
(a) they despair of the cause, but what cause better deserves Divine
aid? (b) they await a General Council; but what use are they, when
the Pope is above them? (c) the time is not ripe, there is still much
for the bishops to reform. Would that they would indeed reform!
(d) some, because they opposed reform are afraid now to join in the
building of the Church; but all is now forgiven them; (e) other
causes there are, but what God complains of by the prophet is that
' every man fell to build his own house, and left the house of God
unbuilded '.[269] (C) We must build only on Christ and the Scriptures.[270] Then in conclusion Jewel urges repentance and further
reformation; we are not changing *enough*![271]

Many of Henry Smith's sermons use this form, but freely and
without undue elaboration. For example, 'A Preparative to
marriage ' does not use a specific text, but after a brief Exordium

[266] *Works*, vol. II, pp. 986–7.   [267] Ibid. p. 987.   [268] Ibid. pp. 987–94.
[269] Ibid. pp. 995–9.   [270] Ibid. pp. 1000–1.   [271] Ibid. pp. 1002–4.

on the occasion of the sermon—a marriage in which the parties have
come to church to enter into a contract and be made one,[272] Smith
proceeds to a Division of the matter: (A) 'First, I will shew the
excellency of marriage '; (B) ' then the institution of it '; (C) ' then
the causes of it '; (D) ' then the choyce of it '; (E) ' then the duties
of it ';(F) ' and lastly, the divorcement of it '.[273] In the Confirmation
there is some subdivision. (A) is confirmed (a) by reference to Heb.
xiii. 4 (' marriage is honourable ') (i) for the author—God; (ii) for
the time—it was the first thing done after man and woman were
created; (iii) for the place—Paradise. (b) Christ honoured marriage
too (i) by His birth, (ii) by His miracles, (iii) by His praises. (c) Three
marriages of Christ are mentioned in Scripture: (i) Christ and our
human nature, (ii) Christ and our soul, (iii) Christ and the Church.
(d) Christ's disciples should then honour marriage too. (e) St. Paul
declares that woman's curse is by marriage turned into a blessing.
(f) Man was born of earth and woman of a bone of man when he was
asleep. This teaches us that as Adam and Eve are figures of Christ
and the Church, (i) in the sleep of Christ the Church was born
(Ephes. v. 14) and (ii) as the bone came out of the first Adam's side,
so blood came out of the Second Adam's side during the Passion.
Further, (iii) Adam slept while his wife was being created, so our
lusts should sleep when we choose a wife, and (iv) Eve was made
from one of Adam's ribs, so a wife should be near her husband's
heart. (g) In all nations the marriage day is reputed the most
joyful.[274] (B) is simply confirmed; a wife is a gift from God,[275] but
(C) has some subdivision: the causes of the institution of marriage
are (a) the propagation of children, (b) to avoid fornication, (c) to
avoid the inconvenience of solitariness.[276] (D) also has subdivision:
(a) our choice should be an understanding wife with (i) godliness,
(ii) fitness: of which there are five marks, (1) the report, (2) the
looks, (3) the speech, (4) the apparel, (5) the companions. (b) There
are two questions regarding choice: may we marry (i) without the
consent of parents? No; (ii) a papist or an atheist? No.[277] In (E)
Smith deals with the duties (a) of man and wife to each other, (b) to
children and (c) to servants. Under (a) he shows that man and wife
should (i) love God and each other, (ii) start well and get to know
each other, (iii) the man should (1) love, (2) share things with, (3)be
tender to his wife, (4) not strike her; while (iv) the woman should be
(1) a good wife, (2) a helper, (3) a comforter, (4) a house-wife, (5) not

[272] *Sermons*, p. 9.   [273] Ibid.   [274] Ibid. pp. 9–12.
[275] Ibid. pp. 12–13.   [276] Ibid. pp. 13–17.   [277] Ibid. pp. 17–27.

shrewish. Smith next deals with (c); both man and wife should be good examples to their household; (i) the man should see to the discipline of the men, (ii) the woman to that of the women. Under (b) he speaks of the duties of parents to children, (i) not to love them inordinately—David's darling Absolom was David's traitor; (ii) the mother's duty is to suckle her children; (iii) the children must be catechised.[278] Finally (F) remains undivided; the only cause of divorcement is adultery.[279]

The Funeral Sermon for the Emperor Ferdinand by Edmund Grindal, Bishop of London (later Archbishop of Canterbury), is also a striking example of this form. The text is ' Therefore be ye also ready; for in such an hour as ye think not the Son of Man cometh ', (Matt. xxiv. 44) and the Division is into three topics: (A) we must prepare to die; (B) the causes that ought to move us to this preparation; (C) the true ways and means to prepare to die; with the addition, 'And by the way I intend somewhat to speak of the cause of this solemn assembly '.[280] The members (A) and (C) are confirmed without elaborate subdivision,[281] but in (B) occurs the praise of the Emperor, where Grindal, like Fisher, uses the topics of the classical orators:[282] (a) his high birth, (b) his great estate—as Emperor, these both being passed over; (c) his gifts of mind and virtues, seen in: (i) his wars against the Turks, (ii) his peaceable government, (iii) his chastity; (d) his noble progeny: (i) his daughters have made fine marriages, (ii) his son was crowned before his death.[283] In (B), Grindal also answers three possible objections to the funeral service: (a) the Emperor was a Catholic. True, he was not a Protestant, but: (i) he was crowned without a Mass; (ii) he was not crowned by the Pope; (iii) his ambassador made an oration at the Council of Trent urging that the laity receive Communion under both kinds.[284] (b) In the

[278] Ibid. pp. 27–45.
[279] Ibid. pp. 45–7. Other sermons by Smith which use a modified version of the 'modern style' are as follows: *Sermons:* 'A Treatise of the Lords Supper in two Sermons,' 'The Examination of Usury in two Sermons,' 'The pride of Nebuchadnezzar,' 'The fall of Nebuchadnezzar,' 'The Restitution of Nebuchadnezzar,' 'The trial of the Righteous.' 'The Pilgrims wish,' 'The godly mans request,' 'A Glasse for Drunkards,' 'The Art of Hearing, The first Sermon,' 'The heavenly Thrift,' 'The Magistrates Scripture,' 'The Ladder of Peace,' 'The betraying of Christ,' 'The Petition of Moses,' 'The Dialogue between Paul and Agrippa,' 'The humility of Paul,' 'A Looking-glass for Christians,' 'Food for new-born Babes,' 'Satans compassing the earth,' 'The poore mans Tears,' 'An allarum from Heaven,' 'Jacobs Ladder, or the way to Heaven;' *Twelve Sermons:* 'The Sinners Conversion,' 'The Sinners Confession,' 'The Rebellion of Jonah,' 'The sinful mans Search,' 'Noahs Drunkennesse.'
[280] *The Remains of Edmund Grindal,* ed. W. Nicholson (Cambridge, 1843) P.S., pp. 5–6.
[281] (A) is confirmed, ibid. p. 6; (C) ibid., pp. 29–31.
[282] See *ante,* p. 86.   [283] *Remains,* pp. 11–19.   [284] Ibid. pp. 19–23.

service there is no prayer for the Emperor's soul, but: (i) there is no
command about this in Scripture; (ii) there is no example of this in
Scripture; (iii) there is no sacrifice for the dead in the Old Testament;
(iv) the oldest Fathers do not speak of praying for the dead.[285] (c)
This service is too Romish, but: (i) in Joshua xxii we learn that when
' the tribes of Reuben and Gad, and the half tribe of Manasseh, had
received their portion beyond Jordan, at their return home they
builded a piece of work like a great altar; which when the rest of the
Israelites heard of, they intended war against the two tribes and the
half, and sent messengers unto them, burdening them with apostasy
and revolting from God's religion, for they had builded another
altar besides the altar in the tabernacle, which was the only altar
appointed by God. The two tribes and the half answered, and that
with calling of God to witness, that they meant no such thing, nor
ever intended to offer any sacrifice upon it; but only builded it for
a bounder and for a testimony, both for them and their children,
that the bounds of their possessions reached so far. The rest of the
Israelites were with this answer very well satisfied and contented,
and abstained from any war making against them. So I do not doubt,
but those who think this action to have any affinity with the superstitious abrogated ceremonies (if any such men be) when they shall
understand that there is no such thing neither done nor meant, they
will be likewise satisfied '; (ii) the Queen has this service celebrated
' for amity '.[286]

Hooker too in his sermons adopts this version of the modern
style approximating to the classical form. Usually his employment
of it is without undue elaboration, although the sermon on Pride
shows an unwonted wealth of subdivision. Here the text is from
Habbakuk: ' Behold, his soul which is lifted up is not upright
within him: but the just shall live by his faith ' (Hab. ii. 4). The
Exordium points out that people obey a law better if they see that it is
reasonable; that God's laws are the expression of Supreme Reason
and therefore men should wish to obey them. On this occasion
Hooker declares that he will go deeper than to remark in the text the
condemnation of the Babylonian's pride, and the happiness of the
righteous even if troubled.[287] Rather: (A) let us consider in the
first part of the text, ' what this rectitude or straightness importeth,
which God denieth to be in the mind of the Babylonian '. This
' rightness ' is right direction to man's true end, to heaven; the
Babylonian, on the contrary, is directed in the wrong direction

---

[285] Ibid. pp. 23–7.   [286] Ibid. pp. 27–9.   [287] *Works*, vol. III, pp. 597–8.

away from this end.[288] So consideration of his pride leads to the subdivisions: (a) ' the nature of this vice '; (b) ' the dangers to be discovered which it draweth inevitably after it, being not cured '; (c) ' the way to cure it '.[289] Then comes (B); in the second part of the text ' but the just shall live by his faith ', Hooker speaks of: (a) ' the promise of life'; (b) ' their quality to whom life is promised ', which is Justice; (c) ' that dependency whereby the life of the just is here said to hang on their faith '.[290] In (a) consider: (i) ' the fountain, the cause original and beginning, whereof spiritual life proceedeth ', (ii) ' in what manner we do here live the life of God ', (iii) ' how this life shall in the world to come be perfected '.[291] In (b) consider: (i) ' the nature of justice in general ', (ii) ' that justice which is of God ', (iii) ' that whereby we ourselves being just are in expectancy of life here promised in the sentence of the prophet, " By faith the just shall live " '.[292] Of these, (i) is further subdivided: (1) ' that in God, there is this divine virtue called Justice '; (2) ' in what sort God doth exercise that virtue in the regiment of his creatures '; (3) ' what injury we do to God for want of right understanding how he doth justice to us '; (4) ' what honour unto him, and us what benefit, the true knowledge of his justice addeth '.[293] Unfortunately the text of the sermon breaks off during the amplification of (3).[294]

Thomas Playfere also adopts this modified version of the ' modern style ', although in an early sermon, *The Meane in Mourning* (1595), he shows a tasteless over-elaboration in the Division, which runs to eight parts! The text is ' Weep not for me, but for your-selves ', (Luke xxiii. 28); and in the Exordium Playfere declares that there were four sorts of people about Christ at His Passion: (1) ' of the first sort were executioners, which tormented him '; (2) ' of the second sort were *Iews*, which mockt him '; (3) ' of the third sort were *lookers on*, which markt him '; (4) ' of the fourth sort were *wel willers*, which lamented him '. Of these, more women wept than men, so Christ spoke the words of the text, ' Weep not for me ', etc.[295] Then follows the Division: ' In which sentence we may observe, so many wordes, so many parts, Eight words, eight parts '. (A) ' The first, *Weepe not* '; (B) ' the second, *But weepe* '; (C) ' the third, *Weepe not, But weepe* '; (D) ' the fourth, *For mee* '; (E) ' the fifth, *For your selues* '; (F) ' the sixth, *For Mee, For your selues* '; (G) ' the seventh, *Weepe not for mee* '; (H) ' the eighth, *But weepe for your selues* '.[296] The

---

[288] Ibid. pp. 598–602.   [289] Ibid. p. 602.   [290] Ibid. p. 610.
[291] Ibid. p. 611.   [292] Ibid. p. 617.   [293] Ibid. p. 623.   [294] Ibid. p. 642.
[295] *The whole Sermons*, 'The Meane in Mourning,' pp. 1–3.   [296] Ibid. pp. 3–4.

Confirmation carries on this ingenuity: (A) *Weepe not*, forbids immoderate weeping;[297] (B) *But weepe*, shows the need for repentance;[298] (C) *Weepe not, But weepe*, shows the need for the mean in weeping;[299] (D) *For Mee*, teaches us not to weep too much for Christ's death; for it is the death of death;[300] (E) *For your selues*, warns us not to weep too little for our own lives: we are all subject to sin;[301] (F) *For Mee, For your selues*, teaches us that we should not weep too much for Christ and too little for ourselves;[302] (G) *Weepe not for Mee*, teaches us to consider three virtues in Christ: (a) wisdom —*Weepe not*; (b) benignity—*Not you*; (c) magnanimity—*Weepe not for Mee*;[303] (H) *But weepe for yourselues*, teaches us to consider three virtues which should be in ourselves: (a) devotion—*But weepe*; (b) compunction—*But you;* (c) compassion—*But for your selues.*[304] After this Development comes the Peroration—a recapitulation and conclusion; in heaven Christ will say *Weepe not for mee, and weepe not for your selues*: *Reioyce for mee, and reioyce for your selues.*[305] However, in his later sermons Playfere gives up this over-elaborate division, and divides his text into the usual number of three parts.[306]

The elaboration of Andrewes is quite different from that of Playfere; from a Division of usually three parts, stems an ordered ramification of subdivisions, reminiscent of the formal symmetry of the ' modern style ' in its medieval fulness. The first sermon on the Passion (1597) will provide an admirable early example of his method. The text is 'And they shall look upon Me, Whom they have pierced ' (Zech. xii. 10), and the arrangement is as follows:

Exordium.

The eunuch (Acts viii. 34) asked St. Philip about whom a similar text in Isaiah was written [' he was led as a sheep to the slaughter ', etc., Isa. liii. 7], and was told that it referred to Jesus. So this text in Zechariah refers also to Him; did He not quote these words in His Passion when His side was pierced? (John xix. 37). We shall do well to put this ' piercing ' with the beginning of Psalm xxi, (Vg.) as do the ' ancient writers ', for in the title Christ is compared *cervo matutino*, to the morning hart: ' that is to a Hart roused early in the morning, (as from His very birth He was by *Herod*) hunted and chased

---

[297] Ibid. pp. 5–9.   [298] Ibid. pp. 10–20.   [299] Ibid. pp. 21–6.
[300] Ibid. pp. 26–54.   [301] Ibid. pp. 54–67.   [302] Ibid. pp. 67–77.
[303] Ibid. pp. 77–92.   [304] Ibid. pp. 92–106.   [305] Ibid. pp. 106–21.
[306] This is his practice in the latter part of *The whole Sermons*, in the collection 'Nine Sermons preached by that eloquent Diuine of famous memorie, Th. Playfere Doctor in Diuinitie' (Cambridge, 1621) which is bound together with the earlier sermons to form the complete volume.

all His life long, and this day brought to His end, and, (as the poore Deer, stricken and pierced thorow side, heart and all).' There is no part of Christ's life which is not worthy to be looked upon, but here His piercing is commended to our view, as an act of grace. St. Paul too (Heb. xii. 2) wills us to 'look unto Jesus' and especially in His Passion. On this day above all others (Good Friday) we should look upon His piercing.[307]

Division.
    (A) The sight itself—*Quem transfixerunt.*
    (B) The act of seeing—*Respicient in Eum.*[308]

Confirmation.
    (A) The object is: (a) *generally*, Christ. But why is He here referred to by the circumlocution *Quem transfixerunt?* (i) 'the better to specifie and particularize the *Person* of CHRIST, by the kinde, and most peculiar circumstances of His death': (1) Isaiah had said *Morietur*, (Isa. liii. 10) He shall die; (2) Daniel tells us *Occidetur* (Dan. ix. 26), He shall die a violent death; (3) the Psalmist describes it: 'They pierced My hands and My feet' (Ps. xxi. 17, Vg.) which is only proper to the death of the cross; (4) the prophet in the text says not *crucifixus* but *transfixus*; not only His hands and His feet, but his Heart also should be pierced.[309] (ii) 'In CHRIST Himselfe, and in His Person, to sever from the rest of His *doings* and *sufferings*, what that is, that chiefly concerneth us, and we specially are to *looke to*: and that, is this dayes worke, CHRIST PIERCED'.[310] The object is (b) *specially*, (i) the Passion itself (*quid*); (ii) the agents (*a quibus*).[311] In (i) consider: (1) the degree—'for *transfixerunt*, is a word of *gradation*: or *suffixerunt*, or *confixerunt*, either'; it expresses the highest degree of piercing even to the heart; (2) the extent— 'upon Me' wholly: α in body, β in soul, by sorrow, by reproach, by ingratitude.[312] In (ii), consider that not only the soldiers and the Jews pierced Christ, but also we ourselves, for He died for our sins.[313] (B) In the act of looking, consider that we are moved thereto by: (a) nature, (b) grace, (c) the invitation of Christ, (d) our own profit, (e) our own danger—for if we do not look upon Him now, God will not avert His eyes from our sins to His Son's face.[314] Further, consider that in this act three things are enjoined: (a) 'That

[307] *XCVI Sermons*, pp. 333–4.   [308] Ibid. p. 334.   [309] Ibid. p. 335.
[310] Ibid.   [311] Ibid. p. 336.   [312] Ibid. pp. 336–8.
[313] Ibid. pp. 338–9.   [314] Ibid. p. 340.

we do it with *attention*: for it is not *Me*, but *in Me*: not only *Vpon* Him, but *Into* Him '; (b) ' That wee doe it oft, againe and againe; with *iteration*; for, *Respicient* is *re-aspicient* '; (c) ' That we cause our nature to do it, as it were, by vertue of an *Injunction*, *per actum elicitum*, as the *Schoolmen* call it. For in the *Originall* it is in the *commanding Conjugation*, that signifieth, *facient se respicere*, rather than *Respicient*.'[315] So, subdividing (a) *Respicient in Eum* implies: (i) looking upon the outside; (ii) looking into the very entrails.[316] Further, subdividing (i): (1) '*Vpon* Him, if wee *looke*, we shall see so much as *Pilate* shewed of Him, *Ecce Homo*, that He is a Man. And, if He were not a *man*, but some other *unreasonable creature*, it were great ruth to see Him so handled.' (2) 'Among men we lesse pitie *Malefactors*, and have most compassion on them that be *innocent*. And, He was innocent, and deserved it not (as you have heard) His enemies themselves being His Judges.' (3) 'Among these that be innocent, the more *noble* the person, the greater the griefe, and the more heavy ever is the spectacle.'[317] But if, (ii) we look ' *into Him*, we shall see yet a greater thing, which may raise us in comfort, as farre as the other cast us downe. Even the bowels of *compassion* and tender *love*, whereby Hee would and was content to suffer all this for our sakes.'[318] Then, subdividing (b); let us look often upon Christ, for in diverse sorts, ' we may with profit behold and looke upon Him, whom thus we have pierced ': (i) *Respice et transfigere*, ' *Looke upon Him that is pierced*; and with looking upon Him, bee pierced thyself '—look lament; (ii) *Respice et transfige*, ' Looke upon Him, and *pierce*: and *pierce* that in thee, that was the cause of CHRIST'S piercing: (that is) sinne and the lusts thereof '; (iii) *Respice et dilige*, ' Look and be *pierced* with *love* of Him that so *loved* thee, that He gave himself in this sort to be pierced for thee '; (iv) *Respice et crede*, 'And, well may we *beleeve* and Trust Him, whom looking a little before, we have seene so constantly *loving* us '; (v) *Respice et spera*, ' Look upon Him, and His heart opened, and from that *gate of hope* promise thyselfe, and looke for all manner of things that good are '; which expectation is twofold: α ' *the deliverance from the evill* of our present misery '; β ' the restoring *to the good* of our primitive felicitie '; (vi) *Respice et recipe*, Receive the water and blood which issue from that pierced side; (vii) *Respice et retribue*, Let us give ' thoughts of thankfulnesse '.[319] Finally, (c) force is necessary to make us look, for ' to *flesh* and *bloud* it is but a dull and *heavy spectacle* '. Yet look we

---

[315] Ibid. pp. 340–1.   [316] Ibid. p. 341.   [317] Ibid.
[318] Ibid.   [319] Ibid. pp. 342–6.

must upon Him, for the words of the text are applied in two ways: (i) ' By Saint Iohn to CHRIST, at His first comming, suffering (as our Saviour) upon the Crosse', (John xix. 37); (ii) 'By CHRIST to Himselfe, at His second comming, sitting (as our Judge) upon His Throne, in the end of the world. *Behold He commeth in the Clouds, and every eye shall see Him, yea even they that pierced Him: et plangent se super Eum omnes Gentes terrae*' (Rev. i. 7).[320]

Conclusion.

How long shall we continue to look upon Him? (a) ' *Donec totus fixus in Corde, qui totus fixus in Cruce* '; (b) ' Or if that be too much or too hard, yet *saltem* at the least, *respice in Illum, donec Ille et respexerit*. Looke upon Him, till Hee looke upon you againe. For, so He will. He did upon PETER; and with His look, melted him into *teares.*'[321]   When shall we know when Christ looks upon us as a Saviour? 'Then truely, when fixing both the eyes of our meditation *upon Him that was pierced* (as it were) one eye, upon the grief; the other upon the love wherewith He was *pierced*, we find by both, or one of these, some motion of *grace* arise in our hearts: the consideration of His *griefe*, piercing our hearts: with sorrow; the consideration of His love, piercing our hearts with mutuall love againe.'[322]

Perry Miller suggests the influence of the Dane Keckermann's *Rhetorica Ecclesiastica* upon the form of Andrewes's sermons.[323] However, the first edition of this manual appeared in 1600,[324] and the form adopted by Andrewes is the same before and after this date.[325]   It is however probable that the precepts of the manual confirmed Andrewes in the practice he had already adopted. In any event the scheme advocated by Keckermann admirably describes Andrewes's method: the three parts of the sermon: *Exordium*, *Tractatio intermedia*, and *Epilogus seu Peroratio* (as Keckermann explains them),[326] are found in the sermons of the English master

---

[320] Ibid. pp. 346–7.   [321] Ibid. p. 347.   [322] Ibid. pp. 347–8.
[323] *The New England Mind: the Seventeenth Century*, p. 337.
[324] The edition to which I have had access is the third: *Rhetoricae Ecclesiasticae, siue Artis Formandi et Habendi Conciones Sacras, Libri Duo* (Hanover, 1606), but the dedication is signed 1600 (ibid. p. 6).
[325] I have analysed an early sermon particularly to show that Andrewes had developed his sermon scheme by 1600. This scheme remains constant to the end of his career: it is beautifully indicated in the early editions by typographical devices—numerals, marginal notes, italics, capitals, and in particular the band of ornament which divides the Exordium and Division from the main body of the sermon. It is unfortunate that the reprint by J. Wilson [vols. I–V in Andrewes's *Works*, Library of Anglo-Catholic Theology (Oxford, 1841–3)] should omit the italics and the band of ornament.
[326] *Rhetorica Ecclesiastica*, pp. 97–104.

preacher, for what better describes the middle section of an Andrewes's sermon, than the Dane's definition of this part—*Tractatio est quae propositi textus explicationem, amplificationem, et applicationem principaliter continet*[327]—or the conclusion, than the definition of *Peroratio*, as *enumeratio* (recapitulation) and *concitatio* (the arousing of the hearers)?[328]

[327] Ibid. p. 100.
[328] Ibid. p. 102. There is a striking parallel also between Keckermann's places of Invention (ibid., p. 38) and Andrewes's practice: the five parts in the Dane's manual —(1) 'Praecognitio textus'; (2) 'Partitio propositi'; (3) 'Explicatio verborum'; (4) 'Amplificatio'; (5) 'Applicatio' (explained at length, pp. 39–97)—are easily recognisable in any sermon by Andrewes.

CHAPTER III

STYLE (Elocutio)

AFTER the disposition of the material, the preacher must further ensure that it will make its full effect by being expressed in a suitable style. The functions of ' delighting ' and ' moving ' are particularly dependent on style (or *elocutio* in rhetorical parlance) and ' teaching ' itself can be aided not only by clarity and force of discourse, but also by illuminating illustrations or *exempla*, which are of course often emotive too.[1] These *exempla* are a notable feature of medieval preaching,[2] and as will be seen they play an important part also in sixteenth century preaching. The word *exemplum* itself is a generic term, and includes the ' figure ' which is a simile or metaphor, the ' narration ' which is a story with human actors, and the ' fable ' which is a story where the actors are animals.[3] I shall employ these terms throughout in the senses explained here.

In general three main styles may be differentiated within the whole period of this study: first the plain but uncolloquial style, which uses few *exempla*, and the rhetorical schemata (artificial word patterns) only occasionally and then not for display, but as an aid to cogent expression; secondly, the colloquial style, which uses a racy and pungent speech idiom, and avoids the schemata, but is enriched by frequent homely *exempla*; and thirdly, the ornate style, which is highly embellished by the schemata, employs many *exempla* (often from literary sources) and aims distinctly at oratorical display. Of course not every important figure to be dealt with can be fitted at all points into these Procrustean beds; nevertheless these styles do run in distinct lines throughout the period, and they provide the most definite and illuminating grouping which the material makes possible.[4]

[1] See St. Augustine's *rationale* of the use of eloquence in preaching, *De Doctrina Christiana*, lib. IV, cap. x–xiii, *P.L.*, xxxiv. 99–102.

[2] See J. Th. Welter, *L'exemplum dans la littérature réligieuse et didactique du moyen âge* (Paris, 1927), Owst, *L. & P.M.E.*, pp. 149–209. J. A. Mosher, *The Exemplum in the early Religious and Didactic Literature of England* (New York, 1911).

[3] See Owst, *L. & P.M.E.*, p. 151.

[4] R. W. Chambers (*On the Continuity of English Prose from Alfred to More and his School*, London, reptd., 1950, E.E.T.S., p. cxxii) distinguishes two styles in the late fourteenth, fifteenth and sixteenth centuries. First, 'an English conscious of its inferiority to the Latin or French which it is seeking to replace, trying to assert its dignity by "augmenting itself," "struggling once more for expression in apologetic emulation of its betters," ' (found for example in Hall's *Chronicle*). Secondly, 'the traditional English of the *Ancren Riwle*—surviving in the works of Rolle or of Hilton, in the *Cloud*, in

I

THE PRE-REFORMATION CATHOLIC PREACHERS, INCLUDING THE CONSERVATIVE HENRICIANS (1450-1547)

Amongst the preachers of this time all three styles are to be found. First, the plain style occurs in the *De Tempore* series of the late fifteenth century, which show, as would be expected, the simplest and least sophisticated mode within this period. In MS. Hatton 96 is found an extremely elementary narrative and expository manner; the sentences are of loose and often clumsy structure, as in this narrative from the Christmas Day sermon:

And sche bare hure swete sonne in hur armes Iesu Crist, and lapped him in cloþes and layd hym yn þe cracche on a lytull heye, bytwyne þe ox and þe asse. And a none þe ox and þe asse worchipped oure Lorde and kneled to hym, and for reuerans of him þei wolde not touch þe heye þat he lay on: þe w[h]iche heye Seynt Eleyne þe qwene bare to Rome. And a none in hys holy burth come many legyons of angels and songon ' Ioye and worchippe to God on heyþ and pes to men on erth of good will.'[5]

The quality of the exposition in the following passage from the Candlemas sermon is typical:

Þe þrid fest of þis day is called Candelmasse day by cause þat we bere candels in oure hondes and þei ben brynnyng for many skylles: to for do an erroure in Rome, for folks of Rome did sacrifice that day to a fende þat was callyd Februus. And when þei did þis sacrifyce, all a day and a nyȝth þei bare taper and oþer lyȝthes in her hondes, þat he schuld graunt to here children the victori of here enmys. Also þei did sacrifice in þe same monthe to anoþer fende þat vas called dame Februe with lyȝth brennyng, þat [s]he schuld haue mercy on her sowles. To fordo this errorre, seynt Gregory the pope ordened þat day we schulde bere lyȝth in þe worschip of oure Lady seynt Mary. Also þe lyȝth schewe the clennes of oure lady as holy church

Nicholas Love or in Thomas More—an English which, while not despising ornament, or eschewing the coupling together of synonyms, never makes that excessive use of tricks which marks those who seek to enrich the English language.' Similarly, Miss E. J. Sweeting (*Early Tudor Criticism: Linguistic and Literary*, Oxford, 1940, pp. 8–19) speaks of the opposition in prose and poetry of the aureate and the plain style. For preaching it is best to speak of three styles, for in addition to the 'plain style' and the fully 'ornate style' the 'colloquial style' can be clearly isolated—although in each chronological section (with the exception of Mary's reign) I have found only one preacher who makes use of this last.

---

[5] MS. Hatton 96. f. 10ᵛ.

said, sothly: ' Blessed lady þou art all faire, al bryȝth, all schynyng as þe sonne . . . .'[6]

This series is quite unadorned with *exempla*, except for occasional narrations which are lifted straight from the *Legenda Aurea*, the source of most of its material.[7]

However the more elaborate set of sermons in the late fifteenth century revision of Mirk's *Festial* in MS. Harleian 2247, not only exhibits a firmer sentence structure, but also is embellished with various kinds of *exempla* of the stock medieval types, which are always apt and often beautiful. The need for contrition is illustrated by this delightfully human simile; the case is:

> As it is of noris and her sowkyng childe, that as longe as þe childe sleepith & is in pees, she gothe hir way. But a non, as þe childe wakith and cryeth and wepith, þe noris rennyth to it, and yevith it souke, and after singeth it to pees it & berith it in hir armes. Right so our souereyn Saviour Christe Ihesu, as longe as synful man slepith obstinatly in synne, then Criste gothe from him; but when þe synner wepith for his synne, and is sorowfull, anon þat mercifull lorde Criste Ihesu is þere redy as a tendir noris to yeve hym sowke.[8]

Similarly pleasing is another simile drawn from the ways of children, which comes ultimately from St. Anselm, but is found in the fifteenth century compendium, the *Destructorium Viciorum* of Alexander Carpenter:

> It is of them þat trusten in worldes worship & rycches, as it is of wanton childre þat breke in to a mannes gardeyn to gadder applis, peris, nuttes or other frute. Sum gone in, & sum stand withoute & dare not entir the gardeyn for betyng or rebuking. And þei þat be within cast applis & such frute as þey haue to þem þat be withoute. But atte laste comyth þe owner or keper of þe gardeyn & fyndith þem þat be within breking his gardeyn. He takith from þem all þe frute þat þei haue gaderid & leve þem not oon. Nor noon þey shall haue, but if þey woll gife þem eny þat stande withoute. . . .[9]

The garden is the world, and the owner God; the keeper is death, who takes away temporal goods, so that the worldly man can then

---

[6] Ibid. ff. 22[r-v].

[7] For example, ibid., ff. 23[v]–4[r], the story is related of the lady who was unable to go to Mass on Candlemas Day, but dreamed she was present at a service, where the celebrant was Our Lord, the deacon St. Lawrence, and the subdeacon St. Vincent. She refused to offer her taper, and when servants came to take it from her, it broke, and she awoke to find herself lying with a piece of candle in her hand, at the foot of the image of the Virgin. (Cf. *Jacobi a Voragine Legenda Aurea*, ed. Th. Graesse, 3rd edn., Bratislava, 1890, pp. 165–7.)

[8] MS. Harl. 2247, f. 52[v].   [9] Ibid. f. 210[v].

profit by his wealth only if his executors have masses said for his soul.[10] Death too, who takes sometimes those older or younger than ourselves, sometimes our friends and relatives, but finally ourselves ' may be assembled & likenyd vnto a yonge archer or a schoter: sum tyme he shotyth over þe butt, sumtyme vndir & sumtyme on þe side & sumtyme he hittith þe prik with þe garlond '.[11] Then in Nicholas Bozon's manner of using the natural properties of things as symbols of spiritual states and processes [12] the preacher declares: ' I fynde, *secundum naturales*, þat þe cristall stone, whan it is sett in brasse, latton, copper, or in any oþer vile metall, it yevith no vertu ', so unworthy reception of the Blessed Sacrament brings no spiritual benefits.[13] Similarly the need for Confession is enforced by reference to the habits of an animal:

A certeyn best called a gott, [goat] lyvith moste by vnclene herbis, & som tyme, but if he ete hony or sum sweete herbis, he shall dye. So þat man or woman þat is synfull & woll not forsake his syn, but live vncleanly, but if he take þe precious herbe of contrition with þe swete hony of confession & satisfaccion, he shall dye gostely for a tyme in his soule.[14]

An aspect of history, the need in medieval times for a strong and competent monarch, is used to illustrate the unhappy and confused spiritual condition of man, before Christ's Advent:

Experiens sheweth, that in þe absence of a kyng, or elles if a kyng be not in reputacyon & fauor of the peple as such a soueryne oweth to be; oftymes þere growes & enkreses moche malice, & shortly to speke of, falshede, syn, and vntrewthe haue than grete dominacion. For there [are] þe spoliacions, robereis, deceyts, treasons & many wronges done withoute correction. And this causeth oft tyme þe peple to rebell & rise ageyn the pees, as it was like to haue bene in this reem within fewe yeres, had not Gode shewed to vs of his gode grace.[15]

The compiler of the additional sermons in this series uses fitting narrations (not grouped together at the end as in Mirk himself, but

[10] Ibid. f. 211ʳ. Cf. Alexander Carpenter, *Summa que Destructorium viciorum appelatur* (Nuremberg, 1496) iv, 2c, sig. f5ᵛ (noticed in Owst, *The Destructorium Viciorum of Alexander Carpenter*, p. 25). *Exempla* drawn from the ways of children belong of course to the great common store of the sermon handbooks. See further, MS. Harl. 2247, f. 14ʳ; a child does not harbour resentment; although beaten, 'als son as ye shewe hym a fayre floure or ells a rede appyl, he hath forryette all þat was done to hym beforn. And he woll cum rennyng with his halsyng armys to plese the & kysse the.' Cf. the version of this noted by Owst, *L. & P.M.E.*, p. 34.

[11] MS. Harl. 2247, f. 211ᵛ; cf. Alexander Carpenter, *Destructorium viciorum*, v, 12 c, sig. t5ᵛ. The figure is attributed to Hugh of St. Victor.

[12] See *Les Contes moralisés de Nicole Bozon* . . . ed. L. T. Smith and P. Meyer (Paris, 1889).

[13] MS. Harl. 2247, f. 97ᵛ.   [14] Ibid.   [15] Ibid. f. 1ʳ.

occurring in the main discourses), as this on the destructive power
of death from the second Funeral Sermon, where the rhymed
messages would stick in the memories of simple listeners:

> I rede in a story, how on a tyme þere was a myghti & a
> stronge tiraunt þat longe tyme beseged a kyng in his castell
> where he lay. Whan þe tyraunt perceyved þe kinge wolde not
> yelde vp his castell to hym, he ordeyred gunnes and engynes &
> dyd þem lose vnto þe castell, & at euery stroke of the engynes
> he cast in a lettre writen to þe kyng. The first scripture &
> writing was þis:

> Kyng be þou redy, wach, and wake,
> Or þou be ware, I woll þe take.

[The second was:]

> Though þou be stronge, noble & gay,
> Thou shalt yelde þe castell yf I may!

The þird tyme he wrote þus:

> O thou kyng aslake þi boste,
> For deth is ny to take þi goste.[16]

The king in the castle is man's soul in the body; death the tyraunt
sends three warnings: in youth sickness; in middle age ' tribula-
cyons, disese, sclandrys '; finally in old age, the sternest monitors,
the tokens of physical decreptitude, enumerated here, as so often in
medieval sermons, with terse vividness, and enforced by the use of
the schemata (alliteration and assonance), the signes ' þat þou
maiste well knowe þat þou art at þe pyttes brynk: þat is to say, whan
þi hands quaketh; þi lippes blaketh, thyne hede rokkyth, þy nose
droppith, þy shynnes sharpith, þi synewes starkith, þi brest pantith,
þy breth wantyth, thy tethe rattlyth, thi þrote rotelyth; anon þou
thenkkest þyn hert wolde brast for þy life may not laste '.[17]

The style of the *De Tempore* collection in MSS. Lincoln Cathedral
Library 50 and 51 is very similar to that in MS. Harleian 2247—
plain, but occasionally using apt *exempla*. For example, the preacher,
following ' Bartolomeus Anglicus ' declares that the noble falcon
after capturing its prey, wants only the heart, so Our Lord wants
only the hearts of men;[18] while (in the sermon for Trinity VII) he
gives the traditional comparison of the seven deadly sins to various
beasts; pride to the lion, covetousness to the hedgehog, wrath to the
wolf, envy to the hound, sloth to the ass, gluttony to the bear and
lechery to the hog.[19] Narrations are found also in this collection, for

---

[16] Ibid. f. 211ᵛ.
[17] Ibid. f. 212ʳ. This is a favourite theme of the pre-Reformation preachers; see
post, pp. 234–5.   [18] MS. Linc. Cath. Lib., 51, ff. 49ᵛ–50ʳ.
[19] MS. Linc. Cath. Lib., 50, ff. 205ʳ–10ᵛ.

example an *exemplum terrible* telling of a swearer, who when lying ill saw a lady come to him carrying a wounded child. When asked what he who did this thing deserves, the swearer replies that damnation is merited. He is then himself carried off to damnation, the wounded child having represented the injuries done to Christ by swearers.[20] On another occasion, to illustrate the validity of Penance no matter how heinous the offence, the preacher draws a story from the *Dialogues* of St. Gregory the Great, of a daughter who sins with her father then kills her mother, her children and her father. Having gone away, she hears St. Augustine preaching on repentance, and moved by his words, confesses her sins. She dies, but three roses grow out of her mouth showing that her sins are forgiven.[21]

Not only uncultivated preachers however, adopt the plain style: it has its votaries amongst the learned also. Fitzjames and Baron, who use the full elaboration of the ' modern ' schematic form,[22] are nevertheless quite plain in style. The form itself is so complex that to superimpose an elaborate style upon it would make the whole so cumbrous as to be a weariness to the hearers. The logical terseness of the following passage on rebellion from Fitzjames, is typical of his brief and ' pointed ' manner; the use of rhetorical ' progression ' lends a cold and formal beauty:

> The cause whi comynly men rebell agenst theyr heedys & souereynes, is pryde & highe mynde. Now our sauyour taught mekenesse. Lerne ye of me sayth he to al his folowers. that I am meke & humble of spyryte. the XI chapytre of Mathu. Mekenes ledyth to obedience & obedyence to patience. Thenne where lackyth mekenes lackyth both obedience & patience: Thenne followeth rebellyon & where men be vnable to rebell: oft they distroy themselfe for malyce.[23]

Doubtless it was not only in his old age as Bishop of London that Fitzjames read his sermons; the careful elaboration of his thought and his calculated style would demand constant reference to writing to refresh his memory, if his effects were to tell.[24] Only occasionally does he employ *exempla*, and these are to aid the thought, not to appeal to the emotions, as this simile on God's image in man: ' Yf a man steppe in snowe or sonde: after his departyng remayneth a steppe. So after the acte of creacion remayneth behynde the hond werke of god in the creature.'[25] Similarly Baron's style is bare and

---

[20] Ibid. ff. 114ᵛ–15ʳ.   [21] MS. Linc. Cath. Lib. 51, ff. 19ʳ–21ʳ.
[22] See *ante*, pp. 78–80.   [23] *Sermo die lune in ebdomada Pasche*, sig. Giiiʳ.
[24] See Erasmus, *The Lives of Jehan Vitrier . . . and John Colet*, p. 40: (*Opus Epistolarum* vol. IV, p. 524).
[25] *Sermo die lune in ebdomada Pasche*, sig. Ciiiᵛ.

terse, eschewing *exempla*, but enforcing the points by frequent quotations of relevant passages of Scripture, *dicta* of the Fathers and School Doctors, and as we shall see, of certain classical authors.[26] This passage on the preciousness of time is typical:

De primo, *Ecclesiastici*. 4: *Fili, conserua tempus*. Temporis preciositas apparet ex fructus sublimitate; quia quasi in momento temporis, vel in quarta parte hore, homo potest delere culpam, recuperare gratiam & promereri gloriam. Dicit apostolus, 2 *Corinthios* 6: *Ecce nunc tempus acceptabile, ecce nunc dies salutis*. O quam preciosum est tempus, in quo lucrari possumus eternitatem! Ideo Seneca *ad Lucillum* dicebat: ' Omnia mi Lucille, aliena sunt; tempus tamen nostrum est.' Ex hoc Hieronimus sic scribit ad Eustochium: ' Omne tempus in quo te meliorem non senseris, existima perdidisse.' Et Bernardus, videns ociosorum incredibilem numerum,in *Libro De Contemptu Mundi* sic loquitur: ' Heu! Heu! Nichil preciosius tempore & nichil hodie vilius reputatur.'[27]

Baron does of course, in common with all who adopt the ' modern ' scheme, enunciate the divisions and subdivisions with rhyme and assonance.[28]

Colet too uses the plain style; in the Convocation Sermon his manner is clear, direct and powerful, but he makes no use of *exempla*, and but little use of the schemata.[29] Erasmus tells us that the dean read the best English authors to acquire a good style,[30] so it is particularly unfortunate that his sermon collections mentioned by Pits[31] should be now lost. Although in the Oxford Lectures his style is austere and undecorated, it would have been most interesting to see if in his addresses from the pulpit of St. Paul's, he had used any of the popular ornaments, or if another of the attractions of his preaching for the Lollards was that plain manner recommended by Wiclif.[32]

A group of late Henrician preachers also adopts the plain style. The style of Taverner's *Postils* is plain and colourless; it is clear and serviceable, but of no literary interest. However Tunstall occasionally decorates his usual plainness by parison and similes, as in the following passage on the union of the Father and the Son in the Blessed Trinity:

[26] See *post*, pp. 210–11.   [27] *Sermones*, f. 3[r].   [28] For example, see *ante*, p. 78.
[29] He does use rhetorical questions ('Convocation Sermon,' Appendix C, in Lupton, *Life of Colet*, p. 295), apostrophe (ibid. p. 296), paragraphs beginning with the same words (ibid. pp. 300–3).
[30] *The Lives of Jehan Vitrier . . . and John Colet*, p. 23: (*Opus Epistolarum*, vol. IV, p. 515).
[31] *Relationum Historicarum de Rebus Anglicis, tomus primus*, p. 694.
[32] See G. P. Krapp, *The Rise of English Literary Prose*, p. 48.

> As the bryghtnes is in the fyre, and as the image or print is in a seale, and as a worde is in the mynde, so the sonne of god is in the father. For the bryghtnes is as soone as the fyre is, and the printe is within the seale, as soone as the seale is, And the worde that men wyll expresse is in the mynde, as sone as the mynde hath conceyued it.[33]

or in this passage on how the virtuous man does not fear to humble himself:

> He that is pore in vertue feareth to humble hym selfe, leste he shulde fall from his feynd & dissembled height. And he that is rych in vertue, doth humble hym selfe, knowynge that he hath in hym vertue, wherby he shall be exalted. Whiche vertue can not be hyd. As a candell bournyng can nat be hyd in a darke house, nor a swete smel hydde in any corner, but it wyll by the good flauour therof disclose where it is, and allure menne to take vp the thynge that so smelleth.[34]

However all human humility pales beside the example of Christ's humility in the Incarnation and the Passion: '. . . the humilyte and obedience of Christe, doth surmount all examples of humilitie and obedience of the olde testament, as farre as the bryghte shynynge of the sonne is aboue the dymme lyght of an olde lanterne.'[35]

Chedsey and Scott too are predominantly plain in style. However Chedsey employs an extended simile drawn from the habits of the viper to provide a striking exordium[36] on the nature of malice:

> The naturall philosopher Plinius in the X boke of his naturall historye, describinge the generation of the Viper, and the maner how she bryngeth forthe hyr yongeons, sayth, that the male engendering putteth his heade in the females mouth: whiche heade she for very pleasure bytyth of. And within iii dayes after hauyng yongeons in hyr bely, maketh haste to bring them forth. But by reason of her slacknesse, they can not abyde within her, and gnawynge hyr belly and sydes, violently breketh forth with slaughter of theyr mother.[37]

So the Devil puts his head, the seed of malice, into man's heart, and man foolishly devours this poison. However, although the viper keeps her young three days in her body before they eat her belly, ' the enuious person maketh more spede: he conceyueth no sooner,

---

[33] *A Sermon . . . made vpon Palme sondaye*, sig. Aiii[r].
[34] Ibid. sig. Biii[r-v].   [35] Ibid. sig. Biii[v]-iv[r].
[36] The use of exordia containing a striking figure or narration is recommended by Erasmus, *Ecclesiastes*, II, xxx. pp. 215–17. These openings are found first in the sermons of the Greek Fathers, who imitated the exordia of the orators of the 'Second Sophistic', as Libanius; (see Mitchell, *English Pulpit Oratory from Andrewes to Tillotson*, p. 95).
[37] *Two notable sermones lately preached at Paules crosse*, sig. Bi[r].

but incontinent he feeleth such a gnawynge about his harte & sydys, that yf he kepe one hower or ii his venemous babe within him, he wyl braste belly, harte & all together '.[38] Scott embellishes his exhortations with a few *exempla* in the usual medieval manner; thus the end of those who will not obey the Commandments is illustrated by reference to a man who ' setteth a tree in his garden, wyllyng that it shall growe there manye yeares for to bringe forth fruyte, now within a fewe yeares when he seeth that it wyll bringe furth none, he commandeth by and by contrary to his first wyll, to cutte it downe sayeng, where vnto doth it occupye the grounde? '[39] Many do not walk in the way of virtue, they never progress in holiness, ' but do runne as it were in a circuit, and maye be lykened to a dogge that runneth in a whele, whiche styll goeth and laboureth & when he maketh an ende, he is euen where he begonne '.[40] Men grow old, but they do not become better; on the contrary they ' do as vittelars vse to do, whiche take bread and drincke of bakers and brewers, to a daye, not payenge money in hande, but tayle [tally] with them: & when the day of payment cometh, they paye theyr money, & strike of the olde tayles, and begynne agayne to tayle of newe '.[41] So each Lent we go to confession, and receive Communion at Easter, but then once more we ' begyn euen to tayle of newe, and fall agayne to our olde kynde of lyuynge '.[42] Once in a delightful simile Scott appeals to the experience of his audience: men stop their ears against the voice of the preachers and will not hear their warnings ' lyke vnto the people of London, which do heare after a sorte the belles of Paules, when they rynge to Matyns at Midnyght; the belles do sounde in theyr eares, yet they wyll not ryse, but rather wyl tourne them on thother syde, and slepe agayne, for they thynke the daye is not yet neare '.[43]

The colloquial style has, within this period, a notable exponent in Edgeworth. At Bristol he had a popular audience, and although a highly learned man, being a Doctor of Divinity, he is able to speak to this audience with a homely vigour which remains unusually pleasing to the modern reader. Thus, expounding Luke vi. 25, [' Woe unto you that are full for ye shall hunger '], he paraphrases the Latin text into an energetic native English:

> *Ve qui saturati estis, quia esurietis.* Wo be to you that be farced, stuffed, and ful fed, for you shal be a hungred at your iudgement, when ye shall beg refreshing, and none shalbe giuen you. . . .[44]

[38] Ibid.   [39] Ibid. sig. Kii^v.   [40] Ibid. sig. Kv^v.   [41] Ibid.
[42] Ibid.   [43] Ibid. sig. Kiii^r.   [44] *Sermones*, f. 7^r.

Frequently his racy colloquialism resembles that of Latimer, as in this pungent passage on Our Lord's patience:

When he was rayled agaynste, and called heretike and tray-toure, a benche-whystler, a blowboll, a felowe with ribalds, knaues, whores, and drabbes, all this wynde shoke no corne, all this moued hym not, but euer styll he proceded in his godlye purpose and for yl wordes gaue to them agayne blessed wordes of godlye exhortation, and good counsayle.[45]

Similarly vigorous is this denunciation of the sensualist:

. . . he that is geuen to the pleasure of the bealy, shall not auoyd the filthiness of lecherye, *Commesationibus*, in extra-ordinarye refections, banketynges, breakefastes, afternone meates, reresuppers, and such other lewde and vnseasonable wanton bealyglee. All these feedeth lechery, and so doth all other potations, and bibbinge, and bollynge, and reuellinge and so doth dronkenes folowynge of the same.[46]

Also, he is able to present a dramatic scene, with the very accent of conversation. The following passage on the difference between an image and an idol shows this very clearly:

I woulde you shoulde not ignorauntelye confounde and abuse these termes, takynge an Image for an Idolle, and an Idolle for an Image, as I haue hearde manye doe in this citye, as well of the fathers and mothers (that should be wise) as of theyr babies and chyldren that haue learned follyshnesse of theyr parentes. Nowe at the dissolucion of Monasteries and of Freers houses many Images haue bene caryed abrod, and gyuen to the chyldren to playe wyth all. And when the children haue theim in theyr handes, dauncynge them after their childyshe maner, commeth the father or mother and saythe: What nasse, what haste thou there? the child aunswereth (as she is taughte) I haue here myne ydoll, the father laugheth and maketh a gaye game at it. So saithe the mother to an other. Iugge, or Thom-mye, where haddest thou that pretye Idoll? Iohn our parishe clerke gaue it me, saythe the childe, and for that the clerke must haue thankes, and shall lacke no good chere.[47]

Also Edgeworth has many *exempla*, which have a delightful fresh-ness, and a measure of individuality. Many of his most characteristic figures are drawn from the ways of animals; he uses the mole as an emblem of self-centred worldly wisdom, but gives a personal twist to his presentation:

---

[45] Ibid. f. 230ᵛ. Cf. Latimer, *Sermons*, p. 130, 'For some said he was a Samaritan, that he had a devil within him, a glosser, a drinker, a pot-companion.' On Latimer's style in detail, see *post*, pp. 142–53.
[46] *Sermons*, f. 234ʳ.   [47] Ibid. f. 40ʳ.

One of these three noughtie wisdomes S. Iames calleth earthyle wisdom [see Jas. iii. 15] and that is it that couetous men be combred with all, whych be euer like wantes or Moles moiling in the grounde, and when they shuld ascend aboue such worldlines to godly meditacions, as to here sermons or diuine seruice, they be as blinde as the Molle. Either they cannot perceiue any thing of godly or heauenly counsail, or if they perceiue it, yet they haue no swetenes in it, but down they would headlong to their lucre and advantages againe, like as a Molle if a man would feede her with wine and wastel, she will none thereof, but downe againe to the grounde she will, and there she is more strong then a Lion, and after her maner wiser then anye other beast.[48]

In similar fashion Edgeworth flays those who are niggardly in good deeds:

The murmurer & grudger with his well doing hath the property of a hog, which slepyng in his stye, & waking and going abroad to his fedyng, vseth to grunt and [is] as it were one neuer pleased, but thinkinge all to muche that he dothe be it neuer so little.[49]

Edgeworth draws on the scenes and actions of common life to provide a homely group of similes. Thus ' like as the pitchers that be whole & sound be made faster, harder and stronger by the fyre; so they that be cracked or broken, flyeth in peces ', so the good are strengthened by trouble, but the unsteadfast are broken by impatience.[50] Servile fear is the beginning, charity the end of wisdom; but fear is the way to bring in charity,

lyke as when a manne soweth in cloothe, the nedle goeth afore and maketh the way for the threde to come after, not because the nedle shall sticke there still in the clothe, but shall passe and go throughe, that the threde may come after and bide still there. And when a man soweth in leather, the threde hathe a bristle, or a harde heere, craftely set and ioyned to the former ende of the threede. After the Nall [awl] hathe made the waye, then afore the threde the sayde heere goeth, not because it shall there abide still, in the hoole, but because it shall leade and gyde the threede that commeth after and muste there remaine styll.[51]

Edgeworth's illustration for the different reactions of the good and

---

[48] Ibid. f. 6[r].
[49] Ibid. f. 262[r]. Cf. too ibid. f. 122[r], 'For he that gyueth ouer and ceaseth to do well afore he haue proued the vttermost of it, or be come to the ende, is lyke an Ape, whose condition is, when he tasteth the vtter [outer] hull or huske of a nutte, and perceiueth it soure and bitter, casteth away the nutte afore he hath tasted the swetenes of the curnell.'
[50] Ibid. f. 124[r].   [51] Ibid. f. 64[v].

the bad to adversity is characteristically homely; the bad complain, the good are patient, ' as if a man chafe in his hand, or els against the fyre talow or greace, it giueth an horrible stinckinge smell, where as if you likewise chafe by the same fyre an pleasant oyntment, it giueth a fragraunt and swete sauour '.[52] The ways of children, that popular source of *exempla* in the middle ages, [53] provide Edgeworth with a lively figure for those who are so uninstructed that they swallow the preaching of heresy, indiscriminately with sound doctrine: ' as yonge infantes many times will sitte moylynge in the axen [ashes], & put erth or coles in to their mouthes, and other things that may do them hurt, as sone as that shal do them good '.[54] Occasionally Edgeworth anticipates the secular euphuists as well as the Elizabethan euphuistic preachers by using a string of *exempla*, as these on the shining of the righteous in an evil world: ' a goodlie Rose springeth up amonge the thornes, and a goodlye Oke amonge the roughe bryer bushes. A candle geueth best lyghte in the darke, and the starres sheweth fayrest in the night.'[55]

In a pleasing group of similes Edgeworth appeals to the experience of his audience, to the farmers, fishermen, merchants, and sailors to be found amongst it. One notes, for example, this passage (possibly derived from St. John Chrysostom) on the need for a preacher to continue his labours, even if (as too often happens) he seems to have but little effect: [some may remember the preacher's words the next time they are in the tavern; the strong may be strengthened, and] . . .

The third profit, although I haue not perswaded men to daye, yet to morowe I maye peraduenture, and if not to morow, I may the next day after, or the fourth day, or in tyme to come. Example we may take of a Fisher and the fish that longe nibleth at his bayte, yet at the last he is taken and cast on lond. Likewise as a husbandman, if he wold giue of going to ploughe, because he seeth distemperaunce and troublous weather many times, and looseth hys labour and cost, we shoulde all dye for hunger. Lykewise the shypman or the merchaunt, if for one storme or twayne, or one losse or twayne, he should abhorre and giue of goyng to the sea, there would at the last no man auenture to the seas, and then farewell this citye of Bristowe, and all good trade of marchaundyse and occupying by sea. The husbandman often laboreth and breaketh one peece of grounde, and little or nothing gayneth, yet at last recouereth in

[52] Ibid. f. 241r.
[53] See *ante*, pp. 115–16; and Owst, *L. & P.M.E.*, pp. 27, 34–5, 37.
[54] *Sermons*, f. 151v.   [55] Ibid. f. 178v. Cf. *post*, pp. 192–3, 197–202.

one yeere the losse of many yeres afore. And the Marchaunt man although he hath had losse by shipwracke diuers times, yet he abstaineth not to passe and seke out straunge portes, and manye times auentreth on hys olde busynes with a Cabao, [i.e. Cabow, a venture in the coast carrying trade], gathered of borrowed money, and dothe full well, and cometh to great substaunce and riches.[56]

Again, some worldly people cannot abide the sweetness of preaching as ' they that be vsed to stinking sauours can not liue in Bucklersbury, or in the poticaries shoppe '.[57] In this group come Edgeworth's most deeply felt and personal figures which are drawn from farming and gardening; these show a real sympathy for growing things and animals. In the early sixteenth century it was of course possible, because of the predominantly agricultural state of the country, for even a highly learned man like Edgeworth to have considerable farming lore. This comes out very clearly in the following treatment of the ' passions ', which must be controlled rather than utterly destroyed:

They be *vbertas quedam animorum*, a certaine batilnes or frutfulnes of the soul which shuld not be destroyed, but rather wel husbanded & bated, as if a ground or a garden be to ranke, it is not best clene to destroy that ranknes, but rather to bate it with sand or grauel, or such like, or els the herbes, the graffes, and trees, that be there set, wil canker and be nought. So it is of these iiii affections (after these Philosophers) that they must not be cleane destroyed but moderate and kept subiect to reason. . . .[58]

Similarly clear is the sympathy in this delightful image expressing the necessity for preachers to give their flocks sound doctrine:

They muste wyth discrete solicitude and studie prouide such pasture and feedinge for them, as shall be good and holsome, & not driuing them to ranke feeding that will bane them: to corrupte ground, as to a certayne spire white grasse, that growith in some grounde, or to groundes that be morish, maresh or otherwise vnholsome, & like to coothe [give sheep rot to] the flocke, for suche the flocke desyreth, And yf they be let run at ther own liberte, to suche feedinge they wyll drawe, rather then to holsome pasture.[59]

Then in a figure which is almost an anticipation of Hopkins's, ' sheer plod makes plough down sillion/Shine ',[60] (' The Windhover ', ll. 11–12) Edgeworth speaks of the noble utility of toil:

[56] Ibid., f. 13ᵛ. cf. St. John Chrysostom, 'Concio prima de Lazaro,' *P.G.*, xlviii. 965–6.

[57] *Sermons*, f. 130ʳ.   [58] Ibid. f. 56ʳ.   [59] Ibid. f. 295ᵛ.

[60] *Poems of Gerard Manley Hopkins*, 3rd. edn., by W. H. Gardner (Oxford, 1948) p. 73.

The plowmans share or culter of his plow, if it be well occupied, it sheweth faire and bryght and doth much good; if it lye vnoccupied in a corner, it rusteth and cankereth to nought, and doth no manne good. So with labour a man shall be shininge and bright before God and man, and shal do muche good; where the slothfull man shall be euer vnprofitable and nothing set by, like the weuyll in the corne, and a verye spill paine.[61]

That it was necessary in his day to defend the use of narrations in preaching, against the Protestant-minded, is shown by Edgeworth's interesting polemic:

I reade a narration of two crafts menne. But yet because (I heare) that some younge menne be daungerous and will peraduenture contemne or dispise such narrations as wel as some other thinges whiche they canne not amende, somewhat to comforte theim that woulde heare examples for theyr learnynge, you shall note what the Apostle saith. *iiii Ephe[seos] Omnis sermo malus ex ore vestro non procedat: sed, si quis bonus ad edificationem fidei, vt det gratiam audientibus.* Let no yll speache or talkinge passe out of your mouthe, but if you haue anye good talkynge to edifie and healpe our fayeth that it maye geue a grace to the audience. Sainte Ambrose expoundinge the same wordes saieth *Bonae enim & sobrie fabulae dant gratum exemplum audientibus.* Good & sober tales geueth pleasant examples to the hearers. Sober tales (he saith) suche as be neither wilde nother wanton. But suche as a manne maye take good and pleasant examples of, as Esopes fables and such other. . . . A feete or proper tale is no more but a mery wrappyng in or coueryng of some truth, inuented and sette foorthe for mennes profite, and for their pleasure, to allure them better to remember the matter that is spoken of.[62]

Edgeworth is, however, sparing of narrations proper,[63] and he does not give personal reminiscences in the manner of Latimer.[64]

A bridge between the exponents of the plain style and those of the fully ornate is made by the sermons of Bishop Alcock. In form he favours, as we have seen, comparative simplicity;[65] nevertheless in style he is predominantly elaborate, although he does not disdain the use of certain popular devices. At times he employs ' augmented ' terms, which resemble the aureate diction found in certain late

---

[61] *Sermons*, f. 174ᵛ.

[62] Ibid. f. 61ᵛ.

[63] An exception is the story of Edgeworth's patron, St. Cuthbert entertaining 'a poore wayfarynge man' who turns out to be an angel (ibid. f. 261ʳ).

[64] See *post*, pp. 147–50.

[65] See *ante*, pp. 74–5.

medieval religious lyrics,[66] and uses ' word-pairs ', (synonyms, one being usually a Latin derivative, the other native English) as in this passage on a favourite theme of his, the glory of consecrated virginity:[67]

It is desyrous to loke and see a bewteuous & a fayre felyshyp of virgyns & maydens semblid togyder, whose bewte the integryte of theyr soules and bodyes togyder, not fyled, con- serueth theyr playsaunt bewte. And [they] ben lykened to the rose rutilaunt and the whyte lely, whyche floures ben preferred in syght & in odour [to] al other floures: for neyther seyr Katheryn, saynt Margarete, nor the fayre lady Cecyly wer neuer more bewteuous in colour of al partyes of theyr bodyes, than these blessed virgyns, men of relygyon & seraunces of god.[68]

The religious life is indeed a heaven upon earth for:

There ben fayre & delycate roses of charyte, the bewteuous lelyes of chastyte in body & soule; the odoryferous & swete vyolettes of all obedyence & humylyte, with herbes and flowers sanatyf to remedy al syknesses, heuynes & malyncoly.[69]

Occasionally too Alcock uses the schemata, as anaphora[70] and antistrophe,[71] but he is not averse to the employment of mnemonic verses, a device of the popular homilists: in an exhortation to the clergy, he gives his priests these aids to flee the temptations of women:

Ne fugias tactus, vix euitabitur actus.
Hos ergo vita, ne moriaris ita.

Est mulier dicta morbus me tangere noli.

Pungit enim vultu, visu, risu, cute, cultu.
Ab eius vultu, quantum potes, esto procul tu.[72]

Like Baron, Alcock studs his sermons with citations from the Fathers,[73] especially St. John Chrysostom,[74] St. Jerome,[75] St.

---

[66] Cf. *Religious Lyrics of the XVth Century*, ed. Carleton Brown (Oxford, 1939) nos. 38 and 56; also *The Poetical Works of John Skelton*, ed. A. Dyce, 2 vols. (London, 1843) vol. I. pp. 139–40; 'Prayer to the Father of Heauen,' 'To the Seconde Parson,' 'To the Holy Gooste.'

[67] See *post*, pp. 258–9.   [68] *Mons Perfectionis*, sig. Eii^r.   [69] Ibid. sig. Cv^r.

[70] *Desponsacio virginis christo*, sig. Avi^{r-v}; the passage beginning, 'ye muste be pacyent amonge your systers . . .' (quoted in the text, *post*, p. 259).

[71] Ibid. sig. Aiv^r: [Christ was served in heaven by the angels, who are virgins, and on earth by virgins too] . . . ' his moder was and is perpetuall virgyne. Iohan Euangelyste his secretary a virgyne. Iohan the Baptyst a virgyne. Ieremy the prophete a virgyne, and angelles in heuen virgynes. . .'

[72] *Gallicantus in sinodo apud Bernwell*, sig. Biii^r.

[73] See *ante*, p. 119.

[74] *Desponsacio virginis christo*, sig. Aiv^v; *Mons Perfectionis*, sig. Aii^r, Bv^v, Ei^r.

[75] *Desponsacio virginis christo*, sig. Aiii^v, Av^v.

Augustine[76] and St. Bernard,[77] but he differs from the learned Franciscan in that he frequently embellishes his matter with *exempla*. The hoary stock similes about the necessity for the religious to remain in their monastery are still valid for him:

> Saynt Anthony saith, right as a fyshe may not lyue without water, but in short time is deed: Ryght so a monke beynge without his celle is deede in the syght of God. . . .[78]

> . . . right as a henne that passeth from her egges & suffre[th] them to be colde, bryngyth forth no chekens: Ryght so a man religion leuynge his celle bryngeth forth no fruyte to the pleysure of god. A tree ofte transplanted from one place to an other loseth his fruyte: Ryght so a monke goynge from place to place for his pleysure, it taketh not awaye his temptacyon.[79]

However the bishop does on occasion use fresher similes, as this from everyday life, (although indeed it is found in Bromyard's *Summa Predicantium*):

> This felyshyp that speketh and malygneth agenst the chirche, in theyr resonynge & argumentes to oppresse the auctoryte thereof, may wel be lykned to a dogge when the mone shyneth fayre & bryghte, he barketh & bayeth euen agenst it as he wolde destroye it: & yet he neyther vnderstondeth what it is, nor it lyeth not in his power to hurte it. And this dogge thus barkynge letteth other men of theyr reste, & seaseth not tyll he be rapt on the heed & so slayne & throwen in a dyche.[80]

Narrations of the usual medieval kind abound in Alcock's pages. Stories of the ascetical prowess of the Desert Fathers and holy women are very much to his taste. By her shining virginity, ' Saynt Margarete hadde the deuyll vnder hyr feete and bounde hym, and he cryed & sayd: Leue ye yonge mayde ye destroye me ';[81] similarly St. Juliana ' bette hym and putte hym to grete rebuke, and therefore the deuyll worshypped virgynyte '.[82] Again, a monk tempted as far as the door of the monastery, stopped there and made the sign of the cross, and ' cryed to the deuyll, Thou hast pulled me

---

[76] *Mons Perfectionis*, sig. Bvi^r; *Sermo. . .Qui habet aures audiendi audiat*, sig. Biv^v.

[77] *Desponsacio virginis christo*, sig. Aiv^r; *Mons Perfectionis*, sig. Cv^r.

[78] *Mons Perfectionis*, sig. Cv^v; see too *Desponsacio virginis christo*, sig. Aiv^v-Bi^r. Cf. *Vitae Patrum*, lib. I, 'Vita Beati Antonii Abbatis,' cap. 53, P.L., lxxiii. 164; ibid. lib. V, 'Verba Seniorum,' P.L., lxxiii. 858, Gratian, *Decreti Secunda Pars*, causa xvi, q. 1, cap. 8, *Corpus Iuris Canonici*, ed. A. Friedberg, 2 vols., (Leipzig, 1879–81) vol. I, p. 763.

[79] *Mons Perfectionis*, sig. Cv^r; see too *Desponsacio virginis christo*, sig. Bi^r. Cf. *Vitae Patrum*, lib. V, 'Verba Seniorum,' P.L., lxxiii. 895.

[80] *Sermo . . .Qui habet aures audiendi: audiat*, sig. Di^r. The simile occurs in Bromyard under 'Conscientia'; noticed by Owst, *L. & P.M.E.*, p. 27, n. 9.

[81] *Desponsacio virginis christo*, sig. Aiv^r.

[82] Ibid. sig. Aiv^v. See too, ibid. sig. Av^v-Avi^r; (reference to the story of St. Agnes).

hyder, pulle me now ferder & thou canst: but it shall neuer lye in thy power'.[83] He tells his audience too of the monk whom St. Anthony commanded to bear naked upon his back pieces of flesh, so that the birds and beasts pulled him down and wounded him, 'And Saynt Anthony sayd vnto hym, Ryght so the deuylls wyl devoure that relygyouse man whiche kepeth ony moneye with hym contrary to his professyon, as thou haste done syth thou entred into thy relygyon'.[84] Obviously too, Alcock believed in the efficacy of the *exemplum terrible*, that favourite device of the popular homilists;[85] those which he gives are typically medieval in their primitive fierceness. Thus:

> Iohn Andrewe in the boke called *Ieronimanum*, sayth that ther was a Greke an heretyke whiche dysputed with a catholycall preest in the chirche of Ierusalem and the sayd preest alledged to the heretyke saynt Ierom, and the heretyk sayd to hym agen. Thy Ierom, whiche thou alledgest lyeth falsely, & euen forth with his tongue was taken from him & he spake neuer after. And in lyke wyse, one of the secte of Arianis sayd that saynt Ierom was false and his wrytynges were not true. And incontynent the deuyll entred in hym, and he cryed euer, *Ieronime, Ieronime*, & so deyed in wretchednesse.[86]

The fully ornate style has two notable exponents in this period, Fisher and Longland. Just as in form Fisher shows some influence of the classical orators,[87] so in style, he emulates the periods of Cicero. Unfortunately there is no true articulated complexity, rather the usual effect is one of clumsiness, as in these sentences:

> Is not the grete mercy & mekenes of almyghty god gretely to be magnyfyed and spoken of that he shewed to Dauid, after so great benefytes gyuen vnto hym after his greuous offences and very grete vnkyndnesse soo soone for to gyue hym mercy and forgyuenesse?[88]

> What thynge myght he then trust to haue, but onely the punysshement of god whiche he gretely ferynge was meruaylously penytent and knowledged hymselfe greuously to haue offended our lorde god askynge hym mercy, made this psalme

[83] Ibid. sig. Bi^r.
[84] *Mons Perfectionis*, sig. Dii^r. Cf. *Vitae Patrum*, lib. V, 'Verba Seniorum,' *P.L.*, lxxiii. 888.
[85] See *ante*, p. 118.
[86] *Sermo . . . Qui habet aures audiendi: audiat*, sig. Ciii^v. See too ibid. sig. Cv^r, where dicers are warned by the cautionary story of one who said: 'I woll playe at the dyse in spyte of Ierom, Austen decrees and all other that bordeth it: and forthwith the deuyll slewe hym and bare hys body awaye thrugh the rouffe of the howse, and lete the bowels stynking there.'
[87] See *ante*, p. 86.
[88] *English Works*, Pt. I, pp. 6–7.

K

with grete contrycyon & sorowe in his soule, whereby agayne
he obteyned forgyuenes.[89]
Indeed the Ciceronian period is not handled with complete mastery
in English preaching until the resonant and shapely elaboration of
Hooker.[90] In his later sermons however, Fisher has greater success
when he uses the schemata more in the medieval manner than in the
classical. As Morris W. Croll and Harry Clemons remark in their
edition of Lyly's *Euphues*: in classical authors, ' the word schemes
occur, when they occur at all . . . with comparative infrequency, and
always in a subordinate relation to the other elements in the composition, especially the rhythmic design and periodic structure,
which they are meant to reinforce and illustrate '. On the other hand,
in medieval writers, ' the figures give the style its pattern and
structure . . . they appear not occasionally, but in sentence after
sentence, paragraph after paragraph. They are also used in different
ways. The schematic ornament is constantly made more obvious in
one of two ways. Either a single figure is repeated over and over in
a succession of short members with something of the effect of a magic
incantation . . . or else different schemes or different forms of the
same one are woven together in a complicated pattern within a
period or a paragraph.'[91] Thus in Fisher we find this series of
rhetorical questions coupled with anaphora (on the Passion of Christ):

> Is it not a wonderfull thyng, that he whych is most to bee
> dreade and feared, would be in so much feare, that for verie
> feare and dread of payne hee had to suffer, he swet water and
> bloud[?].

> Is it not a wonderfull thyng, that he that was most inestim-
> able in price, and most precyous, would suffer hys bodie to bee
> solde for so little pryce, as for the value of thyrtye pence?

> Is it not a wonderfull thyng, that hee that is the Lorde of
> heauen and earth, and all other creatures, woulde suffer him
> selfe to be bound of those vyllaynes wyth ropes lyke a theefe?[92]

—and so on throughout a series of eleven questions.[93] Like Alcock,
Fisher uses word-pairs,[94] while a Latin flavour is at times imparted

---

[89] Ibid. p. 7.   [90] See *post*, pp. 188–9.
[91] *Euphues the Anatomy of Wit, Euphues and his England by John Lyly*, ed. Morris W.
Croll and Harry Clemons (London, 1916) pp. xxxiv–xxxv.
[92] *English Works*, Pt. I, p. 389.
[93] Ibid. pp. 389–90. A similar series occurs, ibid. p. 400. See too the use of *repetitio*,
ibid. p. 404: 'And not onely she [St. Mary Madgalene] giueth the example of sorrowe,
but his blessed mother abundantly then sorrowed at his death. Sainct John sorrowed,
Sainct Peter sorrowed and wepte bitterly. All the Apostles were in sorrow.'
[94] As ibid. e.g. p. 105; 'grete and innumerable', 'couer and hyde', 'make open and
accuse', 'lawe and custome', 'captyuyte and thraldom', 'pardoned and forgyuen', etc.
For Alcock's use of this device, see *ante*, pp. 126–7.

to his exhortations by the use of past participles which retain their Latin form, and are not accommodated to English.[95]

Like Baron and Alcock, Fisher frequently quotes the Fathers;[96] St. Anselm,[97] St. Ambrose,[98] St. Augustine,[99] St. Bernard,[100] St. Cyprian,[101] St. John Damascene,[102] St. Gregory,[103] St. Jerome,[104] St. John Chrysostom,[105] and Origen,[106] are all cited. However (unlike Baron), only four times does Fisher refer to the schoolmen; once to St. Bonaventure,[107] once to St. Thomas Aquinas,[108] and twice to Guillaume Perauld.[109]

The most felicitous aspect of Fisher's ornamentation is his very frequent use of similes. These are not different in kind from those current in the sermon handbooks, but in their context they have a freshness and indeed a certain individuality, which is peculiarly delightful. Many of the most pleasing are drawn from natural phenomena, especially the life of plants, and the sun, its rays and nurturing effects. The sinner who produces contrition and confession, but not satisfaction is compared to a tree which brings forth buds and flowers, but no fruit.[110] The impossibility of the coming of Christ, the sun, without the dawn, the Blessed Virgin, preceding Him, is illustrated by the fact that: 'An apple whiche first is grene waxeth not sodeynly yelowe, but fyrste it is somewhat whyte bytwene grene and yelowe indyfferent'.[111] The soul needs grace, just as a herb withers without moisture;[112] spiritual fruits can grow only in that soul which has been sowed with God's word; although even then, only virgins bring forth few or no weeds, the married and widows still are partly unproductive,[113] for:

> Ye se that though the grounde in the feeldes, by the dyly-
> gence of men, be neuer so well broken and seasoned, yet if
> there be no good sede sowen in it, it bryngeth nothynge forth
> of it selfe but weedes, and all his naturall moysture tourneth in
> to weedes: But whan some good sede is caste into hit, than
> that sede by his naturall vertue, and by the influence of the
> heuens, so mightily draweth that erthely moysture of the
> grounde, and chaungeth it, and assembleth it in to his own

[95] See the list collected by Mayor, ibid., p. xxix.   [96] See *ante*, pp. 119, 127–8.
[97] *English Works*, Pt. I, pp. 67, 230. (These and the following references supplied by Mayor, ibid., p. xxviii.)
[98] Ibid. e.g. p. 319.   [99] Ibid. 245, 273, 318, 327–8, 334, 341, 344, 428.
[100] Ibid. e.g. pp. 230, 401, 411.   [101] Ibid. p. 320.   [102] Ibid. p. 334.
[103] Ibid. pp. 114, 306, 319, 428.   [104] Ibid. e.g. pp. 151, 152, 320, 334.
[105] Ibid. e.g. pp. 287, 320.   [106] Ibid. pp. 177, 209, 320, 333.
[107] Ibid. p. 297.   [108] Ibid. p. 177.   [109] Ibid. pp. 40, 80. See *post*, p. 135.
[110] Ibid. pp. 26.   [111] Ibid. p. 47.   [112] Ibid. p. 148.
[113] On the depreciation of marriage and the exaltation of virginity in this period, see *post*, pp. 258–60.

substaunce: in so muche that in some well prepared erthe there spryngeth nat one weede, but all the moysture of the grounde is tourned into corne. In some other be fewer or mo weedes, accordynge to the goodnes of the erthe, or better or lesse diligence in preparyng of the same.[114]

Good works are the only sure index of the possession of grace; ' we be not yet sure that any tree is aliue to than we se some puttynge forthe of buddes or lefes out of the same tree '.[115] The diseased eye cannot bear the sun's rays, the healthy eye delights in them, so God is terrible to the sinner, but a friend to the just.[116] He can no more with-hold grace from the soul prepared to receive it, ' than the sonne may withstande his bemes out of wyndowes when they be open '.[117] God works on man's soul and the Church, as the sun shines on the earth, bringing forth new life from that which seemed dead; the holy bishop responds with delicate sensitiveness to the miracle of growth:

> . . . what meruaylous vertue what wonderful operacyon is in the bemes of the sonne which as we se this tyme of the yere spred vpon the grounde dothe quycken & make lyfely many creatures the whiche before appered as deed. who that vewed and beheld in the wynter season the trees whan they be wydred and theyr leues shaken from them and all the moystour shronke in to the rote & no lust of grenenes nor of lyfe appereth outwardly. yf he had had none experyence of this mater before he wold thynke it an vnlyke thyng that the same trees sholde reuyue agayn & be so lustely cladde with leues & floures as we now se them. And yet this is done by the sybtyll operacyon and secrete workynge of the sonne bemes spred vpon the grounde.[118]

Animals provide the subjects of another group of similes, the hungry lion lying in wait for its prey resembles sinners waiting for occasions of sin;[119] the ape which imitates the action of the hunter and puts on the shoes laid ready for it, falls from the trees and is taken; so the devils tempt men to a life of more rigorous virtue than they can support.[120] The dog returns to its vomit, and the sow to the clay where it has been wallowing, so sinners return to their evil ways.[121] The horse weltering in mud cannot rise when at length it wishes to do so; similarly the habitual sinner cannot leave his sin when he would.[122] Mastiffs are gentle to those they know, but ' ragyously and furyously gape and ryse ' against strangers; so the

---

[114] *English Works*, Pt. I, pp. 467–8.   [115] Ibid. p. 324.   [116] Ibid. pp. 8, 11.
[117] Ibid. p. 82.   [118] Ibid. p. 323. Cf. too, ibid. p. 148.
[119] Ibid. p. 67.   [120] Ibid. p. 79.   [121] Ibid. p. 88.   [122] Ibid. p. 204.

pains of hell often remembered and set before the mind's eye in life, cannot terrify at the hour of death.[123]

Other similes are drawn from the objects and occupations of daily life. Rubbing makes rusty iron bright, so the tears of penitence wash the soul;[124] our eyes must look first on pictures painted on a wall, and not upon the wall itself, so God must look first on the sins ' painted ' on our soul.[125] It is more difficult to bring the soul disordered by habitual sin into good order, than to mend or bring into the right course a clock which has long continued out of its right order;[126] in hell the intense cold will merely make the heat more unbearable, ' as in the forge of a Smith, the colde water when it is caste into the Fyer, causeth the Fyer to be much more fearse and violent '.[127]

The stock medical similes illustrating the need for recourse to the Sacrament of Penance are found in Fisher's pages; confession is compared to the lancing of a wound,[128] while the longer the penitent delays, the more his soul putrifies; ' as we se a byle or botche full of matter and fylth the more & the lenger it be hyd, the more groweth the corrupycon & venemous infeccion of it, & also perceth to the bones & corrupteth them.'[129]

However, the most deeply felt similes, showing Fisher's observant compassion, come from the miseries of the poor, and the plight of prisoners. Men have pity on ' the beggers or poore folkes that be payned & greued with hungre & colde lyenge in the stretes of cytees or good tounes full of sores ', especially when they hear ' the waylynges, cryenges, & lamentable noyses that they make', so *a fortiori* God shows mercy to those who call upon Him.[130] Again, ' a poore man peraduenture gooth into a pryson where he seeth many prysoners sore punysshed with fetters & other engyns', and 'by that syght he is moued with pyte and mercy, notwithstandynge he hath not wherwith to helpe them ': however almighty God is well able to redeem the world from the ' prison and captyuyte of the deuyll '.[131] The illusory pleasures of the world, ' be lyke to the pleasures that a pore man hathe in his dreme, when he dremeth that he hath gotten a fayre wife & innumerable goods with her, he thynketh hym selfe cladde in precyouse garments, and that he doth handell the golde and syluer and the goodly plate, some of syluer,

---

[123] Ibid. p. 278.   [124] Ibid. p. 17.   [125] Ibid. p. 116.
[126] Ibid. p. 117.   [127] Ibid. p. 424.   [128] Ibid. p. 127.
[129] Ibid. p. 27.; cf. *Jacob's Well*, Pt. I, ed. A. Brandeis (London, 1900) E.E.T.S., o.s. 115, pp. 178–9.
[130] *English Works*, Pt. I, p. 140.   [131] Ibid. p. 228.

som of golde; he seeth houses, gardeyns, feldes, of his owne, and
hath many pleasures. But whan he dothe awake out of his dreme,
and fyndeth none of all these thynges, he is a sory man.'[132] The
Cherubim are strict examiners, and will not let those who are not
clad in the garment of righteousness into Paradise, as the porters
before the Court refuse admittance to the ragged.[133] The soul
deformed by many sins appearing before the majesty of God will
tremble, as when ' a pore man cometh to a prince not accustomed to
shewe hymselfe in the presence of noble men, anone he is smyten
with fere, waxeth pale in the face, quaketh for drede, & is as sore
abasshed that in maner he woteth not what to saye, his spyryte
begynneth to fayle hym '.[134] In the same manner as these similes are
the examples full of tender pity which Fisher uses to arouse the rich
and comfortable to a sense of gratitude to God: let them remember
those less fortunate than themselves ' suche as are streyghtly kept in
pryson, set in a stynkynge derke dungeon, bounde with fetters of
yren and for lacke of meet lyke to dye for hunger, naked without
clothes, in the sharpe colde wynter no fyre to socour them '.[135]
Similarly the healthy should be grateful when they contrast their
lot with that of the diseased, when they perceive: ' how many lye in
stretes & hye wayes full of carbuncles & other vncurable botches
. . . how many be crucyfyed in maner by intollerable aches of bones
& Ioyntes with many other infyrmytees ':[136] and when they do not
forget those ' whiche be vexed with the frensshe pockes, poore, and
nedy; lyenge by the hye wayes stynkynge and almoost roten aboue
the grounde, hauynge intollerable ache in theyr bones. . . .'[137]

On two occasions Fisher uses a striking exordium containing a
figure: the sermon on Ps. l (Vg.) opens with the comparison of the
state of the sinner to that of a man suspended by a slender cord, held
by one whom he has offended, over a pit full of wild beasts;[138] while
the sermon of 1521 against Luther begins with the comparison of
the rise of heresies in the Church and the havoc which they wreak,
to the obscuring of the sun by a dark cloud and the coming of a
tempest which affrights the ignorant.[139] Erasmus, as has been
noticed, approved of such exordia;[140] and as his *Ecclesiastes* originated
in conversations with Fisher,[141] perhaps he was influenced to some
extent in this matter by the bishop's testimony to the effectiveness of

[132] *Hereafter ensueth two fruytfull sermons*, sig. Ei^v; this from Bromyard? cf. Owst,
L. & P.M.E., p. 28, n. 7.
[133] Ibid. sig. Giv^r.   [134] *English Works*, Pt. I, pp. 252–3.   [135] Ibid. p. 239.
[136] Ibid. p. 240.   [137] Ibid.   [138] Ibid. pp. 90–1.
[139] Ibid. pp. 311–12.   [140] See *ante*, p. 120, n. 36.   [141] *Ecclesiastes*, pp. 6–7.

a device which doubtless he used in many other sermons of which no record survives.

Narrations of the usual medieval type occur at times in Fisher's exhortations; especially incidents from the lives of the saints. The audience hears of St. Anthony asking Our Lord where He was during a particularly severe temptation, and being answered, ' I was here with thee ';[142] of the clever but sinful priest spoken of by ' the noble doctour perisiense ' (Guillaume Perauld), who, after he was made a bishop, was so overwhelmed by God's forbearance and goodness, that thereafter he tried never to depart from Him again.[143] Again, the hearers are edified by the example of St. Edward, King of England, and St. Louis of France, who preserved their virginity even in marriage, and despised honours and riches.[144] Then in one peculiarly fine passage, (which surely deserves to become an anthology piece), Fisher draws on his experience of the ' Field of the Cloth of Gold ' (1520) to provide a glittering picture of worldly glory:

> I doubte not but ye haue herde of many goodly syghtes which were shewed of late beyonde the see, with moche Ioy and pleasure worldly. Was it not a great thynge within so shorte a space, to se thre great Prynces of this worlde? I meane the Emperour, and the kyng our mayster, and the Frenche kynge. And eche of these thre in so great honour, shewyng theyr ryalty, shewyng theyr rychesse, shewyng theyr power; with eche of theyr noblesse appoynted and apparellyd in ryche clothes, in sylkes, veluettes, clothes of golde, & such other precyouse araymentes. To se thre ryght excellente Quenes at ones togider, and of thre great realmes. . . . And euery of them accompanyed with so many other fayre ladyes in sumptuouse & gorgeouse apparell; suche daunsynges, suche armonyes, such dalyaunce, and so many pleasaunt pastimes, so curyouse howses and buyldynges, so precyously apparayled, such costely welfare of dyners, souppers, and bankettys, so delycate wynes, soo ryche and goodly tentys, such Iustynges, suche tourneys, and suche feats of warre.[145]

However the winds and tempests came and sullied this magnificent display: it ended as does all worldly glory:

---

[142] *English Works*, Pt. I, p. 89. See too ibid. pp. 283–4: 'Saynt Anthony sawe by reuelacyon that all the worlde was full of snares, and he asked this questyon. Blessed lorde sayd he who shall passe these daungers? It was answered hym *sola humilitas*, onely humbleness and lowlynesse.'

[143] Ibid. p. 40. See too ibid. p. 80, for another story from Perauld—that of one who quelled fleshly temptations by saying 'Fy, fy, fy.'

[144] Ibid. pp. 35–6.   [145] *Here after ensueth two fruytfull Sermons*, sig. Aii.r.

The gownes of veluet, and clothe of golde were full of dust, the ryche trappers of horses were full of dust; hattes, cappes, gownes, were full of dust; the here and faces of men were full of dust. . . . The wyndes blewe downe many tentes; shakyd sore the houses that were buylded for pleasure, and let dyuers of them to be buylded. Sometyme agayne we had raynes and thunders so vnmeasurably that noo man myght styre forth to se no pleasures. Sometyme whan men wolde longer haue dysportyd them at the Iustes, cam the nyght & darkenes vpon them & interruptyd theyr pleasure.[146]

Longland, hitherto virtually neglected as a stylist,[147] surpasses Fisher in his mastery of consciously elaborated rhythms, although to obtain these effects he uses the schemata only in the medieval manner.[148] Also, he uses but few ' augmented ' terms, and is without Fisher's occasional Latinisms.[149] His most striking device is his frequent and felicitous use of *rogatio*, (question and answer), as in the following exposition of a text from St. Paul: *Propter nimiam caritatem suam, qua dilexit nos,* [*Deus,*] *cum essemus mortui peccatis, convivificavit nos in Christo* (Eph. ii. 4–5; ' for his exceeding charity wherewith he loved us even when we were dead in sins, [God] hath quickened us together in Christ ', Douay). Having said that God allowed Christ to die for love, Longland proceeds:

What loue? For the loue he bare to hym selfe? Nay, Nay. It was the inestimable loue he bare vnto vs, *Propter nimiam (inquit) charitatem qua dilexit nos.* What dyde he by this loue? *Conuiuificauit nos CHRISTO.* He reuyued vs agen in Christe, frome death to life. Howe? *Christo.* In Christe and by Christe.[150]

This is simple exposition made more forceful; the device is also used for emotive effect, as in the following cumulative passage on the power of the devil, where, as often, it is coupled with anaphora and iteration:

For if he mought haue his swynge, if he mought haue as much libertye and power ouer the synner as his desior is: who shulde escape his hands? who shulde liue till to morowe? who shulde goo free? fewe, fewe, fewe or noon. Our lyuynge is suche, our wretchednesse is soo grette, our deadys ar soo synneful in the syght of god: that if itt were nott for his defendynge mercy, we shulde be sone att a poynte, sone destroyed, sone rydde out of this worlde.[151]

---

[146] Ibid. sig. Biᵛ.
[147] He receives brief mention by F. E. Hutchinson, in *C.H.E.L.*, vol. IV, ch. xii, pp. 228–9.
[148] See *ante*, p. 130.   [149] See *ante*, pp. 130–1.
[150] *Sermond at Grenwiche*, 1536, sig. Aiiᵛ.   [151] *Sermond at Rychemunte*, 1535, sig. Ciiʳ.

He can use a series of rhetorical questions at great length, but with striking power, as in this passage of set eloquence on the observance of Good Friday, which incidentally shows that although joyful festivals were celebrated with great pomp and display, nevertheless a rigorous asceticism was found at this season among some at least of the courtiers themselves:

> If it be so hygh a day, where are the sygnes & tokens of the feaste? where is the solempne ryngynge of belles to matyns, to masse, to euensong, to diuine service? Where are the solempnytyes of the masses sayd & songe as in other festyuall dayes? Where are the solempne songes of discant, pricked song, faburden, square note, regalles & organs? Where are your warblynge voyces, reeches & pleasant reportes in your syngynges? Where are the ryche ornaments of the aulters, the ryche vestimentes, coopes plaate and iewels, wont vpon such dayes to be set vpon the aulters? Where is the great welfare, the great dynners, the double seruyce, the delicate meates & drynkes on suche festiuall dayes wonte to be vsed? Where are your musicall Instrumentes of all sortes, and youre blowynges to dynner with trumpettes? Where are your harpes, your lutes, your cymballes, your flutes, your tabrettes, your drumslades and dowcymers? Where are your vialles, your rebeckes, your shakebushes: and your swete softe pleasant pypes? Where are your merye communicacyons, your mery iestes, fables and taales wonte to be had at your table for merye pastyme on soche dayes? . . . This day for precyous apparell, some weareth sacke clothe, some heere next vnto theyr bodyes. Some gothe wolwarde, some baare legges, baare footed lyke great penitents, & not lyke as men gothe a holydayes in precyous apparell. But blacke, blacke: in blacke in token of our synnes, for which Chryst dyed.[152]

The simple diction of the above will have been noted; in the following passage there is a subtle breaking up of a scriptural text, [*Proprio filio suo non pepercit sed pro omnibus nobis tradidit illum.* Rom. viii. 32; ' He . . . spared not his own son, but delivered him up for us all ', Douay] which anticipates the mode of Andrewes, but the physical cruelty of the Jews is conveyed with colloquial immediacy:

> And he saythe, *Tradidit.* He dyde traade and gyue hym. This *tradere*, is more than *dare.* For *dare*, is to gyue, but *Tradere* is *dare in potestatem. Tradere* is to gyue into a mannes power, to vse the thynge that is gyue[n] at his or theyr own pleasures to whome it is giuen, to do with it euen what they wyll: as ye wyll

---

[152] *Sermonde at Grenewiche*, 1538, sig. Kiii[r]: cf. too *Sermond at Rychemunte*, 1535, sig. Eii[r], (on the signs of the end of the world); also *Quinque Sermones*, f. 104[v], and *Sermones*, f. 98[v] (on the power of the sun).

saye, to make or marre, to vse at libertie. And so dyde the fadre of heuen for our sake, he gaue his sone Christe into the handes & power of the Iewes, to vse hym and do with hym what they wolde: to handle: to treate, to haale, to lugge, to beate, to scourdge, to cutte, to mangle, to crucifie, and cruelly to put to deathe. And so for this cause *Tradidit illum*. He put hym holly into theyr handes for our saluacyon, to do with hym what they wold, and so they dyde.[153]

It was well for Longland that together with the schemata he adopted such a vernacular diction, for although Fisher and Alcock were moderately successful with Latinized forms,[154] lesser men could produce such tasteless inflation as the following passage on the Incarnation, from a manuscript sermon of this period:

Butt when euerythynge was in extreme distresse, and disparede [despaired] return to light: our blissede savior Ihesu Crist, which is the very light of trawth, procedyde by temporall nativite from the wom of hys immaculat moder Mary. Wher advmbrat þe light of his dyvyne nature inaccessible, he sconsede his high mageste by thassumpcion of our humanite; by the whych as thorough a lantern, he exhibyt the beamis of his eternall veritie. So with rutylant splendour of his infinyt mercy, *visitauit nos oriens ex alto illuminare his qui in tenebris et vmbra sedent*.[155]

The pages of Longland's sermons, like those of Fisher are studded with quotations from the Fathers;[156] St. John Chrysostom,[157] St. Augustine,[158] St. Jerome,[159] St. Ambrose,[160] St. Gregory,[161] and St. Bernard[162] provide suitable *dicta*; but in addition, like Baron, Longland alleges also the authority of the schoolmen[163]—St. Thomas Aquinas[164] and Duns Scotus[165] have their place too in his exhortations.

Again, like Edgeworth and Fisher, Longland uses many

---

[153] *Sermond at Grenwiche*, 1536, sig. Aiii^r.

[154] For Fisher, see *ante*, pp. 130–1, for Alcock, pp. 126–7.

[155] MS. Harl. 3118, f. 117^v-18^r; other notably inflated passages occur on ff. 115^r, 120^v, 123^v.

[156] See *ante*, p. 131.   [157] e.g. *Tres Conciones*, f. 7^r; *Quinque Sermones*, f. 68^v.

[158] e.g. *Quinque Sermones*, ff. 55^v, 56^r, 57^r, 59^r, 60^r, 61^v; *Sermones*, e.g. f. 371^r; *Sermonde at Grenewiche*, 1538, sig. Fi^v.

[159] e.g. *Tres Conciones*, f. 48^v; *Quinque Sermones*, f. 63^v; *Sermond at Grenwiche*, 1536, sig. Giv^r.

[160] e.g. *Quinque Sermones*,ff. 55^r. 63^v,

[161] e.g. *Tres Conciones*, f. 35^v; *Quinque Sermones*, f. 61^r.

[162] e.g. *Quinque Sermones*, ff. 60^v, 62^v; *Sermones*, f. 19^r; *Sermond at Rychemunte*, 1535, sig. Bi^r; *Sermond at Grenwiche*, 1536, sig. Aiii^r.

[163] See *ante*, p. 119.

[164] e.g. *Quinque Sermones*, f. 57^r; *Sermones*, ff. 6^r, 7^v, 56^v, 59^r, 60^v.

[165] e.g. *Sermones*, f. 2^v.

similes,[166] although he too is comparatively sparing of narrations.[167] On the whole Longland's similes are less individual than those of Fisher or Edgeworth, and are more obviously culled directly from the great common store of the sermon handbooks. However they are always extremely apt, as this moralization of ' natural ' history:

> Let us not then usurp God's office, nor mete out the most extreme punishments, as some are wont to do, not unlike the sea monster which after it has killed a man, listens for a long time afterwards in case he is still breathing, lest by chance it should leave him alive.[168]

Similarly apt is this figure of the different reactions of the worldly and the spiritual to tribulations:

> How do you know if a glass is full of wine, or empty? Assuredly you know it is empty if it rings when struck with the finger: if however, the blow makes no sound, you will find that it is full. So if you murmur when stricken with troubles and adversities, if you complain and blaspheme, and blurt out curses, you show yourself to be void of the wine of the Holy Spirit.[169]

Also, he almost always makes these illustrations fully his own, as in the following exhortation to frequent confession lest the habits of sin grow strong:

> Example we may take by twoo pure syluer basons. Fyll them bothe full of filthe, and euery day voyde the filthe out of oon of them & washe hym clene, & agen fyll hym full of fylthe, & agen washe hym, and soo often, and yet at the yeres ende, thy bason shall by thy often washing be clene. But the other bason whiche standeth all the yere full of fylth and not clensed, caste it out at the yeares ende, and washe hym, rubbe him scower hym, & doo thy beste: and yet thou shalt not make hym clene. For by longe lyinge of the fylthe in it, hit cankers and fretes in to the bason, soo that rubbynge and scourynge wyll not fetche it awaye.[170]

So too in this expansion of the Apostles being accounted of no reputation, *abjectissimi*:

[16.] For Edgeworth's use of similes, see *ante*, pp. 122–6, for Fishers' pp. 131–4.

[167] For Edgeworth's narrations, see *ante*, p. 126, for Fisher's pp. 135–6. One of the best instances of Longland's use of narrations is the dream of the rich benefactor of convents and monasteries who is asked by Christ, 'But what did you suffer for me?' and his terrified confusion; (*Sermones*, f. 780ʳ;) another is the vision of Christ in the Blessed Sacrament vouchsafed to the king, taken from the 'History of Edward the Confessor,' (ibid. f. 346ʳ).   [168] *Sermones*, f. 387ʳ. See too ibid. f. 500ʳ.

[169] *Quinque Sermones*, f. 85ʳ. Cf. too *Sermons*, f. 673ᵛ, a good man is like a jar full of spices and perfumes, a bad man like a jar full of evil smelling liquid. When the wind of adversity blows over the former, it omits a choice fragrance, but the latter gives off a vile stench so that all cry 'fy, fy.'   [170] *Sermond at Rychemunte*, 1535, sig. Kiiiʳ.

. . . reputed butt as a rotten parte or as the parying of an aple, or as the duste that is swept out of the house & throwen in to a corner behinde the doore to be caste to the dunghill.[171]

Sometimes, we catch, perhaps, a more personal note, as in this delightful picture of the well-spring of the mercy of God:

> For he euer contynually floweth, he euer issueth, he bub-bullys and sprynges, & dothe euer abundantly runne out of hym mercy & propiciation: so that euery man, euery woman may resorte to hym, and fyll ther pottes and fyll ther vessels as often as they wyll. And yet shall they neuer draw drye this abundante sprynge, thys plentefull welle of the mercy of God, unless yt be *propter ingratitudinem*, for vnkyndenes.[172]

—or in this other figure of the Divine forgiveness:

> Thou mayste fill a vessell soo full of lycour, thatt it may swell aboue the brynke; ye call itt in Englishe brynkfull, whenne it is readye to ronne ouer, whenne it is soo full that with a fyllype, with the leeste touche thou canst touche, it runnes ouer. So god, god is soo full of mercy, that he is brynkfull. And soo full that thou canst not fyllippe hym neuer soo little, touche hym neuer so lightly by desiour, by prayour or humble suyt, but he runnes ouer: mercy floweth, mercy moysteth, mercy worketh.[173]

Similarly fresh in this illustration of how a sinful life bars out the effects of the redemption:

> They do as he that is in a house, wher the wyndous are open & the sone beams shynynge mooste clere in to the house, and gyues lyght to all that are within: whiche wylfully dothe shute the wyndous, & shute the sone beames, by reason wher of, he is left darke in the hous.[174]

Only occasionally do Longland's figures seem to be drawn from scenes of contemporary life. A notable exception is his spirited description of a hunt; the clamour, the sounding of the horns, the urging on of the dogs, the rigours willingly borne ' for a negligible prey '.[175] Again, in the following passage the description of the habits of city children may proceed from personal observation. Sinners who weary themselves in the pursuit of sin:

> . . . act not unlike boys who run incessantly through the streets all day long, who play amongst slime and mud, although tired,

---

[171] *Sermond at Grenwiche*, 1536, sig. Fi[v]. For an earlier parallel to the dust being swept behind the door, cf. Owst, *L. & P.M.E.*, p. 31.
[172] *Sermond at Rychemunte*, 1535, sig. Bi[r].   [173] Ibid. sig. Aiii[v].
[174] Ibid. sig. Hi[r]. See too ibid. sig. Oi[r]: 'The breuytie and shortenes of mannes lyffe, is but a moote in the sone beame, in comparyson of the hoole sphyer of the worlde.'
[175] *Qunique Sermones*, f. 82[v].

weary, hungry and thirsty. Nevertheless, thus they amuse themselves with these trifling pursuits so long as any light glimmers in the sky, nor do they stop when dark night comes: they cease not with the greatest toil to dirty themselves in this way, with the result that, returning home worn out at night, and filthily dirtied, they are beaten by their parents.[176]

Like Fisher, Longland gives two striking exordia.[177] Of these one is unsuccessful; in the first of his Lenten Sermons his use of St. Ambrose's reference to the habits of bees is over-elaborated and rather confused in application. The ' king ', which has a sting which it does not wish to use, represents Christ, who does not wish any soul to be lost: the bees which sting themselves and so die, after they have offended their king, stand for sinners who die spiritually when they offend or ' sting ' God by mortal sin.[178] The other is however more pleasing; in the exordium to the sermon on Ps. vi the bishop, echoing St. John Chrysostom, compares Scripture to a garden rich in beautiful flowers, where the Penitential Psalms are medicinal herbs.[179]

Finally, the ornate style is used at the end of Henry VIII's reign by William Peryn in his extremely rhetorical sermons on the Blessed Sacrament. His manner lacks the distinction of Fisher and Longland; it represents the hardening of the style into a strained artificiality, as in this passage on the ordered glory of the creation and man's dull response to it, where he uses Latinisms, word-pairs, alliteration and eponalepsis:

> What els, vnto vs declareth the hyghe and huge heauen the tegument and couert, of all worldlye thinges, so thycke paynted and powdered, with so many coruscante starres? What the mouable spheres with their continuall motions, and liuely influens, causing generation and corruption, in all thinges subiect vnto chaungeablenes & alteracton? But, (as the prophet saieth) the heauens sheweth forth the glory of God, and the firmament declareth the worke of his handes. What dothe to vs signify, the delectable harmony of all thynges, in

[176] *Sermones*, f. 796ᵛ.   [177] For Fisher's exordia, see *ante*, pp. 134–5.
[178] *Quinque Sermones*, f. 55ʳ. The passage on the habits of bees occurs in St. Ambrose's *Hexameron*, lib. V, cap. xxi, *P.L.*, xiv. 249.
[179] *Sermones*, f. 1ᵛ; (cf. St. John Chrysostom, first 'Homily on the Statues,' *P.G.*, xlix. 17) Longland's essential bookishness is well illustrated by his references to flowers (see further e.g. *Tres Conciones*, f. 22ʳ; *Sermones*, f. 358ʳ⁻ᵛ): he does seem to have an affection for them as tokens of the handiwork of a benevolent creator, but his flower lists—his roses, lilies, violets, crocuses and narcissi—owe something at least to St. Jerome's commentary on *Considerate lilia agri* [Matt. vi. 28] (see 'Commentarium in Evangelium Matthei,' *P.L.*, xxvi. 47); he has none of Edgeworth's sympathy with real growing things. (Cf. *ante*, pp. 125–6.)

course continual, and order certayne? Saue onely the magnificent power, and vnsearchable wysdome of their creatour & maker, as the wise men saith. By the greate and wonderfull comlynesse and bewtie of the creature, might plainely and euidently, be perceiued and knowen, the creator and maker of them. Breuely to conclude, where is any more manifest token, of the diuine power, then (the wonder of the worlde) man, who alone is a whole worlde of myracles, and hath almost as many wonders in himself, as he hath powers and partes. Yet such is the vntowardnes, of our rechles nature, prone and proclyue, vnto blinde ignoraunce, that notwithstandinge that both, within vs, and also without vs, there is almoste nothynge voyde, of goddes singular power & myracle, (the whole worlde fylled full with wonders) yet neglygente ignoraunce, and ignoraunte neglygens, doth growe so fast vpon vs, that the admirable wonder of the creation, conseruation, and administration of all the brode worlde is almooste (as saint Augustine saith) by assyduite and cottidian custom, out of all estimation and meruell, and the power of God herein wyped out of memory.[180]

This ornate mode was not, however, destined to be heard at Paul's Cross again until Mary's reign, when as we shall see, it became one of the predominant preaching styles.[181]

II

THE EARLY REFORMERS (1547–1555)

In this period only the plain and the colloquial styles are found; the Reformers in their fiery zeal to change the religion of England until it accords with the simplicity of ' the Gospel ' eschew the mannered elaboration of the ornate style.

Latimer, by far the finest stylist among them, is the greatest pulpit exponent of the colloquial style in the century. In diction he uses, like Edgeworth, a pungent and racy speech idiom.[182] He draws upon the same resources of language as does Skelton in his satiric poems, but is, of course, without the Laureate's obscenity. Thus the vigorous expansion of the Pharisees' *Num et vos seducti estis*, (John vii. 47) ' What, ye brain-sick fools, ye hoddy-pecks, ye doddy-pouls, ye huddes, do ye believe him? are you seduced also? '[183] can be paralleled in ' Why come ye not to Court ':

[180] *Thre godlye and notable Sermones, of the moost honorable and blessed sacrament of the Aulter*, f. 2ᵛ.
[181] See *post*, pp. 157–61.
[182] For Edgeworth, see *ante*, pp. 121–3.
[183] *Sermons*, p. 136.

He sayth, thou huddypeke,
Thy lernynge is to lewde. . . . (ll. 326–7)[184]
Wherat moche I wonder,
How suche a hoddypoule
So boldely dare controule. . .. .(ll. 669–71)[185]

The use of humorous compounds is the main device by which Latimer attains his characteristic homely vigour. Apart from the famous references to ' purgatory pick-purse ',[186] flatterers are called ' claw-backs and flibbergibs ',[187] Adonijah, David's son, is ' a stout-stomached child, a by-walker ',[188] and the monks and friars are ' merit-mongers '.[189] Similarly, bribery is denounced in these terms: ' Wo worth these gifts! They subvert justice everywhere. *Sequuntur retributiones*: " they follow bribes ". Somewhat was given to them before, and they must needs give somewhat again: for Giffe-gaffe was a good fellow: this Giffe-gaffe led them clean from justice. " They follow gifts." '[190] The Devil may feign to flee from a friar's coat, but ' he can give us an after-clap when we least ween '.[191] Some wish to hinder the progress of the reformation, ' now they have their shifts and their put-offs '.[192] The bishops should be ' preachers not bell-hallowers ',[193] while amongst those who pretend to be Protestants, ' some are card-gospellers; some are dice-gospellers; some pot-gospellers '.[194] Quoting Scripture against the worldly advisers of the king, Latimer asks: ' Where are these word-lings now, these bladder-puffed-up wily men?'[195] On the mingling of Protestant and Roman doctrines and practices, he declares: ' They say in my country, when they call their hogs to the swine trough, " Come to thy mingle-mangle, come pur, come pur ": even so they made a mingle-mangle of it.'[196]

Latimer employs other devices with humorous effect; occasionally he employs paronomasia, as when admonishing the king that he must read the Bible, he continues: ' But how shall he read this book? As the Homilies are read. Some call them homelies, and indeed they are homely handled.'[197] Or again, speaking of a priest who took the part of a bishop who was objecting to his use of the term, ' the Lord's Supper ', Latimer declares: ' There stood by him a dubber, one Doctor Dubber: he dubbed him by and by, and said that this term was seldom read in the doctors.'[198] Latimer

---

[184] *The Poetical Works of John Skelton*, vol. II, p. 37.   [185] Ibid. vol. II, p. 47.
[186] *Sermons*, pp. 36, 50.   [187] Ibid. p. 124.   [188] Ibid. p. 113.
[189] *Remains*, p. 200.   [190] *Sermons*, p. 140.   [191] Ibid. p. 29.   [192] Ibid. p. 132.
[193] Ibid. p. 176.   [194] Ibid. p. 286.   [195] Ibid. p. 121.
[196] Ibid. p. 147.   [197] Ibid. p. 121.   [198] Ibid.

uses alliteration too with comic effect as when denouncing worldly prelates:

> They hawk, they hunt, they card, they dice; they pastime in their prelacies with gallant gentlemen, with their dancing minions, and with their fresh companions, so that ploughing is set aside: and by their lording and loitering, preaching and ploughing is soon gone.[199]

Latimer's use of proverbs frequently lends a colloquial pungency to his sermons, as they had done to those of the medieval popular homilists.[200] Speaking of the different ages at which men die, he quotes 'There do come as many skins of calves to the market as there do of bulls or kine'.[201] Only those with guilty consciences are stung by the denunciations of the preacher; 'as when a horse is rubbed on the gall, he will kick: when a man casteth a stone among dogs, he that is hit will cry'.[202] However Latimer is not content to allow the worldly wisdom of some proverbs to remain unchallenged; as of 'Young saints, old devils', he declares, 'this proverb is nought: for look commonly, where children are brought up in wickedness, they will be wicked all their lives after; and therefore we may say thus "Young devil, old devil; young saints, old saints".'[203] A country audience is warned against the dictum, 'when a man will be rich, he must set his soul behind the door';[204] and on another occasion Latimer points out that it is not true to say 'everything is as it is taken', for 'everything is as it is, howsoever it be taken'.[205]

Like Edgeworth Latimer can catch the accents of conversation with happy accuracy,[206] as in this humorous narration:

> A good fellow on a time bade another of his friends to a breakfast, and said, 'If you will come, you shall be welcome; but I tell you aforehand, you shall have but slender fare: one dish, and that is all.' 'What is that,' said he? 'A pudding and nothing else.' 'Marry', said he, 'you cannot please me better; of all meats that is for mine own tooth; you may draw me round about the town with a pudding.'[207]

or in this narration of a man who was imprisoned in the Castel Sant' Angelo:

> It was heard of, and every man whispered in another's ear, 'What hath he done? Hath he killed any man?' 'No.' 'Hath he meddled with alum, our holy father's merchandise?' 'No.'

---

[199] Ibid. p. 66.   [200] Cf. Owst, *L. & P.M.E.*, pp. 41–6.   [201] *Sermons*, p. 416.
[202] *Remains*, p. 40.   [203] *Sermons*, p. 431.   [204] *Remains*, p. 42.
[205] Ibid. p. 140.   [206] For Edgeworth, see *ante*, p. 122.
[207] *Sermons*, p. 140.

' Hath he counterfeited our holy father's bulls? ' ' No.' For
these were high treasons. One rounded another in the ear, and
said *Erat dives*, ' He was a rich man ': a great fault.[208]
However Latimer is not merely colloquial, he can at times attain
to a certain emotive eloquence, for example this passage on the folly
of placing ' voluntary works ' before ' obligations ':

> Again if you list to gild and paint Christ in your churches,
> and honour him in vestments, see that before your eyes the
> poor people die not for lack of meat, drink and clothing. Then
> do you deck the very true temple of God, and honour him in
> rich vestures that will never be worn, and so forth use your-
> selves according unto the commandments: and then finally set
> up your candles, and they will report what a glorious light
> remaineth in your hearts; for it is not fitting to see a dead man
> light candles.[209]

Latimer uses many *exempla*; he is a master of homely simile
and metaphor; as on the feigned good cheer of an alienated friend,
' I grant you may both laugh and make good cheer, and yet there
remain a bag of rusty malice, twenty years old, in thy neighbour's
bosom '.[210] The ignorant, and hardened sinners alone fear death, as
there are but two kinds of people who fear sleep:

> . . . the first be the children, which weep and grieve when they
> shall go to bed, because they know not that sleep refresheth a
> man's body, and maketh him to forget all the labours which he
> hath had before: this the children know not, therefore they go
> with an ill will to bed. The other be drunkards, which be
> given to great drinking; they care not though they be all night
> at it, and commonly the sleep doth them harm, for it maketh
> them have heavy foreheads.[211]

With a real countryman's knowledge, and an interest akin to that of
Edgeworth[212] in rural occupations, he remembers the farm-life of
his youth to point the parallels between preachers and plough-
men:

> And well may the preacher and the ploughman be likened
> together first for their labour of all seasons of the year; for
> there is no time of the year in which the ploughman hath not
> some special work to do: as in my country in Leicestershire, the
> ploughman hath a time to set forth, and to assay his plough, and
> other times for other necessary works to be done. And then they

---

[208] Ibid. pp. 180–1.   [209] Ibid. p. 24.
[210] Ibid. p. 20. See too ibid., pp. 34–5; the Parable of the Unjust Steward is aimed at
the clergy: 'Ye shall perceive that God by this example shaketh us by the noses and
pulleth us by the ears'; and further, ibid. p. 62; the Word should be frequently preached,
for 'Scripture calleth it meat; not strawberries that come but once a year.'
[211] Ibid. pp. 548–9.   [212] See *ante*, pp. 124–6.

also may be likened together for the diversity of works and variety of offices that they have to do. For as the ploughman first setteth forth his plough, and then tilleth his land, and breaketh it in furrows, and sometime ridgeth it up again; and at another time harroweth it and clotteth it, and sometime dungeth it and hedgeth it, diggeth it and weedeth it, purgeth and maketh it clean: so the prelate, the preacher, hath many diverse offices to do. . . . He hath then a busy work, I say, to bring his flock to a right faith, and then confirm them in the same faith: now casting them down with the law, and with threatenings of God for sin; now ridging them up again with the gospel, and with the promises of God's favour: now weeding them, by telling them their faults, and making them forsake sin: now clotting them, by breaking their stony hearts, by making them supple-hearted, and making them to have hearts of flesh, that is, soft hearts, and apt for doctrines to enter in. . . .[213]

Then again, the Turkish menace to Europe gives added colour to the stock figure of the Castle of Faith besieged by angry passions; ' but alas, for pity! the Rhodes are won and overcome by these false Turks; the strong castle Faith is decayed, so that I fear it is almost impossible to win it again '.[214] On one occasion Latimer parodies the decorated sermon style; some had alleged that he compared the Blessed Virgin to a saffron bag, and were offended at it, but having denied using this figure, he continues:

For I might have said thus: as the saffron-bag that hath been full of saffron, or hath had saffron in it, doth ever after savour and smell of the sweet saffron that it contained, so our blessed lady, which conceived and bare Christ in her womb, did ever after resemble the manners and virtues of that precious babe that she bare.[215]

On another occasion too, he uses a visual example; to drive home that the king must choose his wife and officers with godly fear, he produces one of the new shillings:

We have now a pretty little shilling indeed, a very pretty one: I have but one, I think, in my purse: and the last day I had put it away almost for an old groat: and so I trust some will take them. The fineness of the silver I cannot see: but there in is printed a fine sentence, that is TIMOR DOMINI FONS VITAE VEL SAPIENTIAE.[216]

[213] *Sermons*, pp. 61–2.
[214] Ibid. p. 13. On the figure of the Castle, see Owst, *L. & P.M.E.*, pp. 77–85.
[215] *Sermons*, p. 60.
[216] Ibid. p. 95. On the use of visual aids in medieval preaching, see Owst, *P.M.E.*, pp. 349–52.

However, the most memorable of Latimer's *exempla* are his very frequent personal reminiscences. These are merely an individual development of one of the types of medieval narration,[217] but Latimer tells his audience much more about himself and his experiences than previous English preachers had done; indeed his stories give illuminating glimpses of all the periods of his life. Thus in a justly famous passage he speaks of his yeoman father and the simple prosperity of the days before enclosures:

> My father was a yeoman, and had no lands of his own, only he had a farm of three or four pound by year at the uttermost, and hereupon he tilled so much as kept half a dozen men. He had a walk for a hundred sheep; and my mother milked thirty kine. He was able, and did find the king a harness, with himself and his horse, while he came to the place that he should receive the king's wages. I can remember that I buckled his harness when he went unto Blackheath field. He kept me to school, or else I had not been able to have preached before the king's majesty now. He married my sisters with five pound, or twenty nobles apiece; so that he brought them up in godliness and fear of God. He kept hospitality for his poor neighbours, and some alms he gave to the poor. And all this he did of the said farm, and he that now hath it payeth sixteen pound by year, or more, and is not able to do anything for his prince, for himself, nor for his children, or give a cup of drink to the poor.[218]

He speaks too of the admirable exercise which shooting with the bow provides, a sport which in his youth he had enjoyed:

> In my time my poor father was as diligent to teach me to shoot, as to learn me any other thing; and so I think other men did their children: he taught me how to draw, how to lay my body in my bow, and not to draw with strength of arms, as other nations do, but with strength of the body: I had my bows brought me, according to my age and strength; as I increased in them, so my bows were made bigger and bigger; for men shall never shoot well, except they be brought up in it: it is a goodly art, a wholesome kind of exercise, and much commended in physic.[219]

In an amusing passage he refers to the sharp practices of the rustics:

> I have known some that had a barren cow: they would fain have had a great deal of money for her; therefore they go and take a calf of another cow, and put it to this barren cow, and so come to the market, pretending that this cow hath brought that calf; and so they sell their barren cow six or eight shillings

---

[217] See Owst, *P.M.E.*, pp. 60–4. and *L. & P.M.E.*, pp. 169–72.
[218] *Sermons*, p. 101.   [219] Ibid. pp. 197–8.

dearer than they should have done else. The man which bought
the cow cometh home: peradventure he hath a many of children,
and hath no more cattle but this cow, and thinketh he shall have
some milk for his children; but when all things cometh to pass,
this is a barren cow, and so this poor man is deceived.[220]
Again, in his fight against the superstitions engendered by the old
religion, Latimer recalls an incident which occurred when he had
recently taken his Master's degree:

> I was once called to one of my kinsfolk (it was at that time
> when I had taken degree at Cambridge, and was made master of
> arts). I was called, I say, to one of my kinsfolk, which was very
> sick, and died immediately after my coming. Now there was
> an old cousin of mine, which, after the man was dead, gave me
> a wax candle in my hand, and commanded me to make certain
> crosses over him that was dead: for she thought the devil
> should run away by and by. Now I took the candle, but I could
> not cross him as she would have me to do; for I had never seen
> it afore. Now she, perceiving that I could not do it, with a
> great anger took the candle out of my hand, saying, ' It is a
> pity that thy father spendeth so much money upon thee ': and
> so she took the candle, and crossed and blessed him, so that he
> was sure enough. No doubt she thought that the devil could
> have no power against him.[221]

Of his time at Cambridge, he tells of his conversion to Protestant
doctrine by Bilney, and how together they would visit the prisoners
in the Castle.[222] On one occasion they found a woman accused of
murdering her own child, but finding that she steadfastly denied it,
and that her husband had tired of her, Latimer secured Henry VIII's
pardon for her. However although Latimer and Sir John Cheke's
wife were godparents to another child which she bore in prison, he
did not show her the pardon until he had weaned her away from the
superstition that she would be damned if she died without purification.[223] Latimer tells also of Bilney's spiritual anguish after he had
recanted, and his final patient death for his principles.[224] The perils
of being a Court preacher under Henry VIII are touched upon;
Latimer tells of how he had to defend himself against an accusation
of sedition by contrasting what he would preach concerning the
king's duty before him, and what he would say ' at the borders of
the realm '.[225] The sinister intrigues of this time are illustrated by

---

[220] Ibid. pp. 400–1. Cf. too the trick of putting good corn at the bottom and the
top of the bag, and inferior in the middle. (Ibid. pp. 401–2.)
[221] Ibid. p. 499.   [222] Ibid. pp. 334–5.   [223] Ibid. pp. 335–6.
[224] Ibid. p. 222.   [225] Ibid. pp. 134–5.

Latimer's story of his examination before the bishops, when he heard ' a pen walking in the chimney behind the cloth ', and knew that his answers were perilous indeed.[226] To his time as bishop, belongs the famous anecdote of a village celebrating Robin Hood's day, and not regarding his episcopal office, when he arrived on visitation:

> I came once myself to a place, riding on a journey homeward from London, and I sent word over night into the town that I would preach there in the morning, because it was an holiday's work. The church stood in my way, and I took my horse and my company, and went thither. I thought I should have found a great company in the church, and when I came there, the church door was fast locked. I tarried there half an hour and more: at last the key was found, and one of the parish comes to me and says, ' Sir, this is a busy day with us, we cannot hear you; it is Robin Hood's day. The parish are gone abroad to gather for Robin Hood: I pray you let them not.' I was fain there to give place to Robin Hood: I thought my rochet should have been regarded, though I were not; but it would not serve, it was fain to give place to Robin Hood's men.[227]

Again, he humorously alludes to the fact that under Edward he was no longer a bishop, when he recounts the incident of that bishop who thought very little of his preaching; particularly on the theme of unpreaching prelates, as reported by the bishop's chaplain:

> ' Nay,' quoth the bishop, ' he made so indifferent a sermon the first day, that I thought he would mar all the second day: he will have every man a quondam as he is. . . .'
>
> This bishop answered his chaplain: ' Well,' he says, ' well, I did wisely today; for as I was going to his sermon, I remembered me that I had neither said mass nor matins, and homeward I gat as fast as I could; and I thank God I have said both, and let his unfruitful sermon alone.'[228]

In his attack on Seymour, the Lord Admiral, he relates a tale of a harlot who, led to execution, died desperately, and named the Admiral as her first highly-placed seducer.[229] To illustrate the difficulty of deciding whether a man dies well or not, Latimer recounts a tale that he once heard ' of a thing that was done at Oxford twenty years ago '; a condemned robber steadfastly maintained his innocence on the scaffold, but his companion, who died second, confessed his guilt, and implicated the other—so ' Now who can judge whether this fellow died well or no? '[230] Very few

[226] Ibid. pp. 294–5.   [227] Ibid. p. 208.   [228] Ibid. pp. 154–5.
[229] Ibid. p. 164.   [230] Ibid. p. 163.

who once give up their faith recover it again; Latimer tells of one
who did regain it, but adds 'I have known many since God hath
opened mine eyes to see a little; I have known many, I say, that
knew more than I, and some whom I have honoured, that have
afterwards fallen from the truth; but never one of them, this man
except, that have returned to grace and to the truth again.'[231]

Latimer's sermons abound too in the other types of narration
used by the medieval preachers. It is interesting to note that before
his work, the *facetiae* beloved of the late fifteenth century Continental
preachers as Gabriele Barletta, Olivier Maillard, Michael Menot,
and Johann Geiler,[232] are not found in any profusion in English
sermons. G. R. Owst has suggested that this is because only the
more serious sermons survived the destruction of Catholic books at
the Reformation,[233] and it may be that Latimer had some distinguished predecessors in this field, whose efforts have been lost.
However, unlike the stories of the Continental preachers, Latimer's
merry tales are neither obscene nor scurrilous, but humorously
amusing. He tells of a bargain between two friends about a horse;
'the owner promised the other should have the horse if he would;
the other asked the price; he said twenty nobles. The other would
give him but four pound. The owner said he should not have him
then. The other claimed the horse, because he said he should have
him if he would. Thus this bargain became a Westminster matter:
the lawyers got twice the value of the horse; and when all came to
all, two fools made an end of the matter.'[234] We hear of a priest
who, desiring a benefice, sends a dish of apples to the patron. They
are not appreciated; the patron declares: 'Tush, tush, this is no apple
matter; I will have none of his apples; I have as good as these, or
as he hath any, in mine own orchard.' However the priest requests
that he should try one:

> He cut one of them, and found ten pieces of gold in it.
> 'Marry,' quoth he, 'this is a good apple.' The priest standing
> not far off, hearing what the gentleman said, cried and answered,
> 'They are all one apple, I warrant you sir; they grew all on one
> tree, and have all one taste.' 'Well, he is a good fellow, let
> him have it,' quoth the patron.[235]

He tells of a gentlewoman of London, asked by her neighbour
'Mistress whither go ye?' who replied 'Marry, I am going to St.

---

[231] Ibid. pp. 266–8.
[232] For some account of these preachers see E. C. Dargan, *A History of Preaching*,
2 vols. (New York, 1905) vol. I, pp. 323–8. There is a useful selection from Menot:
Sermons Choisis de Michael Menot (1508–1518), ed. J. Nève (Paris, 1924).
[233] *L. & P.M.E.*, p. 162.   [234] *Sermons*, p. 89.   [235] Ibid. pp. 186–7.

Thomas of Acres to the sermon; I could not sleep all this last night, and I am going now thither: I never failed of a good nap there.'[236] Similarly we hear of the bishop who, being offended that the great bell did not ring him into a town, and signifying his annoyance to the chief men of the parish was given this excuse:

' It was a chance,' said they ' that the clapper brake, and we could not get it mended by and by; we must tarry till we can have it done; it shall be mended as shortly as may be.'

But one steps forward and rebukes the bishop:

' Why, my lord,' saith he, ' doth your lordship make so great a matter of the bell that lacketh his clapper? Here is a bell,' said he, and pointed to the pulpit, ' that hath lacked a clapper this twenty years. We have a parson that fetched out of this benefice fifty pound every year, but we never see him.'[237]

We hear too of ' Friar John ten Commandments ' whose only sermon was on the Decalogue: asked by his servant to choose another subject, (as that worthy did not like his master to be derided), the friar answers:

' Belike then thou kennest the ten Commandments well, seeing thou hast heard them so many a time.' ' Yes,' said the servant, ' I warrant you.' ' Let me hear them,' saith the master. Then he began, ' Pride, Covetousness, Lechery,' and so numbered the deadly sins for the ten Commandments.[238]

Occasionally Latimer follows the medieval preachers by giving an *exemplum terribile*,[239] as that of the unjust judge, whose skin Cambyses caused to be laid on the chair of judgment as a warning to succeeding holders of the office;[240] or again that of the worldly rich man who dies desperately:

He cried out, ' What shall I die? ' quoth he. ' Wounds! sides! heart! Shall I die and thus go from my goods? Go fetch me some physician that may save my life. Wounds and sides, shall I die? ' Within a very little while he died indeed; and then lay he like a block indeed. There was black gowns, torches, tapers and ringing of bells; but what is become of him, God knoweth, and not I.[241]

Also, especially in his later sermons to country audiences, and in the series on the Lord's Prayer delivered before the Duchess of Suffolk, Latimer gives some historical narrations. His simple listeners hear (from Hall's *Chronicle*) of the intrigue into which Andrew D'Amaral entered with the Turks, against the fortress of

---

[236] Ibid. p. 201.   [237] Ibid. p. 207.   [238] Ibid. p. 524.
[239] See *ante*, p. 129, for Alcock's use of this device.
[240] *Sermons*, p. 146.   [241] Ibid. p. 277.

Rhodes, because he had not been made Grand Master: and of his subsequent detection and frustration.[242] The Duchess and her household hear of the end of the empires of the past, of that of the Babylonians, that of the Persians, that of the Greeks and that of the Romans; all overthrown because of sin.[243] The audience in Lincolnshire hears of the fall of Jerusalem in the time of Titus,[244] of the vain attempt of the Jews to wrest their city back from the hands of the emperor Hadrian,[245] and of the foiling (by wind and earthquake), of the attempt to rebuild the temple in the time of Julian the Apostate.[246]

In these country sermons, as well as in those preached before the Duchess, Latimer rather surprisingly gives hagiographical narrations. It is interesting to note that in the later years of Edward's reign, he should turn in this way to such traditional illustrative material. Of course, as he belongs to the first generation of the Reformers, these stories would be familiar to him from his youth; but as they are largely absent from his earlier sermons,[247] it would seem that their use in the later sermons represents a certain mellowing in his outlook, or at least the conviction that as illustrations they are harmless, if carefully selected.[248] Thus the country audience is told the story (from the *Vitae Patrum*!) of the holy man, who when dying, being assured by his disciples that he will go to heaven, yet realizes that he can never deserve heaven: ' though I have lived uprightly, yet for all that, it will not help me: I lack something yet '.[249] Similarly, a story of St. Anthony (also from the *Vitae Patrum*) is related to the Duchess of Suffolk and her household. The Saint, priding himself on his strict life in the desert, asks God to tell him who will be his companion in heaven. He is commanded to go to Alexandria, where he will find a poor cobbler who is to be his fellow in bliss. He goes, and finding that the cobbler and his wife lead an honest yet busy life, puts away his pride and pre-

---

[242] *Remains*, p. 33.   [243] *Sermons*, p. 356.
[244] *Remains*, pp. 45–7.   [245] Ibid. pp. 47–8.
[246] Ibid. pp. 48–9.
[247] A rare earlier instance occurs in the first sermon before Edward: the king is exhorted not to listen to the ill counsels of those who advocate fleshy indulgence, but to remember the example of St. Louis, who, when this advice was given to him as he lay sick unto death during his journey to the Holy Land, refused it, saying 'he had rather be sick unto death than he would break his espousals.' (*Sermons*, pp. 95–6.)
[248] It will be noticed that in the examples which I quote, there is nothing specifically Roman; indeed the doctrine enshrined in them could not offend the most zealous Protestant. Contrast the stories in support of consecrated virginity and the monastic life quoted by Alcock, *ante*, pp. 128–9.
[249] *Remains*, pp. 73–4. See *Vitae Patrum*, lib. III, 'Verba Seniorum,' § 161, lib. V, 'Verba Seniorum,' § 9, *P.L.*, lxxiii. 793, 955.

sumption in his ascetical prowess.[250] Surprisingly too, on one occasion Latimer repeats a very medieval devil story[251] to his audience at Grimsthorpe, (although indeed he does not offer it as true):

> We read a story (take it as you will; though it be not a true story): The devil came once into the church whilst the priest was saying mass; and when he was at these words, *Et homo factus est*, the devil looked about him, and seeing no man kneel down, or bow his knees, he strake one of them in the face saying, ' What! will you not reverence him for this great benefit which he hath done unto you? I tell you, if he had taken upon him our nature, as he hath taken upon him yours, we would more reverence him than you do.'[252]

Apart from Latimer, there is no exponent of the truly colloquial style in this reign; all the other Reformers favour the plain style. There are indeed occasional near-colloquial passages in the ' First Book of Homilies ',[253] but the predominant style of these sermons is plain and yet not inelegant. Sometimes the writers employ the schemata to enforce their teaching, as in the following passage (on the light estimation of whoredom), Thomas Becon uses antithesis and parison:

> . . . this vice is grown into such an height, that in a manner among many it is counted no sin at all, but rather a pastime, a dalliance, and but a touch of youth: not rebuked, but winked at; not punished but laughed at.[254]

Sometimes also, there occur word-lists, (a piling up of nouns in the manner of St. Paul in his Epistles; whence the device is probably derived):[255] as in this passage by John Harpesfield on the movement of concupiscence even in the converted; a just man

> . . . weigheth rightly his sins from the original roots, and spring head; perceiving inclinations, provocations, stirrings, stingings, buds, branches, dregs, infections, tastes, feelings, and scents of them to continue in him still.[256]

[250] *Sermons*, pp. 392–3. See *Vitae Patrum*, lib. II, 'Verba Seniorum,' § 130; also lib. VII, 'Verba Seniorum,' cap xv, *P.L.*, lxxiii. 785, 1038.
[251] For examples of medieval devil stories, see Owst, *P.M.E.*, pp. 175–7, 271; *L. & P.M.E.*, pp. 111–13, 162–3, 169, 243, 270, 398, 412, 424, 511–16.
[252] *Remains*, pp. 109–10. For this story Corrie refers to Ludolph Saxo, *de Vita Christi*, par. I, c. xviii. h, Lugdun., 1510, 'among other places.'
[253] There is, for example, in the 'Sermon against Contention' (probably by Latimer) this imaginary objection of a layman exhorted to be patient under abuse: 'If I be reviled, shall I stand still, like a goose, or a fool, with my finger in my mouth? Shall I be such an idiot and dizzard, to suffer every man to speak upon me what they list, to spew out all their venom against me at their pleasures?' (*Certain Sermons appointed by the Queen's Majesty*, p. 138).   [254] Ibid. p. 118.   [255] Cf. for example, Gal. v. 19–23.
[256] *Certain Sermons appointed by the Queen's Majesty*, 'A Sermon of the Misery of all Mankind,' p. 14. See also ibid. 'An Exhortation concerning good Order, and Obedience to Rulers and Magistrates,' p. 104.

There is too in the ' Homilies ', quite frequent patristic citation:
St. Ambrose,[257] St. Anselm,[258] St. Augustine,[259] St. Basil,[260] St.
Bernard,[261] St. John Chrysostom,[262] St. Cyprian,[263] Fulgentius,[264]
St. Gregory,[265] St. Hilary,[266] St. Jerome,[267] Origen,[268] St. Prosper,[269]
and Theophylact;[270] all are quoted or at least referred to.

However the most delightful aspect of the style of these sermons
is the use of homely and pungent figures, drawn from such simple
things as farming and gardening, eating and drinking, and family
life. Without grace we are nothing: 'For', says John Harpesfield,
' of ourselves we be crab-trees, that can bring forth but weeds,
nettles, brambles, briars, cockle and darnel.'[271] It is necessary that
the righteous suffer in this life, to be made perfect; only abandoned
sinners have no tribulations:

> As long as a man doth prune his vines, doth dig at the roots,
> and doth lay fresh earth to them, he hath a mind to them, he
> perceiveth some token of fruitfulness, that may be recovered in
> them: but when he will bestow no more such cost and labour
> about them, then it is a sign that he thinketh they will never
> be good. And the father, as long as he loveth his child, he
> looketh eagerly, he correcteth him when he doth amiss: but
> when that serveth not, and upon that he ceaseth from correction
> of him, and suffreth him to do what he list himself, it is a sign
> that he intendeth to disinherit him and to cast him away for
> ever.[272]

The study of the Scriptures is a joy to those who really wish to do
God's will; only hardened sinners, says Cranmer, find the sacred
writings tedious:

> . . . as drink is pleasant to them that be dry, and meat to them
> that be hungry; so is the reading, hearing, searching and study-
> ing of holy Scripture to them that be desirous to know God or
> themselves, and to do his will . . . but . . . As they that are sick
> of an ague, whatsoever they eat or drink, though it never be
> so pleasant, yet it is as bitter to them as wormwood—not for
> the bitterness of the meat, but for the corrupt and bitter humour
> that is in their own tongue and mouth—even so is the sweetness
> of God's word bitter, not of itself, but only unto them that

[257] Ibid. pp. 24, 47.   [258] Ibid. p. 24.
[259] Ibid. pp. 7, 8, 9, 24, 36, 38, 45, 46, 47, 91.   [260] Ibid. p. 23.
[261] Ibid. p. 24.   [262] Ibid. pp. 2, 3, 7, 8, 24, 36, 48, 72.
[263] Ibid. p. 24.   [264] Ibid. p. 3.
[265] Ibid. p. 197.   [266] Ibid. p. 23.
[267] Ibid. p. 72.   [268] Ibid. pp. 24, 79.
[269] Ibid. p. 24.   [270] Ibid. p. 73.
[271] Ibid. 'A Sermon of the Misery of all Mankind,' p. 15.
[272] Ibid. 'A Sermon how dangerous a thing it is to fall from God.' p. 84.

have their minds corrupted with long custom of sin and love of this world.[273]

Perhaps the most striking figure of all, however, is drawn from the medieval bestiary: we have nothing to feed our inordinate pride, in reality, declares John Harpesfield, man is wretched and in misery: ' Let us look upon our feet, and then, down peacock feathers, down proud heart, down vain clay, frail and brittle vessels.'[274]

The style of Bradford also is plain, and is allied to that of the ' Homilies '. He too uses word-lists, as in this passage on those who look in God's law and see how far short they fall:

> . . . there is none that looketh well herein, but though he be blameless to the world and fair to the shew, yet inwardly his face is foul arrayed, and so shameful, saucy, mangy, pocked and scabbed, that he cannot but be sorry at the contemplation thereof.[275]

He achieves comic vigour by the use of alliteration, rather in Latimer's manner:

> So that blind buzzards and perverse papists they be, which yet will prate our merits or works to satisfy for our sins, in part or in whole, before baptism or after.[276]

Again, he obtains a pungent satirical effect by the use of word-pairs (that device used on the contrary to achieve gradiosity by Alcock and Fisher):[277] as of the doctrine of Transubstantiation he declares that it turned the Communion into a private action, ' and a matter of gazing and piping, of adoring and worshipping the work of men's hands.'[278]

The occasional figures which Bradford employs are homely, as the following metaphors (drawn from farming life) on St. Paul's list of the fruits of the flesh (Gal. iv. 19–21).

> If these apples grow out of the apple trees of your heart surely the devil is at inn with you, you are his birds, whom when he hath well fed, he will broach you and eat you, chaw

---

[273] Ibid. 'A Fruitful Exhortation to the Reading of Holy Scripture,' p. 1. See too the fully flavoured passage from this sermon by Cranmer, quoted *ante*, p. 63.

[274] Ibid. 'A Sermon of the Misery of all Mankind,' p. 15: quoted by Corrie in note m, from the 1547 edition. For this property of the peacock see Alexander Neckham, *De Naturis Rerum*, ed. T. Wright (London, 1863) p. 92; *Speculum Laicorum*, ed. J. T. Welter (Paris, 1914) c. lii, ' De Mortis Memoria,' Tale 389, p. 76. [I owe these references to *The Sermons of Thomas Brinton, Bishop of Rochester* (1373–1389), ed. Sister Mary Aquinas Devlin, 2 vols. (London, 1954) C.S., Third Series, nos. LXXXV–VI, vol. I, p. 10.]

[275] *The Writings of John Bradford*, vol. I, p. 56. See too ibid. pp. 43, 59.

[276] Ibid. p. 49. See too Krapp, *The Rise of English Literary Prose*, p. 175, where further examples are given.

[277] Cf. *ante*, pp. 127, 130.

[278] *The Writings of John Bradford*, vol. I, p. 88.

you and champ you; world without end, in eternal woe and misery.[279]

The style of Lever also is predominantly plain, although occasionally, as Croll points out, he employs the schemata;[280] as antithesis and homoioteleuton in the following passage:

> Yes but what mercyes of God haue we refused, or what threatenynge of God haue we here in England not regarded: whyche haue forsaken the Pope, abolyshed idolatrye and supersticion, receyued goddes worde so gladly, reformed all thynges accordinglye therto so spedily, and haue all thinges most nere the order of the primitiue churche vniuersallye? Alas good brethren, as trulye as all is not golde that glystereth, so is it not vertue and honesty, but very vice and hipocrisie, whereof England at this day dothe moste glory.[281]

or in this passage, *rogatio* and anaphora:

> Do ye see that they which be in authorite haue not ben regarded and obedientli serued? Then the common people haue not done theyr dutyes, dysobeying any man placed in authoryty by gods ordynaunce. Do ye se the people haue hadde iniuries and yet theyr complaintes neglygently heard and long delayed? then haue the higher powers omytted ryghteousnes and iudgement, whiche wyl be required at theyr handes of the Lord.[282]

The few figures which Lever employs are usually metaphors drawn from Scripture, as:

> For all those that wyll not creepe vnder the merciful wings of God, as the chikynnes of Christ, shalbe caught and deuoured of puttockes, haukes and kytes, as a prey for the deuyll.[283]

or,

> Feigned Christians are . . . clouds without any moisture of gods grace, tossed about wyth contrarye wyndes of straunge doctryne, trees passyng sommer tyme without any frutes of good workes, twyse dead without felynge the corrupcion of synne, or lokynge to be graffed in the stock of grace, yea rooted vp from amongst the vynes of the Lord, wilde waues of the sea frothyng forth vnshamefast brags, and wandryng starres without constancie in iudgement and opinion vnto whom the dungeon of darknes is ordeyned for euerlastyng dampnacion.[284]

---

[279] Ibid. p. 79. See too ibid. p. 77: 'Will such a one, as knoweth by faith Christ Jesus to have his blood to wash him from his sins, play the sow, to walter in his puddle of filthy sin and vice again?'

[280] *Euphues*, p. xlix–l.   [281] *Sermons*, p. 22.   [282] Ibid. p. 108.

[283] Ibid. p. 56. For 'wings of God', cf. Ps. xvii. 8, xxxvi. 7, lvii. 1, lxi. 4, lxiii. 7, xci. 4; for 'chickynnes of Christ', cf. Matt. xxiii. 37, Luke xiii. 34.

[284] *Sermons*, p. 105: cf. Jude, 12–13.

The style of Bernard Gilpin is fervid but direct; indeed the main interest of his only extant sermon lies in the themes, rather than in the expression.[285] However, he occasionally uses word-lists,[286] and he retails the well-known story of Bishop Hatto as an *exemplum terribile* against covetousness.[287]

The style of Hooper is distinctly bare; he makes frequent use of scriptural quotation, but employs short unschematic sentences,[288] and gives very few *exempla*. His only memorable *exemplum* is the personal narration which introduces his version of the ' figure ' of the ship as the commonwealth,[289] in which all must perform their proper office in accordance with law:

> I was once in the Race of Britaine with a fore wind and contrary flood, the seas in that place going both hollow, and that by reason of a multitude of rocks in the same place. The master of the ship to conduct her the better, sat upon the main yard to see the seas aforehand, and cried to him that steered the stern, always upon which side he should steer the ship, to break best the danger of the sea. The wind blowing high, whereas the master cried a larboard, he that steered mistook it, and steered a starboard; and the once mistaking of the master's law had almost cast us under the water.[290]

III

THE PREACHERS OF MARY'S REIGN (1553–1558)

In this reign all three styles are found. However, what is most noteworthy is that the ornate style, in a form akin to the strained artificial manner found in the late Henrican preacher William Peryn,[291] flourishes anew under Mary. At the beginning of the reign, Brooks in his Paul's Cross sermon amplifies the theme of the persecution of the Church by the use of rhetorical questions, epanorthosis, antithesis, anaphora, and the heaping up of examples, together with a *dictum* of St. Augustine:

[285] See *post*, pp. 267–8, 269, 271–3, 268, n. 211, 269, n. 214.

[286] *A Godly Sermon preached in the Court of Greenwich*, p. 34: 'I pass over much infidelitie, Idolatrie, socerie, charming, witchcrafts, coniuring, trusting in figures, with suche other trumpery, which lurke in corners, and began of late to come abroad only for lacke of preaching': ibid. p. 44: 'For all the while that men gather goods vniustly by polling, pilling, vsurie, extorsion and simmonie, and therewith seeke to climbe with bribes and bying of offices, it is scarse possible to haue wholsome magistrats.'

[287] Ibid. p. 56.

[288] I have noted only one use of a scheme by Hooper: the parison in the following: 'In external goods may a man offend three manner of ways: in evil getting of them; in evil keeping of them; and in evil spending of them.' (*Early Writings*, p. 555.)

[289] See Owst, L. *&* P.M.E., pp. 67–76.   [290] *Early Writings*, p. 497.

[291] See *ante*, pp. 141–2.

What persecutions hath she suffered, first in tholde time before the commyng of Christe, when she was rather a Synagog then a churche: rather kept vnder by bonde feare, then directed by burnyng Charitie: rather taughte by darcke shadowes, then by bright veritie, by figurative promises, then by manifest performance: by the sleying letter then by the quickenyng spirite. What persecution (I said) suffred she then, being continuallye afflicted, one time by the Canaanites, an other time by the Moabites, then after by the Madianites, againe by Thamonites, sometyme by the Philystians, now by one nation now by another? What persecutions hath she suffered againe sins that time, sins the coming of Christ, what by Nero, what by Domitian, what by Seuerus, what by Diocletian, what by Maximian, what by the Gothes, what by the Hunnes, what by the Vandales, & other? Of whose cruel torments may wel be verified that S. Austen writeth. *Ligabantur: includebantur: caedebantur: torquebantur: urebantur: laniabantur: trucidabantur.* The Christians they were bounde, imprisoned, whipped, racked, broyled, mangled, & otherwise bereft of their life.[292]

Again, in the following passage on the boldness with which the ignorant set themselves up as interpreters of Scripture, Brooks uses parison and antithesis, although in the appended narration he does inject a little colloquial vigour:

For in these matiers we se commonlie, the more blinde, the more bold: the more ignoraunt the more busie: the lesse wittie the more inquisitiue: the more fooles, the more talkatiue: yea, and wil take on them stoutlie, presumpteously, and arrogantly the iudgement & decision of any matter in controuersie: none amisse to them & Whose malapertnes, I cannot see, howe it maie be more aptly repressed then with that, or the like taunt whiche one Demosthenes seruant, and cooke to the Emperor Valens, was ones quailed withal: Who, what time S. Basil was conferring with the Emperoure of Scripture maters, pertly precing in vncalled, dasshyng out textes, and chopping in lumpes of scripture beselye, as it were to reprehende that profound learned doctor, was sharplie rebuked, and chastened of the same, after thys sorte. *Tuum de pulmentarijs cogitare, non dogmata diuina decoquere.* Sir cooke (saith he) it is your Office to see to pottage makyng, to Cater of the Kitchine, and Cookerie, and not to controule Goddes doctrine, neither to entrecounter againste holie writte. As whoe should saie: what you choppelogike, how long haue you been a chopper

292 *A Sermon very notable, fruicteful and Godlie,* sig. Aiv^r–Av^r.

of Scripture? Meddle with chopping of your hearbes and leaue
your choppyng of Scripture hardely.[293]
Brooks's taste in the choice of figures is far from impeccable; he uses
this inelegant simile to illustrate why Christ veils Himself in the
Blessed Sacrament before the faithful receive Him:

Like as thinfante eateth the very selfe same foode in substaunce, that the nource eateth, but vnder another forme, for
the infant can not away with harde meate, but must be fedd
with milke, and therfore the foode is first qualified of the nurce,
chawed and swallowed downe of the noursse, incarnat and
incorporat in to the bodye of the noursse, and parte thereof by
vertue of her pappes, turned into milke of the nursse, which
milk is a foode apte & meete for thinfante to receiue to suke
& feede vpon, Euen so we christians do receiue the very same
bodie and bloude in substance that was crucified for vs here
in earth. But because we are all as infantes in this behalfe at
least, and can not a waye with suche harde meate, nor can abide
for lothsomnes to eate Christes bodye & drinke his bloude
vnder the fourmes of flesh and bloud, oure Sauioure Christe
therfore (lyke a good nource) he qualifieth his bodie and bloude,
he altereth it, he transformeth it he exhibiteth it, vnder another
forme, vnder the forme of breade and wyne, and so maketh it
to vs infantes as mylke, as a gentle familiar foode, apte and mete
to be receaued, with out horror, of euerye christen man and
woman.[294]

Pollard also is inflated in style; he uses a series of rhetorical
questions and the heaping up of examples of hierarchies in the
natural world, to bring home to his audience the need for Papal
Supremacy:

. . . is it not certayne that in heauen there be many orders of
Aungels and eche of them hygher than other, and onely
almyghty god the hygheste and aboue all other? Do ye not se
in the firmamente dyuers bryghtnes to be in the starres, and yet
the sonne to be the bryghtest of them al? Are there not degrees
amongst the fowles: and yet the Eagle kynge of them all? Do
not the beastes one excell another, and are not they all vnder
the Lyon? What shulde I speake of the Cranes when they flye,
haue they not theyr Capitayne and guyde: is there not amongst
the bees one master bee, vnto whom all the residue be obedient?
In the bodyes both of man and beastes, is there not one principal
part commonly called the head? And where haue ye sene any
common wealth wel gouerned where there hath not bin one
heade? Euen so, good Christen men and women, hath god

[293] Ibid. sig. Bvi^v-Bvii^v.   [294] Ibid. sig. Eviii^v-Fi^r.

done and styl dothe appoynte one to be heade and gouernoure in his Church.[295]

However, unlike Brooks, the figures which he uses are apt; although they are purely illustrative of the thought and carry no emotive charge as do those of Fisher[296] and Longland.[297] Thus the emergence of holy orders in the body of the Church is compared to the development of a chicken in an egg:

> . . . at the fyrst there is no distinction of members, as we se dayely in an egge that is to be hatched into a chycken. At the fyrst there is no becke, there is no foote, there is no wynge, no eye, nor tongue, neyther is it possible for any, but for hym that maketh the chicken to say that this part of the egge shalbe suche a member, and this such, but god taketh one part of the egge, maketh it an eye, & geueth it power onelye to se, an other a foote, and giueth it habilitie to go and so forth, and no diuersitie is there before that they be placed, and haue receaued of gods gyftes agreable vnto theyr places. Euen so good people, before the sacrament of orders receaued, they that be to be ordered and the residue be as one. But after the orders receaued, lyke as they haue other places and romes then they had before, so haue they other vertues and gyftes gyuen to them by the holy ghost to worke and to do those thinges that apperteyne vnto theyr duties.[298]

Bishop Watson, (although in his sermons on the Sacraments he adopts the plain style)[299] in his sermons on the Mass, before the queen, shows that the ornate manner is at his command. Indicating that his aim is to combat the Devil's power, he uses periods, word-lists, word-pairs, anaphora and paramoion:

> The ende of thys my matter is, to destroye the kyngedome of synne, for whych purpose Gods sonne was incarnate, to bryng whyche things to passe in vs, was al the lyfe, the example, the passion, the resurrection of Chryst, and al the doctryne & Sacraments of Christe. Like as contraye, to erecte and establishe thys kingdome of sinne, is all the trauayle and temptacion of the deuil, now fawninge lyke a serpente, transforming himselfe into an angel of lyght, to intrappe & seduce the simple and vnware; now ragynge like a lion to ouerthrowe the feble and feareful, and not only is it his trauayle, but also it is the whole labour & practise of hys children by imitation, as

---

[295] *Fyue homilies*, sig. Giii^v–Giv^r, as marked; counting from the first page, sig. Iiii^v–Iiv^r.

[296] Cf. *ante*, pp. 131–4.   [297] Cf. *ante*, pp. 138–41.

[298] *Fyue homilies*, sig. Gi^v–Gii^r as marked; counting from the first page, sig. Iiii^v–Iiii^r.

[299] See *post*, p. 164.

Infideles, Iewes, heretikes, scismatikes, false brethren, counter-
fayte christians both in liuinge and learninge labouringe night
and daye with all witte and wyll to destroy the fayth of Christ,
the Sacramentes of Chryste the Sacrifice of Christ, as much as
in them lyeth, whyche thre be special means to destroye the
kingdome of sinne, which they wyth all their power set vp and
mayntayne.[300]

However in these formal court sermons Watson uses a homely figure
to illustrate the falsity of Protestant reasoning against the Real
Presence:

> The lyke argumente they make agaynst the real presence. It
> is a sygne, ergo not the thynge whereof it is a sygne. The
> folyshnes of thys reason eueri baker can tel who setteth one
> loofe vpon his stall to signifye there is breade to sell within
> hys house. Whyche lofe is both a signe of breade to be solde
> it selfe of the same bakyng the other is. Euen so the body of
> Christ in the Sacrament is Christes very body in dede, and also
> a sygne of the same bodye, as saynt Augustine sayeth.[301]

The ornate style is found also in Latin sermons of this time:
Weston, in his oration to the Synod, attempts to outdo Cicero in the
self-conscious and ortund self-abnegation of his exordium:

> Cum Demosthenes, totius Graeciae lumen, ante Philipum
> Macedoniae regem verba facturus, obmutuerit, cum Theo-
> phrastus philosophorum doctissumus, et oratorum eloquentissi-
> mus, multum animo consternatus, inter dicendum saepius
> conticuisse feratur, cum ipse denique Marcus T. Cicero,
> Latinae facunidae parens, et timorem quendam naturalem
> insitum habens, meticulose orationum principia solitus sit
> exordiri, mirum fortasse vobis videbitur, ornatissimi praesules,
> doctissimique viri, qua effraeni audacia (ne dicam audaci temeri-
> tate) ego, qui neque usu multum neque doctrine satis, et ingenio
> parum valeo, in hunc celeberrimum coetum dicturus, prodire
> ausim, ubi ante oculos, quocunque inciderint, clarissima hujus
> regni lumina undique observantur.[302]

John Harpesfield too is florid in his Latin sermon, particularly in his
overwrought praise of the queen, which has already been noticed
in the first chapter.[303]

The plain style is used by a few preachers of this reign. It is
found at its most distinguished in the sermons of John de Fecken-

---

[300] *Two notable Sermons*, sig. Aiii^r.   [301] Ibid. sig. Tviii^v.

[302] 'Oratio coram patribus et clero', Strype, *Ecclesiastical Memorials*, III. 2, pp. 182–3.

[303] *Concio . . . habita coram patribus et clero in Ecclesia Paulina Londini*, sig. Aiii^{r-v};
(noticed *ante*, p. 57) the passage beginning, 'Cessauit religio in Anglia, quieuit donec
surgeret Maria . . .' is particularly inflated.

M

ham, whose diction is simply English, and who does not use the
more showy of the schemata. In the exordium to his first sermon on
the Creed, when he employs isocolon and word-pairs, he is nevertheless brief and pithy:

> Dearly beloued and seruantes of our lord God, I haue here
> in hand this day to read and set furth vnto you the right and
> perfit knowledge of God, to be learned and gathered out of our
> common Crede, the same being vnto vs (as it were) an abridge-
> ment, or a brief collection of all thinges necessary to be beleued
> or knowen of God. Lyft vp your hartes therefore and prepare
> yourselves, like beneuolent and attentiue hearers, to receiue the
> same: Considering with yourselues, that the tyme of your
> partes spent in lernyng thereof, shalbe but shorte: the labour
> therein taken, can not be great: the fruite and profite of know-
> yng God, is life euerlasting.[304]

His style, however, is not colourless; he can attain a chastened
eloquence, within a logical progression of thought; as in this praise
of Christ as saviour, priest and king. He is on our part:

> ... worthely to be beleued and called Iesus, that is to saye, our
> annoynted kynge and priest: And to be called Lorde, that is to
> say, our redemer and gouernour: when for our sakes he hath done
> & fulfylled the very office of a sauiour, of a priest, and of a
> lorde and kynge. Of a Sauiour, in that he hath (accordynge as
> the angel sayde) saued hys people from their synnes. Of a
> priest, in that he hath offered vp his owne bodye in sacrifice
> vpon the altar of the Crosse for vs. In the whiche oblation he
> was both the priest, and the sacrifice it selfe. And of a kynge
> and Lorde, in that he hathe lyke a moste myghtye conquerour
> ouercome and vtterly oppressed hys enemyes, and hathe nowe
> spoyled them of the possession of mankinde, which they wonne
> before by fraude and deceyte, by lyenge and blasphemynge, and
> hathe broughte vs now into his possession & dominion, to
> reigne ouer vs in grace and mercy lyke a moste louyng Lorde
> and gouernour. And therefore sythen he is our Iesus and
> sauiour, our Christ, priest, and sacrifice, our Lorde, kynge
> and gouernour, let vs put our whole trust and confidence in
> hym. *For he is the lambe of God whiche taketh awaye the sinnes*
> *of the worlde.* He is our resurrection, health, life and saluation.
> He is the waye, trueth and life: no man cometh to the father, but
> by him. He is the good shepherd, by whom we must be saued
> from the wolfe: & the dore by whom we must enter into
> by grace. He is the vine, in whom we being ingraffed, must
> nedes bringe furth much fruite. He is our wisdom righteous-

---

[304] *Two homilies vpon the first, second, and third articles of the Crede*, sig. Ai^r.

ness, iustification and redemption. He is our peace, our medi-
atour and aduocate, and finallie he is alpha and omega, that is
the beginning and ending of our saluation.[305]
Feckenham is sparing in his use of *exempla*, but on one occasion he
speaks of Death the bowman, becoming yearly a more accurate
marksman; that dread figure which we have noticed in a late
medieval sermon[306] is still ready to bring terror to the audience:

And whereas death at the beginning was no vnripe and
vnprofitable a bowman, that he firste shootinge and lousyinge
his dartes at oure firste father Adam, it was nine hundred and
thirtie yeres: (whose age was no fewer yeares in numbre)
before he coulde strike him. And whereas he bare his bowe
dailie bent against his sonne Seth it was nine hundred and
twelue yeares, before he coulde hit him.

And whereas he daylye laie in waite to ouerthrowe with his
dart Mathusalem, Enoches Sonne, it was nine hundred thre-
score and nine yeares before he could ouerthrow him. Yet
within a certen space after, by daily custome and exercise of his
hands he began to waxe a more perfitte bowemanne, euerye
daye shootynge more nere his marke than other, in so muche
that by the time & dayes of kynge Dauid, he got him suche a
redinesse and stedfastnesse of shotynge, that he would not haue
failed (for the more part) to strike his marke within the space of
LXX or LXXX yeres.[307]

The style of Bonner's 'homilies' also is plain, enlivened by
occasional simple illustrative figures. Fire may consume the Sacred
Host, but it cannot harm Our Lord: similarly:

The sonne beames . . . many tymes do shyne on thynges
impure & vncleane, yet are they no whyt thereby defyled. The
bodye of man is with greater vnion ioyned to the soule, then
are the formes of bread and wyne, to the body and bloude of
our sauiour Christe, in the Sacrament of the aultar, and yet we
know that mortification, putrifaction, and other suche lyke
thyngs chauncyng to our body, the soule hath in it no suche
passion, for that it is immortal.[308]

Although God does not *dwell* in temples made with men's hands, but
in heaven, he can *be* in the temples in the Blessed Sacrament, for:

. . . there is a greate difference betwene beynge, & dwelling in
a place, for a great manye of you (I doubt not) haue bene bothe
in the cheape syde, in Paules churchyarde, yea and Paules
churche to, where ye haue not, with moste due reuerence, vsed,

---

[305] Ibid. sig. Biii[r].   [306] See *ante*, p. 166.
[307] *A notable sermon*, sig. Bi[v].
[308] *A profitable and necessarye doctrine with certayne homelies adioyned therevnto*, f. 69[r].

and behaved yourselves and yet I am sure that ye dwell not there.[309]

Watson too is plain in his ' Sermons on the Sacraments ', (which were of course aimed at popular audiences); but frequently he illustrates his points with apt figures, usually culled with acknowledgement from the Fathers. The indulgence in trifling sins gradually corrupts the soul; the final result is as disastrous as the sudden capitulation to a grave temptation:

> For what difference is it to haue a mans shippe drouned at once with one great surge & waue of the sea, or to suffer the water to enter into small holes by little and little till the shyp by contemning to draw the poompe be full, and so sink and be drowned?[310]

The sinner must repent and confess his sins to the Divine Physician of souls:

> For he that would haue his dysease healed and be brought into healthe, let him put out of mynde all worldlye cares, and wyth repentaunce go to GOD the Phisician, and before hym poure foorthe hys warme teares, and with muche diligence confesse hys synnes agaynst hymselfe, and brynging stedfaste faythe with him, let him truste and put his confidence in the arte and connying of the Phisician. . . .[311]

In the Christian life we cannot expect never to fall, but we must never surrender to the Devil: a soldier 'if perchance hys foote slyppe and he fall (as oftentymes the condition of warre is) he maye not by and by dispayre for shame of a fall, but hee muste remember that thys is the lawe of fyghtyng, not neuer to fall, but neuer to yeelde, for men do not call him ouercommed that oft falleth, but hym that a last yeeldeth '.[312]

Hugh Glasier also adopts the plain style; his Paul's Cross sermon, although interesting as regards themes,[313] is rather undistinguished in style, and has no particular passages worthy of note from this point of view.

The style of Pole, although diffuse, is probably best designated as plain. The cardinal's sermons are distinctly disappointing stylistically: the friend of Contarini[314] and Vittoria Colonna,[315] the

[309] Ibid. ff. 73r-v.

[310] *Holsome and Catholyke doctryne concerninge the Seuen Sacraments*, f. 83r: cf. St. Augustine, Epist. CCLXV, new numbering; CVIII, old numbering; *P.L.*, xxxiii. 1089.

[311] *Holsome and Catholyke doctryne*, f. 110: cf. St. John Chrysostom, 'Hom. XX in Genesim,' *P.G.*, liii. 170.

[312] *Holsome and Catholyke doctryne*, f. 87v. Watson does not give a patristic source for this figure.   [313] See *post*, pp. 280, 287-9.

[314] See W. Schenk, *Reginald Pole Cardinal of England* (London, 1950) pp. 46-7.

[315] Ibid. pp. 86, 90-4.

initiator of the *Reformatio Angliae*[316] and the defender of the unity of the Church against Henry VIII,[317] is not a distinguished vernacular preacher. His sentences (if indeed the manuscript accurately preserves his manner) are long, confused and repetitive, and make no use of the schemata, as may be illustrated by this passage on the significance of the Pallium:

> And so to begin to speke of the declaration of the ceremonie of the Pallio; this yow must furste vnderstand, that by the auncyent ordre of the Church it is not permitted that anye Patriarke or Archbusshoppe, which haue their iurisdiction ouer the busshopes and prouincials, [to] vse their authoritie afore thei haue receiued [the] Pallium from the high Busshope and Patriarke of Rome, taken of the bodye of S. Peter. This is the ordinance obserued in the Church; and reading the old writers making mencion thereof in their worke, amongst other I fynde that Athanasius Magnus, Patriarke of Alexandria in Egypt, a man of most famous memorye for hys sanctitie and learning, writ here of himself, how he haueng recieued his Pallio from Rome, by that entred to vse his full authoritie. And this is the thing that is so signified by the Pallio taken of the bodye of S. Peter: that is to saye, the complement of his power, called in Latin *plenitudo potestatis*; for to whom the Pallio is sent to him is geuen full authoritie to use the power graunted to his ordre & not afore.[318]

The cardinal uses very few *exempla*, and these are not always well applied,[319] but once at least he is successful in his use of a simile drawn from the ways of children. During the schism the people had no spiritual meat, but took the material fruit of Church lands; after the restoration of Catholicism they were allowed to keep this fruit, as a concession to their weakness; the Church:

> ... made promesse yt sholde not be taken from you, and so yt was lefte yn your hande, as yt were an aple in a childes hande, gyven by the moother, whiche she perceyvinge him to feade too much of, and knowynge yt sholde doo him hurte, yf he himselfe sholde eate the hoole, wolde haue him gyve her a lytyll pece thereof, whiche the boye refusinge, and where as he

---

[316] Ibid. pp. 142–9.   [317] Ibid. pp. 70–4.   [318] MS Vat. Lat. 5968, f. 281ʳ.

[319] The following figures on the hidden faith given to the Jews, while the rest of the world lived in ignorance are trite and feeble: the spiritual generation of the righteous, 'dyd neuer lacke, but itt was not so openlie knowen, who thei were, afore Chryste came openlie hymselfe to plant thys faith yn the face of the world. And yett many thousand yeares afore it was planted yn the world, but lyke a plant that was newlie sett yn the grounde, and yet helde as yt were vnder grounde, it was not well known to them that lyued vpon the grounde, but onelie vnto them that were in the viniarde that God had made for himselfe; as it were in a gardein, separating the same from the rest of the world, and that was the viniarde of the people of Israel. . . .' (Ibid. f. 424ʳ.)

wolde crye out yf she wolde take yt from him, lettythe him aloone therwyth: but the father her husbande commynge yn yf he shulde see howe the boye wyll not lett goo one morcell to the mother, that hathe gyuen him the hoole, she askinge yt wyth so fayre meanes, he may peraduenture, take the aple out of the boyes hands, and yf he crye, beate him also, and caste the apple out of the wyndowe. This may Chryste the husbande doo, yf you shew suche unkyndenes to your moother, whiche ys his spouse.[320]

The colloquial style[321] is found in the Boy Bishop's sermon preached at Gloucester Cathedral, which has a delightful raciness and humour. Speaking of the negligence of parents in correcting the lying and swearing of their offspring, the ' bishop ' continues:

And what is the matter? a folysh affection and a fond opinion in the parentes, which very fondly seke the love of ther childe that knoweth not what love or dutye meaneth, and that he may say ' I am father's boy ' or ' I am mother's boy ',and ' I love father (or mother) best '; to wyn this word, and love of the child, the parentes contend who shall make most of the child, and by these meanes no partye dare displease hym, say he or do he never so ongraciously, but both partyes dandill hym and didill hym and pamper hym and stroke his hedd and sett hym a hye bence, and gyve hym the swetyst soppe in the dish even when he lest deserve it: this marrs the child, it makes hym to thynke he does well when he do stark nought.[322]

Similarly, speaking of the choristers, the youthful dignitary warns his audience not to follow them, if they would be innocent:

. . . for I have experience of them more then of the other. Yt is not so long sens I was one of them myself but I kan remembre what shrewdness was used among them, which I will not speake of now; [a] but I kan not let this passe untouched how boyyshly thei behave themselves in the Church, how rashly thei cum into the quere without any reverence; never knele nor cowntenaunce to say prayer or Pater noster, but rudely squat downe on their tayles, [b] and justle wyth their felows for a place; a non thei startes me owt of the quere agayne, and in agayne and out agayne, and thus one after an other, I kan not tell how oft nor wherfor, but only to gadd and gas abrode, and so cum in

[320] 'Cardinal Pole's speech to the citizens of London,' Strype, Ecclesiastical Memorials, III. 2, p. 483.

[321] Edgeworth's three extant sermons from Mary's reign are colloquial in the same manner as those of his Henrician days; a quotation from one of them is given, ante, p. 125, (ref. in n. 59).

[322] Sermon of the Child Bishop, pronownsyd by John Stubs, Querester, on Childermasse Day, at Gloceter, 1558, ed. J. G. Nichols, Camden Society Miscellany, vol. VII, p. 26.

agayne and crosse the quere fro one side to another and never rest, without any order, and never serue God nor our lady with mattyns or with evensong, no more than thei of the Grammar scoles. . . .[323]

Perhaps the audience might think one of the choirboys was like the child which Jesus called to Him as an example of innocence:

Such a one this litill one in the mydes here appereth to be that he myght be thought worthy to be sett in the mydes for an example unto yow of pure childhode, mekness, and innocency. Loke in his face and you wold think that butter wold not melt in his mouth; but, as smothe as he lokes, I will not wysh you to follow hym if you know as much as I do. Well, Well! all is not gold that shynes, nor all are not innocents that beare the face of childer.[324]

Turning to schoolmasters, the boy bishop admonishes them to correct vice in their scholars; for ' yow ought to regard them all as your childer, and your selfes as their fathers, for Quintilian, the flower of scolemasters, termeth you to be *tertios parentes* '.[325] They neglect the spiritual welfare of their pupils, although as he humorously points out, they are very concerned about their academic misdemeanours:

Yf a scoler of the song scole syng out of tune, he is well wrung by the ears, or else well beatyn. Yf a scoler in the gramer scole speak false Lattyn or Englysh forbyddyn, he is taken withall of one or the other and warnyd custos to be beatyn.[326]

In the peroration there is an unusually delightful blend of humour and seriousness, depending on the contrast between the dignity of the preacher's office and the youth of his person: but this renders the spiritual wisdom of the message the more compelling:

Perhaps some will think hurt in ther myndes that I am very bold to fynde so many faltes with so many parties—fathers, mothers, scolemasters, childre, scolers, and no scollers; and take upon me to reforme my elders, I beyng so yong in age as I am, and to reprove other wherein I am not all clere my selfe, as some wil judge that knew me in my childhode. Well! if we all amend we shalbe never the worse; and I confesse to them that I was sumtyme, as yet the most of them are, shrewd ynough for one; but I paid well for it, and have now left it, and I may

---

[323] Ibid. pp. 24–5; [a] As first written: 'what fighting, lying and mooching and forgyng of false excuses was among them, beside that, where thei are brought up specially to serve God in the church, thei do nothing lesse in the church then serve God.' [b] 'which lak twynggyng'; erased.
[324] Ibid. p. 25.   [325] Ibid. p. 28.   [326] Ibid.

now alledge for my self the wordes of S. Paul, *Cum essem parvulus, sapiebam ut parvulus, cogitabam ut parvulus, loquebar ut parvulus) nunc autem factus sum vir evacuavi ea quae erant parvuli:* ' When I was a chyldysh boy, my discrecion was therafter, my wordes and dedes were thereafter, the fansys and desires of my hart were therafter; but, now that I have cum to be a man, I have cast off all boy's touches ', that is to say, all shrewdness of childhod, as I wold all you had don, retayning the puritie of your childhod, that it may [endure] with yow togyther with age and years, and no doubt that will cause you to grow unto honestie and worshippe (as you see in me this day), and also bring you to the honor and felicitie of the kingdom which is promised to pure and innocent childer. . . .[327]

IV

THE ELIZABETHAN PREACHERS (1558–1603)

In this period also, all three styles are found. The plain style has many exponents and three distinct forms of it may be differentiated: first an extremely bare and austere form; secondly a less colourless form, employing tropes but not schemata; and thirdly, a moderately decorated form, employing tropes, and occasionally schemata also.

In the latter part of the reign, certain of the extreme Puritans, doubtless inspired by the example of Calvin, advocate and use the first extremely austere and consciously colourless style, which has little literary interest. Bartimaeus Andrewes declaims against the use of rhetorical devices together with the citation of the Fathers and the classical authors, on the grounds of evangelical simplicity:

... there are some which thinke Christe too base to bee preached simply in him selfe, and therfore mingle with him too much the wisdome of mans eloquence and thinke that Christe commeth nakedly, vnlesse cloathed with vaine ostentation of wordes. Others esteem him too homely, simple and vnlearned, vnlesse he bee beautified and blazed ouer with store of Greeke or Latin sentences in the pulpits: some reckon of him as solitarie, or as a priuate person with out honor and pompe, vnlesse he bee brought foorth of them very solemnly, accompanied and and countenaunced, with the auncient Garde of the fathers and Doctors of the Churches to speake for him: or els he must be glossed out and painted with the frooth of Philosophie, Poetry or such like.[328]

[327] Ibid. p. 29.
[328] *Certaine verie godly and profitable Sermons, vpon the fifth Chapiter of the Songe of Solomon* (London, 1583) p. 26.

Similarly John Stockwood, Headmaster of the Grammar School at Tonbridge, Kent, disdains the help of a striking exordium to win attention; his message, he feels is enough:

I wil vse no fore-speech or entraunce garnished and set out with some Rhetoricall florishe, to winne at your handes heedfull harkening vnto that which vpon these places in the fear of God I am to deliuer vnto you, or to purchase your fauourable hearing with my plaine and simple handling of this Texte, without curious and picked out words & termes. For this cause being, not Mans, but Gods, worthelye chalengeth the greatest attention: and as for painted, labored, and of purpose sought for eloquence, I leaue it vnto them, that seeke rather the praise of men, than the glorie of God, knowing that the worde of the Lorde simply and plainly handled, is able without the help of persuading speeche of mans wisdome, to pierce euen to the hart, & to diuide betweene the thoughtes and the reines. . . .[329]

William Perkins too advises against eloquence, for it seems to savour of presumption; ' the hearers ought not to ascribe their faith to the gifts of men, but to the power of God's word '.[330] Although human learning is useful in preparation, the carnality of rhetoric should be avoided in delivery for ' the speech is *spirituall* which the holy Spirit doth teache. . . . And it is a speech both simple and perspicuous, fit both for the peoples understanding, and to expresse the Majestie of the spirit '.[331] Further, he warns that:

. . . neither the words of arts, nor Greeke and Latine phrases and quirkes must be intermingled in the sermon. 1. They disturb the minde of the auditors, that they cannot fit those thinges which went afore with those that follow. 2. A strange word hindereth the understanding of those things that are spoken. 3. It draws the minde away from its purpose to some other matter. . . Here also the telling of tales and all profane and ridiculous speeches must bee omitted.[332]

In accordance with these precepts, the sermons of Bartimaeus Andrewes, Stockwood and Perkins, are quite undecorated in style. Equally bare are those of some other Puritans: Laurence Chaderton, Stephen Egerton, William Fulke, George Gifford, William Kethe, John Keltridge, John Knewstub, Eusebius Pagit, Hugh Roberts,

[329] *A Sermon Preached at Paules Crosse on Barthelmew Day* . . . 1578 (London, 1578) p. 4.
[330] 'The Art of Prophecying,' *Works*, vol. II, p. 670.   [331] Ibid.
[332] Ibid. pp. 670-1. John Udall, another Puritan, also condemns eloquence; for him it panders to the natural man and thus militates against the repentance which it should be the aim of the preacher to arouse. (*Amendment of Life, Three Sermons Vppon Acts* 2 *verses* 37. 38 . . . London, 1588, sig. Biiᵛ.)

Thomas Sparke, John Udall and Thomas White. However the sermons of a few preachers belonging to the central Anglican school are similarly lacking in ornament; such are those of John Beatniffe, William Cupper, Simon Harward, Richard Porder and Archbishop Whitgift.

Not all the Puritans are completely colourless in style however; some use the second form of the plain style which may be differentiated, employing tropes but not schemata. This is probably due to the influence of the Ramist *Rhetorica* of Talon[333] which contains the tropes, but only a few of the schemata; and also to the fact that the tropes were considered legitimate aids to obtain clarity of meaning, while the schemata were felt to savour of mere oratorical display.[334] Thus Cartwright makes use of simple illustrative similes; as when dealing with men's solicitude for worldly things and their neglect to pray for faith and love, he declares that this is ' as if a man should be careful for the hangings of a house, and have no care for a house to put them in; and for the bosses of the bridle, and not the bridle; for the traps of the horse, and have never a horse to ride upon '.[335] A lie is often more probable than truth, as ' the fruit that groweth now in Sodom hath a more excellent show than other fruit; and yet, come to feel it, it goeth to froth and wind and that loathsome. Again, in gold, before it be tried that which is not gold may have a greater colour and show than the true gold.'[336] Cartwright also gives a historical narration of a king: ' which his son by adultery having transgressed the law, and should have lost his eyes, by the importunity of the people was entreated not to do it; yet because the king would not have the law broken, he found out a way to keep the law, and because he would not have them to have a blind king, he put out one of his son's and one of his own eyes. Where was justice, in that the king would execute the law, and mercy in sparing his son; but this was imperfect justice and mercy.'[337] This contrasts with the supreme justice and mercy of God, but Cartwright, afraid that readers of the sermon should pay too much attention to the narration, adds a note: ' This similitude is warily to be used.'[338] Similarly Thomas Gybson, Rector of Ridlington in Rutland, to illustrate his contention that preaching is necessary in church, not merely the reading of Scripture, uses a series of simple similes:

    . . . bare reading is as though one shoulde cast a whole loafe,

---

[333] *Institutiones oratoriae* (1544?; many subsequent editions).
[334] See Perry Miller, *The New England Mind: the Seventeenth Century*, pp. 355–7.
[335] *A Dilucidation or exposition, of the Apostle St. Paul to the Colossians*, p. 6.
[336] Ibid. p. 31.   [337] Ibid. p. 17.   [338] Ibid.

before them which want strength to cut it, Preaching is a cutting and diuiding of the breade of life, that euery one may haue his seuerall portion.[339]

. . . bare reading is as one shoulde offer good treasures, and yet such as were hid, shut vp and fast locked, and coulde not be come by: Preaching is an opening of the treasures, to the ioy of Gods children. Reading is like to fire couered with ashes, which doth smally profit them that stand by it: Preaching is an opening and discouering of the fire.[340]

Anthony Anderson, another Puritan, prefers however grander similes drawn from natural phenomena: to show how true Faith carries holiness and reverence with it, he refers to the sun, ' whiche hath his Globe, his light and his heate so conioyned, that whereso-euer the one shyneth, the other cannot but warme '.[341]

Again, Christ the Sun alone gives light to the Church, the Moon:

. . . as one shyning Sunne serueth the vniuersall worlde, and is the onely Fountayne of light to all lightes in the same: So the bright sonne of God our righteousnesse Christ, is the onely author of spirituall light, whome the Father of lights hath onely giuen to the whole worlde, And he dothe *lighten euerye man that commeth into the worlde*, neyther will he admit any copemate to be ioyned with him, but keepeth the whole Regimente in and to himselfe. For as the Moone . . . receyueth at the handes of the Sunne her lighte, and is much darkned, as she wanteth of his brightnesse: So the Churche of God, not kept with the coun-tenance of Christs shyning face and Gospell, is wrapped in the wayne of darknesse, but lightened by his truth, she is most gloryous, and her natural spottes shall not deface her.[342]

Similarly, Anderson refers to the revolution of the seasons, the alternation of day and night, and the sequence of tempest and calm, to illustrate how the Church suffers periods of persecution, and then enjoys periods of prosperous tranquillity, as the glorious era of Queen Elizabeth—which latter should be used gladly as an easy opportunity to grow in holiness:

. . . this is natural that after Winter commeth Sommer, after stormy tempest, serenious season, and after the darknesse of the night, the bright shining day. So is it also the spirituall course of God in his Christ, from time to time, as the testimony thereof in the scriptures is most apparante. We nowe are with ioye of heart to imbrace the *Halcion* dayes, our Sommers warmth, this quyet raigne, the shyning countenance of Gods good

---

[339] *A fruitful sermon preached at Occham* (London, 1584) sig. Biii[r].
[340] Ibid. sig. Biii[v].   [341] *The Shield of our Safetie*, sig. Ci[r].
[342] Ibid. sig. Ri[v].

fauour to vs, mauger the malice of al Romanists at home and abroad, and with effect (but not in vayne) to receyue the light of the gospell, yet plentifully casting his blessed beames, least we haue greater cause to saye, when we see darknesse againe to shadow the sunne beames of righteousnesse: Lord that we were with Symeon dead in peace, from the miserable deaths we are lyke to feele, in the sworde of thy wrath.[343]

This second form of the plain style is found too among the more central Anglican preachers. Becon in his *Postils* occasionally gives a narration as that (from the *Vitae Patrum*) of the holy man who stood for three days in the one place, wailing and mourning with eyes lifted to heaven. Asked by his disciples why he does this, he replies: ' I feare death.' When against this they urge his strict life, he answers that this does not help: ' For although . . . I have kept gods preceptes very straightly, yet I can not be without the feare of death: for I knowe that gods iudgement is not lyke vnto mans.'[344] Bishop Curteys heaps up examples and metaphors drawn from trees to show that we should not swerve from the profession of our faith:

> The figtree would not leaue his sweetnesse, the oliue tree his fatnesse, the vyne his wine, wherewith he dyd cheare both God and man: neyther shoulde we leaue the sweetnesse of vnitie, the wine of obedience, which do please both God and man, and be caried away with the brambles of infidelitie and confusion.[345]

Richard Maddoxe in a delightful sermon for sailors, following the old advice of the preaching manuals to have respect to the audience,[346] draws many metaphors from ships and seafaring life. We must, he declares, sail through the sea of life:

> . . . beeing full fraught with humility, bound for the land of promise, hauing our sayles of heauenlie hope, fylled with the winde of Gods spirite, being dyrected by the roother of wisedome, with the anchor of faith, and the mainemast of an vpright conscience and smothe conuersation in Christ Iesu.[347]

The venerable ' figure ' of the ship[348] is found yet again in this nautical sermon: first Maddoxe uses it to symbolize the commonwealth:

[343] Ibid. sig. Miiiʳ.   [344] *A new postil*, ff. 14ᵛ–15ʳ.

[345] *A sermon preached before the Queens Maiestie at Greenwiche*, sig. Civᵛ–Cvʳ.

[346] See e.g. the remark from Waleys's *De Modo Componendi Sermones*, quoted by Owst, *P.M.E.*, p. 331: 'Auditorum etiam condiciones ponderande sunt, et juxta has proferendus est sermo.'

[347] *A learned and godly sermon, especially for all marryners* (London. 1581) sig. Biʳ.

[348] See Owst, *L. & P.M.E.*, pp. 68–76.; also *ante*, p. 46.

[In the state] . . . the Windes be those whisperers that styrre vp stryfe, and spreade debate betweene man and man: the waues be such ambicious desyres, as doo trouble the peace of the Cittie, and make mennes mindes inordinately to swell in pride, in vainglorie, in emulation, in debate: so wrastling and strugling togeather as one byllowe dasheth against an other: which all doo fyll the Cittie with the water of theyr garreboyles, shaking it so sore, tyll it be readie to sincke againe.[349]

He uses this figure also to symbolize man's voyage through the world:

This body of ours is lyke vnto a Shippe, wherein the reasonable soule, lyke a marriner sayleth: this world is naught else but a sea of wickedness: and the prouokementes of the flesshe are tempestous windes, which of our selues wee are not able to asswage: which if they be not in tyme appeased, will bring vs in daunger to be eaten vp of the Sea, and so to make a myserable shipwracke.[350]

Maddoxe does not confine himself however to nautical similes. To illustrate Christ's desire to hear our morning prayers, he humorously alludes to habits of comfort impossible to seafarers: ' Christe is not like one of these testie Squiers, or those nice Dames that can abyde no noyse in the house, for breaking theyr morning sleepe: no, Christe would be awaked with our early prayer, yea with our earlie and earnest calling vpon him.'[351] Again, says Maddoxe, tribulations purify us as, ' Syluer is not syluer tyll it be blowne and purged in the fyre: Golde commeth to no honour, tyll by long hammering and chasing, it be forged into a vessell meete for the Kinges seruice: the corne is grounde in a rough myll, and baked in a hoate ouen, before it become good bread.'[352]

The third form of the plain style, which may be differentiated, which uses tropes and occasionally schemata also, is found in a further group of Puritan preachers. Richard Greenham combines simple illustrative similes from farming, with antithesis, parison, and climax, to show how the Holy Ghost brings full spiritual life only to the elect:

Some corne is sowen and neuer riseth: some springeth and yet shortly withereth: some groweth vp to an eare, and yet then is stricken or blasted: and othersome (at his good pleasure) doth come to a timely ripeness. In like manner, some trees are

[349] *A learned and godly sermon, especially for all marryners,* sig. Ci[v].
[350] Ibid. sig. Cii[v].   [351] Ibid. sig. Bv[v].
[352] Ibid. sig. Biv[r]. See too ibid. sig. Biii[r]: Christ alone forgives us; the saints do not, as: 'At the head of the spring, fayre water is sweetest, and at the fountayne of mercie, mercie is receyued with most pleasure.'

planted and neuer take roote: some take roote, but yet not blossome: some blossome, and yet neuer bring forth fruite: and othersome through his goodnesse doo bring forth fruite in good season.[353]

Similarly Arthur Dent, Rector of South Shoebury, Essex, in a passage on those whose repentance is only perfunctory, uses antithesis, paromoion, word-pairs, parison and homoioteleuton:

> But alas it is a worlde to see how the blinde Bussards, and crooked cancrewoormes of this worlde goe awrye from this rule, deceiuing them selues with the bare title and naked name of repentance. Manie in deede can talke of it, but few walke in it. Manie speake of it, but fewe feele it. Manie describe it, but fewe know it. It is hidde and locked vp from the worlde, and reuealed only to Gods children.[354]

Again, to show that the preacher must be severe with sinners, Dent combines homely similes with isocolon:

> Because ye are full of olde festered woundes, you must haue Corasiue Salues, for that is the beste for you, and the speediest way to recouer your healthe, and for as much as you be rough Horses, you must haue a rough Rider, and harde knobbie timber, must haue harde wedges, and strokes with a beetle.[355]

Similarly, Stephen Gosson, the author of *The School of Abuse*, and now Rector of Great Wigborough, Essex, combines similes with antithesis and parison:

> The people are grown like to springes in summer, the more heat without, the more colde within, the more preaching the lesse deuotion. They may be compared to the pinnacles of the belfry, begin to ring, they beginne to quake; as if they were afraid, continue ringing, they stand still, their feare is past.[356]

This form of the plain style is found too in the ' Second Book of Homilies ', just as it is in the first.[357] The same kind of homely similes occur: to illustrate that evil men may appear virtuous, a simile from fruit is used; here too appearances are deceptive: ' so doth the crab and the choke-pear seem outwardly to have sometime as fair ə red, and as mellow a colour, as the fruit which is good indeed. But he that will bite and take a taste, shall easily judge betwixt the sour bitterness of the one, and the sweet savouriness of the other.'[358]

---

[353] *Workes*, p. 55.
[354] *A sermon of repentance* (London, 1583) sig. Biv[v].
[355] Ibid. sig. Cii[r].
[356] *The trumpet of warre, a sermon* (London, 1598) sig. Evi[r].
[357] See *ante*, pp. 153–5.
[358] *Certain Sermons appointed by the Queen's Majesty*, 'An Homily of Alms Deeds,' p. 393.

A simile from farming is employed to admonish the young husband to be patient with his wife's faults; he should strive to amend them, for:

> Dost thou not see the husbandmen, what diligence they use to till that ground which once they have taken to farm though it be never so full of faults? As for example, though it be dry; though it bringeth forth weeds; though the soil cannot bear too much wet; yet he tilleth it, and so winneth fruit thereof. . .[359]

In addition, the ' Homily against Disobedience and Wilful Rebellion ' gives two narrations. First, as an example of obedience, the story of the Blessed Virgin's journey to Bethlehem is told with great delicacy:

> [She obeyed the divine command] . . . neither grudged she at the length and tediousness of the journey from Nazareth to Bethlehem, from whence and whither she must go to be taxed; neither repined she at the sharpness of the dead time of winter, being the latter end of December, an unhandsome time to travel in, specially a long journey for a woman being in her case.[360]

Secondly the historical narration of King John and the legate Pandulphus is related in the polemic against the Pope's absolution of Queen Elizabeth's subjects from allegiance to her.[361]

Occasional schemata are found as before: a word-list and alliteration are used (probably by James Pilkington) to castigate pampered over-dressing:

> . . . most commonly he that ruffleth in his sables, in his fine furred gown, corked slippers, trim buskins, and warm mittens, is more ready to chill for cold then the poor labouring man, which can abide in the field all the day long, when the north wind blows, with a few beggarly clouts about him.[362]

Word-pairs are used liberally in the exordium of the ' Homily against Rebellion ':

> As God the Creator and Lord of all things appointed his angels and heavenly creatures in all obedience to serve and to honour his majesty; so was it his will that man, his chief creature upon the earth, should live under the obedience of his Creator and Lord: and for that cause, God, as soon as he had created man, gave unto him a certain precept and law, which he, being

---

[359] Ibid. 'An Homily of the State of Matrimony,' p. 512.
[360] Ibid. p. 569.   [361] Ibid. p. 595.
[362] Ibid. 'An Homily against Excess of Apparel,' p. 311. See too ibid. 'An Homily against Disobedience and Wilfull Rebellion,' p. 552; Adam and Eve by their sin brought upon their posterity 'sorrows of their minds, mischiefs, sickness, diseases, death of their bodies. . . .'

yet in the state of innocency, and remaining in paradise, should observe as a pledge and token of his due and bounded obedience; with denunciation of death, if he did transgress and break the said law and commandment.[363]

Then again, parison and antithesis are used (probably by Pilkington) to denounce the possession of too many clothes:

We must have one gown for the day, another for the night; one long, another short; one for winter, another for summer; one through furred, another but faced; one for the working day, another for the holy day; one of this colour, another of that colour; one of cloth, another of silk or damask.[364]

Yet further, in polemic against images, climax is used with a short period (by Jewel):

To conclude: it appeareth evidently by all stories and writings, and experience of times past, that neither preaching neither writing, neither the consent of the learned, nor authority of the godly, nor the decrees of councils, neither the laws of princes, nor extreme punishments of the offenders in that behalf, nor no other remedy or means, can help against idolatry, if images be suffered publicly.[365]

This ' Second Book of Homilies ', like the first, is studded with patristic citations, drawn from an even larger number of Fathers than before.[366]

Most of the earlier Anglican prelates also employ this third form of the plain style. Archbishop Sandys usually restricts himself to the tropes: exhorting the judges to take care to be good examples to others, he uses metaphors from the moon and stars: ' Be bright stars, and not misty clouds. If an eclipse fall amongst you, the rest of England will be darkened with it.'[367] He expands the ' stony soil ' of the Parable of the Sower to refer to those Protestants who had been proved great talkers, but idle workers; ' These our times, dear brethren, have marvellously tried what ground we be, what root God's word hath taken in us. Much gravelly ground doth now

---

[363] Ibid. p. 551. See too ibid. 'An Homily against Peril of Idolatry and superfluous decking of Churches,' [by Jewel, influenced by Bullinger] p. 253: 'churches and temples', 'profit or benefit', 'peril and danger', 'hurt and destruction'.

[364] Ibid. 'An Homily against Excess of Apparel,' pp. 311–12.

[365] Ibid. 'An Homily against Peril of Idolatry,' p. 245.

[366] See 'Index of Writers quoted or referred to,' (ibid. pp. liii–lvi): in the second book occur *dicta* from or references to St. Ambrose, St. Athanasius, Arnobius, St. Augustine, St. Basil, St. Bede, St. Bernard, Cassiodorus, St. John Chrysostom, St. Clement, St. Cyprian, St. Cyril, St. John Damascene, Didymus Alexandrinus, St. Epiphanius, Eusebius (Emissenus), St. Gregory, St. Ignatius, St. Irenaeus, St. Isidore, St. Jerome, Justin Martyr, Lactantius, St. Optatus, Origen, Paulinus Pontius, St. Prosper, Prudentius, Rabanus Maurus, Tertullian, Theodoret.

[367] *Sermons*, p. 232.

appear, which before we thought to be sound and battle.'[368] From farming he draws similes to admonish the gluttonous: ' as the ground, if it receive too much rain, is not watered, but drowned, and turned into mire, which is neither fit for tillage nor for yielding of fruit; so our flesh overwatered with wine, is not fit to admit the spiritual plough, or to bring forth the celestial fruits of righteousness.'[369] However the archbishop also on occasion makes excellent use of the schemata, as parison with antithesis in the following passage on the sad mutability of human life:

[Man never continues in one state]: To-day in his princely throne, to-morrow in his dusty grave; to-day placed in great authority, to-morrow cast out of countenance; to-day in high favour, to-morrow in high displeasure; now rich, now poor; now in wealth, now in woe; now sound, now sick; now joyful, now full of sorrow; to-day a man, to-morrow nothing.[370]

He too adds further colour by patristic citation; St. Ambrose,[371] St. Augustine,[372] Bede,[373] St. Bernard,[374] St. Cyprian,[375] St. John Chrysostom,[376] Eusebius,[377] St. Gregory Nazianzen,[378] St. Hilary,[379] St. Irenaeus,[380] St. Jerome,[381] Lactantius,[382] Origen,[383] Polycarp,[384] Tertullian,[385] Theodoret,[386] and Theophylact,[387]—all are quoted.

Bishop Jewel also, as A. F. Herr points out, sporadically employs the schemata,[388] but he very seldom uses the tropes. However he too gives colour by copious patristic citation.[389]

[368] Ibid. p. 301. [369] Ibid. p. 393.

[370] Ibid. p. 170. See too ibid. p. 257, where Sandys uses anaphora and a word-list when speaking of the 'background' of Cornelius (Acts x): 'If we look on this man's country, if we consider his calling and vocation, if we call to remembrance in what place he lived, and with whom he was conversant; we shall behold nothing but rape, robbery, murder, mischief, spoil, blood-spilling; we shall see nothing but lewdness, profaneness, wicked manners, and cursed company.'

[371] Ibid. pp. 16, 44, 136, 137, 140, 153, 156, 316, 455.

[372] Ibid. pp. 11, 14, 41, 46, 72, 87, 88, 95, 132, 133, 145, 148, 166, etc.

[373] Ibid. pp. 357, 366. [374] Ibid. pp. 117, 168, 170, 210, 214.

[375] Ibid. pp. 4, 222, 334, 455, 457.

[376] Ibid. pp. 71, 87, 147, 148, 152, 200, 229, 231, 322, 332, 339, etc.

[377] Ibid. pp. 38, 109, 130, 218, 248.

[378] Ibid. pp. 53, 93. [379] Ibid. pp. 15, 16, 24. [380] Ibid. p. 453.

[381] Ibid. pp. 117, 138, 216, 222, 223, 368, 454, 455. [382] Ibid. p. 157.

[383] Ibid. pp. 392, 414. [384] Ibid. pp. 217, 218.

[385] Ibid. pp. 80, 283, 371, 453, 455.

[386] Ibid. pp. 72, 73, 109, 129, 183, 224, 455.

[387] Ibid. p. 320.

[388] The Elizabethan Sermon, pp. 93, 96.

[389] As St. Augustine, Works, vol. II, e.g. pp. 982, 983, 996, 1000, 1019; St. Bernard, e.g. pp. 992, 1021; St. Basil, e.g. p. 1059; St. John Chrysostom, e.g. pp. 982, 985, 989, 997, 1021, 1042; St. Cyprian, e.g. pp. 998, 1042; St. Cyril, e.g. pp. 1014, 1021; Eusebius, e.g. p. 998.; St Jerome, pp. 991. 1038; St. Gregory Nazianzen, e.g. p. 1007; St. Gregory the Great, e.g. pp. 791, 992; Hilary, e.g. pp. 994, 1023; St. Irenaeus, e.g. p. 988; Lactantius, e.g. p. 983; Origen, e.g. pp. 994, 1007; Tertullian, e.g. pp. 997, 1000, 1031.

N

   · Edmund Grindal makes sparing use of the schemata, as anaphora and parison, in this passage on the invincibility of death:

> If strength could have preserved from death, Sampson had yet lived: if wisdom, Solomon; if valiancy, David; if beauty Absolom; if riches Croesus; if largeness of dominion, Alexander the Great had yet remained alive.[390]

He gives too a lively *exemplum terrible*, which purports to be a reminiscence:

> I knew a priest who had rapped together four or five benefices, but was resident upon never a one of them. All this sufficed him not; and therefore he longed for a prebend also, there to spend at ease the milk and fleece of the flocks which he had never fed. At length by mediation of money he obtained a prebend: and when his man brought him home the seal thereof, cast into a marvellous joy, he burst forth into these words of the psalm, taken out of his portesse, which was all his study: *Haec requies mea.* ' This is my rest, (saith the priest) this is my place of quiet; here intend I to make merry so long as I live.' What followed hereof? Assuredly *nulla requies*, ' no rest '; but within a few days after he was stricken with a palsy, that he could not stir himself, and besides bereft of all his wits and understanding, that where before he was accounted a worldly wise man, afterwards, he was altogether foolish, and not long after died.[391]

   Robert Humston, later to be Bishop of Down and Connor, also adopts this form of the plain style; he gives a piquant example of climax: the fact that ' God warmeth ' is:

> a short but verie sweete lesson, and sweeter than the Lute to driue dumps from the heart, and to abandon in wealth wickedness, in health wantonnes, in mirth forgetfulnes, in want distrustfulnes, in losse pensiueness, and in death fearfulnes.[392]

Later in this sermon, (when warning the rich against extravagance), in a series of antitheses he uses paromoion coupled with anaphora and homoioteleuton:

> O take heed that many fare not hardly for thy superfluitie: that many go not a begging for thy polling and incroching and inclosing: that many sit not mourning for thy merry makings, that manie go not full bare, for thy going so braue.[393]

   The pungent colloquial style of Edgeworth[394] and Latimer[395] is carried on in this reign by John Bridges, Fellow of Pembroke College, Cambridge, later Dean of Salisbury and a noted controver-

---

[390] *Remains*, p. 10.   [391] Ibid. p. 9.
[392] *A Sermon preached 22. Sept.* 1588 (London, 1589) f. 13ᵛ.
[393] Ibid. f. 23ʳ.   [394] See *ante*, pp. 121–6.   [395] See *ante*, pp. 142–53.

sialist, who ended his life as Bishop of Oxford. Unfortunately only one of his sermons is extant, but in it he gives in generous measure the attractive characteristics of this manner. In declaiming against an imagined Catholic opponent who would have man partly *merit* salvation, Bridges refers to what seems to be a popular tale: ' Ha suttle foole, Sim-Suttle deceued himself, thinkest thou thus to mock God? '[396] His use of paronomasia is racy:

> Compare we now this endlesse ende of perdition, to the vayne pleasures that ende so soone, of this transitorie life, and put them altogether: What hast thou gotten if thou hadst gayned al the world, (sayth Christ) & lost thine owne soule?[397]

Proverbs occur with pleasing frequency:

> *Al runne in a race,* (sayth S. Paule) *but all get not the garlande.* All would haue it, but they refuse the meanes wherby they shoulde obteyne. Wishers and woulders, were neuer good householders, theyr wishing is but a vaine woulding, either they know not what they would, or they would not what they should.[398]
>
> . . . howe could the olde Crabbe teache the young Crab to goe, but a byas?[399]
>
> Where are such maisters and seruants now become? nay it is now the old prouerbe vp & downe, trim tram, such maister, suche man, suche cuppe, suche couer, neyther barrell better herring, bothe maister and man may go in a line together, for a great many of men and maisters now a dayes.[400]

In a lively passage against the ' cockering ' of children, Bridges refers to the Londoners' nickname of Cockneys, and their reputation in Catholic times for being unsuccessful, although this latter, says the preacher, has given way in these happy Gospel times to a prosperous industry:

> We are through out all the Realme called cockneys that are borne in London, or in the sounde of Bowbell. . . . It had wont to be an olde saying, that fewe or none but were vnthrifts, and came to nothing, that were cockneys borne, for so are we termed abroade. But God be praised, this is nowe a false rule, and hath ben a good while since, chiefly since the Gospels light shined on this noble citie, it hath brought for the many worthy gouernors, notable preachers, godly pastors, wise counselors, pregnant wits, graue students, welthy citizens, and is ful of maruellous towardes youth God blesse them. . . .[401]

---

[396] *A Sermon preached at Paules Crosse* (London, 1571) p. 74.
[397] Ibid. p. 7.   [398] Ibid. p. 9.   [399] Ibid. p. 105.   [400] Ibid. p. 109.
[401] *A Sermon preached at Paules Crosse*, p. 104.

Bridges too, like Edgeworth and Latimer, can give racy and convincing conversation,[402] as in his version of a fable from Aesop
about two frogs:

> ... that in a dry Sommer sought for water, and when they came
> to a deepe pit: Here sister (sayth the one) is a good place for
> vs to abide in, there is water inough: nay softe (quod the other
> Frog), let vs viewe a little ere we leape in, if water shoulde
> faile here also, howe should we got out again?[403]

Further, homely and humorous figures abound in Bridges's sermons.
He uses a lively and miscellaneous succession of similes to show
that as the Romanists place the cause of man's salvation to such a
large extent within himself, ' the cause in God is cleane swalowed vp
lyke a drop in the sea, a beane in a Monks hoode, a mouse in a
cheese, nay rather a ciphre in Algorisme[404] [Algebra] '. He draws a
figure from the difference between the gentlenes of a fox-cub and
its later fierce predatoriness, to illustrate that to be saved we must
reject all notion of natural goodness: we must kill the Old Adam
lest he wreak our eternal destruction; false sympathy has no place
here, for:

> A young cubbe can play prettily like a little whelpe, it
> will not bite, the henne may goe by it, it wil not hurte one
> chick, O it is a pretie foole, Alacke who would kil it? but for
> all that kill it say I, else it wil kill chicken, hen, cock and all,
> and it may come by them.[405]

He draws a figure from a dying fire when imagining that the Romanists are pleading with him to allow their doctrine of the co-operation
of man's free will with God's grace in the process of Justification:

> It is but a little that we require, God wot a very small
> sparke, and that so ouercomed with the ashes of synne and
> corruption, that it can neuer giue of it selfe, any light or heate
> of a fier, except the ashes be blowne away, & some stickes
> layd to, to kindle the fyre ... we demaund at the least but this,
> that ye graunt man to haue no more goodnes of himselfe, than
> sutche small sparkes of election, free will, disposition, and
> preparation, as God seeing them peepe out, and giue but a
> glimpse vnder the ashes of synne, with his worde he bloweth
> the ashes away, and putteth too matter for vs to worke our owne
> saluation vpon.[406]

But all this is in vain, the Romanists will never solve the mystery of
salvation until they realise that man has no goodness of himself, nor

---

[402] Cf. *ante*, pp. 122, 144–5.
[403] *A Sermon preached at Paules Crosse*, p. 4.
[404] Ibid. p.77.   [405] Ibid. p. 86.   [406] Ibid. p. 81.

can he do anything to cause his justification; to enforce this, Bridges refers to an old riddle:

> In deede Papist, thou haste runne rounde about the wood, and haste assayed at manye a gappe to enter, but canste not get in, lyke to the olde riddle, what is that that runneth rounde aboute the tree, and neuer entreth in? They hadde wonte to say, it is the barke of the tree: but it is a blind Papist, that sticking only to the trees rinde and barke, looketh altogether on the outwarde appearance of man, and searcheth to fynd in the visyble creature the cause of the highest workes of the inuisible Creator.[407]

Like the older colloquial preachers Bridges too uses narrations;[408] in his case cautionary tales against disobedient children. From Nicholas Selneccerus he takes the story:

> . . . that is written of credible authors to be done in Germanie, within these twentie yeres: of a father, that hauing bidden his chylde goe on his errand, when the chylde stoode still and would not goe, the vnaduised father in his fumish anger cursed him, and said, Standest thou still? stand still then, & so still standing, I pray God thou mayst abide. And euen sodeinly so soone as the curse was spoken the childe stode still, and so standing there aboade till the day of his death.[409]

Similarly parents are admonished to correct naughty children, and to: ' Remember the Fable of the chylde that bitte of his mothers nose, when hee went to hanging, bicause she would not bite his breche with a good rod, when he went to filching.'[410]

Henry Bedel, Vicar of Christ's Church, London, although not so purely colloquial in style as Bridges, nevertheless deserves to be set with him, for his frequently racy idiom, and generous use of proverbs. All must give alms, he says: ' so that neyther the ritch in defiyng the poore say, away with this Begger, go whip me this slaue, this stincking rascal, this lousy wretch, being his own image: neither on the other side none say, I am so poore I cannot help, I neede help my selfe, for God loueth glad hartes & cheereful geuers.'[411] Against those who talk about the miseries of the poor but do not actively help them, Bedel declares: ' many are good to the poore, as we commonly

---

[407] Ibid. p. 63.
[408] For Edgeworth's use of narrations see *ante*, p. 126; for Latimer's pp. 147–53.
[409] *A Sermon preached at Paules Crosse*, p. 101.
[410] Ibid. p. 103. This is a perversion of a story from the pseudo-Boethius, 'Liber de Disciplina Scholarium,' cap. ii, (*P.L.*, lxiv. 1227) which was much to the taste of the medieval preachers—it occurs in Jacques de Vitry and the *Speculum Laicorum*, as well as two manuscript collections, (See Owst, L. & *P.M.E.*, p. 468).
[411] *A Sermon exhorting to pity the poore* (London, 1572) sig. Div.

saye, but they will geue them nought, then I say great boast, and small roast maketh vnsauerye mouthes.'[412] Some wish the poor well, but never help them: ' to such wishers I say as the Begger to the Bishop is reported to say that if their wyshings were worth a half peny, I doubt they would not be so liberal.'[413]

A group of four preachers, George Abbot, Ralph Tyrer, John King and Henry Smith, whose richly coloured style reaches out towards the fully ornate mode, form a bridge between it and the plain style. Abbot defends the use of ornament by reference to the practice of Christ in His parables:

> The Ministers of the Gospel, who have a general warrant to be imitators of Christ in anything that they may, may . . . behold the liberty which is left unto them in the performance of their calling, not only nakedly to lay open the truth, but to use helps of wit, of invention and art (which are the good gifts of God), so to remove away all disdain and loathing of the word from the full hearts of the auditory—similitudes and comparisons, allusions, applications, yea parables and proverbs which may tend to edification and illustrating of the word; for they have to do with weak ones as well as with the strong —with some of queasy stomachs, with some who must be enticed and allured with a bait of industry and eloquence, of pretty and witty sentences.[414]

Strengthened by this, he does not hesitate on occasion to use parison and antithesis, coupled with a series of examples from natural history, somewhat after the manner of the secular euphuists, in this passage on the diverse effects of preaching:

> . . . as the sun being one, doth give light to many, and doth harden the clay and yet soften the wax, and maketh the flowers to smell better, and dead carrion to savour worse, and cheereth the springing plants, and cherisheth other growing things, with an influence which cannot be described, so the word of God, uttered by one man, doth serve a multitude of great numbers, and fitteth every one according to his need.[415]

Abbot has too a taste for historical narrations, as that (from Jovianus Pontanus) of the wicked priests, who during the struggle between Aragon and France for Naples, with the intention of rousing a tempest and thus warding off an attack on a fortified town in Campania, throw a crucifix into the sea, sing a dirge for an ass to which they give Communion, and then bury the animal before the

---

[412] Ibid. sig. Ci^v.   [413] Ibid. sig. Cii^r.
[414] *An Exposition upon the Prophet Jonah*, vol. II, p. 331.
[415] Ibid. vol. II, pp. 44–5.

church door. The tempest breaks as desired, and the attack is thwarted; but Abbot is at pains to add that the storm comes, not because the wicked priests have power over the elements, but only by God's permission, to harden their reprobate hearts.[416]

Tyrer, like Abbot, occasionally uses parison, antithesis, and the heaping up of examples in the euphuistic way, as when illustrating that the devil never destroys more souls than when posing as an angel of light, and that hypocrites are never viler than when pretending to be virtuous: ' Crocodiles neuer hurting more than when they weepe most, *Syrenes* neuer harming more then when they singe sweetest, serpentes no where rather lurking then where the grasse is greenest.'[417] However his taste is not always perfect, as is shown by this combination of alliteration with word-pairs within a tediously expanded simile:

Euen as the mightie kings and Keysers, the greatest states and potentates of the world do vsually giue to their counsellors and courtiers, to their seruants and subiects, gold and siluer, chaines and bracelets, lands and liuings, offices and honours, and other princely preferments according to their desire and desert, and vpon their suite and seruice; but yet reseruing his casket of precious pearles and peerelesse iewels, his rich treasurie and exchequer, his royall crowne and dignitie, his Princely throne and chaire of estate, and all his glorious kingdomes and dominions vnto his owne sonne the Prince and Heire apparant, which is to succede him in his soueraigne rule and gouernment. Semblably dealeth the Lord God with those that are *Dilecti &* *electi Dei* his chosen children, his darlings and delight. . . .[418]

On the other hand, King, (whose sermons were, he tells us, painfully elaborated),[419] reaches out towards the wit of Andrewes. Having related the story of Alcmoeon, (who, being allowed by Croesus to take away as much gold as he could carry, wore a garment down to his feet, which he stuffed as full as he could), King comments, using chiasmus and paronomasia:

Here is an heart set upon riches, and riches set upon an heart, heaps of wealth, like to the hills that wants [i.e. moles] cast up, *cumuli, tumuli*, every hill is a grave, every heap a tomb to bury himself in.[420]

[416] Ibid. vol. I, pp. 53–5.
[417] *Five godlie sermons* (London, 1602) p. 287.   [418] Ibid. p. 79.
[419] *Lectures upon Jonah*, p. 311: 'There be that run away with a lecture as horses with an empty cart; I cannot do it. It is but a mote with them to read thrice in a week, and twice in a day sometimes. I will not dissemble my wants. It was a beam to my back to make it my weekly exercise.'
[420] Ibid. p. 39.

He draws many illustrations from Scripture; as, on the folly of those who seek temporal and neglect spiritual goods, he declaims:

Do ye not see the change that worldings make: corn for acorns; a state of innocency, immortality, incorruption, for an apple; the prerogative of birthright, with the blessing that belongeth unto it, for a mess of pottage, belly cheer, as Esau did; a kingdom upon earth, and the kingdom of heaven also, for oxen and asses, and sheep, as Saul did; Christ, his gospel, his miracles, his salvation, for a herd of swine with the Gadarenes, God for idols, mercy for vanity, the comfortablest nature that ever was created, for that which profiteth not.[421]

On one occasion too he gives an unusually effective succession of similes to illustrate how our love of creatures should be subordinate to our love of the Creator:

[We must love others] . . . with a kind of obliquity; our friends, and the necessaries of this life in God as his blessings, our enemies for God as his creatures: so that whatsoever we love besides God may be carried in the stream of his love, our love going in a right line, and as a direct sunbeam to a certain scope, our love to others, either persons or things, coming as broken and reflexed beams from our love to God.[422]

There has been some controversy whether Henry Smith is a plain or an ornate preacher; G. P. Krapp finds him predominantly plain,[423] but A. F. Herr and Fritz Pützer see him as ornate.[424] The truth surely lies between these extremes, for although his diction is simple, and often his use of the schemata is, as Herr says, ' stolid ';[425] nevertheless his sermons are given rich and varied colour by very frequent masterly similes, which are often combined in a series, each member of which throws some illumination on the subject.[426] One of the finest of these series is the following on the ease with which we fall into sin. Having shown that even if we avoid sin, we can only say, ' so neare we have glided by sin, like a ship which rides upon a rock, & slips away, or a bird which scapes from the Fowler when the net is upon her ', Smith continues:

There is no salt but may lose his saltnesse, no wine but may lose his strength, no flower but may lose his scent, no light but may be eclipsed, no beauty but may be stained, no fruit but may

---

[421] Ibid. p. 185: for the 'apple' see Gen .iii; for Esau, Gen. xxv. 29–34; for Saul, 1 Sam. xv; for the Gadarenes, Luke viii. 26–36.
[422] Ibid. p. 325.　[423] The Rise of English Literary Prose, p. 198.
[424] The Elizabethan Sermon, p. 99; Prediger des englischen Barock, pp. 29–36.
[425] The Elizabethan Sermon, p. 99.
[426] Herr (ibid.) finds Smith's sermons 'dull'. I cannot agree with this judgement; the quotations which I give will in themselves, I think, sufficiently indicate the beautiful and interesting qualities of Smith's work.

be blasted, nor soule but may be corrupted, we stand all in a
slippery place, where it is easie to slide, and hard to get up, like
little children which overthrow themselves with their cloaths,
now up, now downe at a straw, so soone we fall from God, and
slide from his word and forget our resolutions, as though we
had never resolved.[427]

The homely simile from the ways of children, (that favourite source
of illustrations for the medieval preachers),[428] will have been noticed;
in general Smith's similes fall into two groups: first a series drawn
from direct observation, usually of domestic scenes and country life,
and secondly a series drawn from literary sources, usually with
subjects from ' natural ' history. In the first group falls this rather
earthy simile from the nursing of children:

> Because we are naturally given to love the world, more than
> is good for us, therefore God hath set an edge of bitterness upon
> it, to make us loath it; like a Nurse which layeth Mustard upon
> her breasts to wean the Child from the Dug; so, *Many are the*
> *troubles of the righteous*, to wean us from the dug of the world.[429]

On occasion Smith goes further than this, and is not afraid to draw
a simile from indigestion: 'As the meat which is not digested with
exercise doth rumble in the stomach: so the knowledge which is not
digested with *sobrietie*, troubleth the brain.'[430] He draws too upon
the kitchen task of basting, and the liking of some dogs for filth to
illustrate how men not only defile themselves by sin, but also lead
others astray: ' . . . we begge of every unclean spirit, untill we have
bumbasted our selves up to the throat, filling every corner of our
hearts with all uncleannesse, and then we are like the Dogge that
cometh out of the sinck, and maketh everyone as foul as himselfe.
. . .'[431] On the other hand some of Smith's most delightful similes
from observation are drawn from birds; the audience must hear the
preacher with simplicity: 'As the little birds pirk up their heads
when their damme comes with meat, and prepare their beaks to take
it, striving who shall catch most (now this looks to be served, and
now that looks for a bit, and every mouth is open until it bee filled:)
so you are here like birds, and we the damme, and the Word the food;
therefore you must prepare a mouth to take it.'[432] The godly do not
require material riches, nor piping and dancing for their happiness:
' If there be but a prayer, and a thankfulness, and a meditation, there
are instruments enow for them, and they can be as merry as birds

[427] *Sermons*, p. 500.   [428] See *ante*, pp. 115–16, 124, 140–1.
[429] *Sermons*, p. 236.   [430] Ibid. p. 442.
[431] *Twelve Sermons*, p. 785.   [432] *Sermons*, pp. 315–16.

in May.'[433] Mothers who refuse to suckle their infants must not be surprised if their children prove unnatural, for they only follow their mother, who was unnatural first, and committed them forth ' like a Cuckow to be hatched in a sparrows nest '.[434] Men will not renew their minds, and are therefore ignorant of many things they would like to know; until they follow the ' word ' they will never understand it, but ' buz and grope at it like Owls, which pry at the sun out of a barn '.[435] In the lark Smith sees, not a symbol of aspiring prayer, as Jeremy Taylor was to do,[436] but the type of most of us, who fall back spiritually much more easily than we advance:

> ... like a lark, that falls to the ground sooner than she mounted up: at first she retires as it were by steps, but when she cometh nearer the ground, she falls down with a jump: so we decline at first, & waver lower and lower till we be almost at the worst, and then we run headlong, as though we were sent post to hell. . . .[437]

Then again, from the country scene comes this simile against gluttony: 'As the moist and waterish grounds bring forth nothing but frogs and toads: so the belly and watrish stomack that is stuffed like a tun, bringeth forth nothing but a drowsy minde, foggy thoughts, filthy speeches and corrupt affections.'[438] Smith draws further homely similes from trees and farming; let rulers and teachers take particular heed lest they fall, for they will pull many others down with them, ' as when a great Tree is hewne downe, which is a shadow to the beasts, and a nest to the birds, many leaves and boughes, and twigges fall with it '.[439] The man who desires godly children should choose a godly wife, ' as he which soweth seed chooseth a fit ground, because they say it is good grafting upon a good stock '.[440] Sawing timber provides an illustration of how the ignorant flounder among theological problems: ' Commonly the simplest men busie their heads about the highest matters: So that they meet with a rough and crabbed question, like a knob in the tree, and while they hacke and hew at it with their own wits, to make it plain, their saw stickes fast in the cleft, and cannot get out again. . . .'[441] Again, Smith draws on the alternation of night and day, seed time and harvest, to show how we must accomplish our essential tasks when young, for: ' Youth is like the day, to do all our works in. For when the night of age

---

[433] Ibid. p. 373.   [434] Ibid. p. 42.   [435] Ibid. p. 253.
[436] See *The Whole Works of the Right Rev. Jeremy Taylor*, D.D., ed. R. Heber, 15 vols. (London, 1828) vol. V, p. 70.
[437] *Sermons*, p. 501.   [438] Ibid. p. 163.   [439] Ibid. p. 501.
[440] Ibid. p. 20.   [441] Ibid. p. 450.

cometh, then every man saith, I might have been like him, or him, but the Harvest was past before I began to Sow, and Winter is come, now my fruit should ripe.'[442] On one occasion too Smith uses a very striking figure drawn from London life; like Shakespeare (*As You Like It*, Act II, Scene vii, ll. 139–66) he uses the stage of the theatre as a symbol for the life of man; there:

> ... every man hath a part, some longer, and some shorter: and while the Actors are at it, suddenly Death steps upon the Stage like a Hawk which separates one of the Doves from the flight; he shoots his Dart; where it lights, there falls one of the Actors dead before them, and makes all the rest agast, they muse and mourn, and bury him; and then to the sport again. While they sing, play, and dance Death comes again and strikes another; there hee lies, they mourn for him, and bury him as they did the former, and play again: so one after another, till the Players be vanished, like the accusers which came before Christ, and death is the last upon the stage, *so the figure of this world passeth away*.[443]

Smith's more literary similes are predominantly of the euphuistic ' unnatural natural history' type. The difference between sinners who yet have faith, and those who lack it is that ' they which have no faith, fal like an Elephant, which, when he is down riseth not again; they which have faith, do but trip and stumble, fall and rise again '.[444] Godliness brings peace to any heart, 'As the Vnicornes horne, dipped in the Fountaine, makes the waters which were corrupt and noysome clear and wholsome upon the sudden '.[445] Men should be careful how they regard things, for ' The wise eye is like the Bee, which gathereth hony of every weed: the foolish eye is like the Spider, which gathereth poyson of every flower.'[446] Sometimes these illustrations are more extended, as when Smith compares the drunkard to the harpy:

> I have read of a bird which hath the face of a man, but is so cruell of nature, that sometimes for hunger she will set upon a man and slay him; after, when she comes for thirst unto the water to drink, seeing the face in the Water, like the face of him whom she devoured, for griefe that she had killed one like her self, takes such sorrow, that she never eateth nor drinketh after, but beats and frets, and pines herself to death. What wilt thou do then which hast not slain one like thy self, but thy selfe,

[442] Ibid. p. 223.   [443] Ibid. p. 350.   [444] Ibid. p. 496.
[445] *Three Sermons*, p. 15.   [446] *Sermons*, pp. 286–7.

thy very selfe with a cup of Wine, and murderest so many vertues and graces in one houre?[447]

With these ' literary ' figures must be set a rare but striking instance of the use of a conceit which reaches out towards the mode of the seventeenth century ' witty ' preachers:

. . . as Christ when he had blessed the bread, brake the bread; so Christ when he had filled his body with most precious graces, brake it up like a rich Treasure-house; his hands by the nails, his back by the stripes, his head by the thorns, his side by the spear; that out of every hole a river of Grace and goodness might issue and flow forth unto us.[448]

The works of the ' silver tongued ' preacher can indeed still provide considerable literary pleasure; perhaps it is not so difficult as Herr thinks, to understand his great popularity in his own day.[449]

The fully ornate style is found among the Elizabethan preachers in two distinct forms: first in the truly classical manner of Hooker, whose use of the schemata is classical,[450] and who successfully reproduces the Ciceronian period in English; and secondly in the fundamentally medieval manner of those preachers who adopt in the pulpit a style which resembles in varying degrees of closeness, that of the secular euphuists.[451]

It is extremely easy in the sermons of Hooker to pick out masterly periods, in which the rhetorical devices, although present,

---

[447] *Twelve Sermons*, p. 843. This property of the harpy is found in the medieval sermon hand-books, e.g. in the collection of stories in MS. Harl. 268, f. 41 (noted in J. A. Herbert, *Catalogue of Romances in the Department of Manuscripts in the British Museum*, vol. III, p. 128, no. 81 [Holcot's *Convertemini*]. (See too ibid. pp. 56, 176, 572.)

[448] *Sermons*, p. 52.

[449] See *The Elizabethan Sermon*, p. 101. The praise of Nashe, who contrasts Smith's coloured style with the drab austerity of the exponents of the first form of the plain style (see *ante*, pp. 168–70) is still worth noticing: 'I myselfe haue been so censured among dul-headed Diuines: who deeme it no more cunning to wryte an exquisite Poem, than to preach pure *Caluin*, or distill the iuce of a Commentary in a quarter sermon. . . How admirablie shine these Diuines aboue the common mediocritie, that haue tasted the sweete springs of *Pernassus*? Siluer tongu'd *Smith*, whose well tun'd stile hath made thy death the general teares of the Muses, queintlie couldst thou deuise heauenly Ditties to Apolloes Lute, and teach stately verse to trip it as smoothly as if *Ouid* and thou had but one soule. Hence alone did it proceed, that thou wert such a plausible pulpit man, that before thou entredst into the rough waies of Theologie, thou refinedst, preparedst, and purifidest thy minde with sweete Poetrie. If a simple mans censure may be admitted to speake in such an open Theater of opinions, I neuer saw aboundant reading better mixt with delight, or sentences which no man can challenge of prophane affection sounding more melodious to the eare or piercing more deepe to the heart.' ('Pierce Penilesse,' *The Works of Thomas Nashe*, ed. R. B. McKerrow, 5 vols. London, 1904–10, vol. I, pp. 192–3.)

[450] On the distinction between the classical and the medieval ways of using the schemes, see *ante*, p. 130.

[451] Croll has convincingly demonstrated the medieval ancestry of the euphuistic style, both in the use of the schemes, and in the use of similes from 'natural' history (*Euphues*, pp. xvi–xvii, xxiv–lxiv).

are not obtrusive, and the logical sequence of thought flows unin-
terruptedly to its satisfying conclusion. A particularly pleasing
example is the following on the two-fold reason why we cannot
fully appreciate the ordered wisdom of the cosmos:

> What good the sun doth, by heat and light; the moon and
> stars, by their secret influence; the air and wind and water, by
> every their several qualities: what commodity the earth, receiv-
> ing their services, yieldeth again unto her inhabitants: how
> beneficial by nature the operations of all things are; how far the
> use and profit of them is extended; somewhat the greatness of
> the works of God, but much more our own inadvertency and
> carelessness, doth disable us to conceive.[452]

Then again, in the following passage, the use of anaphora within the
period concentrates attention with force and clarity upon the key
word:

> Justice, that which flourishing upholdeth, and not prevailing
> disturbeth, shaketh, threateneth with utter desolation and ruin
> the whole world: justice, that whereby the poor have their
> succour, the rich their ease, the potent their honour, the
> living their peace, the souls of the righteous departed their
> endless rest and quietness: justice, that which God and angels
> and men are principally exalted by: justice, the chiefest matter
> contended for at this day in the Christian world: in a word,
> justice that whereon not only all our present happiness, but in
> the kingdom of God our future joy dependeth.[453]

Hooker's style is distinctive also in his striking use of emotive
figures,[454] drawn neither from contemporary life and pursuits nor
from natural history, but from general human experience and from
Scripture, especially the Psalms and the Prophets. These give a

---

[452] *Works,* vol. III, p. 617. Herr quotes another typical period (*The Elizabethan Sermon,* p. 97) and Mitchell gives the example which most appeals to him. (*English Pulpit Oratory from Andrewes to Tillotson,* p. 65).

[453] *Works,* vol. III, pp. 616–7.

[454] I have noted only one occasion when Hooker uses a purely illustrative simile; to illustrate the difference between the just, whose wills are directed to God (even if at times they waver), and the impious, whose wills are directed away from God, he uses an unemotive simile from the drawing of lines in different directions: however an emotive colouring is added before the close of the period in which it is contained: 'there is not only this difference between the just and the impious, that the mind of the one is right in the sight of God, because his obliquity is not imputed; the other perverse, because his sin is unrepented of: but even as lines that are drawn with a trembling hand, but yet to the point which they should, are though ragged and uneven, neverthe-less direct in comparison of them which run clean another way; so there is no in-congruity in terming them right minded men, whom though God may charge with many things amiss, yet they are not as those dismal and ugly monsters, in whom, because there is nothing but wilful opposition of mind against God, a more than tolerable deformity is noted in them, by saying that their minds are not right.' (Ibid. p. 601.)

peculiarly soft yet rich colouring to his chastened eloquence, as when (drawing upon a common physical experience) he compares preachers who find little sweetness in religion to expectant mothers who have unusual longings:

> We ourselves are like those women which have a longing to eat coals, and lime and filth; we are fed, some with honour, some with ease, some with wealth; the gospel waxeth loathsome and unpleasant in our taste; how should we then have a care to feed others with that which we cannot fancy ourselves?[455]

A notable instance of Hooker's use of figures from the Psalms occurs when he represents the just man reproaching the preacher for dwelling on the reward of virtue, when on the contrary the material prosperity of the wicked, in which he does not share, is such a painful fact:

> Thus we think, looking upon others, and comparing them with ourselves, their tables are furnished day by day; earth and ashes are our bread; they sing to the lute, and they see their children dance before them; our hearts are heavy in our bodies as lead, our sighs as thick as a swift pulse, our tears do wash the beds wherein we lie: the sun shineth fair upon their foreheads; we are hanged up like bottles in the smoke, cast into corners like the shards of a broken pot: tell not us of the promises of God's favour, tell such as to reap the fruit of them, they belong not to us, they are made to others. The Lord be merciful to our weakness, but thus it is.[456]

Similarly in his answer to this, showing how the wicked may have wealth and comfort, but lack interior peace, Hooker again echoes the Psalms, and quotes directly from Job:

> Though wickedness be sugar in their mouths, and wantonness as oil to make them look with cheerful countenance; nevertheless if their hearts were disclosed, perhaps their glittering estate would not greatly be envied. The voices that have broken out from some of them, ' O that God had given me a heart senseless, like the flint in the rocks of stone ', which as it can taste no pleasure so it feeleth no woe; these and the like speeches are surely tokens of the curse which Sophar in the book of Job poureth upon the head of the impious man, ' He shall suck the gall of asps, and the viper's tongue shall slay him '.[457]

[455] Ibid. p. 697.
[456] Ibid. p. 479. cf: Ps. cii. 9, 'I have eaten ashes like bread. . .'; Ps. vi. 6, '. . . I water my couch with my tears'; Ps. cxix. 83, 'I am become like a bottle in the smoke. . .'; Ps. xxxi. 12, 'I am like a broken vessell. . .'
[457] *Works*, vol. III, p. 646: cf. Ps. civ. 15, 'And wine that maketh glad the heart of man, and oil to make his face to shine'; also Job xx. 16.

Again, in the following passage Hooker couples the scriptural figures with a series of rhetorical questions to provide an unusually powerful dissuasive from sin, both from consideration of our shameful neglect of preparation to receive the Divine Guest into our souls, and from the recollection of the fate of the wicked:

> Which of you will gladly remain or abide in a misshapen or a ruinous house, or a broken house? And shall we suffer sin and vanity to drop in at our eyes, and at our ears, at every corner of our bodies, and of our souls, knowing that we are the temples of the Holy Ghost? Which of you receiveth a guest whom he honoureth, or whom he loveth, and doth not sweep his chamber against his coming? And shall we suffer the chamber of our hearts and consciences to lie full of vomiting, full of filth, full of garbage, knowing that Christ hath said, ' I and my Father will come and dwell with you? '[458]

Hooker is equally successful with gentler scriptural figures coupled with questions; this passage on God as our refuge is instinct with his fragrant piety:

> Where should the frighted child hide his head, but in the bosom of his loving father? Where a Christian, but under the shadow of the wings of Christ his saviour? ' Come my people,' said God in the Prophet, ' enter into thy chamber, hide thyself,' etc. But because we are in danger like chased birds, like doves that seek and cannot see the nesting holes that are right before them, therefore our Saviour giveth his disciples these encouragements beforehand, that fear might never so amaze them, but that always they might remember, that whatsoever evils at any time did beset them, to him they should still repair, for comfort, counsel and succour.[459]

Frequently Hooker gives suggestive poetic touches, as when he refers to St. Peter's repentance:

> My eager protestations made in the glory of my ghostly strength, I am ashamed of; but those crystal tears, wherewith my aim and weakness was bewailed, have procured my endless joy; my strength hath been my ruin, and my fall my stay.[460]

The tears, like the crystal, are not only shining but precious and full of ' virtues ' also.[461] Finally in this passage on the necessity for the

---

[458] *Works*, vol. III, p. 686: cf. 1. Cor. vi. 19, 'Know ye not that your body is the temple of the Holy Ghost. . . ?' Isa. xxviii. 8, 'For all the tables are full of vomit and filthiness, so that there is no place clean.'
[459] *Works*, vol. III, p. 652.   [460] Ibid. p. 610.
[461] For these 'virtues' of the crystal, see e.g. *Bartholomeus de proprietatibus rerum*, tr. J. Trevisa (London, 1535) f. 228ᵛ. See too also, for poetic effects, Hooker, *Works*, vol. III, p. 473: speaking of the question whether or not Habakkuk, by his thought 'The law doth fail' (Hab. i. 4), lost grace because of the weakness of his faith, Hooker

Christian to follow our Lord in His sufferings, the very centre of Hooker's spiritual message,[462] the similes although simple, impart a certain imaginative glow, which renders the exhortation unusually persuasive:

> For, though to have no feeling of that which merely concerneth us were stupidity, nevertheless, seeing that as the Author of our salvation was himself consecrated by affliction, so that way which we are to follow him by is not strewed with rushes, but set with thorns, be it never so hard to learn, we must learn to suffer with patience even that which is almost impossible to be suffered; that in the hour when God shall call us unto our trial, and turn this honey of peace and pleasure wherewith we swell into that gall and bitterness which flesh doth shrink to taste of, nothing may cause us in the troubles of our souls to storm and grudge and repine at God, but every heart be enabled with divinely inspired courage to inculcate unto itself, Be not troubled; and in those last and greatest conflicts to remember it, that nothing may be so sharp and bitter to be suffered, but that still we ourselves may give ourselves this encouragement, Even learn also patience, O my soul.[463]

Unlike the other ornate preachers however, Hooker does not stud his sermons with *dicta* from the Fathers; the personal ' inwardness ' which is his most characteristic note would receive no help from such a practice, which would on the contrary detract from its concentrated effectiveness.

In contrast to this classical eloquence is the style of the euphuistic preachers: ' H.B.', Thomas Drant, James Bisse, Edward Bush, Francis Trigge, Edward Topsell, John Carpenter and Thomas Playfere. The marks of euphuism proper are: first, the almost unremitting use of a combination of isocolon, parison and paromoion (whether alliteration or homoioteleuton, or both) usually with antithesis in the thought, and occasionally with the addition of paronomasia and polyptoton; secondly, the heaping up of examples or similes from ' natural ' history,[464] often taken not directly from Pliny, the *Physiologus*, or Bartholomaeus Anglicus, but

continues (pointing out that many entertain thoughts similar to the Prophet's): 'Forasmuch therefore as the matter is weighty, dear, and precious, which we have in hand, it behoveth us with so much the greater chariness to wade through it, taking special heed both what we build, and whereon we build, that if our building be pearl, our foundation be not stubble. . . ' Here 'pearl' suggests the gleaming attractiveness of the doctrine, 'stubble' the flimsiness and easily destructible nature which the premises may have.

---

[462] See *post*, p. 319.   [463] *Works*, vol. III, p. 647.
[464] See Croll, *Euphues*, pp. xv–xvii, C. S. Lewis, *English Literature in the Sixteenth Century excluding Drama* (Oxford, 1954) pp. 312–13.

from the convenient and very popular *Similia* of Erasmus.[465] The
most illuminating way of considering the style of these preachers is
to examine, first their use of the schemes; and secondly, of the heaped
examples and similes, together with any other tropes which they
may employ.

It must be stated at the outset that in none of these preachers is
there that almost constant use of the euphuistic devices found in
Euphues itself; rather 'patches' of euphuism occur with varying
frequency in a style which is certainly ornate in an unclassical way,
but not purely euphuistic.

'H.B.' is the least truly euphuistic of this group; he does indeed
at times employ certain of the schemes beloved of the euphuists, but
seldom does he use them in the characteristically euphuistic combination. Thus he employs alliteration and homoioteleuton in
isolation:

> The princely Prophet *Dauid*, being himself aduanced by the
> goodnesse of God to be king ouer Israell, by dayly experience
> plainly saw, how common a thing it is, that the great and
> mighty, the rich and wealthie men of this world doe many times
> forget both themselues what they be, and their God from whom
> they be. And glorying in nobilitie, and swelling in authoritie,
> and swimming in worldly wealth, do trust in their treasures, and
> seeke their own pleasures, and think themselues Gods.[466]

Then on a rare occasion when he does use a combination of isocolon,
paronomasia, alliteration and antithesis, the effect is more diffuse
than in true euphuism:

> *Nymrod* and his confederates thought themselues safe, when
> they builded their Babell vp to the heauens: but all their high
> Babell was but a bable, that is a verie vaine deuise, and came
> soon to confusion.[467]

Drant and Bisse make more use of the euphuistic schemes in
combination than does 'H.B.', but they do not closely confine
themselves to them; rather they play like delighted children with
many of the schemes to be found detailed in the current rhetorical
handbooks. Thus on occasion Drant (like the euphuists) does indeed
employ parison, homoioteleuton and antitheses in the following:

> The bytyng of a Snake may be cured with the herbe Dittany.
> The biting of a mad Dog may be cured with a Crabfishe; but

---

[465] See the numerous parallels between Lyly and the *Similia* pointed out by Croll in
the notes to *Euphues*.
[466] *A verie profitable sermon*, p. 1.
[467] Ibid. p. 14.

O

the bytyng of a Vsurer is so chargeable, that it is almost vncurable.[468]

But also we find him using antithesis and apostrophe in isolation, in a
very obvious and distinctly mechanical way in this passage on the
contrast between the fading physical beauty of a human face, and the
constantly renewed spiritual beauty of the Church, the Spouse of
Christ:

> This woman therefore must needes be fayre, and fayrest of
> all women. Oh fayrenes of man's face, of womans face. Oh
> treasure for a tyme. Oh fayre foolishe vanitie. A lyttle colde
> dooth pinche, a little heat dooth partch thee, a little sicknesse
> dooth match thee, and a little of sores doth marre thee. But the
> fayreness of Christe in this woman, or in his elect, maye be
> soyled, but it will be washt: it may be blacke, but it will keepe
> a good sauour: it may be made red as scarlet, but it will be
> renued wool white, and snow white.[469]

Then on another occasion he allows apostrophe quite to run away
with him:

> O all ye men, all ye that drawe breath vnder the cope of the
> skyes, ye spring vp like Lilies, and goe downe like Lilies, ye
> florish like Lilies, and deflower like Lilies, Pindarus sayd thrise,
> *Mammea, Mammea, Mammea*, Ieremy cryed thryse, Earth, Earth,
> Earth: so I, Lilies, Lilies, Lilies, and the second time, Lilies,
> Lilies, Lilies, and for that I would haue it remembered, I cry
> againe, Lilies, Lilies, Lilies, and then thus, O men, O Lilies,
> O men, O Lilies, O men, O Lilies, O field grasse, O flowers of
> decay.[470]

Also he finds *rogatio* congenial, but is more tasteful in his use of this
device:

> For what hast thou, which is not subiect vnto casualtie?
> Hast thou gemmes, iewels, and pearles? Theeues may burst in,
> and steale them. Hast thou golde, siluer, wine, plate, and
> mettals? Rust may freate them, or theeues may steale them.
> Hast thou tapestrie, silkes, cloathes, waredrops, mothes may
> eate them: and of themselues they will waxe olde. Hast thou
> great flocks of Sheepe, they may be burnt from heauen as Iobes
> were. Hast thou oxen, cattel, horse: enemies may take them
> away.[471]

Drant feels perfectly justified in this liberal use of the schemes:
indeed he defends eloquence in preaching against the sour plain
Puritans,[472] by reference to Scripture itself, in which he, like St.

---

[468] *Three godly and learned Sermons*, sig. Nii^r.   [469] Ibid. sig. Cv^r.
[470] Ibid. sig. Fii^v.   [471] Ibid. sig. Lvii^r.
[472] For their views, see *ante*, pp. 168-9.

Augustine, finds not a homely lack of artifice, but rather the consummate employment of the rhetorical devices:[473] paronomasia in Isaiah, anaphora in Jeremiah, epiphonema and *reticentia* in the Psalms, *exclamatio*, anatistasis and sarcasmos in St. Paul, and metaphors throughout the sacred volume.[474]

Bisse goes even further than Drant in his tasteless over-employment of the schemes; indeed sometimes his work reads merely like a series of examples from a rhetorical handbook, as in this instance of the ludicrous over-working of epanorthosis:

> There was neuer more eating and drinking, I meane neuer more surfetting and drunkennesse: neuer more buying and selling: neuer more planting, I might truely say, neuer more supplanting, one of an another: neuer more marying, I woulde to God I might not iustly say, neuer more whoring, to conclude neuer more building, I meane not building of Colledges, of almes houses, of schooles, there was neuer lesse: I pray you mistake me not, I say, neuer more building of priuate houses, which we think shall continue for euer, and call our houses and our landes after our owne names.[475]

He is however more felicitous when using the euphuistic schemes in combination as in this passage on the effects of the Redemption:

> We were chaf, but now we are wheat; we were drosse, but now we are golde; we were rauens, but now we are doues: we were goates, but now we are sheep: we were thornes, now we are grapes: we were thistels, now we are lillies: we were straungers, now are we citizens: we were harlots, now are we virgins: hell was our inheritaunce, nowe heuen is our possession; we were the children of wrath, we are the sons mercie: Finally we were bondslaues to Satan, but nowe we are heires of God, and coheires with Iesus Christ.[476]

On one occasion too his use of these devices (including in this case paronomasia also) is strikingly effective; in this very beautiful sentence they combine to give a richly 'witty' description of hypocrites:

> For euen, they, these holy men, or rather holow trees (I would they were holie trees; which are always greene;) are like

---

[473] Drant declares that: ' the eloquence of Scripture is as fit for holiness as the wordes of Cicero for peace, or the wordes of Catullus for wantonnes.' (*Three godly and learned Sermons*, sig. Mvi[r].) Cf. St. Augustine, *De Doctrina Christiana*, lib. IV, cap. vi–vii, *P.L.*, xxxiv, 92–8.

[474] *Three godly and learned Sermons*, sig. Mvi[v].

[475] *Two sermons preached the one at Paules Crosse, the other at Christes Church* (London, 1581) sig. Aiv[v]. See too the example of the use of these devices noted by Herr, *The Elizabethan Sermon*, p. 94.

[476] *Two Sermons*, sig. Cviii[r].

the faire redd morning, which bringeth rayne at noone: like the
calme water, which is most deepe: like the greene grasse, where
the venemous snake lieth, and the filthy curre maketh his
vrine.[477]

Bush, Carpenter, Topsell, Trigge, and Playfere, however, restrict
themselves more closely to the euphuistic schemes than do the
three preachers just considered. Thus Bush uses parison and
paromoion to point the contrast between Catholic and Protestant
times:

> ... for the light of the Gospel, we had the light of candels, for
> the holy bible, bables and banners, for Gods word, many
> trifling traditions, for preaching, massing, and for our free
> iustification by the mere merite and grace of God in Christ
> Iesus through faith, mans merits and righteousnesse estab-
> lished.[478]

Again Carpenter uses antithesis, parison and homoioteleuton with
considerable skill:

> Although the holy Church is as a bush in fire burning, yet is
> it not consumed: though as a ship tossed, yet not ouerturned:
> though as a Vyne pruned, yet neuer starued.[479]

Topsell is equally felicitous in his employment of those figures:

> For carnall minded men, see no more grace in a church than
> in a tauerne, and no more delight in a Christian than in a
> ruffian; nor esteeme any whit better of a preacher than a craftes-
> man; or finde any more sweetenesse in a sermon than a plaie:
> or take any more delight in the Gospell than in a little pedlars
> french.[480]

while Trigge is particularly forceful and pointed:

> It is not thy muske whereof thy garments smel, but mercy;
> not thy heaps of golde, whereof thy chests are full, but good
> deeds: not thy rings plate & iewels, wherewith perchance thy
> cupboard is furnished but pure religion vndefiled, which *Iames*
> speaketh of, that pleaseth God.[481]

Playfere, the most accomplished stylist in the whole group of
euphuistic preachers[482] is similarly ' pointed ' and witty in his use of

---

[477] Ibid. sig. Bi[r].
[478] *A Sermon preached at Paules Crosse on Trinity Sunday* 1571, by E.B. (London, 1576)
sig. Eii[r]. See too ibid. sig. Dii[r]: 'And therefore wher the good and Godly be punished,
or the wicked spared, ther is neither iust iudgement nor good gouerment.'
[479] *Remember Lots wife. Two godly and fruitfull Sermons*... (London, 1588) sig. Ciii[v].
[480] *Times Lamentation*, p. 396.
[481] *A godly and fruitful sermon preached at Grantham* (Oxford, 1594) sig. Bvii[r].
[482] Nashe was impressed by Playfere's gifts, and concerned about his lack of pre-
ferment: ' Mellifluous PLAYFERE, one of the chief props of our aged, and auntientest,
and absolutest Vniuersities present flourishing, Where doe thy supereminent gifts shine
to themselues, that the Court cannot be acquainted with them? Few such men speake

these schemes, as may be seen in this example of chiasmic parison with homoioteleuton:

> . . . as certaine apples haue a sourish sweetnesse, and some old wines haue a sweetish sournesse: so *both our sorrow must be ioyfull, and our ioy must be sorrowful.*[483]

However these last preachers also range beyond the purely euphuistic schemes more frequently than does Lyly himself: for example, on occasion Topsell enploys *rogatio*:

> . . . hast thou rode long iourneys for thy profit? then thou must do the like for the Lord: hast thou spent liberally on thy wife, children, haukes, hounds ,and other vanities? then thou must do the like for the Lord: hast thou watched many nights at cardes, dice, dauncing, and dalliance? thou must do as much in prayer. . . .[484]

Playfere uses alliteration to give added punch to a *dictum* of St. Cyprian:

> When the spirit of man sendeth out sighes, in praier, then the spirit of God giues grace.[485]

while Bush attempts a period, within which however, he makes extensive use of parison:

> For whether wee be persecuted by open enemies, or molested by those that haue seemed to be our friendes, who haue gone vp into the temple with vs, & haue taken sweete counsel together, or whether we be greeued with sicknes, or troubled with the feeling of our synnes, or in what other soeuer perplexity or distresse we be, we may sucke out of thys booke of the Psalmes most sweete and comfortable doctrine, either for the amendment of our lyues, or the comfort of our consciences.[486]

To turn now to the use of tropes by these euphuistic preachers, we find that the employment of heaped examples and similes from ' natural ' history can be illustrated copiously from the sermons of all of them except ' H.B. ', who uses very few tropes of any kind. Thus Drant, declaiming against the avarice of magistrates amplifies his theme by a series of examples drawn from animals:

out of Fames highest Pulpits, though out of her highest Pulpits speake the purest of all speakers. Let me adde one word, and let it not bee thought derogatorie to anie. I cannot bethinke mee of two in England in all things comparable to him for this time. Seldome haue I beheld so pregnant and pleasaunt wit coupled with a memorie of such incomprehensible receipt, deepe reading and delight better mixt than in his Sermons.' (' Strange Newes of the Intercepting Certaine Letters,' *Works*, vol. I, p. 314.)

[483] *The whole Sermons*, ' The Meane in Mourning,' p. 22: see too ibid. p. 55: ' Nay our very reason is treason, and our best affection is no better than an infection.'

[484] *Times lamentations*, p. 113.

[485] *The whole Sermons*, ' The Meane in Mourning,' p. 18.

[486] *A Sermon preached at Paules Crosse on Trinity Sunday* 1571, sig. Aii^v.

The strength of the Eliphante is in his snoute. Of the Boore in his tuske, of the Lyon in his pawes, of the Dogge in his iawes, of the Horse in his hoofe, of the Bull in his hornes, of the Hare in her feete, of the Vrchen in his prickes, of the Cocke in his spurres, of the Hauke in her tallentes and of these Magistrates in their money.[487]

like Lyly, Drant culls many of his examples from the *Similia* of Erasmus, as when he amplifies the theme of the influence of the planets:

The Mallow and the Marigolde and the herbe called Heliotropium apply themselues to the presence or absence of the sunne. The Bittell according to the forme of the moone, commeth out and goeth in with one course. The Pisemyre in the full moone, worketh day and night. Cucumbers in the full moone be more full, in the wayning of the moone more empty. Shell fishes followe the course of the moone. . .[488]

or when he denounces the papists who keep the people in ignorance of the Scripture:

They be like to that Painter that Plutarch speaketh of, that had euill fauouredly proportioned a painted Hen, and therefore chased away the liuelie Hennes, least that his euill workmanship should be perceiued: those chase away Gods word lest theyr fancie be discouered. . . . If they see, and will not let others see, then they be as churlishe as a dog, who when he is smit of a Serpent, will not eate the herbe Canaria, in the sight of man, lest that man in such distresse should be thereby releued.[489]

To show how the creatures teach man wisdom Drant uses a series of examples from Scripture, piled up in a purely euphuistic way; his effort quite lacks the subtlety and emotional colouring of Hooker's scriptural similes:

The Camell at a needles eie, is the Image of a couetous man, at heauens gate. A Bullock being led to slaughter, dooth signifie a young man followinge a harlotte. An Hinde, desiring

---

[487] *Three godly and learned Sermons*, sig. Mi^v.

[488] Ibid. sig. Kvi^v: cf. Erasmus, 'Parabolae sive Similia,' *Opera Omnia*, vol. I, 605F: '. . . heliotropium herba, semper in eam spectat partem, qua sol est, & eo condito florem contrahit . . .'; also ibid. 609D: '. . . conchylia crescente luna augescunt, decrescente macrescunt. . .'

[489] *Three godly and learned Sermons*, sig. Bvi^v: cf. *Similia*, 566C: 'Quidam male pinxerat gallos gallinaceos, jussitque puera, ut veros gallinaceos procul abigerat a tablua, ne collatione deprehenderetur . . .'; also ibid. 605B: 'Herbam canariam canis ita mandit, ut homo cernat nisi depastam & percussus a serpente aliam quandam petit, sed eam non decerpit inspectante homine. . .' Doubtless it was the use of such similies which caused Gabriel Harvey to describe Drant's style as 'curious'. (See G. Gregory Smith, *Elizabethan Critical Essays*, 2 vols., Oxford, 1904, vol. II, p. 281.)

to drinke, dooth put vs in minde of the separation that shalbe in the days of Iudgement.[490]
Unfortunately Drant's taste in the use of this device is not impeccable; his amplification of the theme that nothing is more fragrant than ' the smell of a good life, rysing from a good beleefe ' is clumsy and over-elaborated:

> Whole Grocers shops of spicery, all the flowers in Priapus garden, all the flowers that Naiades, and Draiades, and Satyrus, that is, all the flowers in hilles, and flowers in dales, and flowers in many a greene forrest, are not so delightful and smelling. The Violet hath not the lyke sauor, the Rose hath not the lyke sauor, the Lilie the like smell, the Giliflower the like sent, as good lyfe through good faith yeeldeth to Gods nostrels.[491]

Carpenter, on the other hand, is neat in his handling of such similes:

> The *Syrenes* sing sweetly, the *Lamaei* shine beautifully, the Serpent suggesteth subtiltie, the deuill promiseth al the glorie of the world to them that worship him.[492]

His use of scriptural examples to show that there will always be good and bad Christians in the Church is succinct and effective:

> While the net is in the Sea, the bad fishes wil be taken together with the good: whiles the Mustard seed growth vp to a tree, the birds of all sorts rowst vnder the same.[493]

Sometimes too he adds a colloquial vigour to his heaped similes, as when dealing with the trepidations of the Devil in the world:

> . . . he rageth horribly, and stormeth sturdely, because his time expireth shortly: As *Leuiathan* in the Sea without a hooke in his nostrels: as Behemoth in the wildernes, hauing no bridle in his Iawes, and as a Lyon rampingly he walketh and stalketh, hippeth and skippeth from one coast to another, seeking to deuour.[494]

Bisse is not always so pithy as Carpenter in his use of this device; he can however give to it a certain poetic richness of texture, as when speaking of the ' dunging of the figtree ', England, by the preachers, he declares:

> Behold that hath been doone, and yet this figge tree bringeth foorth small fruite, wee are like trees that haue their heades in the grounde, and sucke all their iuice from the earth: wee are like bruite beastes, who turne their faces to the grounde: wee are not like men, who shoulde turn our countenances towards heauen, thence to fetch our meate and all good thinges, which

---

[490] *Three godly and learned Sermons*, sig. Niiiʳ: cf. Mark x. 25; Prov. vii. 22; Ps. xl. 1. Drant does violence to the sense of Scripture here: the verse runs: 'As the hart panteth after the water brooks, so panteth my soul after thee, O God.'
[491] *Three godly and learned Sermons*, sig. Eiiʳ.   [492] *Remember Lots wife*, sig. Givʳ.
[493] *Remember Lots wife*, sig. Fvʳ.   [494] Ibid. sig. Bivʳ.

by promise we may haue for the asking. We are like the corne growing on the house top, which withereth before it bee plucked vp, whereof the mower filleth not his hand, nor he that bindeth vp the sheaues, his bosome.[495]

Trigge also imparts a poetic richness to this device, together with emotive power, as in this passage on the coming of old age, the herald of death:

> . . . smoke alwaies goeth before fire, to declare that fire is in kindling, & the whirlwinde before the tempest, to tell when that the storme is in breeding: so the swallowes before the spring to signifie that the spring is coming: so the fall of the leaues of trees to testifie and forewarne that winter is approaching. And euen so also is death it selfe, in the winter of our age, he sendeth tokens before thereof euident & manifest, that olde age is now in coming, and that death standeth at the dore, and that winter is at hande. . . .[496]

Then again Bush heaps up a copiously miscellaneous series of examples to show that Protestants should eat meat with a good conscience whenever they choose:

> Smal thinges may do much hurte, a graine of a grape is but a smal thinge, and yet it killed Anacreon the Poet, a haire is but a very smal thinge, and yet it choked one Fabius a senator of Rome, a flee is but a smal thing, and yet it strangled a proude Pope, yea the proudest I think that euer was Adrian the iiij a country man of our owne, a smal mote may hurt the eye, a smal thinge may trouble a good conscience, a smal deale of Leauen wil Leauen a whole lump, to eate meate is but a smal thing, yet if a man eate it with a douting and repining conscience he is condemned because he eateth not of faith.[497]

On the other hand, the most characteristic mode of Playfere is more complicated: he makes some plant, bird, or animal utter a moral sentiment drawn from one of its natural properties; this property is then allegorized after the medieval manner of Bozon's *Metaphors*,[498] and finally a series of corroborating similes is added, often given extra force by the use of strict parison and homoioteleuton. The total effect is rich and pleasing, as when dealing with Christ's victory over death, Playfere amplifies:

> Now the *Phoenix* though sitting in his nest among the hot spices of *Arabia* he be burnt to ashes, yet still he sayes, I die not,

---

[495] *Two sermons*, sig. Civ[r]: the final figure is from Scripture, see Ps. cxxix. 6–7.
[496] *A godly and fruitfull sermon preached at Grantham*, sig. Ciii[v].
[497] *A Sermon preached at Pauls Crosse on trinity Sunday* , 1571, sig. Fiv[v].
[498] See *ante*, p. 116, for late medieval examples of this allegorizing of natural properties.

but old age dieth in mee. And so Christ the true *Phoenix*, though lying in his graue among the hot spices wherewith *Nichodemus* did embalm him, hee was neuer like to rise from death to life againe: yet died not, but mortality died in him, and immortalitie so liued in him that euen in his sepulcher hee did most liue when hee seemed most to be dead. As the Laurell is greenest in the foulest Winter, and the lime is hottest in the coldest water: and the glow-worme shineth brightest when the night is darkest: and the swan singeth sweetest when his death is nearest.[499]

Sometimes however Playfere is simpler, and merely allegorizes the natural property, for which however he always carefully gives the original source, as in this passage on the new spiritual life which attends on repentance:

Pliny writeth that the tears of the vine-branches doe cure the leprosie. And so the teares of those vine-branches which are grafted into the true vine, doe cure the leprosie of sinne. *S. Austin* witnesseth that the Eagle feeling his wings heauy, plungeth them in a fountaine, and so reneweth his strength: After the same sort a Christian feeling the heauy burden of his sins, batheth himself in a fountaine of teares, and so washing off the old man, which is the body of sinne, is made young againe, and lustie as an Egle.[500]

Fountains with unusual properties have a special appeal for Playfere, as symbols of the tears of repentance; in the following passage he manages to correlate scriptural expressions with these marvels:

Austin reporteth, that there is a fountain in *Epirus* which not onely putteth out torches that are lighted, but also lighteth torches that are put out. *Fulgosus* likewise reporteth, that there is another fountaine neere *Grenoble*, a Citie in *France*, which although it haue not hot waters, as a Bath, yet oftentimes together with bubbles of water, it casteth vp flames of fire. The fountaine of teares that is in our eies must be like these two fountaines. As the Psalmist witnesseth. *When my sorrow was*

---

[499] *The whole Sermons*, ' The Meane in Mourning,' p. 39. See too this delightful instance, ibid. p. 38: ' Now the palm tree, though it haue many weights at the top, and many snakes at the roote, yet still it sayes, I am neither oppressed with weights nor nor distressed with the snakes. And so Christ the true palm tree, though all the iudgements of God, and all the sinnes of the world, like vnsupportable weights, were laid vpon him; yea though the cursed Ieues stood beneath like venemous snakes hissing and biting at him, yet hee was neither so oppressed with them, nor so distressed with them, but that euen vpon his crosse he did most flourish, when he was most afflicted: As peny-royal being hung vp in the larder house, yet buds his yellow flower: and Noahs oliue tree being drowned vnder the water, yet keepes his greene branche: and Aarons rod being clung and dry, yet brings forth ripe almonds; and *Moses* bramble-bush being set on fire, yet shines, and is not consumed.'

[500] Ibid. ' The Meane in Mourning,' p. 12.

stirred (sayes he) *my heart was hot within mee, and while I was musing, the fire kindled. When my sorrow was stirred.* There is the first fountaine, *My heart was hot within mee.* There is the Torch lighted. *And while I was musing.* There is the other fountaine. *The fire kindled.* There is the flame burning.[501]

Often the collocation of Playfere's examples is ' witty ' in a euphuistic if not a metaphysical way. This is seen clearly in the flow of ideas in the following passage against immoderate weeping:

> *In nature* the earth when it reioyceth, as in Summer time, then it is couered with corne; but when it hath too too forlorne and sorrowfull a countenance, as in the Winter time, then it is fruitless and barren. The water when it is quiet and calme, bringeth in all manner of Merchandise, but when the sea stormes and roares too much then the very ships doe howle and cry. The aire looking clearly and cheerefully, refresheth all things, but weeping too much, that is rayning too much, as in Noah's flood, it drowns the whole world. . . . The eye it selfe (as Anatomists write) hath twice as many dry skins, like sluces, to damme vp the course of the teares, as it hath moist humors, like chanels, to let them flow forth.[502]

Finally, Playfere can use scriptural similes euphuistically, but (like Hooker) with emotive power, as when speaking of the comforting love of Christ:

> As the cities of refuge, which saue the sinner: as the holes of the rock, which defend the doue; the shadow of the iuniper tree, which receiueth the wearied; as the doore of the Arke, which preserueth the world; as the lure of the soule, which calleth home the Shulamite: as the pot of Manna, which nourisheth the Israelite: as the well of Iacob, which refresheth the thirstie: as the poole of Bethesda, which healeth the sicke: as the arms of the shepheard, which gather his lambs: as the wings of the eagle, which beare vp her birds. So doe the hands and side of Christ comfort his friends.[503]

However, not all of these preachers confine themselves in their use of the tropes to heaped examples and euphuistic similes. Drant gives a striking and felicitous extended simile drawn from an imagined orchard scene, to illustrate the crazed pursuit of material goods by the worldly:

> I cannot not but compare, the great busines, dealynges and struglynges in this world, vnto a company of all kynde of

---

[501] Ibid. pp. 24–5.   [502] Ibid. ' The Meane in Mourning,' pp. 5–6.
[503] Ibid. ' Christs wounds our health,' p, 109: see Gen. xix. 20–2; Jer. xlviii. 28; 1 Kings xix. 4–5; Gen. vii–viii; Can. vi. 13; Exod. xvi. 15, 33, 35; John iv. 6–14; John v. 2; John. x. 14; Exod. xix. 4.

people, watchynge about an apple tree, leapyng and snatching about it for apples. Wheresoeuer apples fall, there they snatch and there they are . . . oftentimes, they beate the tree to much, to soone, and to many wayes. Neither care they, whose the tree is, or whose the apples bee, or whence they droppe, so that they may ouertake them. For the apples of the mouth, young and foolish boyes will aduenture all hazardes for the apples of the eyes, and the apples of the purse, this whole foolishe age of ours is most aduenturous.[504]

Then again, Carpenter gives brief vigorous similes from country life in the manner of Henry Smith's homely similes:[505]

This is the subtilitie of Satan: first to pull out faith from mans heart, which being once gone, he knoweth that man is neither able to resist him, nor to quench his fierie dartes. He doth therein as the Rauen, which first pickes out the sheepes eyes, and after-ward deuoureth his bodie. . . .[506]

Playfere too occasionally uses longer similes, as when he draws upon the pranks of those who dress up as ghosts to illustrate that death is less terrible than it seems:

Those which will needes play the hobgoblins, or the night-walking spirits (as we call them) all the while they speak vnder a hollow vault, or leape forth with vgly vizard vpon their faces, they are so terrible, that he which thinks himselfe no small man, may perhaps bee affrighted with them: But if some lusty fellow chance to steppe into one of these, and cudgell him wel-fauouredly, and pull the vizard from his face, then euery boy laughes him to scorne. So is it in this matter. Death was a terrible bulbeggar, and made euery man afraide of him a great while; but Christ dying, buckled with this bulbegger, and coniured him (as I may say) out of his hollow vault, when as the dead comming out of the graues, were seene in *Ierusalem*, and puld the vizard from his face, when as he himself rising, left the linnen clothes which were the vizard of death behind him.[507]

He also at times employs homely similes, as the following from the ways of children (although indeed a comment of St. Gregory suggests it):

You see little children what paines they take to rake and scrape snowe together to make a snowe-ball: right so, they that scrape together the treasure of this world, haue but a snowe-ball

---

[504] *Three godly and learned Sermons*, sig. Mviii[r].
[505] See *ante*, pp. 184–7.
[506] *Remember Lots wife*, sig. Fvi[r].
[507] *The whole Sermons*, ' The Meane in Mourning,' pp. 27–8.

of it; as soone as the sun shineth, and God breatheth vpon it, and so entreth into it, by and by it comes to nothing.[508]

Like Longland, Playfere draws a homely simile from the cleansing of vessels to illustrate the topic of penitence:

> For euen as a vessel that hath bin tainted with poison or some infectious liquor, will not be cleane with once washing, but must often be scaled, & thoroughly washed, before it will be sweet, so hauing heretofore possessed my vessell in impuritie though I nowe wash me with niter, and take mee much Isope, yet mine own vncleannes is still marked before thee, onely thou O lord canst wash me throughlie.[509]

On another occasion Playfere follows a simile from the dyeing of cloth by a typical schematic sentence:

> For as they which die cloth, doe not immediately change one contrary into another, but first turn a white into an azure, and then make a puke of it: so we can neuer hold colour, as a good puke, except first our white be turned into an azure: that is as Syrinensis saith, except first we do well to *forget*, that which we did ill to get, except first we do happily vnlearne, that which wee did vnhappily learne.[510]

Then again, Playfere gives frequent historical narrations, particularly from British history; as that from Holinshed of ' the bodie of Cadwallo an auncient king of the Brittaines ', which ' being embalmed and dressed with sweete confections was put into a brazen image, and set vpon a brasen horse ouer Ludgate, for a terrour to the Saxons ';[511] or that from Stowe of King Arthur's body, which when exhumed more than six hundred years after his death, ' was knowne to be his by nothing so much, as by the prints of tenne seuerall woundes which appeared in his skull '.[512] He refers to Canute vainly ordering the tide to halt,[513] and to the motto of the city of Waterford, *Intacta manet*, given because ' since it was first conquered by King Henry the second, it was neuer yet attainted, no not so much as touched with treason '.[514] Then from Continental history, comes the story culled from Zieglerus, of a noble Bohemian, who at the siege of Belgrade, saved the city by seizing round the

---

[508] Ibid. ' Glorie waighes downe the Crosse,' p. 45. Just before the words quoted Playfere refers to St. Gregory: 'For as S. Gregorie vpon those words of Iob; who entreth into the treasures of snowe; sheweth that earthly treasures are treasures of snow.'

[509] Ibid. ' The sicke-mans Couch,' p. 17; for Longland's use of this figure, see *ante*, p. 139.

[510] Ibid. ' The Meane in Mourning,' p. 139.

[511] Ibid. ' Christs wounds our health,' p. 92.

[512] Ibid. p. 75.

[513] Ibid. ' The felicitie of the faithfull,' p. 199.

[514] Ibid. ' The Meane in Mourning,' p. 55.

waist a Turkish captain who had got upon the walls, and crashing to death with him.[515]

Playfere also makes very frequent use of patristic citation; in one sermon alone he refers to Theophylact,[516] St. Jerome,[517] Alcuin,[518] St. Augustine,[519] St. Clement,[520] St. Prosper,[521] Synesius,[522] St. Gregory,[523] Fulgosus,[524] Fulgentius,[525] St. John Damascene,[526] Arnobius,[527] St. Bernard,[528] Cassianus,[529] Lactantius,[530] St. Ignatius,[531] Prudentius,[532] St. Anselm,[533] St. Irenaeus,[534] Epiphanius,[535] and Optatus.[536]

Although, because of his celebrated Senecan brevity and point, together with his occasional colloquialisms, Andrewes does not belong in every respect with the fully ornate preachers, nevertheless he is most fittingly considered with them because of his unusually conscious and elaborate verbal art. The main characteristics of his style, apart from those just mentioned, are well known—the frequent neat handling of the schemata, the metaphysical wit, the intellectual use of paronomasia, the sensitive re-creations of the Christmas and Easter scenes, the liberal use of patristic citation[537]—and it would not be profitable to re-examine them here. However one notable feature has, so far as I know, hitherto passed unremarked, and this is the frequent masterly use of emotive figures. Sometimes (like Hooker) Andrewes draws these from Scripture, as in the following beautiful and cogent passage on the fall of Lot's wife (Gen. xix. 26), the first distressing aspect of which is that ' she *fell*, after she had stood *long* ':

> Touching the first. These *winter brookes* (as Iob termeth flitting desultorie Christians) if they *drie*; these *Summer* fruits (as AMOS) if they *putrifie*; these *morning clouds* (as HOSEA) if they scatter; these *Shallow rooted corne, if they wither* and come to nothing, it is the lesse griefe. No man looked for other. PHARAO with his *fits*, that at euery plague sent upon him, is godly on a sudden, and O *pray for mee now*; and when it is gone, as prophane as ever hee was; beginning nine times, and nine times breaking off againe; hee moves not much. To goe

[515] Ibid. p. 34. [516] Ibid. ' The Meane in Mourning,' p. 2. [517] Ibid. p. 9.
[518] Ibid. p. 11. [519] Ibid. p. 12. [520] Ibid. p. 13. [521] Ibid. p. 16.
[522] Ibid. [523] Ibid. p. 22. [524] Ibid. p. 25. [525] Ibid. [526] Ibid. p. 37.
[527] Ibid. p. 51. [528] Ibid. p. 54. [529] Ibid. [530] Ibid. p. 56.
[531] Ibid. p. 83. [532] Ibid. p. 88. [533] Ibid. p. 91.
[534] Ibid. p.105. [535] Ibid. [536] Ibid. p. 106.
[537] See Krapp, *The Rise of English Literary Prose,* pp. 109–207; Herr, *The Elizabethan Sermon,* pp. 103–5; Mitchell, *English Pulpit Oratory from Andrewes to Tillotson,* pp. 149–63; T. S. Eliot, *For Lancelot Andrewes,* pp. 13–22; G. Williamson, *The Senecan Amble: a study in prose from Bacon to Collier* (London, 1951) pp. 231–2: 237–41; D. Bush *English Literature in the Earlier Seventeenth Century* 1600–1660, pp. 300–2.

further: *Saul* that for *two* yeares; Iudas that for three; Nero, that for five kept well, and then fell away, though it be much, yet may it be borne. But, this woman had continued now thirtie yeare (for, so they reckon from ABRAHAMS going out of *Vr*, to the destruction of *Sodome*): This, this is the griefe, that she should *persist* all this time, and after all this time fall away. The rather, if wee consider further, that not only shee *continued* many yeares, but *sustained many things* in her continuance, as being companion of *Abraham* and *Lot*, in their exile, their travell and all their affliction. This is the grief, that after all these stormes in the broad *Sea* well she should in this pitiful manner, be wracked in the *hauen*. And when shee had been in *Aegypt*, and not poisoned with the superstitions of *Aegypt*: when lived in *Sodome*, and not defiled with the *sinnes* of *Sodome*: Not fallen away for the *famine* of *Canaan*, nor taken harme by the *fulnesse* of the *Citie of the Plaine*; and after all his she should lose the fruit of all this, and doe and suffer so many things all in vaine: this is the first: *Remember* it.[538]

The sparkling flow of Andrews's figures when they range further afield than Scripture is as 'witty' as the flashing brilliance of the verbal conceits; in the following passage from a Whitsunday sermon on the ' oil ' of the Holy Spirit, which is so necessary to the preacher, each figure throws a fresh ray of light on the theme:

No no: the *Spirit makes* none of these drie *missions*; sends none of these same *inuncti*, such as have never a feather of the *Doves* wing, not any sparke of the fire of this day, not so much as a drop of this *ointment*. You will *smell them* straight, that have it; the *Myrrhe, Aloes, and Cassia will make you glad*. And you shall even as soone finde the others. Either they want *odor*: *Annointed*, I cannot say, but besmeered with some *unctuous stuffe* (goe to, be it oyle): that gives a *glibnesse* to the *tongue* to talke much and long, but no more *sent* in it, than in a drie sticke; no *odors* in it at all. Either *odors* they want (I say) or, their *odors* are not layd in *oile*. For if in *oile*; you shall not smell them so for a few set

---

[538] *XCVI Sermons*, pp. 303–4: cf. Job. vi. 15; Amos viii. 1–2; Hosea vi. 4; Matt. xiii. 20; Exod. viii. 8. See too this succession of scriptural figures on death as a ' fall ': ' This then we know first; That *death* is not a *fall* like that of *Pharao*, into the Sea, that *sunke downe* like a lumpe of leade into the *bottome*, and never came up more: but a fall like that of *Ionas*, into the *Sea*, who was received by a *Fish*, and after *cast up againe*. It is our SAVIOUR CHRISTS owne *similie*. A fall, not like that of the *Angels*, into the *bottomlesse pit*, there to stay for ever: but like to that of men into their *beds*, when they make accompt to *stand up* againe. A *fall*, not as a *logge* or *stone*, to the *ground*, which where it falleth, there it lyeth still; but as of a *Wheate-corne*, *into* the *ground*, which is *quickened* and *springeth up againe.*' (Ibid. p. 386: cf. Exod. xv. 10; Jonah i. 17, ii. 10; Matt. xii. 40, xxv. 41; Isa. xxvi. 19; 1 Cor. xv. 36.) See further ibid. p. 499: 'And, such is the *Water of our regeneration*) not from the *brooks of Teman* (in Job vi.) that *in Summer*, will be drie; but the water of *Iordan*, a running river.' (Cf. Job vi. 15–20; Matt. iii. 13.)

sermons; if they be *annointed*, not *perfumed* or *washed* (for, such *Divines* we have). If it be but some *sweet water*, out of a *casting-bottle*, the *sent* will away soone; *water colors* or *water odors* will not last. But, if layd in *oile* throughly, they will: feare them not. To them that are *stuffed* (I know) all is one: they that have their senses about them, will soone put a difference.[539]

The final homely metaphor from the common cold gives to the clinching point an admirable force. Then again the old figure of the Divine Physician is lent a new power by a typical ' witty ' touch: ' the Physitian slaine; and, of His flesh and bloud, a receipt made, that the patient might recover!'[540]

However, Andrews's most deeply felt figures are drawn from the renewal of the life of the earth in the Spring. Just as the holy mind of Fisher delights in the nurturing power of the sun and in the growing plants,[541] so the devout spirit of Andrewes responds with a delicate joy and wonder to the yearly miracle of the springing shoots and opening flowers, which he sees as a symbol of Christ's resurrection and of man's spiritual regeneration:

> . . . There goeth from *His resurrection* an *influence*, which shall have an operation like that of the *dew* of the spring; which when He will let fall, *the earth shall yeeld her dead*, as at the falling of the *dew*, the *herbes* now rise and shoot forthe againe. Which terme therefore of *regenerating* was well chosen, as fitting well,with His *rising*, and the time of it. The *time* (I say) of the *yeare*, of the *weeke*, and (if he will) of the *day* too. For, He *rose* in the *dawning*: then is the *day regenerate*: and *in prima sabbati*, that, the *first begetting of* the *Weeke*: And, in the *spring*, when all that were winter-sterved, withered, and dead, are *regenerate* againe and *rise* up anew.[542]

It is, alas, true that the glory of flowers and men fades and dies: ' Straight, of it selfe, doth the Rose *marcere*, and the Violet *livere*, wax pale and wan. Their best, their flourishing estate they hold not long; neither the *flowers*, that are *worne*, nor they, that weare them neither: they, nor we: but decay we doe (GOD wot) in a short time.'[543] Yet the transient freshness of Spring is eternal in Heaven: ' Now, nothing *fades*; but all springs fresh and greene. At this time, here; but, at all times there: A perpetuall spring; no other Season, there, but that.'[544] Christ the Gardener not only brings forth the flowers of grace in this life in the garden of our souls, but ' shall garden our bodies too: turne all our graves into garden-plots: Yea, shall one

[539] Ibid. p. 703.   [540] Ibid. p. 59.   [541] See *ante*, pp. 131–2.
[542] *XCVI Sermons*, p. 500.   [543] Ibid. p. 501.   [544] Ibid. p. 502.

day turne lande and sea and all into a great garden, and so husband them, as they shall in due time bring forth live bodies, even all our bodies alive againe.'[545] Once also Andrewes, with a sensitiveness akin to that of Fisher, draws on the power of the sun to scatter clouds and mist, to provide a figure for the sudden bringing of comfort and joy to the weeping Magdalene on Easter morning:

> A cloud may be so thicke, we shall not see the Sunne thorow it: this one word these two syllables [*Mary*] from His mouth, scatters it, all. No sooner had His voice sounded in her ears, but it drives away all the mist, dries up her teares, lightens her eyes, that she knew Him straight, and answers Him with her wonted salutation, *Rabboni*.[546]

The spiritual depth of this passage is of course its most notable quality, and in the last analysis the greatest sermon stylists are not those who seek first for artistic effects, but those to whom the message is of the utmost urgency, and who yet do not disdain to use the devices of style to allow this message to make its most effective appeal.

[545] Ibid. p. 539. Mitchell (*English Pulpit Oratory from Andrewes to Tillotson*, p. 155) has noticed Andrewes's fondness for figures drawn from conduit pipes. Once he combines this favourite illustration with a figure from gardens to produce a singularly beautiful *exemplum* for the conveying of grace to the faithful, even through unworthy priests: '. . . they that by the *Word*, the *Sacraments*, the *Keyes*, are unto others the *conduits* of *grace*, to make them fructifie in all good workes; may well so be, though themselves remanie unfruitfull as doe the pipes of *wood* or *lead*, that transmitting the water, make the garden to beare both herbes and flowers, though themselves never beare any.' (*XCVI Sermons*, p. 696.)

[546] Ibid. p. 541.

CHAPTER IV

THE USE OF CLASSICAL ALLUSION

THE practice of referring in sermons to classical literature and history was already time honoured at the outset of the period we are examining. St. Augustine had admitted the use of pagan writers in Christian instruction,[1] and in the Middle Ages it was common for the sacred orator to ' enrich the Hebrews with the spoils of the Egyptians ',[2] by using moralized classical narrations and apt *dicta* of the ancients[3]—drawn not from first hand reading of the classical authors, but from various sermon hand-books,[4] and through such *media* as Solinus, Orosius, St. Isidore, and Rabanus Maurus.[5] The classical *exempla* used by the medieval preachers show however little appreciation of the true spirit of the ancient writers,[6] and they are employed in quite the same simply illustrative manner, and often in conjunction with *exempla* from later history, Scripture and the Fathers. As the late fifteenth and sixteenth centuries witnessed the rise of humanism in England, it is interesting to examine the use which the preachers of this period make of the classical material at their disposal, and to see if they show any greater appreciation of the pagan writers than do the medieval preachers.

[1] *De Doctrina Christiana*, lib. II, cap. xi, *P.L.*, xxxiv. 63.
[2] Ibid. quoted by Bromyard in the Prologue to the *Summa Predicantium*; (*Summa Praedicantium . . . Auctore Ioanne Bromiardo*, Antwerp. 1614, p. 2). Just before this the learned Dominican alleges a remark of Peter of Blois on the same subject: ' Nunquam (inquit) frater in verbis vim faciam, de qua facultate sumantur, dummodo aedificant ad salutem. Nam nec de herbis quaeritur, in qua terra, vel cuius hortulani cura vel cultura adoleuerint, dummodo vim habeant sanatiuam.' [' Never, brother', he said, ' do I make ado about words, from which source they come, provided they tend to salvation. For neither do we ask from what ground herbs come, or from which gardener's care or tending, provided they have a healing virtue.']
[3] See the examples of classical allusion from the sermons of Fitzralph, Rypon, Waldeby, Mirk and various anonymous preachers, given by Owst, *L. & P.M.E.*, pp. 181–8.
[4] Apart from the well-known *Gesta Romanorum*, there is the *Book of Moralizations of the Metamorphoses of Ovid* produced by an anonymous Franciscan author; Holcot's *Moralitates*, as well as his *Liber Sapientie Salomonis* abound in classical *exempla*; Bromyard too has many references to the classics, as has the *Speculum Laicorum* (Owst, *L. & P.M.E.*, pp. 180–2). Further, in addition to these authorities, there are the collections of *Flores Doctorum* or ' Proverbys of Phylospherys' where the sayings of the ancients are conveniently arranged in the same manner as the sayings of the Fathers in the *Flores Patrum*. (Ibid. p. 183; typical manuscript examples of these are detailed in notes 4, 5 and 6.)
[5] See Owst, *L & P.M.E.*, p. 182.
[6] This appreciation of the classical spirit is the hall mark of true humanism—see R. R. Bolgar, *The Classical Heritage and its Beneficiaries* (Cambridge, 1954), pp. 265–8.

P

I

THE PRE-REFORMATION CATHOLIC PREACHERS, INCLUDING THE CONSERVATIVE HENRICIANS (1450–1547)

The unlearned preachers of this time make little use of classical allusion, and that little is thoroughly medieval in manner. For example, in an Ash Wednesday sermon in the late fifteenth century revision of Mirk's *Festial* contained in MS. Harleian 2247, the narration is found (from the *Gesta Romanorum*) of how Socrates marries the king's daughter on condition that he will not outlive his wife; and how, when she is sick unto death, the philosopher goes into the forest and gathers medicinal herbs with which he heals her malady and so saves his own life. The king is God, the king's daughter man's soul, and Socrates mankind; the forest is the Church and the healing herbs Confession—so necessary at the beginning of Lent.[7] Similarly, in a sermon for Passion Sunday the homilist of MSS. Lincoln Cathedral Library 50 and 51 relates the story (also from the *Gesta Romanorum*) of the brazen head at Rome made by Virgil which reports the evil doings of the citizens. A young man declares that he will break it if it tells about his misdeeds; so people repine against the preachers of painful home-truths.[8] In this same collection, in the sermon for Trinity XII, to illustrate the blindness of the sinner who does not recognise his sin, the homilist quotes a *dictum* of Seneca: ' Initium salutis cognicio est peccati '. (' The knowledge of sin is the beginning of salvation.')[9]

On the other hand, the learned preachers make considerable use of classical allusion, but again in the medieval manner. Fitzjames refers to the suicide of Cato Uticensis as an example of sinful pride, but his source is St. Augustine's *De Civitate Dei*.[10] Stephen Baron liberally mixes citations from classical authors with others from Scripture and the Fathers; as when expatiating on the preciousness and transience of time, he quotes in conjunction with St. Paul, Job, Lamentations, Wisdom, St. Jerome and St. Bernard, the sayings from Seneca's *Epistles*, ' Omnia mi Lucille [sic] aliena sunt, tempus

---

[7] MS. Harl. 2247, f. 52ʳ; cf. *The Early English Versions of the Gesta Romanorum*, ed. S. J. H. Herrtage (London, 1879), E.E.T.S. e.s. xxxiii, pp. 436–8.

[8] MS. Lincoln Cath. Libr. 50, ff. 128ᵛ–9ᵛ; cf. *The Early English Versions of the Gesta Romanorum*, pp. 27–34.

[9] MS. Linc. Cath. Libr. 51, f. 6ᵛ; cf. Seneca, *Epistulae Morales*, XXVIII. 9 (ed. and tr. R. M. Gummere, 3 vols., London, 1917–25, Loeb, vol. I, pp. 202–3.)

[10] *Sermo die lune in ebdomada Pasche*, sig. Giiiʳ; cf. St. Augustine, *De Civitate Dei*, lib. I, cap. xxiii, *P.L.*, xli. 36–7.

tantum nostrum est ', (' Nothing Lucilius, is ours, except time ')[11] and ' Quotidie morimur, quotidie demitur aliqua pars vite: & tunc quoque cum crescimus, vita decrescit '. (' Every day a little of our life is taken from us; even when we are growing, our life is on the wane '.)[12] In the same passage also, the learned Franciscan gives snatches of Ovid, ludicrously torn from their context: ' Labitur occulte fallitque volatilis etas ', (' Time glides by imperceptibly and cheats us in its flight, and nothing is swifter than the years ') a line from the *Metamorphoses*,[13] which refers to the swift passage of time between the birth of Adonis and his growing to manhood; and ' Nec que preterijt hora redire potest ', (' The hour that is gone by cannot return ') a line from the *Ars Amatoria*,[14] which occurs in a passage advising women to have sport when young, before old age removes their beauty and their lovers.

Longland's classical allusions are similar in kind to those of Baron. Snatches of Juvenal, Horace and Virgil are used merely in illustration of a point which the preacher is making. To illustrate the difference between appearance and reality in the moral sphere, the bishop quotes ' Curios simulant, Bacchanalia vivunt ' (' They ape the Curii and live like Bacchanals ') from Juvenal;[15] against anything inordinate he cites Horae:

est modus in rebus, sunt certi denique fines,

quos ultraque nequit consistere rectum.

(' There is measure in all things. There are, in short, fixed bounds, beyond and short of which right can find no place ');[16] the passage on the ' ages of man ' in the *Ars Poetica* is expanded in a tirade on the vanity and sinfulness of human life;[17] while to provide an illustration of how easy it is to merit hell, from which there is no escape, Virgil's *Aeneid* is laid under contribution:

facilis descensus Averno:

noctes atque dies patet atri ianua Ditis;

sed revocare gradum superasque evadere ad aures

hoc opus, hic labor est.

[11] *Sermones*, f. 3ʳ: see *Epist. Moral.*, I. 3 (Loeb edn., vol. I, pp. 4–5); quoted by Thomas Hibernicus, *Flores omnium fere Doctorum* (Venice, 1550) f. 511ʳ.

[12] *Sermones*, f. 3ᵛ: see *Epist. Moral.*, XXIV. 20 (Loeb edn., vol. I, pp. 176–7); quoted by Thomas Hibernicus, *Flores Doctorum*, f. 336ᵛ.

[13] *Sermones*, f. 3ᵛ: see Ovid, *Metamorphoses*, X. 520 (ed. and tr. F. J. Miller, 2 vols., London, 1916, Loeb, vol. II, pp. 100–1).

[14] *Sermones*, f. 4ᵛ: see *Ars Amatoria*, III. 64 (Ovid, *The Art of Love and other Poems*, ed. and tr. J. H. Mozley, London, revised 1929, Loeb, pp. 122–3).

[15] *Quinque Sermones*, f. 93ʳ: see Juvenal, *Sat.*, II. 3 (*Juvenal and Persius*, ed. and tr. G. G. Ramsay, London, revised 1940, Loeb, pp. 16–17).

[16] *Quinque Sermones*, f. 103ᵛ: see Horace, *Sat.*, I. i. 106–7 (*Horace, Satires, Epistles and Ars Poetica*, ed. and tr. H. R. Fairclough, London, 1926, Loeb, pp. 12–13).

[17] *Sermones*, ff. 393ʳ⁻ᵛ; see *Ars Poetica*, II. 153–78 (Loeb edn., pp. 462–4).

(' Easy is the descent to Avernus: night and day the door of gloomy
Dis stands open; but to recall thy steps and pass out to the upper
air, this is the task, this the toil! ')[18] Then again, the sentiment of
' the Philosopher ' (Aristotle) that he who prefers to live alone must
be ' either a beast or a god ' is quoted to show how angelic a life is
that led by solitaries;[19] while a sentence from the *Nicomachean
Ethics*, ' the most terrible thing of all is death ', is alleged to bring
home to the audience how fearful is the ' first death ', (that of the
body), although the ' second death ', (that of the soul), is far more
terrible than the pagan sage could realize.[20] Yet, further, the story of
the minotaur in the labyrinth is used merely as an illustration of the
hopeless entanglement of the guilty conscience.[21]

  Occasionally too Longland borrows from the *Adagia* of Erasmus,
that very popular sixteenth century source book for classical proverbs,
but the use which he makes of it is similar to that which the medieval
preachers made of the contents of the sermon handbooks current in
their day. Thus he quotes *bis pueri senes* in a passage on the sadness
of old age, with the sour addition that old men are however unlike
children in that they nurse grudges.[22] Equally medieval is the
bishop's use of the *dictum* of Simonides that the more he thought
about God, the less he could understand about Him, which is
employed to point the contrast between empty Gentile theorizing,
and the fulness of Catholic truth on the nature of the Deity.[23] On
several occasions indeed, Longland exults in the superiority of the
Faith over the wisdom of the ancients; the dead virtues of the sages
are as nothing compared with the supernatural virtues of the
Christian;[24] the mistaken ideas of Juvenal and Sallust on Fortune,
and the imperfect notions of the Stoics on Providence, are as foolish-
ness compared with the revealed certainty of Divine Providence;[25]
while puny indeed is the prowess of the pagan conquerors of cities—
Alexander, Hercules, Jason, Pompey or Mark Anthony—compared
with that of the Christian who conquers his own soul!26

 [18] *Sermones*, f. 128[r]: see Virgil, *Aeneid*, VI. 126–9 (*Virgil*, ed. and tr. H. R. Fairclough,
2 vols., London, revised 1933–4, Loeb, pp. 514–15).
 [19] *Quinque Sermones*, f. 69[v]: see Aristotle, *Politics*, I. i. 12 (1253a) (ed. and tr. H.
Rackham, London, 1932, Loeb, pp. 12–13).
 [20] *Quinque Sermones*, f. 58[v]: see Aristotle, *The Nicomachean Ethics*, III. vi. 6 (ed. and
tr. H. Rackham, London, new edn., 1934, Loeb, pp. 154–5).
 [21] *Quinque Sermones*, f. 81[r].
 [22] *Sermones*, f. 704[r]: the passage quoted *post*, pp. 234–5.
 [23] *Tres Conciones*, f. 19[r]: see Cicero, *De Natura Deorum*, I. xxii. 60 (*Cicero, De Natura
Deorum, Academica*, ed. and tr. H. Rackham, London, 1933, Loeb, p. 58).
 [24] *Quinque Sermones*, f. 70[v].
 [25] *Sermones*, ff. 353[r]–9[r]: cf. ibid. f. 736[r]–Aristotle knew the First Cause, but he
understood less about it than the simplest Christian. [26] *Sermones*, f. 588[r].

Fisher's sermons also are studded with classical allusions, which he uses precisely in the same way as does Longland. He makes a little more reference to Greek authors, but he shows no true appreciation of the Greek spirit. Thus from Plato's ' Georgicke '(Gorgias) the bishop quotes the reply of Socrates to Polus, (who had asked the sage whether Archelaus, king of Macedonia, were happy or not): ' If thou wylte . . . that I tell the whether this man be blyssed or wretched, shewe me his soule, & anone I shall assoyle thy questyon, for the demonstracyon of this mater dependeth of the soule.'[27] However he immediately turns to Scripture to apply this saying: ' Truly a soule subiecte to synne is wretched which our prophete Dauyd wytnesseth sayenge *Miser factus sum*.'[28] Similarly, the habit of the Pythagoreans—every morning ' to here the sounde of an harpe, wherby theyr spyrytes myght be more quyke & redy to receyue theyr studyes, thynkynge no thynge more profytable than it vnto the free & noble excytynge of theyr myndes '—is used merely to introduce an exhortation to Christians to ' turne agayne vnto these swete melodyes of our prophete Dauyd whiche somtyme he sange with his godly harpe, wherby we may chase & put away all sluggysshenes & slouth put in to vs by wycked spyrytes '.[29] Then again, Fisher quotes, from Aulus Gellius or perhaps from the *Prouerbiorum libellus* of Polydore Vergil, a saying of Demosthenes, which he follows immediately with a part of the psalm he is expounding:

A certayne phyolsophre called Domesthenes what tyme he desyred to haue the presence & company of a certayne euyll dysposed woman, & she asked a grete somme of money. He answered that his lernynge was not to bye penaunce so dere. Sygnefyenge that after the fylthy volupty of the flesshe no thynge remayneth but sorowe & penaunce, for the whiche he wolde not gyue so moche money. Our prophete consyderynge this addeth sayenge. *Tota die contristatus ingrediebar*.[30]

To illustrate the power of the living voice to move the hearer, and thus to show how God hears the prayer of the truly penitent, the bishop recounts a story about Aeschines and Demosthenes which he found in St. Jerome:

Thyn holy doctour saynt Iherome sayth thus. The effecte of the worde spoken by a mannes owne mouth hath a meruaylous

---

[27] *English Works*, Pt. I, p. 62: see *Gorgias*, 470D, E (*Plato, Lysis, Symposium, Gorgias*, ed. and tr. W. R. M. Lamb, London, revised 1932, Loeb, pp. 338–40).
[28] *English Works*, Pt. I, p. 62.   [29] Ibid. p. 70.
[30] Ibid., p. 63: see Aulus Gellius, *Noctes Atticae*, I. viii (*The Attic Nights of Aulus Gellius*, ed. and tr. J. C. Rolfe, 3 vols., London, 1927–8, Loeb, vol. I, pp. 42–4); also Polydore Vergil, *Prouerbiorum libellus* (Venice, 1498) sig. bvii^v–bviii^r.

preuy and hyd effycacy or strength, so meruaylous that I can not
tell what it sholde be called, whiche he proued by the wordes of
Eschynes a certayn oratour that was exyled and caused to flee
vnto the rodes by his aduersary called Domesthenes [sic] an
oratour also, & there redde an oracion, vnto his scollers made
by the sayd Domesthenes his aduersary, they also praysynge the
same oracyon gretely by his redynge, he toke vp a grete
syghynge & sayd, what yf ye had herde this my cruell enemy
Domesthenes spoken these wordes hymselfe, as who sayth, a
mannes entent or mynde spoken by his owne mouth moueth
more the herer than it were shewed & spoken by ony other.[31]

Fisher's use of the Latin moralists and poets is quite similar; he
quotes Cicero on a favourite late medieval theme, the brevity of life:
' O fallacem hominum spem fragilemque et inanes nostras conten-
tiones que medio in spacio sepe franguntur et corrunt ';[32] ('Ah, how
treacherous are men's hopes, how insecure their fortunes! How
hollow are our endeavours, which often break down & come to
grief in the middle of the race ') while from Seneca ' in his epystles '
he quotes ' Bonam vite clausulum impone ', (' Only see to it that the
closing period is well turned ') as a prelude to Ezekiel's *iusticia iusti
non liberabit eum in quacunque die peccauerit & impietas impij non nocebit
ei in quacunque die conuersus fuerit ab impietate sua*: (Ezek. xxxiii. 12;
' The justice of the just shall not deliver him, in what day soever he
shall sin: and the wickedness of the wicked shall not hurt him, in
what day soever he shall turn from his wickedness ', Douay) which
the bishop expounds as indicating the dread power of one unrepented
mortal sin to effect the damnation of a man hitherto righteous, and
the validity to secure salvation of the death-bed repentance of a
hitherto abandoned sinner.[33] Similarly to illustrate how forgiveness
is the proof of a noble mind (and therefore that God, who is the
Supreme Nobility, never refuses forgiveness to the penitent sinner),
Fisher quotes Ovid's *Tristia*:

corpora magnanimo satis est prostrasse leone,
    pugna suum finem, cum iactet hostis, habet:
at lupus et turpes instant morientibus ursi
    et quaecumque minor nobilitate fera.

('For the noble lion 'tis enough to have overthrown his enemy;
the fight is at an end when his foe is fallen. But the wolf, the

---

[31] *English Works*, Pt. I, p. 140.
[32] Ibid. p. 285: see Cicero, *De Oratore*, III. ii. 7 (ed. and tr. E. W. Sutton, completed
H. Rackham, 2 vols., London, 1942, vol. II, pp. 6–7).
[33] *English Works*, Pt. I, p. 270: see *Epist. Moral.*, LXXVII. 20 (Loeb edn., vol. II,
pp. 180–1).

ignoble bears, harry the dying—and so with every beast of less nobility.')[34]

Again, an example of pagan sorrow at death is coupled with a scriptural instance, to show how all must mourn the death of Henry VII:

The cruell warryour Hanyball he pyteed the deth of his enemyes Paulus Emilius, Tiberius Graccus, Marcus Marcellus, whan he saw theyr bodyes lye deed before hym. And in holy letters also kynge Dauyd, whan it was tolde vnto hym the deth of his enemyes, at dyuerse tymes he wepte ryght pyteously as at the deth of Saul, Absolon and Abner. If they so grete & noble men soo moche pyteed the deth of theyr mortall enemyes, We sholde moche rather tender and pyte the deth of our kyng & souerayne.[35]

Edgeworth also makes occasional use of classical allusion, but again in the medieval manner. From the *Adagia* of Erasmus he borrows Terence's ' Sine cerere et baccho friget venus ', (*Eunuchus*, IV, v. 6; 'Without Ceres and Bacchus Venus is a-chill ') when declaiming against gluttony,[36] while to show how ' trouble teaches patience' he takes, from the *Apophthegmata*, the saying of Socrates (after Xantippe, who has been quarrelling with him, empties the contents of a chamber-pot over him through the window): ' Facile diuinabam, post tantum tonitra secuturam pluuiam.' ('I easily divined that after such thunder rain would follow.')[37] In a borrowing from Cicero's *De Officiis*, when dealing with modesty, Edgeworth shows lack of comprehension of the *mores* of the Greeks, for which he substitutes a reference to the habit of his own age in the staging of plays; [the praetors Pericles and Sophocles]:

... were on a time in counsel together about a cause concerninge theyr office, & by chaunce there came by them a wellfauoured & faire childe, then Sophocles in the middle of theyr matter said, *O puerum pulchrum Pericle*, O brother Pericles, lo yonder is a faire childe; the other answered him: *pretorem, Sophocle, decet non solum manus sed etiam oculos abstinentes habere*, It besemeth a Pretor not onelye to haue his handes abstaining from bribery, but also hys eyes from wanton concupiscence. If Sophocles had said those words in a time when men wer about to chuse men to do a feate, as is used with vs to play in an interlude, to play a

---

[34] *English Works*, Pt. I, p. 161: see Ovid, *Tristia ex Ponto*, III. v. 33–6 (ed. and tr. A. L. Wheeler, London, 1924, Loeb, pp. 122–3).
[35] *English Works*, Pt. I, p. 280.
[36] *Sermons*, f. 234ᵛ: see Erasmus, 'Adagia ', (*Opera Omnia*, II, 521F).
[37] *Sermons*, f. 204ᵛ: see Erasmus, 'Apophthegmata,' (*Opera Omnia*, IV. 161C). See too Richard Taverner, *The Garden of Wysdome* (London, 1539) Bk. I, sig. Bviiiʳ⁻ᵛ.

virgins part or a woers part, or suche like, when men vse to
chuse fayr and welfauored yong men for their purpose, the said
Sophocles shoulde a deserued none suche checke, but then in the
middle of an earnest matter to speake of such light facions or
fansies, because his sayinge was not well placed, he lacked
Modestie that we speake of nowe, and was to be blamed.[38]
Other references in Edgeworth are in the same medieval manner: the
saying of Aristotle, from the *Nicomachean Ethics*, that young men
are unfit to study moral philosophy is used to discourage the laity
from criticizing doctrine,[39] while the narration (from Valerius
Maximus) of Codrus the Athenian, who, in a war with Sparta
allowed himself to be killed, because the oracle had declared that
the Spartans would win only if he was not killed, is used to illustrate
piety for one's country.[40]

Chedsey quotes from the *Apophthegmata* of Erasmus, yet again
using his citations in the medieval manner. The saying of Anacharsis
on the laws: ' Laws be like to the cobweb that the spiders make,
they holde fast little fleas & such small beastes; but the greater
beestes break through them and be not letted '—is used in a complaint against illegal enclosures and greedy landlords,[41] while
Alexander's remark on a wound which he received—' Omnes iurant
me esse filium Iouis, sed vulnus hoc hominem me esse clamat ' ('All
swear that I am the son of Jupiter, but this wound declares me to be
a man ')—is used to expose the vanity of flattery.[42]

II

THE EARLY REFORMERS (1547–1553)

There is a moderate amount of classical allusion in the preaching
of the Reformers, but again it is medieval in kind. The *Adagia* and
the *Apophthegmata* of Erasmus once more prove themselves useful;
Latimer quotes a form of *bis pueri senes* when dealing with the
rebellion of Adonijah in King David's old age (1 Kings i). The
king:

[38] *Sermons*, f. 213ᵛ: see Cicero, *De Officiis*, I. xl. 144 (Loeb edn., pp. 146–7); also in
Erasmus, 'Apophthegmata,' (*Opera Omnia*, IV. 246E).
[39] *Sermons*, f. 299ʳ: see Aristotle, *The Nicomachean Ethics*, I. iii. 5 (Loeb edn., pp. 8–9).
[40] *Sermons*, f. 49ʳ: see Valerius Maximus, *Facta et Dicta Memorabilia*, V. vi. ext. 1 (ed.
C. Halm, Leipsig, 1865, p. 257); this narration is found too in the Latin *Gesta Romanorum*, ed. H. Oesterley (Berlin, 1872), p. 340.
[41] *Two notable sermones lately preached at Pauls crosse*, sig. Eii: see Erasmus, 'Apophthegmata,' (*Opera Omnia*, IV. 330F).
[42] *Two notable sermones lately preached at Pauls crosse*, sig. Divᵛ: see Erasmus, 'Apophthegmata,' (*Opera Omnia*, IV. 197F–8A).

... being in his childhood, an old man in his second childhood, (for all old men are twice children, as the proverb is, *Senes bis puer* ' an old man twice a child ',) it happened with him, as it doth oftentimes, when wicked men of a king's childhood take occasion of evil.[43]

To show how necessary it is for the young to be brought up to be godly, he quotes a saying from one of Horace's epistles, found in the *Adagia*:

quo semel est imbuta recens, servabit odorem testa diu.

(' The jar will long keep the fragrance of what it was once steeped in when new.')[44]

Similarly from Terence Hooper cites *Obsequium amicos, veritas odium parit*, (' It's complaisance that makes friends and truthfulness is the mother of unpopularity '), also found in the *Adagia*, after having indulged in some plain speaking about the ' Jonases ' who bring the ship of the commonwealth into peril.[45] Gilpin, in his denunciation of the greed of the rich quotes from the *Apophthegmata* the saying of the poor pirate to Alexander: ' We rob but a few in a ship, but thou robbest whole countries and kingdomes.'[46]

Classical references from other sources are used similarly by the Reformers; in a passage against the corruption of justice, Latimer cites, from Valerius Maximus, the story of the unjust judge whom Cambyses caused to be flayed alive and his skin laid on the chair of judgment as a warning to his successors.[47] In the ' Homily against Contention ' Latimer uses examples of pagan patience drawn from Plutarch, to shame Christians into neighbourly forbearance:

> Histories be full of examples of heathen men, that took very meekly both opprobious and reproachful words and injurious and wrongful deeds. And shall those heathen excel in patience us that profess Christ, the teacher and example of all patience? Lysander, when one did rage against him, in reviling of him, he was nothing moved; but said ' Go to, go to, speak against me as much and as oft as thou wilt, and leave out nothing; if perchance by this means thou mayst discharge thee of those

---

[43] *Sermons*, p. 113: see, in addition to 'Adagia ' (*Opera Omnia*, II. 195C), *Prouerbes or Adagies gathered out of the Chiliades of Erasmus by Richard Taverner* (London, 1545) f. 17r.

[44] *Sermons*, p. 431: see Erasmus, 'Adagia,' (*Opera Omnia*, II. 529F); Taverner, f. 37r; also Horace, *Epist.*, I. ii. 69–70 (Loeb edn., pp. 266–7).

[45] *Early Writings*, p. 468: see Erasmus, 'Adagia,' (*Opera Omnia*, II. 675A); Taverner, f. 47v.

[46] *A Godly Sermon preached in the Court of Greenwich*, p. 48: see Erasmus, 'Apophthegmata,' (*Opera Omnia*, IV. 200E). This saying is found too in the Latin *Gesta Romanorum*, p. 505.

[47] *Sermons*, p. 146: see Valerius Maximus, *Facta et Dicta Memorabilia*, VI. iii. ext. 3, pp. 292–3. Cf. further, Latimer, ibid. pp. 92, 287, for similar use of *dicta* from Horace and Terence respectively.

naughty things, with the which it seemeth thou art full laden.'
Many men speak evil of all men, because they can speak well of
no man. After this sort this wise man avoided from him the
reproachful words spoken to him, imputing and laying them to
the natural sickness of his adversary. Pericles, when a certain
scolder or railing fellow did revile him, he answered not a
word again, but went into a gallery; and after, toward night,
when he went home, this scolder followed him still raging more
and more, because he saw the other to set nothing by him; and
commanded one of his servants to light a torch, and to bring
the scolder home to his own house. He did not only with
quietness suffer this brawler patiently, but also recompensed a
evil turn with a good turn, and that to his enemy. Is it not a
shame for us that profess Christ, to be worse than a heathen
people, in a thing chiefly pertaining to Christ's religion?[48]
Similarly, in the 'Homily of Faith' Cranmer refers to Caesar's
Commentaries merely to illustrate the difference between a dead and
a lively faith:

> ... as he that readeth Caesar's Commentaries believing the same
> to be true, hath thereby a knowledge of Caesar's life and notable
> acts, because he believeth the history of Caesar, yet it is not
> properly said, that he believeth in Caesar, of whom he looketh
> for no help nor benefit: even so, he that believeth that all is
> spoken of God in the Bible is true, and yet liveth so ungodly
> that he cannot look to enjoy the promises and benefits of God;
> although it may be said that such a man hath a faith and belief
> to the words of God; yet it is not properly said that he believeth
> in God, or hath such a faith and trust in God, whereby he may
> surely look for grace, mercy and everlasting life at God's hand,
> but rather for indignation and punishment according to the
> merits of his wicked life.[49]

III

THE PREACHERS OF MARY'S REIGN (1553–1558)

There is very little classical allusion in the preachers of Mary's
reign. However one instance of its use is humanistic. Dr. Weston,
in his Ciceronian oration to the synod, refers (in a passage already
quoted) to the nervousness of Demosthenes, Theophrastus and

---

[48] *Certain Sermons Appointed by the Queen's Majesty*, pp. 142–3: see Plutarch, *Moralia*,
'Apophthegmata Laconica,' Lysander, 13 (229F) (ed. and tr. F. C. Babbit, etc., 14 vols.,
London, 1927–39, Loeb, vol. III, pp. 376–7); also Plutarch's *Lives*, 'Pericles', v. 2–3
(ed. and tr. B. Perrin, 11 vols., London, 1914–26, Loeb, vol. III, pp. 12–13).
[49] *Certain Sermons*, pp. 32–3.

Cicero in the delivery of their speeches, to allow him to introduce *his* rhetorical self-abnegation before the assembled clergy.[50] The manner of the passage is that of the Renaissance humanists, not that of the medieval preachers.

On the other hand, the other classical allusions of this reign are thoroughly medieval in manner. In the peroration to his Paul's Cross sermon at the beginning of the reign, Brooks recounts (from Livy) the story of the embassy of Quintus Fabius to expostulate with the Carthaginians, for the breach of a league. He gathered his gown in his lap, and in a brief speech declared that in his lap was peace or war: let the Carthaginians choose which they would have! When they laughed, he cast open his gown and gave them war. So Brooks declares that he brings benediction or malediction to the English (who have broken the league of Baptism into the Catholic Church), so let *them* choose which they will have![51] Glasier in his Paul's Cross sermon, quotes from Sallust, ' Concordia parue res crescunt, discordia, maxime res dilabuntur ', ('Harmony makes small states great, while discord undermines the mightiest empires ') and applies it to the recent schism in England.[52] Then again, Bishop White, when expounding *Melius est canis vivus, quam leo mortuus*, (Eccles. ix. 4; 'A living dog is better than a dead lion', Douay) quotes—to illustrate his conception of the lively dog as not only a ' vigilant minister in the church ' but also a ' provident governor ' in the State—Ausonius, ' Non auxi, non minui rem ' (' I neither increased nor lessened my estate ') which such a governor will be able to say when he dies; and as a description of his character, the sentence of Herodianus, ' Quum omnium plurimum, erat omnium pauperrimus.' (' Though he had been trusted with greater Commands than any of the rest, he was notwithstanding the poorest Officer in the Army.')[53]

[50] ' Oratio coram patribus et clero '; Strype, *Ecclesiastical Memorials*, III. 2, pp. 182–3. See *ante*, p. 161.

[51] *A Sermon very notable, fruiteful and Godlie*, sig. Iviii[r] et seq., see Livy, *History*, XXI. xviii. 12–14 (ed. and tr., B.O. Foster, F. G. Moore, E. T. Sage, etc., 14 vols., London, 1919–51, Loeb, vol. V, pp. 52–3).

[52] *A notable and very fruictefull sermon made at Paules crosse*, sig. Bii[v]. See Sallust, *Jugurtha*, X. 6 (*Sallust*, ed. and tr. J. C. Rolfe, London, 1921, Loeb, pp. 148–9).

[53] 'A sermon preached at the funerals of Queen Mary '; Strype, *Ecclesiastical Memorials*, III. 2, p. 545. See Ausonius, *Opuscula*, III. iv (ed. and tr. H. G. Evelyn White, 2 vols., London, 1919–21, Loeb, vol. I, pp. 44–5); Herodianus, *Historia*, II. iii (with a Latin tr. by Politian, Oxford, 1699, p. 48; *Herodian's History of His Own Times, or the Roman Empire after Marcus*, tr. J. Hart, London, 1749, p. 61).

IV

THE ELIZABETHAN PREACHERS (1558–1603)

It might be thought that the Elizabethan age would show in its sermons some true appreciation of classical literature and civilization. Very occasionally this is so. Tobias Bland avers that Scripture is better literature than the classics, but this does not seem to be merely the old exultation over the blind heathens; rather it is based, one feels, on a knowledge of the different qualities of both:

I dare saie, that Tullie himselfe is not more familiar in his Epistles, than the Apostles in theirs, neither were the Philosophers so stately in their Gymnacie, as were the Prophets in the gates of the Citie. Yea, I dare compare, & doe prefer the Psalms of Dauid, before the hymnes of Orpheus, and the one song of Salomons, before al the odes of Pindarus.[54]

Tyrer contrasts the earthly crowns of the pagans with the heavenly crown of the Christian, in a passage which depends on a true grasp of the contrasting world views:

But if we shall then receiue a crowne, what manner of crowne shall it be? For there is divers sorts of crownes: there is *Ciuica corona* a crowne made of Oaken bowes, which was giuen of the Romans to him that saued the life of any citizen in battel against his enemies. Secondly *Obsidionalis* which was of grasse giuen vnto him that deliuered a town or citie from siedge. Thirdly *Muralis* which was of gold, giuen vnto him that first scaled the wall of any towne or castle. Fourthly, *Castrensis*, which was likewise of golde, giuen vnto him that first entred the campe of the enemie. Fifthly, *Naualis*, and that also of gold, giuen vnto him that first by valour bourded the shippe of the enemy. Sixthly, *Oualis*, which was of Mirtle, which was giuen to those captaines that subdued any towne or Citie, or that woon any fielde easily without losse or shedding of bloud. Seuenthly and lastly *Triumphalis*, which was of Laurell giuen to that chiefe Generall or Consul, which after some notable victorie and conquest came home triumphing. But all these, or the most of them were rather garlands then crownes, yea the verie best of those that were of gold, rather coronets then crowns, and if crowns, rather crowns of honor then of glorie.

This crowne therefore that our chiefe shepheard shall giue . . . differeth from all other crownes in two respects. . . . As first, in that it is a crowne of glorie; and secondly, in that it is incorruptible.[55]

[54] *A baite for Momus*, p. 5.   [55] *Five godlie sermons*, p. 58.

It is interesting to note that the ' Homily against Peril of Idolatry ' uses classical allusion for polemical purposes. Following Bullinger (*De origine Erroris in Divorum et Sacrorum cultu*), Jewel equates the Catholic worship of the saints with the cults of the pagan divinities. The patron saints of countries are like the *Dii Tutelares*, those of cities like the *Dii Praesides*, those to whom temples and churches are built, and altars erected, are like the *Dii Patroni*.[56] Further:

> . . . where one saint hath images in diuers places, the same saint hath divers names thereof, most like to the Gentiles. When you heard of our lady of Walsingham, our lady of Ipswich, our lady of Wilsdon, and such other; what is it but an imitation of the Gentile idolaters? Diana, Agrotera, Diana Coryphea, Diana Ephesia, etc. Venus Cypria, Venus Paphia, Venus Gnidia. Whereby is evidently meant that the saint for the image sake should in those places, yea, in the images themselves, have a dwelling which is the ground of their idolatry.[57]

Again, under Catholicism:

> . . . the sea and waters have as well special saints with them, as they had gods with the Gentiles, Neptune, Triton, Nereus, Castor and Pollux, Venus, and such other; in whose places be come St. Christopher, St. Clement, and divers other, and specially our lady, to whom shipmen sing *Ave, maris stella*. Neither hath the fire scaped the idolatrous inventions. For, instead of Vulcan and Vesta, the gentiles' gods of the fire, our men have placed St. Agatha, and make letters on her day for to quench fire with.[58]

and furthermore:

> Every artificer and profession hath his special saint, as a peculiar god. As for example, scholars have St. Nicholas, and St. Gregory; painters, St. Luke; neither lack soldiers their Mars, nor lovers their Venus, amongst Christians. All diseases have their special saints, as gods, the curers of them; the pocks St. Roch, the falling evil St. Cornelius, the tooth-ache St. Apollin, etc. Neither do beasts and cattle lack their gods with us; for St. Loy is the horse-leech, and St. Anthony the swine-herd, etc.[59]

Similarly, saints regarded as intercessors are like the pagan *Dii Medioximi*, for: ' So did the Gentiles teach, that there was one chief

---

[56] *Certain Sermons appointed by the Queen's Majesty*, pp. 224–5. Erasmus too on several occasions points out the parallel between popular saint worship and the cult of the pagan gods: see ' Enchiridion Militis Christiani,' cap. viii. can. 4 (*Opera Omnia*, V, 26E–7A); Μωρίας 'Εγκώμιον (ibid. IV, 443D), ' Colloquiae Familiares,'—' Naufragrium' (ibid. I. 713A, B).
[57] *Certain Sermons appointed by the Queen's Majesty*, p. 225.
[58] Ibid. p. 226.   [59] Ibid.

power working by other, as means; and so they made all gods subject to fate or destiny; as Lucian in his Dialogues feigneth that Neptune made suit to Mercury, that he might speak with Jupiter.'[60]

However the vast majority of the Elizabethan preachers continue in the old medieval way merely to quote moral *dicta* and examples in illustration of their themes. The *Adagia* of Erasmus yet again proves popular; ' H.B. ' quotes *Homo bulla* in a passage on the vanity of life;[61] Thomas White, Vicar of St. Dunstan in the West, and later Canon of Christ Church and of Windsor, cites *Veritas odium parit* before exposing ' intollerable abuses ' to his audience at Paul's Cross,[62] while Tyrer (who *can* as we have seen exhibit on occasion some appreciation of classical values) uses *Tempus edax rerum* in a passage dealing with the transience of all glory except that of heaven,[63] and *Sero sapiunt Phryges* when pointing out that although it was disgraceful that the Jews were not wise in time, it is even worse for Christians to lose their chance of present salvation.[64] The *Apophthegmata* too is still useful, the saying of Anacharsis that the laws are like cobwebs,[65] occurs in Andrewes,[66] Humston[67] and Sandys,[68] while Playfere, dealing with the death and resurrection of Christ, quotes the saying of Epaminondas when he met his noble death, ' Nunc enim Epaminondas nascitur, quia sic moritur.' (' Now is Epaminondas born, because he dies thus.')[69]

Certain sermons of the ' Second Book of Homilies ' abound in moral sayings culled from various sources. That 'Against Gluttony and Drunkenness ' (probably by Pilkington, and mostly a translation of Peter Martyr's *Commentary on the Book of Judges*) quotes in translation three ' sentences ' from Seneca on the plight of the drunkard; ' Men overcome with drink are altogether mad ';[70] ' Drunkenness discovereth all wickedness, and bringeth it to light; it removeth all shamefacedness, and increaseth all mischief. The proud man, being drunken, uttereth his pride, the cruel man his cruelty, and the envious man his envy, so that no vice can lay hid in a drunkard ';[71]

---

[60] Ibid. p. 227.   [61] *A verie profitable sermon*, p. 18: the passage quoted *post*, p. 315.

[62] *A sermon Preached at Pawles Crosse on Sunday the thirde of November*, 1577, *in the time of the Plague* (London, 1578), p. 1.

[63] *Five godlie sermons*, p. 64.   [64] Ibid. pp. 71–2.   [65] Cf. *ante.*, p. 216.

[66] *XCVI Sermons*, ' Certaine Sermons Preached at Sundry Times, vpon severall occasions,' 'A Sermon Preached at St. Maries Hospital,' p. 1 (sig. Aaaaa3r).

[67] *A Sermon preached* 22 *Sept.*, 1588, f. 23r.   [68] *Sermons*, p. 85.

[69] *The Whole Sermons*, ' The Meane in Mourning,' p. 40: see Erasmus, 'Apophthegmata,' (*Opera Omnia*, IV. 253C).

[70] *Certain Sermons appointed by the Queen's Majesty*, p. 301: see Seneca, *Epist. Moral.*, LXXXIII. 16 (Loeb edn., vol. II, pp. 268–9).

[71] *Certain Sermons*, etc., p. 306: see *Epist. Moral.*, LXXXIII. 20 (Loeb edn., vol. II, pp. 270–1).

and 'If any man think that he may drink much wine, and yet be well in his wits, he may as well suppose that when he hath drunken poison, he shall not die'.[72] Plato also is alleged on this topic; 'Excessive drinking is most intollerable in a magistrate or a man of authority, for a drunkard knoweth not where he is himself.'[73] The intemperance of Alexander provides a notable *exemplum* of the vice being castigated:

> The great Alexander, after that he had conquered the whole world, was himself overcome by drunkenness, insomuch that being drunken, he slew his faithful friend, Clitus, whereof when he was sober he was so much shamed that for anguish of heart he wished death. Yet notwithtanding, after this he left not his banqueting; but in one night swilled in so much wine, that he fell into a fever; and when as by no means he would abstain from wine, within few days after in miserable sort he ended his life.[74]

In the same manner in the ' Homily against Excess of Apparel ' (also probably by Pilkington) the sentiments of the pagans are quoted to shame Christian women into the use of modest attire,[75] and in the ' Sermon of the State of Matrimony ' (partly from a homily by St. John Chrysostom, partly a translation of an address by Veit Dietrich, a Lutheran of Nuremberg) the patience of Socrates provides a notable instance of connubial forbearance.[76]

Yet in the same way, Grindal in his funeral sermon for the Emperor quotes the famous lines of Horace about death, after a text of similar meaning from Ecclesiastes: ' The wise man saith: *Moritur doctus simul et indoctus* . . . [Eccles. ii. 16; ' the learned dieth in like manner as the unlearned ', Douay] . . . The ethnicks also did very well express this necessity of death. For Horace saith thus:

> Pallida mors aequo pulsat pede pauperum tabernas
> Regumque turres.

[' Pale Death with foot impartial knocks at the poor man's cottage and at princes' palaces.'][77] The bishop too, quite in the medieval manner quotes proverbs from Cicero on old age: ' Nemo est tam senex qui non putet annum se posse vivere ', (' No-one is so old as to

---

[72] *Certain Sermons*, etc., p. 307: see *Epist. Moral.*, LXXXIII. 27 (Loeb edn., vol. II, pp. 274–5).
[73] *Certain Sermons*, etc., p. 306: see Plato, *The Republic*, IX. 573B, C (ed. and tr. P. Shorey, 2 vols., London, 1930–5, Loeb, vol. II, pp. 342–3).
[74] *Certain Sermons*, etc., p. 303: see Seneca, *Epist. Moral.*, LXXXIII. 19 (Loeb edn., vol. II, pp. 270–1).
[75] *Certain Sermons*, etc., pp. 317–18.   [76] Ibid. p. 513.
[77] *Remains*, pp. 6–7: see Horace, *Odes*, I. iv. 13–14 (ed. and tr. C. E. Bennett, London, revised 1946, Loeb, pp. 16–17).

think that he cannot live one more year',) and 'Aegroto anima dum est, spes est' ('A sick man has hope as long as he has breath ').[78] Pliny and Valerius Maximus provide a catalogue of unexpected deaths to illustrate the uncertainty of the time of death:

> Pliny, in the seventh book of his Natural History, hath a whole chapter entitled De mortibus repentinis; and the like chapter hath Valerius Maximus: where they write, that many upon most light causes suddenly have died. One at Rome, as he went forth at his chamber door, did but strike his finger a little on the door cheek, and immediately fell down dead. Another did but stumble as he went forth, and died forthwith. An ambassador of the Rhodians, after he had declared his message to the senate, departing forth of the council chamber, fell down by the way suddenly, and there died. Aeschylus the poet lying in sleep bareheaded near the sea, a great sea-fowl, thinking his head to be a stone whereon he might break the shell fish which he carried, let it fall on his head, wherewith he was killed out of hand.[79]

Similarly, Henry Smith, dealing with man's lack of desire to persevere all the way to heaven, compares him to a horse which likes short journeys, and then adds a classical illustration of his point:

> When one told Socrates, that he would very fain go to Olympus, but he feared that he should not be able to endure the pains: Socrates answered him, I know that thou usest to walk every day between thy meals, which walk continue forward in thy way to Olympus, and within 5. or 6. daies thou shalt come thither. How easy was this: & yet he saw it not. . . . If men did bend themselves as much to do good, as they beat their brains to do evil, they might go to heaven with less trouble than they go to hell.[80]

Equally medieval is Playfere's reference to Horace and Virgil in his treatment of part of a verse from one of the Penitential Psalms: ' I water my couch with my tears ' (Ps. vi. 6):

> Augustus Caesar was much delighted in the companie of learned men. Especially of two famous Poets which liued in his time, Virgil and Horace. Of the which, Virgil was so much giuen to groaning and sighing, that commonly hee was called

---

[78] Remains, pp. 3–4: see Cicero, De Senectute, VII. 24 (ed. and tr. W. A. Falconer, London, 1923, Loeb, pp. 32–3) and Letters to Atticus, IX. 10 (ed. and tr. E. O. Winstedt, 3 vols., London, 1912–18, Loeb, vol. II, pp. 228–9).

[79] Remains, p. 7: see Pliny, Natural History, VII. liii. 180–6 (ed. and tr. H. Rackham and W. H. S. Jones, 10 vols., London, 1938, Loeb, vol. II, pp. 626–31); also Valerius Maximus, Facta et Dicta Memorabilia, IX. xii. pp. 469–75.

[80] Sermons, p. 548; cf. ibid. p. 36, Phidias painted a woman sitting under a snail's shell, indicating that she should carry her house on her back.

Suspirabundus: and *Horace* was borne bleare eyed. Therefore vpon a time *Augustus* sitting in the middest between *Virgil* and *Horace*, and one that might bee bolde asking what hee did: marie saies hee, I sit heere betweene groanings and *teares*. Our Augustus, King Dauid I meane sitteth not between groanings and *teares*, but lieth sicke in his bed, very sore troubled and even almost overwhelmed with them both.[81]

Also he mingles classical references with scriptural in the old manner, as when recommending ' the mean in mourning ';

Yea *Niobe* be ouer much weeping was tourned into a stone; euen as *Lots* wife by looking backe was turned into salt. It was one of *Pythagoras* poesies, not to eate the heart; which is expounded thus: As a moth fretteth the garment, and a worm eateth the wood; so heauinesse hurteth mans heart.[82]

Playfere also uses classical allusions to form some of his extended euphuistic similes, as when illustrating how during His earthly life Christ surrendered some of His majesty:

Pliny reporteth, that there was a Diall set in *Campus Martius*, to note the shadowes of the sun, which agreeing very well at the first, afterwards for thirty yeares together did not agree with the sun. All the time of those thirty yea three and thirty yeares that Christ liued in his humiliation here vpon earth, you might haue seen such a Diall: In which time the shadow of the Diall did not agree with the shining of the Sun.[83]

Sometimes the Elizabethan preachers range further afield for their classical quotations than did those of earlier times, yet their use of them is the same. Holland quotes Euripides and Hesiod in Greek, but merely to supply moral *dicta*. In illustration of his point that virtue, learning and wisdom are found in some women, he quotes from the *Medea* of Euripides:

> ἀλλὰ γὰρ ἔστιν μοῦσα καὶ ἡμῖν,
> ἥ προσομιλεῖ σοφίας ἕνεκεν.
> πάσαισι μὲν οὔ· παῦρον δὲ γένος-
> μίαν ἐν πολλαῖς εὕροις, ἂν ἴσως-
> οὐκ ἀπόμονσον τὸ γυναικῶν.

> (. . . Should woman find
> No inspiration thrill her breast,
> Nor welcome ever that sweet guest
> Of Song; that uttereth Wisdom's mind?

[81] *The whole Sermons*, ' The sicke mans Couch,' pp. 39–40.
[82] Ibid. ' The Meane in Mourning,' p. 8.
[83] Ibid. pp. 49–50.

Q

Alas! not all! Few, few are they,—
Perchance amid a thousand one
Thou shouldest find, for whom the sun,
Of poesy makes the inner day.)[84]

Similarly when dealing with the need for princes to uphold justice he quotes from Hesiod's *Works and Days*:

ἀθάνατοι φράзονται, ὅσοι σκολιῇσι δίκῃσιν
ἀλλήλους τρίβουσι θεῶν ὄπιν οὐκ ἀλέγοντες.
τρὶς γὰρ μύριοί εἰσιν ἐπὶ χθονὶ πουλυβοτείρῃ
ἀθάνατοι Ζηνὸς φύλακες θνητῶν ἀνθρώπων·
οἵ ῥα φυλάσσουσίν τε δίκας καὶ σχέτλια ἔργα
ἠέρα ἑσσάμενοι, πάντη φοιτῶντες ἐπ' αἶαν.

(' The deathless gods mark all those who oppress their fellows with crooked judgements, and reck not the anger of the gods. For upon the bounteous earth Zeus has thrice ten thousand spirits, watchers of mortal men, and those keep watch on judgements and deeds of wrong as they roam, clothed in mist, all over the earth.')[85]
Tyrer, in spite of the instance of deeper appreciation of classical life noticed earlier, quotes from Euripides' *Phoenissae*:

τί τῆς κακίστης δαιμόνων ἐφίεσαι
Φιλοτιμίας, παῖ; μὴ σύ γ'· ἄδικος ἡ θεός·

(Why at Ambition, worst of deities,
Son, gropest thou? Do not: she is Queen of Wrong)
but only to illustrate his treatment of ambition,[86] while in another passage he blends Homer, Virgil, the *Adagia* and Scripture to show how we must disdain this world and strive towards heaven; let us be detached:

As whose heroicall spirits should disdain al their temporarie and transitorie trash, and trumperie, toies and trifles, but to crie and say εκ ιερειην ουδε βοιειην [' For no slight or sportive prize they seek '] as *Achilles* when he followed *Hector* in *Homer*, and againe *Neque enim leuia aut ludicra petuntur*, [' For it was not for beast of sacrifice or for bull's hide that they strove '] with *Aeneas* pursuing *Turnus* in Virgil; for seeing all the faithfull are Eagles (as the Scripture tearmeth them) they must neither creepe

---

[84] Πανηγυρις *D. Elizabethae*, sig. Eiv^r: see Euripides, *Medea*, ll. 1085–9 (*Euripides*, ed. and tr. A. S. Way, 4 vols., London, 1912, Loeb, vol. IV, pp. 368–9).
[85] Πανηγυρις *D. Elizabethae*, sig. Gi^r: see Hesiod, *Works and* Days, ll. 250–5 (*Hesiod, the Homeric Hymns and Homerica*, ed. and tr. H. G. Evelyn-White, London, 1914, Loeb, pp. 20–1).
[86] *Five godlie sermons*, p. 11: see Euripides, *Phoenissae*, ll. 531–2 (Loeb edn., vol. III, pp. 386–7).

on the earth with the Serpent, not sit on the dunghills with the Rauens, but soare aloft for their pray, and where the carkasse is, thither must they resort. . . . For as it is in the Prouerb, *Aquila non capit muscus*: *The eagle will catch no flies*, that is regard little and light things, but as he is the Prince of birds, so will he be crowned as a King and soueraigne.[87]

Then finally at the end of the reign, going behind the humanistic Renaissance, the old notion of the power of the Devil in the pagan world is found in Abbot, who points out the parallel between the stories of Jonah and Arion, and declares that the Evil One invents fables similar to the truth of Scripture.[88]

---

[87] *Five godlie sermons*, p. 57: see Homer, *Iliad*, XXII. 159 (ed. and tr. A. T. Murray, 2 vols., London, 1924–5, Loeb, vol. II, pp. 466–7); Virgil, *Aeneid*, XII. 764 (Loeb edn., vol. II, pp. 350–1): Erasmus, 'Adagia,' (*Opera Omnia*, II. 761E).

[88] *An Exposition upon the Prophet Jonah*, pp. 12–20.

CHAPTER V

THEMES

A N examination of the preaching themes within the various periods of this study will, by an indication of the characteristic attitudes expressed, not only provide an interesting comment on the tone and temper of the religious life of the times, but also suggest something of its quality. The pattern which emerges is, I think, of first-rate importance for an understanding of the inner changes wrought by the English Reformation, while the real distinction of Hooker and Andrewes, as preachers of the early Anglican maturity, is much enhanced by the knowledge of what went before them.

I

THE PRE-REFORMATION CATHOLIC PREACHERS, INCLUDING THE CONSERVATIVE HENRICIANS (1450–1547)

The evidence contained in the numerous sermons of this time, both manuscript and printed, supplements the account of the piety of the ' Eve of the Reformation ' given by historians who stress unduly the somewhat mystical devotional and instructional books— as the Brigittine of Sion Richard Whitforde's *Werke for Householders*, William Bonde's *The Pylgrimage of perfection*; or the ever popular *Scala Perfectionis* of Walter Hilton[1]—which manuals show only one aspect of the situation.

What then is the most characteristic note of the sermons of this time, especially before the controversy over the Roman Primacy in Henry VIII's reign? Significantly it is the lament over the transience of earthly things, and an admonition about the vanity of trusting in them. The most deeply felt and imaginatively eloquent passages are variations on the *ubi sunt* theme. As when the western Roman Empire was crumbling, the closing years of the old religious order in England re-echo with the sad declamations of the preachers on the melancholy consideration that ' the world passes ', and all the glory and the beauty of life ends in dust and ashes. The homilist of MS. Harleian 2247 declares:

[1] See e.g. Janelle, *L'Angleterre Catholique à la veille du Schisme*, pp. 22–5; H. M. Smith, *Pre-Reformation England* (London, 1938), pp. 339–41; P. Hughes, *The Reformation in England*, vol. I, p. 101; F. A. Gasquet, *The Eve of the Reformation* (London, new edn., 1900), pp. 274–7.

Lat þem be þi mirroure þat be dede & passed oute of þis worlde, and þere þou shall vndirstond what þou art, & what þou shalt be; for beaute, fayrnes, wisdam, frendeship, ricches, delites, honours, dignyties & all such be toke from þe in þi dethe. For þi body is but stynking careyn þat from þe erthe it come, and to þe erthe it shall turne ageyn.[2]

One of the most striking passages of Fisher's eloquence is a threnody over the mortality of earthly glory:

Where be now the kynges & prynces that somtyme regned ouer all the worlde, whose glory & tryumphe was lyfte vp aboue the erth. Where is now the innumerable company & puysaunce of Xerses & Cesar, where is now the grete rychesse of Cresus & Crassus. But what shall we say of them whiche somtyme were kynges & gouernours of this realme, where be they now whiche we haue knowen and seen in our dayes in so grete welthe and glory, that it was thought of many they shold neuer haue dyed, neuer to haue ben out of mynde, they had all theyr pleasures at the full bothe of delycyous and good welfare, of hawkynge, huntynge, also goodly horses goodly coursers, greyhoundes and houndes for theyr dysportes, theyr palayses well and rychely beseen, stronge holdes & townes without nombre, they had grete plente of golde and syluer, many seruauntes, goodly apparayle for themselfe and for theyr lodgynges, they had the power of the lawe to proscrybe, to punisshe, to exalt & set forthwarde theyr frendes and louers, to put downe and make lowe theyr enemyes, & also to punysshe by temporal dethe rebelles and traytours. Euery man helde with them, all were at theyr commaundement, euery man was vnto them obedyent, fered them, lauded also & praysed them, & ouer all shewed theyr grete renowne and fame. But where be they now, be they not gone and wasted lyke vnto smoke of whome it is wryten in an other place. *Mox vt honorificati fuerint et exaltati, quemadmodum fumus deficient* [Ps. xxxvi. 20. (Vg.), ' presently after they shall be honoured and exalted, (they) shall come to nothing and vanish like smoke ', Douay].[3]

This is a favourite theme also with Longland; his treatment too is characteristically rhetorical, but of great emotive force. Preaching before Henry VIII at Richmond, the bishop quotes St. John, *mundus transit* (1 John ii. 17), and continues:

[2] MS. Harl. 2247, f. 213ᵛ. Cf. MS. Lincoln Cath. Libr. 51, ff. 84ᵛ-5ʳ, where the preacher quotes St. Augustine, that man's life is like a glass which can be broken with a hammer. (The reference as given is *De Civitate Dei*, lib. III, but it would seem that the passage actually referred to is ' Sermones ad Populum,' sermo cix, cap. 1, *P.L.*, xxxviii. 636).

[3] *English Works*, Pt. I, pp. 145–6.

And he that settis mooste by hit, shall percaase synnyst goo from hit, synnyst wax wery of hit. Wery of eatynge & drynkynge, wery of sporte & play, wery of daunsynge, syngynge and long lyynge a bede, wery of huntynge & hawkinge & other lyyke tryfullynges. And yet we make asmuche of hit, as thoughe hit shuld neuer ende, as thoughe we shulde neuer dye. And yet we dye, we dye and passe away with the worlde, and with his concupiscensys and figure. *Ecce morimur* (saythe Scripture) *& quasi aqua dilabimur* [2 Reg. xiv. 14. (Vg.)]. Loo, loo, we dye & slyyd forthe as the water doys. A streme of watur, be hit neuer so styll, yet euer hit runnys, hit runnythe, & passithe secretly, and soo secretly that annethe hit kan be perceuyd: and yet hit passithe. Soo we, we slyyd away, our lyffe goythe frome vs, our yerys passithe, our infancy is waastyd, our childehodde is spente, our adolescency is goon, our youghthe is past, our age shall a way, and we shall a way with itt. We waaste and dekay, we wex more feble euery daye then other, and yet wyll not we be a knowen ther of. For many oon dothe say, euyn when they ar veray agyd, myn yye sighth is as good as euer hit was, I am as stronge and as lustye as euer I was, I can caste the barre as fare as euer I kowde, & drawe as stronge a bowe, and shoote as farre, ryyd, goo and runne as lustely as euer I dyde: and wyll not be a knowne of her owne debilitie, nor howe they dekay in nature, lytyll and lytyll, thoughe hit be skarcely parceptible: and yet at lengthe hit is perceyued, at lengthe hit is openly knowen.[4]

Then showing that five ages of the world are past, and that men are now living precariously in the sixth and last, Longland concludes:

And Christe dyyed, Peter is paste, the apostilis ar goon. The grete emperours Iulius Ceasar, Octauianus Augustus,Tiberius, Caius, Claudius, Nero, Vaspasianus, Titus, Domicianus, Traianus, And all the other tyll nowe our tyme, they all ar paste and goon. And all nowe lytyll memory of them. Who remembrithe nowe William the conqueroure of England? who saythe oons, god haue mercy oon his soule? Wher is kynge Arthure, Where is Godfray of Boleyn & the IX Wurthyys? And of this age is paste MCCCCCXXXV yeres: and howe longe hit shall endure, god oonly knowys.[5]

Edgeworth expatiates too on this theme; in this presentation of it we notice the lack of elaborate rhetorical pattern, but in place of this he offers an individual treatment with vivid pictorial effect: the

[4] *Sermond at Rychemunte*, 1535, sig. Diii[v].
[5] Ibid. sig. Ei[r]. Cf. too *Sermones*, ff. 502[r] 393[r], 519[r], 394[r-v] (a sustained lament) and *Quinque Sermones*, f. 56[v].

following extract is surely one of the most beautiful in early Tudor prose:—after quoting St. Peter on the Christian's hope of entering heaven, ' Into an inheritance that is incorruptible, vndefowled, and neuer fadynge ', (1 Pet. i. 4) he continues:

The inheritaunce of Heauen, (as the Apostle saythe here) hathe three excellente properties, whyche wee maye ymagine by three contrarye properties, whyche no purchaser wyll haue in anye Patrimonie, manour, or Lordshippe that he shoulde bye or purchase for himselfe to inhabite or dwell in. Firste if it be a rotten grounde where all thynge anone moulleth, [moulders] the tenauntes, and mortises of tymber buyldynge rotteth oute and loseth their pynnes. The walles or rouffes gathereth a mosse or a wylde Fearne, that rotteth out the Lyme and Morter from the stones. And where the Sea or fresh water weareth out the ground: so that all things that there is, in shorte space commeth to nought. Hee is not wyse that wyll bestowe hym selfe or hys money on suche a grounde. Second if there bee in the Lande or House any infectyue or pestylent Ayre, disposynge menne to manye infirmityes, and genderynge adders, snakes, or todes, or these stingyng scowts or gnats, that will not suffre men to slepe, a man shoulde haue litle ioye to dwell in such a manour. Third, if it be suche a grounde where al thinge withereth, and dryeth awaye for lacke of moysture, where hearbes proueth not, and trees growth not to theyr naturall quantitie, where the leues waxeth yelowe and falleth at Lammas tyde, where men soweth a bushel and reapeth a peck, and for redde wheate reapeth like rye or otes, that is bestowed on suche a purchase, is but caste awaye. The inheritaunce of thes transitorye worlde hathe all these noughty properties rehearsed, and manye worse, townes and towres, castels and manours decayeth continuallye, and where noble men haue dwelled, nowe dwelleth dawes and crowes, the vawtes and rouffes be so ruinous, that no man dare well come vnder them. Where is Troye? where be the olde Emperies and monarchies of the Assirians, of the Caldeis, Medes, Persies, and of Rome, whose Emperours had vnder them in maner all the worlde, for theyr tyme? . . . All thinge waxeth olde and decayeth in processe of time, so that corruption and deathe is the ende.[6]

The preachers of this time, in the tradition of Middle Ages, take a mournful view of human life; its vanities, its besetting temptations, its pains and sorrows visibly increasing in these latter evil days; as Edgeworth pessimistically declaims:

[6] *Sermones*, ff. 120[r-v].

. . . how frequent and many infirmities raigneth: we see dayly
infections of pestilence, pockes great and small, & these newe
burninge agues, and innumerable others, more then the Phisicions
haue written of in their bookes. These contaminate and defow-
leth mens bodies by infections, aches and paines euen to death.
And what corruption and infection of maners commeth
to the soule, by euill example, ill wordes, and suche other
occasions, it were to long to be spoken of nowe. . . . The comon
sterilitie and barenes of the grounde, the greate scarsitie of
all maner of vitall [victuals] and of fruites of the earth, we
feele it so many times to our great paine and discomfort, that
it nede not be declared.[7]

With exaggerated pessimism Longland admonishes the courtiers to
place a low value on life:

. . . would that you, flattered by the world in your least whim,
would consider with yourselves how troublesome is this present
life, how fragile and wearisome; how full it is without distinction of every affliction and stumbling block, how fading,
miserable, deceitful, guileful and fraudulent it is.[8]

Doubtless in all these passages the aim of the preachers is to break
down man's natural inordinate attachment to the world and created
goods, but in manner and effect there is something which is definitely
morbid. Although the Christian does not seek his supreme felicity
in created goods (' for here we have no continuing city, but we seek
one to come', Heb. xiii. 14), nevertheless he need not, one feels,
utterly deny their positive value. However, in these preachers with
their overwrought *contemptus mundi*, there is little notion of how,
although the creation may indeed be disordered by sin, it is yet
fundamentally and of its nature good; how there are natural virtues,
which are far from negligible even if irrelevant to salvation; how
natural joys may be fleeting but are quite real, and certainly need not
be sinful; how both the world and human life are *redeemed*, how
common things may be sanctified; how each human relationship and
activity may be irradiated and supernaturalized by grace. On the
contrary (to borrow the language of Philip Hughes when dealing
with the *Bishops' Book* of 1537)[9] it seems in the sermons of this time
as though men were living in the ages before the coming of Christ,
as though the Devil actually ruled all created things, as though the
average man were a wholly abandoned sinner. The view of life expressed in these sermons has indeed almost more affinities with Neo-

[7] Ibid. f. 121[r].   [8] *Sermones*, f. 805[v].
[9] *The Reformation in England*, vol. II, pp. 44–5.

Platonism and later Stoicism than with the central truths of Christianity. Sometimes with sad earnestness, sometimes with bitter censoriousness the preachers regard ordinary life as a mere collection of miseries and sins. The infant wails helplessly in its cradle dependent for all things upon its parents or nurse, the boy is changeable and inconstant, the young man glories in bodily beauty, strength and birth:[10] ' He spends all the day from the first light of dawn to the evening in lasciviousness and sensual delights; nor does he recognise any other felicity beyond carnality and the gratification of the body; he thinks it is beautitude to melt away in filthy pleasures and obscenity.'[11] The attitude to the body found in these preachers is almost more Manichaean than Christian. Longland at times exhibits a dark hatred of the body *per se* and even declares ' This bodye is the greatest enemye than man hath, and sonest dothe brynge man vnto dampnacion ',[12] and in another place, ' The body is the food of the Devil: the body is the snare of the Devil, the body is the trap of the Devil, with which he sets an ambush for the soul, which latter he catches as with a hook. The body is an engine with which he throws to the ground the soul's virtue: it is a battering ram with which he stoutly shakes the soul's walls.'[13] The senses by our persistent misuse of them become regarded merely as gates leading to sin:

> We turn our eyes to vile and vain sights, through multifarious occasions to sin. We often use our ears to listen to detractions and empty words. We catch with our nostrils scents, aromatic odours, the fragrance of wines, and perfumes of balsam. For our mouth we prepare sumptuous food, seasoned with various spices. The tongue utters the greatest wickedness, it sows discords and quarrels between friends.[14]

In his zeal that all should adopt a detached attitude to the world with its alluring ' siren voices ',[15] Longland at times shows a jealousy

---

[10] *Sermones*, f. 393ʳ: cf. too *Quinque Sermones*, f. 56ᵛ.
[11] *Sermones*, f. 704ᵛ: cf. too Baron, *Sermones*, f. 3ʳ.
[12] *Sermonde at Grenewiche*, 1538, sig. Diiiʳ.
[13] *Sermones*, f. 147ʳ: cf. Fisher, *English Works*, Pt. I, p. 17: ' . . . synne is caused and cometh of the vnlawfull pleasures of the body.'
[14] *Sermones*, f. 150ᵛ: for an earlier instance of this utter distrust of the senses, see *Jacob's Well*, Pt. I, p. 2: ' . . . ȝit, whanne ȝoure pytt is scowryd clene fro the watyr of curs, & fro the wose of dedly synnes, the V. watyrgatys, that is ȝoure V. wyttes, muste be stopped, that the watyr of the grete curs, and the wose of dedly synnes entre nozt in to ȝoure pytt aȝen': also ibid. pp. 216–20. Longland may say, shortly after the words quoted in the text, that we ' can and ought to use properly and honourably [the powers of the body] to the honour and in the just service of God, to our merit and future crown ', but his ideal is obviously singularly repressive, and in any event we do *not* do this; on the contrary, ' we derange and degrade [these bodily powers] into instruments of evil works, and give them up to folly and madness.' (*Sermones*, ibid.)
Sermones, f. 4ᵛ. Cf. St. Jerome, Epist., XXII, *P.L.*, xxii. 405.

of the natural vigour and gaiety of youth, which he constantly regards as a time of mere vanity and filthy servitude to the vile body:

Who are they that are greued, burdened, weryed & fynde faulte with this bodye? the iolye huffaas and ruffelers of this worlde? The yonge galandes of the courte? The lusty Iuuentus youthe? Noo, noo, noo. None of these. For there is nothynge in thys worlde more pleasaunte more acceptable to them than the bodye. For all there study is howe to please this bodye, how to take the ease of this bodye, the pleasure of this bodye. Euery man sekynge and inuentinge how to follow the voluptye and carnall desires of this bodye. We se howe they studye to set forthe this bodye, to fashon it, to make it appeare more gorgyous, more syghtlye & better in makynge and shape then God made it. Nowe with this fashion of apparel, now with that. Nowe with this cutte, and that garde.[16]

However, such wicked service of the body can last only for a little while; there is almost vindictive rejoicing over the ultimate fate of beauty and strength:

This fayre bodye of thyn that thou makeste somoche of, that thou dekkest so preciously, that thou settest somoche by, itt shall awaye, itt is butt *terra & cinis, puluis & esca vermium.* It is but earthe, ashes, duste & wormes meate. *Serpentes hereditabunt illud.* Serpentes shall enheryte thy bodye as thou doest naturally thy fadre his landes. Euen so serpentes wormes and toodes shall gnawe, eate and deuoure thy beawtyfull face, thy fayre nose, thy clere eyes, thy whyte handes, thy gudly bodye.[17]

If youth is sensual and forgetful, age is tortured by physical miseries; these preachers are never more eloquent than when detailing the debilities of old age; ' then because of the infirmity of the feet and arms a staff is needed, then man loses his teeth, the stomach becomes weak, the eyes dim, the ears become deaf, the head grows white and shaky; the tongue stammers, the courage and vigour of youth slips away; every part of the body testifies weakness ';[18] but alas! wisdom does not come, rather we find covetousness, irritability and morosity: 'And although the proverb says of the aged, *bis pueri senes,* nevertheless in this one thing they are quite different, that whereas young children easily forgive and condone injuries: old people, on the contrary, are found to be entirely unforgiving, so full

---

[16] *Sermonde at Grenewiche,* 1538, sig. Dii^v.
[17] *Sermond at Grenwiche,* 1536, sig. Eii^r. Cf. also *Sermones,* f. 32^v, and the similar harsh passages from earlier preachers quoted by Owst, *P.M.E.,* pp. 343–4.
[18] *Quinque Sermones,* f. 56^v. Cf. too *Sermones,* f. 393^v. For earlier passages on the physical miseries of old age, see Owst, *P.M.E.,* p. 342. Probably such passages owe much to St. Jerome, Epist., LIV, *P.L.,* xxii. 557.

are they of anger, and a certain senile malice.'[19] But inevitably, to all comes death, that stern and invincible tyrant; the sure signs appear, the changing colour and expression of the face, the darkening eyes, the loss of hearing and difficulty of speech.[20] The preachers use all the powers of their lugubrious eloquence to show how this grim enemy sends before him prognostications:

> . . . of whiche one is Age, whiche daielye creapeth vppon vs, aduertisynge vs of oure ende to which he dailye driueth vs, as by lacke of naturall heate, and by colde folowynge of the same. And this commeth to manye menne by longe continuynge in thys lyfe, and by multitude of yeres. To other it commeth afore their tyme accedentallye, and in a manner vyolentlye, as by syckenesse, paynes, and aches, and to others by vnmeasurable solicitude and care of minde. Eccle[siasticus] XXX. *Cogitatus ante tempus senectam adducit.* And to others by ouermuche studye and watchynge for to get learnynge and knowledge.[21]

Even more disquieting messengers are 'sicknesses soores and malenders [pustules], as weaknes of complexion, disposition to many feuers & to be now & then vexed with one feuer or another, hedach, colick, the stone, gowts & runninge legges dropsye and palsye'.[22] However death comes not only to the aged, for 'life forsakes all unexpectedly. From time to time, how many infants, daily how many children, how many flowering youths, how many robust young men, how many in the full strength of manhood, how many chaste virgins and honourable wives are borne with weeping and great grief to the tomb?'[23] Even kings die, says Longland, preaching before Henry VIII; death conquers even the mightiest emperors; who like the lowliest of their subjects, 'are born nakyd and baar, and as baarely shall they agen departe this worlde. Baare, naked wythoute clowte or clothe: unless itt be that the grette man shall percase haue a fyner wyndynge shete thenne shall the poore man, but bothe be mortall, bothe shall dye, bothe shall rotte, bothe shalbe forgotten, bothe be *Terra & cinis, puluis & esca vermium, quos hereditabunt serpentes*'.[24]

[19] *Sermones*, f. 704r. Cf. too ibid. f. 703v.   On the vices of age, cf. too Baron, *Sermones*, f. 3r.

[20] *Quinque Sermones*, f. 88r: see too MS. Lincoln Cath. Libr. 50, f. 46r (quoted by Owst, *P.M.E.*, p. 342, n. 5).

[21] Edgeworth, *Sermons*, f. 238r.   [22] Ibid. f. 239r.

[23] Longland, *Sermones*, f. 398r.

[24] *Sermond at Grenwiche*, 1536, sig. Eiir. Cf. too Fisher, *Hereafter ensueth two fruytfull sermons*, sig. Biiir: 'Kynges & Emperours, all be but men, all be but mortall. All the golde & all the precyouse stones of this worlde, can not make them but mortall men. All the ryche apparell that can be deuysed, can not take from theym the condycyon of mortalyty. They be in them selfe but erthe & asshes, & to earth they

How terrible too is death to abandoned sinners; to those who have never remembered their end: ' till they be so taken that they can nother stirre hande nor foote, and can scarsely speake or heare. As we haue knowen of these hel houndes ruffians or riatours that by their life time had neuer deuotion toward god, nether regarding masse nor other diuine seruice, nother the sacrament[s] of Christes churche, which when they haue been taken with feruent sicknes that they could not by the helpe of phisitions recouer, haue fallen to raginge, blasphemyng & swearing, and so died desperatly.'²⁵

After death, the soul faces the dread Judgement, when all worldly goods and honours are as dust, and only the (so frequently) pitiably few ' gode werkes ' avail anything.²⁶ Those who escape the eternal torments of hell, with its exulting and horrible demons,²⁷ have before them an excruciating imprisonment in purgatory, treated typically by Longland and Fisher as a second hell, with little mention of the aspects of purification, hope, and even joy in suffering stressed by the best Catholic writers, as St. Catherine of Genoa.²⁸ On the contrary, the souls there suffering ' pain ' and ' loss ' cry out piteously to the living for a suffrage of prayers, satisfactory works, and masses, so that their torments may be shortened.²⁹ The faithful are urged also to procure indulgences for the departed; as a preacher at Syon abbey, a favourite place to seek pardons, puts it:

must retourne, & all theyr glorye well consydered & beholden with ryght iyen, is but very myserable.' For the medieval preachers' treatment of the death-theme, cf. Owst, L. & P.M.E., pp. 527–33.

---

²⁵ Edgeworth, Sermons, f. 239ʳ: for earlier parallels to this account of a ' bad death ' see Owst, L. & P.M.E., pp. 430–1.
²⁶ MS. Harl. 2247, f. 210ᵛ.
²⁷ See Longland, Sermones, f. 4ʳ; Quinque Sermones, ff. 58ᵛ–9ʳ; Edgeworth, Sermons, f. 77ʳ; also MS. Harl. 2247, f. 43ʳ. For the account of hell given by the medieval preachers, see Owst, P.M.E., pp. 337–40; L. & P.M.E., pp. 293–4, 522–4.
²⁸ See Saint Catherine of Genoa, Treatise on Purgatory, The Dialogue, tr. C. Balfour and H. D. Irvine, (London, 1946) ' The Treatise on Purgatory,' pp. 17–35, passim.
²⁹ Longland, Sermones, ff. 6–7. Cf. Fisher, Hereafter ensueth two fruytfull sermons, sig. Ciiʳ⁻ᵛ: ' Oh, we see many paines in this world, and we fele many, and yet our thought may deuyse many moo. It is a great payne of the hed ache, it is a great payne of the tothe ache, it is a great paine of the gowte. It is a great and dolorouse payne of the stone, colyeke and strangury, who may knowe or thynke his frende to be in any of these paynes and be nat sory for them, nor take any compassion vpon him, or haue wyll to releue and help hym yf he myght so do [?]'—so should we help those in purgatory; ' For doubtlesse the paynes of that place (as saynt Austyn sayth) be so great, that one day there semeth to be a thousand yeres for payne. And as many Doctours holde oppynyon, the paynes of Purgatory haue no dyuersyte in greuousnes (saue onely they be nat euerlastyng and perpetuall) but as the paynes of Hell be.' Cf. further, Fisher, English Works, Pt. I, pp. 10–11; MS. Harl. 2247, ff. 210ʳ⁻ᵛ, C. S. Lewis rightly stresses the darkness of the picture of purgatory given by Fisher and More, and the sense of liberation from this horror felt by the Reformers. . . (English Literature in the Sixteenth Century, pp. 163–4, 172–3).

... we rede in the reulacions of S[aint] B[ridget] that oon of
the remedies that our lorde tellyth to help a soule that was in
purgatori was that some of his frendyse schuld go for hym to
places of pardon. ... And of þis we rede diuers examples, in
special of a knyʒt that for to gete suche pardon þat was graunted
in that forme to his fadrys soule, labored in warre for the
defensse of holi churche alle a lent tyme. And than his fadur
appered to hym in marvelous light and clernes, and thankyd
hym, for by þat pardon ... he was delyvyrd from purgatory
and brought to endles blis.[30]

The themes of moral complaint which bulk large in the sermons
of this time are largely traditional,[31] but they are presented by the
learned preachers after 1500 with a literary skill and effectiveness
not found previously in English vernacular preaching. The chronic
complaint of the cleric that the preacher himself is all too little
heeded reverberates throughout these sermons. Longland with
characteristic severity declaims:

> For we, to whom has been assigned by God the lot of
> preaching the Gospel, are observed to have performed our
> function, whenever we show how detestable are the perils of
> sin, tell of the infestations of demons, the punishments of hell,
> and the mansions of heaven. Also, we set forth those things
> which are necessary for the soul's health; how great a store of
> merit follows upon good works, and what great evils male-
> factors deserve. But how few, I ask, are there who heed our
> counsels and exhortations? What result follows from so many
> sermons? How few who wish to amend their lives in accord-
> ance with our preaching? Who takes the trouble to alter his
> corrupt life? And this is what we should expect, for men are
> none other than cruel, voluptuous, unteachable, rebellious, of
> hard and intractable heart, not fearing God, nor living according
> to His word, but wholly negligent of themselves, and the care of
> their souls.[32]

Edgeworth too has no illusions about the effect of his exhortations: he testifies to the smouldering hostility, sometimes found
among the audience, which they are not afraid to express openly in
the tavern:

> When you be on your Ale benche or in your bankets at the
> whot and strong wine, you spot your owne soules and spotteth
> others by your euill tonges and yll examples, teaching youthe
> to be as euill as you bee. Then haue at the preachers, then they

[30] MS. Harl. 2321, f. 53[r-v].

[31] On the topics of complaint in the medieval preachers, in general, see Owst,
L. & P.M.E., chs. v–vii, ' The Preaching of Satire and Complaint,' pp. 210–470.

[32] Sermones, f. 617[r]. Cf. Bishop Brunton's earlier complaint on this topic, Owst,
P.M.E., pp. 19–20.

hurte men with their rayling tongues, and more hurt they woulde do with their handes if it were not for feare of the kinges lawes. You hadde nede to amend this maner, you muste be content to heare your fauts tolde you, that you mai so amend them, for feare lest the deuill leade you still in your affectate and blinde ignoraunce, till he haue brought you to the blinde exterior darknes in hell, where he woulde haue you.[33]

Nevertheless, he is convinced that preachers must continue to labour diligently and unselfishly, even if there is little apparent effect; let them carry on:

For we se by experience that the veynes of waters floweth and runneth, although no manne drwe vp water at them, yet they sprinkleth, boileth and welleth vp. And brookes, although neither man nor beaste drinke of them, yet neuer the lesse they keepe their course and floweth. So he that preacheth must lette his veyne of sapience flow and runne among his audience, although no man drinck of it, take hede of it, or receiue it.[34]

In one delightful passage Edgeworth appeals to the better nature of his audience using his favourite farming imagery; let the hearers listen to the preachers' words and live as they exhort them:

That they maie be glad of their labours taking among you, like as a husbandman which is glad to do his work when he seeth the trees of his setting & graffing proue well, & bear fruites, when he seeth the fields of his tillynge beare plentifullye suche Corne or grayne as hee hath sowne, then he perceiueth that he hath not laboured in vayne, bende his backe, and galled his handes in vayne, and that he hath not without some cause suffered and borne the heate of Somer, and the colde of Winter: he is gladde of his paines taking, this shal make him glad and merie so to do another time.[35]

Other old topics of complaint continue to be vigorously repeated; bad and ignorant priests are still a scandal to their calling;[36] how far do they fall below the requirements of the *Regula Apostolica* (1 Tim. iii. 2–6), says Alcock; alas! ' in these days the clergy so mis-behave themselves that their life is vastly inferior and more despised than that of the laity. For today, as Jerome says, the lay people are as saints compared to the clergy.'[37] If it was said of Judas, ' Woe

---

[33] *Sermons*, f. 218ᵛ. Cf. MS. Lincoln Cath. Libr. 50, ff. 128ᵛ–9ᵛ.
[34] *Sermones*, f. 12ᵛ: cf. St. John Chrysostom, ' Concio prima de Lazaro,' *P.G.*, xlviii. 963. [35] *Sermons*, f. 298ʳ.
[36] For earlier complaints against the clergy, see Owst, *P.M.E.*, pp. 25–47, 73–9, 248–54; *L. & P.M.E.*, pp. 242–86; *The Destructorium Viciorum of Alexander Carpenter*, pp. 38–40.
[37] *Gallicantus in sinodo apud Bernwell*, p. 1ᵛ; (signature numbers begin on the second page).

unto that man by whom the Son of Man is betrayed ', then, says Alcock, ' so much the more, woe unto those who plunder and ravage the Spouse of Christ not only as regards dignity, sanctity and honour, but even by their deeds, speech and evil examples, turn her, as far as in them lies, into a harlot.'[38] William de Melton exhorts ordinands to remember the dignity of the priesthood and the need for personal sanctity.[39] Although only mediocrity of learning is demanded for ordination, those who do not get so far before ordination, very seldom progress after, but remain stupid and stolid until old age. The vulgar say that there are some priests of manifest ignorance, and this is a scandal to the whole order.[40] Not only Colet warns the clergy against ' conformity to the world ';[41] Fisher in language of the greatest beauty rebukes those who see the ' wealth ' of the Church more in material riches than in virtue; contrasting Apostolic times with his own day the bishop declares:

> Truly it was a more glorious sight to se saynt Poule whiche gate his lyuynge by his owne grete labour in hungre, thurst, watchynge, in colde, goynge wolward, & berynge aboute the gospell & lawe of cryst bothe vpon the see & on the londe than to beholde nowe tharchebysshoppes & byshoppes in theyr apparayle be it neuer so ryche. In that tyme were no chalyses of golde, but than was many golden prestes, now be many chalyses of golde, & almoost no golden prestes, truly neyther golde precyous stones, nor gloryous bodyly garments be not the cause wherfore kynges & prynces of the worlde sholde drede god & his chyrche, for doubtles they haue ferre more worldly rychesse than we haue, but holy doctryne, good lyfe & example of honest conuersacion be the occasyons wherby good & holy men, also wycked & cruel people are moued to loue & fere almighty god.[42]

Alcock finds it necessary to give a word of admonition to priests who wear secular clothes, for ' if thou se a preest go lyke a lay man, with his typpet, slyppers & grete sleues, it is to presume that he repenteth hym that euer he forsoke the habyte of a layeman & therfore he vseth it ';[43] while Longland is particularly frank on the main evil which he sees rampant in the Church of his day, simony:

> Choppynge and chaungynge, bying & sellynge of benefices and of spirytuall gyftes and promocyons. And noo better marchandyse is now a dayes, then to procure vousons of patrons for benefyces, for prebendes, for other spirituall lyueloode:

---

[38] Ibid. sig. Ai[r] (p. 2[r]).   [39] *Sermo exhortatorius*, sig. ai[r]–aii[r].
[40] Ibid. sig. aiii[r-v].   [41] ' Convocation Sermon,' Lupton, *Life of Colet*, pp. 295–9.
[42] *English Works*, Pt. I, p. 181.
[43] *Sermo . . . Qui habet aures audiendi: audiat*, sig. Dii[v].

whether it be by sute, requeste, by letters, by money, bargayne
or otherwyes, yee whether it be to bye them or sell them thou
shalt haue marchandes plentye, marchandes ynoughe for it.
These vousons are abroode here in this citye: In wnicne citye?
In mooste parte of all the greate citye[s] of this realme. In the
shoppes, in the streetes a common marchandyse. And they
that do come by theyr benefyces or promocions vnder soche
maner, shall neuer haue grace of god to profete in the churche.[44]
Then again, Longland is severe on the decay of the religious life in
his day owing to worldliness:

> If they have magnificent furnishings, precious ornaments,
> tables decorated with all the craftsman's skill, laden with sumptu-
> ous dishes and exquisite feasts, piled up with second or third
> relays of courses, even with dessert (in case anything should be
> lacking): if they strive after coloured trappings for horses, and
> constantly indulge in fowling, hunting, secular pursuits, irreligi-
> ous wanderings: if they adopt curiousness and softness of dress,
> and other things of this sort: are these things not considered
> the portion of secular lords and wordly men rather than of
> monks?[45]

By the end of Henry VIII's reign, owing to the ' submission of the
clergy ' and the infiltration of Protestant ideas, the esteem in which
priests were held had sunk disquietingly low; as Scott declares, ' the
hole order of presthode, which was wonte to be had in great reputation, as the worthincsse of the thyng doth requyre, is so ronne in
contempte, that it is now nothing elles but a laughynge stocke for the
people '.[46] Edgeworth laments that even good priests are now mocked:

> . . . if a priest saye his mattens and euensonge, with other diuine
> seruice dayly, according to his bounden dutye, he shall be
> mocked and iested at, yea, and not onely of lighte braynes of
> the layte, but also of men of oure owne cote and profession,
> leude and folysshe priestes, that nother serue God deuoutly, nor
> the world iustely nor diligently, but geue themselues to walkinge
> the stretes, and beatinge the bulkes with theyr heeles, clatteringe
> lighte and leude matters, full vnseeminge for theyr profession,
> and some of them more geuen to reading these folishe englishe
> bokes full of heresies, then anye true expositours of holy
> sciptures.[47]

Yet sometimes the preachers defend their own order against lay
critics. Scott declares that those lay people who criticize the less
worthy clergy are usually bad themselves,[48] and he lays the blame

---

[44] *Sermonde at Grenewiche*, 1538, sig. Fiiʳ.   [45] *Tres Conciones*, f. 7ʳ.
[46] *Two notable sermones lately preached at Paul's crosse*, sig. Giʳ.   [47] *Sermons*. f, 273ᵛ.
[48] *Two notable sermones lately preached at Paul's crosse*, sig. Gvʳ.

upon lay patrons for the moral decay of the clergy; some indeed may be bad in themselves:

> . . . yet this I wyll say agayne; that a greate sorte mo do runne amysse, by the meanes of temporall men: for yf a preest can flatter smothly, yf he wyll keape you company at bankettynge, disynge and cardynge, runne with you of huntynge and hawkynge, whiche thynges draw after them al kind of vices, he shall be called a good felowe, & on suche ye wyll bestowe your benefices, yf money wyll let you gyue them frely.[49]

Then again, Alcock, whose severe castigation of the clergy, preached *ad clerum*, has been noticed;[50] nevertheless declares to the laity:

> . . . truly brethren I am sure that in no maner reame in crystendom, be so many noble clerkes of Curates in all maner facultees & vertues also as be in this realme of Englonde. And though all be not so perfyte as they sholde be, yet loue & worshyp the other that ben good. For Peter, Iohan & other of the apostles ought not to be despysed by cause of Iudas that was apostle; & saynt Austen sayth, Blame not my house yf there be one therein not good, for I can not make my house beter than Abrahams house.[51]

In secular society, the preachers still find the same vices as in the Middle Ages, and the same stereotyped complaint is poured out, although the expression may be more polished. Women with their taste for finery and cosmetics, and their wanton ways, so much decried by the medieval preachers,[52] arouse Edgeworth's stern disapproval:

> Because Saint Peter hadde bidde al wiues please ther husbandes with obedience and due subiection, lest they shoulde thinke thys subiection and pleasynge of ther husbandes to stande in trimmyng and dressynge their bodies curiously and wantonlye for their husbandes pleasures, he declareth that he meaneth nothing lesse & biddeth theim that they vse not to make ther heere for the nonce, settyng it abrode smothly stickt, to make it shine in mens eyes or curiously platted in traces, or as gentlewomen vse nowadaies purposely neglected, hanging about their eies, as it were saiyng: I care not how my heere lye, and yet while they do so, when they take vppon them to care least then they care most for their heere. Some there be that can not be contente with their heere as God made it, but dothe painte it and set it in another hue, as when it was white hoore, they dye it fayre and

---

[49] Ibid. sig. Gvᵛ.   [50] See *ante*, pp. 238–9.
[51] *Sermon. . . Qui habet aures audiendi: audiat*, sig. Bivᵛ.
[52] See Owst, *P.M.E.*, pp. 5, 71, 115, 122, 123, 170–4, 183, 188, 190, 217–18, 295, 344; L. & *P.M.E.*, pp. 376–404; *The Destructorium Viciorum of Alexander Carpenter*, p. 29.

R

yelowe or if it be blacke as a crowe, it muste be set in some
lighter colour, as browne or aburne or redde: And so muste
ther browes and the bryes of ther eye lyddes be painted pro-
porcionably.[53]

Fisher too has a word against the vanity of women; they are ashamed
of a black spot on their faces or mud on their clothes, but are they
ashamed of the spots of sin on their souls?[54] Longland warns his
audience against the dangers of female company, with all his usual
distrust of anything savouring of ' the flesh ':

Thou canst not possyblye lyue chaast as longe as thou hast
pleasure to be conuersaunt with women, as longe as thou
delytest wantonly to iangle and talke with them. As longe as
thou haste pleasure in vncleane touchyngs, in wanton halsenge,
wanton enbrasynge, or in wanton kyssynge.[55]

However, in spite of such admonitions the sins of the flesh are all too
prevalent, and merit the severest reprobation. Longland finds that
cities have become mere sinks of impurity: if God looked down upon
them now:

What abhominacyons shuld he fynde in them worthye
extreme punyshment? What fornicacyons, what aduoutryes
what stupour, what deflourynge of virgyns, Sodomitical and
vnnatural synnes? What scortuous houses, lecherous beddes,
aduo[u]terous chambers, flesshly concupyscencyes, surfettynges,
dronkenes, glotonous lyuynge with soche other therunto
belongynge? . . . He shulde fynde, he shulde fynde in a great
sorte cityes, burghes, tounes and houses: stynkynge lecherous
beddes I feare farre beyonde home, farre beyonde the abhomin-
acyon of the Sodomes.[56]

Chedsey laments the increase in impurity at the end of Henry VIII's
reign:

To speake of the cryme of horedome and aduoutery was
neuer so much neede: for the vice was neuer so muche vsed.
This was so detestable in S. Paules conscience that he wode not
haue it ones named amonge vs. Let fornication (sayth he) and
all vnclenlynes be not ones named amonge you, as it becommeth
saintes. And we to haue the fylthy communication of it styll in
our mouthes, count it mery bordyng. The synfull acte of it is
wynked at, no man doth pounyshe it, and therefore no man dothe
feere it.[57]

---

[53] *Sermons*, f. 198ᵛ. Later in this sermon (f. 200ᵛ), Edgeworth warns women not to
dispute with God's handiwork by the use of cosmetics. Cf. also, ibid. f. 53ʳ. This is
an ancient theme; see St. Jerome, Epist. LIV, CVII, *P.L.*, xxii. 553, 872.
[54] *English Works*, Pt. I, p. 402.
[55] *Sermonde at Grenewiche*, 1538, sig. Eiʳ.   [56] Ibid. sig. Giʳ.
[57] *Two notable sermones lately preached at Pauls crosse*, sig. Eiiᵛ.

Also, he is not at all at ease about the civil permission of brothels, for they provide youth with an easy occasion of sin, and militate against the natural checks of fear and shame.[58]

Vanity and extravagance of dress in men, again a traditional complaint,[59] is still worthy of rebuke. Longland finds this false gorgeousness ' outrageouslye, excessyuely, and excedyngly out of ordre ';[60] but never is it more sinful than in those who dress above their station, ' in especyall meane men, seruynge men, bestowynge vpon one payre of hoses, in maner as moche as his half yeres wages cometh vnto. Alas, how can this be borne? How can this contynue, vnlesse they haue lyueloode to mayntayne it, as they haue not?'[61] The lower orders do not merely dress above their condition, they act above it too says Scott, preaching at the end of Henry VIII's reign:

> . . . may we not see a seruynge man, hauynge not past foure nobles, or XL s[hillings] wages to liue vpon, so gorgiously appareled in his gesture, and behauoure of his bodye, in his paase, and goynge so vse him selfe, as yf he were a man of substaunce, yea an Esquier or a knyght, and if a man wolde haue experience further of his maners & conditions, he shall fynde hym stoute in wordes, lyberall, ye, prodigall in expenses and all together gyuen to prefere himself vnto other man. . . .[62]

Apprentices will not keep obedient to masters, adds Scott, particularly those who are averse to the old religious order:

> . . . these specially wyll haue in their handes the new testament, and they wyll talke much of the scripture, goodes word, and yet wyll not learne thereof to be obedient and gentle vnto theyr maysters: they wyll talke muche of Paul, and yet it doth nothinge moue them that Paule in so many places doth beate and incoulcate in, that seruauntes sholde be obedient, and faythful vnto their maysters. . . .[63]

Again, taking another old topic of complaint, Longland declares that the misuse of holy days is worse than ever before: '. . . we daley, we playe, we ryyd, we labour, we vse outragious games. We commyte more synne in oon holidaye, then in twentye workynge dayes. For now we bestowe it all in voluptie, all in pleasur, in carnalyte, in luxus liuinge & wanton passe tyme.'[64]

---

[58] Ibid. sig. Ev[r].
[59] See Owst, *P.M.E.*, pp. 170–1; *L. & P.M.E.*, pp. 404–11, *The Destructorium Viciorum of Alexander Carpenter*, p. 29.
[60] *Sermonde at Grenewiche*, 1538, sig. Diii[r].   [61] Ibid.
[62] *Two notable sermones lately preached at Pauls crosse*, sig. Hiii[r].   [63] Ibid. sig. Hiv[r].
[64] *Sermonde at Rychemunte*, 1535, sig. Cii[v]. Cf. too *Sermonde at Grenewiche*, 1538, sig. Ii[r]. For ealier complaints on this topic see Owst, *L. & P.M.E.*, pp. 98, 161, 359, 362, 364, 388, 393–5, 423, 435–8, 483–4.

Swearing and blasphemy, also much lamented by the medieval preachers,[65] were never more prevalent; as Longland puts it: 'The olde man nowe blasphemythe god, the yonge man, the woman, the childe, the infante, the noble man, the ryche man, the poure man. And doo not only blaspheme his holy name, butt doo blaspheme hys harte, hys soule, hys armes, hys bodye, hys woundes, hys passyon, hys dethe: and hys mooste precyous bloode. . . .'[66]

The greed and dishonesty of merchants, another stock theme,[67] still must be castigated: Edgeworth attributes it to presumption: 'Why doth one neighboure deceiue another nowe in this fayre time; by false weightes or measures, by false lyghtes, by false oothes? because they feare not God that hath forbid vs to do so.'[68] He sees a new capitalist venture, the floating of a company, as an example of covetousness: 'You haue in this citie erect a certaine confederacie, which you call the companye, I pray God it may do well, but I perceiue a certaine mundanitie in it, a worldlye couetous caste to bring the gaines that was indifferent & comon to al the merchants of this citie into the handes of a fewe persones.'[69] Scott knows well the tricks of the London drapers, how they break the girdle of truth: if a man desires to buy a ' peece of clooth or chamlet ', the merchant will immediately show him one, and declare ' that that ys for hym '. If the purchaser ask to see a better, the wily merchant replies ' with great oathes ' that it is ' cleare the beste in his shoppe, and that there is not a better in London '. The customer buys, and if he should meet a friend, who, liking the cloth, goes to the shop to ask for a similar piece, the merchant will again immediately produce a piece of cloth and praise it as before; and if this second purchaser refer to the piece sold to his friend, and ask to see a better, the merchant now ' wyll answer with grete othes & say: this is worth thre of thother '.[70]

Another traditional theme appears in Scott who complains about the ' common officers ' who should learn of St. John the Baptist who executed his office in accordance with his Master's will:

> . . . but officers in these our dayes, be of a contrarye sorte, for they doo not regarde nor requyre an office, but for this ende, that they may promote and exalte their frendes, enlarge theyr patrimonie, lyue idely, fare dylycately, be appareled gorgiously, & to bringe these thynges to pas, they flatter greate menne,

---

[65] See Owst, *L. & P.M.E.*, pp. 414–25.
[66] *Sermond at Rychemunte*, 1535, sig. Ciii[r].
[67] See Owst, *P.M.E.*, pp. 17, 20, 80, 123, 124, 163, 182, 264, 265; *L. & P.M.E.*, pp. 352–61.
[68] *Sermons*, f. 135[v].   [69] Ibid. f. 211[r].
[70] *Two notable sermones lately preached at Pauls crosse*, sig. Iii[v].

they contempne, ye and polle poore men, if a ryche man of eny parte do his dewtie, that he is commaunded to do, of his lorde, or kynge, by them he shalbe praysed, yea and well rewarded, but if the poore man do it with neuer so greate dylygence, there shall no worde be spoken of it, agayne if the poore man therein offende, he shall be streyghtly punyshed, if the riche man omitte the hole, eyther the offycers mouthes shalbe stopped with a bribe, or els for feare of displeasure, they wyll let it slyp, so that in them it shall not be punysshed.[71]

However two new themes of complaint appear towards the end of Henry VIII's reign. First, the decay of the universities and grammar schools arouses the apprehensions of the preachers under the stern régime of the aged Supreme Head. Edgeworth sadly declares:

. . . verye pitie moueth me to exhorte you to mercye and pitie on the poore studentes in the vniuersities Oxforde & Cambridge, which were neuer fewer in number, & yet they that be lefte, be ready to runne abrode into the world and to leaue their study for very nede. Iniquite is so aboundaunt that charitie is all colde. A man would haue pitie to heare the lamentable complaintes that I heard lately, being among which wold god I were able to releue. This I shal assure you, that (in my opinion) ye cannot better bestowe your charitie.[72]

Chedsey is concerned about the future of the Christian faith itself:

The vniuersities decaye: Grammer scoles be desolated: The olde trees by reason of age ware away and dy: there is nother slyppes nor graffes newe planted: it is to be feared that the fayth wyl away.[73]

Secondly, the decay of ' hospitality ' and the alarming increase of ' engrossing ' in the countryside, causes Chedsey to declaim:

Wo to you that ioyne house to house, and couple fylde to fylde, pasture to pasture, that the poore can get no grounde amonge them, shal you dwell alone in the myddle of the earth? In tyme paste were actes made agaynst decayenge of houses & dwellynge places, and for a tyme was well obserued & kepte: and now a dayes many for feare of the statute kepe vp the house: but as for the house holdyng they maynteyne so, that nother mouse nor sparowe wyll abyde there. Actes also & statutes hath ben made to stynt men from great engrossyng of farmes, and a certayne number of shepe to be kept, and no men to passe that: but the lawes be oftentymes as the philosopher Anacharsis

---

[71] Ibid. sig. Iviv–Iviir. For earlier complaints on this topic see Owst, *L. & P.M.E.* pp. 341–7.
[72] *Sermons*, f. 54r.   [73] *Two notable sermones preached at Paules crosse*, sig. Fiiv.

was wont to say: *Leges aranearum telis similes in quibus infirmiora animalia herent valentiora autem perrumpunt.* ['The laws are like spiders' webs in which the smaller creatures are caught, but through which the stronger break.']⁷⁴ [74]

Similarly Edgeworth deprecates the hospitality of the rich, 'with diuersitie of exquisite disshes, dasshed with spices and delicate wynes and vsed for kynredde and friendes, and suche as can requyte lyke agayne: If poore people haue anye thynge it is those scrappes that be nexte the dogges meate.'[75]

In all this volume of complaint, new as well as traditional, it is noteworthy that the preachers never deal with specific and individual cases of the evils they denounce, as Latimer was to do in Edward's reign;[76] rather they content themselves with broadly general declamations on the topics which give offence. Of course even by the mid-fourteenth century the traditional subjects of complaint had become thoroughly stereotyped in treatment,[77] and although the author of a preaching manual like Thomas Waleys would allow reflections on particular individuals if they were public enemies and notorious sinners, and if it were expedient or necessary for the Church or people,[78] nevertheless what was possible in the way of free speech from the pulpit in Edward's time, was probably hopelessly imprudent under Henry VIII.

It is little wonder that with so many sins to complain about the preachers should find it necessary to exhort their audience to Penance. It is not by chance that Fisher and Longland choose the Penitential Psalms as the basis of a series of sermons! The state of sin is indeed fearful, for ' within vs is the moost stynkynge abhomynacyon of our synne, wherby the ymage of almyghty god in vs is very foule defourmed, and by that we be made vnto hym verye enemyes '.[79] Hardened sinners who abstain from confession merely increase their wretchedness, for then ' we prouoke the goodnes of almyghty god to punysshe vs bycause of our sturdynes, & wyll not turne to hym by doynge penaunce, and in maner we gyue hym occasyon to shewe vengeaunce & destroy vs bothe body & soule. For truly ouer our hedes hangeth a swerde euer mouynge & redy by the power of god, whose stroke whan it shall come shall be so moche

---

[74] Ibid. sig. Eiiʳ: cf. too ibid. sig. Dviiiᵛ.
[75] *Sermons*, f. 203ʳ.   [76] Cf. *post*, p. 268–9, 269 n., 213, 270 n., 223.
[77] See Owst, *P.M.E.*, p. 308, especially the quotation from Richard de Bury (1334); also ibid. p. 251. The situation was even worse by the late fifteenth century; see Owst *The Destructorium Viciorum of Carpenter*, pp. 3, 29, 31.
[78] See Charland, *Artes Praedicandi*, p. 337 (Waleys).
[79] Fisher, *English Works*, Pt. I, p. 93.

more greuous that we so longe by our grete & manyfolde vnkyndnes haue caused almyghty god and prouoked hym to more dyspleasure.'[80] The man lying in the ' triple death ' of sin,[81] loses too his store of merit, so laboriously laid up; one mortal sin will kill the life of grace no matter how ' good ' he has been; while the whole creation accuses him of his wickedness, and presents a hostile front to him, until he returns to God by Penance.[82] It is interesting to note that the ' contrition ' which these preachers recommend, is not merely a penitent will; rather it is an exaggerated, emotional, tearful sorrow which is desiderated. 'We must', says Fisher, ' eyther wepe & wayle in this lyfe with profytable teres wherewith the soule is washed and made clene from synne, elles shal we wayle & wepe after this lyfe with vnprofytable teres whiche intollerably shall scalde & brenne our bodyes.'[83] Similarly Longland approvingly cites the example of St. Peter, who after his denial of his master, ' as saynt Clement writeth of hym, he dydd frome that tyme forwarde customable euery nyght, frome cocke crowynge tyll the houer of matens contynue in prayer, wepynge plentyfully, this hys denyall of his master Christe: ye in somuche that hys face was scorched & sthriuelde with the contynuance of the trykelynge down of the sayd teares by his chekis.'[84] However although Penance may be bitter, God is merciful to the penitent, who may always bear away his vial full of the precious water of forgiveness from that never failing Well-Spring.[85]

Themes of controversy make their appearance in Henry VIII's reign. A preliminary skirmish between the defenders of the old order and the supporters of the new spirit of reform occurred in 1515 when Parliament was about to renew an act of 1513 which took ' benefit of clergy ' (the right to be tried in an ecclesiastical court) from all clerics not yet subdeacons, who were accused of murder or felony. Richard Keydermyster, abbot of Winchcombe, protested in a sermon at Paul's Cross but was answered by Henry Standish,

[80] Ibid. pp. 28–9.   [81] Longland, *Quinque Sermones*, f. 56ʳ.
[82] Longland, *Sermones*, f. 20ʳ; Fisher, *English Works*, Pt. I, pp. 244, 270.
[83] *English Works*, Pt. I, p. 31; cf. too ibid. p. 16.
[84] *Sermonde at Rychemunte*, 1535, sig. Iiiiᵛ–Iiivʳ; cf. Fisher *English Works*, Pt. I, p. 120; also ibid. p. 114 (the example of the weeping St. Mary Magdalene). On the desire of the late Middle Ages for the 'gift of tears', see W. James, *The Varieties of Religious Experience*, (London, reptd., 1952) p. 264; H. O. Taylor, *The Medieval Mind*, 4th edn., 2 vols., (London, 1925) vol. I, pp. 383–8, 478–9; J. Huizinga, *The Waning of the Middle Ages*, (London, reptd., 1952) p. 174.
[85] Longland, *Sermond at Rychemunte*, 1535, sig. Biʳ, quoted *ante*, p. 140. Cf. too Fisher *English Works*, Pt. 1, pp. 97, 138–9, 161–3; MS. Harleian 2247, ff. 50ʳ⁻ᵛ, 52ʳ⁻³ʳ; MS. Lincoln Cath. Libr. 50, ff. 90ᵛ⁻5ʳ.

guardian of the London Franciscans, who approved of the new legislation, and having won court favour, was in due course made Bishop of St. Asaph's (1518).[86]

However it was the Lutheran revolt which called forth the major efforts of the traditionalists in defence of Catholic doctrines and in attack upon Luther and his heresies. It is noteworthy that the defenders give little real theological argument:[87] Fisher's two sermons depend on allegoric interpretations of Scripture[88] and the alleging of a few *dicta* of the Fathers;[89] Longland is content to join the contemporary heretic's name with those of former centuries —with Arius, ' Manicheus ', Pelagius, Origen, Jovinian, Helvidius, Nestorius, Donatus, Wyclif, Hus and others; and to indulge in a tirade of personal denunciation.[90] Edgeworth indeed defends Ceremonies in an interesting and well worked out homily,[91] but more usually he deals in mere debater's points: as that it is foolish not to accept the doctrine of purgatory because the word does not occur in Scripture, for where do we find the word Trinity?[92] Or again, the folly of Lutheranism is dismissed by a picture of its ludicrous practical results in Germany; there they:

> . . . confounde and deface all good order of diuine and humaine thinges, allowing the women to serue the altar, and to say masse while the men tarry at home, and keepe the children and wash theyr ragges and clothes: and as well they might allow the women to be captains of their warres and to leade and gide an army of men in battel, while theyr husbandes tary at home to mylk the Cowe, and serue the Sow, and to spynne and carde.[93]

An anonymous preacher expounds the right use of images, as books

---

[86] See Constant, *The Reformation in England*, vol. I, p. 23.

[87] Owst points out: ' on its purely doctrinal side, the English pulpit of the waning Middle Ages has little inspiration to offer', (*L. & P.M.E.*, p. 54) while Hughes (*The Reformation in England*, vol. I, pp. 97–8) interestingly, and, one feels with justice, stresses that this theological weakness in English piety was one of the main reasons why the dogmatic revolution was effected with only isolated protest.

[88] See *ante*, pp. 17–19.

[89] *English Works*, Pt. I, pp. 318–21 (*dicta* from St, Augustine, St. Ambrose, St. Gregory the Great, St. Jerome, St. Cyprian, St. John Chrystosom and Origen); p. 327 (St. Augustine); p. 333 (Origen); p. 341 (St. Jerome, St. Augustine). Of course a deeper treatment of controversial issues is given by Fisher in his Latin treatises, *Sacri Sacerdotii Defensio Contra Lutherum* (1525), Eng. tr. by P. E. Hallet (London, 1935) and *De Veritate Corporis et Sanguinis Christi in Eucharistia* (1527).

[90] *Tres Conciones*, ff. 41^v–2^r: ' If you commit the works of this one man to the flames you will kill the whole hydra of heresies, you will subdue with certain victory the beast of many heads. It is your heresy I mean, O Luther, Luther: all we faithful people want your opinion changed, you lying man, you wretched impostor, you most unfaithful minister of God and equally of the whole Christian world! Our desire and wish is to destroy your bundle of most unfaithful opinions with a bundle of wood. . . .'

[91] *Sermons*, ff. 88^r–98^r. [92] Ibid. f. 20^v.

[93] Ibid. f. 165^v.

for the laity and aids to devotion,[94] but proceeds to allegorize the commandment against idolatry.[95] William Peryn defends the doctrine of Transubstantiation, but it is noteworthy that instead of defending it on rational grounds, he emphasises the miraculous element in the Real Presence, and castigates the Protestants for being rationalists;[96] he even states that the Catholic doctrine is against both sense and reason.[97] Adopting such an extreme Occamist position to the mysteries of the Faith, Peryn relies on typology,[98] some *dicta* of the Fathers,[99] and the consideration that in view of Our Lord's promises to the Church it cannot be that she has erred for so many years![100] However he does clear up some misunderstandings, as that it is incorrect to say that the priest makes God; he is but the minister, whose words occasion the descent of Christ on to the altar;[101] and that if a mouse should eat the Blessed Sacrament, it gnaws only the outward appearance, while Our Lord remains inviolate.[102]

An element of the ludicrous enters the defence of Catholic doctrine in the person of William Hubberdin (an opponent of Latimer) about whose ' sermon of dancing ' Foxe tells in his incomparable manner:

> ... the said Hubberdin, after his long railing in all places against Luther, Melancthon, Zuinglius, John Frith, Tyndale, Latimer, and all other like professors, after his hypocritical open alms, given out of other men's purses, his long prayers, pretensed devotions, devout fastings, his woolward-going, and other his prodigious demeanour,—riding in his long gown down to the horse-heels like a pharisee, or rather like a sloven dirted up to

[94] MS. Bodley, 119, ff. 1ʳ–4ʳ; the pictorial details of the old images themselves are interesting: St. Paul with his sword and book, St. Laurence with his gridiron, St. Catherine with her wheel, St. Andrew with his cross. (Ibid. ff. 1ᵛ–2ʳ.)

[95] Ibid. ff. 4ʳ–10ʳ: see *ante*, pp. 7–8.

[96] *Thre godlye and notable Sermons, of the moost honourable and blessed sacrament of the Aulter*, f. 6ʳ.

[97] Ibid. f. 9ᵛ. ' This miracle in this sacrament is not wroughte (as I haue saide) to perswade faith ... but this doth presuppose and require a constante faithe ... For in this sacrament, naturall experience contendeth openly against faith, and not onely reason, but also, all oure senses are ledde captiue, against all naturall experience, into the soole and onely worde of god. And that not in one miracle, but in many, whiche are deprehended, onely by constant fayth.'

[98] See *ante*, p. 19.

[99] *Thre godlye and notable Sermons, of the moost honourable and blessed sacrament of the Aulter*, e.g., f. 66ᵛ (St. John Chrysostom); f. 67ʳ (Irenaeus); ff. 67ᵛ–9ʳ (various *dicta* from St, Cyril); ff. 96ᵛ–111ʳ (a *catena* of authorities: Irenaeus, St. Ignatius, Tertullian, St. Cyprian, Juvencus, Hilary, St. Basil, St. Gregory Nazianzen, St. Ambrose, St. Jerome, St. John Chrysostom, St. Augustine, St. Cyril of Alexandria, St. John Damascene, Cassianus, St. Athanasius, Cassiodorus, Fulgentius, St. Gregory the Great, Sedulus, Bede, Haymo).

[100] Ibid. ff. 73ᵛ–4ʳ.   [101] Ibid. ff. 139ʳ–42ʳ.   [102] Ibid. f. 144ᵛ.

the horse belly,—after his forged tales and fables, dialogues, dreams, dancings hoppings and leapings, with other like histrionical toys and gestures used in the pulpit, and all against heretics: at last riding by a church side, where the youth of the parish were dancing in the churchyard, suddenly this Silenus, lighting from his horse, by the occasion of their dancing came into the church, and there causing the bell to toll in the people, thought instead of a fitte of mirth to give them a sermon of dancing. In the which sermon, after he had patched up certain common texts out of the Scriptures, and then coming to the doctors, first to Augustine, then to Ambrose, so to Jerome and Gregory, Chrysostome and other doctors, had made them every one (after his dialogue manner) by name to answer his call, and to sing after his tune for the probation of the sacrament of the altar against John Frith, Zuinglius, Oecolampadius, Luther, Tyndale, Latimer, and other heretics (as he called them); at last, to show a perfect harmony of all these doctors together— as he had made them before to sing after his tune, so now to make them dance also after his pipe—first he calleth out Christ and his apostles; then the doctors and ancient seniors of the church, as in a round ring all to dance together, with ' pipe up Hubberdin '. Now dance Christ; now dance Peter, Paul; now dance Augustine, Ambrose, Jerome. And thus old Hubberdin, as he was dancing with his doctors lustily in the pulpit against the heretics, how he stampt and took on I cannot tell, but ' crash ', quoth the pulpit, down cometh the dancer, and there lay Hubberdin, not dancing, but sprawling in the midst of his audience; where altogether he brake not his neck, yet he so brake his leg the same time, and bruised his old bones, that he never came in pulpit more, and died not long after the same.[103]

Another opponent of Latimer, Prior Buckenham of the Cambridge Dominicans, was scarcely more successful than Hubberdin; after Latimer's famous ' Sermons of the Card ', the prior, relates Foxe:

... brought out his Christmas dice, casting there to his audience *cinque* and *quatre*; meaning by the *cinque* five places in the New Testament, and the four doctors by the *quatre*; by which his *cinque quatre* he would prove that it was not expedient the Scripture to be in English, lest the ignorant and vulgar sort through occasion thereof might haply be brought in danger to leave their vocation, or else to run into some inconvenience: as for example, the ploughman, when he heareth this in the gospel, ' No man layeth his hand on the plough and looketh back, is meet for the kingdom of God ', might peradventure hearing

[103] *Acts and Monuments*, vol. VII, pp. 477–8.

this, cease from his plough. Likewise the baker, when he heareth that a little leaven corrupteth a whole lump of dough, may percase leave our bread unleavened, and so our bodies shall be unseasoned. Also the simple man, when he heareth in the gospel, ' If thine eye offend thee, pluck it out, and cast it from thee ', may make himself blind, and so fill the world full of beggars.[104]

It was easy for Latimer, in reply, to point out that figurative phrases ' were not so diffuse and difficult, as they were common in the Scripture, and in the Hebrew tongue, but also most commonly used and known: " and not only in the Hebrew tongue, but also every speech hath its metaphors and like figurative significations, so common and vulgar to all men, that the very painters do paint them on walls and in houses " '.[105]

It should be remembered here that the defence of certain Catholic principles was carried on into Edward's reign by Gardiner and Bonner in sermons which cost them their freedom. Preaching at Paul's Cross on St. Peter's Day (29th June) 1548, Gardiner did indeed declare that he was against the Roman primacy, religious orders, pilgrimages, and palms; also that he approved of Communion under both kinds, but he opposed the marriage of the clergy, and preaching against the Mass and the Blessed Sacrament.[106] He affirmed that Christ ' was the bishop that offered for our sins, and the sacrifice that was offered. . . . And like as his sacrifice then made was sufficient for us, to deliver us from our sins, and to bring us in favour with God, so, to continue us in the same favour of God, he ordained a perpetual remembrance of himself. He ordained himself for a memory of himself, at his last supper, when he instituted the sacrament of the altar.'[107]   Gardiner is against the idea of satisfaction or new redemption in the Mass, but approves of praying for the dead during it.[108]   Although this sermon is extant only in a summary, quoted by Foxe, nevertheless it is clear that it represents a statement of belief rather than an argued defence of doctrine. Bonner, when ordered to preach at Paul's Cross in 1549 on certain points (against rebellion; that inward devotion is necessary for Communion; that externals in religion are not very important; and that the Royal power is in the youth of the monarch equal to that in his maturity), actually, says Foxe, ' did spend most part of his sermon about the gross, carnal, and papistical presence of Christ's body and blood in

[104] Ibid. pp. 449–50.   [105] Ibid. p. 450.   [106] Ibid. vol. VI, pp. 89–93.
[107] Ibid. p. 93.   [108] Ibid. p. 90.

the sacrament of the altar '.[109] Although the text of this sermon is not extant, it seems likely that it too would be more assertive than argumentative. It remains true that the greatest English Catholic apologist and controversialist of the earlier sixteenth century, as far as the popular front was concerned, was a layman, More; little of solid value was offered by the clergy until Mary's reign, with the theological preaching of Bishop Watson, his set of sermons on the Sacraments, and the Homilies set forth by Bonner.

The question of the Royal Divorce is reflected in pulpit controversy. William Peto, a Greenwich Observant, and Provincial of the Order ('another Micheas' as Stowe calls him), preaching on Ahab in the Convent Chapel before the king on 1st May 1534, alluded to Henry's 'illegitimate marriage' to Anne Boleyn, and those who had driven him like 'the four hundred prophets of Israel, by a lying spirit, [seeking] to deceive him'. Although Henry pretended not to understand, the next Sunday a royal chaplain, Richard Curwen, preached there and called Peto a 'dog, slanderer, rebel and traitor'. Peto had been summoned to Canterbury, and was not present, which enabled Curwen to declare: 'I speak to thee, Peto, who makest thyself Micheas, that thou mayest speak evil of kings, but now thou art not to be found, being fled for fear and shame, as being unable to answer my arguments.' At this, Elstow, Warden of the Convent, called out: 'Good sir, you know that father Peto is . . . not fled for fear of you, for tomorrow he will return again. In the meantime I am here as another Micheas and will lay down my life to prove all those things true which he hath taught out of the holy scripture. . . . Even unto thee, Curwin, I speak, who art one of the four hundred prophets into whom the spirit of lying is entered.' Brought before the Council, Elstow and Peto were told by Lord Essex 'that they had deserved to be put in a sack and cast into the Thames'; to which Elstow answered: 'With thanks to God we know the way to heaven as ready by water as by land.'[110]

Another aspect of the Divorce question is mirrored in the sermon against Elizabeth Barton, the 'Holy Maid of Kent', preached at Paul's Cross on 23rd November 1533 by Dr. Capon, Bishop elect of Bangor. In this he tries to destroy the impression that she was a saint and a prophet. At the beginning of the illusion, says Capon, Elizabeth was a servant with Thomas Cobb, the Archbishop of Canterbury's farmer at Aldington, Kent. After a seem-

[109] Ibid. vol. V, pp. 745–6.
[110] See Constant, *The Reformation in England*, vol. I, p. 132, n. 183.

ingly miraculous cure of an impostume in the stomach, she entered a nunnery at Canterbury. Hearing Dr. Bocking, her Confessor, speak of the ' King's matters ', she spoke too, declaring that God commanded her to say to Wolsey and Warham (the Archbishop of Canterbury) that if they married or furthered the design of the king to marry Anne Boleyn, they would be destroyed. When it seemed that the prelates believed her, she then said that if the king married Anne Boleyn, he would not reign a month after. This opinion was disseminated by ' religious men '. After events proved the falsity of this prophecy, the Maid declared that one month meant one month in the sight of God. She then said that her revelations were only to be declared openly when Dr. Bocking had knowledge from God that it was time. He read to her from St. Brigit and St. Catherine of Siena, and from this she feigned her revelations. Her impostures went further than this however, she burned her veil and said that the Devil did it; she burned brimstone to make a smell when she maintained the Devil was with her; also she said that the Devil vexed her at nights, to the intent that the other nuns would be afraid to stir at night and she could walk abroad as she wished. As the Maid has confessed her many deceits, says Dr. Capon, he hopes that people will not *now* oppose the king's marriage![111]

The most important theme of controversy, however, is that of the primacy of the Pope. There is no doubt of course that the Roman primacy was commonly taught until the time of the ' King's Proceedings '; as Alcock declares: ' the chirche of Rome *sedes apostolica* is our moder, & we are all generat by her *vera fide* & dyspoused *in castitate* to Chryste Ihesu.'[112] The pulpit attack on the papal primacy was a matter of deliberate Government policy. In late 1533 the Council ordered that no one was to preach at Paul's Cross without declaring that the authority of the Bishop of Rome was no greater than that of any other foreign bishop.[113] In the ' Order for the bidding of the beads ' of 1534 issued by the Council, the Pope was said to be the enemy of England, and his power a corruption which no man was to defend.[114] On 1st June 1535 Letters General were issued to the bishops that they were to preach the sincere word of God and the new title of the king, and that the

---

[111] See L. E. Whatmore, ' The Sermon against the Holy Maid of Kent and her Adherents, delivered at Paul's Cross, November the 23rd., 1533, and at Canterbury December the 7th., ' *E.H.R.*, lviii (1943) pp. 463–75.

[112] *Sermo. . . Qui habet aures audiendi: audiat*, sig. Cvi[r].

[113] M. Maclure, *The Paul's Cross Sermons*, 1534–1642, p. 25.

[114] P. Hughes, *The Reformation in England*, vol. I, p. 264.

lower clergy were to do the same every Sunday and feast day.[115]
The first Royal Injunctions of Henry VIII (1536) ordered that for a
quarter of a year parsons were to declare ' once every Sunday, and
after that at the leastwise twice every quarter, in their sermons and
other collations, that the Bishop of Rome's usurped power and
jurisdiction, having no establishment nor ground by the law of God,
was of most just causes taken away and abolished; and therefore they
owe unto him no manner of obedience or subjection, and that the
king's power is within his dominion the highest power and potentate
under God, to whom all men within the same dominion by God's
commandment owe most loyalty and obedience, afore and above all
powers and potentates in earth.'[116] Although, according to Chapuys,
the French Ambassador, the preachers against the Pope at Easter
1534 acquitted themselves ' desperately ',[117] Simon Matthew,
preaching in St. Paul's Cathedral on 27th June, 1535, deprecates
scurrility in preaching against the primacy, as equating the Pope
with the whore of Babylon;[118] but he speaks sharply against Fisher
and More (martyred in June and July of this year) as traitors to the
king.[119] Cranmer however, preaching at Paul's Cross on 6th February 1536, ' approved ', says Charles Wriothesley, ' by scripture and
by the decrees of the Popes lawes, that the Bishop of Rome, otherwise called Pope, was Anti-christ, and also brought divers expositions of holie sainctes and doctors for the same; and how craftelie,
and by what meanes, and how long, he had taken upon him the
power of God and the aucthoritie above all princes christened, and
how his aucthoritie and lawes was contrarie to scripture and the
lawe of God. . . .'[120] Tunstall, preaching at the Cross on 27th
February 1536 (Quinquagesima) in the presence of Cranmer, and
before four Carthusians who had denied the Royal Supremacy,
'declared the profession of the Bishop of Rome when he is elected
Pope, according to the confirmation of eight universall general
counsells, which were congregate for the faith of all Christendome;
and everie Pope taketh an othe on the articles, promising to observe,
keepe and hould all that the said counsells confirmed, and to dampne

[115] R. W. Dixon, *History of the Church of England from the Abolition of the Roman
jurisdiction*, 6 vols. (London, 1878–1902) vol. I, p. 255.
[116] H. Gee and W. J. Hardy, *Documents illustrative of English Church History* (London,
1896) no. LXII, p. 270.
[117] Maclure, *The Paul's Cross Sermons*, p. 184.
[118] *A sermon made in the cathedrall churche of Saynt Paule* (London, 1535) sig. Di[r-v].
[119] Ibid. sig. Cvii[r]–Cviii[r].
[120] Charles Wriothesley, *A Chronicle of England during the reigns of the Tudors, from*
A.D. 1485–1559, ed. W. D. Hamilton, 2 vols. (London, 1875–7) C.S., new series, nos.
XI and XX, vol. I, pp. 33–4.

all that they dampned; and how he, contrarie to his oth, hath usurped his power and aucthoritie over all Christendome; and also how uncharitably he had handled . . . King Henrie the Eight, in marying [him to] his brother's wife, contrarie to God's lawes and also against how owne promise and decrees, . . . and also how everie Kinge hath the highe power under God, and ought to be the supreame head over all spirituall prelates. . . .'[121] The attack as conducted later is however less a reasoned assault on the old position, than a castigation of the pride of the Pontiffs in exalting themselves over the whole Church. Preaching at Greenwich on Good Friday 1538 Longland declares that Christ is the only Universal Bishop, and that the Pope outrageously steals some of his honour;[122] while Tunstall, preaching on Palm Sunday 1539, gives a little sketch of an item of procedure at the Papal Court, which he maintains is quite inordinate. Having mentioned how the sinful woman washed Our Lord's feet with her tears,[123] the bishop continues:

> . . . And fete be washed to no man, but whan they be naked, so that it appereth, that Christis feete than washed with teres and kyssed were bare. But the byshop of Rome offreth his fete to be kyssed, shod with his shoes on. for I se my selfe being than present. xxxiiii. yere ago, whan Iulius than bishop of Rome stode on his fete, and one of his chamberlaynes helde vp his skyrt, bicause it stode not as he thought with his dignitie, that he shulde do it hym selfe, that his showe myght appere, whiles a noble manne of great age dyd prostrate hym selfe vpon the grounde, and kyssed his shoo. Whiche he stately suffered to be doone as of duetie. where me thynke I sawe Cornelius the Centurion, capitayne of the Italions bande spoken of in the tenth chapiter of the actes, submyttyng him selfe to Peter, and moche honourynge hym. but I sawe not Peter there to take hym vp, and to byd hym ryse, sayenge. I am a man as thou arte. as saynte Peter dyd saye to Cornelius. so that the byshoppes of Rome, admyttynge suche adoration dewe vnto god, do clymme aboue the heuenly cloudes. that is to saye, aboue the apostels sent into the worlde by Christe, to water the erthly and carnalle hartes of men, by their heauenly doctrine of the worde of god.[124]

Another point of attack on the old religious order was provided by exposure of ' miraculous ' images and relics. On 24th February 1538 the Rood of Grace, from Boxley Abbey, Kent, was brought to

[121] Ibid. pp. 34–5.   [122] *Sermonde at Grenewiche*, 1538, sig. Bii[r].
[123] *A sermon made vpon Palme sondaye*, sig. Bviii[r].
[124] Ibid. sig. Bviii[v]–Ci[r]. Luther speaks against this kissing of the Pope's foot; *An appeal to the Ruling Class of German Nationality, as to the amelioration of the state of Christendom*, (Woolf, *Reformation Writings of Martin Luther*, vol. I, pp. 151–2).

Paul's Cross, and as Wriothesley relates, ' their at the sermon made by the Bishopp of Rochester [John Hilsey], the abuses of the graces [vices?] and engines, used in old tyme in the said image, was declared, which image was made of paper and cloutes from the legges upward ech legges and armes were of timber, and so the people had bene deluded and caused to doe great idolatrie by the said image, of long contynuance. . . .'[125] Hilsey went on to declare that images cause idolatry and should in general be done away with. If any wish to offer to images, then let them rather do it to the poor people. Twenty years previously, he avers, he heard the confession of a miller's wife from near Hailes, where the relic of the Holy Blood was kept. The woman said that she had received jewels from the abbot, which had been offered to the Holy Blood. When, owing to feelings of conscience, she had been about to refuse a stone, the abbot told her not to be so foolish as the relic was only duck's blood. After this sermon the Rood of Boxley was publicly broken up.[126] In a sermon later the same year however (24th November), Hilsey declared that the Holy Blood of Hailes was in fact not duck's blood, but ' hony clarified and coloured with saffron, and lyinge lyke a goume. . . .'[127]

In the last years of Henry's reign, many must have yearned for the old consent in doctrine, when no matters of faith were questioned; Chedsey nostalgically declaims (in 1544):

The tyme hath ben, when that those whych haue occupyed this place, haue laboured & endeuoured themselues with al the grace geuyn to them to haue pacified & sette at quyet the weake and feble conscyences of their audyens. And nowe (the more it is to be lamented) singularytye so ruleth; that he that can best dispute and reason a new matter in the pulpyt, he is the beste preacher. Simplicitye than dyd edyfye and made peace. Singularytye now doth destroy and setteth men at varyaunce. Then was preachynge swete melodye, whan the pypes were in tune, Nowe it is an vnswete noyse: for the pipes yarryth. Then men endeuered them selues to fulfyl that in lyfe, which the other preached, herde or redde by worde. Nowe al our study is to here new & straunge thynges to speke and set them forth galantly, and lytel or nothynge to do. . . .[128]

But the preaching of controversy was to loom large indeed in the succeeding reigns of the century![129]

In conclusion, it must be asked: what were the positive values

[125] Wriothesley, *Chronicle*, vol. I, p. 75.   [126] Ibid. p. 76.   [127] Ibid. p. 90.
[128] *Two notable sermones, lately preached at Pauls crosse*, sig. Ciii[v].
[129] See *post*, pp. 263–7, 279–88, 292–300.

which the preachers of this time offered amongst so much pessimism and denunciation? First, there is the glorious example of the saints, those who have used the appointed means of prayer and the sacraments to acquire heroic virtues, and to become the lights of the world in their several generations. Unfortunately they are all too often presented as mere wonder-workers to be marvelled at by simple audiences.[130] For example in the *De Tempore* collection in MS. Hatton 96, St. Wulfstan is remembered for a miracle which he performed when removed from his bishopric by William the Conqueror, as being unworthy of that dignity. The saint declares that he is indeed not worthy of his office, so will return his cross to him who gave it him: ' þan vent Volftone to seynt Edward tombe and in the merbull stone he put ys cros like as on myʒth a don in a litill clay and a none Volftone vent is way.'[131] The new bishop tries to remove the cross, but ' he myʒth neþer meve it ne stere it no more þan it had bene a hous.'[132] William and his bishops hasten in awe to behold this wonder, which they all declare is ' a myracle of god ';[133] so Wulfstan is reinstated, and after his death, ' at ys tombe many meracles oure lorde did for ys loue '.[134] Many of the crude hagiographical panegyrics found in the series from which this sermon is taken, are based on the *Legenda Aurea*, that favourite medieval source book; but even more than in the case of Mirk, the sensational elements of the original are seized upon, and the more spiritual and morally edifying neglected. Thus in the account of St. John the Evangelist, we hear how, ' after þe Ascension, he preched in Asie and þere he did many myraclis, for þere he turned the grauell of þe see into precious stones and gemmys and þe bowes and spray of the wode into pure gold ':[135] how at the behest of Aristodamus, the priest of Diana, he drank venom unharmed,[136] and how after his death ' þei founde nouʒth else in ys sepulcur bot manna, all þe grounde as whyte as floure, for þer was no more left on ys body on erth, þan was of our lady seynt Mary '.[137] However, this simple homilist omits other parts of the account of St. John given in the *Legenda*, as his sermon against riches,[138] his reclaiming of his young convert who had lapsed and become the captain of a band of thieves,[139] his wise recommendation of recreation,[140] and his insistence on the central importance of charity.[141]

[130] For similar earlier treatment of the saints, cf. Owst, *P.M.E.*, pp. 245–6; *L. & P.M.E.*, pp. 145–8.
[131] MS. Hatton 96, f. 16ᵛ.   [132] Ibid.   [133] Ibid. f. 17ʳ.   [134] Ibid.
[135] Ibid. ff. 11ᵛ–12ʳ.   [136] Ibid. f. 12ʳ.   [137] Ibid.   [138] See *Legenda Aurea*, p. 58.
[139] Ibid. p. 60.   [140] Ibid. pp. 60–1.   [141] Ibid. p. 61.

S

In these unpolished sermons there is too the praise of a morbidly exaggerated asceticism; St. Wulfstan ' was a man of gret abstinence. For þre days in þe weke he neyþer ete ne dronke, nor with no man wolde speke, and oþer þre days he wolde ete bot a lytyll and þat at he ete was brede and wortys ';[142] St. James the Less 'vas called Iamys þe ryghtful, for his holynes; he vas neuer out of ys bedes, for he kneled an hundreþ syþes on þe day and as often on þe nyȝth vnto þe fadur of heuen. Ys knes ver as ruȝth and as þike for knelyng asse it had be the hyde of a best ';[143] St. Mary Magdalene, as a satisfactory penance for her fleshly sins, lived alone for thirty years in the wilderness, seeing neither man nor woman, and eating no earthly food.[144] However, even in the least spiritual presentation, the saints do represent the victory of the children of light over the powers of darkness; and although most men may misuse their lives, the preachers are consoled because some at least have fought the good fight and conquered; as Longland says:

Could the deuyl, thynke you, overcome saynt Katheryn, saynt Margarite, which were but of xiiii and xv yeares of age or there aboutes? Nay, nay nay. Noo neyther the deuyll, nether the worlde, neyther the prysons, neyther the yngyns of wheles, neyther the fyre, neyther the sworde coulde ouercome these two yonge daemysels: but strongly they dyd ouercome the deuyll and all his bende as maye appeare to those that wyll reede there lyues which are red in the church. . . .[145]

Although these pre-Reformation Catholic and Henrician preachers seldom deal with the happier, more triumphant, or tenderer aspects of the Christian religion (and this is, of course, a grave criticism of the religious temper of the time),[146] nevertheless when they do so, their words have a power and an appeal which comes partly from the very paucity of such passages, but also from a certain inherent intensity of feeling; that even if most men blindly disregard these values, they are to those who have understanding, the most precious in the world. Alcock and Longland are still fired by the monastic and ascetical ideal; the religious life is a new paradise, says Alcock, for as Adam had grace, immortality and the lordship over all creatures, so have men in religion;[147] they despise the world

[142] MS. Hatton 96, f. 16r.   [143] Ibid. f. 38r.
[144] Ibid. f. 50v.
[145] *Sermonde at Grenewiche*, 1538, sig. Kir: cf. too Alcock, *Desponsacio virginis christo*, sig. Aivr (St. Margaret); ibid. sig. Aivv (St. Juliana); ibid. sig. Av–Avir (St. Agnes). Cf. further, Baron, *Sermones*, f. 4r (St. Lucy, St. Agnes, St. Louis of Marseilles).
[146] This is fully within the late medieval tradition; cf. Owst, *L. & P.M.E.*, p. 22.
[147] *Mons Perfectionis*, sig. Biiiv.

quasi nichil habentes, et omnia possidentes (2 Cor. vi. 10; ' as having nothing, and possessing all things ', Douay),[148] and valiantly they conquer the beasts of temptation. Longland's praise of the religious life as it should be lived (in language borrowed from St. Jerome) comes but twenty-seven years before the dissolution of the monasteries[149]:

> Happy is your conscience, happy and blessed your virginity, if on account of the love of Christ (which is wisdom, chastity, obedience, and the other virtues) no other love is admitted into your heart. This love shuts out the love of the world, as one key in a lock keeps out another. You must keep to the chosen path, you must go forward through the scorpions and adders of the world, you must make your journey through the snares and perils of this life with girded loins and sandalled feet, grasping your staff in your hands; that, having a pure conscience you may truly say with the prophet, *Domine dilexi decorum domus tuae, et locum habitationis gloriae tuae. Unam petii a te, hanc requiram, ut inhabitem in domo domini omnibus diebus vitae meae.* [Ps. xxv. 8 (Vg.); ' I have loved, O Lord, the beauty of thy house; and the place where thy glory dwelleth', Douay; Ps. xxvi. 4 (Vg.); ' One thing I have asked of the Lord, this will I seek after; that I may dwell in the house of the Lord all the days of my life', Douay]. Then at length you will be able to reach those sweet streams of the Jordan, to enter into the promised land, to go up to the house of God.[150]

Such a life may not be easy to live; Alcock warns the nuns that they must be unquestioningly obedient,[151] and further:

> . . . ye muste be pacyent amonge your systers & suffre theym, ye muste be meke ye muste ete and drynke suche metes and drynkes as ye be commaunded, and whan ye haue not half slept ynough ye must ryse, ye must synge in your course and ordre with your systers, and take no hede though your voyce be not moost swettest and clere, so ye haue a swete deuocyon, ye must serue your systers and wasshe theyr feet, for Cryste Iesu to whome ye shall be spoused vnto was obedyent to his fader and suffred deth, and he god and man wasshed also the feet of his dyscyples poore fysshers.[152]

Marriage is not unusually exalted; this is the state, says Fisher, in which spiritual fruit is brought forth but thirtyfold.[153] However it

---

[148] Ibid.   [149] Ibid. sig. Biv^r-v.
[150] *Tres Conciones*, f. 11^r; cf. St. Jerome, Epist., XXII. *P.L.*, xxii. 395, 410; Epist., CXXX, *P.L.*, xxii. 1123.
[151] *Desponsacio virginis christo*, sig. Avi^r.
[152] Ibid. sig. Avi^r-v.
[153] *English Works*, Pt. I, p. 468.

is refreshing to find Tunstall not only praising the mystical and spiritual side of marriage,[154] but stressing the human solace of a wife and children in sickness and old age,[155] together with the natural joys of parenthood: ' How great', he declares, 'is the joy of a father when his little ones recognise him, and come to him with smiles, when in their first attempts to speak they utter ridiculous sounds in their effort to mimic our words, when, with quick spent anger, they contend for nuts like kings for kingdoms.'[156]

The Catholic Church itself, the Ark of Salvation, kindles the imagination of Longland; against that Divine Society the gates of hell will never prevail; having spoken of the ' figure ' of Solomon's Temple, the bishop proceeds, speaking of the Church:

> It is built of living and four-sided stones. Four-sided are those men who are polished by the four cardinal, and the other virtues. They are ' hewn out ' who do not leave the faith of the Church because of torments, bruises and oppression: they are regarded as brighter and more sparkling than pearls and every precious stone, because of faith, hope and charity. They shine most radiantly with chastity of body and integrity of spirit. They have not the perishable nature of the cedar, but endure for ever. They are shaped, they are coloured, they are carved by the daily exercise of good works and humble prayer. The temple made with hands fell, the Church which is not made with hands will never fall. The temple has been demolished from the very foundations, the Church can never be destroyed.[157]

Then in passages of Grünewald-like intensity, the physical details of the Passion are brought before the eyes of the audience (although there is little mention of the mental and spiritual agony); and re-echoing the sorrowful questions of the *Impropreria*, the ' fragrant appeal '[158] of the love of the Crucified Redeemer is heard with all its persuasiveness: in Edgeworth's words:

> The crosse layd downe on the grounde extendeth his partes towarde the foure partes of the worlde, East, West, North and Southe, and so did the body of Christ when he was nayled on the crosse, lying on the grounde in signe and token that his loue extended to all partes of the worlde, and that for theyr sakes he suffered so great paines as he did. . . . Then consider how his head was bobbed and beaten and pricked with sharpe thornes, his handes & feete bored through and torne with greate nayles.

---

[154] *Cuthberti Tonstalli in laudem matrimonii oratio, habita in sponsalibus Mariae Potentissimi regis Angliae Henrici octaui filiae, et Francisci Christianissimi Francorum regis primogeniti* (London, 1518) sig. Aii^v–Avii^v.

[155] Ibid. sig. Bi^r–Bii^r.   [156] Ibid. sig. Bi^r.

[157] *Tres Conciones*, ff. 22^r-v.   [158] Cf. Owst, *P.M.E.*, p. 348.

And after that, the crosse, and he hanging on it, hoysed vp, & let downe into the mortess made for it, and to be shiogged and shaken, hauying no stay but this own sinowes, fleshe and skynne rent and torne in his handes and feete. Thys was a payne of all paynes, speciallye in that pure complexioned and tender body.[159] Fisher, urging his audience to hear the sorrowing cry of the Saviour, *O vos omnes qui transitis per viam attendite et videte si est dolor sicut dolor meus* (Lam. i. 12; ' O all ye that pass by the way, attend, and see if there be any sorrow like to my sorrow ', Douay), is moved to exclaim: 'Alas to see so noble a man, so gentle & so innocent, so cruelly intreated in euery parte of his most delicate body. And to here him so pitiously complayninge, who shall not be sory? Surely none, except hys harte be harder than any flynte stone or Adamant stone.'[160] The Christian is therefore exhorted to suffer with Christ; Longland urges:

> Haue therfore compassion on thy lorde God, and heyre his lamentable complaynte. Shewe pytye vpon hym, putt not this heuye crosse to hym ayen to beare, ease hym of his heuye burden. Suffre with Chryste, beare this crosse wyth hym. Suffre paciently for his sake suche aduersytye as he dothe sende, whedre itt be sycknes or pouertye, myserye or hungre, thyrste, contumelye or shame. whedre it be rebuke of the worlde, tortures, passions aduersytyes, or other paynes. Suffre, suffre wyth hym. He was an innocente and deserued it not, thou arte a synner and doste deserue itt.[161]

Suffering too, Longland points out, can have remedial effects if borne willingly; ' the sick man cries out under the hand of the physician, the wounded under the surgeon's hand ', but the end is the soul's health; a child weeps in his mother's arms, but ' she washes him, rubs him, anoints him, so that she may have him clean and healthy '.[162]

Finally the preachers of this time present the goal of the Christian

---

[159] *Sermons*, f. 79^r. Cf. also Longland, *Sermond at Grenwiche*, 1536, sig. Fii^v: ' They crucified hym, they nayled him throughe handes and feete to the crosse. They extended, haalyd and strayned, his blyssyd bodye soo extremely on the crosse that his synous and vaynes crakket: that thou moughtyste haue numbred his bones and Ioyntes.' Cf. further, Longland, *Sermond at Rychemunte*, 1535, sig. Oiii^v, Pii^v, Riv^r; also MS. Harl. 2247, ff. 88^r-v, Fisher, *English Works*, Pt. I, p. 400. For similar treatment of the Passion by earlier preachers, see Owst, *L. & P.M.E.*, pp. 508–9.

[160] *English Works*, Pt. I, p. 403.

[161] *Sermond at Grenwiche*, 1536, sig. Giv^r: cf. also *Sermones*, f. 19^r (where Longland acknowledges the influence of St. Bernard's preaching on the Passion). The loving contemplation of the Passion has remained one of the most characteristic features of post-Tridentine Catholic devotion; see e.g. St. Alphonsus Liguori, *The Passion and Death of Jesus Christ*, ed. E. Grimm (Brooklyn, N.Y., 1927), pp. 207–9.

[162] *Sermones*, f. 22^r.

life, heaven; the *patria* after the weary and dangerous pilgrimage through this world, the *via*;[163] in passages of great power. It is not easy to win; as Longland puts it speaking of Christ's death:

> Hee entrede the heuens with payne, & thynkest thou to come thydre wyth Ioye and worldly pleasure? *Nemo hic gaudere in mundo, & regnare cum Christo in celo.* saithe saincte Ierome . . . Heuen is not wonnen wyth eatinge and drinkinge, with dalyinge and playinge, with sportinge and hoytinge; but with payne and penaunce, with mysery & pouertye, with aduersitye and tribulacion.[164]

Nor must we, says Edgeworth, think of it in terms of sensual delights:

> Carnall, fleshlye, or beastlye in knowledge be they, that of almightye God and heauenlye thinges, imagineth and iudgeth by corporall phantasies, as of God that he is a faire olde man with a white beard, as the painters make him, and that the ioyes of Heauen standeth in eatynge and drinkynge, pipinge and daunsinge.[165]

Men may even despise their true home; as Edgeworth puts it: ' yet to this daye it is reputed as a wyldernes, or a thing forsaken of the most part of people, that will not walk in the streyght way that bringeth a man to heauen, but had leauer keepe the brode way of pleasure, easelye hopping and dauncing to hell, and therefore to them heauen is a wildernes.'[166] However in imagery of delicate beauty, Edgeworth vindicates its joys; for ' in the wooddes of the wyldernes there be many birdes that singeth swetely, with many and diuers swete tunes: so in heauen where the inhabitaunts shall prayse our Lorde God worlde without ende. There be also in [the] wyldernes many swete and pleasant floures, and so in heauen the red roses of Martyrs, the violets of Confessours, the lilies of Virgines. . . .'[167] There too the Christian, as Longland expresses it, feeds on ' the bread of angels ', on God Himself; like the blessed spirits, he is ' held within His vision, satisfied by the possession of Him '.[168] Then at the General Resurrection the souls of the just will receive their risen bodies, no longer to be distrusted as enemies, but now glorious partners in beatitude; in Edgeworth's glowing words:

> . . . for euer stil from the time of mannes conception in his mothers body, tyll he be buried, he maye take hurt, and may be

---

[163] See Edgeworth, *Sermons*, f. 172ʳ.
[164] *Sermond at Grenwiche*, 1536, sig. Givʳ. Cf. St. Jerome, Epist., XIV, *P.L.*, xxii. 354.   [165] *Sermons*, f. 151ᵛ.   [166] Ibid. f. 192ʳ.
[167] Ibid. Cf. St. Jerome, Epist., LIV, *P.L.*, xxii. 557.
[168] *Tres Conciones*, f. 25ʳ: cf. Fisher, *English Works*, Pt. I, pp. 112–13, 134–5, 198.

corrupt, but he shall rise agayne vncorruptible, by the dowrye or gyfte of *impassibilitie*, neither fyre weapon, syckenes, neyther anye other thinge can hurte him. Lykewyse in this life mannes body is dymme and darke, and geueth no light, but it shall rise in glorye, clearenes, and brightnes, by the gyft of *clearnes*. Mannes body is now dul and heauy, and longe a mouinge, and not able to styrre it selfe withoute laboure, but it shall ryse nymble and quicke, able to moue from place to place (how farre distant soeuer they be) in a twinkelinge of an eye, by the will and commaundement of the soule, and this shall be by the dowry or gifte of *Agilitie*: Our body is nowe grosse and no more able to be present with an other bodye, then the body of a brute beaste, but it shall rise so spiritual fine and pearcing, that it may go thorough an other body and be present in one place with an other body by the gifte of *Subtilitie*. . .[169]

II

THE EARLY REFORMERS (1547–1553)

It is most noticeable when we approach the sermons of the Reformers, that several of the dominant themes of the preceding years disappear. Gone is the sad expatiation over transience, and the vanity of life;[170] gone is the morbid preoccupation with old age, death and decay;[171] but gone too is the loving contemplation of the Passion,[172] and in large measure also the expectant raptures over heaven.[173] The keynote is rather zeal for reform of the Church and society into something more akin to what the reformers take to be God's plan. The first step in this regenerative process is the reform of the doctrines and practices of the Church. The most striking theme of these preachers is the vigorous, often bitter attack on Catholicism. Although, unlike Bilney and Barnes,[174] Latimer does not directly attack Catholic doctrine until the time of Edward, nevertheless, probably inspired by the example given by Erasmus, and to some extent by that of Luther, he begins his assault on abuses and super-stitions in Henry's reign with his insistence on the primacy of ' necessary works ' over ' voluntary ', with an exposure of the folly of presenting vestments to churches and of decorating images, while

---

[169] *Sermons*, f. 86ᵛ: cf. Fisher, *English Works*, Pt. I, pp. 262–3.
[170] See *ante*, pp. 228–34.   [171] See *ante*, pp. 234–6.
[172] See *ante*, pp. 260–1.   [173] See *ante*, pp. 261–3.
[174] For their careers, see Foxe, *Acts and Monuments*, vol. IV, pp. 619–56; vol. V, pp. 414–38.

the living temples of Christ, the poor, die of starvation.[175] In the
famous Convocation sermon of 1537, Latimer reiterates his attack
on voluntary works,[176] and castigates the current teaching on
purgatory—that the souls there imprisoned have most need of our
help, and can have no aid but of us in this world. The first of these
propositions he boldly declares is uncertain, the second false,[177]
while with his usual humour he exposes the money-making side of
the current teaching: ' purgatory pick-purse ',[178] ' that fiery furnace
that hath burned away so many of our pence '[179] is shown to be ' a
pleasant fiction, and from the beginning so profitable to the feigners
of it, that almost . . . there hath no emperor that hath gotten more by
taxes and tallages of them that were alive, than these, the very right-
begotten sons of the world, got by dead men's tributes and gifts.'[180]
Other abuses of the sort that angered Erasmus are exposed; ' pardons
and these of wonderful variety, some stationaries, some jubilaries,
some poculuries for drinkers, some manuaries for handlers or relicks,
some pedaries for pilgrims, some osculuries for kissers ';[181] burials
in Franciscan habits to escape the fourth part of one's sins;[182] false
and scandalous relics and images.[183] The clergy are rebuked too for
with-holding Scripture from the laity,[184] and they are reminded that
there have been many consultations for reformation, but virtually
nothing has been done.[185]

Then in Edward's reign comes the full assault on the traditional
Catholicism. The doctrine of the Sacrifice of the Mass is vigorously
assailed by Latimer and Hooper. It evacuates the Sacrifice of the
Cross, says Latimer,[186] while Hooper stresses that the only propitia-
tory sacrifice is that once made at the Crucifixion.[187] Transubstantiation too is fiercely attacked by Hooper, who urges the historical

[175] *Sermons*, pp. 23–4: cf. Erasmus, e.g. ' Enchiridion Militis Christiani,' cap. xiii
Opera Omnia, V, 63E, F. For Luther's attitude to voluntary works, see e.g., *An appeal
to the Ruling Class of German Nationality* (Woolf, *Reformation Writings of Martin Luther*,
vol. I, pp. 153–5).
[176] *Sermons*, p. 37.   [177] Ibid.   [178] Ibid. p. 50.
[179] Ibid. p. 36.   [180] Ibid. p. 50.
[181] Ibid. pp. 49–50: cf. Erasmus, Μωρίας 'Εγκώμιον, *Opera Omnia*, IV, 444A. See
further Luther, *Letter to Staupitz* (Woolf, *Reformation Writings of Martin Luther*, vol. I,
pp. 58–9) *The Ninety-Five Theses* (Ibid. pp. 32–43).
[182] *Sermons*, p. 50: cf. Erasmus, ' Colloquia Familiaria,' ' Exequiae Seraphicae,'
Opera Omnia, I, 866E–73B.
[183] *Sermons*, pp. 53–5; cf. Erasmus, ibid. ' Peregrinatio Religionis ergo,' *Opera
Omnia*, I, 774C–87E, *passim*.   [184] *Sermons*, p. 38.   [185] Ibid. pp. 45–6.
[186] *Sermons*, pp. 72–3; cf. ibid. p. 445. For further attacks on the Mass, see *Remains*,
pp. 58, 60, 192. Luther is against the idea of sacrifice in the Mass (although the words
of the canon contain it) *The Pagan Servitude of the Church*, a First Enquiry (Woolf *Reformation Writings of Martin Luther*, vol. I, pp. 247–51).
[187] *Early Writings*, p. 500.

argument against it; it was not found in the ancient Church, he declares, but after sound learning was lost, it was brought in by the monks.[188] In the typical railing mode of the Reformers (who find a great weapon in making Catholic doctrines appear in a ludicrous light) he refers to certain authorities who aver that the consecration is not complete until the ' um ' of ' Hoc est corpus meum ' has been pronounced; so he declares: 'After this their wicked and idolatrical doctrine, this syllable (*um*) in this oration, *Hoc est corpus meum*, to say, ' This is my body ', hath all the strength and virtue to change and deify the bread! But I pray you, what syllable is it that changeth and deifieth the wine? '[189] Bradford too rails against the corporal presence of Christ in the Sacrament; a doctrine which he sees as lying behind the power of the priests;[190] He is there indeed, says the Reformer, but only by faith[191]—so in interesting contrast to Peryn's stressing of faith against sense and reason in his defence of Catholic doctrine,[192] Bradford is enabled to declare:

> Alas! that men consider nothing at all, how that the coupling of Christ's body and blood to the sacrament is a spiritual thing; and therefore there needs no such carnal presence as the papists imagine. Who will deny a man's wife to be with her husband one body and flesh, although he be at London and she at York? But the papists are animal men, guided by carnal reason only: or else would they know how that the Holy Ghost because of our infirmity useth metaphorically the words of abiding, dwelling, eating and drinking of Christ, that the unspeakable conjunction of Christ with us might something be known.[193]

Some of the attacks on Transubstantiation are of a grossly popular kind; at the beginning of the reign ' was moche spekyng agayne the sacrament of the aulter, that some callyd it Jacke of the boxe, with divers other shamfulle names ',[194] while in a lecture on 1st September 1549 John Cardmaker, a reader in St. Paul's, asks ' if God were a man he was a vj or vij foote of lengthe, with the bredth, and if be soo how canne it be that he shuld be in a pesse of brede in a rownde cake on the awter?'[195]

Then in the ' Homily of Good Works annexed unto Faith ', Cranmer makes a wholesale assault upon the characteristic elements of the traditional piety, which he sees as corrupt accretions upon the primitive purity and simplicity of Christ's religion:

---

[188] Ibid. pp. 520–7.   [189] Ibid. p. 523.   [190] *Writings*, vol. I, p. 84.
[191] Ibid. p. 95.   [192] Cf. *ante*, p. 249.   [193] *Writings*, vol. I, p. 99.
[194] *Chronicle of the Grey Friars of London*, ed. J. G. Nichols, (London, 1852), C. S., no. LIII, p. 55. See too ibid. pp. 56, 57.
[195] Ibid. p. 63.

What man, having any judgment or learning, joined with a
true zeal unto God, doth not see and lament to have entered
into Christ's religion such false doctrine, superstition, idolatry,
hypocrisy, and other enormities and abuses; so as by little and
little, through the sour leaven thereof, the sweet bread of God's
holy word hath been much hindered and laid apart? Never
had the Jews, in their most blindness, so many pilgrimages unto
images, nor used so much kneeling, kissing, and censing of
them, as hath been used in our time. Sects and feigned religions
were neither the fortieth part so many among the Jews, nor
more superstitiously and ungodly abused, than of late days they
have been among us. Which sects and religions had so many
hypocritical and feigned works in their state of religion, as they
arrogantly named it, that their lamps, as they said, ran always
over: able to satisfy not only for their own sins, but also for all
other their benefactors, brothers and sisters of religion, as most
ungodly and craftily they had persuaded the multitude of
ignorant people: keeping in divers places, as it were marts or
markets of merits; being full of their holy relics, images,
shrines, and works of overflowing abundance ready to be sold.
And all things which they had were called holy,—holy cowls,
holy girdles, holy pardons, beads, holy shoes, holy rules, and
all full of holiness.[196]

The religious life itself, with its vows of obedience, chastity and
poverty is attacked also,[197] while the whole matter is summed up in
a passage of extraordinary denunciatory vigour:

. . . let us rehearse some other kinds of papistical superstitions
and abuses, as of beads, of lady-psalters and rosaries, of fifteen
O's, of St. Bernard's verses, of St. Agathe's letters, of purgatory,
of masses satisfactory; of stations and jubilees, of feigned relics,
of hallowed beads, bells, bread, water, palms, candles, fire, and
such other; of superstitious fastings, of fraternities or brother-
hoods, of pardons, with such like merchandise; which were so
esteemed and abused to the great prejudice of God's glory and
commandments, that they were made most high and most holy
things, whereby to attain to the everlasting life, or remission
of sins.[198]

Stowe recounts that ' one Sir Stephen, curate of St. Katherine
Christ's church ' preaching at Paul's Cross attacked the maypole
outside St. Andrew Undershaft, which had in the past been used on
May-day. He declared that ' this shaft was made an idol, by naming
the church of St. Andrew with the addition of " under that shaft " ':

[196] Certain Sermons appointed by the Queen's Majesty, pp. 55–6.
[197] Ibid. pp. 56–8.   [198] Ibid. p. 58.

and ' persuaded therefore that the names of churches might be altered; also that the names of days in the week might be changed; the fish days to be kept any days except Friday and Saturday, and the Lent any time, save only betwixt Shrovetide and Easter.' This sermon had a practical effect: ' for ', says Stowe, ' in the afternoon of that present Sunday, the neighbours and tenants . . . over whose doors the said shaft had long lain, after they had well dined, to make themselves strong, gathered more help, and with great labour raising the shaft from the hooks, whereon it had rested two-and-thirty years, they sawed it in pieces, every man taking for his share so much as had lain over his door and stall, the length of his house; and they of the alley divided among them so much as had lain over their alley gate. Thus was this idol (as he termed it) mangled, and after burned.' Sir Stephen seems to have been somewhat of an eccentric, for, recounts Stowe: ' I have oft times seen this man, forsaking the pulpit of his . . . parish church, preach out of a high elm-tree in the midst of the churchyard, and then entering the church, forsaking the altar, to have sung his high mass in English upon a tomb of the dead towards the north.'[199]

Certain abuses in the old order which had survived into the Church as then reformed, arouse the indignation of the preachers. Latimer is never more racily eloquent than when denouncing ' un-preaching prelates '[200] and the scandal of ecclesiastics holding secular offices,[201] while Hooper urges bishops and priests to preach, adding that if a bishop cannot preach, he should obtain a helper who can.[202] Lever is concerned about non-residents[203] and the buying of benefices,[204] while Gilpin details the abuses which he declares have not yet been sent back to Rome: ' I meane of dispensations for pluralities, and tot quots with dispensations for non-residents, which auarice & Idlenes transported hither from Rome: But for that they sauour sweete for a time to carnall men, they haue so many patrones they can not be driuen away with other abuses. . . .'[205] Dis-pensations for non-residence, says Gilpin, ' haue brought forth farming of benefices to gentlemen, lay men, wherein they haue founde such sweetnes and wordly wealth, that preachers can not haue them, they will be perpetual farmers '.[206] Also, even in these

[199] *Survey of London*, introd. by H. B. Wheatley (London, revised 1956) Everyman, p. 130.
[200] *Sermons*, pp. 67, 158, 193, 202, 207, 232, 275: *Remains*, p. 24.
[201] *Sermons*, pp. 68, 176: *Remains*, p. 120.   [202] *Early Writings*, pp. 507–8.
[203] *Sermons*, pp. 30, 64–5.   [204] Ibid. pp. 109–10.
[205] *A godly sermon preached before the court at Greenwich*, p. 21.
[206] Ibid. p. 28: see too ibid. p. 32.

Gospel times, ' Patrons see that none doe their duetie, they thinke as good to put in asses as men. The Byshops were neuer so liberall in making of lewde priestes, but they are liberal in making lewd vicars.'[207] Simony too continues; and Gilpin, as is the habit of the Reformers, gives a particular instance of the abuse he is castigating: ' I could name the place where a liuing of a hundreth markes by yere, if I say not poundes, hath here sold for many yeares, I suppose an 100 saue one, & so continueth still.'[208] With all these abuses choking the spiritual life of the church, it is little wonder that Gilpin too must complain about the lack of preaching: 'A thousand pulpits in England are couered with duste, some haue not had four sermons these XV or XVI yeares, since Friers left their limitations, and a fewe of those were worthy the name of sermons.'[209]

A considerable proportion of the preaching of the Reformers consists of complaints on secular topics, but unlike their Catholic predecessors the preachers of this reign are not content to give broadly general denunciations;[210] on the contrary as we have just noticed in the case of Gilpin, they frequently give particular instances and examples. First, they are deeply concerned about the administration of civil justice; magistrates and judges who take bribes and favour the rich are mercilessly castigated.[211] Both Latimer and Hooper quote approvingly the story of the hanging up of the skin of the judge who took bribes;[212] while Latimer frequently brings cases of the miscarriage of justice to the king's notice, always related with his delightful vigour, as:

> I can tell where one man slew another in a township, and was attacked upon the same: twelve men were impanelled: the man had friends: the sheriff laboured the bench: the twelve stuck at it, and said, ' Except he would disburse twelve crowns, they would find him guilty '. Means were found that the twelve crowns were paid. The quest comes in, and says ' Not guilty '. Here was ' not guilty ' for twelve crowns. This is a bearing, and if some of the bench were hanged, they were well served. This makes men bold to do murder and slaughter. We should

---

[207] Ibid. p. 29: cf. Scott's complaint about those preferred to livings by lay patrons, *ante*, pp. 240–1.

[208] Ibid. p. 32, in margin, ' Crostwaite & Cheswicke.' See too ibid. p. 30: ' I dare say, if suche a monster as Deruell Gatherel the idole of Wales brent in Smithfield coulde haue bene well conueied to come & set his hand to a bil to let the patrons take the greatest part of the profits, he might haue had a benefice.' Cf. Longland's complaint on this topic, *ante*, p. 239–40.

[209] Ibid. p. 40.   [210] See *ante*, pp. 246.

[211] See Latimer, *Sermons*, pp. 128, 140, 145, 171, 193; Hooper *Early Writings*, pp. 482–3; Gilpin, *A godly sermon preached before the court at Greenwich*, p. 47.

[212] Latimer, *Sermons*, pp. 146, 181, 260; Hooper, *Early Writings*, p. 483.

reserve murdering till we come to our enemies, and the king bid us fight: he that would bestir him then were a pretty fellow indeed. Crowns! if their crowns were shaven to the shoulders, they were served well enough.[213]

The Reformers complain too about the lack of upright conduct in public officials; just as sacred offices are bought, so are secular, and those who obtain positions of responsibility in this way cannot be expected to wield them honourably.[214] Corruption permeates public life, poor suitors are not heard,[215] self-aggrandizement is the aim of officials,[216] even the Lord Admiral (Seymour) is shamefully involved in a fraud at the Mint.[217]

Lying behind such offences is the root evil of covetousness, the sin most castigated by the preachers of this time. As Gilpin puts it:

> Couetousnesse is the roote of all. Euery man scratcheth & pilleth from other, euery man would sucke the bloud of other: euery man encrocheth vpon an other. Couetousness hath cut away the large winges of charitie, and plucketh all to her selfe, shee is neuer satisfied, she hath chested all the olde gold in England & much of the newe: she hath made that ther was neuer more Idolatry in England, than at this day.[218]

Covetousness shows itself most shockingly in the practice of usury,[219] and in the conduct of landlords, who enclose, engross, and shamefully rack-rent their tenants. Preaching before the king, Latimer declares:

> The poorest ploughman is in Christ equal with the greatest prince that is. Let them therefore, have sufficient to maintain them, and to find their necessaries. A plough-land must have sheep; yea, they must have sheep to dung their ground for bearing of corn; for if they have no sheep to help fat the ground, they shall have but bare corn and thin. They must have swine for their food, to make their veneries or bacon of: their bacon is their venison, for they shall now have *hangum tuum*, if they get any other venison; so that bacon is their necessary meat to feed on, which they may not lack. They must have other cattle: as horses to draw their plough, and for carriage of things to the markets; and kine for their milk and cheese, which they must

---

[213] *Sermons*, p. 190: see further, ibid. pp. 128, 190–1.
[214] Latimer, *Sermons*, p. 185; *Remains*, pp. 26–7. See too Gilpin, *A godly sermon preached before the court at Greenwich*, p. 44; Hooper, *Early Writings*, p. 481.
[215] Latimer, *Sermons*, pp. 255, 273–4.
[216] Ibid. p. 261.   [217] Ibid. pp. 161–4, 181–4.
[218] *A godly sermon preached before the court at Greenwich*, p. 65; see too ibid. pp. 52, 64. In denunciation of covetousness, see further, Latimer, *Sermons*, pp. 184–5, 241–2, 246, 247, 280; *Remains*, pp. 107, 155.
[219] Latimer, *Sermons*, p. 279; *Remains*, p. 42.

live upon and pay their rents. These cattle must have pasture, which pasture if they lack, the rest must needs fail them: and pasture they cannot have, if the land be taken in, and enclosed from them.[220]

In similar vein Lever laments:

. . . alas, here in England, superfluous gorgeous building is so much prouided for ryche mens pleasures, that honest houses do decay, where as labouryng men ought to haue necessary lodgyng. It is a commen custome with couetous landlordes, to lette their housynge so decaye, that the fermer shalbe fayne for a small rewarde or none at all, to gyue up his leasse, that the takynge the groundes into their owne handes, may turne all to pasture: so now Olde Fathers, poore Wydowes, and yong Chyldren lye beggyng in the myrie stretes.[221]

Of course, there were economic forces at work which the pulpit orators did not comprehend, but they see the rise of a new rural economy purely in terms of personal greed. The sermon complaints on this last form one of the most deeply felt themes of the reign;[222] and it is interesting to note that (as usual) the preachers denounce specific instances of this evil. For example, Lever declaims:

I haue heard howe that euen this last yere, ther was certayn Acres of corne growyng on the ground bought for. viii. poundes: he that bought it for. viii. sold it for. x. He that gaue. x. pounds, sold it to an other aboue. xii. poundes: and at last, he that caryed it of the ground, payde. xiiii. poundes. Lykewyse I hearde, that certayne quarters of malte were boughte after the pryce of. iii. shyllynges. iii. pence a quarter to be delyuered in a certayne markette towne vpon a certayne daye. Thys bargayne was so oft bought and solde before the daye of delyueraunce came, that the same Malte was solde to hym that shoulde receyue it there and carrye it awaye, after. vi. s. a quarter. Looke and se howe muche a craftes man or anye other honeste man that muste spend corne in his house, by this maner of bargaynynge, payeth, and howe littel the housbande manne that tylleth the ground, and paieth the rent, receyueth: Then ye may se and perceyue it must needes be harde for eyther of theim to kepe a house, the cra[f]tes man payinge so muche, and the husbandman takynge so lytle.[223]

The decay of the grammar schools and universities (already lamented

---

[220] *Sermons*, p. 249; see too ibid. p. 279.

[221] *Sermons*, p. 77; see too ibid. pp. 37, 82, 84, 128–9; Hutchinson, *Works*, p. 301. Cf. the earlier complaint on this topic by Chedsey, *ante*, pp. 245–6.

[222] See R. H. Tawney, *Religion and the Rise of Capitalism* (London, reptd. 1943), pp. 137–50.

[223] *Sermons*, pp. 128–9; see too ibid. p. 82; also Latimer, *Sermons*, p. 248.

in Henry VIII's reign)[224] is still more complained of in Edward's; it is a further manifestation of covetousness, coupled with the unscrupulous subversion of funds. Lever speaks with great feeling about the decay of Cambridge; addressing the laity, he declares:

> ... before that you did beginne to be the disposers of the kinges liberalitye towardes learnynge and pouerty, there was in houses belongynge vnto the vnyuersytye of Cambryge, two hundred studentes of dyuynyte, manye verye well learned: whyche bee nowe all clene gone, house and manne, young towarde scholers and old fatherlye Doctors, not one of them lefte: one hundred also of an other sorte that hauyng rych frendes or beyng benefyced men dyd lyue of theym selues in Ostles [Ostries] and Innes be eyther gon awaye, or elles fayne to crepe into Colleges, and put poore men from bare lyuynges. Those bothe be all gone, and a small number of poore godly dylygent studentes nowe remaynynge only in Colleges be not able to tary and contynue theyr studye in the vniuersitye for lacke of exibicion and healpe.[225]

He is concerned too about the grammar schools, and has a glaring instance of injustice to expose:

> There was in the North countrey, amongest the rude people in knowledge (which be most readye to spend their lyues and goodes, in seruyng the Kyng at the burnyng of a Beacon) there was a Grammer schole founded, hauyng in the Vniuersitie of Cambridge, of the same foundacion. viii. scholarships, euer replenyshed with the scholers of that schole, which scole is now solde, decayed and loste. Mo there be of lyke sorte handled: But I recyte thys only, because I knowe that the sale of it was once stayed of charitie, and yet afterwards broughte to passe by bribrye, as I hearde say, and beleue it bicause that it is only bribyre, that customablye ouercometh charitie.[226]

Gilpin and Latimer too complain on this subject, for like Chedsey before them, they see that the decay of learning will result in the decay of Christianity.[227]

[224] See *ante*, p. 245.

[225] *Sermons*, pp. 121–2. Lever is indignant that money from the dissolved monasteries and chantries should not have gone to the maintenance of Learning: ' If ye hadde anye eyes ye shoulde se and be ashamed that in the great aboundaunce of landes and goods taken from Abbeis, Colleges and Chauntryes for to serue the kyng in all necessaryes, and charges, especially in prouision of relyefe for the pore, and for mayntenaunce of learnynge the kynge is so dysapoynted that bothe the pore be spoyled, all mayntenaunce of learnyng decayed and you only enryched.' (Ibid. p. 120; see too ibid. p. 32.) Cf. further the denunciation of a particular misappropriation of money, ibid. p. 80.

[226] Ibid. p. 81.

[227] *A godly sermon preached before the court at Greenwich*, p. 37: ' Looke vpon the two welles of this Realme, Oxforde and Cambridge, they are almost dried vp. The cruell Philistines abrode, enemies to Christes gospell, haue stopped vp the springes of faithful

The times were indeed disappointing; Catholicism was overthrown, but it seemed as if the Gospel still could not flourish in England because of greed and ambition. The bitterest taunt of the preachers is that even the superstitious papists were charitable, albeit in a misdirected way, but those who have the chance of entering into the joy of a purified faith, perversely turn to the degrading worship of Mammon: in Lever's words:

> And now England hauyng occasion, by the abolishyng of Papistrie, to embrace sincere Christianitie, tourned that occasion, to take the spoyle of Papistrie, whiche is the cause that many neglecte, and sclaunder sincere Christianitie. And so haue, and doe tourne all occasions of godly charitable reformation, into worldly couetous corruption.[228]

The Machiavellian politicians and citizens who support the ' Gospel ' merely to enrich themselves deserve the sternest condemnation: covetousness, says Lever, summing the matter up, is the worst idolatry:

> I saye and testyfye vnto you in the word of the Lorde, that so many of you as be couetous, haue no profit by the preachyng of gods word, mynistracion of hys sacraments and the settyng forth of pure religion wythin the realme: no ye be clene from God framyng your selues vnto the fassion of thys worlde, ye can brynge forth no good frutes of charitable workes nourishing the rote of all euyll in youre hartes, ye muste nedes prouoke the wrath and indignacion of god to your vtter destrucion, when as ye kepe the ydoll of couetousnes styll in youre myndes to be honoured and serued in all your doings, and yet pretend a zele and loue vnto the religion of Chryst in your workes and sayinges.[229]

But alas! it is an evil generation; Gilpin is deeply saddened by the absence of the Court from his sermon: public business, he urges, is no valid excuse:

> I am come this day to preach to the king, and to those which be in authority vnder him. I am very sory they should be absent, which should giue example, and encourage other to the hearing of gods word. And I am the more sorie that other preachers before me complaine much of their absence: But you

Abraham. The decay of studentes is so great, there are scarse left of euery thousand, an hundred. If they decay so fast in seuen years more, there shalbe almost none at al, and then may the Diuel make a triumph.' If the king does not stop this, Gilpin declares: ' there is entering into England, more blinde ignorance, superstition and infidelitie, then euer was vnder the Romish Byshop.' (Ibid. p. 38). See too Latimer, *Sermons*, pp. 102, 269, 458. Cf. *ante*, p. 245.

---

[228] *Sermons*, p. 61: cf. too ibid. pp. 73, 113, 119.   [229] Ibid. pp. 102-3.

will saye, they haue waighty affaires in hande. Alas, hath God
any greater businesse then this? If I could cry with the voice of
Stentor, I shoulde make them heare in their chambers: But in
their absence, I will speake to the seates, as if they were present.[230]
However, although the nobility, gentry and magistrates may be
so unworthy, all the preachers have the typical sixteenth century
horror of rebellion. The position which they adopt here is extreme;
as Lever declares:

> It is God that maketh these euyl men to be gentlemen, rulers,
> and officers in the countrey: it is the sinnes of the people that
> causeth God to make these men youre rulers. The man is
> sometymes euyll, but the authoritye from God is alwayes good,
> and God geueth good authoritye vnto euyll men, to punyshe
> the synnes of the euyll people. It is not repynyng, rebellyng, or
> resisting gods ordinance, that wyll amende euyll rulers. For
> [sainct] Paule sayeth, that all powers be of goddes ordinaunce.
> And in Iob it is playne, that euyll menne bee made rulers by
> God: So that who soeuer resysteth the offycers, be the menne
> neuer so euyll that be in office, he resisteth the ordinaunce of
> God, he can not preuayle againste God, but surely he shall be
> plaged of God.[231]

In a sermon attributed to Cranmer, probably occasioned by Ket's
rebellion (Summer 1549), it is declared that the recent seditions are a
plague sent from God for the rejection and abusing of His holy
word, and that they are to entice Englishmen to repentance.[232]

Yet the preachers wish the young king to be an upright and just
ruler; they are particularly concerned to make him aware of and
immune to the dangers of flatterers. Latimer's warning, delivered
in his best manner, may be quoted as typical:

> It is in the text [Deut. xvii. 19], that a king ought to fear
> God: ' he shall have the dread of God before his eyes '. Work
> not by worldly policy: for worldly policy feareth not God.
> Take heed of these claw-backs, these venemous people that will
> come to you, that will follow you like Gnathos and Parasites:
> if you follow them, you are out of your book. If it be not
> according to God's word that they counsel you, do it not for
> any worldly policy; for then ye fear not God.[233]

---

[230] *A godly sermon preached before the court at Greenwich*, p. 26.
[231] *Sermons*, pp. 34–5. Cf. too Latimer, *Sermons*, pp. 247, 371, 496, 538; *Certain
Sermons appointed by the Queen's Majesty*, p. 108. It should be pointed out however that
Lever places conscience above human ordinances—Daniel was forbidden to pray, and
the Apostles to preach: yet Daniel *did* pray and the Apostles preach, although they did
not rebel. (*Sermons*, p. 46).
[232] T. Cranmer, *Miscellaneous Writings and Letters*, ed. J. E. Cox (Cambridge, 1846)
P.S., pp. 197–201. See also ibid. pp. 188–9, (notes for a homily against rebellion).
[233] *Sermons*, p. 124. Cf. too ibid. p. 133; also Lever, *Sermons*, pp. 68, 71, 89.

T

Private morals, alas! must still be censured as before.[234] Indeed
they are if anything worse, says Latimer: 'O Lord, what whoredom
is used now-a-days, as I hear by the relation of honest men, which
tell it not after a worldly sort, as though they rejoiced at it, but
heavily, with heavy hearts, how God is dishonoured by whoredom
in this city of London; yea, the Bank when it stood, was never so
common!'[235] Such an evil, he thinks, requires legislation of an Old
Testament severity: let the Mosaic law on adultery be revived to
check this growing evil:

> Lechery is used throughout England, and such lechery as is
> used in none other place of the world. And yet it is made a
> matter of sport, a matter of nothing; a laughing matter, and
> trifle; not to be passed on, not to be reformed. . . . I look not to
> live long, and yet I trust as old as I am, to live so long as to see
> lechery punished. I would wish that Moses's law were restored
> for punishment of lechery, and that the offenders therein might
> be punished according to the prescription of Moses's law.[236]

In the ' Homily against Whoredom and Uncleanness ' Becon points
out, with great eloquence, how manifold are the evils which attend
upon immorality:

> What beauty, although it were never so excellent, is not
> disfigured with whoredom! Is not whoredom an enemy to the
> pleasant flower of youth, and bringeth it not grey hairs and old
> age before the time? What gift of nature although it were never
> so precious, is not corrupted with whoredom! . . .How many
> consume all their substance and goods, and at the last fall into
> such extreme poverty, that afterward they steal, and so are
> hanged, through whoredom! What contention and manslaugh-
> ter cometh of whoredom! How many maidens be deflowered,
> how many wives corrupted, how many widows, defiled, through
> whoredom! How much is the public and common weal impover-
> ished and troubled through whoredom! How much is God's
> word contemned and depraved by whoredom and whore-
> mongers![237]

However, marriages themselves are not as they should be! how
many are made, declares Latimer, for the wrong reasons! Those
who marry for ' fleshly lust and their own phantasy ' must be rebuked
but unhappily ' there was never such marrying in England as is
now '.[238] Further, says the Reformer:

[234] Cf. *ante*, pp. 242–3.
[235] *Sermons*, p. 196. Cf. too Becon's ' Homily against Whoredom and Uncleanness ',
Certain Sermons appointed by the Queen's Majesty, p. 118.
[236] Ibid. p. 244.   [237] *Certain Sermons, appointed by the Queen's Majesty*, p. 126.
[238] *Sermons*, p. 169.

I hear tell of stealing of wards to marry their children to. This is a strange kind of stealing: but it is not the wards, it is the lands that they steal. And some there be that knit up marriages together, not for any love or godliness in the parties, but to get friendship, and make them strong in the realm, to increase their possessions, and join land to land. And other there be that inveigle men's daughters, in the contempt of their fathers, and go about to marry them without their consent: this marrying is ungodly. And many parents constrain their sons and daughters to marry where they love not, and some are beaten and compulsed. And they that marry thus, marry in a forgetfulness and obliviousness of God's commandments.[239]

Latimer's attitude to women is still that of the medieval preachers;[240] he warns the king:

Christ limiteth unto us one wife only; and it is a great thing for a man to rule one wife rightly and ordinately. For a woman is frail, and proclive unto all evils; a woman is a very weak vessel, and may soon deceive a man and bring him unto evil. Many examples we have in holy scripture. Adam had but one wife, called Eve, and how soon had she brought him to consent unto evil, and to come to destruction. How did wicked Jezebel pervert king Achab's heart from God and all godliness, and finally into destruction! It is a very hard thing for a man to rule well one woman.[241]

He finds it necessary also to rebuke in the traditional manner vanity of dress and extravagant hair styles. St. Paul writes, ' a woman ought to have a power on her head ' (1 Cor. xi. 10) which is, says Latimer, ' a manner of speaking of the scripture; and to have her power on her head, is to have a sign and token of power, which is by covering her head, declaring that she hath a superior above her, by whom she ought to be ruled and ordered: for she is not immediately under God, but mediately. For by their injunction, the husband is their head under God, and they subjects unto their husbands.'[242] But, continues Latimer:

. . . this power that some of them have is disguised gear and strange fashions. They must wear French hoods, and I cannot tell you, I, what to call it. And when they make them ready, and come to the covering of their head, they will call and say, ' Give me my French hood, and give me by bonnet, or my cap'; and so forth. I would wish that the women would call the covering of their heads by the terms of the scripture: as when she would have her cap, I would she would say, ' Give me my

[239] Ibid. pp. 169–70. Cf. too ibid. pp. 243–4.   [240] Cf. *ante*, pp. 241–2.
[241] *Sermons*, p. 94.   [242] Ibid. p. 253.

power.' I would they would learn to speak as the Holy Ghost speaketh, and call it by such a name as St. Paul doth. I would they would (as they have much pricking), when they put on their cap, I would they would have this meditation: 'I am now putting my power on my head.' If they had this thought in their minds, they would not make so much pricking up of themselves as they do now-a-days. But now here is a vengeance devil: we must have our power from Turkey, of velvet, and gay it must be; far fetched, dear bought; and when it cometh, it is a false sign. I had rather have a true English sign, than a false sign from Turkey. It is a false sign when it covereth not their heads as it should do. For if they would keep it under the power as they ought to do, there should not any tussocks nor tufts be seen as there be; nor such laying out of the hair, nor braiding to have it open. I would marvel of it, how it should come to be so abused, and so far out of order; saying that I know by experience that many will not be ruled by their husbands, as they ought to be.[243]

Like Alcock before him, Latimer is constrained to speak against vanity of dress even in the clergy:[244] quoting Our Lord's remark on the austere dress of St. John the Baptist (Matt. xi. 8; ' But what went ye out for to see? A man clothed in soft raiment? behold they that wear soft clothing are in king's houses '), Latimer continues:

. . . Kings and great men are allowed to wear such fine gear; but John he was a clergyman, it behoved not him to wear such gear. . . . But how our clergymen wear them, and with what conscience, I cannot tell: but I can tell it behoveth not unto them to wear such delicate things. . . . I hear say that some of them wear velvet shoes, and velvet slippers. Such fellows are more meet to dance the morrice-dance than to be admitted to preach. I pray God amend such worldly fellows; for else they be not meet to be preachers.[245]

In conclusion, it must be asked, as before, what are the positive values offered? The greatest joy of the Reformers lies in the liberation from the old religious legalism: they feel an exultation in having thrown away what they believe they have discovered to be the worthless accretions upon the primitive simplicity of the faith and practice of Christianity; the Lord's Supper has replaced the Mass,[246]

[243] Ibid. pp. 253–4.   [244] Cf. *ante*, p. 239.   [245] *Remains*, p. 82.
[246] Latimer, *Sermons*, pp. 236–7, 459–61; *Remains*, p. 127; Bradford, *Works*, vol. I, pp. 101–5; Hooper, *Early Writings*, pp. 533–6. Note also that Latimer recalls the scruples which the ceremonial of the Mass raised in his conscience: ' I remember how scrupulous I was in my time of blindness and ignorance; when I should say mass, I have put water twice or thrice for failing; insomuch when I have been at my memento, I have had a grudge in my conscience, fearing that I had not put in water enough.' (*Sermons*, p. 138.)

repentance has replaced penance,[247] purgatory is now recognised as but a fable,[248] and after death the just are received immediately into the joys of heaven.[249] Then preaching itself is exalted, as the appointed means of bringing saving faith to men: 'preaching is necessary,' says Latimer, 'for take away preaching and take away salvation.'[250]

In an attempt to secure the reformed order in religion by the succession of Lady Jane Grey, Ridley preaching at Paul's Cross on 16th July 1553, announcing the death of Edward, declared that Mary and Elizabeth were illegitimate, and were so found by the clergy and acts of Henry VIII's time.[251] However the succession of Mary meant the triumph for a time at least of the Counter Reformation.

III

THE PREACHERS OF MARY'S REIGN (1553–1558)

The first year of Mary's reign witnesses the expression of joy by the Catholic-minded preachers at the return of England to the Catholic faith; a joy the greater as the Catholic party had progressively lost ground during the preceding reign, and its leaders, as Gardiner and Bonner, had suffered imprisonment.[252] Indeed in the first Paul's Cross sermon of the reign (13th August, 1553) Gilbert Bourne, later Bishop of Bath and Wells, condemned Bonner's imprisonment, only to have a dagger thrown at him by one of the crowd, escaping not without danger of manhandling by some, while Bradford asked the audience to calm itself.[253] However, now, says Brooks, the Church in England is revived as was Jairus's daughter;[254] ' God in His goodness ', declares Weston, ' has given to a Virgin Church a virgin queen '.[255] The preachers praise Queen

---

[247] Latimer, *Sermons*, p. 405; *Remains*, pp. 9–13, 50, 179–80, 207; Bradford, *Works*, vol. I, pp. 45–6, 51, 53. Latimer does however leave room for a modified form of voluntary confession (*Remains*, pp. 13, 180).

[248] Latimer, *Sermons*, pp. 426, 550.

[249] Ibid. p. 305; *Remains*, pp. 56, 58, 191; Hooper, *Early Writings*, pp. 561–2 ,566–7.

[250] *Sermons*, p. 155: cf. too ibid. pp. 202, 291, 349, 358, 418, 470.

[251] Foxe, *Acts and Monuments*, vol. VI, pp. 389–90; Wriothesley, *Chronicle*, vol. II, p. 88.

[252] See Hughes, *The Reformation in England*, vol. II, pp. 85–93, 102–5, 120, 122.

[253] Foxe, *Acts and Monuments*, vol. VI, pp. 391–2; Wriothesley, *Chronicle*, vol. II, pp. 97–8; *The Diary of Henry Machyn, Citizen and Merchant-Taylor of London, from* A.D. 1550 *to* A.D. 1563, ed. J. G. Nichols (London, 1848), C.S., no. XLII, p. 41.

[254] Brooks, *A Sermon very notable, fruictefull and Godlie*, sig. Iiiʳ.

[255] Weston, ' Oratio coram patribus et clero,' Strype, *Ecclesiastical Memorials*, III. 2, p. 184.

Mary almost to the borders of blasphemy;[256] she is compared also to
the great Christian Roman Emperors; she is equal to Theodosius;
she emulates Constantine who would not sit on his throne when
churchmen were present; like Jovinianus she has called together the
bishops as she begins her reign.[257] Pole some years later, after the
return of the country to the Roman obedience [1555], reminds his
hearers how they too may exclaim with David, *Laetatus sum in his
quae dicta sunt mihi: in domum domini ibimus* (Ps. cxxi. 1 Vg.; ' I rejoiced
at the things that were said to me: we shall go into the house of the
Lord ', Douay).[258] They had indeed been expelled from the Church
for disobedience, as was Adam from Paradise, but now in their
return they have ' recoueryd bothe as muche as most all creatures can
recouer in earthe, wyth sure hope if [they] contynue thereyn and
obeye the same, to enjoy the eternall felycyte hereafter yn heauen '.[259]

Those who suffered for the Catholic cause are praised; John
Harpesfield speaks of the bishops who held out under Edward: (I
translate):

> Let us commend my most reverend lord, the bishop of this
> diocese [Bonner, Bishop of London] praying that (as he does)
> he may continue diligently to direct both himself and the flock.
> Let us commend the Lord Bishop of Winchester [Gardiner],
> Chancellor of this realm, who both in the beginning of his
> episcopate laboured strenuously in the vineyard of the Lord,
> and in these recent years, bound in the Lord, fought most
> valiantly for the Christian faith, putting forth to our admiration
> his most learned and Christian books; and by the mercy of God
> preserved to us and this kingdom unharmed among so many
> dangers, now by his talents, experience, learning and virtue, he
> vigorously sustains the conduct and business of this realm, and
> the cause of Christ. Let us commend the Right Reverend
> Cuthbert Tunstall, notable among the first not only for his
> grey hairs, but for his talents, piety, learning, experience and
> for his sufferings with Christ.[260]

Pole, preaching to the citizens of London, extols the example of
Fisher and More:

> And here nowe was the provysyon that God made to stay
> the multytude, that they shoulde not so deeply fawle, which
> was the example of these ij great and notable servants of God,
> that rather suffered theyr heedes to be stryken off, than to

---

[256] See *ante*, pp. 56–7, 161.
[257] Weston, op. cit. Strype, *Ecclesiastical Memorials*, III. 2, pp. 184–5.
[258] MS. Vat. Lat., 5968, f. 278ʳ.   [259] Ibid. f. 278ᵛ.
[260] *Concio . . . habita coram patribus et clero in Ecclesia Paulina Londini*, sig. Aivʳ.

consent that the realme shoulde be cut off from the obedyence to the hedde, that Chryste dyd appoynete yn earthe.[261]

Yet they were not alone in their stand:

> For God had selected and chosen owte bothe prystes and religiouse men out of those religiouse howses that were moste refourmede, suche as were most notable for theyr vertue and religion: as owt of the Charterhowses, oute of Syon, and the fryars Observantes, and of St. Francys: *quorum nomina sunt in libro vitae*: that with theyr bludde testyfyede the same, havynge lyfe offered them, yf they woulde have swarved from the staye of the same; but they shewed by the high grace that God had gyven them, that no so cruel deathe coulde be offered them, but they had rather suffer yt, as they dyd, than to have byn browght owt of the bodye of the churche.[262]

Previously, says the cardinal, love of the world prevented the members of his audience from following the glorious example of these martyrs: but now, the prince is on the Catholic side; so let all be more fervent in their religion![263]

If Mary's reign is a new spring-time for the Church, the preachers frequently remember with a shudder the chaos and the manifold evils of Edward's time; Brooks, referring to Polycarp's horror at the religious turmoils of *his* day, continues:

> What wolde this Policarpus say (thinke you) if he were nowe a lyue and harde thenormities of our tyme: if he harde the mariages of priestes, monkes, friers, nonnes; the multitude of diuorses, thorough out al the realme: the swering, periurie, blasphemie, and vsurie of many a one: the bieing & selling of temporall offices: the like marchaundise, & chopping, of spirituall liuings: the bribrie & extorsion of the riche: Their pouling and peeling of the poore: Their dubling & trebling of rentes, & rearing of immeasurable fines: Their letting downe of hospitalitie: thimpacientnes of the poore, altered by rebellion, and tumults: the disobedience, & contempt of the same, towardes the magistrates: If he harde againe the feruor of deuotion so sore coled that it is almost quenched: The pulling downe of gods houses, & hospitals. The defacing of churches, in spoiling their goods & ornamentes: the breaking down of aulters: the throwing down of crosses: the casting out of images: the burning of tried holy reliques: the contempt of holy daies: the annullinge of vigilles: the breaking of Lent faste, & imbring dayes: with a numbre of other enormities moo:

---

[261] ' Cardinal Pole's speech to the citizens of London,' Strype, *Ecclesiastical Memorials*, III. 2, p. 496.

[262] Ibid.   [263] Ibid. pp. 497–8.

of whome, because there is no ende, I will make an ende of
rehersall, If this holy martyr Policarpus, I saye, were now a
liue, and harde all this, he would vndoubtedly stop his eares,
hyde his face and crie oute, *O caelum*: *o terra*: *o tempora*: *o mores*.
O heauen: o earth: o tymes: o manners. Out alas that euer I
was borne, to see this daye.[264]

Henry Pendleton, in his ' Homily of the Authority of the Church '
in Bonner's collection, gives the audience a vivid reminder of the
material miseries and visible sacrileges of the schism, which should
move even those who will not think about the sin of it:

> . . . thoughe you do not consyder the plage of sundry sinnes,
> that hathe in this late scysme possessed many mens soules, yet
> doo not dyssemble, nor forgette the myserye, that we all haue
> suffred outewardlye, synce we were separate from the churche
> of Christe: alas, what Christen bloude within this realme, euen
> by our owne countrymen, hath bene shed? Oh Lorde, how
> many fatherlesse children withour succoure? I leaue here to
> speake of the vnshameles breakynge of the dede mennes testa-
> mentes, and theyr most godly intentes, & ordinances. Abbais
> are poulled down: Collegies, and Chauntrees are overthrowen:
> churches are robbed and poore Christ (that is to saye), the
> hungry, and needeful people, famyshe, and crye oute therefore.[265]

Hugh Glasier, asking for church treasures to be restored, complains
about the state to which the sacred buildings have been reduced:
' Indeed,' he declaims, ' it were a great shame for so many of you to
lie in beddes, & sit vpon quisshins, made out of the church stuffe,
for whiche ye haue payed, either little or nothing at all, and the
temples & churches of Englande, to stande so naked, and so bare as
they do.'[266] Pollard does not hesitate to pronounce that God has
sent various temporal disasters as a punishment for the recent
defection from Catholicism:

> . . . the plages that come by the tempestuousnes of the ayer, by
> the vnfrutefulnesse of the grounde, by myse, rattes and other
> vermine, are not all of these tokens of gods wrath towarde man?
> And therefore it may apere to come that God hath so plaged vs
> Englyshe men of late, bycause we haue offended hym in leauynge
> of oure catholyke and true fayth, and in steede thereof haue
> embraced presumptuous reasonynge vpon his holy mysteries,
> and faythlesse heresie.[267]

However, the spiritual calamity has been even greater: Watson,

---

[264] *A Sermon very notable, fruictefull and Godlie*, sig. Hviiv–Hviiiv.
[265] *A profitable and necessarye doctryne with certayne homelies adioyned therevnto*, f. 41v.
[266] *A notable and very fruictefull sermon, made at Paules crosse*, sig. Divv–Dvr.
[267] *Fyue homilies*, sig. Hivv–Iir (Livv–Liir).

having detailed the blessings flowing from the proper reception of Holy Communion,[268] exclaims:

> O what wonderful effectes be these, which bi this blessed Sacrament be wrought in the worthy receauer, agaynst the deuyll and his temptations, against the fleshe and hir illusions, against the viciouse affections of oure corrupte minde? What conscience had these men, oure late teachers & pastors, destroyers of Christes flocke, to robbe vs of this treasure, which is the cause of so great benefytes, and in the place of that, to plante amonge vs a bare ceremonye of breade and wine to put vs in remembraunce of Chryste in heauen (as they sayde) which neyther by theyr own nature nor yet be any institution eyther of God or man be able to bringe to passe in vs these effectes I haue spoken of. What meant they that toke awaye this armour of Christes flesh and bloude frome vs, but to leaue vs naked and vnarmed agaynste the deuyll, that he shuld preuayle againste vs in all temptations, and that the kyngedome of sinne shuld be erected, and the kyngedom of grace destroyed? & to teache that this blessed Sacrament is nothinge else, but breade & wyne, what is it but to take awaye this armour and harnesse of Christes flesh, and bloude from vs. For breade be it neuer so muche apoynted to signifye thinges absente, is not able to defende vs from the deuyl.[269]

Then again, the traditional ceremonial has been disordered: Edgeworth employs his best satirical vein to ridicule the varieties of Protestant usage in the celebration of the Holy Eucharist:

> . . . how manie manners and dyuerse wayes ministringe the Communion haue we had amonge vs? I haue knowen one whyle the Priest to take the breade vpon the patten of the Chales, and turned his backe to the Aulter, and his face downe to the people, and sayd the wordes of consecration ouer the breade, & then layde it vpon the Aulter and afterwarde donne lyke wise with the Chales & the wine. Then because there seemed to muche reuerence, to be giuen to the Sacrament by this waie, the people were al driuen out of the chauncell except the ministers, that the Communion should not be commonlye sene nor worshipped. And anone that way seemed not best, and therefore there was veils or curtens drawen, yea and in some churches the very Lente cloth or veil hanged vp though

---

[268] *Twoo notable Sermons*, sig. Giii[r]: 'It dryueth away not onlye death, but also al sicknes, it stilleth and pacifieth the raginge law of oure membres, it strenthneth deuotion, it quenc[h]eth the froward affections of the mynde, and those small synnes we be in, it regardeth not, it healeth the sicke, it restoreth the brussed, and frome al falling it lyfteth vs vp.'

[269] Ibid. sig. Giii[r]–Giv[r].

it were with Alleluya in the Easter time to hide it, that no man should see what the prieste did, nor here what he saide. Then this waye pleased not and the aulters were pulled downe and the tables set vp, & all the obseruaunce saide in Englyshe, and that openly that all men might heare and see what was done, and the bread commaunded to be common vsed brede leuende with salte, barme, and such other. And then sone after were all corporaces taken awaye to extenuate the honoure of the sacrament, & it laied downe on the prophane borde clothe. And at the saide tables the Prieste one while turned his face Eastwarde, an other while turned his back Southward, and his face towarde the West as the Iewes vseth to worshippe. And anone by commandement tourned his back Southward, and his face to the north, and finally after the laste boke that was set forth he turned his face to the South. And this boke made swepestake of the blessed sacrament; declaring there to be nothing els but bare bread and wine.[270]

In similar mocking vein, Hugh Weston, preaching at Paul's Cross on 22nd October 1553, compares the Protestant Communion Table to an oyster board.[271]

There is further an interesting group of sermons whose main theme is the denunciation of the Reformers of Edward's reign—of their doctrines and actions. Dr. Richard Smith, preaching at the burning of Ridley and Latimer at Oxford on 16th October 1555, maintained, recounts Foxe, ' that the goodness of the cause, and not the order of death, maketh the holiness of the person; which he confirmed by the examples of Judas, and of a woman in Oxford that of late hanged herself, for that they, and such like as he recited, might then be adjudged righteous, which desperately sundered their lives from their bodies, as he feared that those men that stood before him would do.'[272] Further, ' he cried still to the people to beware of them, for they were heretics, and died out of the church. And on the other side, he declared their diversity in opinions, as Lutherans, Oecolampadians, Zuinglians, of which sect they were, he said, and that was the worst: but the old church of Christ and the Catholic faith, believed far otherwise.'[273] Dr. Henry Cole preaching at the burning of Cranmer at Oxford, sought to justify the proceedings, although Cranmer had recanted, and at this stage it was thought that he would die in the Catholic faith. Pardon and reconciliation are due to Cranmer by the canons, admits Cole, but the queen and

[270] *Sermons*, ff. 312ᵛ–13ʳ. [271] Foxe, *Acts and Monuments*, vol. VI, p. 541.
[272] Ibid. vol. VII, p. 548. [273] Ibid.

her Council have condemned him to death, (in the words of Foxe's summary):

First, that being a traitor, he had dissolved the lawful matrimony between the king her father, and [her] mother; besides the driving out of the pope's authority, while he was metropolitan. Secondly, that he had been a heretic, from whom, as from an author and only fountain, all heretical doctrine and schismatical opinions that so many years have prevailed in England did first rise and spring; of which he had not been a secret favourer only, but also a most earnest defender even to the end of his life, sowing them abroad by writings and arguments, privately and openly, not without great ruin and decay of the catholic church. And further, it seemed meet, according to the law of equality, that as the death of the duke of Northumberland of late, made even with Thomas More chancellor, that died for the church, so there should be one that should make even with Fisher of Rochester; and because that Ridley, Hooper, Ferrar, were not able to make even with that man, it seemed meet that Cranmer should be joined to them to fill up their part of equality.[274]

Cole exhorted the people to beware by Cranmer's example and told Cranmer to take his death well, after which there would be masses and dirges all over Oxford for his soul.[275] However, as is well known, Cranmer denied his recantation, and was hurried to his death.[276] Dr. Andrew Perne, Vicechancellor of Cambridge, preaching during the Visitation of the University by Cardinal Pole's Commissioners on 26th January 1557, after Cuthbert Scott, Bishop of Chester, had commanded the bodies of Bucer and Fagius to be exhumed and degraded from the priesthood, declared that true concord came from the Roman obedience; then says Foxe, ' he passed forth to Bucer, upon whom he made such a shameful railing, that it is not possible to defame a man more than he did, saying, that his doctrine gave occasion of division in the commonwealth; and that there was not so grievous a mischief, which by his means had not been brought into the realm '.[277] Perne claimed that Bucer had privately admitted to him that he held the opinion that ' God was the author and wellspring, not only of good, but also of evil; and that whatsoever was of that sort, flowed from him, as from the headspring and maker thereof ', but that for fear of ' offending divers men's consciences, he durst not put it into men's heads '.[278] Dr. Watson, Bishop of Lincoln, continued this attack on Bucer and

274 Ibid. vol. VIII, p. 85.   275 Ibid. p. 86.   276 Ibid. pp. 87–90.
277 Ibid. p. 280.   278 Ibid. pp. 280–1.

Fagius in a sermon on Candlemas day (2nd February) in which he
said that among other things they had taught men to cast away all
ceremonies. However St. Paul commands all things to be done in
due order (1 Cor. xiv. 40): ' and ', as Foxe reports, ' upon that deed
of the blessed Virgin and Joseph, which was done by them as upon
that day, it was manifestly apparent, that they with our Saviour,
being then a little babe, observed these rites and ceremonies for
catholic men to teach. For he said that they came to the temple the
same time with wax candles in their hands, after the manner of
procession, (as they term it) in good order, with much reverence and
devotion; and yet we were not ashamed to laugh and mock at those
things with the heretics and schismatics.'[279]   Watson preached
again in Great St. Mary's on 6th February, during the burning of the
exhumed bodies of Bucer and Fagius in the market place, taking
occasion to condemn the events of the previous reign; as Foxe narrates:

> What robbing and polling (quoth he) have we seen in this
> realm, as long as religion was defaced with sects; the common
> treasure (gathered for the maintenance of the whole public
> weal) and the goods of the realm shamefully spent in waste for
> the maintenance of a few folks' lust; all good order broken, all
> discipline cast aside; holidays appointed to the solemnizing of
> ceremonies neglected; and that more is, the places themselves
> beaten down; flesh and other kind of prohibited sustenance
> eaten everywhere upon days forbidden, without remorse of
> conscience; the priests had in derision; the mass railed upon;
> no honour done to the sacraments of the church; all estates and
> degrees given to such a licentious liberty without check, that
> all things may seem to draw to their utter ruin and decay.[280]

Although, continues Watson, all was done ostensibly in the name of
the Gospel, yet nothing could have been more opposed to God's
word. The Reformers denied the Real Presence in the Blessed
Sacrament, and taught Predestination: 'As who should say, it skilled
not what a man purposed of any matter, since he had not the power
to determine otherwise than the matter should come to pass. The
which was the peculiar opinion of them that made God the author of
evil, bringing men through this persuasion, into such a careless
security of the everlasting eternity, that in the mean season it made
no matter either toward salvation, or damnation, what a man did in
this life.'[281]

However, to counteract the dogmatic weakness in the pre-
Reformation Catholic piety,[282] the preachers of this reign supply

[279] Ibid. p. 282.   [280] Ibid. p. 284.   [281] Ibid.   [282] Cf. *ante*, pp. 248–52.

reasoned statements of Catholic faith and practice. Mary's Injunctions (1554) ordered that ' by the bishop of the diocese, a uniform
doctrine be set forth by homilies, or otherwise, for the good instruction and teaching of the people '. Bonner's Homilies, which significantly quote Scripture and the Fathers, but not the school doctors,
give a well-knit, clear, and simple exposition of the main points of
doctrine;[283] Pollard's Homilies provide a similar treatment of
certain selected topics;[284] while in Watson's ' Sermons on the
Sacraments ' a detailed and academic explanation of these central
channels of grace is provided. Gone are the days when crude
panegyrics of the saints could be considered adequate instruction in
the parishes,[285] the cogent presentation of reformed doctrine in the
Edwardian Homilies had to be met with an equally satisfying
account of the Catholic position. In particular the teaching on the
Mass is presented fully and clearly; now all were to be taught the
true Catholic doctrine. Watson's second polemical sermon on the
Mass gives the fullest and subtlest exposition:

> . . . we offre Christ misticallye in oure dayle sacrifice of the
> Masse, where Christe is by hys omnipotent power presented to
> vs in the Sacramente, and of vs agayne represented to his and
> our father, and his passyon renewed, not by sufferynge of deathe
> againe but after an vnbloudye maner, not for thys ende, that we
> shoulde thereby deserue remission of our synnes, but that by
> our fayth, deuotion, and thys representation of hys passion we
> mooste humblye praye almyghte God to applye vnto vs by
> Christe that remission which was purchased and deserued by
> his passion before.[286]

[283] John Harpesfield, Archdeacon of London is the author of most of these homilies,
viz. nos. 1, 'An Homelye of the creation and fall of Man '; 2, 'An Homelye of the
miserie of all mankynd, and hys condempnacion to euerlastynge deathe, by his owne
synne '; [this virtually the same as the Edwardian homily of similar title]; 3, 'An
Homelye of the redempcion of man '; 4, 'An Homelye declaring how the redemptyon
in Chryst is appliable to vs '; 6, 'An Homelye declaryng howe daungerous a thyng, the
breach of Charitye is '; 9, 'An Homelye of the primacie or supreame power, of the
highest gouernor of the militant church '; 10, 'An other Homelye of the Primacye ';
11, 'An Homelye declarynge that in the blessed Sacrament of the aultar, is the verye
bodye and bloude of our Sauyour Chryst '; 12, 'An Homelye of Transubstantiation.'
Henry Pendleton is the author of two, viz. nos. 7, 'An Homelye of the churche, What it
is, and of the commodyty thereof '; and 8, 'An Homelye of the authorite of the church,
declarynge what commoditie and profyt we haue thereby.'   Edmund Bonner is the
author of no. 5, 'An Homelye of Christian loue, or Charitie'; [this virtually the same as,
the Edwardian homily of similar title] while no. 13 is anonymous, viz., 'An Homelye,
wherein is answere made to certayne common obiections, agaynst the presence of
Christes bodye, and bloude in the Sacrament of the Aultar.'
[284] The titles are: 1, ' Of the Sacrament of the aultar '; 2, ' Of the Sacryfyce of the
Masse '; 3, ' Of fayth and knowledge of God '; 4, ' Of the primatiue & chiefe auctoritie '; 5, ' Of confession and purgation or clensynge from sinne.'
[285] Cf. ante, pp. 257–8.   [286] Twoo notable Sermons, sig. Rvii[r].

However it was one thing to present Catholic doctrine, another to make the people receive it. Pole labours diligently to form a spirit of child-like acceptance of the teaching of the Church, which he feels is infinitely superior to the conviction of argument.[287] After the recent turmoils he wishes only to bring peace to England, but, he points out, the audience must be *filij pacis,* to receive this peace.[288] To be children of peace is to be children of grace, and that means that each must be ' the chyld of obedience, that chyld that hearing peace offered hym of the messenger of God, doeth giue eare vnto it, doth nott repugne to the same, but gladlier doth accept it.'[289] This obedience consists of accepting Catholic doctrine in the same unquestioning way in which a child receives lessons from its mother.[290] Englishmen must become spiritually *parvuli* if they are to enter again into their religious inheritance, they must, *in simplicitate cordis* accept the true *fides patrum;*[291] ' content to here wythout replyinge, what theyr fathers teche them, as theyr fathers haue doone to theyr fathers afore them ',[292] for the spiritual fatherhood of the Church runs back through the bishops to the Apostles and Christ Himself.[293] If the members of the audience, going behind Cranmer, who ' broughte in thys newe and pernycyous doctryne ',[294] asked Archbishop Warham what was his teaching on the Sacrament of the Altar, he would answer that it was the same as that now restored, and if they questioned him further about where it came from, he would reply that it came from his predecessors in the See of Canterbury, and so was received from St. Augustine, who in turn received it from Pope Gregory, who received it in succession from St. Peter, ' who wyth the other Apostles had the same of Chryste '.[295] The Blessed Virgin submitted her reason and her will to the message of God announced by the angel, so let Englishmen submit their reason and will to the message of the Church announced by Pole; and then, as the Blessed Virgin conceived Christ ' both spirituallye and corporallye ', so each Christian will conceive Christ in his soul.[296] Pollard too uses these simple analogies; Christians must receive the teaching of the Church with the same ' simplicitie ' as children receive instruction from their parents;[297] while the only way for us, 'beinge but as babyes, and God's suckynge chyldren' to avoid 'the cruell daunger of that mischeuous beaste the deuyll', is

[287] MS. Vat. Lat. 5968, ff. 379^r–80^r.   [288] Ibid. ff. 387^r–408^r.   [289] Ibid. f. 412^r.
[290] Ibid. ff. 440^{r-v} [291] Ibid. ff. 299^{r-v}.   [292] Ibid. f. 300^r.
[293] Ibid. ff. 301^{r-v}.   [294] Ibid. f. 301^v.
[295] Ibid. ff. 303^r–4^r.   [296] Ibid. ff. 417^{r-v}.
[297] *Fyue homilies,* sig. Diii^v–Div^r (Fiv^v–Gi^r).

'to keep vs within the house of our father which is the Catholike Church '.[298]

However, declares Feckenham, the people are slow to return to the Catholic faith; little heeding the voices of their shepherds, seduced by the ' straunge voices ' of the ' deceitfull Mayremaides ' [the Protestant preachers], Londoners recompense the patience of the hierarchy and Sovereign with ' most cursed and wycked speak-ynges, blasphemyng God, and reysing vp false lyes and rumors agaynste oure mooste gratious kynge and Quene '.[299] So much is this the case that the preacher is forced to warn his audience, ' that excepte ye shortlye retourne frome youre wycked heresyes into the vnitie of Christes churche agayne. . . . Doutles your euill beleuynge and corrupte lyuynge shall brynge you vnto a miserable and lament-able death and endynge. . . .'[300]

Pole upbraids Londoners for their sloth in works of mercy: the Italians, he avers, are more liberal in alms-giving and in the support of hospitals and monasteries; indeed in Italy, he declares:

> . . . I knowe yn somme cyte to be above iii score monasteryes, as I am sure yn Venyce be; and yn Florence alone above iiii score and the most part founded by the voluntarye almes of the citesyns, one not knowynge another's almesse. If I woulde reherse at Rome, at Bononye [Bologna], at Mylane, what a multitude of holy houses, and hospitals be founded under this manner, yt were a wonder to heare, and a great reproche to you yn this cyte, whereas there are not X places, neyther of hospytalls nor monasteryes yn the cyte, nor aboute the cyte; and yet for you they maye dye for hunger. . . .[301]

Feckenham finds it necessary to upbraid the nobles and gentlemen for their parsimony in causing the number of clergy at St. Paul's to be severely diminished, ' where ', he tells them, ' of the numbre of LVIII or LX priestes, be now left by your prouision, but onely twelue priestes, called Peticanones, here daylie to serue God in the Queere . . .'[302] Hugh Glasier declares that although an order has been taken for tithes in London, yet:

> . . . concerning the countrey in most places, the tithes be wonder-full euyll payed, and some times worse spent. For I my selfe haue a poore lyuinge within twelfe miles of this citie, and rounde about me there are to the numbre of xvi. or xx. parishes,

[298] Ibid. sig. Eiir-v (Giiir-v).   [299] A notable sermon, sig. Cviir-v.
[300] Ibid. sig. Cviiv.
[301] ' Cardinal Pole's speech to the citizens of London,' Strype, Ecclesiastical Memorials, III. 2, p. 507. Cf. too ibid. p. 484.
[302] A notable sermon, sig. Dir

and amongest them all there be not past foure or fiue priestes
that do recyue one tithe sheif [sheaf], for all be impropried (as
they call theim) And somme of those benefices bee worthe an
hundreth markes a yere, some an hundreth poundes, some two
hundreth markes. And some of these parishes bee without a
priest a quarter of a yere together, and some daye thei haue
mattens, & no masse, and some times a shorte euensonge in
stede of both. For the farmers be so deuoute men, that they
passe not muche, if there were no masse sayde in the churche,
tyll our lady had a new sonne.[303]

Other topics of complaint found in this reign are traditional.
Watson, like Latimer, must speak against the wrong motives for
marriage.[304] First, to marry to gratify lust (for ' good love ' as the
young put it), is wrong; for:

> . . . that good loue is moost principallye for to haue their
> sensual appetyte and carnal desyre fulfylled. Whiche maner of
> loue doth neuer long endure betwene them that so marrye, but
> it decayeth and goeth shortly away. And then suche persones
> beginne to mislyke one an others conditions, and to waxe
> werye one of another, and after continuaunce and increase of
> that werynesse, it groweth to bee paineful and greuous, that the
> parties wyshe them selues buried, and no merueyle. For an
> euyl tree such as is carnall concupiscence and fleshely loue, can
> bring forth no good fruyte.[305]

Secondly, to marry for ' goodes and ryches ' is wrong; although,
says the bishop, nothing is so common these days: for let a man be
rich, and it matters not if he lacks virtue and is deformed, or let a
woman have great possessions, and it is of no consequence whether
she is fair or foul, young or old! However, parents who choose
partners for their children for this reason, often provide a life of
misery for them, and may even cause the downfall of their house.[306]
The right reasons for marriage are mutual affection coupled with the
desire of children and posterity by whom God should be more
honoured, and also hatred of fornication and an unclean life.[307]

Glasier declaims against bribery in the traditional manner; he
quotes Isaiah lix. 14: *Corruit in plateis veritas, et iustitia non potest
ingredi* (' truth hath fallen down in the street, and equity could not
come in ', Douay) and continues:

---

[303] *A notable and very fruictefull sermon made at Paules crosse*, sig. Ev^r-v.
[304] Cf. *ante*, pp. 274–5.
[305] *Holsome and Catholyke doctryne concerninge the Seuen Sacraments*, f. 179^v.
[306] Ibid. ff. 180^r-v.   [307] Ibid.

Truth doth fall doune in the streetes, yea, euen of this citie, and few or none there are that wyl take her vp by the hande, and bring her into their shoppes, & *iustitia* can not come in. And why so? For dame briberye kepeth the dore, and will not lette *iustitia* come in: for dame briberie is as busie an officer nowe a dayes as euer she was. Dame briberi is kinne to an agewe: for as an agew is at hande with all diseases, so is dame briberie at hande in all offices, and is readie to picke euerye mannes purse.[308]

In the Boy Bishop's sermon for Gloucester Cathedral appears complaint of the old kind against children, parents and school-masters,[309] although, as we have noticed, it is touched with humour.[310] It is difficult to find an example of innocent childhood in these degenerate days, sighs the youthful bishop, for children are now corrupted.[311] In the city they are irreverent and swearers; those from grammar schools misbehave shamefully when at liberty; choir-boys do not know how to comport themselves fittingly in church—only the little one who runs still on his mother's hand can give the required example.[312] Parents foolishly indulge their children, forgetting that *Qui parcit virgae odit filium* (Prov. xiii. 24), and that ' the rodde breakes no bones '.[313] They refuse to punish them lest they break their ' corage '; but surely the aim of ' good education ' is ' to discorage youth utterly as touching vice and vicious maners, and to bolden and corage them in all probitye and vertue and vertuose maners! '[314] Schoolmasters care about academic attainments and singing in tune, but neglect character-formation; but they should not ignore the moral and spiritual well-being of their charges.[315]

The old lugubrious declamation on senility and death[316] re-appears in this reign in Feckenham's funeral sermon for Queen Joanna of Spain. We might be listening once more to Longland or Edgeworth as the preacher shows how death attacks us in diverse manners:

Sometime he maketh towarde vs as it were with open batayle, sendynge before hym vnto vs diuerse infirmities and sycknesses: and vnto some, hoare heares, blered eies, tremblinge and shakinge handes, stouping shulders and croked backes, as

---

[308] *A notable and very fruictefull sermon made at Paules crosse*, sig. Eiii[r-v].
[309] Cf. Owst., *L. & P.M.E.*, pp. 460–8.
[310] Cf. *ante*, pp. 166–8, where various passages are quoted.
[311] ' Sermon of the Child Bishop,' *Camden Society Miscellany*, VII, p. 23.
[312] Ibid. pp. 23–5.   [313] Ibid. pp. 26–7.   [314] Ibid. p. 27.
[315] Ibid. pp. 28–9.   [316] Cf. *ante*, pp. 228–36.

U

it were messengers or herauldes at armes sent before him. Sometime he commeth priuely creapinge as a thefe, and stealynge
vpon vs like as he dyd vpon the richeman, of whome we rede in
the twelfeth of saincte Lukes gospell [Luke xii. 20], sending to
vs no warninges or messengers at all before him.[317]

How salutary it is, he declares, to contemplate the certainty of death:

> At whose first entrye and breakynge into our houses,
> beholde howe the conscience begynneth to dreade, howe the
> hearte quaketh, the head stoupeth, the witte wasteth, the
> strengthe faileth, the visage waxeth pale, the tonge fombleth,
> the breath goeth awaye, the speche very rare and thynne, all the
> beautie of the body cleane tourned into a grisely and fylthye
> corruption: and after that the bodye is buried, it falleth into a
> cationlyke stenche the fleshe cleane tourned into grubbes
> meate.[318]

Let all come, declaims Feckenham, to behold their own death in the
mirror of the death of this noble lady whose funeral is now being held:

> O ye olde fathers vnto whome deathe beyng very fauour-
> able hathe sent before him, vnto you so many messengers, as
> youre hoare hears, bleared eies, droppinge noses, sogginge
> chekes, your lippes hanging, stowping neckes and shulders:
> come ye hither and beholde your selues and learne at the least
> wayes nowe in your olde age to be wise & vnderstande what
> vaine hope you be in which do loke and make your most vayne
> accomptes, to liue one yeare longer: be ye neuer of so greate
> an age, euer crepynge awrie and sore fearinge to die. O ye olde
> fathers and hoare heares, why feare ye to die at LXX or LXXX
> yeres of age, when all the tyme that ye shal liue after is in
> heuines, in greuous aches, in continual decaiyng, and neuer
> vpright, but rolinge, relinge, and ready to fall in to the graue
> whiche you do so lothe.[319]

Let women, (whom the preacher in the traditional manner reviles for
vanity)[320] come too:

> O ye gentlewomen & faire ladies greatlie deliting in pure
> glasses, forgett not I praye you to beholde youre selues in
> this glasse of al other most profitable, which are so sodenly
> geuen here in this worlde to set forth your selues, wyth youre
> browded heare (whiche is a great abuse) youre fyngers be set
> with ringes, bearing purses full of swete sauoures & smells,
> and bandes aboute youre neckes fynely wroughte wyth silke,
> and beset with pearles, with bracelets ful of gaudies, and such
> other maner of disguisinges.[321]

---

[317] *A notable Sermon*, sig. Biii[r].   [318] Ibid. sig. Bv[v].   [319] Ibid. sig. Bvi[v].
[320] Cf. *ante*, pp. 241–2.   [321] *A notable sermon*, sig. Bviii[v].

With all the old dark asceticism Feckenham admonishes these ladies to ponder deeply the vile state to which the body will come:

> Why do ye therefore make so much of so filthie a carkas, and wast so much time in washinge, kemming and pranking of the same, vnto no smale prid and ostentation; when ye do but loose your laboures, and in so doynge you do nothing els, but floure a fylthye donghyll and garnish a smokie miskin [i.e. mixen—a compost heap], which you shall neuer make sauerie washe him neuer so muche.[322]

To all comes death; St. Paul warns, ' it is appointed unto men once to die ' (Heb. ix. 27); and, continues the preacher, with sombre eloquence:

> Do not we see the order of this present life to be suche, that after infancie commeth childhod, after childhod youth, after youth mans state, age, then olde age, and so at the last death? The whiche order and naturall course can by no law, statute or meanes that man can inuent, be infringed or broken, neither yet once staied or pluckt backe. No not Minos the lawe maker at Crete, nor Lycurgus at Lacedemony, nor yet the wise Solon in his lawes, deuised at Athenes, could make any repeale of this decree and ordinaunce of God. When from the first man Adam, vnto this most noble and gracious queene of Spaine late departed, none hath escaped or can escape this sentence of death. No not Noe for all his righteousness nor Loth for al his hospitalitie, nor yet Toby for all his diligence in buriyng the dead, could escape this rigorous sentence of death. When it was neither the strong and mightie faith of Abraham, nor the supplanting of vices that was in Iacob, or the great mekenes of the prophete Moyses, nor the chastitie of Ioseph, nor yet the holines of the prophet Samuel, that could perswade death to be the more fauourable to them. The great wisdome, riches, might & power, of kyng Solomon, the great strength & force of Sampson agaynst his enemies, the puissance of the king and prophete Dauid, his feates of chiualrie & great might in armes coulde not auaile against the assaultes of death: death beyng fauourable to no man, but like cruel and tirannous to euery man. And therefore I do reade that death was portred and painted of the Paynims with the face and countenance of a tiraunt hauinge in his hande redie bent bow and arrowes to kill, slea, and shote at euerye man withoute all respecte or acception of persons.[323]

Mary's reign, which in the sermons opens in joy,[324] ends in gloom;

---

[322] Ibid. sig. Bviii[v].
[323] Ibid. sig. Aviii[r-v]; cf. too the passage on Death the bowman quoted *ante*, p. 163.
[324] Cf. *ante*, pp. 277–9.

the queen too has succumbed to the common enemy, and although she may be already in heaven,[325] now, warns Bishop White, ' the wolves be coming out of Geneva '.[326]

IV

THE ELIZABETHAN PREACHERS (1558–1603)

The efforts of the preachers of Mary's reign to build up an informed Catholic piety[327] were indeed short-lived, for the reign of Elizabeth witnesses a vigorous and prolonged attack upon almost all the aspects of Catholicism. This attack is at first usually reasoned and doctrinal. In the ' Homily against Peril of Idolatry ' Jewel, following Bullinger, argues against images from Scripture and history: the Bible consistently condemns the making and worshipping of images;[328] they were not in use in the primitive Church, certain of the Fathers disapproved of them, but after St. Gregory the Great permitted them for instructional purposes, they crept into the Western Church under his authority, and then were worshipped.[329] Also (as has been noticed), this homily argues against the invocation of the saints and the veneration of their images by adducing the parallels with the pagan deities and *their* statues;[330] and, adds Jewel, never were the Gentile idolaters so foolish as to worship relics, as have Christians in recent centuries.[331] Again, in his famous ' Challenge Sermon ' preached first at Paul's Cross on 26th November 1559 and repeated at Court on 17th March and again at Paul's Cross on 31st March 1560, he attacks on historical and rational grounds five matters concerning the Roman Mass: the use of Latin and not the vernacular, Communion under one kind, the teaching enshrined in the Canon concerning sacrifice, the adoration of the Blessed Sacrament, and the private celebration. These are perversions of the primitive practice of the Church: use of a tongue not understood by the people meant that, ' of all that holy supper and most comfortable ordinance of Christ, there was nothing for the simple souls to consider, but only a number of gestures and countenances; and, yet neither they nor the priest knew what they meant';[332] for the first six hundred years of the Church, the Communion was

[325] 'A sermon preached at the funerals of Queen Mary,' Strype, *Ecclesiastical Memorials*, III. 2, p. 548.
[326] Ibid. p. 542.   [327] See *ante*, pp. 284–5.
[328] *Certain Sermons appointed by the Queen's Majesty*, pp. 169–82.
[329] Ibid. pp. 182–213.   [330] Ibid pp. 224–34; cf. *ante*, pp. 221–2.
[331] Ibid. pp. 234–6.   [332] *Works*, vol. I, p. 9.

universally administered under both kinds;[333] the doctrine of sacrifice in the Canon is blasphemous, while the prayer *Jube haec perferri per manus sancti angeli tui in sublime altare tuum* (['We humbly entreat thee, Almighty God,] command those things to be carried by the hands of Thy holy Angel to Thy Altar on High [before the sight of Thy Divine Majesty'])[334] is ludicrous; there is nothing in the old Fathers about adoration, nor about Transubstantiation, for they speak of the bread and wine remaining in the Sacrament after the consecration;[335] then again, the private celebration is a recent abuse, it is unknown to the Fathers, and is obviously not intended by the text of the Missal itself.[336] Jewel also ridicules various weak arguments by Roman apologists in defence of the practices of their church, as that of Eck, that because it is written, ' " Give not holy things to dogs "; *ergo*, the priest at mass, and other where, may not speak to the people but in a strange tongue ';[337] or that of Sylvester, that because ' Christ was buried in a shroud of linen cloth; *ergo*, the corporal must be made of fine linen ';[338] or that of various authorities, that as ' many of the lay people have the palsy, and many have long beards; *ergo*, they must all receive the communion under one kind '.[339]

In contrast to this type of theological argument is the violence of one William? Baldwin, who, preaching at Paul's Cross in September 1563, calls for the gallows for the deprived Marian bishops. However, relates Stowe, Baldwin himself died of the plague the week after delivering his sermon.[340]

In these early years the reformed doctrine on key topics is clearly set forth so that the people should be fully weaned away from the old errors: thus in the ' Homily of the worthy receiving of the Sacrament ' Jewel stresses that the Holy Communion should be celebrated and received in the same manner as in the primitive Church, and gives directions for worthy reception;[341] while the ' Homily of Repentance ', following Gualter, explains that after contrition comes the ' acknowledging of our sins unto God ', and

---

[333] Ibid.
[334] Ibid. pp. 9–10. The prayer continues, ' that as many of us as shall by partaking at this Altar, receive the most Sacred Body and Blood of Thy Son, may be fulfilled with all grace and heavenly benediction, through the same Christ Our Lord. Amen.' *The Sarum Missal in English*, (London, 1868,) p. 312.
[335] Ibid. pp. 10–13.   [336] Ibid. pp. 16–20.   [337] Ibid. p. 15.   [338] Ibid.
[339] Ibid.; see further the other arguments quoted, ibid. pp. 14–16.
[340] Maclure, *The Paul's Cross Sermons*, 1534–1642, p. 204; J. Stow, ' Historical Memoranda ' in *Three Fifteenth Century Chronicles*, ed. J. Gairdner, (London, 1880) C.S., new series no. XXVIII, p. 126.
[341] *Certain Sermons appointed by the Queen's Majesty*, pp. 444–56.

then by faith, the laying hold of the promises of forgiveness, with consequent amendment of life, and that whereas the scholastic contrition, confession and satisfaction are found in the sterile repentance of Judas, the reformed procedure is found in the fruitful repentance of St. Peter.[342]

However, after the excommunication and deposition of Elizabeth by Gregory XIII in 1570, together with the arrival in England of the Seminarists, the preachers frequently indulge in bitter, and at times scurrilous, popular polemic against the Roman Church and the English papists. Thus Tyrer, with extraordinary vigour, declares that Catholicism consists merely in outward show; this religion lies:

. . . in fantasies not in veritie, and in circumstances not in substance: . . . in vanitie of vestments in copes & corporasses, albes and amisses in palles and purples, and such like trifles, their prayer being nothing els but lipp labour, in murmuring and muttering manie creeds, Paternosters, and Ave Maries, in blessing & bending, in kneelinge and knocking, in beating their breasts, in groueling on the ground, in houlding vp their hands, in lifting vp their eies to heauen, like the proude Pharisie in the Gospell, the same being in the tongue not in trueth, in voice not in spirit, in externall crying and calling, in bellowing and bawling in sorrowing and sighing, in grieues & growning from the face outward but without remorse of conscience, Heauinese of heart, contrition, of minde, and conuersion of soule: their bapti[s]me standing of water, creame, oile, salt, spittle, sneuill, and such like filthie slauerings, and yet those so necessary, as they dare be bold to say blockishlye & blasphemously; without the which Saluation cannot be obtained. The Sacrament of the supper they make as it were a maske or mummerie by their massing, yea they vse it as heathenish sacrifice by their manifest Idolatrie, yea like a plaie or pageant by their goulden shewes by their bendinges and bowinges, mocking and mowinges, windings and turninges, and such like vnseemly gesture, by their adoration, eleuation, exaltation: the shameless shaueling that celebrateth this Sacrifice or rather committeth this sacri-ledge not without most horrible blasphemie, dealeth with the baked God which they call an host, euen as a cat doth with a mouse, who after they haue dalied with it, dandled it, towsed and tossed it two & fro vpward and downeward, forward and backward, at the last, the iest turning into earnest, he choppeth it vp at one bitte, flesh, bloud, bones and all. To conclude, their whole religion consisteth of nothing els, but of raggs and

342 Ibid. pp. 537–45.

reliques, ringing and singing, censing and sancting, shauing and shriuing, thereby shragging the purses of the poore people, and all this in shew of sanctimonie and sinceritie, and being indeede nothing els but decite & dissembling. . . .[343]

Similarly, with scurrilous *élan*, Bridges attacks Transubstantiation:

. . . they turned Chryst out of his owne likenesse, and made him looke lyke a rounde cake, nothyng lyke to Iesus Christe, no more than an apple is lyke an oyster, nor so mutche, for there appereth neyther armes nor handes, feete nor legges, backe nor belly, heade nor body of Chryst: but all is visoured and dis-guysed vnder the fourme of a wafer, as lyghte as a feather, as thinne as a paper, as whyte as a kerchiefe, as round as a trenchour, as flat as a pancake, as smal as a shilling, as tender as the Priestes lemman that made it, as muche taste as a stycke, and as deade as a dore nayle to looke vpon. O blessed God, dare they thus disfigure our Lord and Sauior Iesus Christ?[344]

In like manner Deringe attacks the ceremonies for ordination:

. . . for, where Christ's ordinance is that his ministers should bee made with prayer and fasting, and with laying on of handes: they, as men, thinking baselie of such simple dealing, adde a great deale more to the making of their priests: they must haue oyle, candels, basens, towels, amices, albes, stoules, gyrdles, maniples, miters, bookes, crosses, linnen, bandes, chalices, patens, singing, cakes, wine and water, flower, and such other thinges, trifled and toyed with all, with so many foolish gestures, as I am perswaded, that any wise man, this day, reading it in their owne bookes, would abhorre it, either as intollerable pride, or vnspeakable foolishnesse.[345]

Purgatory is a fable of evil spirits, says Henry Smith, for: ' They had never heard of Purgatory but for these spirits which walked in the night, and told them, that they were the souls of such and such which suffered in fire, till their Masses, and alms, and Pilgrimages did ransome them out: so these night-spirits begat Purgatory and Purgatory Trentals, as one Serpent hatcheth another.'[346] Anderson scoffs at the very notion of purgatory, and illustrates the manner in which at this time children were taught to mock at prayers and masses for the dead: ' how vayne a thing is it ', he asks, ' to imagine a purgatory, from whence our friends soules are fetched by our sundry deedes for them? As by *Trentals, Diriges, Requiem, and restles Masses, Almes deedes, Popes pardons, and prayers for all christian soules*, with *Aue Maria Amen*. Whose pelfe yong babes can scoffe, and saye in these

[343] *Five godlie sermons*, pp. 302–4.   [344] *A Sermon preached at Paules Crosse*, p. 125.
[345] *XXVII Lectures or readings vpon part of the Epistle written to the Hebrues*, sig. Yii[v].
[346] *Sermons*, p. 263. Cf. ibid. pp. 259–60, *Twelve Sermons*, pp. 649–50.

dayes. *Come tye the Mare Tomboy. A cake, a cake for all christian soules, De profundis, Salue Regina. Godfather.*[347] However, in a graver passage, he contrasts the Protestant's ' assurance of salvation ' with the terrifying doubt of the Catholic:

> They tell him that his friends shall praye for him, and the Church shal be plyed with Trentals, to delyuer him from Purgatory, which doctrine is most troublesome, and so the Papist, for all that Popery can doe, dyeth thereby moste doubtefull of rest, if not moste fearefull of eternall payne. . . . Can this worke peace in the hart, when the best account made, at the foot thereof, he fyndeth an arrearage, which his soule is to aunswere in burning fyre, and flaming brimstone; in a Purgatorie of payne, whence he cannot by all the cunning of Popish arte, know when or how to be delyuered? . . . O poore harte, be wise in God, imbrace his word, beleeue on his Christ, walke in his statutes by the grace of his spirite, so shalt thou be assured that the popish Purgatory is Hell, from whence no man can be delyuered. So shall all terror of death be drawne from thee, . . . no condemnation can come to thee, which by fayth art ingraffed into Christ.[348]

Drant satirises vigorously the scholastic *quaestiones*, by framing some ludicrous ones of his own, as ' whether that Byshopp, that was so fretting fell for the losse of his peacocke pie, did possesse hys soule in patience, or no? '[349] Similarly, he mockingly salutes the medieval doctors:

> . . . should not we take a shrill trumpet and blowe vp from a lofty Theater All hale learned Doctors, Venerable doctors, Reuerent doctors, Doctorall doctors. Doctorly doctors, Irrefragable doctors, Impregnable doctors, Seraphicall doctors, Angelical doctors, Magistral doctors, Illiminate doctors, Autentical doctors?[350]

' But,' he tells his audience, ' see the learning of these doctors in the epistles of obscure men, and in a dialogue between *Reuchlin* and *Erasmus*.'[351] In his best euphuistic manner, Drant declares that there is no sound learning amongst the schoolmen; ' that which Aloes is to the lyppes, which gall is to the tongue, which a carcase smell is to the nose, which a cockatrice to the eyes, which a naked dagger is to the hart, that it is and even that comfort it is, to be conuersaunt in the base barbarismes, and balde solisismes, and bad sillogismes, and whole dungeons of the Dunceries of *Hardings* companions.'[352] On

---

[347] *The Shield of our Safetie*, sig. Gi[v].   [348] Ibid. sig. Iiv[v].
[349] *Three godly and learned Sermons*, sig. Aviii[v].   [350] Ibid. sig. Ciii[r].
[351] Ibid.   [352] Ibid. sig. Bvii[r].

the contrary, ' the world will neuer be so learned *Martin Luther*, but thou shalt be counted learned, thou shalt be called learned *Zuinglius*, and thou excellent well learned *Oecolampadius*, learned *Bucer*, learned *Phagius*, learned *Emmanuel*, learned *Pelicane*, and learned *Pomerane*, and learned *Brentius*.'[353] Furthermore, the contemporary Romanists obtained what learning they possess from Protestants:

Ye groundsels of learning, ye kindlers of lyght, in deede ye be ours. These Papists haue lighted theyr candles at your candles, and whetted theyr weapons at your stones, and sucked vp theyr learning at your feete: Euen so *Thomas Harding* sucked vp his learning at *Peter Martyrs* feete: and *Thomas Watson*, his learning at Syr *Iohn Cheekes* feete: *Baldwinus* his learning at *Caluines* feete, and *Fredericus Staphilus* at *Melancthons* feete: *Sanders* and the Iesuites haue theyr Grecismes and theyr Hebraismes, by imitation of *Musculus*. Our *Erasmus* set Latine a flote, our *Reuchlin* hatched Hebrue, our *Budaeus* a gaged Greeke, our *Melancthon* regendered Artes and Sciences. Papistes, from vs ye haue had it, or by our examples ye haue spied it. It is ours, it is ours, it is all of it ours. Crowes leaue your cackling, or giue you home again your borrowed feathers.[354]

On another occasion Drant does not hesitate to declare that the teaching of the Roman Church is so perverted as to approach the errors of Mohamedanism: ' That euill fauored *Mahomets* woman or church defendeth many wiues; This *Romish* church defendeth stewes and strumpets, curtizans, concubines & boy harlots. Mahomets woman dreameth heauen to be a place of goodly Riuers, pleasaunt Apples, young delycate women, and fayre fruites: The Popes woman dooth say and holde, that S. *Dorathey* made baskettes of Apples that came downe from heauen.'[355]

The attacks on the English Catholics are equally bitter as those on their church. Drant has no faith in their loyalty: ' as it is true', he declares, ' that two & two make foure, that when the sun is in the middest of the heauen, it is noone tyme, that euerie part of the cyrcle differeth equallie from the center, that when the sun ryseth, it is morning: so it is infallible true, that no perfect Papist, can be to any christian Prince a good subiect.'[356] An anonymous preacher upbraids the Recusants for not attending the parish churches: 'Are you soe priuiledged', he asks, 'that you can not bee seduced? Are you so perfect, that you neede not bee instructed? or are wee soe accursed, that the truth of God is a lye, or such castawaies, that the

[353] Ibid.   [354] Ibid. sig. Bvii^v–Bviii^r.
[355] Ibid. sig. Cvi^r.   [356] Ibid. sig. Giv^v.

woorde of God is an abomination in our mouthes? '357   All the
blame for bloodshed rests upon the traitorous papists, declares this
preacher, for ' their neuer fell an heare from your heads, vntill you
strooke at our head, their was neuer one dropp of bloode shedd
before you sought to spill her bloode as water, spilte on the earthe,
w[h]ich can neuer bee gathered vp againe, whose bloode is dearer
vnto vs then the bloode that runneth in our owne vaines, whose life
is dearer vnto vs and ought to bee more deare vnto you then your
owne lifes.'358   Bitter indeed is the rebuke given by William Kethe
to a bishop (' a papistical Prelate ' as he calls him) who in the pulpit
dared to speak mildly about the Pope: ' where men merueyled he
spake no more agaynst the Pope, he did them to vnderstand, that he
knew no hurt by the pope, if he were a good man, he prayed God to
continue him in his goodnesse, if he were an ill man, he prayed God
to amend him '; but, asks this zealous loyalist:

> What wordes were these of a preacher? what subiect is
> there so simple which knoweth not, that that vile *Italian* of
> *Rome* is a traitor to this Realme, who hath of late by his beastly
> Buls sturred the subiectes of this Realme, to rebell agaynst their
> lawfull magistrates, and hath sought what he might, and yet
> doth what he can to pull the crowne from the Queene[s]
> Maiesties head: and is this fit that a Papist which shall speake
> such wordes of the Pope as I haue recited, or the lyke in effect,
> shall yet continue not onely an ordinary ouer a great multitude,
> but also a common preacher (such as he is) in this shyre?359

Stockwood castigates the harbouring by country gentlemen of popish
schoolmasters and old Marian priests:

> . . . we haue in manye Gentlemens houses, and also in the houses
> of others in the countrey of hygher callyng the sweepings of
> the Vniuersities, I meane, suche rotten Papistes, as by the
> broome of godly discipline, as vnprofitable duste, haue bin
> sweeped out thence, are entertayned in the Countrey in priuate
> houses to teach their children. And there they be as safe as
> the Foxe in his borow. For who dare be so bolde as once to
> enquire wherein they instruct their schollers? besides this,
> there are huddled together olde Popyshe persecuting Masse
> Priestes, in some houses foure, in some three, in some two, in
> some one, and they (forsooth) vnder pretence of seruing in
> seuerall offices as some stewardes, some Caters, and so forth,
> peruerte whole famylies. For can it possibly be otherwise,
> that themselues Papistes, and vnder Papistes hauing the gouerne-

---

357 MS. Lambeth 488, f. 85v.   358 Ibid. f. 84r.
359 *A sermon made at Blandford Forum* (London, 1572) f. 13v.

ment of youth, as men chosen for the purpose, shoulde teach any other than Papistrie?[360]
The preachers are zealous in their polemic against all remnants of the old religion still left in the countryside. Speaking of his brother clergy, Gybson avers that still ' there be some amongest vs sacrificing and Massing Priestes, full of manifest superstition and hypocrisie, and in trueth enemies to Christs religion':[361] where the Word is not preached, alas! ' the people are still in ignoraunce and blindnesse, and kept stil in their olde and Popish errours, receiued from their forefathers, they know not the vse of the sacraments, or to what ends they serue, they holde still their Papisticall transubstantiation: some say, they receiue their maker: other saye, they neuer hearde what a Sacrament meant.'[362]   Some in Wales, declares Bishop Davies, ' defende papistrie, supersticion and Idolatrie, pilgrimages to Welles and blinde Chappelles, procure the wardens of churches in tyme of visitacion to periurie, to conceale images, roode loftes and aulters '.[363]
In spite of good laws for the removal of ' Images in the walles & windowes of Churches ', White tells his hearers that either because of covetousness or idolatry these laws are but slenderly executed; ' for Churches keepe their olde colours still though the images haue lost their countenaunce, and though their heads be off, yet they can make somewhat of their bodies: they that can, keepe reliques, and ragges, of coates, hose and shoes, olde bones and duste, to wor-shippe. . . . '[364] Furthermore says White, ' the Diuell is crafty and where he cannot get an Elle, he will be content to take an inche, for he thinkes it is better to haue halfe a loofe than no bread: but where you graunt an inche, he wilbe sure to haue an elle. The Serpent gets his grounde by creepyng, and if his head be once in, he will shifte for himselfe, and soone winde in his whole body.'[365]   There are unfor-tunately many ' poysoned Protestants and maymed professours ' who still accept elements of Catholic faith and practice:

. . . you shall haue a gospeller as he wil be taken, a ioyly felow to retayne and maintayne such patches of popery and infection of Rome, that me thinkes I see the Serpentes subteltie as playne as by the clawe you may iudge the Lion: one holdeth, faith iustifieth and yet workes doe no harme: an other sayth, prayer

[360] A Sermon Preached at Paules Crosse on Barthelmew Day, p. 94. Cf. also Anthony Anderson, A sermon preached at Paules Crosse, sig. Gv[v]–Gvi[r].
[361] A fruitful sermon preached at Occham, sig. Cv[v].
[362] Ibid. sig. Di[r].
[363] A funerall sermon preached at the buriall of Walter Earle of Essex (London, 1577) sig. Dii[r].
[364] A sermon Preached at Paules Crosse . . . the thirde of November 1577, p. 26.
[365] Ibid. p. 29.

for the dead is charitie, and though it doe no good, yet it doth no hurte: what will you haue mee say, the Diuell go with them? . . . Another crosses me his face and nose, and breast; with thombes and fingers, and cannot pray but towarde the east: and some haue not forgotten their *Aue Maria* yet, although their *Pater noster* was forgotten long agoe. . . .[366]

White has no doubt about the character of such trimmers; he is sure ' that . . . halfe Protestants, halfe Papistes, are wholy Diuells: that suche Mermaydes as are half fish, halfe flesh, or Minotaures, that be halfe men halfe bulls, are all beasts, which thinke that God and Idols, the Sacrifice and the Sacraments, Circumcision and Baptisme, the lawe and the Gospell, nay that fleshe and the spirits, and God and man may be ioyned together, are but common pedlers and patchers of Christ[s] coate, which had no seame in deede . . . '[367]

All is not well, however, within the Established Church; many of the old abuses still linger on, and the preachers, as before, raise their voices with indignation against them. There are still many ignorant clergy; simony has not been abolished, patrons still place unworthy persons in livings, and the parishioners are still boorishly content with third rate vicars;[368] as Bartimaeus Andrewes puts it:

> . . . many blinde Dolts of the Country, Ploughmen, and artificers, thorough Symony and corruption steale into the liuings of the Church, that the learned and meete persons in the Vniuersitie which shold be called foorth are fayn to be without place. Which happeneth partly by default of Patrons which make not conscience of the Lordes people, partly by other corruptions: but howsoeuer it be the poore soules of the people are in extreme hazard thereby, and the people for the moste parte see not their owne misery, and therefore pitty not themselues, . . . For if they haue an honest and quiet man (as they term him) and a good fellow, they are best with such a one, though he hath no graces from the Lord meet for that honourable and high ambassage, which is a lamentable case.[369]

Deringe, preaching before Queen Elizabeth, indulges in what proved to be a dangerous piece of straight talking on this topic:

> To reforme euil Patrones, your Maiestie must strengthen your lawes, that they maye rule as wel hye as low, as Esdras said once, so many I say now: The handes of the Princes and Rulers

---

[366] Ibid.
[367] Ibid. p. 32. See further the bitter polemical passages against the Catholics quoted by Haweis, *Sketches of the Reformation and Elizabethan Age*, pp. 178–83.
[368] For earlier complaints on these topics, see *ante*, pp. 238–40, 267–8.
[369] *Certaine verie godly and profitable Sermons, vpon the fifth Chapiter of the Songs of Solomon*, p. 121.

are chiefe in this trespasse. If you wil haue it amended, you must prouide so that the highest may be afraide to offende. To keep back the ignorant from the Ministerie, whom God hath not called to suche a function, take away your authoritie from the Bishops, let them not at their pleasure make Ministers in their Closset, whom so euer it pleaseth them. To stop the inconueniences that grow in the Ministerie by other, who say they are learned and can preach, and yet do not, that are as I said dum Dogs, and wil not barcke, bridle at the least their greedy appetites, pul out of their mouthes these poisoned bones that they so greedely gnaw vpon. Take away Dispensations, Pluralities, Totquots, Non-residences, and such other sinnes. Pull downe the court of Faculties, the Mother and Nurse of all such abominations.[370]

Jewel speaks too against these abuses,[371] while John Dove upbraids those gentlemen who ' cry out for a learned ministerie, whereas in deede they do but picke quarrels with vs, intending nothing lesse then a learned ministerie, for they will willingly present none, but such as are base, ignorant, and beggerly, because such persons will easilie accept of benefices vppon vnlawful conditions '.[372] It is still necessary for Drant to rebuke the clergy for worldliness: ' We thinke it ', he sadly declaims, ' a merie lyfe to be styll in this worlde, and to builde our nestes as high, as warme, and as during as we can.'[373] Eusebius Pagit finds that he must speak against lazy ministers,[374] while Robert Travers and John Keltridge inveigh against the drunkenness and incontinence of some of their order.[375] Then again, Tyrer is compelled to complain about the pride of certain of the dignitaries, ' who ', he declares, ' follow herein the false prophets, Pharises and popish prelates, who care not, nor spare to vse hardly not onely the common multitude, but also the ministrie of the

---

[370] *A Sermon preached before the quenes maiestie . . . the* 25 *day of February, Anno.* 1569 (London, [1569?]) sig. Eiv^v–Fi^v. For a time after the delivery of this sermon, Deringe was inhibited from preaching: see the article on him in *D.N.B.*

[371] *Works*, vol. II, pp. 999, 1011.

[372] *A sermon preached at Pauls Crosse . . . the* 3 *of November* 1594 (London, 1594) sig. Cvi^v. See too the passages on bad patrons and the prevalence of simony, quoted by Haweis, *Sketches of the Reformation and Elizabethan Age*, pp. 70–2.

[373] *Three godly and learned Sermons*, sig. Eiv^r: cf. the complaints of Colet and Fisher on this topic, mentioned *ante*, pp. 239. Drant also rebukes some of the clergy for vanity of dress (Haweis, op. cit., p. 76), much as Alcock had done before him. (See *ante*, p. 239.)

[374] *A Godly Sermon preached at Detford* (London, 1586) sig. Avi^v. Cf. the condemnation of clerical sloth by the medieval preachers, noticed by Owst, *L. & P.M.E.*, pp. 238, 246, 260, 278–9.

[375] Haweis, *Sketches of the Reformation and Elizabethan Age*, pp. 79–80. Cf. the castigation of these vices by the medieval preachers, in Owst, *P.M.E.*, pp. 32, 42, 249–50; *L. & P.M.E.*, pp. 244, 246–7, 252, 258–60, 267, 269, 271, 274, 276.

Church, in not only loftie looking ouer them as the Diuel lookes ouer Lincolne (as we say) but also in laying greater charge and burden vpon them then they are able to beare.'[376] ' But ', he warns, ' would to God these would remember, that for all their superioritie, they are but shepheards. . . .'[377] Further, in the countryside there is still in many places but little preaching; as Bush puts it, there is a ' wonderful great want thereof, that a man may go a great way, and cannot here the word of the Lorde preached '.[378] However he does recognise the superiority of London in this particular: ' Surely,' he declares, ' when I come out of the country hether to the City, methink I come into another world, euen out of darknes into light, for here the word of God is plentifully preached.'[379]

The clergy are still, as in Henry VIII's time, little regarded;[380] Anderson uses bitter language on this subject:

> The holye Ministrie is holden in contempt (Christ and hys
> Father despysed in them) their patrons many, are become
> *Latrons*, and pryue the preachers portion to serue their owne
> prouision (it is ynough for the priest to haue ten powndes by the
> yeare, and for this too, he shal besydes carry a dyshe to his
> maysters Table, or else stande at the dresser, orderly to set out
> the messe of meate, and supply the Clarke of the kytchyns
> place, his seruice and Homilyes he must cut short, and measure
> them by the Cookes readynesse, and dynner dressing; the roste
> neare ready, the kitchin boye is sent to master Parson, to bydde
> hym make haste, the meate is readye, and hys mayster cals for
> dynner; he commeth at a becke, not daring to denye or make
> longer staye, least his delaye might cause the cook to burne the
> meate, and he be called of mayster and men, Syr John burne
> Goose. . . .[381]

The ministers are poor;[382] tithes are shamefully withheld, and yet laymen complain about the lack of clerical hospitality.[383]

---

[376] *Five godlie sermons*, p. 21.

[377] Ibid. Cf. the earlier complaints about the pride of the prelates noticed by Owst, L. *&* P.M.E., pp. 270–1.

[378] *A Sermon preached at Pauls Crosse, on Trinity Sunday* 1571, sig. Fii[r].

[379] Ibid.   [380] Cf. *ante*, p. 240.

[381] *The Sheild of our Safetie*, sig. Tiv[v]–Vi[r]. On the small esteem in which the clergy were held, see too Sandys, *Sermons*, p. 350; Anthony Anderson, *A sermon preached at Paules Crosse*, sig. Div[v], Dv[r]: also Haweis, *Sketches of the Reformation and Elizabethan Age*, p. 71; see further, ibid. pp. 77–9, for the contempt with which the wives and families of the ministers were regarded.

[382] Abbot, *An Exposition upon the Prophet Jonah*, vol. I, pp. 176–7; Topsell, *Times lamentation*, pp. 21–3. Haweis, op. cit., p. 83, points out that the laity, having made the clergy poor, then despised them for their poverty.

[383] Dove, *A sermon preached at Pauls Crosse . . . the* 3 *of November* 1594, sig. Civ[v].

However, the Anglican Church is not only encumbered with these old abuses; there is alas! dissension within. The vestiarian and presbyterian controversies find expression in the pulpit. In Lent 1565 T. Sampson and Laurence Humphrey preached at Paul's Cross against the surplice,[384] as did William Fulke at Great St. Mary's Cambridge in January of the same year, and in the Chapel of St. John's College Cambridge in the autumn.[385] Fulke also attacked the use for Communion of unleavened bread and kneeling for the reception of Communion. He was backed up in his ideas by Richard Longworth, Master of St. John's, but on 1st November 1565, Dr. Robert Beaumont, Master of Trinity and Vice Chancellor, preached against those private individuals who took upon themselves public reformation of the Church.[386] However, as late as January 1587, William Perkins, preaching in Christ's College Chapel, maintains that to kneel when receiving Communion is superstitious and anti-Christian.[387] William Charke preached in December 1572 at Great St. Mary's Cambridge, and declares that bishops and archbishops were introduced into the Church by Satan and that no minister ought to be superior to any other.[388] In the summer of 1573 Richard Crick preached at Paul's Cross in support of Cartwright's presbyterian principles,[389] while on the other side Thomas Cooper, Bishop of Lincoln, had on 27th June 1572 preached in the same place an answer to the Puritan *Admonition to the Parliament*.[390] Richard Bancroft, in his famous Paul's Cross sermon of 9th February 1589, spoke forcefully against the presbyterian party. They pervert Scripture, declares the future Primate, in their desire for a new form of ecclesiastical government;[391] and indeed many of those who are most zealous against the established order are really merely avaricious: 'I am', he announces, 'fully of this opinion that the hope which manie men haue conceiued of the spoile of Bishops liuings, of the subuersion of cathedrall churches, and of a hauocke to be made of all the churches reuenues, is the cheefest and most principall cause of the greatest schismes that we haue at this day in our church.'[392] Further, he declares, the Calvinist system lends itself to tyranny, for the Scotch Assembly is bolder than are the English

---

[384] Maclure, *The Paul's Cross Sermons*, 1534–1642, p. 205.
[385] Porter, *Reformation and Reaction in Tudor Cambridge*, p. 121.
[386] Ibid.   [387] Ibid. p. 181.   [388] Ibid. p. 141.
[389] Maclure, *The Paul's Cross Sermons*, 1534–1642, pp. 208–9.   [390] Ibid. p. 308.
[391] *A Sermon preached at Paules Crosse. . . Anno* 1588 (London, 1588) pp. 8–10. Bancroft o bjects to the presbyterian interpretation of Matt. xviii. 17, Exod. xix. 21–6. Num. xi. 16–17, 24–5, Luke. xix. 14, 27.
[392] Ibid. pp. 23–4.

bishops; indeed their authoritarianism emulates that of the papal jurisdiction![393]

Another controversy which finds pulpit expression, although of a less acrimonious sort, is that concerning ' assurance of salvation '. A University Sermon at Cambridge on 29th April 1595 by William Barret, Chaplain of Gonville and Caius College, maintaining the doubtfulness of salvation, as ' justifying faith may decay and be lost ' was very ill received by the strict Calvinists, and the Heads of Houses got Barret to read a recantation, although Archbishop Whitgift really agreed with Barret's views.[394] In October 1595, William Whitaker, Master of St. John's and Regius Professor of Divinity, preached his last sermon, his *Cygnea Cantio*, and seeks to prove the Calvinist position that in the elect justifying faith cannot be utterly lost, and that consequently they are certain of salvation.[395] However, the future in the Church of England lay with those of views similar to those of Barret. Lancelot Andrewes, preaching at Court in 1594, stresses the dangers of ' security ',[396] while on 12th January 1596, Peter Baro, Lady Margaret Professor of Divinity at Cambridge, in a University Sermon, declares that God wishes to give grace sufficient for salvation to every man, because Christ died for all, and that if men are lost the fault is theirs.[397] In the Spring of 1600, John Overall, Master of St. Catherine's College, and Regius Professor of Divinity at Cambridge, in succession to Whitaker, asserts that repentance is necessary for ' assurance ',[398] and this became the general Anglican position in the early seventeenth century.

Not only are there internal dissensions in the Church, the fabric of many of the church buildings is decaying owing to indifference and neglect; as Jewel in the ' Homily for Repairing and keeping clean of Churches ' exhorts the audience:

> ... forasmuch as your churches are scoured and swept from the sinful and superstitious filthiness, wherewith they were defiled and disfigured, do ye your parts, good people, to keep your churches comely and clean; suffer them not to be defiled with rain and weather, with dung of doves and owls, stares and choughs, and other filthiness, as it is foul and lamentable to behold in many places of this country.[399]

[393] Ibid. pp. 74-9.
[394] Porter, *Reformation and Reaction in Tudor Cambridge*, pp. 344-5.
[395] Ibid. pp. 380-3. There is a useful English translation of this sermon: *Cygnea Cantio or the Swan Song (Being the last Public Discourse) of William Whitaker D.D. ...* translated into English by a Presbyter of the Church of England (London, 1772).
[396] Porter, *Reformation and Reaction in Tudor Cambridge*, p. 335.
[397] Ibid. pp. 380-3. [398] Ibid. p. 402.
[399] *Certain Sermons appointed by the Queens Majesty*, p. 278.

Bishop Howson is concerned about the laziness and niggardliness evinced in the interior furnishing:

> . . . in countrey Villages *Canescunt turpi templa relicta situ*. The Churches are almost become that, which those heretikes *pseudoapostoli* likened them vnto, little better then hog-styes; for the best preparation at any high feast is a little fresh straw vnder their feete, the ordinary allowance for swine in the stye, or at the best *Domus opportuna volucrum* . . . and in cities and boroughes they are not like the Palaces of Princes as they were in the primitiue church, *regijs aulis clariora*, but like a countrey hall, faire whitelined, or a citizens parlour, at the best well wainscotted. . . .[400]

There are too in this reign several new topics of moral complaint on secular subjects. Classical learning is now in some circles taking the place of knowledge of the Christian faith; as Bishop Curteys declares: ' Wee buylde Castles and toures in the ayre to get vs a name. So many heads, so many wittes, so many common wealths. Plato his Idaea, Aristotle's felicitie, and Pythagoras numbers, trouble most mens brayns.'[401] Bishop Cooper finds it necessary to inveigh against those seduced by ' *Heathenish Gentilitie*, which raigneth in the hartes of godlesse persons, Atheistes, and Epicures ', for these ' passe neither for heauen, nor hell, nor for God, nor the Diuell, but thinke those thinges to bee no better than Poeticall fables, or (at the least) Bugges, by policie deuised to feare Babes '.[402] Such reprobates ' iest & scoffe at all Religion, and make themselues merie with talke of Preachers '.[403]

Popular romances, translations of novels of love, and stage plays, those favourite forms of Elizabethan literature for the student of to-day, arouse the deepest anger of some of the preachers of Puritan leanings. Just as their medieval predecessors looked with jaundiced eyes on minstrels, secular love poetry, and tournaments,[404] so these Elizabethan pulpiters find only sin in these (for us) delightful productions. Stockwood, preaching at Paul's Cross, tells us that we should keep godly company, and grow in knowledge and understanding of heavenly truth:

> . . . whereas if we shal be rather delighted in reading of filthie books, as the Baudies de Gall, the Amaudis, I trow it be, the

---

[400] *A second sermon, preached at Paules Cross the* 21 *of May,* 1598, *vpon the* 21 *of Math. the* 12 *and* 13 *verses, concluding a former sermon*. . . (London, 1598) p. 27.

[401] *A sermon preached before the Queens Maiestie at Grenewiche*, sig. Civ^v.

[402] *Certain Sermons wherein is contained the Defense of the Gospell nowe preached, against such Cauils and false accusations, as are objected against the Doctrine it selfe and the Preachers*. . . *thereof, by the friendes* . . . *of the Church of Rome* (London, 1580) p. 189.

[403] Ibid.   [404] See Owst, L. *& P.M.E.*, pp. 10–17, 334–6.

X

great Pallace and the little Pallace of pleasure, with a number
moe of suche filthy bookes, wherwyth this Churchyard swarm-
eth in this cleare light of the Gospell . . . the Deuil of hell will
associate himselfe vnto vs, & creepe at the length so farre into
our hearts, that he wyl roote out of vs al care of vertue, and
godlinesse, and make vs reioyce in our owne shame, that we
may be the more fit vessels of wrath & damnation.[405]

He is quite incensed by plays, which unfortunately are so much more
attractive than sermons: ' Wyll not a fylthye playe,' he asks, ' wyth
the blast of a Trumpette, sooner call thyther a thousands, than an
houres tolling of a Bell, bring to the Sermon a hundred? '[406] He is
certain that plays deprave the young: ' What should I speak of
beastlye Playes,' he asks:

against which out of this place euery man crieth out? haue we
not houses of purpose built with great charges for the maintenance of them, and that without the liberties, as who woulde say,
there, let them saye what they will say, we wil play. I know
not how I might with the godly learned especially more dis-
commende the gorgeous Playing place erected in the fieldes,
than to terme it, as they please to haue it called, a Theatre, that
is euen after the maner of the olde heathenish Theatre at Rome,
a shewe place of al beastly and filthie matters, to the which it
can not be chosen that men should resort without learning
there muche corruption. For if hee that behelde but the filthie
picture of Iupiter in a shower of golden raine descending vnto
Dianae, coulde therby encourage himself vnto filthinesse: shall
we thinke that flocks as of wyld youths of both sexes, resorting
to Enterludes, where both by lively gesture, and voices, there
are allurements vnto whordom, they can come awaye pure,
and not inflamed with concupiscence?[407]

Thomas White sees the theatres as resorts for all kinds of immoral
persons and breeding-places for the plague:

Looke but vppon the common playes in London, and see
the multitude that flocketh to them and followeth them:
beholde the sumptuous Theatre houses, a continuall monument
of Londons prodigality and folly. But I vnderstande they are

---

[405] *A Sermon preached at Paules Crosse on Barthelmew Day.* p. 147. See too Francis
Bradley, *A Godly Sermon preached before the Right Worshipfull Edward Cooke, Esquier,
Atturney Generall* (London 1600) sig. Cii^r. See further the passage from Deringe
Topsell, and William Alley cited by Haweis, *Sketches of the Reformation and Elizabethan
Age*, pp. 146–50.
[406] *A Sermon Preached at Paules Crosse on Barthelmew Day*, p. 23. On the contrary,
declares Stockwood, ' if you resorte to the Theatre, the Curtayne, and other places of
Playes in the Citie, you shall on the Lords Day haue these places, with many other that
I can not recken, so full, as possible they can throng. . .' (Ibid.)
[407] Ibid. p. 133.

nowe forbidden, because of the plague, I like the pollicye well if it holde still, for a disease is but bodged or patched vp that is not cured in the cause, and the cause of plagues is sinne, if you looke to it well: and the cause of sinne are playes: therefore the cause of plagues are playes. . . . Shal I reckon vp the monstrous birds that brede in this nest? without doubt I am ashamed, & I should surely offende your chast eares: but the olde world is matched, and Sodome ouercome, for more horrible enormities, and swelling sins are set out by those stages, then euery man thinks for, or some would beleeue, if I shold paint them out in their colours: without doubt you can scantly name me a sinne, that by that sincke is not set a gogge: theft and whoredome: pride and prodigality: villanie and blasphemie: these three couples of hellhoundes neuer cease barking there, and bite manye, so as they are vncurable euer after, so that many a man hath the leuder wife, and many a wife the shreuder husband by it . . . thou losest they selfe that hauntest those scholes of vice, dennes of Theeues & Theatres of all leudnesse: and if it be not suppresed in time, it will make such a Tragedie, that all London may well mourne whyle it is London, for referring to the plague then raging it is no playing time (and euery man bethinke him wel) but time to pray rather.[408]

The indefatigable Stockwood complains about Machiavellianism, that great popular political bogey of the Elizabethans. The good Cornelius (Acts x) was a magistrate, declares the preacher, and his example overthrows:

. . . the most wicked assertion of the vnpure Atheiste Machiauel, who shameth not in most vngodly manner to teach that princes need make no account of godlyness and true religion, but onely to make an outwarde shewe of it. for that (sayth he) is ynough, albeit in minde they abhore it. And that which is most horrible, he affirmeth further, that the religion of Christians casteth them down into too much humilitie, abateth al courage and towardnesse, and maketh them fit to be wronged & spoiled, whereas the religion of the Gentiles maketh them to be of stout courage & emboldneth them manly to atchieue great matters: yet wyl he forsooth, that Princes pretende religion, the better to kepe their subiectes within the compasse of their dueties, with the feare and reuerence thereof. This poyson and a great deale more suche filth blusheth not this malaperte and pelting Towncleark of Florence to spew out, . . . and yet be the only Court booke,

---

[408] *A sermon Preached at Paules Crosse on Sunday the thirde of November* 1577, p. 46. See also, for similar condemnation of plays and theatres, Rainolds, *The Prophecy of Haggai interpreted and applied in sundry sermons*, p. 28; Topsell, *Times lamentation*, pp. 60, 386.

nay the Alcoran and God of Courtiers, whose diuellish precepts they put in dayly vse, learning to be godlesse.[409] Apart from these new topics of complaint, however, the Elizabethan preachers declaim at length on many of the older subjects. The covetousness of landlords and their wicked enclosures[410] still merit rebuke:

> ... The poore tenants cry out of some, as done to beggery by vnreasonable fynes, racked rents, great enclosures, priuation of their auncient Commons into Parkes and pastures, not for fallows but for well tallowed shamble Deare. Oh vyle debase of noble state, to acquainte themselues with grasing arte, and Butchers skill, or to destroye for woole and Lambe, the Lambes of Christ, bought with the precious blood of the sonne of God.[411]

There is an increased volume of complaint on usury;[412] John Knewstub speaks against those who sell dearer by allowing the purchaser time to pay, ' taking money for time, & making it to increase and adde to the value of their commodities '.[413] But, he warns, ' time is no merchandise. For who dare be so bolde as to say that he hath brought time into the market to sell? Or who hath giuen thee leaue to sell dayes and monethes? '[414] Bishop Curteys lashes the manifest shifts of the capitalistic merchants:

> They will hord vp their corne and wares, vntill the poorer sort hath sold, and then sell it at their owne price, or keepe it vntill it be rotte[n]. They will varnishe their wares, and make them shewe fayre to the eye, though neuer so bad to the vse: or they will leaue their naturall and lawfull trauell, and vse vnnaturall and vnlawfull multiplication of money: or they will set their landes vpon the last, and stretche them from sixe pounde a yere to sixe score pounde a yere. Or they will make all fish that commeth to net by sea or by lande, or they will transporte corne, butter cheese and all kinde of necessaries, and that to them that neyther loue Gods worde, nor this countrey: or they will sell their landes three or foure times to be sure.[415]

---

[409] *A Sermon Preached at Paules Crosse on Barthelmew Day*, p. 59.

[410] Cf. *ante*, pp. 245–6, 269–70.

[411] Anderson, *The Shield of our Safetie*, sig. Siv^r; see too Anderson, *A sermon preached at Paules Crosse*, sig. Fiii^v, also Bush, *A sermon preached at Pauls Crosse on Trinity Sunday 1571*, sig. Bii^r: ' I do know wher of late there hath bene villages mainteyned, able to serue both the prince and cuntry. And now all are wrung out, and turned out, and all is annexed to the demayne of one man, to mainteine an vnsatiable cormorant.' See further, Eusebius Pagit, *A Godly and Fruitefull Sermon made vpon the 20 and 21 verses of the 14 Chapter of the booke of Genesis* (London, 1580?) sig. Bviii^v; also Haweis, *Sketches of the Reformation and Elizabethan Age*, pp. 278–80.   [412] Cf. *ante*, p. 269.

[413] *The Lectures of Iohn Knewstub vpon the twentieth Chapter of Exodus, and certaine other places of Scripture* (London, 1579) p. 145.

[414] Ibid. cf. too the passages cited by Haweis, op. cit., pp. 240–7.

[415] *A sermon preached before the Queens Maiestie at Grenewiche*, sig. Cvii^r.

The universities still do not flourish;[416] Howson avers that they decay because of simony,[417] Jewel because of the subversion of funds intended for the support of learning.[418]

Other complaints are on yet older topics, it is indeed remarkable that the stock themes of medieval moral preaching should persist so strongly even after the dogmatic revolution. The hoary complaint that the preacher is not regarded occurs with extraordinary frequency.[419] Drant expresses it with his usual euphuistic rhetoric:

> The state of England is lyke to chyldren, sitting rechlesse in the market steede. We playe and pipe to them, but they relent not: our sermons are like vnto the Musick which *Aristotle* speaketh of. Which when once doone, there is no remembrance of it. They beleeue Lawiers in lawe matters, and follow them: Phisitians, and follow them: Councellors, and follow them: they heare Preachers, but they doo not follow them.[420]

Bisse amplifies this theme with all the devices of his mannered eloquence:

> Whereas like wise Merchant men, wee shoulde labour and seeke for good pearles, and sell all that we haue to buy that pearle of great price: We, like dogs refuse holy things offered, we turn about and teare them that doe offer them: we like swine, tread pearles vnder our feete, and doe accounte this pearle, this holy thing, the word of life, to be vnto vs as a ring of golde in a swines snoute. For doeth the people delight to heare Gods word? Behold yet they are like the deafe adder, which stoppeth her eares at the voyce of the charmer, charme he neuer so wisely. Or if they with delight doe heare it, doe they vnderstand it? behold yet, they are vntamed colts, & vnweaned heyfers. Or if they doe all these three, heare, vnderstand, obey, can they abide to be rebuked to their faces of their sins?[421]

Henry Smith laments that the Devil schemes so successfully to counteract the efforts of the preachers: ' he labours all that hee can to stay us from *hearing*; to effect this, he keeps us at taverns, at plays, in our shops, and appoints us some other business at the same time, that when the bell calls to the Sermon, we say, like churlish guests:

---

[416] Cf. *ante*, pp. 245, 270–1.

[417] *A Sermon at Paules Crosse the 4 of December* 1597. *Wherein is discoursed, that all buying and selling of spirituall promotion is vnlawfull* (London, 1597) p. 30.

[418] *Works*, vol. II, p. 999. See further Maclure, *The Paul's Cross Sermons*, 1534–1642, p. 206 (reference to a sermon on 13th January 1566 on the mean state of Oxford by John Oxenbridge); Machyn, *Diary*, p. 227 (reference to a sermon on 8th March 1560 on the need to help the universities by Pilkington).

[419] Cf. *ante*, pp. 237–8.

[420] *Three godly and learned Sermons*, sig. Lvi[r].

[421] *Two sermons*, sig. Aviii[r].

we cannot come.'[422] If we come, we do not mark what is said, ' like the birds which fly about the Church '.[423] If we listen attentively, we dislike what is said, or think how little the preacher himself lives up to his teaching; and then alas! we do not think of considering the matter of the sermon until we have forgotten it.[424] In addition, Anderson speaks against those who appreciate the artistry and delivery of a sermon, but completely disregard the message:

> . . . the preachers are to the people as a *merry sounde*, (as the Prophete sayth) of one which syngeth a pleasant song: and so it is nowe. All our endeuour is to marke the Preachers cunning, his Eloquence and synguler gyftes, and when the Sermon is ended, we thinke sufficiently to haue answered all our duetie, if vpon the conceyued delight of his well digested order, and sound delyuery, we can, and doe giue him his due commendations, but the cause wherfore God sent him, or he speake to our amendment we regarde not. . . .[425]

Playfere, with fantastic rhetoric, repeats the old notion that the main duty of the preaching office is the mournful castigation of vice:[426] ' Touching *Preaching*,' he declares, ' the voyce of a Preacher ought to be the voyce of a cryer, which should not pipe to make the people daunce, but mourne to make them weepe. . . .'[427] Drawing a comparison with the Old Law, he continues:

> . . . when they offered vp to the Lord their first borne, who was ordinarily in euery family their Priest or their Preacher, they offered also with him a paire of Turtle doues, or two yong Pigeons; That paire of Turtle doues, did signify a paire of mournefull eyes. These two yong Pigeons did signify likewise two weeping eies. And at that offering they prayed for their first born, that after-ward he might haue such eyes himselfe. For as Pigeons fly to their windowes, so the sincere Preacher hath no other refuge to flie vnto, but onely to his windowes, that is to his eyes, which are glazed with teares, when they weepe for the sins of the people.[428]

Drant is saddened by the timidity of many preachers in this central duty: ' We be lyke *Ely*,' he laments, ' he durste not sharpely enough correct his children, nor we controule our auditors. *Iacob* fell downe seuen times before *Esaus* face, but wee make seuentye seuen lowe downe crouching courtesies to euerie noble man, before we will tell him of his duetie, howe vnduetifull so euer he be.'[429]

---

[422] *Sermons*, p. 300. See too Topsell, *Times lamentation*, pp. 6, 25, 43.
[423] *Sermons*, p. 300.   [424] Ibid. pp. 300–1.   [425] *The Shield of our Safetie*, sig. Tiv^v.
[426] See Owst, *P.M.E.*, p. 334; *L. & P.M.E.*, p. 22.
[427] *The whole Sermons*, ' The Meane in Mourning,' p. 14.   [428] Ibid. p. 15.
[429] *Three godly and learned sermons*, sig. Eiv^r.

The sin of extravagance in apparel, another favourite traditional theme,[430] appears also in many sermons of this reign. 'As for aparell,' John Udall asks Englishmen, ' . . . ordeined onelie for to couer our shame, in a civil decencie, is not our exceeding vanity most monstrously to be seen therin: not onlie, in the excesse and costlines thereof, but in the seuerall formes and fashions also, wherein wee are so apish in imitating all nations, that wee shewe our selues the most inconstant people of all other: yea and for the feeding of our monstrous humour of vanitie, euen in the hyghest degree, howe manie thousands of quarters of the purest wheat, which God ordeined for the food of man, are yearlie conuerted into that most deuelish deuice of starch, it cannot be vnknowen vnto manye.'[431] ' Our World is like a Pageant,' says Henry Smith, ' where every mans apparel is better than himself.'[432] Such is the vanity of the human race, that ' It is a wonder to see, how a gay coat, a gold ring, or a wrought handkerchief can brave a man's mind, that he thinks better of himself that day when he weareth them, than any day else, and speaks and walks, and looks after another fashion than he did before '.[433] Women, as before, are notable offenders in excessive personal adornment;[434] Adam and Eve ' covered themselves with leaves, and God derided them '; but women now, says Smith, 'cover themselves with pride, like Satan which is fallen down before them like lightening: ruffe upon ruffe, lace upon lace, cut upon cut, four and twenty orders, until the woman be not so precious as her apparel....'[435] Further, he declares, this unhealthy attention to appearances proceeds from an impure mind; 'as Herodias was worse for her fine dancing: so a woman may have too many Ornaments. Frizled locks, naked brests, painting, perfume, and specially a rolling eye, are the fore-runners of adultery. . . .'[436] But alas! many *do* take inordinate pains over their toilet: ' This is their work so soon as they rise, to put a pedlers shop upon their backs, and colour their faces, and prick their ruffes, and frisle their hair: and then their day's work is done: as though their office were to paint a fair image every morning, and at night to Blot it out again.'[437]

---

[430] Cf. *ante*, p. 243.
[431] *The true remedie against Famine and warres. Fiue Sermons vpon the first chapter of the prophesie of Ioel. . . Preached in the time of the dearth.* 1586 (London, [1588]) ff. 26ᵛ–7ʳ.
[432] *Sermons*, p. 208.
[433] Ibid. p. 209. See further Pilkington's 'An Homily against Excess of Apparel,' (*Certain Sermons appointed by the Queen's Majesty*, pp. 309–20).
[434] Cf. *ante*, pp. 241–2, 275–6, 290–1.   [435] *Sermons*, p. 38.
[436] Ibid.   [437] Ibid. p. 207.

The extravagance of the rich, and the neglect of the poor, another medieval theme,[438] appears also in the preaching of this reign. Henry Bedel addresses the gluttonous rich in the old satirical manner:

> Ye that eate til ye blow, and feede til your eyes swel with fatnes, that taste first your course meates, and then fal to your fine, that drincke the colde drinkes for your stomackes that are hot, a cup of claret wine, some ale or beare to laye a foundation, then eate till to much make vs blow, & then a good carouse to make good digestion, a cup of sack for the stomacke that is cold, it is good at midlemeale say some, this & that ye haue I know not what the prodigal waster licentiously doth spend . . . [but, pleads Bedel] . . . haue some remorse to the poore in their miserye.[439]

There are, says the preacher, ' good and godly lawes ' appointed for the relief of the poor, ' as ceasements in parishes, and Collectors for the same forfaits for absence from the parish church, and Sidemen for the same, and such others ordayned by authoritie for the comfort of the poore.'[440] ' But', he laments, ' how lewdly this is looked vnto, it appeareth in the treasure of the poore; for euery man plucketh his necke out of the yoke, and no man asked why so: the forfaites is neuer asked, be absent who wyl.'[441] Englishmen are less generous than ever, declaims Bedel, for in Catholic times they at least bestowed gifts misdirectedly on the Church:

> For looke what wastfully our Fathers as fooles did lay forth and bestow vpon shameles Friers that neuer were full, and fat bellyed Monkes whose bellyes were their gods, that now our Niggards cannot lay foorth, distrustyng their states, least they should beg (say they) before we dye, distrusting the prouidence of God, that blesseth their store.[442]

But now in these Gospel times:

> . . . Where is the plentye of gold that garnished the erronious church, the siluer & iewels that so largelye was geuen forth to stockes & stones, the cloth that cloathed the Pylgrime god that felt no colde, the stocke that bought the candles to set before them, that had eyes, and yet saw nought? Were ye so plentifull about such pelfe, and will ye geue nothing to poore Iesus Christ?[443]

---

[438] Cf. *ante*, p. 246; also Owst, *L. & P.M.E.*, pp. 298–306, 313, 320–2, 398, 445, 447–8.
[439] *A Sermon exhorting to pity the poore*, sig. Diiiᵛ.   [440] Ibid. sig. Diiiʳ⁻ᵛ.
[441] Ibid. sig. Diiiᵛ.   [442] Ibid. sig. Biiiᵛ.
[443] Ibid. on the state of the poor, see too the passages cited by Haweis, *Sketches of the Reformation and Elizabethan Age*, pp. 274–7, 281–3.

Luxurious living, as before, arouses the ire of the preachers;[444] White lashes delicate feeding:

> Veale and Mutton is to grosse for our diet, nay, the Sea with all his fishe, the ayer with all his byrdes, and the earth with al hir beasts cannot satisfie our beastly appetities. A cooke among prophane menne was a straunge arte, banished out of some common weales as a superfluous science, to make menne eate more than needes: but in England it is a great occupation, and in London a very riche company.[445]

Anderson castigates the habit of late rising; ' The Country hath receyued the Courtly vice,' he declares, ' night is tourned into daye, and day into night, to bedde at midnight, and vp at noone day. The Sermon Bell doth lull these Babes a sleepe, and Sathan laugheth at their swynishe slumber.'[446]

The evil keeping of holy days, yet another old theme,[447] appears in the Elizabethan preachers as the breaking of the Sabbath. Stockwood reminds his audience of the severe penalty meted out under the Old Law for but gathering a few sticks on the Lord's Day (Num. xv. 32–6), however:

> . . . we notwithstanding on the Lordes daye must haue Fayers kept, must haue Beare baytyng, Bulbaytyng (as if it wer a thing of necessity for the Beares of Paris garden to be bayted on the Sunnedaye) muste haue baudie Enterludes, siluer games, dicing, carding tabling, dauncing, drinking, and what I praye you is the penaltie of the offenders herein, forsooth a flap wyth a Foxe tayle, as if our Sauiour Christe had commen for his day to set vs at lybertie to doe what we liste.[448]

White is equally concerned about the misuse of Sunday; ' on oure Sabbothes', he declaims, ' all manner of games and playes, bankettings, and surfettings, are very rife: if any man haue anye businesse in the world, Sonday is counted an idle day: If he haue none, then it is bestowed in other pleasure. *Trahit sua quemque voluptas.* . . . And the wealthyest Citizens haue houses for the nonce: they that haue

---

[444] See Owst, *L. & P.M.E.,* pp. 442–3.
[445] *A sermon preached at Pawles Crosse on Sunday the thirde of November* 1577, p. 64.
[446] *The Shield of our Safetie,* sig. Tiv^v: cf. Owst, *L. and P.M.E.,* pp. 443–4.
[447] Cf. *ante,* p. 243.
[448] *A Sermon preached at Paules Cross on Barthelmew Day,* p. 50; see too ibid. p. 133: ' There be not many places where the word is preached besides the Lords day (I woulde to God there were) yet euen that day the better part of it is horrible prophaned by diuellishe inventions, as with Lords of Misserule, Morice dauncers, Maygames, insomuch that in some places, they shame not in the time of diuine seruice, to come and daunce aboute the Church, and without to haue men naked dauncing in nettes, which is moste filthie: for the heathen that neuer hadde further knowledge, than the lighte of nature, haue counted it shamefull for a Player to come on the stage without a slop. . . .'

none, make shift with Aleshouses, Tauernes, and Innes, some
rowyng on the water, some rouing in the field, some idle at home,
some worse occupyed. . . .'[449] Hugh Roberts rebukes his audience
for playing football on Sundays; indeed, has there not been a notable
judgement upon it?

> That pestilent play at football vpon the Lordes day hath of
> late beene very fearfully punished among you; euen in a
> neighbour of your next parish, a spectacle sufficient to terrifie
> all, whose heartes are not hardened in sinne. This your neigh-
> bour being (as you know) at play this day fortnight, with
> running against another man, brake his legg so lamentably that
> (as it is reported for truth) the sight thereof made some of the
> beholders ready to faint. This wound could by no means bee
> cured, but his body putrifiing therevpon, it brought him to his
> end, & to his graue this day senight, to the great discomfort &
> vndoing of his poor wife and six children.[450]

Then again, just as Dr. Bromyard looked with disapprobation on
May-games and the revelry of Eastertide,[451] so Roberts admonishes
his audience: ' . . . your May-pole, & May games are the fruit of
ignorance, are after the fashion of the world, and are the works of
darknesse, proceeding from *fleshly lusts*.'[452] Some crafty exponents
of the games, when erecting the maypoles, ' haue set vp with them
the Queenes arms, intending by this colour to intrap such men as
would speake against them, or go about to haue them downe,
as if the Queenes maiesty had allowed her arms to be set on may-
pols.'[453] Setting up may-poles is too a wretched ' abuse of Gods
creatures: for God created not the trees of the woods to be cut
doune and set vp againe for gazing stockes, to no other vse but to
satisfie mens *fleshly lusts*. . . . But vaine and gracelesse men destroy
the most flourishing trees, and set them vp to bee drye and vnfruit-
full like themselues.'[454] However Roberts connects such things
with Catholicism: ' who can tell ', he asks, ' whether the setting vp
of these poles proceedeth not from the leauen of our aduersaries the
Pope & his seminaries? '[455]

Even more striking than the persistence of these traditional
moral themes, is the resurgence in several preachers of the later
part of the reign of the old ascetical world-view.[456] The declining

---

[449] *A Sermon Preached at Pawles Crosse on Sunday the thirde of November* 1577, p. 45.
[450] *The day of hearing: or six lectures vpon part of the thirde ch. of the Ep. to the Hebrewes.
Hereunto is adioyned a sermon ag. certaine mischeuous May games* (Oxford, 1600) sig. Kiii[v].
[451] See Owst, *L. & P.M.E.*, pp. 383–4.   [452] *The day of hearing*, sig. Kv[v].
[453] Ibid. sig. Kvi[v].   [454] Ibid. sig. Kvii[r].
[455] Ibid. sig. Kvii[v].   [456] Cf. *ante*, pp. 229–36, 289–91.

years of the fading Gloriana re-echo, as did those of the toppling Catholic order, with ornate declamations on the transience of the world. Henry Smith asks the old mournful questions:

>   Where is *Alexander* that Conquered all the World, and after sought for an other, because one would not satisfie him? Where is *Xerxes*, which could not number his Army for multitude? Where is *Nimrod* which built his nest in the Clouds? Where is *Sampson* which slew an Army with the jaw of an Asse? Where is *Constantine*, *Nero*, *Caligula*, *Titus*, *Vespatian*, *Domitian*, thunderbolts in their times? A hundred Princes of *England* are dead, and but one alive, the rest have gone to give account how they ruled here when they sustained the person of God.[457]

This ' patheticall ' preacher[458] uses all the resources of his ' siluer tongu'd ' eloquence[459] to bring home to his audience the fragility of life:

>   . . . our life is but a short life: as many little sculs are in Golgotha as great sculs; for one apple that falleth from the tree, ten are pulled before they are ripe; and the parents mourn for the death of their children, as often as the children for the decease of their parents. This is our *April* and *May* wherein we flourish; our *June* and *July* are next when we shall be cut down. What a change is this, that within fourscore years not one of this assembly shall be left alive? but another Preacher, and other hearers shall fill these rooms, and tread upon us where our feet tread now.[460]

The old metaphors for man's vain life are indeed all too clearly justified; as ' H.B. ' declaims:

>   . . . it is a common prouerbe: *Homo bulla*, Man is but a bubble of water, soone vp, soone downe. Man is but grasse, soone withered away: but a flower soone faded away: but a smoke soone vanishing away: but dust soone puffed away: but a shadow suddenly carried away: but a bubble of the water soone sunk away. . . .[461]

Smith touches on the miseries of old age in the traditional manner: ' Long life is like a long night,' he declares, ' when a man cannot sleep: So age is wearisome with sickness, and strives with it self because it cannot walke, nor talke, nor heare, nor see, nor taste, nor sleep, as it was wont: Therefore wisheth often the night were

---

[457] *Sermons*, p. 348. See too H. B., *A verie profitable sermon*, pp. 19–20.

[458] The adjective is Gabriel Harvey's; see G. Gregory Smith, *Elizabethan Critical Essays*, vol. II, p. 281.

[459] So described by Nashe, see *ante*, p. 188.   [460] *Sermons*, p. 274.

[461] *A verie profitable sermon*, p. 18. Cf. too Drant's elaborate and strained comparison of man's life to that of lilies, *Three godly and learned Sermons*, sig. Fi^r–Fii^v, a passage from which is quoted *ante*, p. 194.

gone, that the pain were past.'[462] The world itself is growing old for Trigge:

> The generation of man which now remaineth vpon the face of the earth, is neither so big in stature, nor so strong in body nor of so many yeares in their liues, as were the generations before. The bones which we finde in graues digged vp, which were buried next before our memories, testify the same: our skulls are but shels in comparison of them, our bones are the straws, or little sticks to theirs. And the same strength of procreation, which God gaue to *Adam* in the beginning, is now waxen weake and almost extinguished, like engendering his like, as the Philosophers do say. What speake I of the decay of man? our meadowes, our lands, and our pastures testifie the same: so that euery one may plainly see that the old age of the earth is nowe, and that her force faileth her, and that by and by she shall fall and faide away her selfe.[463]

The world being so decrepit, how foolish are those that dote upon her:

> There was a time when with some reason these earthly thinges which men now so greedily gape after, might haue bin cared for or embraced, when the world was in her youth, at the dawning of the daie: but now in her old age, in her wrinkled visage, at the sunne setting, so greatly to esteem this world, to bestowe such cost vpon a louer whose beauty is past, and which is euen now readie to forsake vs, is folly.[464]

William Cupper dwells on the plague with its terrifying symptoms: '. . . trembling, sadnesse, headach, rauing . . . cholericke distillations from the head to the stomach, ouermuch sleepe or none at all, swelling, giddinesse, rednesse of face, beating of the temples, with infinite other paines both inward and outward (which the Phisitions haue obserued) as the disease taketh a man, whether in the braine or in the heart.'[465] This dread disease brings many to a premature and horrible death; ' they that are taken with it are often times burned and consumed with great and intollerable heate, some begin forth-with to dote, to talke idley, and to raue and rage wonderfully: there haue beene also [those] that haue cast themselues headlong out of

---

[462] *Sermons*, p. 361.

[463] *A godly and fruitful sermon preached at Grantham*, sig. Dii[v].

[464] Ibid. sig. Avi[v]. On the old age of the world, see too Chardon, *A Sermon preached in St. Peters Church in Exceter the 6 day of December last: wherein is intreated of the Second comming of Christ vnto iudgement, and of the end of the world* (London, 1580) ff. 10[r-v]; also Abbot, *An Exposition upon the Prophet Jonah*, vol. I, p. 288.

[465] *Certaine Sermons concerning Gods late visitation in the citie of London and other parts of the land, teaching all men to make vse thereof that meane to profit by Gods fatherly chastisements. Preached at Alphages Church neare Creplegate* 1592 (London, 1592) p. 113.

windowes in their extremitie. . . .'[466] But the plague is not the only ill to which man is subject; the diseases which attack us are manifold, indeed each part of the body has its proper ailments, as Drant puts it:

The head hath the *Apoplexia*, the *Epileptia*, and the turn-about sicknesse, the eyes haue the *Opthalmia* and the *Migrain* the necke hath the Palsey, and the conuulsion, the nose hath the *Polipus*, the pallat hath the *Uuula*, the gummes haue the *Canker*, the teeth haue the toothach, the throate hath the *Angine*, the tongue hath blisters and swelling, the stomacke the motiue cause of the cardiacall passion, & murthering rewmes (the studentes sicknesse), the sides haue colikes, stitches and pricking plurisies, the vaines haue the stone, the legs haue dropsies and crampes, the feete and hands haue the knobbed gout.[467]

However all is not denunciation and gloom; the preachers of ' the spacious days of Queen Elizabeth ' *have* their positive values to offer. First, the queen herself is a topic for rejoicing. Thomas White, preaching in 1589 in thanksgiving for Elizabeth's reign of thirty-two years, asks: ' Did not *Hir Highnes* finde our *Coins*, *Copper*, and our *Religion*, *Superstition*, and through the goodness of God, hath shee not freed our Country from both? '[468] The difference between the times of Elizabeth and Mary, says an anonymous homilist, is even greater than that between the days of Solomon and Herod.[469]

Secondly, Christian marriage at last receives its full meed of praise from Henry Smith.[470] ' House and riches are given of Parents,' he declares, ' but a good wife is given of God: as though a good wife were such a gift, as wee should account from God alone, and accept it as if hee should send us a present from heaven, with this name written on it, *The gift of God*.'[471] Then again, says the distinguished Lecturer at St. Clement Danes: ' Beasts are ordained for food, and clothes for warmth, and flowers for pleasure, but a wife is ordained for man; like little *Zoar*, a City of Refuge to flye to in all his troubles, and there is no peace comparable unto her, but the peace of conscience.'[472] Woe indeed to him who is alone!

Thoughts, and cares, and fears will come to him because he hath none to comfort him, as Theeves steal in when the house

---

[466] Ibid. p. 111.   [467] *Three godly and learned Sermons*, sig. Fii^r.

[468] *A Sermon preached at Paules Crosse the* 17 *of Nouember An.* 1589. *In ioyfull remembrance . . . for peaceable yeres of her Maiesties most gratious Raigne ouer vs, now* 32 (London, 1589) p. 52.

[469] MS. Lambeth 488, f. 83^v. The observance of the ' Queen's Day ' (17th November) lent itself of course to panegyrics of the monarch.

[470] Tunstal's praise of marriage (*ante*, p. 260) is less the praise of connubial felicity than of the joy of parenthood and the consolation afforded by wife and children in sickness and old age.

[471] *Sermons*, p. 12.   [472] Ibid. p. 13.

is empty; like a Turtle, which hath lost his Mate; like one legge when the other is cut off; like one wing when the other is clipt; so had the man been, if the woman had not been joyned to him; therefore for mutual society, God coupled two together, that the infinite troubles which lye upon us in the world might be eased with the comfort and help one of another, and that the poor in the world might have some comfort as well as the rich.[473] There is however need to warn against inordinate affection, let the married remember, says Smith, ' that they may love, and keep love one with another, it is necessary that they both love God: and as their love increaseth toward him, so it shall increase each to other. But the man must take heed that his love towards his Wife be not greater than his love toward God, as *Adams* and *Sampsons* were: for all unlawful love will turn to hatred; as the love of *Amon* did toward *Thamar*, and because Christ hath forbidden it, therefore he will cross it '.[474]

Thirdly, the Church of England is a subject for the praise of Bancroft and Hooker. ' The doctrine of the church of England,' affirms Bancroft, ' is pure and holie: the government thereof, both in respect of hir maiestie, and of our Bishops is lawful and godlie: the book of common praier containeth nothing in it contrarie to the word of God.'[475] The English Church holds the just balance between a stifling authoritarianism in religion and an unrestrained freedom:

> Some forbid the children of GOD to proove any thing. Others command them to be ever seeking & prooving of all things. But neither of them both in a right good sense, do deale therein as they ought to do. A meane course betwixt these two is to be allowed of and followed: which is, that we proove some things and that we receive without curiosity som other things being alreadie examined, prooved and tried to our hands.[476]

Against the Romanists, who deny any virtue to the Church of England, Hooker raises his voice in an eloquent plea:

> I appeal to the conscience of every soul, that hath been truly converted by us, whether his heart were never raised up to God by our preaching; whether the words of our exhortation never wrung any tear of a penitent heart from his eyes; whether his soul never reaped any joy, any comfort, any consolation in Christ Jesus, by our sacraments, and prayers, and psalms, and

[473] Ibid. p. 17.   Contrast the attitude of the earlier preachers to women, *ante*, pp. 241–2, 275–6, also Fisher's comparatively low estimation of marriage, *ante*, p. 259.
[474] Ibid., p. 28.
[475] *A Sermon preached at Paules Crosse. . . . Anno* 1588, pp. 89–90.
[476] Ibid. p. 33.

thanksgiving; whether he were never bettered, but always worsed by us.

O merciful God! If heaven and earth in this case do not witness with us, and against them, let us be razed out from the land of the living! Let the earth on which we stand swallow us quick, as it hath done Corah, Dathan, and Abiram! But if we belong unto the Lord our God, and have not forsaken him; if our priests, the sons of Aaron, minister unto the Lord, and the Levites in their offices; if we offer unto the Lord every morning and every evening the burnt-offerings and sweet incense of prayers and thanksgivings; if the bread be set in order upon the pure table, and the candlestick of gold, with the lamps thereof, to burn every morning; that is to say, if amongst us God's blessed sacraments be duly administered, his holy word sincerely and daily preached; if we keep the watch of the Lord our God, and if ye have forsaken him: then doubt ye not, this God is with us as a captain, his priests with sounding trumpets must cry alarm against you; ' O ye children of Israel, fight not against the Lord God of your fathers, for ye shall not prosper.'[477]

Fourthly, (and of the greatest significance in the history of the religious sensibility in England), the preaching of Hooker and Andrewes exhibits a new wholesomeness of tone, and exudes a peculiarly fragrant spirituality. Little concerned about contemporary manners and morals, Hooker's great mission is to bring peace to the bruised conscience; instead of excoriating the wounds of the soul, he brings precious unguents to soothe and heal them. He knows well the weakness of human nature and the subtlety of the Devil,[478] but he assures his hearers: ' the faith . . . of true believers, though it have many and grievous downfalls, yet doth it still continue invincible; it conquereth and recovereth itself in the end.'[479] The ancient complaint of the righteous, that the wicked prosper, while they themselves are afflicted,[480] is answered satisfyingly: the wicked may indeed flourish in this world, but in the next they will feel God's wrath;[481] even here on earth they often lack interior peace[482]—and moreover suffering itself can have value: ' affliction is both a medecine if we sin, and a preservative that we sin not.'[483] Suffering too has been consecrated by the Passion of Christ,[484] and no calamity can ever separate from the Divine Love ' that mother's child whose faith hath made him the child of God ';[485] therefore the Christian trusting in the Lord, can say:

[477] *Works*, vol. III, pp. 679–80.   [478] Ibid. pp. 475–9.   [479] Ibid. p. 476.
[480] Ibid. pp. 479 (the passage quoted *ante*, p. 236), 629–31.   [481] Ibid. p. 646.
[482] Ibid. (the passage quoted *ante*, p. 190).   [483] Ibid. p. 636.
[484] Ibid. p. 647.   [485] Ibid. p. 481.

I am not ignorant whose precious blood hath been shed for
me; I have a Shepherd full of kindness, full of care, and full of
power: unto him I commit myself; his own finger hath engraven
this sentence in the tables of my heart, ' Satan hath desired to
winnow thee as wheat, but I have prayed that thy faith fail not ':
therefore the assurance of my hope I will labour to keep as a
jewel unto the end; and by labour, through the gracious media-
tion of his prayer, I shall keep it.[486]

Love and Joy are the notes also of the best preaching of
Andrewes; going behind the morbid piety of the late Middle Ages,
he returns to the tender Christmas happiness, the selfless charity of
the Passion, the glorious exultation of the Resurrection, and the
spiritual strengthening of Pentecost, which he found in the Fathers
and St. Bernard.[487] In his treatment of the Passion, the stress, in
contrast to that of the pre-Reformation Catholics, is on the spiritual
anguish, although he does not forget the physical miseries.[488] The
body is no longer regarded merely as the enemy of man,[489] rather it
is clearly shown that by grace it becomes the temple of Christ; and
although men can and do abuse the body, or dedicate it to Ceres or
Bacchus or Venus, nevertheless it is distinctly conveyed that this is,
for the Christian, a wilful perversion.[490] The centre of the Christian
religion is charity, and Andrewes places this holy love at the very
heart of his preaching: we hear of the love manifested in the Incarnation;[491] of the love of Christ Crucified,[492] the love of the Physician
dying for the patient,[493] of the love of St. Paul for souls;[494] of the
love of St. Mary Magdalene at the sepulchre;[495] of the Holy Ghost
' Love it selfe, the essentiall love and love-knot of the two persons of the
God-head, Father and Sonne'; of this Spirit ' shedding abroad His
love '[496] in the hearts of the servants of God, making them ' goe
bound in the spirit, and (as it were) with full saile to Ierusalem (when it is
for His service) '.[497] It may indeed be claimed with justice that the
spirit most akin to that of the Great Exemplar Himself, to be found
up to this time in English vernacular preaching, appears in Hooker
and Andrewes, these truly illustrious fathers of the Church of
England.

[486] Ibid.
[487] On the patristic influence on Andrewes, see Mitchell, *English Pulpit Oratory from
Andrewes to Tillotson*, pp. 9, 141–2, 145, 151–2, 170.
[488] See *XCVI Sermons*, pp. 336–8 (see *ante*, p. 109), 353–4, 370–9. Contrast *ante*, pp.
260–1.
[489] See *ante*, pp. 233–4.   [490] *XCVI Sermons*, pp. 491–2.
[491] Ibid. pp. 5, 30–1, 73, 114.   [492] Ibid. pp. 343–4, 359–60, 363, 370, 378, 381.
[493] Ibid. p. 59, quoted *ante*, p. 207.   [494] Ibid. pp. 321–30.
[495] Ibid. pp. 533–4.   [496] Ibid. p. 619.   [497] Ibid. p. 654.

CHAPTER VI

THE INFLUENCE OF SERMON THEMES ON POETRY AND DRAMA

G. R. Owst suggests the influence of preaching themes on many satirical poems of the late Middle Ages and sixteenth century.[1] He also shows that the mystery and morality plays owe much to the sermons,[2] and that elements in the Elizabethan drama have a preaching ancestry.[3] Therefore it seemed that, having examined the sermons from the middle of the fifteenth century to the end of the sixteenth, it would be interesting to consider what further light is thrown on the relationship between the pulpit oratory and the poetry and drama of the time.

In the case of many traditional themes, I find that where Owst draws attention to parallels between medieval sermons and sixteenth century poems and plays, similar parallels can be drawn from sixteenth century sermons. Also, I discover that within the sixteenth century itself the influence of some of the new sermon themes can be traced. Of course it is impossible to show the influence of specific sermons on particular poems and plays, but I believe that a real, if diffused, influence of certain sermon themes on corresponding themes in verse and drama can be demonstrated. It is difficult, as regards the different themes, to estimate the degree and directness of this influence; as these are doubtless affected by the prevalence of the theme in earlier poetry and drama (a prevalence which is marked in the case of the traditional themes), and the number of possible secondary sources for it; which may mean that the ultimate source in the sermon is not so close as originally thought. However there *are* striking parallels to be observed, all indicating, I believe, the presence of sermon influence, as part of the mental environment of the authors of the poems and plays.

I
1450–1547

The *ubi sunt* and death theme is, as we have noticed, most important in the sermons of the earlier part of this period.[4] The

---

[1] *L. & P.M.E.*, chs. v–vii, pp. 210–470, *passim*.
[2] Ibid. ch. viii, pp. 471–547, *passim*.   [3] Ibid. pp. 234, 529 n. 3, 591–3.
[4] See *ante*, pp. 229–31, 234–6.

Y

parallels in poetry and drama are striking, although this theme is strong in earlier creative writing.[5] It receives deeply felt and beautiful expression in the lyric verse of the late fifteenth and early sixteenth century. Skelton in his lament ' Of the noble prince, kynge Edwarde the forth ' (d. 1483), makes the king say:

> Where is now my conquest and victory?
> Where is my riches and my royal aray?
> Wher be my coursers and my horses hye?
> Where is my myrth, my solas, and my play?
> As vanyte, to nought al is wandred away.
> O lady Bes, longe for me may ye call!
> For I am departed tyl domis day;
> But loue ye that Lorde that is souerayne of all.
> Where be my castels and buyldynges royall?
> But Windsore alone, now I haue no mo.
> And of Eton the prayers perpetuall,
> *Et, ecce, nunc in pulvere dormio!*   (ll. 61–72)[6]

In his stanzas ' On Tyme ', he speaks of the harsh mutability of earthly life:

> Tyme is a thing that no man may resyst;
> Tyme is transytory and irreuocable;
> Who sayeth the contrary, tyme passeth as hym lest;
> Tyme must be taken in season couenable;
> Take tyme when tyme is, for tyme is ay mutable;
> All thynge hath tyme, who can for it prouyde;
> Byde for tyme who wyll, for tyme wyll no man byde.
>   (ll. 1–7)[7]

A poet of the late fifteenth century speaks of the fear of death which troubles him:

> As I me walked in one morning,
> I hard a birde both wepe and singe.
> This was the tenor of her talkinge,
> *Timor mortis conturbat me.*

[5] See E. Gilson, *Les Idées et les Lettres*, pp. 31–8, ' Tables pour l'histoire du thème littéraire *ubi sunt?* ' J. Peter, *Complaint and Satire in Early English Literature* (Oxford, 1956) pp. 72–4. Notable earlier English examples of this theme are: Carleton Brown, *English Lyrics of the XIIIth Century* (Oxford, 1932) nos. 10, 38, 46, 48, 73; *Religious Lyrics of the XIVth Century*, 2nd edn., rev. G. V. Smithers (Oxford, 1957) nos. 9, 43, 81, 106, 134, 135; *Religious Lyrics of the XVth Century*, nos. 152, 153, 155, 156, 158; E. K. Chambers and F. Sidgwick, *Early English Lyrics, Amorous, Divine, Moral and Trivial* (London, 1907), nos. XC, XCIV, CIII, CXV.

[6] *Poetical Works*, ed. Dyce, vol. I, p. 4. The whole poem, pp. 1–5, is on the *ubi sunt* theme. Other poems on this theme of the late fifteenth century are found in Carleton Brown, *Religious Lyrics of the XVth Century*, nos. 149, 154, 157 and 162; pp. 236–7, 243–5, 248, 255–6.

[7] *Poetical Works*, ed. Dyce, vol. I, p. 137.

I asked this birde what he ment.
He said ' I am a musket gent; (noble sparrow-hawk)
For dred of deth I am nigh shent;
    Timor mortis conturbat me.'

Jesu Crist, whan he shuld die,
To his Fader loud gan he crye;
' Fader,' he said, ' in Trinity,
    Timor mortis conturbat me.'

Whan I shall die now I no day,
Therefore this songe sing I may;
In what place or contrey can I not say.
    Timor mortis conturbat me.[8]

Skelton, in ' Vppon a Deedmans Head ', reflects:
            It is generall
            To be mortall:
            I haue well espyde
            No man may hym hyde
            From Deth holow eyed,
            With synnews wyderyd,
            With bonys shyderyd,
            With his worme etyn maw,
            And his gastly jaw
            Gaspyng asyde,
            Nakyd of hyde,
            Neyther flesh nor fell.   (ll. 7–19)[9]

Stephen Hawes, in *The Pastime of Pleasure* (1509), makes the dead
knight Graunde Amour admonish mankind:
        O mortall folke / you may beholde and se
        How I lye here / somtyme a myghty knyght
        The ende of Ioye / and all prosperyte
        Is dethe at last / through his course and myght
        After the day there cometh the derke nyght
        For though the day be neuer so longe
        At last the belles ryngeth to euensonge.   (ll. 5474–80)[10]

The homilist of MS. Harleian 2247 in a funeral sermon is at pains to
show that worldly goods—' ricches ', 'worshippe ', ' delites '—avail
nothing at the hour of death; the deceased person can take only his
' gode werkes ' with him.[11] In preaching of this sort may probably

---

[8] Chambers and Sidgwick, *Early English Lyrics*, no. LXXXIII, p. 150. Cf. too ibid.
no. LXXXII, p. 149.
    [9] *Poetical Works*, ed. Dyce, vol. I, p. 18; cf. the rest of the poem, pp. 18–20.
    [10] *The Pastime of Pleasure*, ed. W. Mead (London, 1928), E.E.T.S., o.s., no. 173, p.
208.   [11] MS. Harl. 2247, f. 210r.

be found the raw material of the famous Morality play *Everyman* (written 1495?) with its theme of death and the inability of earthly goods to help the soul in its last extremity; as in the sermon, only good deeds (in the state of grace) retain their power.[12]

The vanity and sadness of earthly life, which calls forth gloomy declamations from the preachers,[13] inspires poet and dramatist to lugubrious eloquence. Of course, this too is a traditional theme in poetry,[14] but the sermons would no doubt help to keep it in the forefront of the creative writers' minds. The grim speeches of the Seven Deadly Sins over the dead body of Graund Amour in Hawes's *Pastime of Pleasure* stress the emptiness and folly of much human activity,[15] while the whole course of human life is presented in a joyless way by the author of the play *The World and the Child* (1522, written 1508?). The child is wanton until the age of fourteen, then until the age of twenty-one comes the period of ' lust and liking '. At twenty-one comes the time of manhood and servitude to the seven deadly sins. Although for a time Manhood declares that he will follow Conscience, he soon goes off with Folly. Only in old age, is he penitent.[16]

The sermon themes of moral complaint are also faithfully mirrored in poetry and drama. The preacher is not regarded;[17] as Skelton writes in ' The maner of the world now a dayes ':

> So many good lessons,
> So many good sermons,
> And so few devocions,
>   Sawe I never.   (ll. 5–8)[18]

and later in the same poem:

> So much preachinge,
> Speaking fayre and teaching,
> And so ill belevinge,
>   Saw I never.   (ll. 133–7)[19]

---

[12] *Everyman*, reptd. by W. W. Greg from the edition by John Skot preserved at Britwell Court (Louvain, 1904) [W. Bang, *Materialen zur Kunde des alteren englischen Dramas*, vol. IV]. I give the probable date of composition (as in the case of other moralities and interludes) from T. W. Craik, *The Tudor Interlude, Stage, Costume, and Acting* (Leicester, 1958), pp. 140–1.

[13] See *ante*, pp. 231–4.

[14] See Carleton Brown, *English Lyrics of the XIIIth Century*, no. 71; *Religious Lyrics of the XIVth Century*, nos. 28, 53, 133; Chambers and Sidgwick, *Early English Lyrics*, nos. XCI, XCIII.

[15] *The Pastime of Pleasure*, ll. 5425–73, pp. 206–8.

[16] *The World and the Child* (*A Select Collection of Old English Plays. Originally published by Robert Dodsley in the year* 1744. Fourth edn., . . . ed. W. C. Hazlitt, 15 vols., London, 1874–6, vol. I, pp. 243–75.)

[17] For the sermon theme see *ante*, pp. 237–8.

[18] *Poetical Works*, ed. Dyce, vol. I, p. 148.   [19] Ibid. p. 152.

The ignorance and immorality of the clergy, their worldliness and addition to simony, a traditional theme in preaching[20] and in poetry,[21] continues to find expression. This is a theme of some importance in Skelton. Apart from the well known attack on Wolsey in ' Why come ye not to court ' ?[22] the racy poem ' Ware the Hawke ' is directed against hawking and hunting by the clergy. These are not pursuits for men of their calling, says Skelton, but he will tell of a priest who:

> wrought amys,
> To hawke in my Church of Dis.   (ll. 41–2)[23]

He continues in his best satirical vein:

> This fonde frantyke fauconer,
> With his polutid pawtenar
> As priest vnreverent,
> Streyght to the Sacrament
> He made his hawke to fly,
> With hogeous showte and cry.
> The hye auter he strypt naked;
> There on he stode, and craked;
> He shoke downe all the clothis,
> And sware horrible othes
> Before the face of God,
> By moses and Arons rod,
> Or that he thens yede,
> His hawke shoulde pray and fede
> Vpon a pigeons maw.
> The bloude ran doune raw
> Vpon the auter stone;
> The hawke tyrid on a bonne;
> And in the holy place
> She mutid there a chase
> Vpon my corporas face. . . (ll. 43–63)[24]

When the poet rebukes him, this lewd priest threatens to bring his hounds and hunt too:

> Dowtless such losels
> Make the churche to be
> In smale auctoryte:
> A curate in speciall
> To snapper and to fall

---

[20] See *ante*, pp. 238–41.
[21] See J. Peter, *Complaint and Satire in Early English Literature*, pp. 80–4.
[22] *Poetical Works*, ed. Dyce, vol. II, pp. 26–67.   [23] Ibid. vol. I, p. 156.
[24] Ibid. pp. 156–7.

> Into this open cryme;
> To loke on this were tyme.   (ll. 138–44)[25]

However ' mayden Meed ' prevents redress against such ruffians.[26]
In ' Colyn Cloute ' the laureate details the complaints of the laity
against the clergy. The prelates are haughty and care about promotion not souls; they are too concerned with lawsuits; they haunt
the court and neglect preaching owing to laziness and ignorance.
They are cowardly in denouncing vice, and spend their time in
hunting and catching girls.[27] They eat meat in Lent and take too
little care about whom they ordain,[28] so that foolish priests receive
care of souls,

> And woteth neuer what thei rede,
> Paternoster, Ave, nor Crede;
> Construe not worth a whystle
> Nether Gospell nor Pystle
> Theyr mattyns madly sayde,
> Nothynge deuoutly prayde;
> Theyr lernynge is so small,
> Theyr prymes and houres fall
> And lepe out of theyr lyppes
> Lyke sawdust or drye chyppes.   (ll. 236–45)[29]

Simony is rampant yet the bishops oppress the poor laymen with
summons, citations and excommunications.[30] Wolsey's pride and
low birth are castigated:

> For ye loue to go trym,
> Brought vp of poore estate,
> Wyth pryde inordinate,
> Sodynly vpstarte
> From the donge carte,
> The mattocke and the shale,
> To reygne and to rule;
> And haue no grace to thynke
> Howe ye were wonte to drynke
> Of a lether bottell.
> With a knauysshe stopell,
> Whan mamockes was your meate,
> With moldy brede to eate; . . .   (ll. 642–55)[31]

Learned clerks have poor livings;[32] and while Colin does not object
to such men,n evertheless:

---

[25] Ibid. p. 159.   [26] Ibid. p. 160.   [27] Ibid. pp. 314–18.
[28] Ibid. pp. 318–20.   [29] Ibid. p. 320.   [30] Ibid. pp. 322–3.
[31] Ibid. pp. 335–6.   [32] Ibid. pp. 339–40.

> . . . doctour Bullatus,
> *Parum litteratus,*
> *Dominus doctoratus,*
> At the brode gatus,
> Doctour Daupatus
> And bacheler *bacheleratus,*
> Dronken as a mouse,
> At the ale house,
> Taketh his pyllyon and his cap
> At the good ale tap,
> For lacke of good wyne;
> As wyse as Robyn swyne,
> Vnder a notaryes sygne
> Was made a dyuyne;
> As wyse as Waltons calfe,
> Must preche, a Goddes halfe,
> In the pulpyt solempnely;
> More meet in the pyllory, . . .   (ll. 797–813)[33]

Robert Copland, the author of the interesting early sixteenth century poem *The Hye Way to the Spytell House* (written after 1530–1), includes among the wasters who end their days in the hospital,

> Preestes and clerkes, that lyue vycyously,
>   Not carying how they shold do theyr duty,
> Vnruly of maners, and slacke in lernyng,
>   Euer at the alehous for to syt bybyng,
> Neglectyng the obedyence to them dew,
>   And vnto Chrystes flocke take none anew,
> But lyke as wolues, that rauysh the folde, . . .   (ll. 583–9)[34]

These are obviously *confrères* of Doctor Double Ale, who:

> When he his boke shulde study,
> He sitteth there full ruddy,
> Tyll halfe the day be gone,
> Crying, fyll the pot Jone,
> And wyll not be alone,
> But call sum other one
> At Wyndowe, or at fenestre,
> That is an idell minestre,
> As he him selfe is.[35]

[33] Ibid. p. 342.

[34] *Remains of the Early Popular Poetry of England*, ed. W. C. Hazlitt, 4 vols. (London, 1866), vol. IV, p. 51.

[35] ' Doctour Doubble Ale,' ll. 126–34; ibid. vol. III, p. 311. This piece shows Protestant sympathies, but is composed largely of traditional material. (Ibid. pp. 301–21.) Other poetic passages on the theme of unworthy clergy may be noticed here; *Political Poems and Songs relating to English History, composed during the Period from the Accession of EDW. III to that of RIC. III*, ed. T. Wright (London, 1859–61, Rolls series

This theme makes its appearance in drama in *Hickscorner* (written 1513?), when Pity laments the times:

> And yet one thing maketh me ever mourning:
> That priests lack utterance to show their cunning;
> And all the while that clerks do use so great sin,
> Among the lay people look never for no mending.
>
> (ll. 135–8)[36]

Women, with their wanton ways and taste for finery and extravagance, who call down upon themselves the preachers' castigations[37] receive similar traditional treatment at the hands of some of the popular poets.[38] Copland asks the porter of the hospital:

> But hey, las! do none this way trace
>   That do take wyues of small effycace,
>   Which cannot yet bestow, nor yet saue,
>   And to go gay they wyll spend and craue;
> Makyng men wene that they loue them alone,
>   And be full fals unto them echone,
> Spendyng theyr goodes without ony care,
>   Without good gownes, but not of hoodes bare?
>
> (ll. 1016–23)[39]

to receive the answer:

> They must come hyther, for they cannot chuse, . . . (l. 1024)[40].

The author of *The Payne and Sorowe of Evyll Maryage* (1509?) argues against marriage on the grounds of the numerous frailties of women which render wedlock ' an endlesse penaunce '.[41] *The Scole-House of Women* (before 1541) presents a long indictment of the female sex; women are bad to please, loud, obstinate, adulterous and given to gossip. The young complain to the old about their husbands, who advise them to be bold and quarrelsome. They are extravagant in dress and gluttonous, and if they seek to win recognition of their importance by reference to the scriptural account of the creation of Eve from one of Adam's ribs, the poet replies that it is probable that a dog ran off with the bone, and that God took a rib of the dog with which to create Eve![42] Thus:

14) ' On the Corruptions of the Times,' ll. 37–40 (vol. II, p. 236); ' On the Corruptions of the Times,' ll. 11–15, 105–12 (ibid. pp. 238, 241); ' On the Corruption of Public Manners,' ll. 9–24 (ibid. p. 251); ' On the Times,' l. 7 (ibid. p. 253).

[36] *A Select Collection of Old English Plays*, ed. W. C. Hazlitt, vol. I, p. 153.
[37] See *ante*, pp. 241–2.
[38] For the theme in earlier verse, see Peter, *Complaint and Satire in Early English Poetry*, pp. 86–91, 99–102.
[39] *Remains of the Early Popular Poetry of England*, ed. Hazlitt, vol. IV, pp. 67–8.
[40] Ibid. p. 68.   [41] Ibid. pp. 73–80.   [42] Ibid. pp. 105–24.

> Nature she followeth, and playeth the gib,
> And at her husband dooth barke and ba[w]ll,
> As dooth the Cur, for nought at all.   (ll. 508–10)[43]

Little wonder that the poet is able to conclude with a catalogue of bad women—Jezebel, Herodias, the maid who declared that St. Peter had been with Christ, the daughters of Lot, Pasiphae, Messalina, Pyrrha, Fabula, Helen of Troy and many others.[44] *The Boke of Mayd Emlyn* (1525) tells of this worthy who ' had v. husbandes and all kockoldes ', who ends up in the stews and at the end of her life is forced ' to begge her brede '.[45] One of her husbands sums up the general attitude of the poet; he is brought to think:

> That a man can fynde
> A wyfe neuer to late;
> For of theyr properte
> Shrewes all they be,
> And style can they prate.
> All women be suche,
> Thoughe the man bere the breche,
> They wyll be euer checkemate.
> Faced lyke an aungell,
> Tonged like a deuyll of hell,
> Great causers of debate;
> They loke full smothe,
> And be false of loue,
> Venymous as a snake.   (ll. 144–57)[46]

The prevalence of the sins of the flesh, a traditional theme both in preaching[47] and in poetry,[48] continues to merit the rebuke of the popular poets. The author of *A Treatise of a Galaunt* (1510?) stresses this element in the behaviour of the scandalous gallants of his day; sadly he declaims:

> Somtyme we had Fraunce / in grete derysyon
> For theyr hatefull pryde and lothsome vnclennes
> Use we not nowe / the same in our regyon
> And haue permuted our welthe / for theyr gladnes
> Lechery of our people is become a maystres.
> Our gentylnes / for galauntyse haue we lefte there.
> Englonde may wayle that euer it came here.   (ll. 42–8)[49]

---

[43] Ibid. p. 124.   [44] Ibid. pp. 131–46.   [45] Ibid. pp. 83–96.
[46] Ibid. p. 88. Cf. too Chambers and Sidgwick, *Early English Lyrics*, nos. CXIX, CXX, pp. 208–9.
[47] See *ante*, pp. 242–3.
[48] See Carleton Brown, *Religious Lyrics of the XVth Century*, nos. 176, l. 8; 177, ll. 17–20.
[49] *Remains of the Early Popular Poetry of England*, ed. Hazlitt, vol. III, p. 153. See too ibid. ll. 78–84, 148–54, pp. 154, 158.

The porter tells Copland that among those who daily resort to the
Spittle House are:

> Lechours, fornycatours and advouterers,
>   Incestes, harlots, bawdes and bolsterers,
>   Applesquyers, entycers and rauysshers. . . .   (ll. 830–2)[50]

to which Copland replies:

> No marvell of them, and happy they be,
>   If they do and in so honest degre:
> For surely theyr endying is fayrest,
>   If that with pouerte they be supprest:
> For I do fynd wryten of aduoutry
>   That these fyue sorowes ensueth thereby.   (ll. 834–9)

*   *   *   *

> Eyther they shall be poore, or dye sodenly,
>   Or lese by wound some membre of the body,
> Or to be sclaundred to suffre sharpe pryson,
>   Therfore pouerte is fayrest by reason.
> And yet besyde that they be so beaten,
>   That with great pockes theyr lymmes be eaten.
>
>   (ll. 844–9)[51]

Swearing and blasphemy as in the sermons[52] are denounced in the
traditional way by the poets.[53] Hawes's *The Conversyon of Swerers*
repeats the usual complaint of Christ against swearers:

> They newe agayne do hange me on the rode
> They tere my sydes and are nothynge dysmayde
> My woundes they open and deuoure my blode
> I god and man moost wofully arayde
> To you complayne it maye not be denayde
> Ye nowe do tug me / ye tere me at the roote
> Yet I to you am chefe refuyte and boote.   (ll. 85–92)[54]

Among those who deservedly come to the Spittle House are swearers,
as the porter says:

> All rotten and torne, armes, heades and legges,
> They are the moost sorte that ony where begges,
> And be the people that moost annoy us.   (ll. 854–6)[55]

Extravagance of dress in men receives traditional rebuke[56] by Skelton
in *The maner of the world now a dayes*:

---

[50] Ibid. vol. IV, p. 60.   [51] Ibid. p. 61.   [52] See *ante*, p. 244.

[53] See Peter, *Complaint and Satire in Early English Poetry*, p. 103.

[54] *The Conversyon of Swerers: a Joyfull Medytacyon to all Englonde of the Coronacyon of Kynge Henry the Eyght*, ed. D. Laing (Edinburgh, 1865) Abbotsford Club, sig. Aiii[r]. The whole of this poem is parallel to the sermon complaints on this topic.

[55] *Remains of the Early Popular Poetry of England*, ed. Hazlitt, vol. IV, p. 61.

[56] For the sermon theme, see *ante*, p. 243; for the theme in poetry, see Peter, *Complaint and Satire in Early English Poetry*, p. 102.

> So many poynted caps
> Lased with double flaps,
> And so gay felted hats,
>   Saw I never.   (ll. 1–4)[57]

Having mentioned ' gardes, . . . jagged and al to-torne ', (ll. 9–10)
' pranked cotes and sleves ', (l. 21) ' garded hose ', (l. 25) ' cornede
shoes ', (l. 26) ' gay swordes ', (l. 33) ' newe fashyoned daggers ',
(l. 42)[58] it is little wonder that he exclaims:

> So much vayne clothing
> With cultyng and jagging
> And so much bragginge
>   Saw I never.   (ll. 53–6)[59]

Similar denunciation is found in *A Treatise of a Galaunt*,[60] while
extravagance in dress is yet another of the causes which leads men
to the Spittle House.[61]

Corruption among the ' common officers ' is denounced in the
traditional manner[62] in *Vox Populi Vox Dei* (1512–20?):

> . . . pawre men dayly sees
> How officers takes their fees,
> Summe yll, and some yet worse,
> As good right as to pike there a purse:
> Deservethe this not Godes curse?
> There consyenes ys sooe greet
> Thaye fere not to dischare,
> Yf it were as moche more,
> Soe they may haue the stowre.   (ll. 383–91)[63]

The covetousness of landlords; their engrossing and oppression
of the poor is denounced at length in the sermon style in the same
poem.[64] A few now own all, sheep replace arable land, the yeomen
are in distress and upstarts rule the roost.[65]

The exhortations to repentance in the sermons[66] may be paralleled
in drama by the call of Perseverance to Age in *The World and the*

---

[57] *Poetical Works*, ed. Dyce, vol. I, p. 148.
[58] Ibid. pp. 148–9.   [59] Ibid. p. 149.
[60] ll. 22–8, 92–4, 113–61, 176–203; *Remains of the Early Popular Poetry of England*,
ed. Hazlitt, vol. IV, pp. 152, 155, 156–8, 159–60.
[61] ' The Hye Way to the Spyttel Hous,' ll. 601–6, 730–5; ibid. vol. IV, pp. 52,
57.
[62] For the sermon theme see *ante*, pp. 244–5; for the theme in poetry, see Peter, *Complaint and Satire in Early English Poetry*, p. 84.
[63] *Remains of the Early Popular Poetry of England*, ed. Hazlitt, vol. III, p. 281. Cf. too
ll. 701–12, ibid. p. 292.
[64] See *ante*, pp. 245–6.
[65] ll. 1–382, 480–587, 776–824, *Remains of the Early Popular Poetry of England*, ed.
Hazlitt, vol. III, pp. 268–81, 284–88, 295–6.
[66] See *ante*, pp. 246–7.

Child (ll. 842–973),[67] by the taking of Everyman to Confession by Knowledge, and the putting on him of the garment of Contrition (ll. 540–52),[68] and by the admonitions of Perseverance and Contemplation to Freewill in *Hickscorner* (ll. 664–1031).[69]

Themes of controversy appear in poetry and drama, and it is interesting to note the similarity in tone to the treatment of these themes in the sermon. In *A replyccacion agaynst certayne yong scolers abiured of late*, Skelton uses the same method of personal denunciation and ridicule employed by Longland and Edgeworth against Luther and the Lutherans:[70]

> Wolde God, for your owne ease,
> That wyse Harpocrates
> Had your mouthes stopped,
> And your tonges cropped,
> Whan ye logyke chopped,
> And in the pulpete hopped,
> And folysshly there fopped,
> And porishly forthe popped
> Your sysmaticate sawes
> Agaynst Goddes lawes,
> And shewed your selfe dawes!   (ll. 114–24)[71]

Or, one might instance this racy passage:

> Ye soored ourer hye
> In the ierarchy
> Of Jouenyans heresy,
> Your names to magnifye,
> Among the scabbed skyes
> Of Wycliffes fleshe flyes;
> Ye strynged so Luthers lute,
> That ye dawns all in a sute.
> The heritykes ragged ray,
> That bringes you out of the way
> Of holy churches lay
> Ye shayle *inter enigmata*
> And *inter paradigmata*
> Marked in your cradels
> To beare fagottes for fabyls.   (ll. 161–76)[72]

---

[67] *A Select Collection of Old English Plays*, vol. I, pp. 271—5.
[68] *Everyman*, ed. Greg, pp. [19]–[23].
[69] *A Select Collection of Old English Plays*, vol. I, pp. 179–95. The theme of penitence is of course traditional; there are many medieval poems on this subject: see Carleton Browne, *English Lyrics of the XIIIth Century*, nos. 2, 32, 65, 88; *Religious Lyrics of the XIVth Century*, nos. 10, 54; *Religious Lyrics of the XVth Century*, nos. 137–46.
[70] See *ante*, p. 248.   [71] *Poetical Works*, ed. Dyce, vol. I, pp. 212–13.
[72] Ibid. p. 214.

It is further interesting to note that the kind of attack which Bale makes on the pride of the Pope in *King Johan* (written 1535? ll. 1284–1378)[73] is similar to that of Longland and Tunstall in their sermons.[74]

When one turns to the positive sermon themes, one again finds parallels in the poetry, although here there is too a long poetic tradition. The praise of the saints in the sermons[75] is reflected in poems dealing with Our Lady; in the words of a poet of the late fifteenth century:

Haylle be þu quene moste comely,
þat euyr was formyd both fare & nere!
Therefore I hayle þe worschypfully—
In all þe world was neuer þy pere.
Thy sone ys kynge moste worthy & myȝty,
ffor ouer alle thyngus ys his powere.
And welle I wote & lefe fully
he wylle deme þe best prayere;
þerefor þu pray þat blessydfull kynge,
þat þe blys in-with þe may wonne,
þere as þu art euer, with ray schynnyng
Velud rosa wel lylyom.[76]

The Passion of Christ[77] also receives poetic treatment, as in a fine early sixteenth century complaint of the redeemer to mankind:

Then one this crosse thei dyde me strecch & stayn,
And nayled me faste wyth naylles gret & longe,
And hyng me vppe betweene false thevis twayne,
Most shamefully, wyth moche rebuke & wronge.
I called for drynke, my thurst was grevous strong;
Thei gave me aysell, tempred wyth bitter galle,
Which I did taste & dranke therof but smalle.

My visage changed to pale & blew as byse,
My fleshe be-ganne to styff & waxid drye,
My hart lokyd lyke a plomett of Ise,
My lyff was spent, myne owre was come to dye.

[73] *King Johan by John Bale*, ed. J. H. P. Pafford and W. W. Greg (Oxford, 1931) M.S.R. [no. 61] pp. 61–4.
[74] See *ante*, pp. 254–5.
[75] See *ante*, pp. 257–8.
[76] Carleton Brown, *Religious Lyrics of the XVth Century*, no. 24, ll. 37–48, p. 44. See too ibid. no. 47, pp. 76–7. For the poetic tradition see ibid., nos. 11–23, 25–46, pp. 22–42, 45–76: also *English Lyrics of the XIIIth Century*, nos. 3, 16–18, 31, 41, 55, 60, 61, 87; *Religious Lyrics of the XIVth Century*, nos. 16, 32, 33, 111; Chambers and Sidgwick, *Early English Lyrics*, nos. XLVI, XLIX, LII–LVII, LXXXVI.
[77] For the sermon theme, see *ante*, pp. 260–1.

Vnto my father I cryed, ' heli, heli !'
And wyth that worde, I layde myne hede a-syde,
And dolfully gave vp the spret & dyed.

* * * *

Off tendure love, all this I dyd endure;
Love dyde me lede, love dyde me thus constrayne;
And, for my dede & grevous adventure,
More aske I nott but love for love a-gayne.
Brother, be kynde, & for a good certayne,
By-side all this, rewardede shalt thou be
In the blysse of hevyne, where ther ys no pouerte.[78]

II

1547–1553

Polemic against Catholicism in the sermons of this period[79] is
reflected in drama in Robert Wever's *Lusty Juventus* (written 1550?)
when Hypocrisy boasts to the Devil that he has mangled God's
commandments with ' vain zeals and blind intents ' so that they have
been greatly abused; he has:

> set up great idolatry
> With all kind of filthy sodometry,
> To give mankind a fall: (ll. 42–4)

and has introduced superstition ' under the name of holiness and
religion ' to deceive nearly all:

> As holy cardinals, holy popes,
> Holy vestments, holy copes,
> Holy hermits and friars,
> Holy priests, holy bishops,
> Holy monks, holy abbots,
> Yea, and all obstinate liars:
> Holy pardons, holy beads,
> Holy saints, holy images,
> With holy, holy blood,
> Holy stocks, holy stones,
> Holy clouts, holy bones;
> Yea, and holy holy wood.   (ll. 408–19)

---

[78] Carleton Brown, *Religious Lyrics of the XVth Century*, no. 109, ll. 155–68, 190–6,
pp. 174–5. See too ibid. no. 93, pp. 136–8. There is too a long poetic tradition on
this theme: see ibid. nos. 91–2, 94–108, 110, pp. 131–6, 138–69, 175–7: also *English
Lyrics of the XIIIth Century*, nos. 1, 24, (ll. 31–90). 33–7, 45, 49, 56, 64, 84; *Religious
Lyrics of the XIVth Century*, nos. 1–4, 15, 34, 46, 51, 52, 55, 64, 67, 69, 70, 72, 74, 76, 77,
79, 83 (ll. 33–44), 90, 91, 126, 127; Chambers and Sidgwick, *Early English Lyrics*, nos.
LXXVIII–LXXX.

[79] See *ante*, pp. 263–7.

and so throughout twenty four lines more in the manner of the
' Homily of Good Works annexed unto Faith '.[80]

The attack on the doctrine of Transubstantiation in the sermons[81]
is paralleled in the comic poem *John Bon and Mast Parson*,[82] in which
the countryman John is represented as working early to finish by
noon. Complimented by his parson who thinks that he is going to
keep Corpus Christi Eve, John asks:

What saynt is Copsi Cursty, a man or a woman?   (l. 11)[83]

After some argument about the Real Presence, John concludes:

Yea: but mast Parson, thynke ye it were ryght,
That, if I desired you to make my blake oxe whight,
And you saye it is done, and style is blacke in syght,
Ye myght me deme a foole for to beleve so lyght?
                                      (ll. 128–31)[84]

and reveals himself a Protestant in these matters:

By my trueth, mast Parson, I lyke ful wel your talke:
But masse me no more messinges. The right way wil I walke.
For thoughe I have no learning, yet I know chese from chalke,
And yche can perceive your juggling, as crafty as ye walke.
But leve your devilish masse, and the communion to you take,
And then will Christ be with you, even for his promisse sake.
                                      (ll.   150–5)[85]

Themes of complaint are reflected also; the castigation of covetousness[86] plays an important part in the popular poem *The Booke in
Meeter of Robin Conscience* (c. 1550), where Robin argues with his
father who upholds acquisitiveness as a rule of life.[87] The vanity and
extravagance of women receive rebuke in the same poem when
Robin argues with his mother about over rich apparel and with his
sister about wanton dallying.[88] Similar attacks on women are found
in Charles Bansley's *A Treatyse shewing and declaring the Pryde and
Abuse of Women Now a Dayes* (c. 1550),[89] a rollickingly comic piece:

Sponge up youre vysage, olde bounsynge trotte,
    And tricke it with the beste,
Tyll you tricke and trotte youre selfe
    To the devylls trounsynge neste:
Oure trotte, our trotte, our lustye trotte,

---

[80] *A Select Collection of Old English Plays*, vol. II, pp. 64–6. Cf. *ante*, pp. 265–6.
[81] See *ante*, pp. 264–5.
[82] *Remains of the Early Popular Poetry of England*, ed. Hazlitt, vol. IV, pp. 3–16.
[83] Ibid. p. 5.   [84] Ibid. p. 14.   [85] Ibid. p. 15.
[86] For the sermon theme, see *ante*, pp. 269–70.
[87] ll. 1–96, *Remains of the Early Popular Poetry of England*, vol. III, pp. 227–32.
[88] ll. 97–339; ibid. pp. 232–47.   [89] Ibid. vol. IV, pp. 229–44.

> Whyche shoulde be mooste sadde and playne,
> Is nowe become a trickynge one,
> And a wanton trincklet agayne. (ll. 45–52)[90]

Bansley has his theory about the source of vain and wanton dress:

> From Rome, from Rome, this carkerd pryde,
> From Rome it came, dobtles;
> Awaye for shame wyth soch filthy baggage,
> As smels of papery and devylyshness! (ll. 125–8)[91]

III

1553–1558

The praise of Queen Mary in the sermons[92] is paralleled in drama in *Respublica*, an interlude for Christmas 1553 attributed to Nicholas Udall. The Prologue rejoices that Mary is now Sovereign, and will reform the abuses which have been too long neglected.[93] The queen is equated with Nemesis[94] who appears at the end of the play and brings judgement to the rogues, Avarice masquerading as Policy; Adulation as Honesty; Insolence as Authority, and Oppression as Reformation.[95]

The whole of the play up to the fifth act is a satire on the time of Edward, with the depredations of the rogues and the complaints of People who suffer at their hands.[96] James Brooks, preaching at Paul's Cross on 12th November 1553 had spoken against the doings of the previous reign,[97] and no doubt there had been many similar pulpit tirades, which could well have had some influence on the dramatist's presentation of his theme.

The *ubi sunt* and death theme which reappears in the sermons of this reign[98] is paralleled in poetry in some of the items in Tottel's *Miscellany* (1557), as ' Comparison of lyfe and death ', with the sad lines:

> The pleasant yeres that seme, so swifte that runne:
> The mery dayes to end, so fast that flete:
> The ioyfull nightes, of which day daweth so soone:
> The happy howers, which mo do misse, than mete,

---

[90] Ibid. p. 234.   [91] Ibid. p. 240.   [92] See *ante*, pp. 277–8.
[93] *Respublica, an Interlude for Christmas* 1553, *attributed to Nicholas Udall*, re-ed. W. W. Greg (London, 1952) E.E.T.S., o.s. 226, ll. 45–58, pp. 2–3.
[94] Ibid. l. 53, p. 3.   [95] Ibid. Act V, sc. x. ll. 1814–1938, pp. 62–6.
[96] Ibid. pp. 3–40; the following passages may be particularly noticed: Act III, sc. iii, ll. 677–739, pp. 24–6; Act III, sc. vi, ll. 855–966, pp. 30–3; Act IV, sc. iii–iv, ll. 1001–1168, pp. 34–40.
[97] See *ante*, pp. 279–80.   [98] See *ante*, pp. 289–91.

Doe all consume: as snow against the sunne:
And death makes end of all, that life begunne.   (ll. 13–18)[99]
or Lord Vaux's famous ' The aged louer renounceth loue ', sung by
the gravedigger in *Hamlet* (Act V, sc. i, ll. 69 ff.):

I lothe that I did loue,
In youth that I thought swete:
As time requires for my behoue
Me thinkes they are not mete,
My lustes they do me leeue,
My fansies all be fledde:
And tract of time begins to weaue,
Gray heares vpon my hedde.
For age with stelyng steppes,
Hath clawed me with his cowche: [MSS. and later edns.,
And lusty life away she leapes,   ' crutch' or ' crowch ']
As there had bene none such.

*   *   *   *

The wrincles in my brow,
The furrowes in my face:
Say limpyng age will hedge him now
Where youth must geue him place.
The harbinger of death,
To me I see him ride:
The cough, the colde, the gaspyng breath,
Dothe bid me to prouide,
A pikeax and a spade,
And eke a shrowdyng shete,
A house of claye for to be made,
For such a gest most mete.   (ll. 1–12; 21–32)[100]

Similar melancholy considerations are found also in the poems
' Of the mutabilitie of the world ',[101] and ' That length of time con-
sumeth all thinges '.[102] Probably here too we may postulate preaching influence on the mental climate of the times.

IV

1558–1603

The attack on Catholicism and the English Catholics in the
sermons[103] is paralleled in poetry and drama. One of Joseph Hall's

---

[99] *Tottel's Miscellany*, ed. H. E. Rollins, 2 vols. (Cambridge, Mass., 1928–9) vol. I, p. [124].

[100] Ibid. pp. [165]–[6]; cf. *Hamlet*, ed. E. Dowden, 5th edn. (London, 1919) [The Arden Shakespeare] pp. 189–91.

[101] Ibid. pp. [131]–[2].   [102] Ibid. pp. [218]–[19].   [103] See *ante*, pp. 292–300.

z

satires in *Virgidemiae* ([1597–8] Bk. IV, sat. vii) is devoted to the castigation of Romanism. The ' Romish Pageants ', he declares, are subjects for satire; if Juvenal could return to life he would rage that Caesar's throne is now turned to Peter's chair:

> To see an old shorne *Lozell* perched hy
> Crossing beneath a golden *Canopy*,
> The whiles a thousand hairelesse crownes crouch low
> To kisse the precious case of his proud Toe,
> And for the Lordly *Fasces* borne of old,
> To see two quiet crossed keyes of gold,
> Or *Cybeles* shrine, the famous *Panteons* frame
> Turn'd to the honour of our Ladies name.   (ll. 13–20)[104]

Friars collecting rent from the stews, the custom of burial in a Franciscan habit to secure salvation merit rebuke,[105] as does the ' likerous Priest ' who:

> . . . spits euery trice
> With longing for his morning Sacrifice,
> Which he reres vp quite perpendiculare,
> That the mid-Church doth spite the *Chancels* fare,
> Beating their emptie mawes that would be fed,
> With the scant morsels of the *Sacrists* bread.   (ll. 57–62)[106]

Ludicrous legends of the saints; of St. Christopher, St. George, the Seven Sleepers, or St. Peter's well, arouse the satirist's ire, as does the story of ' Pope Joan ' and the new Calender![107] John Marston in *The Scourge of Villanie* ([1598] sat. iii, l. 58) attacks the moral climate of the seminary at Douai,[108] and the doctrine of Transubstantiation:

> *Democritus*, rise from thy putrid slime
> Sport at the madnes of that hotter clime.
> Deride their frenzie, that for policie
> Adore Wheate dough, as reall deitie.
> Almighty men, that can their Maker make,
> And force his sacred body to forsake
> The Cherubines, to be gnawne actually,
> Deuiding *indiuiduum*, really.   (sat. ii, ll. 80–7)[109]

In William Wager's interlude *The Longer thou Livest the more Fool thou art* (c. 1568, written 1564?), Moros the incorrigible fool, although intractable as regards education, nevertheless can ring the sanctus bell and fetch fire (bring the thurible) when they go to

[104] *The Collected Poems of Joseph Hall*, ed. A. Davenport (Liverpool, 1949) p. 72.
[105] Ibid. p. 73, ll. 27–8, 45–6.   [106] Ibid. p. 74.   [107] Ibid. ll. 63–74.
[108] *The Poems of John Marston*, ed. A. Davenport (Liverpool, 1961) p. 113.
[109] Ibid. pp. 108–9.

Matins.[110] Discipline refers to Catholic teaching on the Mass as heresy,[111] while Ignorance declares that he has dwelt with the papists.[112] In the interlude *New Custom* (1573, written 1570?) the old popish priests Perverse Doctrine and Ignorance, posing as Sound Doctrine and Simplicity, plot with Hypocrisy against New Custom, or Primitive Constitution. Cruelty and Avarice lend their support to the Roman faction, reminiscing about their activities in Queen Mary's days. However, in support of the Elizabethan settlement, New Custom and Light of the Gospel convert Perverse Doctrine to their point of view; he becomes Sincere Doctrine and is greeted by Edification and Assurance.[113] Nathaniel Woodes's *The Conflict of Conscience* (1581, written 1572?) deals with the story of Philologus (Francis Spira) who recants his evangelical faith for worldly considerations and dies in despair. At the beginning of the play Satan decides to help his son the Pope as much as possible and sends him two champions, Avarice and Tyrannical Practice.[114] There is mordant satire in the depiction of Caconos, a priest who rejoices at the setting up of popery, and who denounces Philologus as a heretic. He is unable to read the Latin of his breviary, but finds the service of the day by the picture in the ' great gilded letter ' which illustrates the feast—as a babe in a manger for Christmas, or the three kings for Epiphany.[115] His knowledge of which saint to invoke for various needs causes Tyranny to declare that he is well read in the *Golden Legend*, to which Caconos replies:

> Bay may trooth, in readyng any other, ne taym do I spend
> Far that ay ken, bay general caunsell, is canonized
> And bay the hely Pope hymselfe is authorized:
> That Buke farther, is wholly permytted,
> Wharas, the Bayble in part is prohibited.
> And therefore, gif it be lawfull to vtter my conscience,
> Before the New Testament ays giue it credence.[116]

It is obvious that in this play Woodes is reflecting on the events of Mary's reign and seeking to warn against a repetition of them.

The sermon topics of complaint continue to be reflected in poetry and drama. The abuses in the Church of England[117] provide a

---

[110] *The Longer thou Livest the more Fool thou art*, ed. J. S. Farmer (London, 1910) T.F.T. (no. 49) sig. Aiv^r.   [111] Ibid. sig. Bii^r.   [112] Ibid. sig. Eiii^r.

[113] *A Select Collection of Old English Plays*, ed. Hazlitt, vol. III, pp. 4–52.

[114] *The Conflict of Conscience*, ed. H. Davis and F. P. Wilson (Oxford, 1952) M.S.R. [no. 86] ll. 87–93, sig. Aiv^r.   [115] Ibid. ll. 962–77, sig. Div^r-v.

[116] Ibid. ll. 1003–10, sig. Div^v–Ei^r. Cf. too the anti-Catholic propaganda in Lewis Wager's *The Life and Repentance of Mary Magdalene*, ed. J. S. Farmer (London, 1908) T.F.T. [no. 23] sig. Aiii^v–Aiv^r, Biii^v, Li^v, Div^v–Iiii^r.

[117] For the sermon theme, see *ante*, pp. 300–2.

subject for satire to Spenser in *Prosopopoia or Mother Hubberds Tale* ([1590, written 1579–80] ll. 379–574). Ignorant and opportunist clergy together with simony are lashed by the portrait of the ' formal priest ' with his worldly wise advice to the fox and the ape, and by the episode of the fox becoming a parson with the ape as his clerk.[118] Hall, in *Virgidemiae*, satirizes the buying of benefices at St. Paul's (Bk. II, sat. v),[119] and the shabby treatment given to domestic chaplains in the houses of the country gentry (Bk. II, sat. vi).[120] Marston, in *The Scourge of Villanie*, mocks hedge priests (sat. iii, ll. 168–76),[121] and mentions Maurus, who got his gelded vicarage by simony, but will rise to dignities through usury (sat. v, ll. 64–9).[122]

In the play *The Second Part of the Returne from Parnassus* (1601–2) there is an amusing attack on simoniacal appointments to benefices. The squire Sir Raderick, bribed by the farmer Stercutio, prefers his son, the unlearned but cunning Immerito, to a living, while the deserving Cambridge graduate Academico is mocked by Sir Raderick's foolish son Amoretto, because he has no money to advance his fortunes.[123]

The covetousness of landlords and their wicked enclosures, by now a traditional complaint,[124] appears in George Gascoignes's *The Steele Glas* ([1576] ll. 418–47)[125] and in Hall's *Virgidemiae* (Bk. V, sat. i & ii).[126] The custom of ' housekeeping ' is now dead, laments Hall; gentlemen build garish houses for show, but have no fires in them.[127]

This theme is glanced at also in Lewis Wager's interlude, *The Life and Repentance of Mary Magdalene* (1566, written 1566?), when Mary, wondering what will become of her when old, is told by Cupidity that in old age she can oppress her tenants, take fines and raise rents.[128]

In the sermon tradition, usury is satirized by Hall in *Virgidemiae* (Bk. IV, sat. v) as in the person of Tocullio, who:

> . . . was a welthie vsurer,
> Such store of incomes had he euery yeare,

---

[118] *The Poetical Works of Edmund Spenser*, ed. J. C. Smith and E. de Selincourt (Oxford, reptd. 1952) pp. 499–501.

[119] *Collected Poems*, p. 28.   [120] Ibid. p. 29.

[121] *Poems*, pp. 116–17.   [122] Ibid. p. 132.

[123] *The Second Part of the Return from Parnassus*, [Act II, sc. ii–Act III, sc. iii] ll. 583–1250; [*The Three Parnassus Plays* (1598–1601) ed. J. B. Leishman, London, 1949, pp. 263–300.]

[124] For the sermon theme, see *ante*, p. 308.

[125] *The Complete Works of George Gascoigne*, ed. J. W. Cunliffe, 2 vols. (Cambridge, 1907–10) vol. II, p. 154.

[126] *Collected Poems*, pp. 75–83.

[127] Ibid. pp. 79–83.

[128] *The Life and Repentance of Mary Magdalene*, sig. Diiv–Diiir.

By Bushels was he wont to met his coyne
As did the olde wife of *Trimalchion*.   (ll. 39–42)[129]

Human improvidence allows such rogues to prosper:

The ding-thrift heire, his shift-got summe mispent,
Comes drouping like a pennylesse penitent,
And beats his faint fist on *Tocullios* doore,
It lost the last and now must call for more.   (ll. 59–62)[130]

The theme of the evils of covetousness in general[131] is treated in the traditional way in some interludes: Thomas Lupton's *All for Money* (1578, written 1560),[132] William Wager's *Enough is as good as a Feast* (1565?, written 1564?),[133] *The Trial of Treasure* (1567, written 1565?),[134] also possibly by William Wager, George Wapull's *The Tide tarrieth no Man* (1576, written 1576?),[135] Robert Wilson's *The Three Ladies of London* (1584, written 1581)[136] and *The Three Lords and Three Ladies of London* (1590, written 1589?).[137] In these late moralities, the old allegorical method of presentation is used, but they have some dramatic life, and very real earnestness. Bearing these plays in mind, it becomes even clearer that the ' anti-acquisitive ' attitude displayed in the plays of Ben Jonson, especially in his masterpieces *Volpone* (acted 1606) and *The Alchemist* (acted 1610),[138] is fully within the earlier tradition of moral poetry, drama and sermon.

The dishonest shifts of merchants, as in the sermons,[139] receive rebuke by George Gascoigne in *The Steele Glas* (ll. 750–98), where he castigates monopolies, lending wares at unreasonable rates, and oppressive treatment of apprentices.[140]

Extravagance in apparel, another traditional theme in sermon and poetry[141] is also denounced by Gascoigne in *The Steele Glas*:

Our bumbast hose, our treble double ruffes,
Our sutes of Silke, our comely garded capes,
Our knit silke stockes, and spanish lether shoes,
(Yea velvet serves, oft times to trample in)
Our plumes, our spangs, and al our queint aray,

---

[129] *Collected Poems*, pp. 66–7. For the sermon theme, see *ante*, p. 308.
[130] Ibid. p. 67.   [131] For the sermon theme, see *ante*, pp. 308–9.
[132] Ed. J. S. Farmer (London, 1910) T.F.T. [no. 49].
[133] Ed. S. de Ricci (New York, 1920) Huntington Fascimile.
[134] *A Select Collection of Old English Plays*, ed. Hazlitt, vol. III, pp. 257–301.
[135] Ed. J. S. Farmer (London, 1910) T.F.T. [no. 55].
[136] *A Select Collection of Old English Plays*, ed. Hazlitt, vol. VI, pp. 246–370.
[137] Ibid. pp. 372–502.
[138] See the illuminating discussion by L. C. Knights, in *Drama amd Society in the Age of Jonson* (London, 1937) pp. 200–27.
[139] See *ante*, p. 308.   [140] *Complete Works*, vol. II, pp. 162–3.
[141] See *ante*, p. 311.

Are pricking spurres, provoking filthy pride,
And snares (unseen) which leade a man to hel. (ll. 373–9)[142]

Hall, in *Virgidemiae*, devotes a satire to this topic (Bk. III, sat. v) in
the person of a ' lustie Courtier ' with a wig which is blown off by
the wind,[143] while Marston's best mocking vein is called forth in
ridicule of such follies:

O spruce! How now *Piso*, *Aurelius* Ape,
What strange disguise, what new deformed shape
Doth hold thy thoughts in contemplation?
Faith say, what fashion art thou thinking on?
A stitch'd Taffata cloake, a payre of slops
Of Spanish leather? O who heard his chops
Ere chew of ought, but of some strange disguise.
This fashion-mounger, each morne fore he rise
Contemplates sute shapes, & once from out his bed,
He hath them straight full liuely portraied.
And then he chukes, and is as proud of this,
As *Taphus* when he got his neighbours blisse.
All fashions since the first yeare of this Queene,
May in his studdie fairely drawne be seene,
And all that shall be to his day of doome,
You may peruse within that little roome.
For not a fashion once dare show his face,
But from neate *Pyso* first must take his grace.
The long fooles coat, the huge slop, the lugg'd boot
From mimick *Piso*, all doe claime their roote.
O that the boundlesse power of the soule
Should be coop'd vp in fashioning some roule![144]

Ulpian Fulwel in his interlude *Like will to Like* (1568, written 1568?)
makes the Vice Nichol Newfangle declare that the Devil taught him
all kinds of sciences which tend to the maintenance of pride, thus:

I learn'd to make gowns with long sleeves and wings:
I learn'd to make ruffs like calves' chitterlings,
Caps, hats, coats, with all kind of apparels,
And especially breeches as big as good barrels.
Shoes, boots, buskins, with many pretty toys:
All kind of garments for men, women, and boys. (ll. 59–64)[145]

The wanton ways of women, their taste for cosmetics and
provocative attire are satirized by poet and dramatist as well as by

---

[142] *Complete Works*, vol. II, pp. 152–3.
[143] *Collected Poems*, p. 39.
[144] *The Scourge of Villanie*, sat, xi, ll. 156–77 (*Poems*, p. 172). See also *The Meta-morphosis of Pygmalions Image and Certaine Satyres*, sat. iii, ll. 1–32 (ibid. pp. 77–8); *The Scourge of Villanie*, sat. vii, ll. 17–22, 30–1, 40 (ibid., pp. 140–1).
[145] *A Select Collection of Old English Plays*, ed. Hazlitt, vol. III, p. 310.

preacher.[146] Stephen Gosson in *Pleasant Quippes for Upstart New-fangled Gentlewomen* (1595) provides, as he puts it, 'A Pleasant Invective against the Fantastical Forreigne Toyes dayly used in Womens apparel '.[147] With denunciatory vigour he condemns the current fashions in detail, as:

> These perriwigges, ruffes armed with pinnes,
> > These spangles, chains, and laces all;
> These naked paps, the Devils ginnes,
> > To worke vaine gazers painfull thrall:
> > > He fowler is, they are his nets,
> > > Wherewith of fooles great store he gets.   (ll. 73–8)[148]

Marston, in *The Scourge of Villanie* (sat. vii), has a notable passage on this theme:

> *Peace*, Cynick, *see what yonder doth approach*,
> A cart, a tumbrell? *no a Badged coach.*
> What's in't? some man. *No, nor yet woman kinde,*
> *But a celestiall Angell, faire refinde.*
> The deuill as soone. Her maske so hinders mee
> I cannot see her beauties deitie.
> Now that is off, shee is so vizarded,
> So steep'd in Lemons-iuyce, so surphuled
> I cannot see her face, vnder one hood
> Too faces, but I neuer vnderstood
> Or saw, one face vnder two hoods till now,
> Tis the right semblance of old *Ianus* brow.
> > Her mask, her vizard, her loose-hanging gowne
> For her loose lying body, her bright spangled crown
> Her long slit sleeue, stuffe busk, puffe verdingall,
> Is all that makes her thus angelicall.
> Alas, her soule struts round about her neck,
> Her intellectuall is a fained nicenes
> Nothing but clothes, & simpering precisenes.   (ll. 160–79)[149]

Everard Guilpin in *Skialetheia* (1598) devotes an entire satire to the ridicule of such pride (sat. ii): it is useless now, he declares, to rely on cosmetics and extravagant dress in an effort to impress:

> (Madame) you gull your selfe, thinking to gull
> Young puisnes eyes with your ore-varnish'd scull:
> For now our Gallants are so cunning growne,
> That painted faces are like pippins knowne:
> > They know your spirits, & your distillations,

---

[146] For the sermon theme, see *ante*, p. 311.

[147] *Remains of the Early Popular Poetry of England*, ed. Hazlitt, vol. IV, p. 249. The poem is found ibid. pp. 249–62.

[148] Ibid. p. 252.   [149] *Poems*, pp. 145–6.

Which make your eies turn diamonds, to charm passions,
Your cerusse now growne stale, your skaine of silk,
Your philterd waters, and your asses milke,
They were plaine asses if they did not know,
   Quicksiluer, iuyce of Lemmons, Boras too,
Allom, oyle Tartan, whites of egges, & goules
Are made the bawdes to morphew, scurffs & scabs
Then whats a wench but a quirke, quidlit case,
Which makes a Painters pallat of her face?[150]

Lewis Wager in *The Life and Repentance of Mary Magdalene* touches on
this theme when Carnal Concupiscence, Infidelity, Pride and
Cupidity urge Mary to dress her hair in a wanton fashion, to have
recourse to cosmetics when her beauty begins to fade, to dress
provocatively and use alluring perfumes.[151] Hamlet's tirade to
Ophelia on ' painting ' (*Hamlet*, Act III, sc. i, ll. 148–57) is also
recognizably in the old homiletic tradition.[152] Ben Jonson's satur-
nine temperament finds in this theme a congenial subject for satire,
as for example in *Volpone* (Act II, sc. ii, ll. 223–48), when, in the
disguise of the mountebank Scoto of Mantua, Volpone describes the
marvellous properties of a powder which kept Venus perpetually
young, which was given to Helen but lost at the seige of Troy and
now recovered by an antiquary from some ruins in Asia, is offered
to his audience to preserve youth and restore age.[153] Perhaps, however, Jonson's most mordant scene on this topic is in *The Devil is an
Ass* ([acted 1616] Act IV, sc. iv), when, at Lady Tailbush's house,
Wittipol disguised as a Spanish lady details the ingredients of the
finest cosmetics of Spain:

> Your *Allum Scagliola*, or *Pol di pedra*;
> And *Zuccarino*; *Turpentine* of *Abezzo*,
> Wash'd in nine waters: *Soda di leuante*,
> Or your *Ferne* ashes; *Beniamin di gotta*;
> *Grasso di serpe*; *Porcelletto marino*;
> Oyles of *Lentisco*; *Zucche Mugia*; make
> The admirable *Vernish* for the face,
> Giues the right luster; but two drops rub'd on
> With a piece of scarlet, makes a *Lady* of sixty
> Looke at sixteen. (ll. 30–9)[154]

---

[150] *Skialetheia* [1598], (reptd. London, 1931) Shakespeare Association Facsimiles,
no. 2, sig. Cvi[r-v].
[151] *The Life and Repentance of Mary Magdalene*, sig. Ciii[v]–Dii[r].
[152] *Hamlet*, ed. Dowden [Arden] p. 105.
[153] *Ben Jonson*, ed. C. H. Herford, P. and E. Simpson, 11 vols. (Oxford, 1925–52)
vol. V, pp. 56–7.
[154] Ibid. vol. VI, p. 236.

The folly and impurity of the conversation which follows causes Pug the devil to exclaim:

> You talke of a *Vniuersity*! why, *Hell* is
> A grammar-schoole to this! (ll. 71–2)[155]

and Manly to go out with indignation declaring:

> What things they are! That nature should be at leasure
> Euer to make 'hem! my woing is at an end. (ll. 191–2)[156]

Luxurious living (as in the case of the preachers)[157] earns the condemnation of Hall in *Virgidemiae* (Bk. III, sat. iii). in the description of an over elaborate dinner:

> O: *Cleopatricall*: what wanteth there
> For curious cost, and wondrous choise of cheare?
> Beefe, that earst *Hercules* held for finest fare:
> Porke for the fat *Boeotian*, or the hare
> For *Martiall*: fish for the *Venetian*,
> Goose liuer for the likerous *Romane*,
> Th'*Athenians* goate, Quaile, *Iolaus* cheere,
> The *Hen for Esculape*, and the *Parthian Deere*,
> Grapes for *Arcesilas*, figs for *Platoes* mouth.
> And Chestnuts faire for *Amarillis* tooth. (ll. 167–6)[158]

This is a major theme in Ben Jonson; the ironically exaggerated swelling speeches of Volpone when tempting Celia (*Volpone*, Act III, sc. vii, ll. 186–225)[159] or of Sir Epicure Mammon when contemplating the delights which he hopes will be his when the alchemist is successful in his experiments (*The Alchemist*, Act II, sc. ii, ll. 41–94, Act IV, sc. i, ll. 134–69),[160] are clearly influenced by the sermon tradition.

The *ubi sunt* and death theme in the sermons[161] continues to be paralleled in poetry and drama. Some lines in ' Though Fortune haue sette thee on hie, Remember yet that thou shalt die ' in *The Paradise of Dainty Devices* (1576), echo the ancient sentiments:

> Death hath in all the earth aright,
> His power is great, it stretcheth farre:
> No Lord, no Prince, can scape his might,
> No creature can his duetie barre.

---

[155] Ibid. p. 241.
[156] Ibid. Cf. also *The Devil is an Ass*, Act II, sc. viii, ll. 34–6, Act IV, sc. iii, ll. 24–46, ibid., pp. 207, 234. See further, *Sejanus*, Act II, ll. 60–84, 124–31 (ibid. vol. IV, pp. 377, 379); *Volpone*, Act III, sc. iv, ll. 32–8 (ibid. vol. V, p. 72); *Cataline*, Act. II ll. 2–15, 60–75 (ibid. pp. 454, 456).
[157] See *ante*, p. 313.   [158] *Collected Poems*, p. 37.
[159] *Ben Jonson*, vol. V, pp. 83–4.
[160] Ibid. pp. 319–20, 363–4. See too *The Staple of News*, Act III, sc. iv, ll. 45–64 (ibid. vol. VI, p. 342).
[161] See *ante*, pp. 314–15.

The wise, the iust, the strong, the hie,
The chast, the meeke, the free of hart,
The rich, the poore, who can denie,
Haue yeelded all vnto his dart.

Could *Hercules* that tamde eache wight?
Or else *Vlisses* with his witte?
Or *Ianus* who had all foresight?
Or chast *Hypolit* scape the pitte?
Could *Cresus* with his bagges of golde?
Or *Irus* with his hungrie paine?
Or *Signus* through his hardinesse bolde?
Driue back the dayes of Death againe.   (ll. 16–32)[162]

George Gascoigne in *Gascoynes good night* sadly compares going to bed with death:

The stretching armes, the yauning breath, which I to bedward use,
Are patternes of the pangs of death, when life will me refuse:
And of my bed eche sundrye part in shaddowes doth resemble,
The sundry shapes of deth, whose dart shal make my flesh to tremble.
My bed it selfe is like the grave, my sheetes the winding sheete,
My clothes the mould which I must have, to cover me most meete:
The hungry fleas which friske so freshe, to wormes I can compare,
Which greedily shall gnawe my fleshe, & leave the bones ful bare: . . .   (ll. 23–30)[163]

Thomas Nashe, in *Summer's Last Will and Testament* (1600), gives an exquisite lyric on the old theme with the famous stanza:

Beauty is but a flowre,
Which wrinckles will deuoure,
Brightnesse falls from the ayre,
Queenes haue died yong and faire,
Dust hath closed *Helens* eye.
I am sick, I must die:
Lord haue mercy on vs.   (ll. 15–21)[164]

The 'Gravedigger' scene in *Hamlet* ([acted 1601] Act V, sc. i), with the prince's meditations on Yorick's skull,[165] can be recognised

---

[162] *The Paradise of Dainty Devices*, ed. H. E. Rollins (Cambridge, Mass., 1927) p. [40]. See too in the same collection, ' Our pleasures are vanities ' (p. [9]); ' Though Fortune haue sette thee on hie, Remember yet that thou shalt die ' (pp. [39]–[40]).

[163] *Complete Works*, vol. I, pp. 58–9.

[164] *Works*, ed. McKerrow, vol III., pp. 282–4.

[165] *Hamlet*, Arden edn., pp. 187–97.

as the product of a long preaching and poetic tradition. Vindice's profound speeches to the skull of his dead mistress in Tourneur's *The Revenger's Tragedy* (1607) are also obviously in the same tradition:

> Does euery proud and selfe-affecting Dame
> Camphire her face for this, and grieue her Maker
> In sinfull baths of milke?—when many an infant starues
> For her superfluous out-side, all for this?
> Who now bids twenty pounds a night, prepares
> Musick, perfumes, and sweete-meates? All are husht.
> Thou maist lie chast now! It were fine me-thinkes
> To haue thee seene at Reuells, forgetfull feasts
> And uncleane Brothells! sure 'twould fright the sinner
> And make him a good coward; put a Reueller
> Out of his Antick amble,
> And cloye an Epicure with empty dishes!
>
> (Act. III, sc. v, ll. 86–97)[166]

In Ben Jonson the influence of Horace blends with the native tradition as (in *The Devil is an Ass*) in Meercraft's speech to Fitz-dottrell, who aspiring to be the Duke of the Drowned-land declares ' *Drown'd-lands* will liue in *Drown'd-land*! ':

> MER.   Yes when you
>   Ha' no foote left; as that must be, Sir, one day.
>   And, though it tarry in your heyres, some *forty*,
>   Fifty descents, the longer liuer, at last, yet,
>   Must thrust 'hem out on't: if no quirk in law,
>   Or odde *Vice* o' their owne not do it first.
>   Wee see those changes, daily: the faire lands,
>   That were the *Clyents*, are the *Lawyers*, now:
>   And those rich Mannors, there, of good man *Taylors*,
>   Had once more wood vpon 'hem, then the yard,
>   By which they were measur'd out for the last purchase.
>   Nature hath these vicissitudes. Shee makes
>   No man a state of perpetuity, Sir. (Act II, sc. iv, ll. 29–39)[167]

It seems that the ' mutability ' theme in Spenser owes something to preaching and the popular tradition as well as to classical sources. Colin's lament in the November Eclogue of *The Shepherds Calender* (1579) is obviously in an old native tradition:

[166] *The Plays and Poems of Cyril Tourneur*, ed. J. C. Collins, 2 vols. (London, 1878) vol. II, p. 84. See too *The Revenger's Tragedy*, Act I, sc. i, ll. 14–29 (ibid. p. 6).
[167] *Ben Jonson*, vol. VI, p. 199; cf. Horace, Sat. II. 2, ll. 129–32; also generally, Odes. I. iv, I. xxviii. Cf. further, *Volpone*, Act I, sc. ii, ll. 17–21; also *The Devil is an Ass*, Act I, sc. iii, ll. 129–31, and Odes I. xi, ll. 7–8. See the discussion of this theme Horatian influence on Jonson in L. C. Knights, *Drama and Society in the Age of Jonson*, pp. 193–4, 195–8.

O trustlesse state of earthly things, and slipper hope
Of mortal men, that swincke and sweate for nought,
And shooting wide, doe misse the marked scope:
Now haue I learned (a lesson derely bought)
That nys on earth assurance to be sought: . . . (ll. 153–7)[168]

Similarly the poet's sad reflection on Venus's powerlessness to save
her brood from the ravages of Time in the Gardens of Adonis
seems partly prompted by this same tradition:

For all that liues, is subiect to that law:
All things decay in time, and to their end do draw.
(*The Faerie Queene*, III. vi, stanza 40)[169]

The vanity and sadness of life, as in the sermons,[170] is expressed
in poetry and drama. For example, Lord Vaux's poem, 'Beyng
asked the occasion of his white head, he aunswereth thus' in *The
Paradise of Dainty Devices*, exhibits a traditional sadness:

Where wretched woe doeth weaue her webbe,
There care the clewe, can catche and caste:
And floudds of ioye are fallen to ebbe
So loe, that life maie not long laste.
What wonder then, though you doe see,
Vpon my head white heeres to bee.   (ll. 19–24)[171]

The disguised Duke's speech to the condemned Claudio in prison
(*Measure for Measure*, [acted 1604] Act III, sc. i, ll. 6–41) is the handling by the master dramatist of the old commonplaces:

... Reason thus with life:
If I do lose thee, I do lose a thing
That none but fools would keep: a breath thou art,
Servile to all the skyey influences,
That dost this habitation where thou keep'st
Hourly afflict:............................
..........................Thou are not noble,
For all th'accommodations that thou bear'st,
Are nursed by baseness. Thou'rt by no means valiant,
For thou dost fear the soft and tender fork
Of a poor worm: thy best of rest is sleep,
And that thou oft provok'st, yet grossly fear'st
Thy death, which is no more, Thou art not thyself,

---

[168] *Poetical Works*, p. 462.
[169] Ibid. p. 175.   See too *The Faerie Queene*, Bk. VII ['Two Cantos of Mutabilitie']
canto vi, stanzas 1–6, canto vii, stanzas 17–56, canto viii, stanza 1 (ibid. pp. 394–5,
401–5, 406); *The Ruines of Time*, ll. 1–588 (ibid. pp. 471–7); *Daphnaida*, ll. 393–518
(ibid., pp. 532–3); *Astrophel. A Pastorall Elegie*, ll. 49–60 (ibid. p. 549).
[170] See *ante*, pp. 315–17.
[171] *The Paradise of Dainty Devices*, p. [53]. See too Francis Kinwelmarsh, 'All thinges
ar Vaine' (ibid. p. [41]).

For thou exists on many a thousand grains
...............................Thou hast nor youth nor age,
But as it were an after-dinner's sleep,
Dreaming on both—for all thy blessed youth
Becomes as aged, and doth beg the alms
Of palsied eld: and when thou art old and rich,
Thou hast neither heat, affection, limb, nor beauty,
To make thy riches pleasant . . . [172]

When one turns to the happier themes of this time, one notes that the praise of Queen Elizabeth in the sermons[173] is strikingly echoed in poetry and drama, from simple broadside ballads to the mannered eloquence of Spenser's *Faerie Queene* (1590–6) and the courtly compliment of Ben Jonson's *Every Man out of his Humour* (acted 1599).[174] The new wholesomeness of tone and fragrant spirituality in the preaching of Hooker and Andrewes[175] contributes to the development of the distinctively Anglican piety found most notably in the poetry of George Herbert.

It will have been amply demonstrated, I hope, that preaching certainly was an important influence on the minds of the poets and dramatists of the late fifteenth and sixteenth centuries, together with some of the early seventeenth century,and that while it would be mistaken to over-stress this influence, nevertheless it is more pervasive and powerful than has been generally recognized.

[172] Ed. H. C. Hart (London, 1905) The Arden Shakespeare pp. 61–4.
[173] See *ante*, p. 317.
[174] See the numerous passages quoted in E. C. Wilson, *England's Eliza* (Cambridge, Mass., 1939).
[175] See *ante*, pp. 319–20.

BIBLIOGRAPHY

Contents

I. TEXTS OF SERMONS, 1450–c. 1600

[*Note*. Where there is more than one edition of a particular work, the edition listed below is that which has been used in this study. In the case of printed sermons of the Elizabethan period, as there already is the very full and detailed list of these in A. F. Herr, *The Elizabethan Sermon, a Survey and a Bibliography* (Philadelphia, 1940) here I merely supplement this list by giving certain later editions of various preachers which I have found it convenient to use.]

(i) SERMONS IN ENGLISH.
    (*a*) Printed texts.
        1. 1450–1558.

ALCOCK, John, Bp.   [Desponsacio virginis christo. Spousage of a virgin to Cryste.] An exhortacyon made to Relygyous systers in the tyme of theyr consecracyon by the Reuerende fader in god Iohan Alcok bysshop of Ely (Westminster, [n.d.]).
In Die Innocencium Sermo pro Episcopo Puerorum, ed. J. G. Nichols, *Camden Society Miscellany*, vol. VII (London, 1875) C.S. new series, XIV; ' Two Sermons preached by the Boy Bishop, at St. Paul's Temp. Henry VII, and at Gloucester, Temp. Mary,' pp. 1–13.
    [This sermon is attributed to Alcock by the *S.T.C.* (no. 282) but it is probably not by him.]
Mons perfectionis otherwyse in Englysshe the hylle of perfeccyon. Exhortacio facta Cartusiensibus et alijs religiosis per venerandum in christo patrem et dominum Iohannem Alcok Eliensis episcopum (Westminster, 1497).

BONNER, Edmund, Bp.   A profitable and necessarye doctryne, with certayne homelies adioyned therevnto set forth by the reuerende father in God, Edmonde, byshop of London, for the instruction and enformation of the people being within his diocese of London (London, 1555).

BRADFORD, John   The Writings of John Bradford, M.A. Fellow of Pembroke Hall, Cambridge, and Prebendary of S. Paul's, Martyr 1555, ed. A. Townsend, 2 vols., (Cambridge, 1848–53) P.S. [vol. I contains the sermons].

BROOKS, James, Bp.   A sermon very notable, fruictefull, and Godlie, made at Paules crosse the xii daie of Nouembre, in the first yere of the gracious reigne of our Souereigne ladie Quene Marie her moste excellente highnesse, by Iames Brokis Doctor of Diuinitie, and Master of Bailye College in Oxforth . . . (London, 1553).

CHEDSEY, William, and   Two notable sermones lately preached at Pauls crosse. Anno
SCOTT, Cuthbert   1544. . . . Ouerseen and perused by the byshop of London . . . (London, 1545). [The first sermon is by Chedsey, the second by Scott. (Not in the *S.T.C.*, Peterborough Cath. Libr., F. 4. 22)].

COLE, Thomas   A godly Sermon, made at Maydstone the fyrste sonday in Lent (London, 1553).

COLET, John   The Sermon of Doctor Colete, made to the Conuocacion at Paulis (London, [n.d.])
    [Text in J. H. Lupton, *A Life of John Colet*, new edn. (London, 1909) Appendix C, pp. 293–304. This is a translation; the original sermon was delivered in Latin. For that text, see *post*, p. 356].

EDGEWORTH, Roger   Sermons very fruitfull, godly, and learned, preached, and set forth by Master Roger Edgeworth, Dr. of Diuinity, Canon of the Cathedral Churches of Sarisbury, Wells, and Bristow,

EDGEWORTH, Roger *cont.* — Residentiary in the Cathedral Church of Wells, and Chancellour of the same Church . . . (London, 1557).

FECKENHAM, John de [i.e. John HOWMAN] — A notable sermon made within S. Paules church in London, in the presence of certen of the kinges and Quenes moost honorable priuie counsel at the celebration of the exequies of the right excellent and famous Princesse, Lady Ione, Quene of Spayne, Sicilie and Nauarre, etc., the XVIII of Iune, Anno 1555 . . . (London, [1555]).
Two Homilies vpon the first, second, and third articles of the Crede, made by maister Iohn Fecknam. Deane of Paules . . . (London, [1555?]).

FISHER, John, Saint — The English Works of John Fisher, Part I, ed. J. E. B. Mayor (London, reptd. 1935) E.E.T.S., e.s. xxvii.
Here after ensueth two fruytfull sermons, made & compyled by the ryght Reuerende father in god, Iohan Fyssher—Doctour of Dyuynyte and Bysshop of Rochester . . . (London 1532).

FITZJAMES, Richard, Bp. — Sermo die lune in ebdomada Pasche. (Westminster, 1495); facsimile by Francis Jenkinson (Cambridge, 1907).

GILPIN, Bernard — A Godly sermon preached in the Court at Greenwich the firste Sonday after the Epiphanie, Anno Domini, 1552 . . . (London, 1581).

GLASIER, Hugh — A notable and very fruictefull Sermon made at Paules Crosse the XXV day of August, by Maister Hugh Glasier, Chapleyn to the Quenes most excellent maiestie, Perused by the reuerende father in god Edmond bishop of London, and by him approued, commended, and greatly liked: and therefore nowe set furth in print by his auctoritie and commaundement (London, 1555).

HARPESFIELD, John — A notable and learned Sermon or Homilie, made vpon saint Andrewes daye last paste 1556 in the Cathedral churche of S. Paule in London, by Mayster Iohn Harpesfield doctour of diuinitie and Canon residenciary of the sayd churche, Set furth by the bishop of London . . . (London, 1556).

HOMILIES, the First and Second Book of — Certain Sermons Appointed by the Queen's Majesty to be declared and read by all Parsons, Vicars and Curates, every Sunday and Holiday in their Churches . . . ed. G. E. Corrie (Cambridge, 1850).

HOOPER, John, Bp. — Early Writings of John Hooper, D.D., Lord Bishop of Gloucester and Worcester, Martyr 1555, ed. S. Carr (Cambridge, 1843) P.S.

HUTCHINSON, Roger — The Works of Roger Hutchinson, Fellow of St. John's College, Cambridge, and afterwards of Eton College, A.D. 1550, ed. J. Bruce (Cambridge, 1842) P.S.

LATIMER, Hugh, Bp. — Sermons by Hugh Latimer, sometime Bishop of Worcester, Martyr, 1555, ed. G. E. Corrie (Cambridge, 1844) P.S.
Sermons and Remains of Hugh Latimer, sometime Bishop of Worcester, Martyr, 1555, ed. G. E. Corrie (Cambridge, 1845) P.S.
[Although these volumes have different title pages, they form a pair, and the index to both is in vol. II.]

LEVER, Thomas — Sermons, 1550, ed. E. Arber (Westminster, 1895).

LONGLAND, John, Bp.   A sermond made be for the kynge hys hyghnes at Ryche-munte vppon good fryday, the yeare of our lorde MCCCCCXXXVI, by Iohan Longlond, Byshope of Lincoln . . . (London, [1535?]). [The date of this sermon is probably 1535; see *T.L.S.*, 31st Dec. 1931. Not in *S.T.C.*, copies in the libraries of Trinity College, Cambridge, and Christ Church, Oxford.]
A Sermond spoken before the kynge his maiestie at Gren-wiche, vppon good fryday: the yere of our Lord. MCCCCC XXXVj. by Iohan Longland byshope of Lincolne (London, 1536).
A Sermonde made before the Kynge, his maiestye at Grene-wiche, vpon good Frydaye. The yere of our Lorde God. M.D. xxxviij. By Iohan Longlonde, busshope of Lincolne (London, 1538).

MATTHEW, Simon   A sermon made in the Cathedrall church of saynt Paule at London, the xxvii day of Iune, anno. 1535 . . . (London, 1535).

PERYN, William   Thre godly and notable Sermons of the moost honorable and blessed Sacrament of the Aulter. Preached in the Hospitall of Saynt Antony in London by Wyllyam Peryn preest, bacheler of diuinitie . . . (London, 1546).

POLE, Reginald, Card.   Cardinal Pole's speech to the citizens of London, in behalf of religious houses. [incomplete]. In John Strype, *Ecclesiastical Memorials*, 3 vols., (Oxford, 1822) vol. III, pt. 2, 'A Catalogue of Originals,' no. LXVIII, pp. 428–510.

POLLARD, Leonard   Fyue homilies of late made by a ryght good and vertuous clerke, called Leonarde Pollarde, prebendary of the Cathedral Churche of Woster, directed and dedicated to the ryght reuerende father in God Rychard by the permissyon of God byshoppe of Woster his specyall good Lorde . . . (London, 1556) [The signature numbering in this volume is disordered. What should be marked Dii (counting from the first leaf and following the earlier numbering) is marked Ciii; Eii is marked Civ, Eiii^{r} is blank, only the verso being printed; then Eiv is again marked Ciii. After this however the numbers run on consecutively. For this reason in the references to this volume I give two signature numbers, that as marked, and that counting from the first page.]

POSTILS, [anon.]   Title-page missing; the colophon runs: ' The ende of this brefe Postyl, vpon the Epistles and Gospelles of all the Sudayes in the yeare.' [This volume is not in *S.T.C.*; it bears the device of Grafton (R. B. McKerrow, *Printers' and Publishers' Devices in England and Scotland* 1485–1640, no. 88) and is in the possession of Mr. J. I. Bromwich of St. John's College, Cambridge].

POYNET, John, Bp.   A notable sermon concerning the ryght vse of the lordes supper and other thinges very profitable for all men to knowe . . . (London, 1550).

SCOTT, Cuthbert, Bp.   [See above, under William Chedsey, Two notable sermones lately preached at Pauls crosse.]

SERMONS, [anon.]   Sermon of the Child Bishop, pronownsyd by John Stubs, Querester, on Childremasse Day, at Gloceter, 1558, ed. J. G. Nichols, *Camden Society Miscellany*, vol. VII, pp. 14–29.

Aa

SINGLETON, Robert   A sermon preached at Poules crosse the fourth sonday in
                       lent. The yere of our lorde God 1535 by Ro. Singleton
                       (London, 1536).

TAVERNER, Richard   Postils on the Epistles and Gospels compiled and published
                       by Richard Taverner in the year 1540, ed. E. Cardwell
                       (Oxford, 1841).

TUNSTALL, Cuthbert,   A Sermon of Cuthbert Bysshop of Duresme, made vpon
Bp.   Palme sondaye laste paste, before the maiestie of our
                       souerayne lorde kynge Henry the VIII kynge of France,
                       defensor of the fayth, lorde of Irelande, and in erthe next
                       vnder Christ supreme heed of the Churche of Englande
                       (London, 1539).

WATSON, Thomas, Bp.   Twoo notable Sermons, made the thirde and fyfte Fridayes
                       in Lent last past, before the Quenes highnes, concerninge
                       the reall presence of Christes body and bloude in the blessed
                       Sacrament: & also the Masse, which is the sacrifice of the
                       newe Testament . . . (London, 1554).
                       Holsome and Catholyke doctryne concerning the seuen
                       Sacraments of Chrystes Church expedient to be knowen of
                       all men, set forth in the maner of short sermons to bee made
                       to the people . . . (London, [1558]).

WHITE, John, Bp.   A sermon preached at the funerals of Queen Mary: by the
                       Bishop of Winchester. [In Strype, *Ecclesiastical Memorials*,
                       III, 2, 'A Catalogue of Originals,' no. LXXXI, pp. 536–50].

    (2.) 1558–c. 1600—editions used other than in A. F. Herr, *The Elizabethan Sermon, a
Survey and a Bibliography* (Philadelphia, 1940).

ANDREWES, Lancelot,   XCVI Sermons by the Right Honourable and Reuerend
Bp.   Father in God, Lancelot Andrewes, late Lord Bishop of
                       Winchester, 2nd edn., (London, 1632).

CARTWRIGHT, Thomas A Dilucidation, or Exposition of the Epistle of St. Paul the
                   Apostle to the Colossians, deliuered in sundry sermons, ed.
                   A. B. Grosart (Edinburgh, 1864).

GRINDAL, Edmund,   The Remains of Edmund Grindal, D.D., successively
Abp.   Bishop of London, and Archbishop of York and Canterbury,
                       ed. W. Nicholson (Cambridge, 1843) P.S.

HOOKER, Richard   The Works of that Learned and Judicious Divine, Mr.
                       Richard Hooker, ed. J. Keble, 2nd edn., 3 vols. (Oxford,
                       1841) [Vol. III contains the sermons.]

JEWEL, John, Bp.   The Works of John Jewel, Bishop of Salisbury, ed. J. Ayre,
                       4 vols. (Cambridge, 1845–50) P.S. [Vols. I and II contain the
                       sermons.]

KING, John, Bp.   Lectures upon Jonah, delivered at York, in the year of our
                       Lord 1594, ed. A. B. Grosart (Edinburgh, 1864).

PERKINS, William   The Works of that famous and worthy Minister of Christ in
                       the Vniuersitie of Cambridge, M. William Perkins . . .
                       (London, 1631) [The Elizabethan sermons in vol. III.]

PLAYFERE, Thomas   The whole sermons of That Eloquent Diuine, of Famous
                       Memory; Thomas Playfere . . . Gathered into one vollume
                       . . . (London, 1623).
                           This is a composite volume, the contents and pagination
                       being as follows:

PLAYFERE, Thomas
cont.

1. The Meane in Mourning. [Preached 1595, Printed at London, 1623; pp. 1–121.]
2. Pathway to Perfection. [Preached 1593, Printed at London, 1623; pp. 123–232.]
3. Hearts Delight. [Preached 1593, Printed at London, 1617; pp. 1–47.]
4. The Power of Praier. [Preached 1596, Printed at London, 1617; pp. 1–36.]
5. The Sick-Mans Couch. [Preached 1604, Printed at London, 1617; pp. 1–84.]

The next items are in one collection:

Nine Sermons. Preached by that eloquent Diuine of famous memorie. Th. Playfere Doctor in Diuinitie, Cambridge, 1621, pp. 1–261.

6. Gods Blessing is Enough. [Preached 1604, pp. 1–27.]
7. Glorie waighes downe the Crosse. [Preached 1604, pp. 28–52.]
8. God be with you. [Preached 1604, pp. 33–71.]
9. Christs wounds our health. [Preached 1598, pp. 72–112.]
10. Say well, doe well. [pp. 113–42.]
11. The kinges Crowne. [Preached 1605, pp. 143–71.]
12. Good Ground. [Preached 1605, pp. 172–94.]
13. The felicitie of the faithfull. [Preached 1605, pp. 195–237.]
14. Difference betweene Law and Gospel. [Preached 1604, pp. 238–61.]

RAINOLDS, John

The Prophecy of Obadiah opened and applied in sundry sermons, ed. A. B. Grosart (Edinburgh, 1864).
The Prophecy of Haggai interpreted in sundry sermons, ed. A. B. Grosart (Edinburgh, 1864).

SANDYS, Edwin, Abp.

The Sermons of Edwin Sandys, D.D., successively Bishop of Worcester and London, and Archbishop of York . . . ed. J. Ayre (Cambridge, 1841) P.S.

SMITH, Henry

The Sermons of Mr. Henry Smith: Gathered into one Volume . . . and the life of Mr. Henry Smith, by Tho. Fuller, B.D. (London, 1657).
Twelve Sermons, preached by Mr. Henry Smith (London, 1657) [The pagination of this volume is consecutive with that of The Sermons, above.]
Three Sermons made by Mr. Henry Smith (London, 1642).

WHITGIFT, John, Abp.

The Works of John Whitgift, D.D., Master of Trinity College, Dean of Lincoln, etc. Afterwards successively Bishop of Worcester and Archbishop of Canterbury, ed. J. Ayre, 3 vols. (Cambridge, 1851–3) P.S. [vol. III contains two sermons.]

(*b*) Manuscript texts.

MS. Bodley 119.

A sermon on Matt. v. 20, defending the use of images. Early 16th century.

MS. Gough Eccl. Top. 7

Part of a sermon on the plague, wanting the end and perhaps a leaf at the beginning. c. 1600.

MS. Harleian 131.

A sermon by Dr. John Taylor, Master of the Rolls, on Luke ii. 22–4, for Candlemas day 1508.

MS. Harleian 2247.

A late 15th century revision of Mirk's *Festial*, containing many new sermons. [See Lilian L. Steckman, 'A Late Fifteenth-century Revision of Mirk's *Festial*', *S.P.*, xxxiv. (1936) pp. 35–48].

MS. Harleian 2321.

[ff. 16–32]. A sermon at Syon on indulgences. Mid-late 15th century.

MS. Harleian 3118.

[ff. 113–39] A sermon on John viii. 46, containing an attack on Luther. c. 1520?

MS. Hatton 93.

[ff. 10–91]. A series of *De Tempore* sermons. The inclusion of sermons for the feasts of St. Wulfstan and St. Oswald suggest that the series was compiled in the Worcester diocese. Late 15th century.

MS. Lambeth 392.

[ff. 148ʳ–218ᵛ]. A series of *De Tempore* sermons. Late 15th century.

MS. Lambeth 488.

[ff. 46–48]. A sermon on Rom. vi. 3, on Baptism, defending the use of the sign of the cross in the Anglican ceremonial. Late 16th century.
[ff. 74–85]. A sermon on Jude 22–3, against the recusants. Late 16th century.

MS. Vat. Lat. 5968. [MS. microfilm 33, Bodleian Library].

This contains (along with other items) homilies by Cardinal Pole.

MS. Cotton Vitellius E. X.

[ff. 141ʳ–4ᵛ]. A sermon at the opening of Parliament, on Rom. xii. 4. c. 1483.

(ii) SERMONS IN LATIN.
(*a*) Printed texts.
(1450–1558).

ALCOCK, John, Bp.

Gallicantus Iohannis Alcok Episcopi Eliensis ad confrates suos curatos in sinodo apud Bernwell. xxv. die mensis Septembris. Anno millesimo. cccc. nonagesimo octauo (London, [1498]).

BARON, Stephen

Sermones Declamati coram alma vniuersitate Cantabrigiensi per venerandum patrem fratrem Stephanum baronis fratrum minorum de obseruantia nuncupatorum regni Anglie prouincialem vicarium ac confessorem regium, diligenter impressi in achademia parrhisiensi. In quibus imprimendis ordo prioris impressionis non sine consilio quibusdam in locis mutatus extitit (Paris, [after 1508]).

COLET, John

Oratio habita ad clerum in Conuocatione, Anno 1511 (London, 1511).

GARDINER, Stephen, Bp.

Excerpta per R.D. Archdiac. Cantuariensis ex Concione quam Reuerendus D. Episcopus Wintoniensis Cancellarius Regni Angliae habuit prima Dominica Aduentus Londini in Coemeterio D. Pauli in maxima populi frequentia presentibus Sereniss. Lege and Reuerendo Legato (Rome, 1555).

HARPESFIELD, John

Concio quaedam admodum elegans, docta, salubris, & pia, magistri Iohannis Harpesfeldi, . . . habita coram patribus et clero in Ecclesia Paulina Londini. 26. Octobris. 1553 . . . (London, 1553).

LONGLAND, John, Bp. Ioannis Longlondi Dei Gratia Lincolniensis Episcopi, tres conciones reuerendissimo Domino. do. waramo Cantuariensi Archiepiscopo totius Angliae primatie merito nuncupatae (London, [1527?]).

[In the same volume and with consecutive pagination: Quinque Sermones Ioannis Longlondi Theologie professoris, dei gratia Lincolniensis Episcopi, sextis quadragesime ferijs habiti coram illustrissimi regis Henrici octaui, fidei defensoris inuictissimi summa maiestate: cui est a confessionibus. Anno. Do. M.D. XVII.]

Sermones Ioannis Longlondi Theologie professoris, dei gratia Lincolniensis Episcopi, habiti coram illustrissimi regis Henrici octaui, fidei defensoris inuictissimi summa maiestate, cui est a confessionibus (London, [1518–32?]).

This is a composite volume containing sermons on the Penitential Psalms, issued in successive years, but with consecutive pagination. The contents are as follows: ff. 1–52, Sermon on Ps. vi; preached 1518 (Pynson, 1518): ff. 53–109, Sermon on Ps. xxxi (Vg.), preached 1519 (Pynson, [1519?]): ff. 109–98, Sermon on Ps. xxxviii (Vg.), preached 1520 (Pynson, [1521?]): ff. 198–351, Sermon on Ps. l (Vg.), preached partly in 1521, partly in 1522 (Pynson, [1522?]): ff. 351–864, Sermon on Ps. ci (Vg.), preached in parts, 1523, 1524, 1525, 1526, 1527, 1528, 1529 (Redman? [1532?]).

MELTON, William de Sermo exhortatorius cancellarij Eboracensis hijs qui ad sacros ordines petunt promoueri (Westminster, 1508).

TUNSTALL, Cuthbert, Bp. Cuthberti Tonstalli in laudem matrimonii oratio, habita in sponsalibus Mariae Potentissimi regis Angliae Henrici octaui filiae, et Francisci Christianissimi Francorum regis primogeniti (London, 1518).

WESTON, Hugh Magistri Hugonis Westoni, decani Westmonasterii, oratio, coram patribus et clero in synodo congregatis habita. [In Strype, *Ecclesiastical Memorials*, III. 2, ' Catalogue of Originals,' no. VIII, pp. 182–9].

(b) Manuscript texts.

MS. Harleian 3118. [ff. 4–87] A collection of *De Tempore* sermons.
MS. Lambeth 488. [ff. 129–42] A sermon to Convocation on John ii. 17. Late 16th century.

II. WORKS CONTAINING SUMMARIES OR BRIEF NOTICES OF SERMONS REFERRED TO, 1450–c. 1600

[Anon.] Chronicle of the Grey Friars of London, ed. J. G. Nichols (London, 1852) C.S., no. LIII.

FOXE, J. The Acts and Monuments [of Matters happening in the Church], ed. J. Pratt, 4th edn., 8 vols. (London, [1877]).

MACHYN, H. The Diary of Henry Machyn, Citizen and Merchant-Taylor of London, from A.D. 1550 to A.D. 1563, ed. J. G. Nichols (London, 1848) C.S., no. XLII.

MACLURE, M. The Paul's Cross Sermons, 1534–1642 (Toronto, 1958).

STOWE, J. Survey of London, introd. by H. B. Wheatley (London, revised 1956) Everyman.

WRIOTHESLEY, C.   A Chronicle of England during the reigns of the Tudors from A.D. 1485 to1559, ed. W.D. Hamilton, 2 vols. (London, 1875–7) C.S., new series, nos. XI and XX.

III. TEXTS OF REPRESENTATIVE SERMONS OF THE MIDDLE AGES
(i) English.
[Anon.]   Jacob's Well, an Englisht Treatise on the Cleansing of Man's conscience . . . ed. A. Brandeis (London, 1900), E.E.T.S., o.s. 115.

[Anon.]   Middle English Sermons, edited from British Museum MS. Royal 18B. xxiii by W. O. Ross (London, 1940) E.E.T.S., o.s. 209.

MIRK, John   Mirk's Festial: a collection of homilies by Johannes Mirkus (John Mirk) . . . Part I, ed. T. E. Erbe (London, 1905), E.E.T.S., e.s. xcvi.

(ii) Latin.
BRINTON or   The Sermons of Thomas Brinton, Bishop of Rochester
BRUNTON, Thomas,   (1373–1389), ed. Sister Mary Aquinas Devlin, 2 vols.
Bp.   (London, 1954) C.S., third series, nos. LXXXV–VI.

IV. ARTES PRAEDICANDI
(i) Patristic.
AUGUSTINE, St.   De Doctrina Christiana, lib. IV, P.L., xxxiv. 89–122.

(ii) Medieval.
BASEVORN, Robert de   Forma Praedicandi. [In Th. M. Charland, Artes Praedicandi, Contribution à l'histoire de la Rhétorique au Moyen Âge (Paris and Ottawa, 1936)].

HENRY, of Hesse   ' " Henry of Hesse " on the Art of Preaching,' ed. and tr. H. Caplan, P.M.L.A., xlviii. 2 (1933), pp. 340–61.

[Anon.] derived from   'A Brief Forma Praedicandi,' ed. W. O. Ross, M.P., xxxiv,
JOHN, of Wales   (1933), pp. 337–44.

THOMAS, St., Aquinas   'A Late Mediaeval Tractate on Preaching, the Pseudo-Aquinas Tract,' ed. and tr. H. Caplan, in Studies in Rhetoric and Public Speaking in honour of James Albert Winans (New York, 1925), pp. 61–90.

WALEYS, Thomas   De Modo Componendi Sermones. [In Charland, Artes Praedicandi.]
(See further, Chapter II, note 1.)

(iii) Sixteenth and early seventeenth century.
ERASMUS, Desiderius   Desiderii Erasmi Roterodami Ecclesiastae sive de Ratione Concionandi Libri Quatuor, ed. F. A. Klein (Leipzig, 1820).

GERARDUS, Andreas   The practis of preaching, otherwise called the pathway to
(' HYPERIUS ')   the pulpet. . . . Written in Latin . . . by A. H., and Englished by I. Ludham . . . (London, 1577).

KECKERMANN,   Rhetoricae Ecclesiasticae, siue Artis Formandi et Habendi
Bartholomew   Conciones Sacras, Libri Duo: Methodice Adornati per Praecepta & Explicationes . . . Editio Tertia . . . (Hanover, 1606).

LUIS, de Granada   Ecclesiasticae Rhetoricae, siue de ratione concionandi, libri sex (Cologne, 1582).

OSIANDER, Lucas   De Ratione Concionandi . . . (Tübingen, 1582).

PERKINS, William   The Art of Prophecying or a treatise concerning the sacred and onely true maner and method of preaching.... First written in latine by Mr. William Perkins; and now faithfully translated into English . . . by Thomas Tuke (*Works*, 1631, vol. III, pp. 642–73).

POLANUS, Amandus   De concionum Sacrarum methodo (Basel, 1574).
  (See further, Chapter II, note 1.)

V. REPRESENTATIVE MEDIEVAL SERMON HANDBOOKS

[BESANÇON, Étienne de]   An Alphabet of Tales. An English 15th century translation of the Alphabetum Narrationum once attributed to Étienne de Besançon, ed. M. M. Banks (London, 1904–5) E.E.T.S., o.s. 126–7.

BOZON, Nicole   Les Contes moralisés de Nicole Bozon . . . ed. L. T. Smith and P. Meyer (Paris, 1889).
Metaphors of Brother Bozon, a Friar Minor. Translated from a Norman French MS. of the fourteenth century in the possession of the Honourable Society of Gray's Inn, by J[ohn] R[ose], (London, 1913).

BROMYARD, John de   Summa Praedicantium . . . (Antwerp, 1614).

CARPENTER, Alexander   Summa que Destructorium viciorum appelatur (Nuremberg, 1496).

[Anon.]   Gesta Romanorum, ed. H. Oesterley (Berlin, 1872).
The Early English Versions of the Gesta Romanorum, ed. S. J. H. Herrtage (London, 1879) E.E.T.S., e.s. xxxiii.

[Anon.]   Liber Exemplorum ad Usum Praedicantium, ed. A. G. Little (Aberdeen, 1908).

NECKHAM, Alexander   Alexandri Neckham De Naturis Rerum Libri Duo, ed. T. Wright (London, 1863) Rolls series, 34.

[Anon.]   Speculum Laicorum, ed. J. Th. Welter (Paris, 1914).

THOMAS, Hibernicus   Flores omnium fere Doctorum (Venice, 1550).

VI. RHETORICAL TREATISES AND HANDBOOKS

Representative works in Latin and English published in England, and in English published abroad (including translations), 1450–c. 1600.

B[ROWNE], T.   A Ritch Storehouse or Treasurie Called Nobilitas literata, translated by T. B[rowne] (London, 1570) [From the *Nobilitas literara* of John Sturm].

CAXTON, William   The Myrrour and Descrypcyon of the Worlde, with Many Meruayles and the VII Scyences as Grammayre, Rhetorike, with the Arte of Memorye (London, [1480?]).

COX, Leonard   The Arte or Crafte of Rhetoryke (London, [1524?]) ed. F. I. Carpenter (Chicago, 1899) University of Chicago Studies, no. 5.

DAY, Angel   The English Secretorie: also a Declaration of All Tropes and Figures (London, 1592).

FENNER, Dudley (supposed translator)   The Artes of Logike and Rhetorike (Middelburg, 1584) [From the *Dialecticae partitiones* of Ramus and the *Institutiones oratoriae* of Talaeus.]

FRAUNCE, Abraham   The Arcadian Rhetorike or the precepts of rhetorike made plain by examples (London, 1588) [From Talaeus, *Institutiones oratoriae.*]
The Lawiers Logike exemplifying the Praecepts of Logike by Practicse of the Common Law (London, 1588) [A version of Ramus's *Dialecticae partitiones.*]

HARVEY, Gabriel   Rhetor, vel duorum dierum oratio, de natura, arte et exercitione rhetorica (London, 1577).

JEWEL, John, Bp.   Oratio contra rhetoricam, tr. H. H. Hudson, *Q.J.S.*, xiv (1928) pp. 347–92.

MERES, Francis   Palladis Tamia: Wits Treasury, being the second part of Wits Commonwealth (London, 1598).

MUNDAY, Anthony (translator)   The Orator: handling a hundred seuerall discourses, in forme of declamations, written in French by Alexander Siluayn [i.e. Alexander van der Busche and Englished by L. P. i.e. Anthony Munday.] (London, 1596).

PEACHAM, Henry the elder   The Garden of Eloquence, Conteyning the Figures of Grammar and Rhetorick (London, 1577) [From John Susenbrot, *Epitome troporum ac schematum.*]

PUTTENHAM George(?) or Richard (?)   The Arte of English Poesie (London, 1589).

RAINOLDE, Richard   A Booke called the Foundation of Rhetorike (London, 1563) [Translated by Rainolde from an edition of Aphthonius, *Progymnasmata*, by Reinhardus Lorichius (c. 1540)].

SHERRY, Richard   A Treatise of Schemes and Tropes (London, 1550).
A Treatise of the Figures of Grammar and Rhetorike (London, 1555).

TRAVERSANUS, Laurentius Guilielmus   Fratris laurencii guilelmi de soana prohemium in nouam rethoricam (St. Albans, 1480).

WILSON, Thomas   The Arte of Rhetorique, ed. G. H. Mair (Oxford, 1909) [A reprint of the 1585 edn.]

VII. CRITICISM OF SERMONS

(i) General hisories of preaching.

BRILIOTH, Y. T.   Landmarks in the History of Preaching (London, 1950).

BROWN, J.   Puritan Preaching in England (London, 1900).

DARGAN, E. C.   A History of Preaching, 2 vols. (New York, 1905–12).

HERING, H.   Geschichte der Predigt (Berlin, 1897).

KEMPE, J. E.   The Classic Preachers of the English Church: Lectures delivered at St. James's, Westminster in 1877–8, 2 series (London, 1877–8).

KER, J.   Lectures on the History of Preaching (London, 1888).

ROTHE, R.   Geschichte der Predigt, von der Anfängen bis auf Schleiermacher . . . (Bremen, 1881).

SMYTH, C. H. E.   The Art of Preaching. A Practical survey of Preaching in the Church of England 747–1939 (London, 1939).

(ii) Patristic.

AMERINGER, T. E.   The Stylistic Influence of the Second Sophistic on the Panegyrical Sermons of St. John Chrysostom (Washington, D.C., 1921). The Catholic University of America Patristic Studies, vol. V.

BARRY, Sister Inviolata   St. Augustine the Orator. A Study of the Rhetorical Qualities of St. Augustine's ' Sermones ad Populum '. (Washington, D.C., 1924). The Catholic University of America Patristic Studies, vol. VI.

BURNS, Sister M. Albania   St. John Chrysostom's Homilies on the Statues: a Study of their Rhetorical Qualities and Form. (Washington, D.C., 1930) The Catholic University of America Patristic Studies, vol. XXII.

CAMPBELL, J. M.   The Influence of the Second Sophistic on the Style of the Sermons of St. Basil the Great (Washington, D.C., 1922). The Catholic University of America Patristic Studies, vol. II.

DEFERRARI, R. J.   ' St. Augustine's method of composing and delivering sermons,' A.J.P., xliii (1922), pp. 97–127; 193–219.

(iii) Medieval.

CAPLAN, H.   ' Classical Rhetoric and the Medieval Theory of Preaching,' C.P., xxviii. 2 (1933), pp. 73–96.

DEVLIN, Sister Mary Aquinas   ' Bishop Thomas Brunton and his Sermons,' Speculum, xiv. 3 (1939), pp. 324–44.

DOUIE, D. L.   'Archbishop Pecham's sermons and collations,' [in Studies in Medieval History presented to F. M. Powicke (Oxford, 1948), pp. 269–82.]

GILSON, E.   ' Michel Menot et la technique du sermon médiéval,' [in Les Idées et les Lettres (Paris, 1932), pp. 93–154.]

MOSHER, J. A.   The Exemplum in the early Religious and Didactic Literature of England (New York, 1911).

MOURIN, L.   Jean Gerson, Prédicateur Français (Bruges, 1952).

NEALE, J. M.   Mediaeval preachers and mediaeval preaching (London, 1856.)

OWST, G. R.   The Destructorium Viciorum of Alexander Carpenter, a fifteenth century sequel to Literature and Pulpit in Medieval England (London, 1952).
Literature and Pulpit in Medieval England, a neglected chapter in the history of English letters and of the English people, 2nd edn., (Oxford, 1961).
Preaching in Medieval England, an Introduction to the Sermon Manuscripts of the Period c. 1350–1450 (Cambridge, 1926).

SMITH, L. T.   'English Popular Preaching in the Fourteenth Century,' *E.H.R.*, vii (1892), pp. 25–36.

STECKMAN, L. L.   'A late fifteenth century revision of Mirk's Festial,' *S.P.*, xxxiv (1936), pp. 36–48.

WELTER, J. Th.   L'exemplum dans la littérature réligieuse et didactique du moyen âge (Paris, 1927).

(iv) The sixteenth century.

BARING-GOULD, S.   Post-medieval preachers; some account of . . . preachers of the 15th, 16th, and 17th centuries, with outlines of their sermons (London, 1875).

BLENCH, J. W.   ' John Longland and Roger Edgeworth, two forgotten Preachers of the early sixteenth Century,' *R.E.S.*, new series, v. 18 (1954), pp. 123–43.

BRIDGETT, T. E.   ' The Bristol Pulpit in the days of Henry VIII,' *D.R.*, 3rd series, i (1879), pp. 73–95.

CAMPBELL, W. E.   ' Sermons and Religious Treatises,' in E. M. Nugent, *The Thought and Culture of the English Renaissance. An Anthology of Tudor Prose* 1481–1555 (Cambridge, 1956), pp. 305–25.

DONOVAN, M. and   ' The Homilies,' *Theology*, xliii. 257 (1941), pp. 284–95.
VIDLER, A. R.

HAWEIS, J. O. W.   Sketches of the Reformation and Elizabethan Age, taken from the Contemporary Pulpit (London, 1844).

HERR, A. F.   The Elizabethan Sermon, a Survey and a Bibliography (Philadelphia, 1940).

HUTCHINSON, F. E.   ' The English Pulpit from Fisher to Donne,' *C.H.E.L,* 1st edn., vol. IV, ch. xii, pp. 224–41.

KRAPP, G. P.   The Rise of English Literary Prose (New York, 1915), ch. iv. pp. 153–217.

MACLURE, M.   The Paul's Cross Sermons, 1534–1642 (Toronto, 1958).

PARKER, T. H. L.   The Oracles of God. An Introduction to the Preaching of John Calvin (London, 1947).

PÜTZER, F.   Prediger des englischen Barock: stilistisch Untersucht (Bonn, 1929).

STEUERT, Dom Hilary   ' The English Prose Style of Thomas Watson Bishop of Lincoln, 1557,' *M.L.R.*, xli. 3 (1946), pp. 225–36.

(v) The Seventeenth Century.

ELIOT, T. S.   For Lancelot Andrewes, Essays on Style and Order (London, 1928).

MITCHELL, W. F.   English Pulpit Oratory from Andrewes to Tillotson (London 1932).

VIII. STUDIES IN RHETORIC AND PROSE STYLE, AND WORKS
CONTAINING SECTIONS ON THIS TOPIC

(i) General.

BAIN, A.   Rhetoric and English Composition, enlarged edn. (London, 1890).

GRIERSON, Sir H. J. C. Rhetoric and English Composition (Edinburgh, 1944).

(ii) Classical.

ATKINS, J. W. H.   Literary Criticism in Antiquity; a Sketch of its development, 2 vols. (Cambridge, 1934).

BALDWIN, C. S.   Ancient Rhetoric and Poetic (New York, 1924).

CLARK, D. L.   Rhetoric in Greco-Roman Education (New York, 1957).

DILL, S.   Roman Society in the last century of the Western Empire, 2nd edn. (London, 1899).

DUFF, J. W.   A literary history of Rome from the origins to the close of the golden age, ed. A. M. Duff, 3rd edn. (London, 1953).
A literary history of Rome in the Silver Age from Tiberius to Hadrian (London, 1927).

NORDEN, E.   Die antike Kunstprosa (Leipsig, 1898).

VOLKMANN, R.   Die Rhetorik der Griechen und Römer (Berlin, 1872).

(iii) Medieval.

ATKINS, J. W. H.   English Literary criticism: the medieval phase (Cambridge, 1943).

BALWIN, C. S.   Medieval Rhetoric and Poetic to 1400 (New York, 1928).

CHAMBERS, R. W.   On the Continuity of English Prose from Alfred to More and his School (London, reptd. 1950), E.E.T.S.

McKEON, R.   ' Rhetoric in the Middle Ages,' *Speculum*, xvii. 1 (1943), pp. 1–32.

(iv) The Sixteenth Century.

ATKINS, J. W. H.   English Literary Criticism: the Renaissance (London, 1947).

BALDWIN, C. S.   Renaissance literary theory and practice: classicism in the rhetoric and poetic of Italy, France, and England, 1400–1600 (New York, 1939).

CLARK, D. L.   Rhetoric and Poetic in the Renaissance, A Study of Rhetorical terms in English Renaissance literary criticism (New York, 1922).

CRANE, W. G.   Wit and Rhetoric in the Renaissance (New York, 1937).

KRAPP, G. P.   The Rise of English Literary Prose (New York, 1915).

SOUTHERN, A. C.   Elizabethan Recusant Prose, 1559–1582 (London, 1950).

SWEETING, E. J.   Early Tudor Criticism: Linguistic and Literary (Oxford, 1940).

IX.   SCRIPTURAL INTERPRETATION

(i) Representative original texts.

CALVIN, Jean   Commentaries, [in Ioannis Calvini Opera quae supersunt
                        omnia, ed. G. Baum, E. Cumitz and E. Reuss, 59 vols.
                        (Brunswick and Berlin, 1863–1900) *passim.*]

COLET, John   Ioannis Coleti Enarratio in primam Epistolam S. Pauli ad
                        Corinthios: An Exposition of St. Paul's First Epistle to the
                        Corinthians . . . ed. and tr. J. H. Lupton (London, 1874).
                        Ioannis Coleti Enarratio in Epistolam S. Pauli ad Romanos:
                        An Exposition of St. Paul's Epistle to the Romans, delivered
                        as Lectures in the University of Oxford about . . . 1497 . . .
                        ed. and tr. J. H. Lupton (London, 1873).
                        Ioannis Coleti Opuscula Quaedam Theologica. Letters to
                        Radulphus on the Mosaic account of the Creation, together
                        with other treatises . . . ed. and tr. J. H. Lupton (London,
                        1876) [Contains also 'Epistolae B. Pauli ad Romanos
                        Expositio '].

ERASMUS, Desiderius   Novum Testamentum (*Opera Omnia*, vol. VI).
                        Paraphrases in Novum Testamentum (*Opera Omnia*, vol.
                        VII).

HUGH, of St. Cher,   Prima (-septima) pars huius operis: continens textum
     Cardinal   Biblie cum postilla domini Hugonis Cardinalis, 7 vols.
                        (Basel, 1498–1502).

MUSCULUS, Wolfgangus In Epistolam Apostoli Pauli ad Romanos: Commentarii,
                        Wolfgangum Musculum Dusanum (Basel, 1555).

NICOLAS, de Lyra   Textus biblie, cum glosa ordinaria, Nicolai de Lyra postilla,
                        Moralitatibus eiusdem, Pauli Burgensis additionibus,
                        Matthie Thoring. replicis, 6 vols. (Basel, 1506–8).

STANDISH, John   A discourse wherein is debated whether it be expedient
                        that the Scripture should be in English for al men to reade
                        that wyll, 2nd edn., (London 1555).

THOMAS, St. Aquinas   Summa Theologica I 2. 1 a. 10 (*Sancti Thomae Aquinatis
                        Opera Omnia*, 25 vols. Parma, 1852–73, vol. I, pp. 6–7).
                        Quaestiones Quodlibetales, VII, a. 14-16 (ibid. vol. IX, pp.
                        562–5).
                        Catena Aurea (ibid. vol. XI and see next item, below).

TOAL, F. M.   The Sunday Sermons of the Great Fathers, 4 vols. (1957–63)
                        [contains an English translation of the *Catena Aurea* of St.
                        Thomas Aquinas on the Sunday Gospels, together with
                        selected patristic homilies.]

TRENT, the Council of   The Canons and Decrees of the Sacred and Oecumenical
                        Council of Trent, tr. by J. Waterworth (London, 1888)
                        Session IV, pp. 18–19.

TYNDALE, William   Doctrinal Treatises and introductions to different portions
                        of the Holy Scriptures, ed. H. Walter (Cambridge, 1848) P.S.
                        Expositions and notes on Sundry portions of the Holy
                        Scriptures, together with the Practice of Prelates, ed. H.
                        Walter (Cambridge, 1849) P.S.

WHITAKER, William   A Disputation on Holy Scripture against the Papists,
                        especially Bellarmine and Stapleton, tr. and ed. by W.
                        Fitzgerald (Cambridge, 1849) P.S.

(ii) Secondary authorities.

CAPLAN, H.   ' The Four Senses of Scriptural Interpretation and the Medieval Theory of Preaching,' *Speculum*, iv (1929), pp. 282–90.

COULTON, G. G.   The Roman Catholic Church and the Bible, 2nd edn. London, 1921) Medieval Studies, no. 14.

DEANSLEY, M.   The Lollard Bible (Cambridge, 1920).

DUHAMEL, P. A.   ' The Oxford Lectures of John Colet,' *J.H.I.*, xiv. 4 (1953), pp. 493–510.

[ELLIOT]–BINNS, L.   The Reformers and the Bible (Cambridge, 1923).

FARRAR, F. W.   History of Interpretation (London, 1886).

GILBERT, G. Y.   Interpretation of the Bible (New York, 1908).

POPE, H.   St. Thomas Aquinas as an interpreter of Holy Scripture (Oxford, 1924).

SMALLEY, B.   The Study of the Bible in the Middle Ages, 2nd edn. (Oxford, 1952).

X. ECCLESIASTICAL HISTORY AND THE HISTORY OF RELIGIOUS THOUGHT AND EMOTION

ALLEN, P. S.   The Age of Erasmus (Oxford, 1914).

BOUYER, L.   Erasmus and the Humanist Experiment, tr. F. X. Murphy (London, 1959).

BURNET, G., Bp.   A History of the Reformation of the Church of England, ed. N. Pocock, 7 vols. (Oxford, 1865).

CARRÉ, M. H.   Phases of Thought in England (Oxford, 1949).

CONSTANT, G .   La Réforme en Angleterre, 2 vols. (Paris, 1930–9).

COULTON ,G. G.   Art and the Reformation, 2nd edn. (Cambridge, 1953). Five centuries of religion, 4 vols. (Cambridge, 1923–50).

CUTTS, E. L.   Parish Priests and their People in the Middle Ages in England (London, 1914).

DIXON, R. W.   History of the Church of England from the Abolition of the Roman jurisdiction, 6 vols. (London, 1878–1902).

[ELLIOT]-BINNS, L. E.   England and the New Learning (London, 1937). Erasmus the Reformer. A Study in Restatement (London, 1923).

ERASMUS, Desiderius   Μωρίας 'Εγκώμιον. Stultitiae Laus (*Opera Omnia*, IV, 381–504). Paraclesis (ibid., V, 137–40). Opus Epistolarum Des. Erasmi Roterodami, ed. P.S. and H. M. Allen, and H. W. Garrod, 12 vols. (Oxford, 1922–47). Ratio Verae Theologiae (*Opera Omnia*, V, 75–138).

FRERE, W. H.   The English Church in the reigns of Elizabeth and James I (1558–1625) (London, 1904).

GAIRDNER, J.   The English Church in the sixteenth century from the succession of Henry VIII to the death of Mary (London, 1904).

GASCOIGNE, T.   Loci e Libro Veritatum. Passages selected from Gascoigne's Theological Dictionary illustrating the condition of church and state 1403–1458, ed. J. E. Thorold Rogers (Oxford, 1881).

GASQUET, F. A.,   The Eve of the Reformation; studies in the religious life and
Cardinal   thought of the English people in the period preceding the rejection of the Roman Jurisdiction by Henry VIII, new edn. (London, 1900).

GEE, H. and   Documents illustrative of English Church History (London,
HARDY, W. J.   1896).

HUGHES, P.   The Reformation in England, 3 vols. (London, 1950–4).

HUIZINGA, J.   The Waning of the Middle Ages (London, reptd. 1952).

HUNT, E. W.   Dean Colet and his Theology (London, 1956).

HYMA, A.   Luther's Theological Development from Erfurt to Augsburg (New York, 1928).

JACOBS, H. F.   The Lutheran Movement in England during the reigns of Henry VIII and Edward VI, and its Literary Monuments (Philadelphia, 1891).

JAMES, W.   The Varieties of Religious Experience (London, 1952).

JANELLE, P.   L'Angleterre Catholique à la veille du Schisme (Paris, 1935).

JOURDAN, G. V.   The Movement towards Catholic Reform in the early XVIth century (London, 1914).

JUNG, E. M.   ' On the nature of Evangelism in 16th century Italy,' *J.H.I.*, xiv. 4 (1953), pp. 511–27.

LUPTON, J. H.   A Life of John Colet, D.D., new edn. (London, 1909).

MILLER, P.   The New England Mind: the Seventeenth Century (New York, 1939).

MOORMAN, J. R. H.   A History of the Church in England (London, 1953).

PANTIN, W. A.   The English Church in the 14th Century (Cambridge, 1955).

PARKER, T. M.   The English Reformation to 1558 (Oxford, 1950).

PORTER, H. C.   Reformation and Reaction in Tudor Cambridge (Cambridge, 1958).

RICE, E. F., Jr.   ' Erasmus and the Religious Tradition, 1495–1499,' *J.H.I.*, xi. 4 (1950), pp. 387–411.

RUPP, E. G.   Luther's Progress to the Diet of Worms, 1521 (London, 1951).
The Righteousness of God. Luther Studies (London, 1953).
Studies in the making of the English Protestant Tradition (Cambridge, 1949).

RENAUDET, A.   Études Érasmiennes (1521–1529) (Paris, 1939).
Érasme, sa pensée réligieuse et son action d'après sa correspondence (1518–1521) (Paris, 1926).

SCHENK, W.   ' The Erasmian Idea,' *H.J.*, xlviii (1950), pp. 257–65.
Reginald Pole, Cardinal of England (London, 1950).

SEEBOHM, F.   The Oxford Reformers, 2nd edn. (London, 1869).

SMITH, H. M.	Pre-Reformation England (London, 1938). Henry VIII and the Reformation (London, 1948).
SMITH, L. B.	'The Reformation and the Decay of Medieval Ideals,' *C.H.*, xxiv. 3 (1955), pp. 212–20.
SMITHEN, F. J.	Continental Protestantism and the English Reformation (London, [1928]).
SMYTH, C. H. E.	Cranmer and the Reformation under Edward VI (Cambridge, 1926).
SPINKA, M., ed.	Advocates of Reform from Wycliff to Erasmus (London, 1953).
STRYPE, J.	Annals of the Reformation and Establishment of Religion and . . . other occurrences in the Church of England, during the first twelve years of Queen . . . Elizabeth's Reign, 4 vols. (Oxford, 1824). Ecclesiastical Memorials relating chiefly to religion, and the reformation of it, and the emergence of the Church of England with King Henry VIII, King Edward VI, and Queen Mary the First, 3 vols. (Oxford, 1822). Historical collections of the life and acts of J. Aylmer, Lord Bishop of London in the reign of Queen Elizabeth (Oxford, 1821). The history of the life and acts of Edmund Grindal . . . Archbishop of Canterbury (Oxford, 1821). The life and acts of John Whitgift . . . Archbishop of Canterbury, 3 vols. (Oxford, 1822). The life and acts of Matthew Parker, Archbishop of Canterbury, 3 vols. (Oxford, 1821). Memorials of . . . Thomas Cranmer, Archbishop of Canterbury, 2 vols. (Oxford, 1822).
SURTZ, E. L., S.J.	'Oxford Reformers and Scholasticism,' *S.P.*, xlvii (1950), pp. 547–56.
TAWNEY, R. H.	Religion and the Rise of Capitalism (London, reptd. 1943).
TAYLOR, H. O.	The Mediaeval Mind: a history of the development of thought and emotion in the Middle Ages, 2 vols. (London, 1911). Thought and Expression in the sixteenth century, 2 vols. (New York, 1920)
TOMLINSON, J. T.	The Prayer-Book, Articles and Homilies (London, 1897).
WATSON, E. W.	The Church of England, 2nd edn. (Oxford, 1944).
WHITNEY, J. P.	The History of the Reformation, new edn. (London, 1940). Reformation Essays (London, 1939).

XI. THE PAGAN CLASSICS

(i) Sixteenth century collections of classical material.

ERASMUS, Desiderius	Adagiorum chiliades (*Opera Omnia*, vol. II). Apophthegmata Lepideque dicta, principium, philosophorum, ac diversi generis hominium ex Graecis pariter ac Latinis Auctoribus selecta . . . (ibid., IV, 85–380).
TAVERNER, Richard	Flores aliquot sententiarum. . . . The Flower of Sencies gathered out of sundry wryters by Erasmus in Latine and

TAVERNER, Richard   Englished by R. Taverner (London, 1547) [i.e. from the
    cont.   *Apophthegmata* of Erasmus].
    The Garden of Wysdome (London, 1539).
    Prouerbes or Adagies gathered out of the Chiliades of
    Erasmus by Richard Taverner (London, 1545).
VERGIL, Polydore   Prouerbiorum libellus (Venice, 1498).

(ii) Classical learning and the influence of the classics in the Middle Ages and the
    sixteenth century.

BOLGAR, R. R.   The Classical Heritage and its Beneficiaries (Cambridge,
    1954).

BUSH, D.   Classical Influences in Renaissance Literature (Cambridge,
    Mass., 1952).
    The Renaissance and English Humanism (Toronto, 1939).

CURTIUS, E. R.   European Literature and the Latin Middle Ages, tr. W. R.
    Trask (London, 1953).

HYMA, A.   Erasmus and the Humanists (New York, 1940).

SMALLEY, B.   English Friars and Antiquity in the early Fourteenth
    Century (Oxford, 1960).

TAYLOR, H. O.   The Classical heritage of the Middle Ages, 3rd edn. (New
    York, 1911).

INDEX